MANAGERIAL ECONOMICS AND ORGANIZATION

ZOLTAN J. ACS
and
DANIEL A. GERLOWSKI

University of Baltimore

PRENTICE HALL, Upper Saddle River, New Jersey 07458

Library of Congress Cataloging-in-Publication Data

Acs, Zoltan J.
    Managerial economics and organization / Zoltan J. Acs, Daniel A. Gerlowski.
        p. cm.
    Includes bibliographical references and index.
    ISBN 0-02-300292-1
    1. Managerial economics. I. Gerlowski, Daniel A. II. Title.
HD30.22.A27 1996
338.5'024658—dc20   95-31256
                                                                          CIP

Acquisitions Editor: Leah Jewell
Assistant Editor: Teresa Cohan
Editorial Assistant: Kristin Kaiser
Managing Editor: Nicholas Radhuber
Editorial/Production Supervision: Linda B. Pawelchak
Design Director: Patricia Wosczyk
Cover Design: Lorraine Castellano
Cover Illustration: George Abe
Interior Design: Function Thru Form
Interior Line Art: ElectraGraphics, Inc.
Typesetting/Page Makeup: Rainbow Graphics, Inc.
Proofreading: Maine Proofreading Services
Copy Editor: JaNoel Lowe
Manufacturing Buyer: Marie Mcnamara

© 1996 by Prentice-Hall, Inc.
Simon & Schuster/A Viacom Company
Upper Saddle River, New Jersey 07458

Printed in the United States of America
10 9 8 7 6 5 4 3 2 1

ISBN 0-02-300292-1

Prentice-Hall International (UK) Limited, London
Prentice-Hall of Australia Pty. Limited, Sydney
Prentice-Hall Canada Inc., Toronto
Prentice-Hall Hispanoamericana, S.A., Mexico
Prentice-Hall of India Private Limited, New Delhi
Prentice-Hall of Japan, Inc., Tokyo
Simon & Schuster Asia Pte. Ltd., Singapore
Editora Prentice-Hall do Brasil, Ltda., Rio de Janeiro

To our children

Ashley and *Annabel*
and
Danny and *Drew*

Brief Contents

Contents

Preface

The business environment that will carry us into the next century is driven by global competition, quality products, technological change, and the flexibility of organizations. In our rapidly changing world, the diverse field of economics has much to offer in preparing tomorrow's managers.

Traditional economics courses in the nation's business schools are beginning to change. Managerial economics is no exception. The quantitative tools emphasized in most managerial economics courses have increased in scale and scope, very often finding a home in specified "tool courses" and leaving the way open for innovation. Managerial economics courses are being revised from a traditional mix of *quantitative tools and economic theory* toward an understanding of the role of management in economic organizations.

Managerial Economics and Organization is the first textbook to present the economics of organization at the undergraduate level, focusing on how organizations are evolving in today's highly competitive, global, and technology-driven economy. This is the first truly new managerial economics book in twenty years. The pioneering spirit in this endeavor was first embodied in *Economics, Organization, and Management* by Paul Milgrom and John Roberts (Prentice Hall, 1992), which was an instant success. Although it represents a remarkable achievement, the book is written well above the level of most undergraduate and graduate students. Moreover, certain themes that warrant expansion in order to make the subject more applicable in a global economy are missing: international influences are a prime candidate, along with technological change and international comparisons of organizations.

SUBJECT MATTER

Relying on many years of experience in teaching managerial economics, we have created an exciting treatment of managerial economics that is (1) reflective of the changing business environment and (2) more integrated with other traditional business disciplines.

Traditional aspects of our text include a detailed treatment of supply and demand, the theory of the firm, and efficiency in a general equilibrium framework. We also make available to students many of the contributions of economics in the areas of coordination, motivation, organization, and strategy. Therefore, we have provided undergraduate students with a set of tools to manage diverse and rapidly changing business organizations.

Managerial Economics and Organization bridges the gap between traditional approaches to managerial economics with courses of the future. We believe that this framework will be adopted by a large number of our colleagues because of its relevance to the real world, because of its integrative nature, and because of our efforts to tailor the material in terms of content and level toward the prototypical undergraduate at a traditional U.S. business school.

UNIQUE FEATURES

1. *Managerial Economics and Organization* is the first textbook to integrate the economics of organization into undergraduate managerial economics courses. The text starts with the economics of exchange and systematically develops the theory of economic organization. This makes managerial economics much more relevant for management education.

2. The text has five highly original and easy to understand chapters on the economics of organization. Building on transaction cost economics, we examine efficiency and coordination within organizations. We develop the theory of contracting to discuss issues of motivation and discourse. Finally, we develop the theory of distribution. This allows us to explain why firms exist in the first place.

3. The text is written in conversational language. It is easy to read, yet it maintains a high level of rigor and analytic content. The text uses more than one hundred real-world examples drawn from the pages of the popular press and explains them with organizational tools. The students enjoy the text, are more motivated, and find learning rewarding.

4. The text examines organizational issues in a changing environment. Organizational dynamics are examined from historical, technological, and global perspectives. For example, we examine the evolution of the firm from mass production using semi-skilled workers to the high value-added corporation using knowledge workers.

5. Our text is more integrated than traditional managerial textbooks with traditional business disciplines such as finance and human resource management. Drawing on the economics of organization, we study the market for corporate control, human resources, and the changing boundaries of the firm.

ORGANIZATION OF THE BOOK

The book is organized into five sections: The Efficiency of Markets; The Economics of Organization; Organization, Ownership, and Control; Managing Human Resources; and Organizational Structure as a Dynamic Process. There are several inter-related themes that permeate all of the individual chapters in this book. We can only briefly describe these themes to you here:

Theme 1. Exchange. Economic activity is really about exchange. What economists do is focus on the conditions surrounding exchange more than the exchange itself. Many exchanges, or transactions, occur in markets and are well understood. Many take place outside the protective realm of markets. We aim to understand the course of events in these instances as well.

Theme 2. Organization. Firms exist to organize economic activity. A firm is really a series of contracts linking together various parties. The circumstances surrounding these contracts may be termed the *environment of the firm*. Over time this environment changes, which implies that organizations will change as well.

Theme 3. Imperfect Information. Uncertainty and imperfect information exist in all contracts. No contract is made under conditions of complete certainty. Therefore, trust is important.

Theme 4. Opportunistic Behavior. Contracting must address opportunism through the establishment of incentives and provisions for monitoring. Efficiency dictates that contracts will be crafted keeping these factors in mind.

Appreciably, these four themes allow the student to explore managerial issues from an economic vantage point. Drawing on the theory of economic organization, we develop relevant examples from business to study issues of human resource management, financial structure, and organizational dynamics.

■ FOR THE INSTRUCTOR

Managerial Economics and Organization targets undergraduate students at the junior/senior level. In order to fully appreciate the relevance of the topics in this text, it is recommended that students have at least an exposure to principles-level economics. There are no formal requirements that students must have mastered, neither do they have to have learned calculus or statistics. We have had great success in the classroom involving students in discussion rather than simply conducting lectures.

This book represents an exciting and rewarding approach to teaching managerial economics. The material has been classroom tested at the University of Baltimore over a three-year period. We have found that students are genuinely excited about what they learn, acquire the ability to apply the material to their real-world situations, and independently begin to use the concepts in other courses. Students can easily discuss moral hazard, asset specificity, and the principal-agent problem in class.

The wide variety of topics included in *Managerial Economics and Organization* would make it nearly impossible to cover each and every chapter fully. When designing this text, we fully appreciated this constraint and included several redundancies allowing for numerous subsets of chapters to be strung together in a coherent way.

We offer two suggested paths through the book, each of which is appropriate for a different mix of students' skills and interests. Each pathway can be covered in a traditional semester consisting of 14 weeks of instruction.

For business students who may have a relatively weak background in principles-level economics, or who may have taken these courses long ago (a common feature given the changing student demographics), we recommend the following pathway, which is more closely related to the "traditional" economics education:

Chapter Number	Chapter Title
1	Introduction: Firms and Managing Them
2	Competitive Exchange
3	The Neoclassical Theory of the Firm
4	Efficiency, the Price System, and Organizations
5	Property Rights, Ownership, and Efficiency
6	Organizational Tools
7	Contracts: Motivation Through Agreement
8	Contracts: Issues of Discourse
9	Distribution, Rents, and Efficiency
10	Modern Financial Theory
11	Corporate Control and Economic Efficiency
14	The Evolution of the Modern Firm
15	Core Competencies, Organization, and Strategy

The instructor can substitute the labor chapters (12 and 13) for the finance chapters (10 and 11) without any loss of continuity.

The second model course outline is more applicable when students already have a good understanding of the material covered in principles-level economics. It provides more of a managerial perspective and an increased emphasis on how "firms" adapted before, change in response to current forces, and are likely to continue evolving.

Chapter Number	Chapter Title
1	Introduction: Firms and Managing Them
2	Competitive Exchange
5	Property Rights, Ownership, and Efficiency
6	Organizational Tools
7	Contracts: Motivation Through Agreement
8	Contracts: Issues of Discourse
10	Modern Financial Theory
11	Corporate Control and Economic Efficiency
12	The Employment Relationship
13	The Employment Experience
14	The Evolution of the Modern Firm
15	Core Competencies, Organization, and Strategy
16	Organizational Strategy and Strategic Alliances
17	An International Comparison of Organizational Styles

Whether or not you choose to follow one of these two course outlines or create your own, you will find that *Managerial Economics and Organization* is part of a complete package to help you provide students with a sound educational outcome.

The accompanying instructors manual is a powerful resource containing several unique and useful features. Most important, for every chapter, we include a sample lecture and suggestions for teaching the material. Additionally, we provide a brief narrative to remind us of how each chapter fits into the train of thought running through the text. To help in the necessary testing and grading dimensions of teaching, the instructors manual includes answers to the end-of-chapter questions and additional review questions for each chapter.

We will also provide, on request, a database of key articles from academic journals as well as the popular press, including *Business Week*, *The Wall Street Journal*, *The Economist*, and *Fortune*. The database includes more than 500 up-to-date articles. All articles have been key worded and have complete citations and an abstract enabling the instructor to find many examples dealing with, for example, "asset specificity" or "strategic alliances." The whole database comes on disk and can be accessed with *Foxpro*, the leading database management system. This database will be updated on a regular basis and represents a continuing effort to keep *Managerial Economics and Organization* current.

In keeping with our view that the material in the text is innovative, we also follow innovative trends in classroom pedagogy by making available suitable classroom presentations for each chapter. These are available in either a *Powerpoint* or

Freelance Graphics format, organized by chapter and keyed to the material in the text. We encourage you to exploit the flexibility of the information technology available and tailor these presentations to suit your needs.

We also have a computerized test bank with more than 500 multiple choice questions. These questions have been written by the textbook authors and have been classroom tested.

The justification for this book is twofold. First, as we mentioned earlier, the business environment has undergone drastic and fundamental changes: the decline of communism, rapid technological change, organizational evolution. Second, business schools have recognized these trends and, through the American Assembly of Collegiate Schools of Business (AACSB), have expressed a desire for a more applicable, synthesized approach to education. *Managerial Economics and Organization* is rigorous, flexible, and current enough to allow you easily to meet both of these needs in your classroom.

FOR THE STUDENT

This book is written for you. It is written to help you learn about the world in which you live and the organization in which you will work. Every page of the book is filled with information that will be of use to you for years to come. The introductory chapter is your road map to the book. Each part has an introduction to make sure that you will find your way. The sections of each chapter are clearly marked and easy to follow. The text has a complete glossary with clear definitions.

The vocabulary necessary to understand *Managerial Economics and Organization* is boldfaced within the text at the point where the term is introduced and defined. All boldfaced terms are also defined in the glossary at the end of the text.

Using substantial input from students, the authors have written a study guide. The study guide serves three main purposes in enhancing the learning outcome. First, the study guide clearly outlines the importance of each chapter in the logical development of the book. Second, it provides an explanation of the relevant concepts in more of a layperson's terminology. Third, the study guide offers additional examples of some of the concepts illustrated in *Managerial Economics and Organization*.

ACKNOWLEDGMENTS

A project like this does not appear overnight. Our story is also an example of organizations at work. We originally signed our contract with Macmillan Publishers. We would like to thank Jill Lectka, who originally convinced us to sign with Macmillan. As you might know, Macmillan was taken over by Prentice Hall in 1994, and we were sort of acquired. An acquisition is never an easy process: uncertainty abounds as projects are abandoned, people leave, others are fired, and organizations are in transition for quite a while.

During this process, we were constantly kept up to date by Teresa Cohan, who survived the shift from Macmillan to Prentice Hall. She took special care to keep us informed and made sure that we had someone to talk to during the year-long merger. During this time, we had several editors, some for as short as a week. Out of the dust emerged Leah Jewell, Economics Editor for Prentice Hall. We have been very happy with our current, and we hope future, editor. We would like to thank her for the patience and care she took with the manuscript. Our production editor, Linda B. Pawelchak, did a wonderful job. She took our manuscript and turned it into a book. We thank her.

Many people have helped us with this project. First and foremost, we express our gratitude to our students, without whom this project could not have been completed. We are especially thankful to Felix FitzRoy of the University of St. Andrew and Sharon Gifford of Boston University, who read many different versions of the manuscript over the years. We also benefited from comments by Josh Lerner, Harvard Business School; Donald Siegal, Arizona State University-West; Bo Carlsson, Case Western Reserve University; Thomas Klier, Chicago Federal Reserve Bank; Frank Giarratani, University of Pittsburgh; and David Levy, University of Baltimore.

We would also like to thank the following additional reviewers: Henry Cheesbrough, Berkeley, CA; John Conant, Indiana State University; Peter Mattila, Iowa State University; Mo-Yin Tam, University of Illinois; Robert Windle, University of Maryland; Richard A. Zuber, University of North Carolina; and Habib Zuberi, Central Michigan University.

We would also like to thank Janet Zhao and Susan Lei for setting up the database and for their competent assistance on this book.

Finally, there's the group of people who helped us at every stage of the project. Our colleagues at the University of Baltimore and the University of Baltimore administration were supportive throughout the project.

Then there is my wife Jane (Zoltan), who patiently took care of the family while I worked late hours on the book. I thank her deeply. Last but not least we would like to thank our families for their support throughout this project.

About the Authors

Zoltan J. Acs is the Harry Y. Wright Professor of Economics and Finance in the Robert G. Merrick School of Business at the University of Baltimore and Associate Director of the Center for Intentional Business Education and Research (CIBER), College of Business and Management, at the University of Maryland. Dr. Acs has been a Research Fellow at the Wissenschaftszentrum Berlin and Columbia University, and a visiting professor at the University of St. Andrews, the University of Aix-Marseille, and the University of Maryland at College Park. He has lectured extensively and in 1994 was invited to deliver the F. de Vries Lecture at Erasmus University in Rotterdam.

Professor Acs is widely known for his research on innovation and technological change. He has authored, co-authored, or edited nine books and over 75 articles. He is the co-founder and co-editor of *Small Business Economics*, an international journal. He has been a consultant to many international organizations, including the United Nations, the European Community, the OECD, the Ministry of Economic Affairs (the Netherlands), and the National Forum of Brazil and has served as an expert economic witness.

Daniel A. Gerlowski is an Associate Professor of Economics and Finance at the University of Baltimore and a Research Fellow in The France Center. He earned a Ph.D in economics at the University of Pittsburgh. His research has been published in *Land Economics*, *Regional Science*, and the *Journal of Economic History*, and he has consulted to Arthur Anderson. He is a successful and innovative teacher in undergraduate and MBA programs. He has taught managerial economics and econometrics for six years.

Introduction: Firms and Managing Them

The theme propounded here is that modern business enterprise took the place of market mechanisms in coordinating the activities of the economy and allocating its resources. In many sectors of the economy, the *visible hand* of management replaced what Adam Smith referred to as the *invisible hand* of market forces. . . . As modern business enterprises acquired functions hitherto carried out by the market, it became the most influential group of economic decision makers.[1]

Can Economists teach business people anything useful about the day-to-day running of companies? About such meat-and-potatoes problems of managerial life as how to restructure your company, how to motivate and compensate employees, how to outfox your competitors, whether to compete in a new market? For much of its 200-plus-year history, the dismal science has had little to say about such questions, but that's changing fast.[2]

▮ WHAT IS AND WHAT IS NOT A FIRM

One day at a major investment banking house on New York City's famous Wall Street, a well-known economist is speaking about the general economic environment and the earning prospects of General Motors, Microsoft, and IBM. In her discussion, she repeatedly refers to these entities as firms. Everyone in the room, and probably every student in your class, understands what is meant by the term *firm*. Quite possibly however, the economist addressing the investment bankers would be at a loss no smaller than yours if pressed to create a universally accepted definition of firms.

Providing a definition for the term *firm* that is acceptable to everybody is not possible. However, we are not helpless. The word *firm* is used in much the same way as is the word *love*; never defined but intuitively understood by a large enough number of people to be accepted as part of common dialogue. Instead, we offer the following working definition to be used throughout this text:[3]

---

[1]Alfred Chandler, *The Visible Hand: The Managerial Revolution in America* (Cambridge: Harvard University Press 1977), p. 1.

[2]Rob Nortune, "A New Tool to Help Managers," *Fortune*, May 30, 1994, p. 135. © 1994 Time Inc. All rights reserved.

[3]For a working definition of the word *love*, you are referred to the many works of Shakespeare and/or numerous country music songs.

**What Is Included
in Our Definition**

firm: *A conscious, willful effort to organize economic activity that consists of a
collection of contracts when more than one party is involved.*

You may find this working definition somewhat surprising for what it does
and what it does not contain. Primarily, when a firm is created, there is no Dr.
Frankenstein gleefully clasping his hands over his creation and wondering about
his ability to create life. A firm is not a person or any other living thing; it is
merely a legal entity, recognized by law, which is permitted to enter into binding
contracts with other persons and firms.

It is quite important to recognize the implied functionality of firms; they organize economic activity. For this reason, a more general term has evolved in
business for firms: *organizations.* Throughout this book we will use the terms *firm*
and *organization* interchangeably.

The production of a car by General Motors, a farmer bringing the year's
wheat harvest to market, the provision of educational services by your university,
and the furnishing of meals to the indigent in America's inner cities are examples
of economic activity. Each of these activities is organized or arranged in a particular way that depends on a number of forces both inside and outside the firm.
Much of what we have to say in this book concerns the impact of these internal
and external forces on the way in which firms choose to organize economic activity.

The second important component of our definition of firms is that they involve a conscious, willful effort to organize economic activity. This implies two
intuitive points. First, we assign a motive for having organizations in the first
place. Traditional economic analysis focuses to a great degree on profit maximization as the primary force driving firms in their actions. We will adopt the much
broader concept of efficiency. A particular way of organizing economic activity is
said to be **efficient** if it is impossible, given available resources, to implement an
alternative arrangement under which all parties involved are at least as well off.

Also implied by the fact that firms are a conscious, willful effort to organize
economic activity is that there may be a way to organize that same economic activity that is not conscious or willful. We refer here to the possibility that markets
may fulfill these functions through the workings of Adam Smith's famous invisible
hand. The market alternative has attracted much attention as recent history has
witnessed many firms switching from producing inputs inside the firm to acquiring them in markets.

Our working definition of the word *firm* is flexible enough to allow for
changes in the way in which firms opt to organize their activities through time.
The best, or most efficient, way for organizations to meet the needs of society at
any point in time depends on the general economic environment, technology, and
the availability of information. Changes in any one of these three dimensions will
change the way in which different organizations arrange their economic affairs.
Organizational structures are chosen subject to competition as are a firm's pricing
policy, its choice of product offerings, and its investment decision. Failure to
choose the optimal organizational structure may lead to being supplanted by a
more efficient competitor. The dominance of the Japanese automakers is one example of this as is the reemergence of U.S. auto producers in the mid 1990s.

Any organization consisting of more than one person requires that some
"sticky stuff" exists to bind the parties together. In a family, bloodlines serve as
the proverbial "ties that bind." In firms, contracts serve the same purpose. A **contract** is merely an agreement between two or more people that specifies actions
that each will take or assigns decision-making powers. Within organizations, contracts serve two very broad purposes. First, they coordinate the actions of differ-

ent people in a meaningful way. In a restaurant, for example, the cook's contract specifies that he will prepare the food; the server's contract specifies that she will serve as a liaison between the customer and the cook. Second, contracts provide motivation to the parties. Construction firms may receive larger payments for completing work ahead of some specified schedule; likewise, they may be penalized for finishing late (without good reason) or if the project fails any number of technical inspections.

Our understanding of the importance of the contracting process to organizations needs to recognize the important difference between contracts made within the firm and contracts made by the firm with outside parties. **Internal contracts** are those made entirely within the firm such as those between a firm and its employees and are typically vague with some amount of latitude given to each of the involved parties. **External contracts** are those that a firm makes with a party not within the firm; these agreements are, by necessity, more explicit.

**What Is Not
in Our Definition**

Now we should consider what is not said in our working definition of firms. There is no pretense in our definition concerning a set of organizational goals. We could say that a goal for not-for-profit firms (i.e., the United Way, Salvation Army, Red Cross) is to promote the social welfare or, at a minimum, the well-being of some subset of the population. In the for-profit sector, the picture is even more clouded.

The traditional approach of economics is to argue that firms seek to maximize profits, the difference between revenues and costs. If this were so, then we would not, strictly speaking, see corporations active in supporting social causes or building large expensive office buildings in the downtown areas of major cities. Such deviations from profit-maximizing behavior must face constraints in the long run, for, if a business is to be viable, it is under constant pressure to make money.

In the theory of finance, it is often argued that firms seek to maximize the market value of the shares held by their stockholders. The problem with a strict interpretation of this view lies in the tricky, complicated nature of managing firms: typically many parties are involved, each of which has a say in the operations of the firm. Furthermore, each of these involved parties has clear incentives to safeguard and promote its own interests even at the expense of the firm's shareholders.

Another interesting feature missing from our working definition of the firm concerns what the firm actually does. All organizations produce output that has value to others; however, this does not imply that firms actually "make" anything. Many of today's profitable organizations rely on others to actually "make" the products that have made them famous.

In the early 1990s, Chrysler Corporation introduced a new line of cars, the LH Series. As a matter of fact, Chrysler's very survival was at stake in this new product line. How much of these new cars did Chrysler actually produce? Analysts estimate that Chrysler produced about 30 percent of the cars, and other parties produced the rest. At the other extreme, General Motors made about 60 percent of its cars, and Ford about half. In the athletic footwear industry, this way of doing business is even more entrenched. One of the major players in this market, Nike, owns one small factory and Reebok, one of its competitors, owns none. In 1992 both Nike and Reebok earned a return on assets of 16 percent, placing fifth and sixth, respectively, in *Fortune* magazine's list of best service companies in that year.[4]

In short, there may never be a single accepted definition of *firm*. However, it

---

[4]Shawn Tully, *"The Modular Corporation,"* Fortune, February 8, 1993, pp. 106–111.

An Alternative to Firms

is very important to have a feel for what the word means and for how to use it in a meaningful way. It is our purpose in this book to understand the forces that affect organizations as they orchestrate economic activity. In the next section we will consider the importance of firms in our economy, some legalistic definitions concerning the types of firms, and some economic concepts describing the role firms play in a market economy.

At this point, there may very well be some confusion in your mind. Much of the work done by economists in the past two centuries has dealt with the related issues of scarcity and allocation. All resources in existence are said to be scarce, meaning that everyone who wants the resource cannot have as much of it as he or she wishes. Because there is scarcity, an allocation mechanism must work to determine who gets the resources and who does not. In your prior economics courses, the basic principles of supply and demand have undoubtedly been burned deep into your mind. Perhaps you even understand the conditions under which the "market" forces of supply and demand interact in the best interests of society.

The market system in the United States is very well developed and entrenched in business practice. Economists are not ignorant of this, nor has your training to date ignored a sound exposure to the price system as an allocating or organizing mechanism. Herein lies the confusion undoubtedly forming in your mind. If a functioning system of specialized markets exists, why is it necessary for firms to organize economic activity? The answer to this question is not all that straightforward; a detailed answer will appear in later chapters. For now, it suffices to say that in organizing some types of economic activities, firms work better than markets. Further, in most instances, the choice of using firms or markets to organize activity is not one of completeness but one of degree. The examples discussed above concerning the automobile and athletic footwear industries have made it clear that the choice is usually not one or the other but some proportion of each.

■ FIRMS IN OUR CAPITALISTIC ECONOMY

What They Produce

The leaders of any country are very concerned about how much their economy is producing. Roughly speaking, the more that is produced, the higher the number of people who are working and the higher their incomes. A happy populace is very likely to be supportive of any group of leaders. Economists use two concepts to measure the amount of production in an economy; the measures differ according to the openness of the economy to foreign ownership and trade. **Gross domestic product** (GDP) is the total money value of the goods and services produced by the residents of a country in a given time period. **Gross national product** (GNP) is a measure of the incomes of the residents of a country including incomes earned abroad but excluding payments made to those abroad.

Over the past 50 or so years, the United States has enjoyed a steady growth in production by either measure. This growth is evident and well documented elsewhere and is known to have averaged between 2 and 3 percent when **real,** or adjusted for inflation, GDP and GNP are examined. This sustained economic growth is responsible for raising the standard of living for most U.S. citizens. For a student interested in developments in the business world, this period of growth is even more interesting because of the accompanying changes in what types of goods grew in importance over this time and also because of a changing mix of things being produced.

Usually when we think of production, we envision assembly line workers piecing together a car at a GM plant or a technician placing a maze of circuit boards and wires into a computer box at an Apple computer plant. Such thinking was more in line with the state of the world in 1980 than in 1989 and even less in line with business today. Most firms in today's economy produce **intermediate goods,** goods that are subject to later processing by another firm, rather than **final goods,** products or services that are consumed by the ultimate user.

Consider this example. A salvage firm may gather aluminum cans from a variety of recyclers. A smelting operation may purchase the cans from the salvage firm, melt them down to remove impurities, and sell them to a stamping plant that processes them further before selling them to an appliance manufacturer that uses the pieces to make coverings for refrigerators. The refrigerators are then sold to a wholesaler, which, in turn, transfers them on consignment to a retailer. The ultimate user purchases the refrigerator. In this example, the appliance manufacturer is the final goods producer; all the parties prior to that are intermediate goods producers. The wholesaler and retailer in this example act as facilitator; they add value to the process by increasing consumer access to the refrigerator.

Above and beyond the relative increased emphasis placed on intermediate goods production, some sectors in the U.S. economy have clearly grown faster than average while others have actually declined in relative importance. Table 1.1 provides some idea of how the composition of output produced by the U.S. economy has changed over the period 1977 to 1991. Table 1.1 shows, for the beginning and ending years, the percentage of GDP in broadly defined industries. We know, for example, that in 1977 services accounted for about 13 percent of economic activity in the United States. By 1991, however, the service industries were responsible for over 17 percent of output.

Over the 14 years shown in Table 1.1, the relative size of activity in many sectors has decreased. The mining sector's importance, for example, was nearly

Table 1.1	**Gross Domestic Product of the United States, by Industry, 1977 and 1991**	
Industry	**1977 Percentage of Total**	**1991 Percentage of Total**
Agriculture, Forestry, and Fisheries	2.87%	1.92%
Mining	2.76	1.82
Construction	4.78	3.86
Non-durable Goods Manufacturing[a]	9.63	7.58
Durable Goods Manufacturing[b]	14.15	10.41
Transportation, Communications, and Utility Services	9.13	12.41
Wholesale Trade	7.02	6.45
Retail Trade	9.70	9.38
Finance, Insurance, and Real Estate	14.45	17.16
Services	13.02	17.16
State and Local Government	8.03	7.76
Federal Government	4.56	3.84

[a]This group includes food, food processing, tobacco, textiles, clothing, paper, printing and publishing, chemicals, oil and coal, rubber, plastics, and leather.
[b]This group includes lumber and wood, furniture, stone, clay and glass products, metal, machinery, electrical equipment, automobiles and trucks, measuring equipment, and computers.
Source: 1977 data from *Survey of Current Business*, November 1993, Table 6, p. 38; 1991 data from *Statistical Abstract of the United States, 1993*, U.S. Department of Commerce Economics and Statistics Administration, Bureau of the Census (Washington, D.C.: U.S. Government Printing Office), p. 447, Table No. 685.

halved. On the other hand, the finance, insurance, and real estate, and service sectors grew in importance. What we have documented is the shift in U.S. industry to a service economy, one in which there is less importance on actual production and more importance placed on activity in related sectors and the level of demand. As we think of production throughout this book we must, of course, remember traditional blue-collar workers slaving away in mines, fields, and factories; we must also consider men and women sitting at their desks working with pen, paper, and computers.

Types of Firms: Legalistic Definitions

According to the federal and state laws in the United States, there are three main forms of business organization: sole proprietorship, partnership, and corporation. Each of these has the ability to enter into legally binding contracts with other legal entities; however, there are some conceptual differences among them that must be recognized. In terms of numbers, about 80 percent of business firms are operated as sole proprietorships; the remainder are divided equally between partnerships and corporations. A very different picture emerges by dollar value of sales. Corporations are responsible for about 80 percent of sales in the United States, proprietorships account for about 13 percent, and partnerships about 7 percent.[5]

A **sole proprietorship** is a business owned by a single individual. The proprietorship has two important advantages. First, it is easily and inexpensively formed and, once operating, it is subject to few government regulations. Second, the business pays no corporate income taxes; its earnings are taxed at the owner's tax rate. The three organizational drawbacks of the sole proprietorship are that these businesses usually have great difficulty obtaining large sums of capital; the proprietor has unlimited personal liability for business debts; and the life of a business organized as a proprietorship is limited to the life of the individual who created it.

A **partnership** exists when two or more persons associate to conduct a noncorporate business. Partnerships may operate under different degrees of formality, ranging from informal, oral understandings to formal agreements filed with the office of the secretary of the state in which the partnership does business. The major advantages of a partnership are its low cost and ease of formation. Partnerships share many of the disadvantages of the sole proprietor form of business: unlimited liability by the partners, limited life of the organization, difficulty of transferring ownership, and difficulty of obtaining large sums of capital.

A **corporation** is a legal entity, or "person," recognized by the state. The major disadvantage of corporations are the costs and difficulties involved in forming them. Formation may require substantial legal effort and a fair amount of government regulation. This legal form of organization features three major advantages. First, it permits limited liability for its owners who are simply the owners of shares of stock issued by the corporation. Second, it permits easy transfer of ownership because there are rarely conditions placed on selling or buying stock. Third, a corporation has an unlimited life; it can continue to operate with few complications long after its original owners are dead and gone.

The property of limited liability has made possible the large corporations that we know today. Exxon, IBM, GM, and DuPont would likely not exist if it were not for the availability of the corporate form.

Perhaps the most interesting aspect of the corporate organizational form is

---

[5]For a more thorough discussion of the forms of corporate ownership, consult most any introductory finance text. An excellent source is J. Fred Weston and Eugene F. Brigham, *Essentials of Managerial Finance*, 9th ed. (Fort Worth: The Dryden Press, 1990).

the potential for separation of ownership from control in large firms.[6] The owners of the firm are the stockholders. Typically, firms are run, however, by the chief executive officer (CEO), who is accountable not directly to the shareholders but usually to a board of directors, which is a group of individuals that is supposed to represent the interests of the shareholders. At times, the relationship between the CEO (and his or her management teams), the corporate board, and stockholders becomes tense. Perhaps the firm's managers seek to advance their interests at the expense of the stockholders, or perhaps the corporate board fails to monitor the CEO. In later chapters we will discuss some of these situations of conflict, focusing on the role of incentives and information in describing the individual's behavior.

Consider Jose Martinez, who commutes daily from his home in the suburbs to his job at a bank downtown. Because of the heavy congestion and resultant traffic jams, Jose frequently leaves his home early in the morning. Sometimes, in fact, Jose leaves before his newspaper is delivered. On these occasions Jose has to purchase a newspaper on route to his job, an event that costs him an extra three miles and 15 minutes. Jose, is struck with an idea: surely there must be others like him who are annoyed with the lack of a conveniently located newspaper vendor.

After much thought, Jose does a little research on what would be required to open a store to service the daily newspaper needs of a large commuting population. He identifies a currently vacant storefront in an excellent location. Consulting the phone book, he puts himself in touch with equipment suppliers and determines what his needs would be. After several days of research with information provided by the Small Business Association, Jose decides that his store would require all of his working time for the first several years of operations. In total, Jose would need to quit his job at the downtown bank and acquire about $70,000 in start-up capital.

Finally, Jose quits his job, takes his life savings of $30,000 and opens just such a store. What sorts of options are open to Jose in determining the legal form for his business? Let's consider some alternatives.

Along with his own start-up capital, Jose borrows an additional $40,000, signs a three-year lease, purchases storefront equipment and an inventory, and opens business as a sole proprietor. If Jose's business fails, he not only has lost his $30,000 but may also be forced to sell personal property to make good on the bank loan and the remainder of the three-year lease.

An alternative would be for Jose and his brother-in-law, John Vaselenak, to form a partnership to start the news stand of Jose's dream. In this scenario, each partner may provide $20,000 of his savings for start-up capital, and the partnership may borrow the remaining $30,000. In the event of failure, each partner would lose his $20,000 and face personal responsibility for some share of the $30,000 bank loan along with any other expenses involved with setting up the news stand.

If Jose were to organize his shop as a corporation, he could invest his own money, perhaps the full $30,000, borrow some from a bank, and raise the remainder of the $70,000 by selling stock. If he pursues this route, Jose would encounter additional legal costs in forming the corporation, perhaps $2,000, which would be covered by his personal investment of $30,000. Perhaps he could interest John in purchasing shares in his newsstand venture, giving John some element of ownership in the business. In the event of bankruptcy, the corporation's assets will be

---

[6]Many of the problems arising because of the separation of ownership from control were illustrated by A. Berle and G. Means, *The Modern Corporation and Private Property* (New York: Macmillan, 1932).

sold. The monies obtained will go first to those that lent the corporation money (banks and bondholders), and only then will any surplus be given to Jose, John, and any other shareholders. The liability of the shareholders (owners) is then limited to their stake in the firm, but nothing more. Under this option, Jose effectively works for John; if John were unhappy with the way in which Jose managed his business, he may or may not have any recourse, depending on the initial financing plans between Jose and John.

An additional feature of the corporate form for Jose to consider is the relative ease of acquiring additional capital for expansion if his newsstand is successful in its early years.

A corporation seeking capital, either for start-up or for an expansion of operations, has three avenues available. It can borrow funds either from a bank or directly from investors through a bond issue. The corporation may issue new shares of stock. Finally, profitable corporations can be (to an extent) self-financing, that is, by retaining a portion of their earnings rather than by paying them out to its shareholders (owners) in the form of dividends. The best choice of financing a firm's operations depends on many factors and is closely linked with the organizational form chosen. Some economists go so far as to argue that these decisions are made simultaneously with the choice of organizational form.

Four Attributes of Firms

In the developed economies of the world today, the dominant feature on the economic landscape is clearly the existence of firms.

The field of economics has provided a number of theories explaining why these firms exist and, it is hoped, to explain their behavior and future evolution. A brief review of these theories appears in the next section. For now, it is instructive to identify four attributes of firms assigned by Alfred D. Chandler after a lengthy historical study.[7]

* *The firm is a legal entity.*

This is the most general attribute of firms in our society. As explained in the prior section, firms are able to enter into contracts with suppliers, distributors, employees, and customers.

* *Organizations are administrative units.*

Recall our working definition of a firm. The importance placed on the role of firms in arranging economic activity cannot be ignored. Perhaps the basic idea behind large firms is that a group of persons engages in some form of collective behavior; because of the size of the group, each member is able to specialize in some task (or set of tasks) that is a smaller part of the whole job of producing salable output. The benefits of specialization have been well known since the work of Adam Smith in the 1600s. Organizations hope to capture these benefits, at the expense of having to arrange the actions of some group of persons. In this perspective, firms are concerned with coordinating, motivating, and monitoring the actions of others.

* *Once established, a firm becomes a pool of physical facilities, learned skills and liquid capital.*

In the previous section we learned that one aspect of legally recognized corporations is that they exist as their own "person" and that they can outlive their original owners. Once created, several pieces make up this "thing" that we call a firm. First are tangible components such as plants, distribution networks, patents, copyrights, and investment holdings. Second are intangible components to be

---

[7]See Alfred D. Chandler, "Organizational Capabilities and the Economic History of the Industrial Enterprise," *Journal of Economic Perspectives* 6, no. 3, Summer 1992, pp. 79–100.

considered: proprietary technical knowledge, consumer goodwill, reputation, and the personal relationships developed through years of dealing. Third, every firm is a ready liquid source of capital.

- *Major corporations are currently the largest responsible parties in the production and distribution of goods and services and have the added burden of investing in and deciding how goods will be produced and distributed in the future.*

If we categorize all economic activity as coming from three sources—for-profit firms, not-for-profit firms, and government—it is clearly the case that the vast majority of economic activity occurs in the for-profit sector. A rough idea of this was presented in Table 1.1, where government activity amounts to about only 12 percent of the total economic pie. It would be possible to more closely estimate the share of total economic activity occurring in the not-for-profit sector; a more detailed breakdown is available only at greatly increased cost and effort and not in our interest at the current time.

Not only do the large profit-seeking corporations control current production; they also have almost unlimited say in future events as well. After all, the investment of firms involves their money, so they should have the final say in its disposition. In some instances, the government becomes involved in the process, attempting to represent the interests of the public at large; recall the efforts of the Clinton Administration in determining the infrastructure (in conjunction with the health and insurance industry leaders) of our national health plan.

◼ A REVIEW OF TRADITIONAL THEORIES OF THE FIRM

Given the state of economic knowledge today, there are four identifiable, separate, and established theories concerning the existence of firms.[8] The differences among the theories largely concern the unit of analysis, the availability of information, and the operational environment assumed. We now briefly discuss these theories. Please do not try to fully understand them based on this brief discussion; that is not our purpose. Rather, we offer them here as general ideas. In later chapters we will return to these theories of firm organization with fuller, more appropriate detail.

The *neoclassical theory of firm organization* is perhaps the oldest and most established view. Your prior courses in economics probably examined firm behavior from this vantage point. In its simplest form, the firm is able to produce a large variety of output(s) using different combinations of inputs. Every economic agent has **perfect information;** that is, all agents know all production and consumption plans and all prices in every market.

Furthermore, information is distributed symmetrically; that is, every party has access to the same data. The role of managers given their (and everyone else's) full information according to the neoclassical theory is simply to maximize the profits or market value of the firm by choosing the optimal production plan.

The *principal-agent theory of firm organization* introduces asymmetric information into the mix. **Asymmetric information** exists when at least one party to an agreement has better information concerning some dimension of the agreement than some other party(ies). At the heart of the firm is a series of contracts, in many of which a principal hires an agent to act on his behalf. Usually, the agent has better information regarding her own effort level and/or the true prospects for advancing the principal's interests.

---

[8]The number of "unestablished" theories of the firm is undoubtedly very large.

Within the principal-agent theories it is important to understand one very basic difference between the principal and the agent. The principal is best thought of as the "superior party" in the relationship, frequently cast as the owner of the concern. The agent is best thought of as the employee. The principal then bears the underlying risks facing the concern, and the agent is insulated from these risks by the obtained contractual obligations of the principal.[9]

What makes the principal-agent theory attractive to the study of firms is that, in many situations, the interests of the agent do not align with those of the principle.

The unit of analysis in the Neoclassical theory of the firm is exchange. In the principal-agent methodology, it is the firm in relation to itself. In the *transaction cost theory of firm organization*, the unit of analysis is the individual transaction underlying the contractual agreements between parties.

Many of the important elements of the transaction cost theory concern the availability and accuracy of information and the possibility that those involved will act selfishly. The most basic assumption in transaction cost theories is that individuals and organizations have the property of **bounded rationality,** which means that information is costly (perhaps tremendously so) to acquire. As such, agreements are made with less than full information.

From the transaction costs vantage point, it is possible that parties to an agreement will engage in **opportunistic behavior,** that is, act in their own selfish interests at the expense of others.

Exchange in such an environment gives rise to what are called **transaction costs** above and beyond contracted prices including the acquisition of costly information, the costs of monitoring performance, the costs of committing specific assets, and the costs of handling complexity in reaching agreements. The proponents of the transaction cost theory of firm organization argue that transaction costs affect the structure of agreements on which organizations are based; as such, they greatly affect the ultimate organization itself.

By now you have probably come to understand the importance of contracts to the transaction costs theory of firm organization. One of most interesting questions addressed by transaction costs analysis is whether the firm should contract to fill a particular need within the organization or contract to fill that need with a party outside of the organization. Internal contracting will be chosen over external contracting (other things being equal) if the transaction costs of so doing are relatively smaller. This issue is so central to the problems facing managers of organizations that it has come to be called the **make-or-buy decision;** that is, should a firm make an intermediate good in-house or secure the intermediate good in some competitive market?

The *evolutionary theory of the firm* is the newest and least developed of the accepted theories of firm organization. The unit of analysis under this view is clearly the firm and its productive processes.[10] It focuses on three related aspects of organizations: their structure, their strategy, and their **core competency.** A firm is said to have a core competency in a business area if it has an advantage not only in producing a good or service but also in producing new, related products.

---

[9]The principal-agent relationship is so important in modern economics that we devote an entire chapter to it, Chapter 8. For those of you with some background in this area, we now point out that the agent is risk averse toward the underlying risks of the concern. If this were not so, the optimal, or efficient, solution would be to make the agent the residual claimant in the relationship.

[10]For a more in-depth discussion, see Richard Nelson and Sidney Winter, *An Evolutionary Theory of Economic Change* (Cambridge: Belknap Press, 1982).

Firms are able to survive if they change in response to changing market demands and technologies; in short, they must find new productive and valuable outlets for their core competencies, the things they do well.

The evolutionary theory of the firm is dynamic. The purpose is to explain the movement of firms through time. Evolutionary theories stress the process by which firms enter an industry and how they learn about their costs and abilities. Firm survival, according to the evolutionary theory, depends on learning about its costs and abilities relative to other producers.

▮ A BRIEF HISTORY OF FIRMS: U.S. CAPITALISM

To consider the evolution of economic organizations in the United States, it is best to start in the period immediately after the signing of the Constitution of the United States. At that point in time, commerce in the United States had shaken off some of the British influence and also had, for the first time, a stable system of government in which to operate. Moving forward from that time, we will consider major technological advances, changes in the operating environment, and managerial developments as they influenced the structures of the huge corporations that we see today.[11]

In the 1790s, business in the "New America" consisted of a large number of very, very small units. In most instances, that unit was the family. Agriculture was important, and a large percentage of individuals lived in rural areas. The cities were populated with tiny shops (often doubling as homes) selling a variety of goods: textiles, shoes, and even a limited supply of manufactured wares. As an exception, in the southern United States, rice, tobacco, and cotton plantations had developed beyond the family level and employed indentured servants and slaves.

As the heartland of the United States became more heavily populated in the early 1800s, new forms of specialized enterprises sprung up to facilitate trade and transportation from the farms in the interior of the young nation to the domestic and international markets accessible from the larger cities on the eastern and southern coasts.

The growth in industry continued along these lines into the first decades in the 19th century as large enterprises emerged that specialized in finance, transportation, marketing, and distribution. Because of the large sums of capital required, the privately owned of these enterprises were typically organized as corporations, or "joint stock companies" in the vernacular of the day. Also early in the 1800s, a transportation infrastructure began linking points inside and outside of the United States.

Some of the first multiunit firms emerged in the United States between 1810 and 1820. Chandler[12] cites the success of the Boston Manufacturing Company in producing cloth by harnessing the power generated by a nearby passing river. This mill was the largest in the United States at that time and was the first textile operation to integrate the weaving and spinning functions of cloth production at a single location.

A number of new ways of doing business were introduced by the creation of these large mills. These large mills created a new class of entrepreneur, the owner of large mass-producing facilities. More important for our purposes, it created a class of owners and another of managers. Managers were concerned with expand-

---

[11]Much of the material in this section is summarized from the undisputed authority in this area, Alfred D. Chandler, *The Visible Hand: The Managerial Revolution in American Business* (Cambridge: Harvard University Press, 1977).

[12]See *The Visible Hand*, p. 58.

ing output and monitoring the performance of the workers. Second, in a concept that was new at the time, workers relied on a single, full-time job for their wages; in the past, many worked primarily in small, family operations in addition to part-time in agriculture or another small concern.

In addition to the textile industry, at about the same time, the roots of modern corporate enterprise could be found in the gun-making industry. Quite interestingly, only after the integration of production of all parts of the gun within a single establishment was accomplished did these producers specialize into each part of the gun: the lock, stock, and barrel.

1850–1890: The Railroading Industry

According to Chandler, the first modern business enterprises were the railroads, which grew to link the far-flung corners of a young United States. The ability to ship large volumes of product great distances at a reasonable cost would be an important cornerstone in the development of the United States and its industries. These particular firms emerged for both technological and organizational reasons.

The new railroads were quite different from the already established firms that managed the canals, turnpikes, and smaller railroads. These new companies not only owned the right of ways but also operated the common carriers that used them. According to the safety and efficiency dimensions, these new organizations required detailed managerial structures that could coordinate and monitor the geographically dispersed components of the company. Quoting Chandler,

> The railroads were, then, the first modern business enterprises. They were the first to require a large number of salaried managers; the first to have a central office operated by middle managers and commanded by top managers who reported to a board of directors. They were the first American business enterprise to build a large internal organizational structure with carefully defined lines of responsibility, authority, and communication between the central office, departmental headquarters, and field units; and they were the first to develop financial and statistical flows to control and evaluate the work of the many managers.[13]

The developments of the 1850s and 1860s became the standards of the 1870s and 1880s. In the latter, the great railroad companies learned, and provided a model for, corporate cooperation and competition for U.S. business. The individual companies were arguably efficient with their new management practices and technologies; but when considered as a system, the arrangement had many drawbacks. Railroads had different gauges of track and small gaps between two shipping points. The industry learned how to cooperate and when to compete in order to eliminate the snags in the system.[14] Cooperation was necessary to operate a true transportation system spanning the entire country; cooperation was also necessary to control severe price competition. Ultimately, the first type of cooperation was established, but the second never was. Alliances of individual carriers and system building through mergers and acquisitions became the norm.

Distribution: A New Function

The development of the railroad as a means of reliable and economical transportation significantly impacted the distribution systems for goods in the U.S. economy. Also playing critical roles were emerging infrastructures in urban areas, turnpikes, and the telegraph and postal services. The first large distribution firms were more along the lines of wholesalers. This development was facilitated by the establishment of recognized exchanges: the Chicago Board of Trade (1848), the

---

[13]*The Visible Hand*, p. 120.

[14]In 1849 freight moving from Philadelphia to Chicago waited nine weeks for delivery, having to pass through nine transshipments. In 1860, the trip was shortened to three days and no transshipments.

Merchants Exchange of St. Louis (1854), and the New York Produce Exchange (1850). The shipping and communications links greatly facilitated transactions and promoted efficiency in these markets. Large wholesalers emerged to handle the distribution of manufactured goods. Using the railroad and telegraph, a single wholesale jobber could cover an extensive geographic area and keep a much smaller inventory than in the prerailroad days.

In 1880, the mass retailers emerged and began to erode the position of the wholesalers in the distribution chain. Macy's was the first of the large retailers to grow from a small retail establishment rather than as a unit of a large wholesaling enterprise. New York City was the first center in the world to support a collection of truly massive department stores, undoubtedly because it stood at the center of a large urban population and it served as a major transportation center at that time. As the retailing industry spread across the United States with its emphasis on serving the public directly, it gave rise to a new industry: the advertising agency.

By the mid- to late 19th century, an infrastructure for distribution was firmly in place. Organizational and technical developments had made their mark on those entities performing the distribution function in our economic system. The next step in the industrial development of the United States was the spread of the large multiunit business enterprise across many different industries. The manufacturing industries were a little slower than the distribution industries because of the need to overcome technical obstacles before large quantities of output could reasonably be produced.

Historians have characterized the last decades of the 19th century as the Second Industrial Revolution. Its hallmark was the emergence of mass production techniques. The mass production system required four major conditions to attain its potential of providing economic growth: (1) stability and control of the production process within the firm; (2) stability among rivals within the market, ensuring price and quantity control; (3) stabilization of aggregate demand; and (4) reliability and dependability of all inputs, including labor. The invention of scientific management and the corporate hierarchy provided the first condition, government regulatory agencies provided the second and third, and labor unions and a mixture of market accessibility and in-house production provided the fourth.

Mass Production, Scale, and Scope

To economists the key organizational point is that mass production required both a reliable input and a reliable output market. The railroads, steamships, canals, and telegraph contributed to the establishment of each. Business enterprises also often purchased their suppliers if there were problems in coordinating and managing market transactions. **Vertical integration** occurs when one business enterprise gains control over more than one stage in the production and sale of goods and services. In short, firms could secure reliable deliveries of large quantities of inputs and have ready access to large output markets.

The principal benefits of mass production are that the business enterprises are able to enjoy both economies of scale and economies of scope. **Economies of scale** represent the reduction in average unit cost as output expands. **Economies of scope** represent a cost advantage from producing related, yet different goods.

The dominance of these features is made clear by Chandler:

> These potential cost advantages, however, could not be fully realized unless a constant flow of materials through the plant or factory was maintained to assure effective capacity utilization. If the realized volume of flow fell below capacity, then actual costs per unit rose rapidly. They did so because fixed costs remained much higher and "sunk costs" (the original capital investment) were also much higher than in the more labor-intensive industries. . . .

THE STANDARD OIL TRUST: MASS PRODUCTION AT ITS FINEST

In 1882, John D Rockefeller formed the Standard Oil Trust, whose ultimate successor, Exxon, remains the largest oil company in the world today. This alliance was a federation of 40 separate companies, each related to Standard Oil Company.

The trust was probably not an attempt to monopolize the U.S. market for kerosene; the firms in the alliance already accounted for 90 percent of the U.S. kerosene output. Rather, the trust provided the essential legal means that could coordinate the flow of inputs and outputs needed by a mass-producing firm to fully benefit from potential economies of scale. As a result, approximately 25 percent of the world's kerosene productive capacity was put into three refineries, each with a capacity of 6,500 barrels per day. In 1885, the average cost of kerosene in the typical refining plants (daily capacity of 2,000 barrels) was 1.5 cents. The cost of refining kerosene at the trust's facilities was about 0.452 cents. This cost advantage arising out of economies of scale permitted the Standard Oil Trust to have a substantial advantage over smaller-scale producers.

Such coordination did not, and indeed could not, happen automatically. It demanded the constant attention of a managerial team or hierarchy. The potential economies of scale and scope, as measured by rated capacity, are the physical characteristics of the production facilities. The actual economies of scale or of scope, as determined by throughput, are organizational. Such economies depend on knowledge, skill, experience, and teamwork—on the organized human capabilities essential to exploit the potential of technological processes.[15]

The role of managers in this new paradigm was to facilitate the production, distribution, and sale of output. Scientific management, or **Taylorism,** came to be the way in which the human component of these massive firms was organized. The algorithm of mass production was enunciated by Henry Ford: "The net result of the application of these principles is the reduction of the necessity of thought on the part of the worker and the reduction of his movements to a minimum."[16] The underlying rules for management under Taylorism were (1) the specialization of each job through the simplification of individual tasks, (2) predetermined rules devised by management to coordinate the separate tasks, and (3) evaluation of individual performance by management through a detailed monitoring system. Thus was born the boring monotony of the assembly line.

The pattern of large firms dominating the economic landscape in the early 1900s greatly affected the pattern of U.S. industry for many, many years. Many of the large corporate entities with which you are familiar today began at that time. In our abbreviated timeline of the development of the U.S. industrial enterprise, we now take a discrete jump to the early 1970s. This is not to say that important

---

[15]Afred D. Chandler, *Scale and Scope: The Dynamics of Industrial Capitalism* (Cambridge: The Bellknap Press of Harvard University Press, 1990), p. 24.

[16]William J. Abernath, Kim B. Clark, and Alan M. Katrow, *Industrial Renaissance* (New York: Basic Books, 1983), p. 71.

developments did not occur in the first 70 years of this century; they did. However, most of these developments involved further exploitations of the trends already discussed as the mass-producing oligopolistic firms strengthened their positions in the extremely stable environment of that time period.

The great mass-producing firms born during the Second Industrial Revolution clearly dominated the global economy. However, these organizations do not survive in the same form today. They found themselves in a hostile environment buffeted by forces of change both internal and external.

The corporate form adopted by the mass-producing firms followed two principles: functionalization of work into specialized units of activities and the creation of a rigid, hierarchical management to coordinate the activities of the numerous and varied units. Successful firms grew in size by diversifying into new businesses and vertically integrating into their supply sources or means of distribution. With each increase in size and function, additional layers of management were required to coordinate the many different actions of the individual units. As a result, coordination within the firm became a cumbersome process working through a bureaucratic structure in which information transfer became problematic.

On the one hand, management became "out of touch" with itself. On the other hand, management also lost contact with the owners of the firms. In the context of economics, we would say that the separation of ownership and control became more complete. It became nearly impossible for the ownership interests (the stockholders) to monitor and evaluate the performance of management. Furthermore, in many cases, ownership interests could not participate in the strategic, or long-term, planning of the firms they technically owned.

History provides us with the ability to look back and examine the structures of the mass-producing firms. What we see is the emergence of severe problems primarily attributed to the very nature of these organizations—their size. The internal problems facing these firms were, in part, their cumbersome, bureaucratic nature, and, in part, the further separation of ownership from control. The threats to these firms were not only internal. Very severe external problems emerged, and we now turn our attention to them.

Five major categories of external causes interacted to undermine the mass production system and ultimately induced its collapse: (1) shocks in input price and availability, (2) the simultaneous development of foreign competition and evolution of U.S. industries toward the mature and declining stages of the product life cycle, (3) a destandardization of consumer preferences, (4) technological change reducing the minimum efficient scale (MES) in many industries, and (5) the endogenous instability in a system of regulated oligopoly. Ironically, the same political and social forces that were conducive to the success of mass production were also the cause for its breakdown. Those same rigidities that provided stability during the previous 50 years became the catalyst for the crisis facing firms in the 1960s and 1970s.

In 1973 the Organization of Petroleum Exporting Countries (OPEC) raised crude oil prices by about 400 percent. Protein prices also rose rapidly as agricultural markets adjusted to a severe anchovy shortage, affecting the cost of fertilizer. These were major shocks of the period; there were others. As oil prices rose, consumers shifted to natural gas, but the federal regulatory system prevented adjustment in production and distribution to meet the new demand. Great anxiety resulted throughout the economy and translated into higher wage demands.

Foreign competitors emerged as well, at an extremely bad time for U.S. firms that had come to rely on oligopolistic industries populated by a few mass-producing firms. U.S. manufacturing industries were well along and fairly set in

The Breakdown
of the Mass Production
System

their ways, producing goods in the mature and declining stages of the product life cycle. Furthermore, U.S. firms had enjoyed protection from nondomestic producers because of both their geographic isolation and government regulation.

Decades earlier, U.S. firms had been the undisputed leaders in production. Back when product concepts were new, managers would experiment with design in short production runs, responding with changes after gauging consumer demand. As products became well defined and standardized, production evolved from the growth to the mature and declining stages of the product life cycle. In these later stages, technological change slowed and a reliance on very large runs of production with little product differentiation or development was typical. In light of the emergence of Japanese and German competitors, U.S. products were often at a disadvantage.

Perhaps spurred on by the offerings of the foreign firms, consumer tastes shifted to favor both product diversity and customization.[17] To the extent that consumer tastes are destandardized, mass production enterprises no longer maintain a market advantage. When consumers preferred a standardized product at the lowest possible price, large-scale firms prospered and mass production was profitable. In the new economy of the 1960s and 1970s, it was not.

A fourth factor destablizing the mass production system was a general technological shift, reducing the size and, hence, capital requirements for entry into many manufacturing industries. Automation and computerization were no longer the friends of large, static corporations.

Some large U.S. firms responded. The immediate response of the entrenched corporations was an effort to reassert control and stability over the economic environment. These efforts took three forms: multinationalization, conglomeration, and increased protection from more efficient foreign producers via calls for tariffs and quotas. Other firms, some new, some old, undertook fundamental organizational changes. These enterprises came to be highly competitive and sometimes rose from the ashes of their predecessors.

**1980s Merger Mania
and Flexible Production**

Two big forces operated in the U.S. business environment in the decade of the 1980s. The first was the rapid growth in activity in the market for the control of corporations. Economists now view the rash of mergers and acquisitions in the United States during the 1980s as an attempt to close the widening gap separating ownership and control interests. The second was a sizable shift in the productive activities of U.S. corporations to production processes that could be tailored to many different variations of a base product.

Figures 1.1 and 1.2 provide measures of the growth in mergers and acquisitions in the United States through the 1980s. Figure 1.1 shows the number of mergers and acquisitions roughly doubling over the period 1981 to 1988. Figure 1.2 shows the dollar value of mergers involving U.S. corporations in each year from 1980 to 1990. This alternative measure shows an even greater increase in merger activity. The dollar amounts involved showed a marked increase rising by about a factor of 5 between 1983 and 1988.

A number of managerial issues surrounded these changing patterns of corporate control. From an organizational standpoint, it is important to recognize that many of these mergers featured deconglomeration; that is, many of the large conglomerates created in the 1960s were effectively undone. Many of the mergers and acquisitions in the 1980s were followed by bust ups or spin-offs, where divi-

---

[17]An interesting documentation of this trend is found in Michael J. Piore and Charles F. Sabel, *The Second Industrial Divide* (New York: Basic Books, 1984), p. 189; and Alvin Toffler, *The Adaptive Corporation* (New York: Bantam Books, 1985), p. 37.

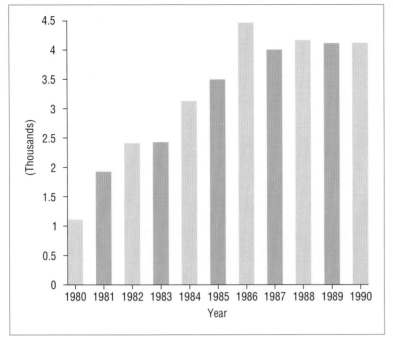

Figure 1.1 Mergers and Acquisitions by Year

sions were either set up as fairly independent companies or sold to other corporations. In a large number of the bust ups, the businesses were acquired by firms engaged in similar business interests.[18]

The threat of takeover is also seen as a discipline device for CEOs and their management teams. Conceivably, a CEO and the management team could be pursuing their own interests at the expense of the corporation for which they work. Say, for example, that they pay themselves huge salaries and lavish themselves with large perks; their corporation therefore could be seen as inefficient and then threatened by a hostile takeover.

The final managerial issue surrounding the waves of takeovers was the rise of debt on corporate balance sheets. A corporation's purchase was often financed by issuing **junk bonds,** bonds with a very high risk of default. Thus, the players in the merger game didn't even need to use their own money; usually this debt was secured against the value of the acquired corporation.

The effect of all of this financing activity on ownership patterns was clear by the end of the decade. Over the period 1980 to 1989, the ratio of stockholders' equity to total assets on the balance sheets of U.S. manufacturing firms fell from 49.6 to 40.5 percent.[19]

The same factors precipitating the breakdown of the mass production system also, in a strange way, formed the incentives for the type of enterprise that would replace them. **Flexible manufacturing systems** were developed that could pro-

---

[18]See Sanjai Bhagat, Andrei Shleifer, and Robert W. Vishny, "Hostile Takeovers in the 1980s: The Return to Corporate Specialization," *Brookings Papers: Microeconomics 1990* 1 (Washington: Brookings Institution, 1990).

[19]See the quote by Henry Kaufman, executive of Salomon Brothers, Inc., in J. Fred Weston, Kwang S. Chung, and Susan E. Hoag, *Mergers, Restructuring, and Corporate Control* (Englewood Cliffs, N.J.: Prentice Hall, 1990), p. 123.

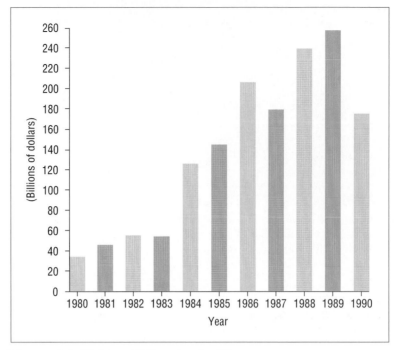

Figure 1.2 Value of Mergers by Year

duce a wide variety of products. Robert Reich provides the best description of firms adopting the new technology, saying that they are "based not on huge volume and standardization, but on producing relatively smaller batches of more specialized, higher-valued product-goods that are precision-engineered, that are custom tailored to serve individual markets, or that embody rapidly evolving technologies."[20] The flexible producer thrives on continuous process and product innovation, the extensive use of computer-based technology, and the software to make the technology function smoothly.

Flexible production required new management practices, which were a marked departure from the remains of Taylorism in the huge mass production firms. This happened because the flexible production firm is organized horizontally with considerable synthesis and overlap among units. By way of contrast, the mass production firm is vertically integrated in a rigid hierarchy. Under flexible production, labor is given much wider ranges of responsibility. Workers are more fluid, doing as required by the changing production process.

The managerial style in flexible production also differs in its relationship to suppliers. Suppliers are useful to mass production firms only to the extent that they provide standardized inputs at minimum cost, but their role takes on a new importance with flexible production. Because of the premium placed on innovation, new development of parts and consultation between supplier and customer (producer) is essential. The Japanese automobile producers were seen as leaders in this regard, having done this years before their U.S. counterparts.

The adoption of flexible manufacturing strategies by a large segment of the manufacturers in any particular industry would have a profound effect on the conduct of business and change forever the relationships between firms and the importance of firms in the market. As we will argue in Part Five, there are four major effects of the evolution of flexible production on market structure.

---

[20]See Robert Reich, *The Next American Frontier* (New York, NY: Times Books, 1983).

SOFT, FLEXIBLE MANUFACTURING

In the mid 1990s the new American factories stand as testimony to flexibility, silicon chips, and advanced software. At a massive IBM plant in Charlotte, North Carolina a visitor would find an assembly line quite unlike any envisioned by Henry Ford or the highly automated Japanese factories. The team on this line will, during the course of a few hours, produce 27 different products, each with a variety of options.

Each team member receives "kits" of parts grouped together by others at the factory for assembly. In front of each worker is a computer screen tied into the factory's network displaying a checklist of parts or help on how to assemble the product to meet the customer's specifications. The factory network meshes customer orders with available inventory and plans activities. At some firms, customers are permitted direct access to the network. At others, firms are electronically linked with suppliers permitting "seamless" exchange of data.

In these advanced manufacturing systems, sometimes called digital factories, automation is not complete. Some tasks, such as final assembly are better done by the hands of an adaptable person whose dexterity and flexibility are not the result of programming code.

Source: "The Digital Factory," Fortune, *November 14, 1994, pp. 92–110. © 1994*

Increased **decentralization,** or a reduction in the importance of a command and control hierarchy and the emergence of more independent business units, was the first major effect on corporations. Industries became more competitive due to decreased **concentration,** a term used by economists referring to the importance of large producers in a market. Partially as a result of the first two effects, organizations became less vertically integrated. And finally, there was a move away from becoming conglomerates.

The decade of the 1990s is a turbulent time for U.S. corporations. During this decade, three fundamental changes in the general business environment occurred that affected nearly all firms, large and small.

1. For starters, the very concept of being a "U.S. corporation" is eroding away. NAFTA, GATT, and the European Common Market have altered the complex web of buyers and sellers in many nations.
2. On the more micro level, all firms have access to technologies that were the basis of science fiction novels even 10 years ago. The computing power that cost $50,000 in 1986 is available for less than $3,000 today and can be used in applications not even invented in 1986.
3. The issues surrounding the concept of "corporate control" raised in the 1980s serve as lessons for the 1990s. A corporation's owners (stockholders) have come to understand their rights to enforce efficiency in the corporations that they own.

These three fundamental changes altered the ways in which corporations chose to organize economic activity. The decade of the 1990s is one of corporate reorganizations and downsizings. Another feature is the emergence of firm cooperation in many in forms of joint ventures. The technological advances of the lat-

1990s Reorganizations, Joint Ventures, and the Role of Small Firms

ter part of the 20th century have had quite the opposite effect of those earlier this century: they have made smaller firms viable competitors.

Before turning to these fundamental changes in the organization of economic activity by firms in the 1990s, we consider three themes that seem to be evident in the changes.

The first theme is an increased emphasis on customer relations. "Give them what they want, where and when they want it, and at a very good price" is a dictum regularly appearing in corporate manifests.

The second theme is a return by corporations to what they do best. This may involve becoming more narrowly focused with their product offerings and breaking with the concept of vertical integration, letting other companies compete for component delivery. In other words, corporate strategies are shying away from being masters of everything. The resulting networks of firms are a marked departure from the functional hierarchy days of the mass producer.

The third theme gaining momentum in the 1990s is the creation of new specialized management service industries as replacements for current staff functions. Departments such as accounting, human resources, and legal services are being downsized or modified so that the organizations may secure these services in fairly competitive markets.

Many U.S. corporations have been forced to reorganize in the 1990s. Basically, the business environment that they had grown used to changed, and change was in order. The recession in the early 1990s may have served to speed this process as owners and managers became more willing to recognize the need for change after several unprofitable years.

Often these reorganizations were supposedly along the lines of **total quality management** (TQM) or **business reengineering,** a phrase that embraces such techniques as work teams, training employees in multiple skills so that they can do more than one job, and some form of worker empowerment, or pushing decision-making authority as far down the organizational structure as possible. Usually these reorganizations involved substantial job loss.

The term *reengineering* was coined by Michael Hammer, a popular management consultant, in 1990. In one sense, business reengineering may be an attempt by firms to reap the massive benefits from earlier investments in information technology. These benefits arise due to increased productivity. Quite often, reengineering implies substantial job loss. This type of trend is not exactly new; for example, U.S. manufacturers employ roughly the same number of employees today as they did in 1946 to produce nearly five times as many goods. What is new is the type of workers being cut from firms. Such white-collar job loss lacks historical precedent. An increased reliance on outside suppliers also contributes to job loss. Reengineering has taught a new lesson: greater productivity from existing employees means the need for fewer employees.

In many instances, after corporations go through a reorganization by way of reengineering, they often eliminate whole divisions and rely more and more on outside suppliers for component production. Once again, we see a further blurring of the boundaries separating markets and firms.

The popular business literature is filled with examples of corporations, large and small, that have experienced massive success after being reengineered. For an account of one of the more widely mentioned examples, see the box "Redoing Hewlett-Packard."

The benefits of reorganization and business reengineering are clear. Economywide productivity, in terms of output per worker, is undoubtedly increased, as is profitability and return on assets for the involved firms. There are obvious questions however. First, what are the macroeconomic effects of the unemploy-

In 1991, Hewlett-Packard, the computer electronics firm, was facing very tough times. The company's PCs were partly incompatible with the IBM industry standard and cost one-third more. Its printers were widely recognized as high quality but were a bit pricy, excluding the lower ends of the market.

The solution for Hewlett-Packard was to reorganize. Its PC division now caters to different market segments by assigning a single empowered team to each segment. It has closed 10 of 12 plants and reduced manufacturing time to a fraction of what it once was.

The company intends to continuously reevaluate its core competencies and to direct its energies in directions parallel to these competencies. Toward this end, Hewlett-Packard will contract out operations that it does not judge to be able to compete with the world's best. It also has entered the electronic notebook market with a variety of product offerings geared to different market segments. Further, the company is moving into the market for "multimedia" products, hardware and software that allows interactive television and communications between cable broadcast systems and personal computers. Each of these products, in theory, represents applications of its electronics expertise in new areas.

Source: "The Metamorphosis of Hewlett-Packard," The Economist, June 19, 1993, pp. 67–69. © 1993 The Economist Newspaper Group, Inc. Reprinted with permission. Further reproduction prohibited.

ment? If corporations keep the most productive and able workers to make the best use of corporate assets, then the displaced will be those least likely to be hired.

Perhaps more fundamentally, reengineering changes the implicit contracts organizations have with their employees and greatly alters corporate cultures that had existed for decades. Although many Japanese firms have become famous for their policy of "lifetime employment,"[21] job security is one of the main reasons people choose to work for big European and U.S. firms. *Liberation Management*, a best-selling book by Tom Peters, envisions a business world in which all corporations have been reengineered. Under this scenario, big firms are effectively nothing more than vast horizontal networks with "empowered" teams of workers who are judged on their performance. Interestingly enough, Peters and other well-known writers such as Michael Hammer have simply assumed that employees will more than welcome these changes. It is difficult to determine just how enthusiastic a worker will be after his or her corporation announces a massive layoff and declares that no one's job is safe.

Also harmed by reengineering in organizations are the so-called "middle managers" who would be eliminated by the reorganization. Within large, diverse organizations, inertia has historically played a large role in firm development and evolution. Quite rationally, these middle managers would begin politicking in an attempt to secure their own futures. We would expect then that two groups in the organization would oppose reengineering: regular workers, who would probably not have a large say in decisions, and middle managers, who may have some say in organizational decisions.

---

[21]In reality, the lifetime employment contracts popularized by the popular business press covered only about one-half of the workforce as of 1992. Furthermore, most employers are seriously rethinking this policy.

Another, more troubling aspect of reengineering is also expected to develop: the very relationship between the units of a multiunit business. Most of the reorganizations of the early 1990s stressed the creation of fairly autonomous divisions. There were strengths here as well to the more vertically integrated hierarchies of earlier years. One profitable division could effectively subsidize a second division needing cash in its early going.

With changing technologies and the opening of a more global economy, most markets are becoming much more risky. A common response to this risk is the emergence of organizations that permit the "pooling" or sharing of this risk. A certain camaraderie is emerging among firms; even historical rivals are seeing the benefits of cooperation.

In some instances, joint ventures and strategic alliances are created as firms seek to enter new industries. Technologies are now emerging that will create whole industries in the years ahead. The corporate form that will organize production, distribution, and marketing in these new industries is emerging as well. In the past, large firms were created via acquisition and internal investment; in these emerging markets, it appears that the major players will be consortiums of firms, each investing in the project so as to bid for entry into the market while avoiding some of the involved risks. The consortiums are usually made up of similar firms, sometimes even competitors. There is a definite pattern of teamwork and mutual trust that was absent in the corporate world of the past.

One example of a number of players participating in a joint venture into a new market is General Magic, Inc., an organization producing handheld communicators and electronic notebooks. It started as a venture by Apple Computer, Inc. The early versions of this product were called Newton. In 1993, General Magic was joined by American Telephone and Telegraph Co., Sony Corp., Motorola, Inc., Phillips Electronics NV, and Matsushita Electric Industrial Co. As an incentive, each member of the alliance would have access to the underlying software (Telescript and Magic Cap) that would likely become the industry standard in a market projected to be worth $3.5 trillion by the year 2000.

One pledge made by General Magic in securing the participation of these industrial giants (some of which compete in other markets) was to keep this technology open to anyone who wants to adopt it. This pledge was somewhat compromised when AT&T obtained exclusive rights to General Magic software over its direct competitors. However, all in all, the credibility of the General Magic pledge was sufficient to acquire many investors.

Competitors emerged quickly. As of 1993, the most promising competitor was EO, another California firm, that shares two principal investors with General Magic: AT&T and Matsushita. Interestingly, by 1994, EO had ceased to exist and was replaced by other alliances and joint ventures. This pattern of strategic alliances forming to access new and growing markets is historically unique in U.S. business. Its hallmark seems to be an atmosphere based on firms exploiting their core competencies and on trust and cooperation. For another example of strategic alliance building to serve a market that did not yet exist at the time of its formation, see the box "High-Density Television: The Grand Alliance." The limiting case of the trend by business toward strategic alliances is an organization pattern referred to as a virtual corporation. A **virtual corporation** is a temporary network of companies that come together quickly to exploit changing market conditions and then, possibly, disband.

A somewhat different rationale for cooperation is emerging as well as cooperation among independent companies is being substituted for a single corporate form. A *value-adding partnership* (VAP) is an important and ongoing form of organizing economic activity. The VAP form is a collection of independent companies

In the early 1990s, a high-stakes race was taking place to establish an industry standard for the technology underlying high-density television (HDTV). The competition was international with firms in the United States, Japan, and Europe vying to become leaders in this, as of then, nonexisting marketplace.

In the early going, it seemed that the Japanese had an advantage with an analogue-based system that was operational at the time. Similar systems were proposed by European firms as well. Both the Japanese and the various European governments heavily promoted their producers' offerings. U.S. firms were concerned more with a less well-developed system based on digital signals, similar to those used in computers.

The Federal Communications Commission sponsored an impartial competition to determine the standards in the U.S. marketplace. Nearly every entrant into the competition itself was sponsored by several firms; thus, the competition was entirely between joint ventures. During the competition, more alliances were formed until only three were left.

Those three entities effectively merged into a single entity that came to be called, somewhat appropriately, the Grand Alliance after they had already agreed to jointly share future royalties from the one chosen system. The members of the Grand Alliance are mostly U.S. companies: AT&T, General Instrument, Zenith, the David Sarnoff Research Center, and the Massachusetts Institute of Technology, along with Holland's Phillips and France's Thomson.

This outcome was attributed both to a desire to avoid the costs of subsequent testing before the FCC, which would reduce future gains for the winner and losses for the losers, and to a fear that the FCC's choice might be challenged in the courts in a lengthy (and costly) legal battle.

jointly managing the flow of goods and services along the value-added chain. The relationship is in stark contrast to the historically prevalent highly vertically integrated corporations because of the many ownership interests involved. The VAP also differs markedly from a single entity hiring outside suppliers to produce the component parts of final goods provided to the consumer. Thus, it represents a true horizontal network of producers involved in production.

Smaller is better. Over the period 1987 to 1992, there was robust growth in small firms in general and small manufacturers in particular. Over that period the 500 largest U.S. companies reduced their number of workers by 1.3 million; meanwhile, there was a tremendous increase in activity in small firms. Whereas the largest firms became smaller over that five-year period, the number of manufacturers with fewer than 100 employees operating in the U.S. economy increased by 483,000 firms. The growth among small manufacturing firms is remarkable in that it represents a net increase at small manufacturing firms of 13.4 percent. As a basis of comparison, growth in the much heralded service sector was slightly over 11 percent.[22]

---

[22]Michael Selz, "Small Manufacturers Display the Nimbleness the Times Require," *The Wall Street Journal*, December 29, 1993, p. A1.

THE VIRTUAL CORPORATION

The increased popularity and success of the current joint ventures and strategic alliances may continuously evolve into its next logical step. In a *virtual corporation*, "companies can share costs, skills, and access to global markets, with each partner contributing what its best at."

Each member of these consortiums will focus its efforts, as part of a group, along the lines of its core competencies. The upside potential of this increased specialization is the formation of a team whose parts are the world's best. Recall that one of the primary functions of a firm is to organize economic activity. The virtual corporation represents an application of Adam Smith's argument centuries ago in favor of specialization in production.

Technological advances in communications could foster the formation of these alliances, as partners in different sections on different continents would have ready, reliable, and relatively cheap access to each other. The potential for self-serving behavior by partners is limited since these alliances are not expected to endure.

Source: For a fuller discussion of the virtual corporation concept, see "The Virtual Corporation," Business Week, *February 8, 1993, pp. 98–102.*

Small firms are more nimble and better able to target products to defined market niches. In larger organizations, new ideas may require the development of a business plan, a budget, an impact analysis, and the approval of many layers of management. In smaller firms, decision making is easier.

In some industries, however, size is still important. Two economists can easily decide to open a firm and print a textbook; they do not have the resources, however, to build multibillion dollar oil refineries or paper production mills. See the box concerning the (still) importance of size.

VALUE-ADDING PARTNERSHIPS

A value-adding partnership, or VAP, is a relatively new application of organizational logic arising in the 1990s in response to changing technologies and markets. A VAP is a group of independent companies participating in the production, marketing, and distribution of goods and services. In a highly vertically integrated firm, divisions or units of a single corporation would manage and perform the functions performed by separate firms in a VAP.

McKesson Corporation, once a wholesale distributor of drugs and healthcare products, is an important example of a VAP in the United States. In positioning itself for competition with large drugstore chains, McKesson has forged closer ties with its customers, independent drugstores, and created partnerships with its suppliers, the insurance companies that process medical claims, and consumers.

Other important examples of VAPs include the U.S. construction industry and the supply *keiretsu* of Toyota, the Japanese auto producer.

Despite the success of small firms in the U.S. economy in the 1990s, there are still industries in which size is a necessity for survival. In each of these industries, large fixed capital investments are clearly required.

Classic Production. Industries: commodity chemicals, paper, oil refining, and concrete. Mass production setting is still important for these standardized commodities. Companies: Dow Chemical, Texaco, Boise Cascade.

Marketing-Distribution Intensive. Industries: beverages, athletic footwear, consumer goods. Brand name and consumer familiarity and loyalty are made important by the existing producers' marketing budgets and distribution networks. Companies: Coca-Cola, Anheuser-Busch, Nike, Procter & Gamble.

Volume Buyers. Industries: automobile manufacturing, food processing, and retailing. Block buying is transferred to lower per unit costs, a distinct advantage to retail outfits and firms buying components for finished products. Companies: Toyota, Kraft, General Foods, Wal-Mart, Toys 'R' Us.

Technology-Intensive Businesses. Industries: semiconductors, pharmaceuticals. Big corporations may have more funds for research and development when product lives may be short. Companies: Intel, Merck, Motorola.

Source: Adapted from James B. Treece, "Sometimes You Still Gotta Have Size," Business Week, *Enterprise 1993, p. 200.*

■ OUR PATHWAY TO AN UNDERSTANDING OF MANAGING ECONOMIC ORGANIZATIONS

What we want to teach you in our book is new, exciting, and, most important, useful in your real life: those years after you graduate from business school. On the down side, we must in fairness point out that much of the material is abstract and only recently fully developed by economists. Further, our approach is different from what has come, as of 1995, to be "accepted" for the economics component of your business education.

Economics is, after all, the science dedicated to exchange. All economic activity results from transactions between multiple parties. Ultimately, such exchanges build on themselves to create things such as partnerships, joint ventures, firms, and virtual corporations. The tools developed in this textbook enable you to understand the way in which transactions are carried out across and within firms. The culmination of this study is valuable insight into the development of corporate strategy, which we argue must reflect both the internal and external environments of organizations.

Several interrelated themes permeate all of the individual chapters in this book. At this point, we can only describe these themes to you; their importance will be demonstrated in latter chapters.

Theme 1: Exchange. Economic activity is really about exchange; this is what economists do. We focus on the conditions surrounding exchange more than on the exchange itself. Many exchanges, or transactions, occur in markets and are well understood. Many take place outside the protective realm of markets. It is our purpose to understand the course of events in these instances as well.

Theme 2: Organization. Firms exist to organize economic activity. We must keep in mind that, to a certain extent, organizations replace markets. What a firm really is, is a series of contracts linking together various parties. The circumstances surrounding these contracts may be termed the *environment of the firm*. Over time this environment changes, which implies that organizations will change as well.

Theme 3: Information Availability. Uncertainty and imperfect information exist in all contracts. No transaction is made under conditions of complete cer-

---

TWO VIEWS OF THE "NEW WAY" OF DOING ECONOMICS

"Unlike most other people, businessmen love not only to give advice, but to take it too. Management gurus proliferate. Consultants earn fat fees. A flood of books on management pour off printing presses every year. And yet the one group of people to whom most businessmen rarely turn are economists. Big firms ask economists to predict the ups and downs of national economies, but when it comes to finding ways to run their own company better, many managers would sooner consult an astrologer.

"In the past this was understandable. Most economists assumed all firms responded in much the same way to incentives and obstacles. To any practising manager it is not the similarities between firms that matter, but the differences—specifically those that explain why some firms succeed and others fail, even though all are seeking to survive and prosper.

"Nevertheless, the gulf between economists and managers should be closing . . ."

Source: "Quacks and Coaches," The Economist, April 17, 1993, p. 65. © 1993 The Economist Newspaper Group, Inc. Reprinted with permission. Further reproduction prohibited.

"What defines business-oriented economics is its focus on what economists call 'the firm'—and the rest of us call 'the company'—as the unit of analysis. Traditional microeconomics, by contrast, is concerned with markets and prices. It looks at the economy or at an industry, but rarely peeks inside the individual enterprise. Indeed anyone who wandered into the usual course in microeconomics would discover only that the firm sells everything it produces at a market price that it does not control. Says Yale economist Bengt Holmstrom: 'There was nothing there for a manager to learn.'

"A series of conceptual breakthroughs in microeconomics and game theory over the past dozen years has set the stage for today's work . . .

"The new ideas tend to be commensensical notions with forbidding-sounding names like 'bounded rationality,' 'asymmetric information,' and 'incomplete contracts.' "

Source: "A New Tool to Help Managers," Fortune, May 30, 1994, p. 136. © 1994 Time Inc. All rights reserved.

tainty; nobody can predict the future. It is difficult for us to monitor the behavior of our contracting partners, and it is always wise for us to have a clear understanding of all commitments made to a given deal. Trust becomes a valued commodity.

Theme 4: Opportunistic Behavior. In framing and carrying out agreements governing exchange, rational parties may engage in self-serving behavior—possibly at the expense of other involved parties. Contracting, because it is the building block of organizations, must address this through the establishment of trust, incentives, and provisions for monitoring. As a guiding principle, efficiency dictates that agreements will be crafted keeping these things in mind.

This chapter introduced the subject and provided a useful starting point for our explorations.

Part I, "The Efficiency of Markets," is the most comfortable part of this text because it is concerned with traditional, neoclassical economic analysis and some of the problems of applying the teachings of this school of thought in the real world. Large parts of Chapters 2, "Competitive Exchange," and 3, "The Neoclassical Theory of the Firm," are probably review to most students. In these chapters are the basic tools of analysis of traditional economics: the functioning of markets and the competitive profit-maximizing firm. We review price determination by supply and demand and highlight some useful managerial implications of demand analysis. What is interesting and unique in our coverage of this material is our emphasis on the underlying assumptions behind the workings of the price system. The profit-maximizing firm is then considered in light of the markets governed by supply and demand.

Chapter 4, "Efficiency, the Price System, and Organizations," is a very detailed, fairly technical treatment of general equilibrium theory. This chapter serves two useful purposes. First, it introduces and summarizes the beneficial aspects of equilibrium in competitive markets. Second, it defines, in the context of the general competitive equilibrium, the notion of efficiency. The underlying message here is, of course, that competitive markets are beneficial to society because they are efficient. The chapter develops an important linkage between market efficiency and social output. An analytical connection is developed between efficient production and an economy's production possibilities frontier. By highlighting this linkage, we are able to unmask and draw attention to some of the restrictive assumptions long held central to economists.

The fifth chapter, "Property Rights, Ownership and Efficiency," explores a rapidly growing literature in economics on property rights, that is, the effects of asset ownership on exchange. We view the approach in this chapter as a bridge between the "new" and the "old" economics. Much of this material is from the work of Nobel Laureate Ronald Coase, who showed the world that even if a market were to fail, an efficient outcome can still occur if all interested parties are able to bargain with each other.

A very different view of exchange is presented in Part II, "The Economics of Organization." We begin framing a different approach to understanding exchange, contracts, and the structure of economic organizations. The logic behind all of Part II centers on transaction costs that represent "frictions" preventing the smooth functioning of exchange. In some markets, transaction costs do not inhibit the functioning of the powerful forces of supply and demand. The emphasis of the Coase theorem introduced in Chapter 5 is clearly that bargaining can lead to an efficient outcome if the costs of doing so are relatively small. The material in Part II is applicable to the huge number of exchanges lacking coverage by either competitive analysis or Coasian bargaining.

Chapter 6, "Organizational Tools," addresses transaction costs and their impact on exchange. We explore the various dimensions of transaction costs in order to provide a useful terminology for later application of these ideas. Students are made aware of two major ways in which transaction costs can arise. Firms in the economy operate with less than perfect information about the exchanges in which they engage. Also, firms have ample reason to hesitate to make a deal from which the other parties can walk away but they cannot.

From a managerial vantage point, this chapter considers what has come to be called the "make or buy" decision in organizations (i.e., should the organization purchase or produce components of its final product?).

Chapter 7, "Contracts: Motivation Through Agreement," is all about the "sticky stuff" that holds organizations together, contracts. It is important to remember that contracts reflect various transaction costs. Usually one thinks of contracts as being highly rigid and legalistic; in practice, contracts are more relational, stressing the underlying dynamics of the relationship between the parties. Contracting problems arise under conditions of asymmetric information and when opportunistic behavior is an option. Opportunistic behavior is acting to advance your own interests at the expense of other party(ies) under an existing contract.

In Chapter 8, "Contracts: Issues of Discourse," we turn to one important issue of discourse in relational contracting, **moral hazard.** A transaction occurs with moral hazard when (at least) one party to the transaction can only imperfectly monitor the behavior of the other party to the transaction. We begin by relating the organization to the property rights material presented in Chapter 5. We need to think about organizations as teams. Two important questions are these: Who should own the team? Who should experience the rewards from good team behavior? We also consider certain types of contracts in which moral hazard is a problem: insurance and employment contracts. Once a firm understanding of the basic issue of moral hazard is in place, we turn to considering how contracts may be structured to eliminate some of the moral hazard and to minimize the risks posed to different parties.

In Chapter 9, "Distribution, Rents, and Efficiency," the importance and role of rents in economic exchange and organizations are made clear. We explore the somewhat difficult concept of **economic rents,** which, for now, can be defined as benefits going to a party engaged in an activity that are in excess of what is required to attract that party to that activity. Thus, in a sense, economic rents represent "something for nothing." Economic rents serve many purposes in our economic system. First, since they are desirable to those receiving the rents, individuals and organizations will strive to earn them. Second, rents provide one way to reward good behavior in a world strewn with transaction costs. In organizations, rents abound and members expend much effort in securing these rents for themselves, an activity termed *rent-seeking behavior*. Usually these efforts are counterproductive to the organization, and we discuss ways to minimize the impact of such behavior.

Parts I and II contain all of the building blocks needed to understand the organizational theory of economics. Economic activity may be organized by markets or by contracts within organizations. Beginning with the premise that all economic activity occurs through exchanges carried out in an environment of imperfect information, firms respond by contracting with their owners, workers, and related firms in very interesting ways. The remainder of this book focuses on these relationships by addressing issues in firm financing, issues arising in relationships with workers, and issues arising in relationships between firms addressed from the strategic alliance vantage point.

In Part III, "Organization, Ownership, and Control," we attempt to gain some understanding of the financing activities of firms. The emphasis here is on a sometimes imprecise relationship between the owners of a firm and those who control it.

Chapter 10, "Modern Financial Theory," concentrates on understanding some basic tools and issues of financial analysis. In the beginning of the chapter, we present one vision of a nearly utopic environment in which all involved parties share the same information and expectations. There is a striking resemblance between this theoretical setting and the traditional neoclassical analysis of economic markets. Not surprisingly, the outcome in this case is efficient, and we present a shortened version of the Miller Modigliani theories. We then begin to drop some of the assumptions guaranteeing perfect information and attempt to analyze behavior when transaction costs cannot be ignored. We explain that the relationship between the owners and managers of the firm is one beset by moral hazard contracting problems. When these issues become prevalent, ownership interests must reassert their control; quite often this implies an ownership change, corporate restructurings, and the selling off of several corporate divisions.

Chapter 11, "Corporate Control and Economic Efficiency," is directly concerned with the establishment of an efficient relationship between the owners and managers of a firm. It centers on the issue of corporate control raised in the previous chapter but greatly enriches this concept in a number of ways. We directly consider the market for corporate control discussing the efficiency aspects of mergers and acquisitions. Other, managerially useful concepts, such as the use of debt and leveraged buyouts to enforce managerial efficiency, are discussed. By far, the most interesting aspect of Chapter 11 for managers is the model of corporate control. This model of corporate control explicitly recognizes the moral hazard contracting problems existing and identifies explicit steps that can be taken to minimize their impact.

Part IV, "Managing Human Resources" applies our understanding of exchange to the management of human resources. Put in the simplest terms possible, employment is a contract; as with all contracts, it is made under conditions of uncertainty, imperfect information, complexity, and imperfect commitment. Employers offer a wage and a certain amount of security; they are concerned with productivity, employee fit, and turning a profit on operations. Workers offer their skills, knowledge, and some degree of loyalty; they are concerned with earning a good living and, presumably, in having a job in the future.

Chapter 12, "The Employment Relationship," is devoted exclusively to establishing the ground rules behind the employment relationship. It begins by questioning the central proposition of classical economics: that productivity is the main determinant of pay levels. For most workers this relationship may not be so direct. We offer an alternative view under which pay is primarily a function of employer screening and job seniority. This interpretation proves very useful in explaining many developments in white- and blue-collar labor markets.

Chapter 13, "The Employment Experience," carries the theoretical construct of the employment relationship into today's business world. Of particular importance in Chapter 13 is the issue of what replaces the employment relationship when the trust on which it is based erodes. We consider much of the logic behind the business reengineerings carried out in the early 1990s. Chapter 13 concludes with an institutional look at executive employment.

Part V, "Organizational Structure as a Dynamic Process" is part visionary, part descriptive. We hope, in this part of the text, to present an accurate picture of current organizational structures in light of the historical organizational schemes that preceded them. The transformation of firms and the industries that they make up is presented in a dynamic context emphasizing the role played by transaction cost considerations and efficiency concerns.

Chapter 14, "The Evolution of the Modern Firm," begins with a review of the rise and fall of America's great mass-producing firms. The student will undoubtedly be reminded of the material in Chapter 1. However, in Chapter 14, we enrich the story by including the role played by transaction costs and how efficiency considerations affect organizational structure. Significant changes in the business environment cause changes to occur in how firms choose to organize economic activity. The new environment is driven by global competition, technological innovation, and flexibility in production.

Chapter 15, "Core Competencies, Organization, and Strategy," presents a more detailed look at how corporations respond to environmental changes by crafting an appropriate organizational strategy. In an ultracompetitive environment in which consumers demand customized products, firms must move their focus "back to basics," or, in other words, pursue their core competencies. Coupled with this movement toward an organization's fundamental strengths is the important role played by flexible manufacturing systems in the organization of industry today. We conclude the chapter by presenting a simplified version of firm behavior under the flexible manufacturing paradigm.

In Chapter 16, "Organizational Strategy and Strategic Alliances," we apply some of the managerial tools developed concerning incomplete contracting and transaction costs to the logic supporting the use of strategic alliances by business. We argue that these increasingly common organizational forms are consistent with the pursuit of efficient behavior by organizations.

"An International Comparison of Organizational Styles," Chapter 17, compares and contrasts the patterns of organizing economic activities chosen by the largest competitors of U.S. firms. In this chapter, we pay extra attention to how cultural and demographic influences affect organizational patterns in light of the problems facing U.S. firms.

OF PARTICULAR INTEREST TO MANAGERS

Just what do economists do at large corporations today? Most frequently, they are asked to forecast movements in interest rates, price levels, or overall economic activity. A smaller number of economists are consulted regarding the impact of various regulatory changes. Among businesspeople, economists are viewed in a special way, very good at working in the abstract realm of theory and somewhat good at predicting the future course of events but rarely consulted for strategic managerial decisions. The purpose of this book is to introduce managers to the many powerful tools available in the so-called "dismal science."

We have presented a fairly brief history of industrial evolution in the United States. The mass-producing firms enjoyed a prolonged period of profitability; however, this is no longer the case. Foreign competition and rapid technological change are causing firms to change the way in which they organize economic activity. Large, hierarchial firms are being replaced by smaller, flatter corporate forms. These new competitors rely on technology and frequently partner with others forming networks, strategic alliances, and virtual organizations to fulfill a growing demand for low-priced, customized goods. It is our aim to study this change at the organizational level. We turn our attention throughout this book to the ultimate building blocks of all economic activity: the exchanges themselves.

Transaction cost analysis provides a powerful lens with which we can view economic activity. However, this approach is hardly new at all; if you notice the list of further readings at the end of each chapter, much of this work is over 25 years old. The implications of this approach are far reaching and widely applicable. It is now time to bring them into the business arena for wider exposure.

asymmetric information
bounded rationality
business reengineering
concentration
contract
core competencies
corporation
decentralization
economic rents
economies of scale
economies of scope
efficient
external contract
final goods
firm
flexible manufacturing systems
gross domestic product

gross national product
intermediate goods
internal contract
junk bonds
make-or-buy decision
moral hazard
opportunistic behavior
partnership
perfect information
real
sole proprietorship
Taylorism
total quality management
transaction costs
vertical integration
virtual corporation

FURTHER READINGS

Abernath, W. J., K. B. Clark, and A. M. Katrow. *Industry Renaissance*. New York: Basic Books, 1983, p. 71.

Acs, Z. J. and D. B. Audretsch. "The Restructuring of U.S. Markets." Wissenschaftzentrum Berlin, Working Paper, January 1986.

Bhagat, S., A. Shleifer, and R. W. Vishny. "Hostile Takeovers in the 1980s: The Return to Corporate Specialization." *Brookings Papers: Microeconomics 1990*. Washington, D.C.: Brookings Institution, 1990, p. 1.

Carnevale, M. L. "HDTV Bidders Agree to Merge Their Systems." *The Wall Street Journal*, May 24, 1993, p. B1.

Chandler, A. D. "Organizational Capabilities and of the Economic History of the Industrial Enterprise." *Journal of Economic Perspectives* 6, no. 3, pp. 79–100.

———. *Scale and Scope: The Dynamics of Industrial Capitalism*. Cambridge: The Bellknap Press of Harvard University Press, 1990, p. 24.

———. *The Visible Hand: The Managerial Revolution in American Business*. Cambridge: Harvard University Press, 1977.

Ermshoff, J. R. "Is It Time to Create a New Theory of the Firm?" *Journal of Economics and Management Strategy* 2, no. 1, Spring 1993, pp. 3–15.

Gleckman, H. "Meet the Giant-Killers." *Business Week*, Enterprise 1993, p. 68.

Johnston, R. and P. R. Lawrence. "Beyond Vertical Integration—The Rise of the Value-Adding Partnership." *Harvard Business Review*, 66 July/August, 1988, pp. 94–101.

Piore, M. J., and C. F. Sabel. *The Second Industrial Divide*. New York: Basic Books, 1984, p. 189; and Alvin Toffler. *The Adaptive Corporation*. New York: Bantam Books, 1985, p. 37.

Reich, R. *The Next American Frontier*. New York, N.Y.: Times Books, 1983.

Selz, M. "Small Manufacturers Display the Nimbleness the Times Require." *The Wall Street Journal*, December 29, 1993, p. A1.

Tully, S. "The Modular Corporation," *Fortune*, February 8, 1993, pp. 106–111.

Weston, J. F., and E. F. Brigham. *Essentials of Managerial Finance*, 9th ed. Fort Worth, Tex.: The Dryden Press, 1990.

———, S. C. Kwang, and S. E. Hoag. *Mergers, Restructuring, and Corporate Control*. Englewood Cliffs, N.J.: Prentice Hall, 1990, p. 23.

I

The four chapters in Part I develop the set of traditional tools students need to examine economic efficiency in market economies. Each focuses on the external market environment of the firm under perfect information. When considered as a part of the remainder of the text, Part I serves as a bridge linking traditional economic analysis to the evolving inquiries based on imperfect information and transaction costs that are developed in Part II.

Four major themes permeate all of the topics in this book: exchange, organization, uncertainty, and opportunism. Part I primarily focuses on the first of these, exchange. However, exchange here is limited to the competitive exchange ideal that populates most of traditional economic analysis. As was hinted in the introductory chapter, the remaining three major themes are largely ignored in the economic analysis with which economists have become so familiar.

Chapter 2, "Competitive Exchange," is probably review to most students. This chapter presents the basic tools of analysis of traditional economics: the supply and demand framework. Price determination, comparative static analysis, and elasticities make up the bulk of the chapter. Our presentation of this material is unique, however, in that we stress the assumptions commonly made but infrequently disclosed in applying the supply and demand model.

Chapter 3, "The Neoclassical Theory of the Firm," extends the traditional, neoclassical view into the competitive firm. From the conventional vantage point, profit maximizing behavior is considered in light of diminishing marginal productivity. In this analysis the firm remains shrouded in its operations acting in markets governed by supply and demand.

THE EFFICIENCY OF MARKETS

I

Chapter 4, "Efficiency, the Price System, and Organizations," is a very detailed, fairly technical treatment of general equilibrium theory. This chapter serves two useful purposes. First, it introduces and summarizes the beneficial aspects of equilibrium in competitive markets. Second, it defines, in the context of the general competitive equilibrium, the notion of efficiency. The chapter develops an important linkage between market efficiency and social welfare. An analytical connection is developed between efficient production and an economy's production possibilities frontier. By highlighting this linkage, we are able to unmask and draw attention to some of the restrictive assumptions long held central by economists.

Chapter 5, "Property Rights, Ownership, and Efficiency," explores a rapidly growing literature in economics on property rights, that is, the effects of asset ownership on exchange. We view the approach in this chapter as a bridge between the "new" and the "old" economics. Much of this material is from the work of Nobel Laureate Ronald Coase, who showed the world that even if a market were to fail, an efficient outcome can still occur if all interested parties are able to bargain with each other.

2

Competitive Exchange

Nobody ever saw a dog make a fair and deliberate exchange of one bone for another with another dog.[1]

▰▰▰ CHAPTER OUTLINE AND STUDENT GOALS ▰▰▰

This chapter explains activity in a competitive market. The forces of demand and supply are explained as representing the activities of many interrelated buyers and sellers whose interaction determines market prices. The perfectly competitive model we describe is important because it is the best understood and most powerful (when used correctly) tool with which to study, explain, and predict activity in the business world. This chapter covers material that you should be familiar with from your introductory economic class.

Exchange is the unit of analysis in this chapter. We consider two types of participants in our analysis: the consumer and the entrepreneur. The consumer is the head of the household; the entrepreneur is the head of the firm. We define a **market** as the interaction of one or more buyers with one or more sellers.

In *competitive markets*, it is competition that limits and guides the behavior of market participants and forms the basis of efficiency on which the whole economy rests.

When competition is present, it is not necessary for governments to intervene. The impersonal forces of supply and demand motivate firms to produce the goods and services people value and to produce them in the most efficient, least costly way. Market reactions, not public policies, eliminate shortages or surpluses. There is no need for government regulatory agencies or bureaucrats to make arbitrary decisions about who may produce what, how to produce it, or how much it is permissible to charge for the product. Within the competitive model, the public good is best promoted by individuals pursuing their own self-interests.

In the impersonal decision-making world of **perfect competition,** neither private firms nor public officials wield economic power. Adam Smith, perhaps the most famous economist of all time, used the metaphor of the "invisible hand" to describe how self-interest led to the social good:

> It is not from the benevolence of the butcher, the brewer, or the baker, that we expect our dinner, but from their regard to their own interest. . . . He intends only his own gain, and he is in this as in many other cases, led by an invisible hand to promote an end which was not part of his intention.[2]

First, this chapter develops the elements of competitive exchange and provides some guidance as to when it is appropriately applied. It is a logical statement about the functioning of the price system. Second, it is also a "set of tools" for lat-

---

[1]Adam Smith, *The Wealth of Nations* (Chicago: The University of Chicago Press), book 1, ch. 2.
[2]Ibid., p. 18.

ter use to help you understand the working of the market environment in which real firms actually exist. These tools have been developed over many years and will be invaluable for understanding the external environment facing firms.

After reading this chapter, you should be able to

- Briefly explain the methodological features of economic analysis.
- Explain in your own words what perfect competition is.
- Explain the difference between supply, demand, and price.
- Understand how market equilibrium works and why markets clear.
- Understand the difference between elastic and inelastic demand.
- Understand the difference between point and arc elasticity.
- Explain the relationship between demand and total revenue.

■ THE METHODOLOGY OF ECONOMICS

The **scientific method** is a way to think about problems and formulate a solution to or explanation of them. We can briefly outline the steps involved in scientific inquiry. A schematic diagram, such as Figure 2.1, may be used to represent these steps in a meaningful way.

The Scientific Method
in Economics

The first step is to observe some phenomenon occurring in the real world. This may amount to something simple, such as the legendary account of Sir Isaac Newton dozing under an apple tree and "discovering" gravity when an apple fell from the tree to the ground. In economics, such an initial observation might be a relationship between the amount of money in an economy and the price level or the so-called flattening organizational restructurings common at large U.S. corporations in the 1990s.

The second step is to consult existing knowledge and logical systems related to the initial observation. The economist might turn to the written literature on a given topic in a variety of academic fields. Further, the economist might, and often does, consider a mathematical representation of the circumstances surrounding the initial observation.

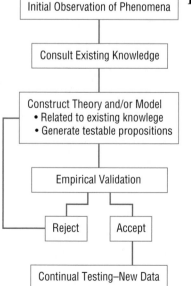

Figure 2.1 Schematic Drawing of Scientific Method

The third step is to construct a *theory* that explains the initial observation and all other related events. A theory, or hypothesis, is nothing more than an attempt at an explanation for some phenomenon. Quite often, a theory is put forth as part of a broader proposition called a *model*, which may be defined as an abstract description of reality. Such a model might be a system of mathematical equations, a series of graphs, or a verbal description. A model might incorporate one or more theories in an attempt to explain, analyze, and predict behavior. The requirements for a model are that it offer an explanation reducible to an existing and known body of knowledge and that it generate testable propositions that can validate or reject the model and/or its underlying theory(ies).

The fourth step in the scientific method is to seek empirical validation, confronting the model and its testable implications with activity in the real world. At this stage, we would then gather data from the real world and use it to prove or disprove the stated theories. Usually such proof is statistical in nature. Unfortunately, it is rather common for the statistical tests to generate ambiguous results that neither completely reject nor completely accept the theory. A good case in point of statistical tests not being able to judge a theory's validity is in macroeconomics, where there is a constant and long-standing difference of opinion between the monetarist and Keynesian views regarding appropriate stabilization policies. If, however, the theory is rejected by the empirical evidence, the scientist should return to step 3 and reexamine the basic assumptions and construction of the theory.

The scientific method also calls for a continuing test of theory by new experience in the real world. Quite often, a theory is originally tested with data from one period or place, and it is found to be less than suitable for another period or place. Again, the scientist should return to step 3 and critically reconsider the development of the theory.

Perhaps you are familiar with this general approach to problem solving from prior coursework in chemistry, biology, or physics. Most of these courses involve a laboratory section in which the experiments done by students have been designed with this type of approach in mind. Many people do not immediately recognize economics as a science; however, the subject is best approached as one. In the next section, we point out some differences between economics and the more commonly recognized sciences.

Some Differences Between the Sciences

Like any science, economics is concerned with the explanation and prediction of observed phenomena. When most people think about science, they relate the concept only to the so-called **hard sciences,** those concerned with the interactions and physical properties of matter: chemistry, physics, and engineering. Economics, like psychology, sociology, and political science, is a so-called **soft science,** one that explains the interactions resulting from human behavior. There are two basic differences between the hard and soft sciences.

1. The hard sciences have the benefit of the controlled experiment. Two chemists can conjecture as to the exact shade of green that will result when certain yellow and blue chemicals are mixed. Their conjectures can be proven in the laboratory. Economists do not have this luxury: for example, it would be inhumane to place a thousand people on a desert island and tinker with various systems that would allocate them food, clothing, and shelter.
2. In the hard sciences, there is a stochastic, or random, component; however it is quite small and can often be identified. In economics, the random component of behavior is usually not negligible. A fact of life is that when the same individual is confronted with exactly the same stimuli, he or she will act differently on different occasions.

These differences have been identified and known for centuries and, as such, greatly affect the way in which economists approach problems vis-à-vis their counterparts in the hard sciences.

The method of inquiry adhered to by most economists is **logical positivism.** According to logical positivism, the basic axioms or assumptions of the theory are not subject to independent empirical verification. However, no theory, whether it be in economics or physics, is perfectly correct. Therefore, it is important to test the deduced hypotheses and thereby to test indirectly the system of axioms underlying economic theory. The usefulness and validity of a theory depends on whether it succeeds in explaining and predicting the set of phenomena that it is intended to explain.

Economists put primary emphasis on the predictive powers of a model. If the predictions derived from one model prove better than the predictions drawn from another model, the former is tentatively selected as preferable. If a subsequent theory is advanced that explains more of the relevant facts, the new theory is deemed superior to the one previously accepted.

The study of managerial economics and organization deals with both **positive** and **normative economics.** Positive questions have to do with explanations and predictions of what is or is expected to be. Normative questions entail some moral or ethical basis within the issues to be addressed, dealing with what ought to or should be.

Positive economics is crucial to economic theory. It tells us what will happen to the price of cars when autoworkers' wages increase, or what will happen to productivity if wages are increased at Ford Motor Company.[3]

There may be times when we, as economists and human beings, want to go beyond explanation and prediction. We may wish to explore the normative implications of certain decisions. For example, what are the consequences of paying competitively determined wages in a developing country? Within this arena of intellectual exchange, we may identify instances in which the predicted outcome of our models may not be what is in the best interests of society.

Though different economists employ different models of the economy, they all use a common, basic set of assumptions as a point of departure. The basic model of the economy has three components: assumptions about how firms behave, assumptions about how consumers behave, and assumptions about the market in which these consumers and firms interact. Underlying much of economic analysis is the basic assumption of **rationality.** This assumption is based on the expectation that individuals and firms will act in a consistent manner, with a reasonably well-defined notion of what they like and what their objectives are and with a reasonable understanding of how to attain those objectives.

For individuals, the rationality assumption is taken to mean that he or she makes choices and decisions in pursuit of his or her own self-interest. Different people have different goals and desires. Bill may want to own a Porsche, have a large house in the country, and work the long hours needed to provide for his family. Andrea prefers a less harried life style. She is willing to accept a lower income for longer vacations and more quality time with her family.

The rationality assumption is taken to mean that firms operate to maximize their profits. The principle of rationality applies to decisions about gathering information as well. Rational firms decide whether to spend money and time to become more informed, for example about new technologies.

**More on the Practice
of Good Economics**

**The Assumption
of Rationality**

---

[3]The art of economics is the application of the knowledge learned in positive economics to the achievement of the goals determined in normative economics. This three-part distinction dates back to John Neville Keynes.

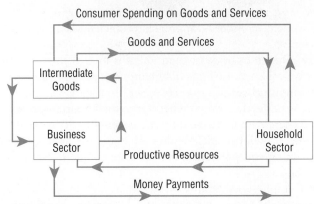

**Figure 2.2 Relationship Between Households
and Businesses in the Economy**

Exchange
and the Circular Flow

Figure 2.2 is a broad schematic diagram showing the economic flows that to-gether constitute a market economy. Goods and services go from the business sector to consumers in exchange for payments labeled consumer spending in Fig-ure 2.2. Consumers provide labor and funds, in the form of labor services and stock purchases, to firms. Money payments are returned to households for these productive resources, providing households with incomes with which they pur-chase more from the business sector.

Figure 2.2 also shows a self-contained loop within the business sector labeled intermediate goods. The importance of this loop is growing by leaps and bounds with far-reaching repercussions for the way in which economic activity is orga-nized. Notably absent from our diagram is government activity. This simplifica-tion enables us to focus on the role of exchange. The consumer spending and goods and services flows result from activity surrounding the exchange in final goods markets. Of course, behind these aggregate flows are many, many individ-ual markets. There is, for example, a market for cars, one for refrigerators, and one for beds. Likewise, the productive resources and money payments flows rep-resent activity in different labor markets and in different capital (money, stock, and bond) markets.

We now more clearly focus on our view of the economy and describe the forces operating in each of these markets.

■ THE MARKET MECHANISM

One of the best ways to appreciate the relevance of economics is to begin with the basics of supply and demand. Supply and demand analysis is a fundamental and powerful tool that can be applied to a wide variety of interesting and important problems.

To appreciate the workings of exchange, we begin by focusing on the case with many buyers and sellers, all buying and selling basically the same thing. This case is termed the *basic competitive model* by economists. Each firm is a price taker, which simply means that because it cannot influence the market price, it must ac-cept that price. On the other side of the market are rational individuals, each of whom would like to pay as little as possible for goods and services. The con-sumers also take the market price as given.

The market economy revolves around exchange between individuals who buy goods and services from firms, and firms, which buy productive resources, in particular labor and capital, from households. Many firms also sell their goods and services to other firms. This intermediate good market is becoming even more important today.

Demand is the quantity of a good or service that customers are willing and able to purchase over a given period of time. For managerial decision making, the primary focus is on market demand. Market demand, however, is merely the aggregation of individual demands, and insight into market demand relations is gained by understanding the nature of individual demand. Individual demand is determined by two factors: (1) the value associated with using the good or service and (2) the ability to acquire it. Both are required for effective individual demand and, hence, for market demand.

There are two basic types of individual demand: direct and derived demand. **Direct demand** is the appropriate concept for analyzing individual demand for goods and services that directly satisfy buyer desires. In this model, the value of a good or service lies not in the product itself but rather in the satisfaction provided by the good.

Other goods and services are acquired not for their direct consumption value but because they are required to produce, distribute, or market other products. Engineers, production workers, natural resources, and airplanes are all examples of goods and services demanded not for direct final personal consumption but for their use in providing other goods and services. We say that their demand is derived from the demand for the products that they help produce. The demand for all inputs used by a firm is **derived demand.**

Regardless of whether a good or service is demanded by individuals for final consumption or as an indirect factor used in providing other goods and services, the fundamentals of economic analysis provide a basis for investigating the characteristics of demand. When we make this relationship explicit and define it over a range of prices, we create a **demand function.** It is customary to view the relationship with price-determining quantity. We could state a demand function as follows:

$$q = f(p) \tag{2.1}$$

where q is the quantity of the good or service demanded and p is the price of the good or service, other things being equal. The law of demand states that there is an inverse relationship between price and quantity.

A distinction must be made between the amount demanded at a given price and the whole schedule of quantities demanded at all relevant prices. In other words, the quantity demanded is a function of price in the short run. If the price of a good or service falls, the quantity demanded increases, but the change in price does not affect the demand schedule. When we say that the quantity demanded is a function of price, we state simply that for every price, there is a corresponding quantity demanded. Will the relationship between price and quantity be a direct one or an indirect one? Although it may not be obvious, it is clear from every business case that if you increase price sooner or later you will sell less. This happens because the consumer's ability and willingness are enhanced by a reduction in the price of a good or service. This is known as the *law of demand*.

How can the relationship between quantity demanded and price be represented? One method is to use a demand schedule. This is a numerical tabulation showing the quantity that is demanded at selected prices. Table 2.1 is a hypothetical demand schedule for computer chips. It lists the quantity of chips that would be demanded at various prices, other things being equal.

A second method of showing the relationship between quantity demanded and price is by an equation. Suppose that the demand curve is given by the following equation:

The Law of Demand

The Demand Curve

Table 2.1	Hypothetical Demand Schedule

Price	Quantity Demanded
$10	0
9	1
8	2
7	3
6	4
5	5
4	6
3	7
2	8
1	9
0	10

$$q = 10 - p \qquad (2.2)$$

where q is the amount demanded and p is the price of computer chips. Instead of a general functional relationship between the amount demanded and the price, we now have a specific relationship between the amount demanded and the price. That is, we now have a specific demand by particular consumers for a given good. By substituting different values of p in equation (2.2), we can determine the amount that would be demanded at any price.

Figure 2.3 Demand Curve

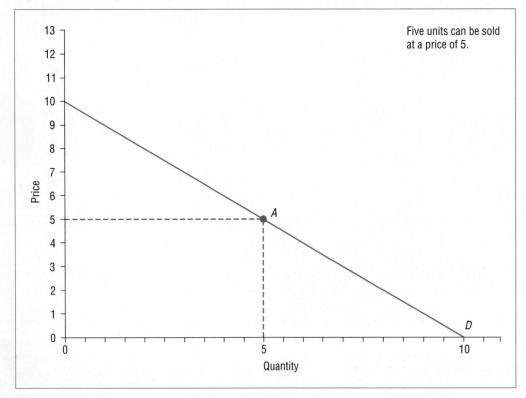

Demand can also be represented geometrically by a **demand curve.** The demand curve in Figure 2.3 represents the complete relationship between quantity demanded and price, other things being equal. A single point (point *A*) on the demand curve indicates a single price-quantity combination. Notice that although any point on the demand curve presents a specific quantity demanded, the demand curve as a whole shows all such combinations.

Before we continue with our study of demand functions, we must make sure we understand what a demand function shows. Consider once again the demand schedule shown in Table 2.1. Basically, we may view the situation as follows: each of nine people is willing to buy one unit of the good at prices ranging from $9 down to $1. Suppose that we could get these nine people to stand in a line with those who value the good the most in front of those who value the good the least.

If we asked the first person in line what value she placed on her unit of the good, she would respond "$9." The second person would value the good at $8. The last, or ninth person in line, would value the good at $1.

We can conclude then that every point on the demand function shows the value placed on one unit of the good by some buyer. This important interpretation of the demand function is frequently overlooked. It will become extremely useful to us in Chapter 5 when we consider externalities and their implication for a smoothly functioning price system.

If q number of computer chips can be sold at price p, then if the price falls to p', the number of computer chips that will be demanded will increase. This variation in the number of chips sold is referred to as a **change in quantity demanded,** defined as a movement along a given demand curve as shown in Figure 2.4a (from point A to point B, or from $p = 8$ to $p = 6$).

Figure 2.4a Movement Along a Given Demand Curve

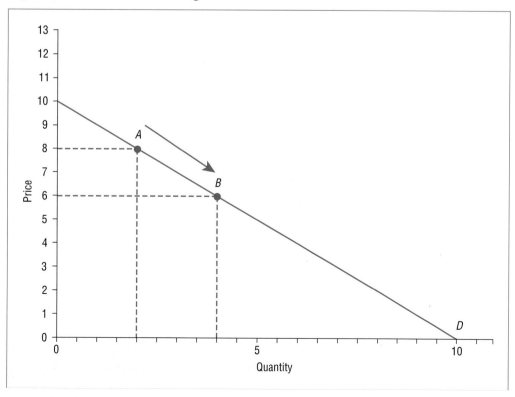

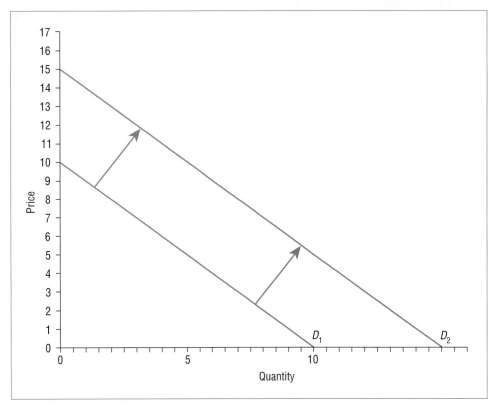

Figure 2.4b Change in Demand

A demand schedule (such as that in Table 2.1) and a demand curve are always stated with the assumption of *ceterius paribus*, a Latin phrase meaning all other things being constant. The other things that are constant are anything else that may affect buyer behavior besides the good's or service's own price being held constant. A change occurs when any of the variables previously held constant shifts the entire demand curve to a new position. A shift to a new demand curve implies that the quantity demanded at each price has changed.

A change in demand, or a shift from one demand curve to another, reflects a change in one of the nonprice determinants of demand: income, the price of other goods, consumer tastes, population, advertising expenditures, and so on. In Figure 2.4b, the rightward shift in the demand curve from D1 to D2 indicates an increase in the quantity demanded at each and every price. Such a shift in the demand function indicates that consumers are willing to pay more for any unit of the good.

A leftward shift in demand is a decrease in demand. A decrease in the demand for a good is consistent with consumers' willingness to pay less for any unit of a good.

Nonprice Determinants of Demand

We should keep in mind that price is not the only factor that influences demand. For most goods and services, there are a number of nonprice determinants of demand that, if changed, will cause a shift in the demand function. Generally speaking, the effects of the nonprice determinants of demand are felt in two ways: a change in the willingness and/or ability of existing consumers to pay or a change in the number of consumers.

After one of the most intense debates in recent years, the House of Representatives approved the North American Free Trade Agreement (NAFTA) on November 18, 1993. The 234 to 200 vote was a huge victory for President Clinton, who pushed for the trade deal with Mexico and Canada that was actually negotiated by his Republican predecessor. A majority of Democrats—156—opposed the treaty, which would eliminate most barriers then in place to the export and import of goods and services among the United States, Canada, and Mexico over the next 15 years. The treaty places 360 million consumers in the three countries, with a total annual economic output of $6 trillion, into a single, open, barrier-free market. The agreement took effect on January 1, 1994. What are the nonprice determinants of demand, and how do they affect the demand curve?

One of the most important effects of NAFTA on demand will be the increase in the number of consumers in the market. Mexico alone adds over 100 million consumers. Mexicans who in 1993 purchased $40 billion worth of U.S. exports will be buying more consumer goods, financial services, autos, and agricultural goods, especially corn, grains, meat, and soybeans. NAFTA integrates the U.S. market with a large and growing Mexican consumer base. This will shift the demand curve to the right for a large number of consumer and capital goods.

Population is also an important determinant of demand. Population growth does not by itself create new demand. The additional people must have purchasing power before demand is changed. Extra people of working age, however, usually mean extra output; and if they are productive, they will earn income. Mexico has a relatively young population that is growing and working. When this happens, the demand for all the commodities purchased by the new income earners will rise. A rise in population will shift the demand curves for goods and services to the right, indicating that more will be bought at each price. Both the additional income of Mexicans and the larger number of wage earners should increase the demand for U.S. products in Mexico.

The Law of Supply

You now have a basic understanding of demand and the behavior of consumers. The other half of the picture is supply and the behavior of sellers. The term *supply* also means something different to the economist from the meaning attached to the word in popular speech. **Supply** is the relationship between amounts of a commodity that sellers would be willing and able to make available for sale and alternative prices during a given time period, all other things remaining the same. As with demand, it is customary to view the quantity determined by price, holding all else constant. It too may be stated in mathematical terms:

$$q = f(p) \qquad (2.3)$$

where q is the quantity supplied and p is price. This expression does not indicate the nature of the price-quantity relationship: it simply says that for any price, a corresponding quantity will be supplied. But this time common sense tells us that the relationship is a direct one. Unlike the demand curve, the supply curve slopes upward from left to right (as price increases). This property illustrates what is known as the *law of supply*.

The general relationship just discussed can be illustrated by a supply schedule that shows various price-quantity pairs. Table 2.2 represents a hypothetical supply schedule for computer chips. No chips will be offered for sale for prices at or below $2.50. We call $2.50 the *reservation price*. We may also consider the **supply function** in an explicit mathematical form. The values in Table 2.2, for example, were created using the following equation:

$$q = 2p - 5 \qquad (2.4)$$

where q is the quantity supplied. The quantity supplied can be obtained by supplying different values for price. For example, at the price of $8.98, 12.96 units per time period would be supplied.

The Supply Curve

The supply schedule can also be represented geometrically as a **supply curve.** The supply curve is the part of the supply function that expresses the relation between the price charged for a good or service and the quantity supplied, holding constant the effects of all other variables.

Before we go on to the more detailed workings of the supply concept, we need to address one frequently overlooked issue of supply functions, namely, when they exist. Interestingly enough, this issue has only been addressed at the higher levels of economic theory, although the ideas are very intuitive.

We now note that sellers hold the idea of the supply price for a given unit of output very near and dear to their hearts. A supply price is, of course, the price shown by the supply function. This supply is important, but it shows only the minimum price at which a unit will be affordable for sale. We know that sellers are greedy, but since this term has a decidedly negative connotation, we instead say that sellers are rational. Why would sellers provide the good at the lowest price? Only if they are pushed.

In short, a supply function exists only under conditions of competition. Consider a market with only one seller. Does he or she have a supply function? No, he or she does not. In a market with a single seller, that seller is concerned with costs only in so far as costs are covered; that seller sets his or her price based solely on what the market will bear.

A shift in the supply curve means that at each price, a different quantity is supplied than previously. As with the demand function, a **change in supply** occurs when the supply function shifts to a new position in response to a change in one of the nonprice determinants of supply. Production, distribution, marketing, and selling are all processes that may affect the supply function in this way. A change in any costs related to actually providing the good or service to consumers causes a change in supply. This is somewhat different from a **change in quantity supplied,** which occurs in response to a price change and involves a movement along a fixed supply function.

An increase in supply is shown as a shift in the supply function downward and to the right. Figure 2.5 shows an increase in supply from *S*1 to *S*2. If we adopt the logic that each point on the supply function shows the amount that producers must be paid to bring a given unit of output to market, then we can claim that an increase in supply (such as shown in Figure 2.5) means that each unit is supplied to the market at a lower price. Similarly, a decrease in supply is shown as an upward and leftward shift, implying that each unit brought to market appears at a higher price.

Nonprice Determinants of Supply

What will shift the whole supply curve? The concept of a supply curve pertains to factors that affect the production, distribution, marketing, and selling costs. If changes occur that decrease the final, total cost of providing consumers with a good or service, this will cause an increase in supply.

Table 2.2	Hypothetical Supply Schedule	
Price		**Quantity Supplied**
$10		15
9		13
8		11
7		9
6		7
5		5
4		3
3		1
2		0

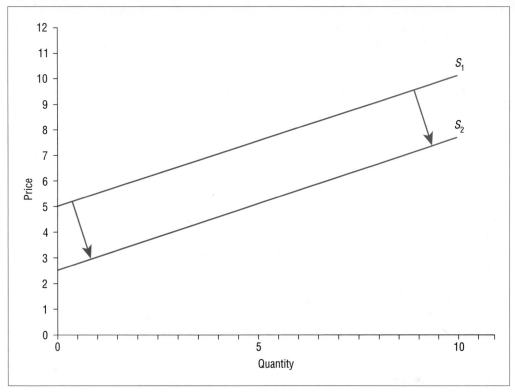

Figure 2.5 Change in Supply

The price paid for a factor of production (or input) is a cost to the firm that uses it. A change in factor prices changes the price that producers will be willing to sell any unit of output because it changes firm profitability. Just as profits are increased by an increase in the good or services price, factor costs remaining constant, so are they increased by a fall in factor prices, the price of the good or service remaining constant. An increase in factor prices reduces the profitability of a commodity at any given price of that good or service.

At any time, what is produced and how it is produced depend on what is known. Over time, this knowledge changes. The enormous increase in production per worker that has been going on in industrial societies for the last 200 years is largely the result of improved methods of production. Discoveries in computers have led to lower costs in the production of many goods and services. The invention of the microprocessor has revolutionized production of televisions, computers, and satellites. Today many companies gather daily sales records so that inventories can be changed and production plans altered nearly as often.

▧ MARKET EQUILIBRIUM

Integrating the concepts of demand and supply establishes a framework for understanding how they interact to determine market price and quantities. When the quantity of a good or service demanded and the quantity supplied are in perfect balance at some price governing exchanges, the market for the good or service is in **equilibrium.** Another way to say that a market is in equilibrium is to say that there is no tendency for price to change.

There is only one price in equilibrium. Table 2.3 brings together the demand and supply schedules from Table 2.1 and Table 2.2. The quantities to be supplied

Surplus and Shortage

and demanded at each price can be directly compared. There is only one price at which the quantity demanded and the quantity supplied are equal. At any price above equilibrium, the quantity supplied is greater than the quantity demanded. This is often referred to as a situation of **surplus** or excess supply. The tendency for buyers to offer, and sellers to ask for, lower prices when there is excess supply implies a downward pressure on price. In many markets, consumers have come to expect excess supply at special times. For example, at the end of summer, retailers often put air conditioners, swim suits, and some sporting goods on sale.

At prices less than equilibrium, the quantity demanded is greater than the quantity supplied and there is a **shortage.** The tendency for buyers to offer, and sellers to ask for, higher prices when there is excess demand implies an upward pressure on price.

Neither surplus or shortage occurs when a market is in equilibrium, since *equilibrium* is defined as a condition in which the quantities demanded and supplied are exactly in balance at the current market price. Surplus and shortage describe situations of market **disequilibrium** because both result in powerful market forces being exerted to change the price and quantities offered in the market. At the equilibrium price, there is no tendency for price to change as long as demand and supply remain unchanged.

The equilibrium price is determined by locating the price at which the quantity demanded is just equal to the quantity supplied. In terms of our algebraic model, we want to determine where the supply and demand functions have the same values for p and q. We can accomplish this by setting the two functions equal to each other and solving for p:

$$
\begin{aligned}
S &= D \\
2p - 5 &= 10 - p \\
3p &= 15 \\
p &= \$5
\end{aligned}
\tag{2.5}
$$

Therefore,

$$Q_d = 10 - 5 = 5, \text{ and } Q_s = 10 - 5 = 5,$$

where q_d is the quantity demanded and Q_s is the quantity supplied.

This situation is depicted in Figure 2.6. The price of $5 is the equilibrium

Table 2.3	Market Equilibrium, Shortage, and Surplus		
Price	**Quantity Demanded**	**Quantity Supplied**	**Market Status**
$10	0	15	Surplus
9	1	13	Surplus
8	2	11	Surplus
7	3	9	Surplus
6	4	7	Surplus
5	**5**	**5**	**Equilibrium**
4	6	3	Shortage
3	7	1	Shortage[a]
2	8	0	Shortage[a]
1	9	0	Shortage[a]
0	10	0	Shortage[a]

[a]There is technically a shortage at prices below 2.5, but no exchange occurs. Similarly, there is no exchange at price equal to $10.

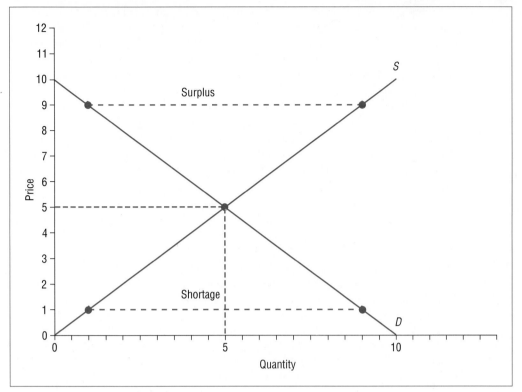

Figure 2.6 Market Equilibrium

price because there is neither excess supply nor excess demand. All other prices are disequilibrium prices and if they occur, the market is not in a state of rest. At prices below the equilibrium, there are shortages and rising prices. At prices above the equilibrium, there are surpluses and falling prices.

Shifts in Demand

Now let us look at the effect of an increase in demand on price and quantity. Figure 2.7 shows an increase in demand caused, for example, by an increase in income. With greater disposable income, consumers can spend more money on any good or service; and some consumers will do so for most goods. If the market price were held constant at P_1, we expect to see excess demand. Facing this shortage, sellers would raise prices toward that level indicated by P_2. In Figure 2.7, this is shown as an increase in demand from D_1 to D_2.

In general, neither price nor quantity remains constant when disposable income increases. Rather, the market responds with a new equilibrium price and quantity, as the new demand force interacts with the existing supply force. In Figure 2.7 at point B, we expect to see consumers pay a higher price, and firms produce a greater quantity as a result of an increase in disposable income.

Shifts in Supply

Now let us look at the supply curve. Suppose that there is a change in technology of production lowering assembly costs. How does that affect supply? Lower production costs make production more profitable, encouraging existing firms to expand production and enabling new firms to enter the market and produce. So if the market price stayed constant at P_1, we expect to observe a greater supply of output than before. In Figure 2.8, this is shown as an increase from A to B. Output increases no matter what the price happens to be, so the entire supply curve shifts to the right, which is shown in the figure as a shift from S_1 to S_2. As a result, the market price drops from P_1 to P_2, and the total quantity produced increases from Q_1 to Q_2. Lower costs result in lower prices and increased sales.

Comparative Statics
Analysis

This approach is referred to as **comparative statics.** That is, the theory is static rather than dynamic. Static theory compares different equilibrium points, for example, the shift from equilibrium point A to B in Figure 2.7. Static theory assumes prompt adjustments to changes in the economic environment; it is not concerned with the time required for changes to take place or the organizational and managerial structure needed for the change. Static theory is concerned with determining the direction in which economic variables move in response to other variables. This is important because economic variables are seldom observable or easily manipulated. The comparison of the original equilibrium with the new equilibrium provides the economist with one of the most powerful tools at her disposal. Comparative statics analysis is designed to provide some of the tools that will assist the economist in her analysis of economic variables.

Algebraic Example
of Shift in Equilibrium

Suppose now that with no change in supply, demand increases because of a change in income of consumers. The new demand function, denoted D', is given by

$$Q_d = 13 - P \tag{2.6}$$

The new demand curve represents an increase in demand since at any price more units will be demanded now than previously. We may then determine the new equilibrium price as before by setting the supply function equal to the new demand function, D', and solving for P.

$$
\begin{aligned}
S &= D' \\
2P - 5 &= 13 - P \\
3P &= 18 \\
P &= 6
\end{aligned} \tag{2.7}
$$

Therefore, $Q_d = 13 - 6 = 7$ and $Q_s = 12 - 5 = 7$.

Figure 2.7 A New Equilibrium: Increase in Demand

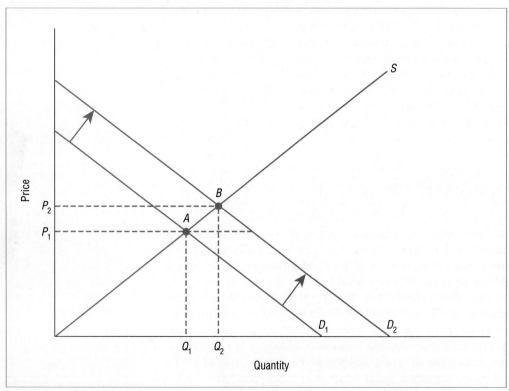

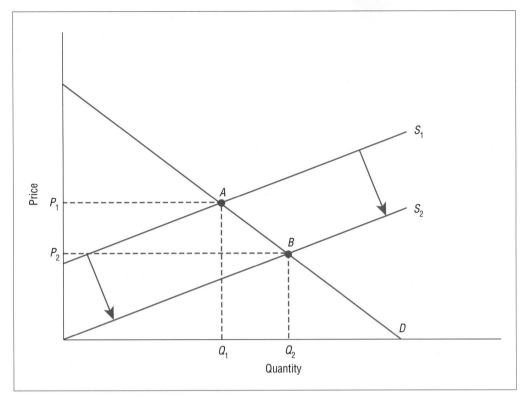

Figure 2.8 A New Equilibrium: Increase in Supply

We can briefly review the concepts of supply and demand. The law of demand states that the quantity demanded of a good varies inversely with its price, other things remaining constant. The law of supply states that the quantity supplied of a good usually varies directly with its price, other things remaining constant. The intersection of the supply and demand curve indicates the equilibrium market price and quantity. A change in demand or a change in supply is represented by a shift of the curve to a new position. Such shifts may occur as a result of changes in any of the nonprice determinants assumed to be constant. Finally, if the demand or supply curves remain fixed, a movement along the curve from one point to another denotes a change in the quantity demanded or a change in the quantity supplied.

ELASTICITY, TOTAL REVENUE, AND MARGINAL REVENUE

As we have seen earlier, the relationship between price and quantity is one of causation. For example, a rise in price causes a decrease in the quantity demanded. It is time that we turn our attention toward describing by how much the quantity demanded changes in response to variations in price.

Elasticity is a general economic concept that measures the change in one variable caused by changes in other, related variables. In short, elasticity measures sensitivity. What is interesting about the concept of elasticity is that it is a pure number, that is, one to which no units are attached.

We can consider and compare elasticity measures for very different commodities. The quantity demanded of both apples and oranges depends on the prices of apples and oranges, respectively. Elasticity enables a useful comparison

Elasticity Defined

49

to be made between the sensitivity of apple demand to changes in the price of apples and the sensitivity of orange demand to changes in the price of oranges.

We will be concerned with three measures of demand elasticity in this section: price elasticity of demand, income elasticity of demand, and cross-elasticity of demand.

Elasticity is a measure of responsiveness of one variable to changes in another. Specifically, it is a number that tells us the percentage change that will occur in one variable in response to a 1 percent change in another variable. Remember that, for example, quantity demanded is a function of price, where price is an independent variable; that is, price determines quantity demanded. We can define a simple mathematical expression quantifying the concept of the price elasticity of demand. This expression is in equation (2.8), with the symbol Δ meaning change in:

$$\varepsilon_p = \frac{\%\Delta \text{ in } Q}{\%\Delta \text{ in } P} \tag{2.8}$$

Since price and quantity demanded are inversely related, ε_p is, technically speaking, a negative number. However, this measure is more easily interpreted if we ignore the minus sign and treat it as a positive entity. Economists consider three cases, depending on the value for ε_p. Shortly, we will explain how numerical values are actually obtained for ε_p; for now, we concentrate on its intuitive meaning.

First, the case of weak percentage response of Q to a change in P is put in the category of **inelastic demand.** The numerator of ε_p is very small relative to the denominator. Thus, for goods with an inelastic demand, ε_p will be a very small number, between zero and one. Put more simply, goods whose demand is inelastic with respect to price are goods whose prices can drastically change with a very small resultant charge in quantity demanded.

For goods with an **elastic demand,** a change in P causes a large change in the quantity demanded. The numerator of ε_p is very large relative to the denominator. Thus, for goods with an elastic demand, ε_p is relatively large: between 1 and infinity. Put more simply, goods whose demand is elastic with respect to price are goods whose quantity demanded changes drastically for some change in price.

The in-between case, where the percentage change in P equals the percentage change in Q, is called **unitary elasticity of demand.** In this case, $\varepsilon_p = 1$.

Equation (2.8) for ε_p is a mathematical equation that can be rearranged to the following:

$$\varepsilon_p = [(\Delta Q)/(\Delta P)] * [P/Q] \tag{2.9}$$

Thus, the price elasticity of demand is the product of two terms. The first term shows the ratio of the change in quantity to the change in price. This concept is similar to that of the slope of a function. In the traditional graphical representation of demand functions, price is put on the vertical axis and quantity is put on the horizontal axis. The expression $(\Delta Q)/(\Delta P)$ is then the inverse (i.e., 1 divided by) the slope of the demand function. The second product in the expression for ε_p is the ratio of price to quantity.

In general, as we move along a given demand curve, the price elasticity of demand changes. Both the price-quantity ratio and the slope of the demand function may change. Therefore, the price elasticity of demand must be measured at a particular point on the demand curve or, at the least, over a very small region of the demand curve.

Beware of a very common mistake. Often the slope of a curve is confused with its elasticity. You might think that a steep slope must mean inelastic demand and that a flat slope must mean elastic demand. This is not quite true. Why not?

Because the slope of the demand curve depends on the absolute change in P and Q, whereas elasticity depends on the percentage of change.

This can be easily demonstrated with a linear demand curve of the form

$$Q = a - bP, \qquad\qquad (2.10)$$

where a and b are numerical constants. As an example, consider the following demand curve ($a = 10$ and $b = 1$):

$$Q = 10 - P \qquad\qquad (2.11)$$

For this curve, $(\Delta Q)/(\Delta P)$ is constant and equal to -1. However, the curve does not have a constant elasticity. As shown in Figure 2.9 as we move down the demand curve, the ratio P/Q falls; therefore, the elasticity decreases in magnitude. Near the intersection of the curve with the price axis, Q is very small; so elasticity is large in magnitude. When $P = 7$, elasticity is greater than 1. When $P = 3$, elasticity is less than 1. As the demand curve approaches the vertical axis, the ratio of P/Q gets to be quite large and elasticity approaches infinity. As the demand curve approaches the horizontal axis, the ratio P/Q approaches 0, causing elasticity also to approach 0. At the midpoint of the demand curve, $(\Delta Q)/(\Delta P) \times (P/Q) = -1$. This is the point of unitary elasticity.

If a demand curve is perfectly **elastic** throughout, or if it has an elasticity of zero at all points, it is not inappropriate to speak of the elasticity of the curve since the elasticity is uniform at all points or between any two points. The case of the perfectly elastic demand curve is an important one for economics, and such a demand curve is shown in Figure 2.10a. It is infinitely elastic. A perfectly **inelastic** demand curve is said to have an elasticity of zero and is shown in Figure 2.10b.

Figure 2.9 Elasticity and Demand Curve

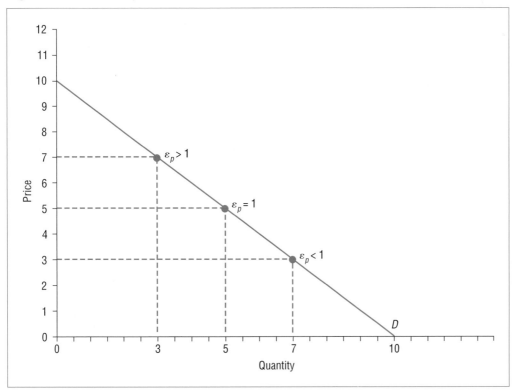

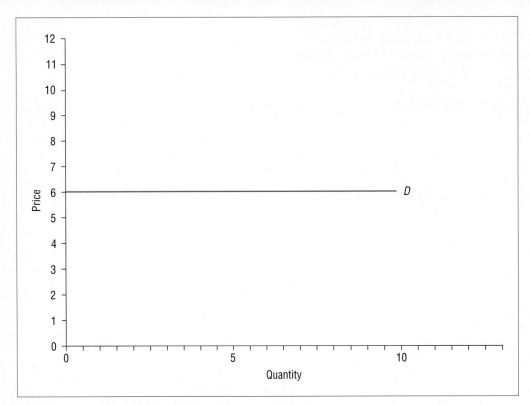

Figure 2.10a Perfectly Elastic Demand Curve

Figure 2.10b Perfectly Inelastic Demand Function

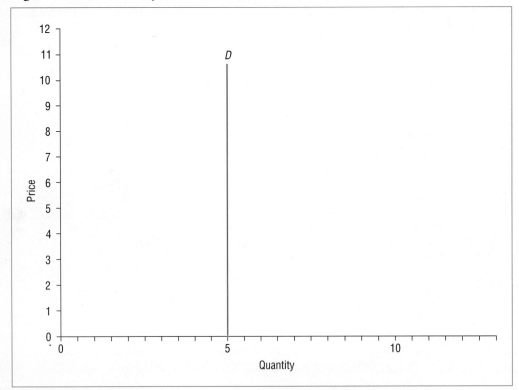

Let's stop for a moment to examine the numerical details of the elasticity of demand calculation. There is always a slight ambiguity about percentage changes. Fortunately, when it comes to very small percentage changes, as from 99 to 100 or from 100 to 101, the difference between 1/99 and 1/100 is hardly worth talking about. For small changes, it matters little how you calculate the percentage change. For larger changes, it may make quite a difference. Unfortunately, no single approach can be declared to be the right one. Elasticity can be measured two different ways, point elasticity and arc elasticity. **Point elasticity** measures elasticity at a given point on a demand function, and **arc elasticity** is a measurement done over a range of a function.

We have already obtained equation (2.9), which can be used to calculate the point elasticity of demand:

$$\varepsilon_p = [(\Delta Q)/(\Delta P)] * [P/Q]$$

Recall that this implies that ε_p is the product of two ratios: the inverse of the slope of the demand function and the price-to-quantity ratio. In Figure 2.11, we show a linear demand function with the equation

$$Q = 100 - 5P \qquad (2.12)$$

To calculate the price elasticity of demand at various points on the demand function shown in Figure 2.11, we need three pieces of information, a price, a quantity, and $\Delta Q/\Delta P$. At a price of 10, the quantity demanded is 50. Also at a price of 10, the $\Delta Q/\Delta P$ ratio is (–5). Thus, the point of elasticity of demand at $P = 10$ is given by $[(\Delta Q)/(\Delta P)] * [P/Q]$, or $[(-5)] * [(10/50)] = -1$. Thus, when $P = 10$, the demand function in Figure 2.11 has unitary elasticity. At a price of 15, the quantity demanded is 25, and the $\Delta Q/\Delta P$ ratio remains equal to (–5). The point elasticity

Figure 2.11 Measuring Point Elasticity

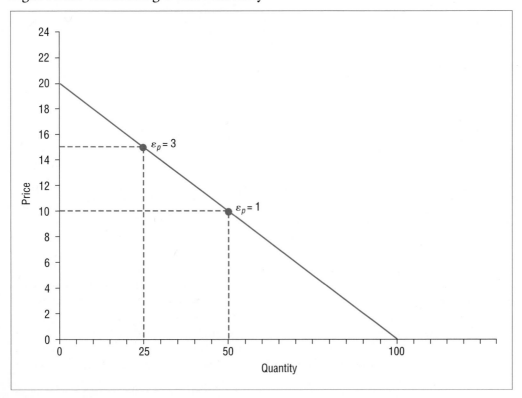

of demand when $P = 15$ is then given by $[(-5)] * [(15/25)] = -3$. At a price of 15, the demand function in Figure 2.11 is price elastic.

In general, for all linear demand curves of the form

$$Q = a - b*P, \tag{2.13}$$

where a and b are numerical constants, the point elasticity of demand can be shown to be equal to

$$(-b) * [P/(a - b*P)] \tag{2.14}$$

Notice that for linear functions, the $\Delta Q/\Delta P$ term is constant, that is, does not vary with P or Q.

Arc elasticity is an alternative measurement of the price elasticity of demand. The calculation of arc elasticity requires far less information than does the calculation of point elasticity.

When calculating arc elasticity, it is important to determine the percentage change based on the averages of the price and quantity ranges. For example, consider the calculation of the elasticity of demand for movie tickets between $8 and $9. If you calculate the percentage of change with $8 as the base, the percentage change is 12.5 percent. However, if you calculate the same change with $9 as the base, the percentage change is 11 percent. A good rule to use is to calculate the price change relative to neither the higher nor the lower of the two prices but to their average. Arc elasticity measures the average elasticity over a given range of a demand curve. We assume then that we know two points on the demand curve. Let those two points be (Q_1, P_1) and (Q_2, P_2). The arc elasticity formula is

$$\frac{\Delta Q/\text{average } Q}{\Delta P/\text{average } P} \text{ or } [(Q1 - Q2)/(P1 - P2)] * [(P1 + P2)/(Q1 + Q2)] \tag{2.15}$$

Arc elasticity can be estimated from the following demand curve:

$$Qd = 30 - 5P \tag{2.16}$$

As shown in Figure 2.12, assume that the price is increased from $2 to $4. At the $4 price, the quantity demanded is 10, and at $2, the quantity demanded is 20. The change in Q, ΔQ is 10, the average Q is $(20 + 10)/2 = 15$; the change in P, ΔP is 2; and the average P is 3. Substituting these values into the equation for arc elasticity yields

$$\frac{10/15}{-2/3}$$

which simplifies to -1.

Which measure, point or arc, to use depends on the problem to be studied and the amount of information available to the decision maker. When the range of change is small and approaches zero, the point elasticity formula is preferred. However, when the range is greater than, for example, 5 percent, it is appropriate to use the arc elasticity formula. We also point out that using the point elasticity formula requires that the analyst know the exact demand function or at least its slope. If it is assumed that the demand function is not stable, that is, has shifted over time, using the arc formula may pose a problem since the analyst might end up comparing two points on two separate demand functions.

**Price Elasticity
of Demand**

What determines the price elasticity of demand for particular goods? It is important to be able to quantify the various measures of elasticity, but a great deal of intuition is involved in finding what factors cause a good to have an elastic or inelastic demand.

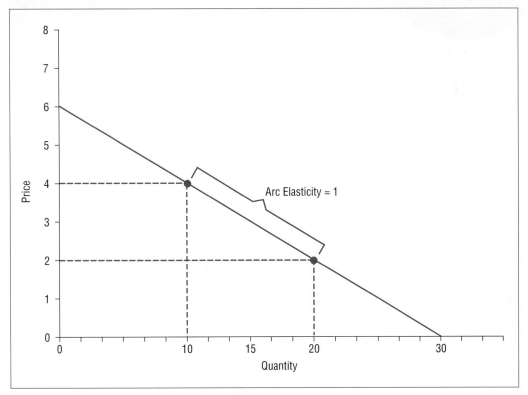

Figure 2.12 Measuring Arc Elasticity

Far and away, the most important factor in determining elasticity is the availability of substitutes for a particular good. As more substitutes are available, demand becomes more and more elastic. As fewer substitutes are available, demand becomes more and more inelastic. The demand for the experimental AIDS drug AZT is probably very, very inelastic. Even though the price of AZT could conceivably increase greatly, there would be little variation in the quantity of the good demanded by AIDS patients. However, if the price of potato chips were to increase substantially, consumers would very likely shift their consumption toward pretzels and nachos.

Also related to the availability of substitutes is the width of the definition used in defining the good. For widely defined goods, demand tends to be more price inelastic than for more narrowly defined goods. For example, the demand for meat is probably price inelastic. The demand for beef or chicken is probably more responsive to changes in the prices of these goods and, hence, more elastic.

A third dimension that affects the price elasticity of demand concerns the percentage of a consumer's budget spent on a commodity. If consumers spend a very small portion of their budget on a commodity, there is a tendency for demand to be price inelastic. We probably spend an almost negligible percentage of our incomes on salt; the demand for salt is likely to be very price inelastic.

One of the most useful features of the concept of price elasticity is that it can be used to predict the effect of price changes on total revenue. Remember that elasticity can be equal to 1, greater than 1, or less than 1. Depending on the degree of price elasticity, a reduction in price can increase total revenue, decrease it, or leave it unchanged. If we have a good estimate of price elasticity, we can estimate quite accurately the change in total revenue.

Recall from your principles of economics course that **total revenue** (*TR*) is

Price Elasticity and Total Revenue

equal to price (P) times quantity (Q). If we change price in one direction, there will be a change in quantity in the opposite direction; the net effect on total revenues depends on which effect dominates. Say, for example, that price increases and quantity decreases. The higher price, by itself, tends to raise total revenues; the lower the quantity sold tends to reduce total revenues. The resolution of these opposing forces on total revenues depends on the price elasticity of demand.

If demand is price elastic, then ε_p is greater than 1, and the %Δ in Q is larger than the %Δ in P. If price increases when demand is price elastic, the impact of the quantity effect dominates the impact of the price effect, and total revenues fall. Likewise, if demand is price elastic, a price decrease causes total revenues to increase.

A summary of the effects on total revenues from price changes is shown in Table 2.4.

A more mathematical treatment of price elasticity of demand and its relationship to total revenues is also possible and is presented in Appendix A at the end of this chapter.

**Income Elasticity
of Demand**

We may be interested in elasticities of demand with respect to other variables besides price. Income is another important determinant of demand. For example, demand for most goods usually rises when income rises. The **income elasticity of demand** measures the responsiveness of demand to changes in income, holding constant the effect of all other variables that influence demand.

The income elasticity of demand is the percentage change in the quantity demanded, Q, resulting from a 1 percent change in income (I):

$$\varepsilon_I = \frac{\%\Delta Q}{\%\Delta I} \tag{2.17}$$

Income and the quantity purchased usually move in the same direction; thus, ε_I is usually greater than zero, although it may conceivably be negative. When ε_I is positive, the good is said to be a normal good; when ε_I is negative, the good is said to be an inferior good. Automobiles, jewelry, and housing are normal goods. Some examples of inferior goods are generic potato chips, public transportation, and beer.

**Cross-Price Elasticity
of Demand**

The demand for some goods is also affected by the price of other goods. For example, because butter and margarine can easily be substituted for each other, the demand for each depends on the price of the other. As the price of chicken rises, so does the demand for beef. The **cross-price elasticity of demand, $\varepsilon_{x,y}$** for goods x and y, refers to the percentage of change in the quantity demanded for a good x resulting from a 1 percent increase in the price of another good or service, y. So, for example, the cross-price elasticity of demand for butter with respect to the price of margarine would be written as

$$\varepsilon_{b,m} = \%\Delta \text{ Quantity of Butter}/\%\Delta \text{ in Price of Margarine} \tag{2.18}$$

Table 2.4	**Elasticity and Total Revenue**			
	The Case of	Implies	Following a Price Increase, Revenue	Following a Price Decrease, Revenue
1.	Elastic demand, $\varepsilon_p > 1$	$\%\Delta Q > \%\Delta P$	Decreases	Increases
2.	Unitary elasticity, $\varepsilon_p = 1$	$\%\Delta Q = \%\Delta P$	Is unchanged	Is unchanged
3.	Inelastic demand, $\varepsilon_p < 1$	$\%\Delta Q < \%\Delta P$	Increases	Decreases

Next we examine how exchange in a free and competitive market leads to gains for both buyers and sellers. Consumers buy goods because the purchases make them better off. However, because different consumers value particular goods and services differently, the maximum they are willing to pay for these goods and services also varies. **Consumer surplus** is the difference between what a consumer is willing to pay for a good and what she or he actually pays. For example, suppose that one consumer values a good much more highly than another. However, they both will pay the same price for the commodity because in perfect competition there is only one price. In other words, some consumers would pay more for a good or service than they had to.

Suppose, for example, that there are two consumers in the market, Danny and Andrea. Danny values the one unit of the good he purchases at $15; Andrea values her one unit of the good at $10. If the market price of the good is $10, then Danny earns a consumer surplus of $5 and Andrea earns no consumer surplus. Andrea is not hurt by the transaction; she will still buy the unit for $10. The total consumer surplus in this market is then $5.

In a more general sense, the consumer surplus in a free, competitive market is all of the area under the demand function and above the market price. In Figure 2.13, the amount of consumer surplus is shown as the area of the right triangle *ABC*. Notice that triangle *ABC* is bounded above by the demand function and below by the horizontal line at the market price.

An analogous concept to consumer surplus exists for the supply curve called **producer surplus.** Producer surplus is the area above the supply curve and below the market price. It is measured by the right triangle *DBC* in Figure 2.13. Some

Figure 2.13 Benefits of Exchange

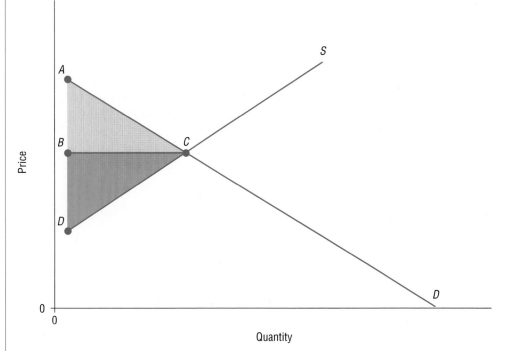

producers are producing goods and services just at the market price. At a lower price, these producers would not be in the market. However, some producers would be willing to produce if the price were below the market price. These producers would sell even if the market price were lower because their costs are lower.

Therefore, consumer surplus and producer surplus measure the welfare benefits of a competitive market. The total gain from exchange is measured by the area between the supply curve and the demand curve.

Considered jointly, consumers and producers are made as well off as possible by exchange in free, competitive markets. Technically, we would say that the sum of producer and consumer surplus is maximized under free, competitive exchange.

▌ CHAPTER SUMMARY AND KEY IDEAS ▌ ▌ ▌ ▌ ▌ ▌

This chapter explained how competitive exchange works. First, we examined the scientific method. Economists rely on the scientific method to study markets. Economists use both normative and positive economics to examine the economy. The economy is organized by markets that facilitate exchange between households and firms.

The main force operating on exchange in the economy is competition. When competition is perfect, government does not have to intervene in the market. The basic competitive model in the economy studies demand, supply, and price. Demand is the quantity of goods or services that customers are willing and able to purchase. Supply is the quantity of goods and services that firms are willing to supply. The equilibrium price occurs when the quantity demanded and the quantity supplied are in equilibrium. If the quantity demanded is greater than the quantity supplied, there is a shortage in the market. If the quantity demanded is less than the quantity supplied, there is a surplus in the market.

A change in demand is a shift from one demand curve to another, reflecting a change in one of the nonprice determinants of demand. A change in supply is a shift from one supply curve to another, reflecting a change in one of the nonprice determinants of supply. The study of two equilibrium points is comparative statics.

Elasticity is a measure of responsiveness of one variable to another. Price elasticity of demand is the percentage change in the quantity demanded of a good resulting from a 1 percent increase in the price of that good. Demand for a good may either be elastic, inelastic, or unit elastic. Two other measured elasticities of demand are income elasticity of demand and price cross-elasticity of demand.

One of the most useful features of elasticity is that it can be used to predict the effect of price changes on total revenue. If demand is elastic, a decrease in price results in an increase in revenue. If demand is inelastic, an increase in price results in an increase in revenue.

Competitive exchange leads to the concept of consumer and producer surplus. These gains from exchange are an important outcome of the market economy.

▌ KEY TERMS

arc elasticity	comparative statics
change in demand	consumer surplus
change in quantity demanded	cross-price elasticity of demand
change in quantity supplied	demand
change in supply	demand curve

demand function
derived demand
direct demand
disequilibrium
elastic
elastic demand
elasticity
equilibrium
hard sciences
income elasticity of demand
inelastic demand
logical positivism
market
normative economics

perfect competition
point elasticity
positive economics
producer surplus
rationality
scientific method
shortage
soft science
supply
supply curve
supply function
surplus
total revenue
unitary elasticity of demand

FURTHER READINGS

Boulding, K. E. *Economic Analysis*, 3rd ed. New York: Harper and Row, 1955.

Robbins, L. *An Essay on the Nature and Significance of Economic Science*, 2nd ed. London: Macmillan & Co., 1935.

Smith, A. *An Inquiry into the Nature and Causes of the Wealth of Nations*. Chicago: The University of Chicago Press, 1976.

Stigler, G. J. *The Theory of Price*. New York: The Macmillan Co., 1952.

QUESTIONS AND PROBLEMS FOR REVIEW AND DISCUSSION

A. Construct (i.e., draw) a supply and demand model to explain the following three situations. Please include with each picture a brief paragraph of explanation.

 1. Consider the market segment for cars that contains the Ford Taurus and Honda Accord. Explain what you expect to happen to the price of Ford Taurus if the exchange rate between the dollar and yen changes substantially. Suppose that the dollar becomes much stronger relative to the yen.

 2. Show the effects in the market for cigarettes if President Clinton's health plan is passed and a tax is imposed on a package of cigarettes that approximately equals its current price.

 3. Show the effects in the market for "lunch" in the area near your university if a new restaurant featuring cheap and fast food opens directly nearby.

 4. Consider the market for generic paper towels. This is the paper towel market for those of us consumers who lack the purchasing power to buy "Bounty" or some other name brand. Suppose that as a result of an economic expansion, real consumer incomes increase by 30%. Show the effects of this increase in real income in the generic paper towel market.

B. Explain whether the following goods and services have a demand that is either price elastic or inelastic. Be sure to clearly explain why you have chosen your answer.

 1. Secretaries.

 2. Strawberries.

 3. Gasoline.

 4. Cigarettes.

C. Advertising serves many goals in our economic system (some of these are noble). One purpose of advertising in consumer goods markets is to differentiate products. There are, for example, about a billion different types of laundry soaps; each is nearly equally able to clean your clothes. Explain, using the concept of the price elasticity of demand, one rationale for this practice. Be sure to use all the relevant concepts and frame your discussion in language that a layperson could understand.

D. Assume for this question that the necessary competitive assumptions are fulfilled and that the market for used cars is blessed with competition among and between sellers. Information is not freely distributed in this market. For any given used car, the seller would have a tremendous informational advantage over any potential buyer. Explain how the supply and demand functions would differ because of this uneven spread of information. In any diagram that you may (should) draw, make one demand and supply function where information is not a problem. On that same diagram (if you draw it), include curves that show the effects in the market of the uneven distribution of information.

E. Suppose that I am selling cans of beer to people on a beach. Since I am concerned about my income (and since I am the only beer seller), I decide to sell the beer in the following way. I will not tell the people on the beach how many cans of beer I have. I will sell the cans of beer individually, or one at a time, to my customers. Each can of beer will go to the highest bidder, and the person who buys the can of beer from me will be required to consume the beer. As such, I am basically holding an auction for the beer. The first can of beer sells for $3.70. The second can of beer sells for $3.40, the third for $3.10, the fourth for $2.80, the fifth for $2.50, and the sixth for $2.20.

    1. In either tabular or graphical form, show the demand for beer function for the consumers on the beach.

    2. If I offer to sell the beer at a single price of $2.80 (i.e., do not follow my auction scheme), how many cans of beer will I sell?

    3. If I sell the beer at a single price of $2.20, what is the consumer surplus in the market?

    4. If I sell the beer individually according to the rules of the auction, what is the consumer surplus?

F. **1.** Draw a supply and demand curve for the beer for people on the beach market of problem (E) if I am going to sell the beer according to rules stated there for the auction.

    2. Is there a supply function? Explain why or why not.

▮ APPENDIX 2A   Price Elasticity, Demand, and Total Revenue

In this appendix we use some of the tools available from mathematics to shed some light on the relationship between the price elasticity of demand and total revenue.

    We begin with a general statement of a demand function that is inverted; that is, it expresses P as a function of Q rather than Q as a function of P. Notice that P and Q are still negatively related and that an increase in Q can be obtained only by a reduction in P.

$$P = a - b*Q \qquad (2A.1)$$

The notation implies that a and b represent any positive, constant values. We will refer to a as the vertial intercept, since it reveals the value for price, P, when Q is zero. Likewise, b is termed the slope of the function since it shows the change in P for a one-unit change in Q. When the demand relationship is written in this way, it is referred to as the *average revenue*, or *AR*, function since it shows the revenue received for each of Q units sold.

Since total revenues, *TR*, are equal to price times quantity, we can multiply each side by *Q* to obtain:

$$TR = AR * Q = P * Q = (a - b*Q)*Q$$
$$\text{or,} \tag{2A.2}$$
$$TR = a*Q - b*Q^2$$

Marginal revenue, *MR*, is defined as the change in total revenue resulting from a one-unit change in output, *Q*. As such, we can write the marginal revenue function, also expressed in terms of *Q* as:[4]

$$MR = a - 2*b*Q \tag{2A.3}$$

Some additional intuition is possible by looking at all of these relationships in a graphical context. This is accomplished in the two panels of Figure 2.14. Panel (a) shows a total revenue function of the form discussed above. In panel (b) you will find the corresponding average and marginal revenue functions. In these displays, the values for *a* and *b* are 100 and 0.25, respectively. Thus, the functions are

Average Revenue or *AR*: $P = 100 - 0.25*Q$
Total Revenue: $TR = P*Q = 100*Q - 0.25*Q^2$
Marginal Revenue: $MR = 100 - 0.5*Q$

In panel (a) of Figure 2.14, notice that total revenues are maximized when $Q = 200$ at point *C*. In the lower panel, notice that marginal revenue equals zero whenever $Q = 200$. A comparison of equations 2A.1 and 2A.3 displayed for the sample values of *a* and *b* in panel (b) yields some insights as well. Both the average revenue and the marginal revenue share the same vertical intercept, 100 in this example and *a* in general. Also note that the marginal revenue is twice as steep as the average revenue function. Thus, given the same starting point, the *AR* function hits the horizontal axis twice as fast as does the *MR* function.

It is also true that total revenues are maximized whenever marginal revenue equals zero. We can easily argue this point without the use of mathematical techniques. First, the marginal revenue function is decreasing. Second, when the *MR* function is positive, additional output causes an increase in total revenues. Likewise, when the *MR* function is negative, additional output causes a decrease in total revenues. Thus, for total revenues to be maximized, *MR* must be zero.

▉ APPENDIX 2B Price Elasticity and Optimal Pricing Policy

A bit of knowledge relating demand, total revenues, and price elasticity can be of great help to managers in determining an appropriate pricing policy. The simple relationship between marginal revenue, price, and point elasticity of demand may be one of the most useful pricing tools managerial economics has to offer. The relationship between marginal revenue, price, and point price elasticity of demand can be stated as follows:

$$MR = P(1 + 1/\varepsilon_p) \tag{2B.1}$$

where ε_p is the point elasticity of demand.

To illustrate the usefulness of this relationship, recall from your introductory course that the firm maximizes profits by producing when $MR = MC$. By equating marginal costs with marginal revenues, the profit-maximizing level of output can be determined.

---

[4]For those who know some calculus, the marginal revenue function is obtained by taking the derivative of the total revenue function with respect to *Q*. If you don't know calculus, take our word for it.

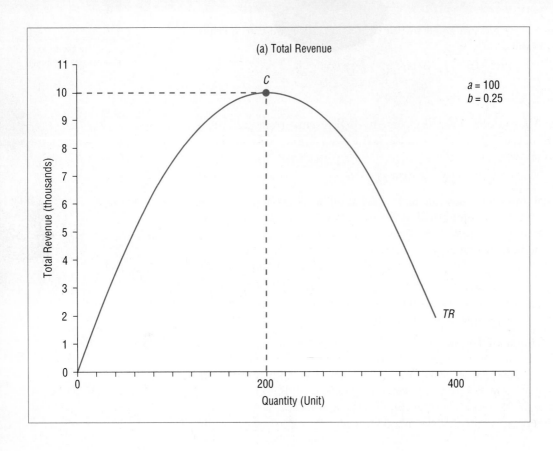

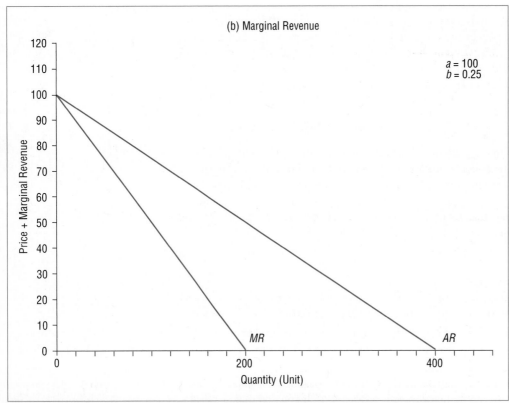

Figure 2.14 Demand and Price Elasticity

Suppose that your local supermarket ran a sale on hamburger last week and found that a 4 percent discount resulted in a 12 percent increase in weekly sales. The point elasticity of demand for hamburger is

$$\varepsilon_p = \frac{\%\Delta \text{ in } Q}{\%\Delta \text{ in } P}$$
$$= 12/-4$$
$$= -3$$

What is the optimal price for hamburger if the supermarket's relevant marginal costs per unit for hamburger is $1.50? Working with equation 2B.1, we can build the following relationship:

$$MC = MR$$
$$MC = P(1 + 1/\varepsilon_p)$$

which implies that the optimal or profit maximizing price, P^*, equals

$$P^* = \frac{MC}{(1 + 1/\varepsilon_p)}$$

With marginal cost of $1.50 and $\varepsilon_p = -3$, the profit-maximizing price is then

$$P^* = \frac{\$1.50}{(1 + 1/-3)}$$
$$= \$2.25$$

Therefore, the profit-maximizing price on the supermarket's hamburger is $2.25 a pound. The preceding equations can be used to calculate profit-maximizing price under current cost and market conditions, as well as under a variety of conditions.

Sometimes managers are interested in maximizing total revenues rather than profits. Equation (2B.1) can also be used to help managers achieve these ends. We can clearly see that if, at the price charged, demand is price elastic and marginal revenues are positive, lowering price will increase total revenues.

In Table 2.5 we display a numerical example drawn from the sample values of Appendix 2A. The demand relationship is shown in the first two columns. A price of $6 in this example is seen to be too high since lowering it to $5 increases total revenues.

Table 2.5 Demand, Total Revenue, Marginal Revenue, and Elasticity

Price (P)	Quantity (Q)	Total Revenue (TR = P*Q)	Marginal Revenue (MR = ΔTR/ΔQ)	Point Price Elasticity ($\varepsilon_p = (\Delta Q/\Delta P)\,\varepsilon_p\,(P/Q)$)
$10	0	0	0	
9	40	360	80	−9.00
8	80	640	60	−4.00
7	120	840	40	−2.33
6	160	960	20	−1.50
5	200	1,000	0	−1.00
4	240	960	−20	−0.66
3	280	840	−40	−0.43
2	320	640	−60	−0.25
1	360	360	−80	−0.11

3

The Neoclassical Theory of the Firm

The firm in the model world of economic micro-theory ought not to call forth any irrelevant associations with firms in the real world. We know, of course, that there are firms in reality and that they have boards of directors and senior and junior executives, who do, with reference to hundreds of different products, a great many things—which are entirely irrelevant for the micro-theoretical model.[1]

CHAPTER OUTLINE AND STUDENT GOALS

The last chapter examined the elements of perfect competition. In this chapter we would like to turn to the supply side of the economy and examine the behavior of firms. We will see how firms determine the optimal level of output, how the cost of production changes as output increases, and how profits are maximized.

In the perfectly competitive economy, there are many firms and each is a price taker responding freely to prices set by the market. No single firm has any market power, or control over the price of its product. Individual producers are passive quantity adjusters who respond to market signals.[2] As the opening quotation makes clear, firms in a perfectly competitive world have very little to do. The impersonal force of the perfectly competitive market produces an appropriate response to all changes, be they in tastes or technology.

Throughout most of this book, you will study the firm from the inside out. We will be looking "under the hood" to understand the functions of the engine and the transmission. The theory of the inner workings of the organization—the principal-agent model and the transactions cost model—is the subject of Chapters 5 through 8. The theory is applied to organizations in the rest of the book. However, before we study the mechanics of the car, we would like to learn a little about how to drive it and how it responds to its environment. We may even be interested in the "highway system" and perhaps about the "regulations" that determine what kind of car can go on the highway, who can drive it, and how fast it can go.

In the neoclassical model the firm is a black box. It is a black box in the same sense that a computer chip is a black box. You may know what it does, but you have very little understanding of how the microprocessor in your computer works. This chapter has four parts: the theory of production, the cost of production, assumptions of perfect competition, and the firm in perfectly competitive markets. The assumption of profit maximization is analyzed for both short-run and long-run equilibrium.

---

[1]Fritz Machlup, quoted in "Theories of the Firm," *American Economic Review* 57, 1967, p. 29.
[2]Ibid.

After reading this chapter, you should be able to

- Understand the difference between short-run and long-run cost.
- Explain how a production function turns inputs into outputs and the difference between total, average, and marginal product.
- Explain profit-maximizing behavior of firms.
- Explain why a firm may be loosing money in the short run and still stay in business.
- Explain why the demand curve for a perfectly competitive firm is perfectly elastic.
- Understand how entry and exit work to cause equilibrium in the long run.

▦ THE THEORY OF PRODUCTION

The theory of production is concerned with the way in which physical resources are employed to produce a firm's products. The concept of production encompasses the production of both goods and services. We can divide inputs into broad categories of labor, materials, and capital. Labor inputs include skilled workers and unskilled workers, as well as the efforts of the firm's managers. The theory of production is also concerned with the level of technology used to produce goods and services. Materials include steel, plastics, electricity, water, and so on. Capital includes buildings, equipment, and inventories.

The relationship between the inputs to the production process and the resulting output is described by a production function. A **production function** is a descriptive statement that relates inputs to outputs. It specifies the maximum output that can be produced for a given number of inputs. The actual production function is determined by the given state of technology (i.e., a given state of knowledge about the various methods that might be used to transform inputs into outputs). Any improvement in technology—for example, a new, faster computer chip—that permits a manufacturing company to produce a given output with fewer raw materials results in a new production function.

The production function describes what is technically feasible when the firm operates efficiently. *Efficiency* refers to the situation in which the firm uses each combination of inputs in a manner that produces the largest possible output. The relationship between the inputs of the production process and the resulting output is described by a production function. A production function indicates the output (Q) that a firm produces for every specified combination of inputs. The basic properties of the production function can be illustrated by a simple two-input, capital (K) and labor (L), model. The production function can be written as follows:

$$Q = F(K,L) \tag{3.1}$$

This function states that the quantity of output (Q) depends on the quantity of the two inputs, capital (K) and labor (L). This production process could describe, for example, the amount of wheat that can be grown with different amounts of land and labor. The production function can be used to describe two different situations. The first situation looks at the relationship between inputs and outputs when all inputs are increased or decreased together. The second looks at how inputs can be combined in different combinations to produce the same output. Note that a highway can be built with either large amounts of machinery and a few operators or with thousands and thousands of workers and very little machinery.

In production it is important to distinguish between the short and the long

Production
with One Variable Input

run. The short run pertains to a period of time in which one or more factor of production cannot be changed. For example, the capital in an automobile plant cannot be changed in the short run since it takes years to build a new plant. However, additional labor can be hired rather quickly. Factors that cannot be varied over this period of time are called *fixed factors*.

Assume that a firm starts with a fixed amount of capital and contemplates applying various amounts of labor to it. The output of the variable and fixed inputs will be the total product. The term *total product* denotes total production from a production system. Total production is identical to the measure Q in equation (3.1). If the inputs of all but one factor are held constant, total product changes as more or less of the variable factor is used. The manager has to decide how much labor to hire and how much output to produce.

The **total product** concept is used to describe the relationship between output and variations in only one input in a production function. Table 3.1 shows this information. The amount of the variable input is shown in column 1. The second column shows the amount of the fixed factor. The third column is to total product. For example, with capital fixed at 20 units, 3 units of labor will produce 60 units of output. When labor input is zero, total product is also zero. You cannot produce without variable inputs. As variable inputs are increased, total product is initially increased but eventually declines because too much of the variable input is added. A classic example is fertilizer applied to an acre of land. A small amount of fertilizer greatly increases total product; however, a great amount of fertilizer will destroy the crops.

For any given production process, it is important to know how production will change as a variable input is changed. The contribution that the variable factor makes to the production process can be described by the average and marginal products of labor.

The **marginal product** of a factor is the change in total product resulting from the use of one more unit of the variable factor, holding all other factors constant. The marginal product can be expressed as

$$\text{Marginal Product} = \frac{\text{Change in Output}}{\text{Change in Labor Input}} = \frac{\Delta Q}{\Delta L} \tag{3.2}$$

Table 3.1	Production with One Variable Input			
(1)	(2)	(3)	(4)	(5)
	Fixed	Total	Average	Marginal
Labor	Capital	Product	Product	Product
L	K	Q	Q/L	$\Delta Q/\Delta L$
0	20	0	—	—
1	20	10	10	10
2	20	30	15	20
3	20	60	20	30
4	20	80	20	20
5	20	95	19	15
6	20	108	18	13
7	20	112	16	4
8	20	112	14	0
9	20	108	12	−4
10	20	100	10	−8

The marginal product of labor is shown in column 5 of Table 3.1. For example, with capital fixed at 20 when labor is increased from 3 to 4 units, total product increases from 60 to 80, creating a marginal product of 20 (80 – 60).

The **average product** of labor is shown in column 4 of Table 3.1. A factor's average product is the total product divided by the number of units of input employed. The average product of labor is shown in Table 3.1 in column 4. At 6 units of labor input, the average product is 16 (108/6).

The relationship between the average-, marginal-, and total-product curves can be seen by looking at Figure 3.1. The marginal product equals the slope of the total product curve, while the average product equals the slope of a line drawn from the origin to a point on the total product curve.

Three important points may be illustrated in Figure 3.1(a). Point A is the inflection point on the total product curve, and it is the point at which marginal product is at a maximum. The marginal product of labor increases until it reaches this point and then decreases until it reaches zero. Technical efficiency rules out the possibility of negative marginal product. The marginal product is at a maximum at point A' in Figure 3.1b.

The second point, B, on the total product curve is where average product is a maximum. The slope of the line from the origin is tangent to the total product curve at point B. The slope of this line measures the average product of labor. Point B is also the point at which the marginal product intersects the average product. The marginal product curve intersects the average product curve from above. That is, the average product is increasing as long as the marginal product is greater than the average. This is illustrated by the fact that the slopes of successive lines drawn from the origin to the total product curve increase until point B, after which their slopes decline. Average product equals marginal product at point B' in Figure 3.1b.

The third point, C, indicates where the slope of the total product curve is zero. At this point, total product is at a maximum and marginal product is zero. When the total product is maximized, the slope of the tangent to the total product curve is zero. Beyond this point, any additional labor inputs will reduce, instead of increase, total product.

In Figure 3.1b, the points on the unit production curves that correspond to points A, B, and C in Figure 3.1a are marked as points A', B', and C'.

The variations in output that result from applying more or less of a variable factor to a given quantity of a fixed factor are the subject of a famous economic law called the **law of diminishing returns.** The law states that if increasing amounts of a variable factor are applied to a given amount of a fixed factor, eventually a situation will be reached in which each additional unit of the variable factor adds less to total product than did the previous unit.

Stated differently, the law of diminishing returns states that the marginal product of the variable factor must eventually decline if enough of it is combined with some fixed quantity of one or more other factors in a production system. The hypothesis predicts only that sooner or later the *MP* curve will decline, but it is not clear when it will decline. The law of diminishing marginal returns is usually applied to the short run. However, it can be applied to the long run.

Consider the issue of a variable number of workers in a manufacturing operation. If there is only one worker, that worker must do all the tasks, shifting from one to another and becoming competent in each. As a second, third, and other workers are added, it is often possible to break the tasks into a large number of separate jobs, with each laborer specializing in one job and becoming expert at it. This process is called the **division of labor.**

The law of diminishing returns applies to a given production technology. Over time, however, inventions and other improvements in technology may allow the en-

The Law
of Diminishing Returns

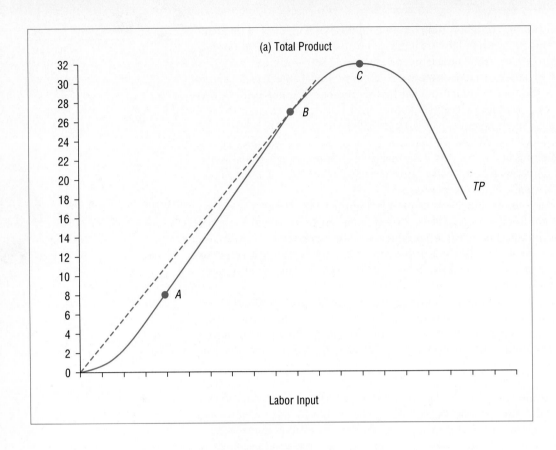

(a) Total Product

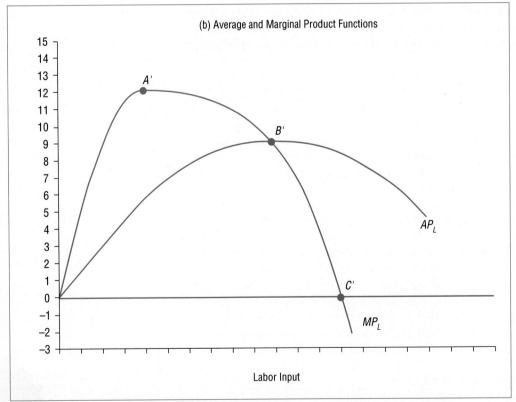

(b) Average and Marginal Product Functions

Figure 3.1 Production Function

tire total product curve to shift upward, so that more can be produced with the same inputs. The shifting of the total product curve hides the presence of diminishing returns and suggests that they need not have any negative long-run implications for economic growth. This issue will be discussed in more detail in Chapter 15.

THE COST OF PRODUCTION

Having examined the firm's production technology, the method by which inputs are turned into outputs, we now turn to the firm's costs. The production technology together with the cost of factor inputs determines the firm's cost of production.

Accountants and economists have different views of costs. Accountants take a historical view. That is, they are concerned with money that has already been spent. Economists, and managers, have a forward-looking view of the firm. Therefore, they are concerned with what costs are expected to be in the future. The cost of a "thing" is what must be given up to acquire it. For example, the cost of a college education is the income that must be forgone while in school. The cost of living in a house you own is the rent that you forgo by not renting it out. This forward-looking view of costs is known as **opportunity cost.** These are costs that are forgone by not putting a firm's resources to its highest use.

Costs are important to managers because profits are the main motivating force in a market economy. Also, profit is the difference between total revenue and total cost:

$$\pi = TR - TC \tag{3.3}$$

where π is profit, TR is **total revenue,** and TC is **total cost.** Opportunity costs are a part of total cost. Opportunity costs are costs associated with opportunities forgone. For example, an owner who manages his or her own business but chooses not to take a salary forgoes an opportunity to earn a salary somewhere else. Although no monetary costs have been incurred and no costs appeared on the accounting statement, an opportunity cost nevertheless has been incurred by forgoing income from another occupation. The **opportunity cost of capital** is the rate of return that one could earn by investing in a different project with similar risk. Another cost of doing business may be the return to one's own funds invested in one's business that could earn an income if invested elsewhere.

From the point of view of the manager, all costs can be classified as either short-run or long-run costs. In the short run, some costs can be varied with the rate of production, while others are fixed.

Total cost (TC) refers to the total cost of producing any given level of output. The total cost of production is divided into two parts: variable cost (VC), and fixed cost (FC). **Fixed costs** are those that do not vary with output. These costs include insurance, plant maintenance, and some staff and will remain the same no matter how much is produced. All costs that vary directly with output, rising as more is produced and falling as less is produced, are called **variable costs.** Variable costs include expenses for wages, raw materials, and utilities.

There are three types of average costs. **Average total cost** (ATC) is the total cost of production, at any level of output, divided by the number of units produced, TC/Q. **Average fixed cost** (AFC) is fixed cost divided by the level of output, FC/Q, and **average variable cost** (AVC) is variable cost divided by Q, VC/Q. Average fixed cost plus average variable cost equals average total cost.

Marginal cost (MC)—sometimes called *incremental costs*—is the increase in total cost resulting from raising production by one unit. Because fixed costs do not change with output, marginal cost is the increase in variable costs that results from an extra unit of output. It can be written as $\Delta VC/\Delta Q$. Marginal cost tells us how much it will cost to expand output by one unit. A hypothetical set of these costs is shown in Table 3.2.

Short-run costs can be summarized as follows:

$$AFC = FC/Q$$
$$AVC = VC/Q$$
$$ATC = TC/Q = (FC + VC)/Q = AFC + AVC$$
$$MC = \Delta TC/\Delta Q$$

Let us look at an algebraic example. These three measures of cost are simply different ways to look at the same phenomenon. They are mathematically interrelated. For example, suppose that we are given the following total cost function

$$TC = Q^3 - 4Q^2 + 8Q + 4 \qquad (3.4)$$

Because the last term, the number 4, is the only term that does not change as Q (output) changes, the fixed cost must be 4.

$$FC = 4 \qquad (3.5)$$

Total cost minus fixed cost is variable cost. The terms in the total cost function that contain the variable Q compose total variable cost:

$$VC = Q^3 - 4Q^2 + 8Q \qquad (3.6)$$

Marginal cost is the derivative of the total cost function, which is also equal to the derivative of the variable cost function. (Students with a background in calculus will see this right away. If you do not know calculus, just take our word for it.) We may write

$$MC = dTC/dQ = 3Q^2 - 8Q + 8 \qquad (3.7)$$

The average cost curves can also be derived by dividing TC, VC, and FC by q:

$$ATC = Q^2 - 4Q + 8 + 4/Q \qquad (3.8)$$

Similarly,

$$AFC = 4/Q \qquad (3.9)$$

and

$$AVC = Q^2 - 4Q + 8 \qquad (3.10)$$

Short-Run Cost Curves

Figures 3.2a and 3.2b plot the cost curves from information in Table 3.2 and the preceding equations. Total costs are shown in Figure 3.2a, and average costs in Figure 3.2b. Fixed cost does not vary with output (Q), and therefore is a horizontal line at $4. Variable cost are zero when there is no output. Therefore, the

Table 3.2	Costs as a Function of Output Q						
Q	FC	VC	TC	MC	AFC	AVC	ATC
0	4	0	4	—	—	—	—
1	4	5	9	5	4	5	9
2	4	8	12	3	2	4	6
3	4	15	19	7	1	5	6
4	4	32	36	17	1	8	9
5	4	65	69	33	0.8	13	13⅘

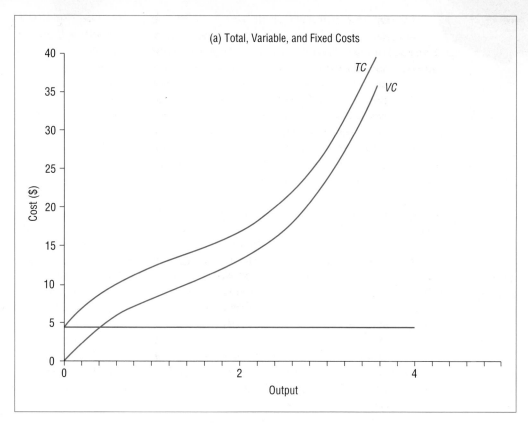

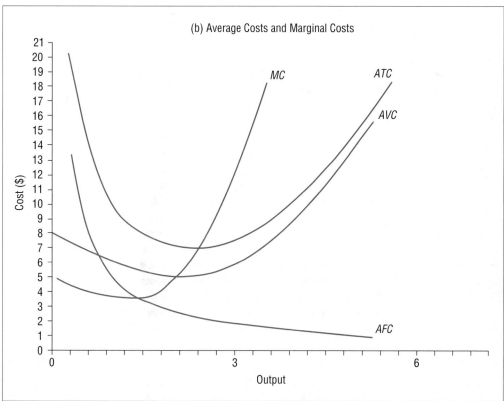

Figure 3.2 Cost Curves

variable cost function goes through the origin. Total cost is variable cost plus fixed cost ($VC + FC$) and therefore sits on top of the fixed cost curve. When output is zero, total cost is also $4. The distance between the two curves always equals 4.

The average fixed cost AFC falls as Q is increased. This happens because as long as the denominator is increasing, AFC is smaller with each additional unit of output. Such a curve is described by mathematicians as a *rectangular hyperbola*. As Q increases, ATC approaches but never reaches the Q axis. It is apparent that if we have large fixed costs—for example, in mass production industries—average fixed costs decrease over a wide range of output. Suppose that the die to stamp out the left front fender of an Acura Legend costs $5 million. If the die is used to produce only one car, the die cost per car is $5 million. If 1 million cars are produced, the die cost per fender is only $5.

Next we turn our attention to the relationship between total variable cost and average variable cost. Variable cost increases with increases in output, first at a decreasing rate and then at an increasing rate. Variable cost will be at a minimum and start to increase when the tangent from the origin is the smallest. The AVC curve corresponds to the variable cost curve in the following way. Average total cost will start out high, fall reaching a minimum, and then start to increase at the point where the tangent to the variable cost (VC) curve is at a minimum. The reason for this is quite simple. With fixed factor prices, when average product per worker is a maximum, average variable cost is a minimum because each additional worker adds the same amount of cost to the firm but a different amount of output. When output per worker is rising, the cost per unit of output must be falling, and vice versa.

The average total cost curve shows the total cost of production. Since the average total cost is the sum of the average fixed cost and the average variable cost, the average total cost declines steadily, and the distance between the ATC and the AVC curve decreases. This happens because the AFC is pulling the ATC down faster than the AVC is rising. This is another way to say that the relationship between the average variable and average total cost is determined by the marginal cost curve. When marginal cost, the cost of producing one additional unit of output, is below ATC, the average total cost declines. As long as it costs less to produce an additional unit of output than the average, average total cost will fall. When marginal cost is greater than the average cost, average cost will rise. When average cost is at a minimum, average cost equals marginal cost. The marginal cost curve also intersects the average variable cost curve at its minimum.

The Determinants of Short-Run Costs

Short-run costs are U shaped. That is, they decrease as output increases, reach a minimum, and then increase. The rate at which they increase depends on the production process and in particular on the law of diminishing returns. Costs are closely related to production. The cost function is the relationship between a firm's cost and its production. Whereas the production function specifies the technological minimum quantity of output that can be produced from various inputs, the cost function combines these data with input price data. In other words, the cost function can be thought of as a combination of production information and factor input prices.

For example, to produce more output, the firm has to hire more labor. If the marginal product of labor decreases as additional labor is hired, more and more expenditures must be made to produce output. This is due to the law of diminishing returns. However, if the marginal product of labor decreases only slightly, then costs will not rise so rapidly.

Long-Run Cost Curves

In the long run, all factors can be varied. When this is the case, there are alternative ways to achieve the same total output and it is necessary to choose among them. Any firm that is trying to survive in a competitive environment must minimize its costs in the long run. Therefore, it must choose to produce at the lowest possible cost. If the level of output is known, along with factor costs, the firm can select the economically most efficient level of output. However, today's variable factors are tomorrow's fixed factors. If the firm does not choose wisely, it may not be at the minimum level of costs. Long-run decisions are among the most important that the firm makes.

For example, a utility executive decides to build a coal-fired plant because the price of coal is expected to be cheaper than oil in the future. The firm is planning to be the low-cost producer. After the plant has been built, there is a strike and the miners demand higher wages. Similarly, peace is achieved in the Middle East, and the price of oil declines significantly. Oil now costs 20 percent less than coal, and the coal-fired utility plant is no longer producing at the lowest average total cost.

A second decision facing managers is the level of future demand and, therefore, the size of plant to build. If the plant that is built is too large, the firm may be saddled with excess capacity and higher short-run average cost. In the long run what is important is the firm's long-run average cost curve. The long-run average cost curve is usually called the *envelope curve*, showing all the possibilities of short-run cost curves. The relationship between long-run and short-run costs curve is shown in Figure 3.3. Assume that the firm is uncertain about the future demand for energy and is considering three alternative plant sizes. The short-run average cost (*SAC*) curve for the three plants is given by SAC_1, SAC_2, and SAC_3. The decision, just like the type of plant to build, is important since once made, it cannot be easily changed.

If the firm believes that it will have long-run demand of Q_1, it can be produced with either SAC_1 or SAC_2. This level of output is least costly for plant 1. It is at the minimum point on SAC_1. However, if the firm increased output too much with plant 1, average cost would be higher than with plant 2. However, neither of these plants achieves the minimum average cost at point *D* with plant 3. To achieve this, the firm would have to build a larger plant.

Figure 3.3 Long-Run Average Cost

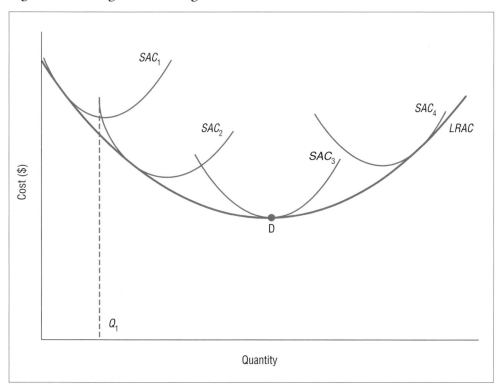

What determines the shape of the long-run average cost curve? The most important determinant is returns to scale. **Returns to scale** refers to the doubling of a firm's inputs and its effect on output. Whether there are increasing, constant, or decreasing returns to scale is a matter of some debate among economists. The long-run average cost (LRAC) typically declines over some range of output because of increasing returns to scale, usually attributed to specialization. Other reasons for the decline in the LRAC are more capital-intensive machinery and better technology. The LRAC curve turns up when it becomes too difficult to manage a very large plant and costs increase. **Decreasing returns to scale** occur when the doubling of inputs causes output to increase by less than a factor of 2.

■ PERFECTLY COMPETITIVE MARKETS

Having looked at a firm's cost and production technology, we would now like to examine under what condition some firms will survive and under what conditions others will not. To sort out the question of who is competing with whom and in what sense, it is useful to distinguish between the behavior of individual firms and the type of market in which the firm operates.

Economists use the term *market structure* to refer to the market type. The degree of competitiveness of the market structure refers to the extent to which individual firms lack market power over price. The degree of competitive behavior refers to the degree to which individual firms actively compete with one another. Perfect competition is an exacting concept forming the basis of the most important model of business behavior. The essence of the concept is that the market is entirely impersonal. There is no rivalry among suppliers in the market and buyers do not recognize their competitiveness with one another. Before we examine the behavior of firms, it is important to look at the assumptions of perfect competition.

**Large Number
of Small Firms**

The number of buyers and sellers in the market is so large that no single seller can affect the price. The demand curve confronting the individual firm is perfectly elastic. The firm can sell in the market period any quantity it wants at the market price. However, it cannot affect the market price. Both seller and buyer are price takers in a competitive market.

Homogeneous Output

The products sold in a perfectly competitive market must be identical. That is, the product of one firm is in no way differentiated from the product of other sellers in the market. The term *perfectly competitive* is used very strictly. Every feature of the product must be the same. If the product is not homogeneous, the producer has a degree of control over the product.

**Freedom of Entry
and Exit in Product
and Factor Markets**

All factors of production have perfect mobility. Workers can move promptly and quickly from low-wage to high-wage jobs, and land will be quickly diverted from low-rent to high-rent uses. Moreover, firms will not face any barriers to either entry or exit from an industry.

All producers, factors of production, and consumers in a perfectly competitive market have perfect information of present and future prices. A worker, for example, would not accept a lower wage because of his or her ignorance of the going market wage rate, and consumers would never pay more than the current market price. Information is costless and free to everyone.

**Perfect Information
of Present
and Future Prices
and Costs**

One must be careful not to confuse the individual firm's demand curve under perfect competition with the market demand curve for the product. In Figure 3.4a the market demand curve is downward sloping. In perfectly competitive markets, the price of the good or service is determined exclusively by the intersection of its market demand curve and its market supply curve. The perfectly competitive firm is then a price taker and can sell any amount of the good or service at the estab-

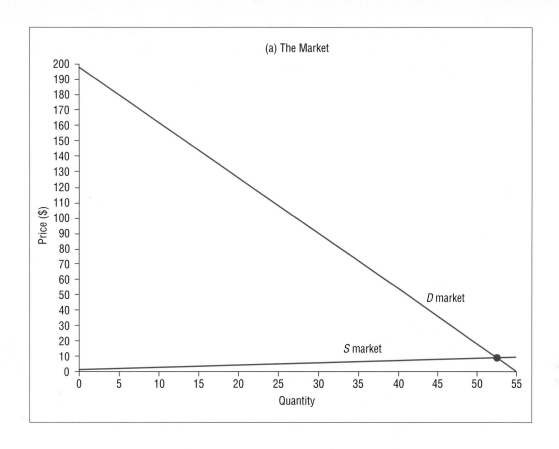

(a) The Market

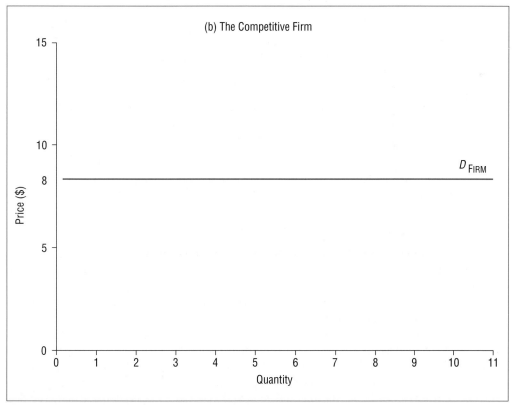

(b) The Competitive Firm

Figure 3.4 Competitive Supply and Demand

lished price. Because the firm is a price taker, the demand curve facing an individual firm is a horizontal line over the range of output we need to consider. The implication of the horizontal demand curve for the firm is that its actions cannot change its price.

In Figure 3.4b, the firm's demand curve corresponds to a price of $8 for a computer chip. The horizontal axis measures the quantity of chips that the firm can sell and the vertical the price that it can charge. Figure 3.4a shows conditions in the chip market. The market demand curve indicates how much all consumers are willing to buy; at lower prices, they buy more. The demand curve facing the firm is horizontal because the firm's sales have no effect on price. If the firm increases its sales of chips from 100 to 200, the increase has no effect on the market because the total market for chips is in the millions. Under perfect competition, a firm can sell an additional unit of output without lowering its cost. Therefore, its average revenue curve is the same as its marginal revenue curve. If the firm sells an additional chip, its total revenue will go up by $8. Its **marginal revenue** is then $8. Therefore, for the firm, average revenue is the same as marginal revenue and price along the demand curve.

THE FIRM IN A PERFECTLY COMPETITIVE MARKET

A firm is defined as a unit that employs factors of production to produce goods and services that it sells to other firms, to households, or to the government. First economists assume that each firm makes consistent decisions, as though it were a single individual. Thus, economic theory ignores the internal problems of who reaches particular decisions and how they are reached. In doing this, economists assume that the firm's internal organization is irrelevant to its decisions. Second, economists assume that most firms make their decisions with a single goal in mind: to make as much profit as possible. Before examining perfect competition, it is useful to deal with the rules of behavior common to all firms that seek to maximize their profits, independent of market structure.

The first rule of profit maximization is to decide whether to produce or not. If a firm produces nothing, it will have a loss equal to fixed cost. If the firm decided to produce, it will add the variable cost of production to fixed cost. If at some point the level of revenue, $P \times Q$, exceeds variable cost, it pays the firm to produce. If however, revenue is less than variable cost, it does not pay to produce. The first rule of profit maximization is that the firm should produce if the revenue from selling its product exceeds the variable cost of production.

If the firm decides to produce, it must decide how much to produce. The second proposition of profit maximization is that the firm must produce to the point where marginal revenue equals marginal cost.

$$MR = MC \tag{3.11}$$

Marginal revenue is the addition to total revenue attributable to one extra unit of sales. Marginal cost is the addition to total cost resulting from adding one unit to output. Thus, it should be evident that profit increases when marginal revenue exceeds marginal cost and diminishes when marginal cost exceeds marginal revenue. Profit must, therefore attain its maximum when marginal revenue and marginal cost are equal.

As shown in Figure 3.5, the marginal revenue curve for a perfectly competitive firm is a horizontal line. The fundamental proposition is that at market price OP, the firm attains a profit-maximizing equilibrium at point E, corresponding to the output of $0Q$ units. Marginal revenue and marginal cost are equal at output $0Q$. If the level of output were less than $0Q$, say $0Q_1$, marginal revenue would exceed

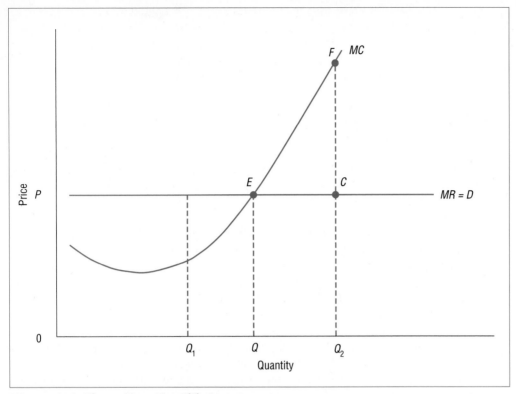

Figure 3.5 Short-Run Equilibrium

marginal cost. Increasing output would add more to revenue than to cost. The firm should expand output as long as marginal cost is less than or equal to marginal revenue. On the other hand, suppose that the rate of output exceeded $0Q$. At $0Q_2$, marginal cost would be greater than marginal revenue by the distance FC. As is clear from the graph, profit is reduced by adding the extra unit of output.

Let us examine the profit maximization decision in more detail. Consider the example in Table 3.3. The first two columns of the table give the demand curve

Table 3.3	Revenue, Cost, and Profit for a Perfectly Competitive Firm				
Output and Sales	Marginal Revenue or Price	Marginal Cost	Average Total Cost	Unit Profit	Total Profit
1	$5.00	$2.00	$17.00	-$12.00	-$12.00
2	5.00	1.50	9.25	-4.25	-8.50
3	5.00	1.00	6.50	-1.50	-4.50
4	5.00	1.25	5.19	-0.19	-0.75
5	5.00	1.50	4.45	+0.55	+2.75
6	5.00	2.00	4.04	+0.96	+5.75
7	5.00	3.25	3.93	+1.07	+7.50
8	5.00	5.00	4.06	+0.94	+7.50
9	5.00	8.00	4.50	+0.50	+4.50
10	5.00	12.00	5.25	-0.25	-2.50

for the perfectly competitive firm. Market price is $5 per unit. The firm can sell as many units as it chooses at this price. The product of column 1 and column 2 gives total revenue. Column 3 and 4 give marginal cost and average total cost, respectively. Unit profit, the difference between column 2 and 4, is shown in column 5, and total profit is in column 6. It is clear from the table that the maximum profit, $7.50, is earned when 8 units are produced.

The profit function can be derived using the total revenue and total cost curves. If the firm produces Q units of output, its total revenue will be price $\times Q$. Total revenue equals the price of the good or service, P, times the number of units sold, Q. In other words, total revenue equals the number of units sold times the price of each unit. The cost of production also depends on the level of output Q. Profit is the difference between total revenue (TR) and total cost (TC):

$$\text{Profit} = TR - TC \tag{3.12}$$

To maximize profits, the firm selects the level of output for which the difference between total cost and total revenue is the greatest.

This is demonstrated graphically in Figure 3.6. For a perfectly competitive firm, total revenue is price times quantity. Price is a constant. Therefore, the total revenue function is a straight line through the origin with a constant slope. That is, for a perfectly competitive firm, the total revenue curve is linear and passes through the origin with a slope equal to price. The typical total cost function has been drawn. The total cost function will be positive at zero level of output since fixed cost must be paid whether production takes place or not.

Total revenue intersects total cost at two points. At both of these intersections, profit equals zero. These are known as *breakeven points*. As output increases, profits eventually become positive. Total profit is a maximum when the distance

Figure 3.6 Profit Maximization (*TR–TC*)

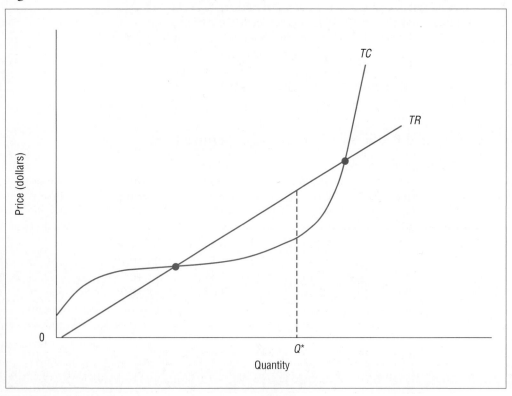

between total revenue and total cost is at a maximum. Notice that the vertical distance between these two curves is the greatest at output level Q^*. Beyond Q^* level of output, marginal revenue is less than marginal cost and profit falls, reflecting the rapid increase in the total cost of production.

How should the manager of a profit-maximizing firm choose a level of output over the short run? Remember that in the short run, the firm operates with a fixed amount of capital and must adjust its variable cost to maximize profits. The market determines the highest price at which the firm can sell its product. The firm picks the quantity of output that maximizes its profits. This is the output for which price equals marginal cost. If the firm is maximizing its profit, it has no incentive to change its output unless price changes. The firm is said to be in **short-run equilibrium.** In perfect competition, the firm is a mere quantity adjuster. It pursues its goal of profit maximization by increasing or decreasing quantity in response to changes in the market price. However, as we shall see shortly, the market price to which the perfectly competitive firm responds is itself set by the forces of supply and demand.

While the firm may be in short-run equilibrium, we wish to know how it is doing in relation to its costs. In other words, does the firm have the staying power to remain in the industry? Figure 3.7 shows the "representative" firm's average total cost, average variable cost, and marginal cost curves.

Alternatively, the firm faces three different demand and marginal revenue curves. Each one results in a different situation for the firm. We will analyze each one separately in descending order. If the market price is P_3, the optimum level of production is at point A, at which $MR = MC$. If the firm sells at a price lower than P_3, any economic profit it currently enjoys decreases. If the firm sells at a price higher than P_3, its sales drop to zero because customers switch purchases to one of

**Short-Run Equilibrium
of the Firm**

Figure 3.7 Profit Maximization (*MR=MC*)

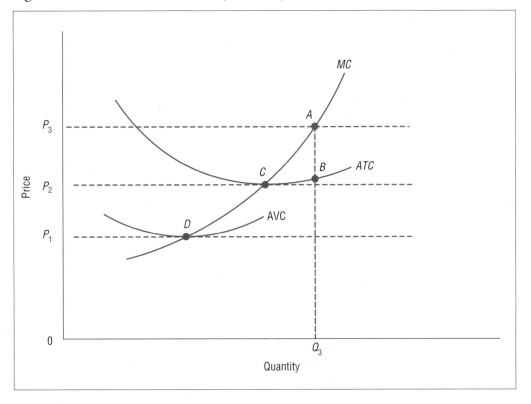

the many other sellers. You will notice that at price P_3, price is above the average total cost curve. The firm earns a short-run economic profit at this price. Economic profit per unit of output equals the distance AB. Total profit equals OQ_3 times AB.

On the other hand, suppose that the market price is established at P_2. The firm maximizes profits by producing at point C, where $MR = MC$. At point C, the demand curve is exactly tangent to the average total cost curve. At this price, the firm is exactly covering its average total cost and is earning no economic profit. In other words, each unit of output costs exactly the same to produce as the market price. For example, if the market price is $30, the ATC is also $30. Therefore, economic profit is zero.

The final situation occurs when price is equal to or below average variable cost at point D. When price is equal to average variable cost, the firm is no longer covering its average variable cost and it will reduce losses by shutting down. This is known as the **shut-down point.** In other words, the firm will minimize its losses by shutting down.

A firm need not always make an economic profit in the short run. Why would a firm operate at a loss in the short run? It might do so because it expects the market price to change. In other words, it fully expects to make a profit in the future and, therefore, will operate at a loss in the short run. The firm has two choices here. It can continue to operate at a short-run loss, or it can shut down. If price is above average variable cost and below average total cost, some production is appropriate. It is cheaper to operate the firm than to produce no output because price exceeds average variable cost. In other words, the firm can minimize losses by continuing to produce at a loss.

**Short-Run Supply
Curves**

Using the proposition just discussed, it is possible to derive the short-run supply curve of an individual firm in a perfectly competitive market. The supply curve of the firm tells us how much will be produced at every possible price. The firm's marginal cost curve gives the marginal cost corresponding to each level of output. For prices below AVC, the firm will supply zero output. For any price greater than minimum AVC, the profit-maximizing output can be read directly from the graph. The firm's supply curve is its marginal cost curve above the point of minimum average variable cost. In perfect competition, the firm's supply curve has the identical slope as the firm's marginal cost curve above AVC. The reason for this is the same as for increasing marginal cost, the presence of diminishing returns to a fixed factor of production. This is illustrated in Figure 3.8a.

Having derived the firm's short-run supply curve, we can now illustrate the derivation of the industry's short-run supply curve. If there are two firms, A and B, then at any price P the industry supply curve will be the total output of firm A and B at that price. In perfect competition, the industry supply curve is the horizontal sum of the marginal cost curves above the level of average variable cost of all firms in the industry. This is illustrated in Figure 3.8b.

**Long-Run Equilibrium
of the Firm**

In the short run a firm may break even or earn an economic profit or loss. In the long run, however, all of these prices are not possible equilibrium positions. The keys to **long-run equilibrium** under perfect competition are entry and exit. We have seen that when firms are in short-run equilibrium, they may be making profits or losses or just breaking even. Since costs include the opportunity cost of capital, firms that are just breaking even are doing as well as they could if they had invested their capital elsewhere. Thus, there will be no incentive for existing firms to leave the industry. Neither will there be an incentive for new firms to enter the industry, for capital can earn the same return elsewhere in the economy. This can be illustrated as follows. The firm's economic profit is π equal to its revenue total

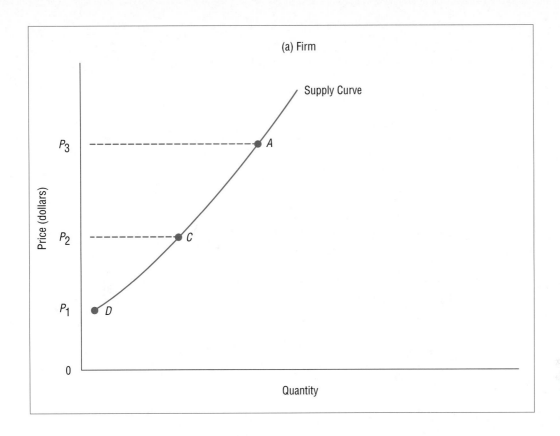

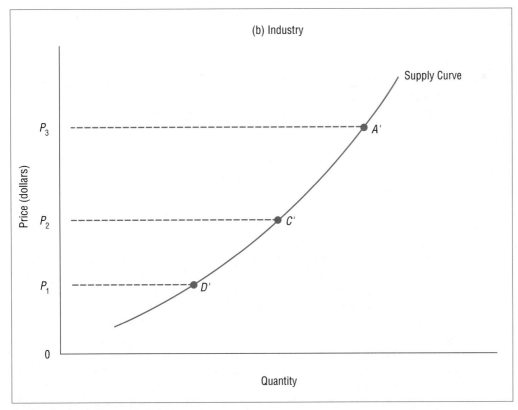

Figure 3.8 Short-Run Supply Curve

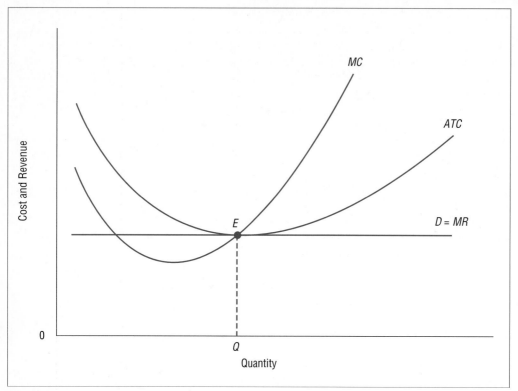

Figure 3.9 Long-Run Equilibrium in a Competitive Market

minus its variable costs, wL, and minus its opportunity cost of capital rK, measured by what it could rent the capital for in the market. Therefore,

$$\pi = R - wL - rK = 0 \qquad (3.13)$$

If existing firms are making a negative economic profit, they should consider leaving the industry since higher returns can be earned elsewhere. If existing firms are earning positive economic profits, new capital will enter the industry. Firms that are earning zero economic profits need not go out of business because zero economic profit means that firms are earning a competitive return. Of course, entrepreneurs would like to earn economic profits. Indeed, that is what motivates them. In competitive markets, profits serve their function of allocating resources among the industries of the economy.

If economic profits are being earned in the industry, price is above average total cost, encouraging entry into the industry. Over time, the industry supply curve will shift to the right. Remember that the industry supply curve is the summation of the supply curve of all firms in the industry. Thus, if entry occurs, the supply curve will shift to the right and price will fall as total quantity increases. This will put downward pressure on prices, thereby competing away economic profits in the long run.

If the industry is suffering from overcapacity and firms are experiencing an economic loss, over time, some firms will exit the industry. As firms exit the industry, the industry supply curve shifts to the left as the number of firms in the industry shrinks. As firms leave the industry, prices rise and, over time, economic losses in the industry are eliminated.

Remember that in the long run all factors of production and all costs are variable. Therefore, a firm remains in business in the long run only if it can obtain the appropriate size plant and therefore the appropriate level of output. The best level of output in the long run is given by the point where the demand curve (marginal revenue) is tangent to the long-run average cost curve and the short run average cost curve as seen in Figure 3.9.

The only conceivable point of long-run equilibrium occurs at point E in Figure 3.9. Here firms in the industry receive neither pure profit nor pure loss. They all earn zero economic profit. There is no incentives for further entry or exit because the rate of return in this industry is the same as the opportunity cost of capital in all other industries.

Figure 3.10 shows the derivation of the long-run supply curve for a constant cost industry. Assume that we start from a position of short-run equilibrium for the perfectly competitive firm and industry. The industry demand is D_1 and the industry supply is S_1, as shown in Figure 3.10. The firm faces the perfectly elastic demand curve at price P_1.

Suppose that the market demand for computer chips increases from D_1 to D_2. The market price will increase from P_1 to P_2, and the new short-run market equilibrium is at point B. At the new equilibrium level, each firm supplies more chips at the higher price and moves up its short-run marginal cost curve. Remember that to get firms to produce higher levels of output, prices must be higher. The higher level of price and the subsequent economic profits earned by the producers in the industry attract other firms into the industry.

We well know that entry into an industry causes an increase in the market supply; this is shown as a movement from S_1 to S_2 in Figure 3.10. The new equilibrium moves from point B to point C. Notice that the price associated with the

Long-Run
Supply Curves

Figure 3.10 Long-Run Equilibrium in a Constant Cost Industry

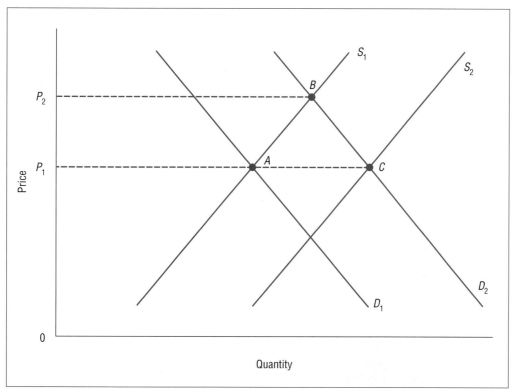

new equilibrium is the same price associated with the original equilibrium, P_1. Why is this the case?

In a constant cost industry, the additional inputs necessary to produce the higher output can be purchased without an increase in their price. Since the price of inputs has not changed, the new producers can produce with the exact cost-output relationships as the original producing firms. Thus, the market entry will move the market price back to P_1. The new market equilibrium is shown in Figure 3.10 as point C.

▌ CHAPTER SUMMARY AND KEY IDEAS ■ ■ ■ ■ ■

This chapter examined the neoclassical theory of the firm. According to the neoclassical theory, the firm is a black box. The firm is described by a production function in which inputs are turned into outputs. The production function specifies the maximum amount of outputs that can be produced with given inputs.

We first looked at production with one variable input to examine total product, average product, and marginal product. The production function is characterized by the law of diminishing returns. The law states that if increasing amounts of a variable factor are applied to a given amount of a fixed factor, eventually a situation is reached in which each additional unit of the variable factor adds less to the total product.

Next we examined the cost of production. Costs are divided between short-run costs and long-run costs. Short-run costs can be varied with the cost of production. Total cost is the cost of producing any given level of output. Costs are important because they are used to calculate profits. Profit is the difference between total revenue and total cost. A firm maximizes profit by producing when marginal revenue equals marginal cost.

Economists use the term *market structure* to refer to the type of market in which the firm produces. In a market where firms are price takers, markets are referred to as being perfectly competitive. Perfectly competitive markets are characterized by a large number of firms, homogeneous output, easy entry and exit, and perfect information.

In short-run equilibrium, firms will produce when marginal revenue equals marginal cost. Under these conditions, a firm may earn excess economic profits or may incur short-run losses. In long-run equilibrium, a firm earns zero economic profits.

In the long run, all inputs are variable. Therefore, a firm will stay in business only if it is the appropriate size and can produce the appropriate level of output. In the long run, firms adjust to changes in supply and demand by either entering or exiting an industry.

▌ KEY TERMS

average fixed cost	marginal revenue
average product	opportunity cost
average total cost	opportunity cost of capital
average variable cost	production function
decreasing returns to scale	returns to scale
division of labor	short-run equilibrium
fixed cost	shut-down point
law of diminishing returns	total cost
long-run equilibrium	total product
marginal cost	total revenue
marginal product	variable cost

FURTHER READINGS

American Economic Association. *Readings in Price Theory*, ed. G. J. Stigler and
K. E. Boulding. Homewood, Ill.: Richard D. Irwin, 1952.

Baumol, W. J. *Economic Theory and Operations Analysis*, 4th ed. Englewood Cliffs,
N.J.: Prentice Hall, 1977.

Kreps, D. *A Course in Microeconomic Theory*. Princeton, N.J.: Princeton University
Press, 1990.

Machlup, F. "Theories of the Firm." *American Economic Review* 57, 1967.

Marshall, A. J. *Principles of Economics*, 8th ed. London: Macmillan, 1922.

Pindyck, R. S., and D. L. Rubenfeld. *Microeconomics*. New York: Macmillan, 1992.

Scherer, F. M., and S. Ross. *Industrial Market Structure and Economic Performance*.
Chicago: Rand McNally, 1980.

QUESTIONS AND PROBLEMS FOR REVIEW AND DISCUSSION

A.

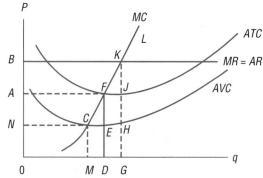

Based on the preceding diagram, circle the correct answer in each instance:

1. Most profitable output: *OA, OB, OM, OG.*

2. Market price: *BK, AF, GK, MC.*

3. Average revenue: *OB, BK, OG, DF.*

4. Marginal revenue: *OA, AF, GK, DF.*

5. Average total cost at most profitable output: *OB, OD, MC, GJ.*

6. Average variable cost at most profitable output: *GH, GJ, MC, DF.*

7. Profit per unit at most profitable output: *AB, JK, HJ, EF.*

8. Average fixed cost at most profitable output: *EF, JH, AB, MC.*

9. Long-run equilibrium output: *OD, OM, OG, ON.*

10. Short-run supply curve: *OM, CI, AF, BK.*

B. Given:

$$TC = x^3 - 4x^2 + 8x + 4$$
$$TR = 4x$$

1. What is the equation for the firm's average
revenue curve? _____

2. What is the equation for the firm's marginal
revenue curve? _____

3. What is total revenue at $x = 4$? _____

4. What is the equation for marginal cost? _____

5. What is the equation for the average total cost curve? _____

6. What is the firm's total fixed cost? _____

7. What is the firm's average fixed cost at $x = 5$? _____

8. What is the firm's total variable cost at $x = 3$? _____

9. What is the y-intercept of the firm's demand curve? _____

10. What is the equation for the firm's total profit? _____

11. What is the most profitable output? _____

12. At what price can the most profitable output be sold? _____

13. What is the elasticity of demand at the most profitable price? _____

14. What is marginal revenue at the most profitable output? _____

15. What is total revenue at the most profitable output? _____

16. What is total variable cost at the most profitable output? _____

17. What is total cost at the most profitable output? _____

18. What is total profit at the most profitable output? _____

19. What is total profit at $x = 2\frac{1}{2}$? _____

20. In what kind of market does this firm sell? _____

C.

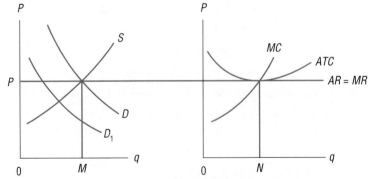

In the preceding figure, the market price is established at OP, the industry is producing OM units of output per time period, and each firm is selling ON units. Assume that market demand shifts from D to D'.

1. Indicate on the figure the new market price as OP', the new output of the industry as OM', and the new output of each firm as ON'.

2. Each firm is now (making a profit, suffering a loss, breaking even), and as a result there will be in the long run (an entry of new firms into the industry, an exit of firms from the industry, no change in the number of firms); this will result in a shift in the industry's short-run supply curve to the (right, left).

3. Assume that this is a constant cost industry. Draw the short-run supply curve that will reestablish long-run equilibrium. Label it S'.

4. The new long-run equilibrium price is _____.

5. The output of each firm under the new equilibrium condition is _____.

6. The output of the industry under the new equilibrium is (equal to, less than, greater than) the original equilibrium output because the number of firms has (increased, decreased, remained the same).

7. Label the long-run supply curve LRS.

D. The owner of a small retail store does her own accounting work. How would you measure the opportunity cost of her work?

E. The supply curve for a firm in the short run is the short-run marginal cost curve (above the point of minimum average variable cost). Why is the supply curve in the long run NOT the long-run marginal cost curve (above the point of minimum average total cost)?

F. In long-run equilibrium, all firms in the industry earn zero economic profit. Why is this true?

G. What assumptions are necessary for a market to be perfectly competitive? In light of what you have learned in this chapter, why is each of these assumptions important?

4

CHAPTER

Efficiency, the Price System, and Organizations

The greatest improvements in the productive powers of labor, and the greatest part of the skill, dexterity, and judgement with which it is anywhere directed, or applied, seem to have been the effects of the division of labor.[1]

Imagination is baffled when it tries to appreciate the vast multiplicity of commodities which must enter tomorrow in order to preserve the inhabitants from falling prey to the convulsions of famine, rebellion, and pillage. . . . Yet all sleep, and their slumbers are not disturbed for a single minute by the prospects of such a frightful catastrophe.[2]

CHAPTER OUTLINE AND STUDENT GOALS

Chapter 2 introduced the elements of perfect competition—supply and demand and price—and Chapter 3 developed the neoclassical theory of the firm under perfect competition. Both of these chapters were developed in a partial equilibrium framework. In other words, Chapter 2 examined activity in one market in isolation from all other markets. Similarly, Chapter 3 emphasized the behavior of one firm in isolation from the rest of the economy.

When individuals specialize in production, their activities must be coordinated so that they produce the right things and are able to exchange their output for the goods and services they wish to consume. The need to achieve coordination arises from the division of labor. Separate, yet interconnected, markets coordinate the activities of millions of individuals and firms in the economy. Economists refer to the collection of related markets in a capitalistic economy as the *price system*. The price system achieves coordination by answering three basic economic questions concerning what to produce, how to produce it, and for whom to produce it. One basic criterion used in determining the adequacy of the price system is whether the allocation of resources obtained by the price system happens efficiently.

Put very simply, efficiency is the process of getting more for less. For example, today many people are interested in the efficiency of their appliances, such as their refrigerator, furnace, or car. They want to make sure that they get as much heat from their furnace as possible for a given unit of input. An economy is efficient when it is impossible to get more output from existing resources. Efficiency

---

[1]Adam Smith, *The Wealth of Nations* (Chicago: The University of Chicago Press, 1976).
[2]Frederick Bastiat, commenting about the Paris of his day, as quoted in C. E. Ferguson, *Microeconomic Theory* (Homewood, Ill.: Richard D. Irwin, 1972).

is what all economic systems strive for whether they are individuals, organizations, or countries. How a system of related competitive markets (the price system) achieves economic efficiency is the subject of this chapter.

The study of the interrelationship of all markets is known as *general equilibrium theory*. In this chapter we will examine the concept of efficiency in a general equilibrium framework.

The most common reasons for markets not achieving efficient coordination are market power, imperfect information, increasing returns in production, and externalities. When any of these conditions prevail, the market may be inefficient. When people found that markets were inefficient in coordinating economic activities, they often organized firms. Recall the functional component in the definition of firms presented in Chapter 1: they organize economic activity.

The fundamental question of why firms exist was first asked by Ronald Coase. According to Coase, there are costs of carrying out transactions in a market setting. These are different depending on the product, industry, or the market. To achieve efficiency, the tendency is for activities to be carried out so that the costs of conducting transactions and/or the costs of coordinating individuals' activities are the lowest. Coase argued that production is coordinated within markets when the organization costs are low, and in firms when the costs of using the market are high. This, in and of itself, is an interesting concept and we will return to it in Chapter 6, "Organizational Tools."

After reading this chapter, you should be able to

- Explain the difference between partial equilibrium and general equilibrium.
- Discuss the various ways in which economic efficiency is achieved.
- Understand the importance of achieving efficient ways to organize economic activity.
- Intuitively explain and use the graphical devices isoquants and isocost lines.
- Interpret the efficiency condition using a cost minimization criteria.
- Understand how to use a production possibilities frontier to discuss questions of efficiency.
- Understand what is meant by market failure.
- Understand why market failure leads to organizations.

ECONOMIC EFFICIENCY

Ukraine, a country of 52 million people, gained independence from the former Soviet Union in 1991.[3] At that time, its prospects seemed promising, to say the least. After all, it was the breadbasket of the former Soviet Union, rich in natural resources, and possessed a warm water port on the Black Sea. However, it hasn't worked out that way. After two years, the country's economic and social systems appeared in deep collapse with inflation running at 70 percent a month, bread lines in Kiev, and fuel so scarce that many factories had shut down. Indeed, Ukraine made other "new" nations such as Poland and Russia seem to be success stories.

---

[3]Two recent articles present a good picture of the confusion gripping Ukraine's political and economic system: "Ukraine's Prospects, Once Bright, Grow Dim as Its Economy Falters," *The Wall Street Journal*, November 13, 1993, p. 1; and "Ukraine, The Birth and Possible Death of a Country," *The Economist*, May 7, 1994, a collection of separate stories beginning after page 60.

Two causes of the misfortunes of Ukraine's economy can be identified. First, the economic environment had changed. When Ukraine declared independence, it severed long-standing ties with Russia, forcing a push toward a new and unfamiliar equilibrium in the economy. Oil and gas became much more expensive than before, and markets for exports dried up. With a new equilibrium, the basic questions of what to produce, how to produce it, and for whom to produce had to be answered again.

Second, and perhaps much more important, the country inherited an ideology from its former communist rulers that assumed that people are fundamentally good; but, unfortunately, they are not—*they are fundamentally selfish.*[4] Prior to its independence from the Soviet Union, the Ukraine had a system of government in place with the lines of authority set up to suit the convenience of party officials. As of 1994, there was no clear rule of law or effective banking system, and huge unprofitable state enterprises dependent on state subsidies played a major role in the Ukraine economy.

Trying to avoid the shock therapy that President Yeltsin had applied in Russia, the country failed to restructure its economy. Privatization, for example, was almost nonexistent. Market prices and market incentives that come with privatization were also nonexistent. The economy was seen to be hopelessly inefficient, in part because the prices needed to coordinate economic activity were nonexistent.

The Concept of Efficiency

The concept of *efficiency* is related to the concerns and well-being of those in the economy. Efficiency is to be judged by the ability of the system to satisfy the wants and needs of individual human beings. Efficiency is therefore important for **resource allocation.** Resource allocations that have the property that no one can be made better off without someone else being made worse off are said to be efficient. If someone can be made better off without making someone worse off, then the system is inefficient. When economists refer to *efficiency*, this is what they usually mean. We offer the following definition:

> efficient: *An economic arrangement is said to be efficient if it is impossible, given available resources, to implement an alternative arrangement under which all parties involved are at least as well off.*

The concept of efficiency can be easily illustrated. If two individuals with different endowments specialize in production and agree to trade thereafter, each will be better off than before. Individual A specializes in farming and individual B in hunting. They both like bread and meat equally. Allowing these two people to trade makes both better off. In other words, if individuals are willing to specialize according to their comparative advantages and trade according to their preferences, each has the capability to become enriched beyond what he or she could accomplish on his or her own.

Coordination and Motivation

Ever since Adam Smith, and even before, it was known that wealth can be increased if people specialize in production and then exchange their output for the actual goods and services they need. Most people in the economy specialize. For example, the computer programmer specializes in writing and maintaining software systems. However, he probably does not consume very much programming on a weekly basis. Therefore, his specialized output of lengthy binary code must be exchanged for food, shelter, and entertainment.

Specialization arising from the division of labor makes possible a larger output than if each person worked alone and were self-sufficient. However, when each person specializes and is not self-sufficient, the economy must either be

---

[4]Gerlinde Sinn and Hans-Werner Sinn, *Jumpstart* (Cambridge: The MIT Press, 1994).

planned by some central agency or some other mechanism must accomplish the same goal. Since the information needed to coordinate the activities of millions of individuals simply doesn't exist in any one place, the price system provides one mechanism for *coordinating* economic activity. Imagine, for example, that all transactions would take place between individuals in markets. There would be no need for organizations. The other extreme would be a system in which there was only one firm and all decisions would be made by the central planning agency.

Historically speaking, nations with a communist or socialistic government structure were, and are, prone to coordinate economic activity within a framework of central planning. By all accounts, these attempts have failed time and again. The information requirements of a centrally planned economy are almost unthinkable: even if enough information could be gathered, there is no way to process it.

There used to be a riddle in communist societies: Why can't you have socialism in every country? The answer is that you need one country to set the prices. Of course, no economy approaches either one of these extremes relying on only the market or the state. The U.S. government dabbles in setting prices. Even the communist economies left some decisions to individual consumers.

Is the price system an efficient mechanism for achieving coordination? The answer appears to be yes. The daily shortages that plague socialist countries are deemed news items when they occur in capitalist countries. Moreover, the market economy achieves this result with a minimal amount of information. The system requires less information than any other system to achieve efficiency. *Knowing only local information and systemwide prices is enough for each producer and consumer to make the choices required for efficiency.*

Like the DNA in our bodies that carries all the genetic information to create life, prices carry all the necessary *economic* information for organizing an economy. As Milgrom and Roberts point out,

> There is no need to transmit detailed information about preferences, technological possibilities, resource availabilities, and the like that would be needed to achieve a centralized solution because the prices summarize all the relevant information. Furthermore, when conditions change detailed local knowledge of these changes need not be transmitted to achieve effective responses.[5]

What motivates individuals? The second remarkable feature of the price system is that it provides the incentive for individuals to help themselves in a socially beneficial way. As Adam Smith put it in his famous metaphor from the "Invisible Hand" to describe how self-interest led to social good: "He intends only his own gain, and he is in this as in many other cases, led by an invisible hand to promote an end which was no part of his intention."[6]

People pursuing their own self-interest promote the public interest. They do not have to be artificially induced or forced to work in a well-functioning economy. People led by impersonal market forces will take the actions necessary to achieve efficiency. Economics has progressed a long way since Adam Smith, but his fundamental argument has had great appeal over the past two centuries.

A few years ago airports all over the United States installed carts on which people could carry their luggage. They could be rented for $1 and used throughout the airport. When they were returned, the customer would receive a 25¢ refund. They were an instant success. Most people used them to take their luggage

---

[5]Paul Milgrom and John Roberts, *Economics, Organization & Management* (Englewood Cliffs, N.J.: Prentice Hall, 1992), p. 27.
[6]Smith, *The Wealth of Nations*, book 1, ch. 2, p. 18.

Coordination
Through Markets

to the parking lot. A difficulty arose, however, when individuals did not return them to the vending machine. The parking lot was littered with abandoned carts. The 25¢ refund was not enough of an incentive to return the cart. Whereas very few executives returned the cart for the reward, dozens of people found it profitable to spend the whole day at the airport collecting carts. Indeed, it was a common sight at Kennedy Airport in New York City to see people pushing up to 50 carts.

In Chapter 2 we examined events in separate, isolated markets and did not consider, for example, that events in the pretzel market could impact all other markets in the economic system. Economists term this type of analysis **partial equilibrium** analysis because it examines one small piece of a larger system in which all markets must be in equilibrium. For some problems partial equilibrium analysis is perfectly adequate, but interdependence often makes partial equilibrium analysis overly simplistic. Demand and supply in one market depend on prices determined in other markets. **General equilibrium analysis** takes into account all of the interactions and interdependencies between the various parts of the economy. For example, general equilibrium analysis seeks an understanding of the wages, interest rates, and prices at which the markets for labor, capital, and goods and services clear simultaneously. In general equilibrium analysis, all markets must clear simultaneously for equilibrium to be achieved. For all markets to clear, the economy must meet three conditions: exchange efficiency, production efficiency, and product mix efficiency.

Exchange efficiency analyzes the behavior of consumers who can trade goods between themselves. In an efficient allocation of goods, no one can be made better off without making someone else worse off. **Production efficiency** looks at the economy from the perspective of inputs into the production process. A particular allocation of inputs into a production process is technically efficient if the output of one good cannot be increased without decreasing the output of another good. **Product mix efficiency** requires that the goods produced are those that consumers want at the right prices or, in other words, that all markets clear.

The basic assumptions of the model are that rational, perfectly informed households interact with rational, profit-maximizing firms in competitive markets, and in an environment free of **market failures.** Market failure is defined as a malfunction in the market mechanism that results in a misallocation or an unproductive use of resources. In the rest of this chapter, we focus on production efficiency, also known as *technical efficiency*. The reason for this is that production efficiency is the first step toward achieving efficiency in the economy.[7]

Production
with Two Variable Inputs

■ EFFICIENCY IN PRODUCTION

We introduced the concept of production in Chapter 3 when we examined the production process in the short run; that is, we constrained our analysis to the case in which there is only one variable input whose level of usage must be determined by the firm. In this section we consider production in a setting in which two (or more) inputs must be chosen. We then say that a **production function** shows the maximum output (Q) that a firm produces for specific combinations of inputs of capital (K) and labor (L). In this section, we analyze efficient behavior for a single firm; in the next section, we analyze efficiency across multiple firms.

To gain a full understanding of the concept of productive efficiency, we need to adopt several tools from standard microeconomic analysis: isoquants and iso-

---

[7]Exchange efficiency is examined in Appendix 4A, and the material need not be covered to understand the logic of the argument. Product-mix efficiency is discussed in the section Assumption of General Equilibrium Theory; however, it is not covered in great detail.

cost lines. The term **isoquant**—derived from *iso*, meaning equal, and *quant*, from quantity—refers to all of the possible combinations of inputs K and L that yield the same output. Traditionally, isoquants are shown in graphical form with the amount of capital input, K, on the vertical axis and the amount of labor input, L, on the horizontal axis. **Isocost** lines are drawn in a graph relating units of labor to units of capital as well; however, isocost lines show combinations of inputs that cost the firm the same amount.

Hypothetical production data are represented in Table 4.1.[8] In this table, the amounts of capital (K) and labor (L) inputs required to produce three output levels ($Q = 55$, $Q = 60$, and $Q = 65$) are shown. It should be remembered that the input amounts shown in Table 4.1 represent the minimum amounts of inputs required to produce each level of output or, in other words, that production is technically efficient.

As will be discussed shortly, however, technical efficiency is not enough to determine the "best" way to produce because several alternative input combinations may produce the desired level of output. Choosing the "best" way to produce a given level of output is a question of productive efficiency.

The numbers in Table 4.1 show, for example, that 50 units of output can be produced with either 10 units of labor and 391 units of capital, or with 19 units of labor and 206 units of capital.

The data in Table 4.1 can be used to create isoquants. In Figure 4.1, we show an isoquant that corresponds to the production of 50 units of output. Notice that if the firm decides to produce 50 units of output, it must choose a mix of L and K from among those shown on the isoquant in Figure 4.1 labeled Q_{50}.

With two inputs, managers want to substitute between inputs, perhaps as one input becomes relatively more expensive than another. Isoquants provide a unique way to analyze this substitution. The slope of each isoquant is in terms of $\Delta K/\Delta L$, that is, change in K divided by the change in L. Economists refer to the slope of an isoquant as the **marginal rate of technical substitution** of labor for capital, or $MRTS_{lk}$.

The $MRTS_{lk}$ provides a measure of the amount of capital that must be added (substituted) when one less unit of labor is used so as to keep output constant. It is always negative, although, for simplicity, we will ignore the negative sign. This relationship can be stated as follows,

$$MRTS_{lk} = \Delta K/\Delta L \qquad (4.1)$$

where ΔK is a small change in capital and ΔL is a small change in labor for a fixed level of Q.

The $MRTS_{lk}$ is not constant but diminishes as you move down (left to right) the isoquant. Or, put another way, the isoquant becomes flatter. In a bit more precise language, we say that isoquants are convex, that is "bowed in" toward the origin. This is an important point and explaining, or proving, it will add greatly to our understanding of what economists mean when they speak of productive efficiency.

In Chapter 3 we discussed the concept of diminishing marginal productivity. We argued there that because a factor of production is added to the production process, and all other factors are fixed, that the contribution to output of additional units of the added factor must diminish. As will be explained later, the principle of diminishing marginal productivity plays an important part in explaining the shape of isoquants.

**The Marginal Rate
of Technical Substitution**

---

[8]The data in Table 4.1 are based on a production function with the mathematical representation $Q = 0.8*K^{.5}*L^{.5}$. The exact values in the table are obtained by substituting in the given values for output, Q, and solving for the required capital amounts for the listed values for the labor input.

Table 4.1   Hypothetical Production Data

Q = 50		Q = 55		Q = 60	
L	K	L	K	L	K
10	391	10	473	10	563
11	355	11	430	11	512
12	325	12	394	12	469
13	300	13	364	13	433
14	279	14	338	14	402
15	260	15	315	15	375
16	244	16	295	16	352
17	230	17	278	17	331
18	217	18	263	18	313
19	206	19	249	19	296
20	195	20	236	20	281
21	186	21	225	21	267
22	178	22	215	22	256
23	170	23	206	23	244
24	163	24	196	24	235
25	156	25	189	25	225

Consider the input substitution that occurs as we move (rightward) along an isoquant, that is, holding output level constant. A rightward movement involves an increase in the amount of labor available to the firm; this should work to increase output. However, a rightward movement along an isoquant involves a decrease in the amount of capital available to the firm and, hence, a reduction in output. As long as we remain on a given isoquant, the increase in output must be balanced by the associated decrease in output.

Intuitively, then, the increase in output caused by having more labor available for production equals the number of units that labor is increased times the amount produced by those added units. Mathematically,

$$\Delta Q = MP_L \times \Delta L \qquad (4.2)$$

where ΔQ represents the change in output, MP_L is the marginal productivity of labor, and ΔL equals the number of units that L is changed.

This increase in output does not occur in isolation, however. Recall that we are moving along a given isoquant and that capital must decrease so as to keep output constant. The reduction in output attributable to the lower amount of capital can be written as

$$\Delta Q = MP_K \times \Delta K \qquad (4.3)$$

where MP_K represents the marginal productivity of capital and ΔK, the change in the number of units of capital.

Recall that the definition of an isoquant requires that output be constant all along the curve. The increase in output caused by the greater amount of labor must then be offset by the reduction in output caused by the lower amount of capital. Put another way, we may take the two previous mathematical expressions, add them together, and set the result equal to zero.

$$MP_L \times \Delta L + MP_K \times \Delta K = 0 \qquad (4.4)$$

In Figure 4.1, we have drawn an isoquant with the capital input on the vertical axis and labor on the horizontal axis. As such, the slope of the isoquant will be

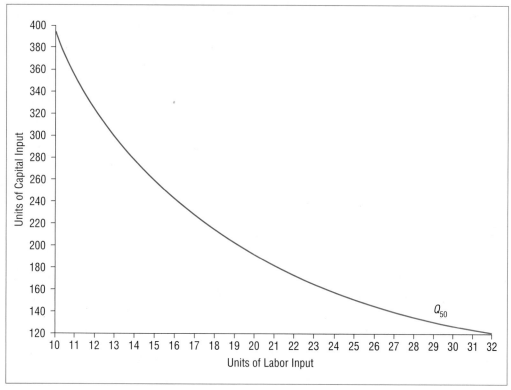

Figure 4.1 An Isoquant

$\Delta K/\Delta L$. The preceding equation may be solved for $\Delta K/\Delta L$, which will be the slope of an isoquant, or the marginal rate of technical substitution of labor for capital:

$$MRTS_{lk} = MP_L/MP_K = \Delta K/\Delta L \qquad (4.5)$$

Similar relationships exist for isoquants representing other levels of output. In Figure 4.2, the three production relationships of Table 4.1 are shown in isoquant form. The isoquant labeled Q_{50} shows all of the possible technically efficient combinations of capital and labor that can produce 50 units of output. Similarly, the curves labeled Q_{55} and Q_{60} show the K and L combinations that can produce 55 and 60 units of output, respectively.[9]

The standard definition of productive efficiency for a single firm used by economists includes a cost minimization dimension. In fact, productive efficiency means that a firm is getting the most output given what it spends on inputs or, put another way, that the firm cannot rearrange its input usage to produce more output at the same cost. To help us identify and characterize producer equilibrium we will need an **isocost line**, a graphical tool that shows all the different combinations of labor and capital that a firm can purchase for a given sum of money.

The total cost, C, by definition must be equal to the sum of the amounts spent on each input. Since we are considering the case of two inputs, total cost, C, will equal the dollar expenditures on labor L plus dollar expenditures on capital K. We assume that each unit of labor costs the firm w and that each unit of capital costs the firm r.[10] If the firm hires L units of labor, then total expenditure on the

Producer Equilibrium

---

[9]The equations used in creating the images in Figure 4.1 are those on which the figures in Table 4.1 were created.

[10]This follows the language developed by economists in the historical development of these ideas where w refers to a wage rate and r refers to a rental rate.

labor input equals w^*L. Likewise, total expenditure on the capital input equals r^*K. The total costs, C, may then be written as

$$C = w^*L + r^*K \qquad (4.6)$$

Suppose, for example, that a firm has $1,000 to spend on inputs, that the price of labor is $100, and that the price of capital is $200. Then the firm can purchase 4 units of capital and 2 units of labor, 3 units of capital and 4 units of labor, or any one of a number of combinations of labor and capital that involve a $1,000 expenditure. In Figure 4.3, we show the isocost line, C_{1000}, that corresponds to these prices for labor and capital.

With the basic concepts of an isocost line derived, we can now move on to two more important issues: the isocost line's slope and its position. Equation (4.6) can be rearranged to yield:

$$K = C/r - (w/r)L \qquad (4.7)$$

which says the same thing but in a different form. We have written the equation with the variable measured on the vertical axis on the left-hand side. On the right-hand side is the variable on the horizontal axis, L, multiplied by the expression $-w/r$. If you are familiar with basic geometric concepts, then you know that the expression C/r represents the vertical intercept of the line and $-w/r$ represents the line's slope.

The isocost line's position is determined solely by the level of total cost, C. Consider our example isocost line discussed earlier for which the total cost was said to be $1,000. How many units of capital could the firm buy if it bought only

Figure 4.2 Three Isoquants

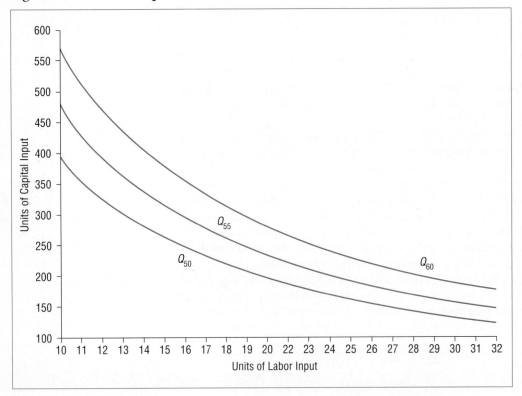

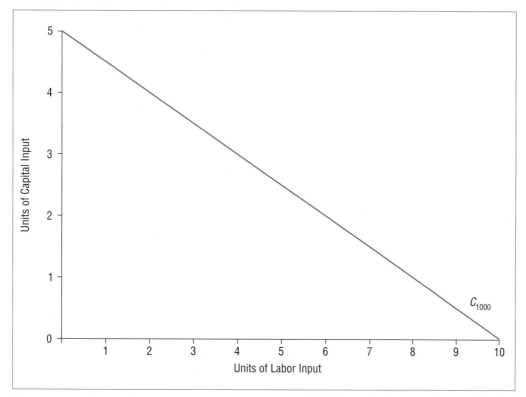

Figure 4.3 Example Isocost Line C = 1,000

capital? The answer is $1,000 divided by the unit cost of capital, $1,000/$200, or 5 (in general, this would be C/r). If the firm bought only labor, it could purchase $1,000 divided by the price of labor, $1,000/$100, or 10 (in general, this would be C/w). Clearly, if the firm were to increase its total expenditures on inputs to, say, $2,000, then it could purchase 10 units of capital and 20 units of labor. If total costs increase, the isocost line shifts outward and parallel to itself. This situation is shown in Figure 4.4. In Figure 4.4, C_{1000} shows all combinations of K and L that can be purchased for a total outlay of $1,000. Similarly, C_{2000} shows all combinations of K and L that can be purchased for a total outlay of $2,000.

The position of the isocost line depends on the level of total expenditure by the firm; its slope is determined by the ratio of the input prices.

Let's continue with our previous example in which the price of labor is $100, the price of capital is $200, and total expenditures are $1,000. What would happen if the price of labor were to increase to $125? If the firm bought only capital, it could purchase 5 units, just as many as it could before the price of labor increased. On the other hand, the firm could now purchase only 8, $1,000/$125, units of labor. The isocost line representing the new price of labor will connect the two points (5 capital, 0 labor) and (0 capital, 8 labor). The effect of this change is shown in Figure 4.5.

In more general terms, the slope of the isocost line is equal to $-w/r$. As labor becomes more expensive relative to capital, the isocost line becomes steeper. The opposite is true for capital. Notice, however, that if the prices of both inputs increase by the same percentages, the isocost line slope is unchanged.

Regarding our productive efficiency puzzle, we now have two of the major pieces of the puzzle and it is time to put them together in a meaningful way.

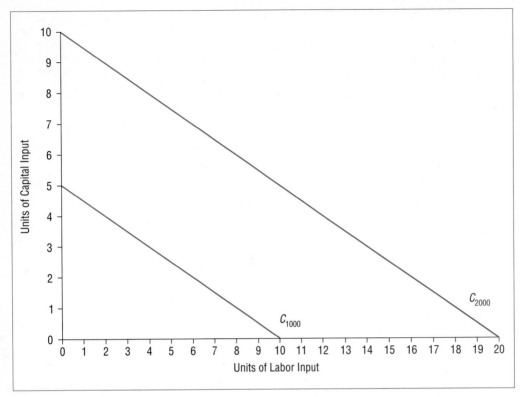

Figure 4.4 Isocost Lines: Alternative Total Cost

The manager of the firm wishes to produce Q units of output at the lowest possible cost. Suppose further that the firm wishes to spend a fixed amount of money. The problem facing the manager is shown in Figure 4.6.[11]

In Figure 4.6, equilibrium in production occurs at point E, where the isocost line C_{1260} intersects isoquant Q_{55}. We must develop an understanding as to why point E is an equilibrium and why it is efficient.

Definitionally, we say that a firm is in *productive equilibrium* when it maximizes output for a given cost outlay. In this example, the isocost line IC_{1260} shows all combinations of capital and labor that the firm can purchase for its total outlay of $1,260 (the price of labor, w is $42, the price of capital, r, is $2). Notice that the firm could purchase the combination of inputs associated with point F and use them to produce the output associated with Q_{50}, or 50 units. However, this outcome would be neither efficient nor an equilibrium.

Notice also that the firm would like to attain point G on Q_{60} and produce 60 units. However, this combination of inputs would require an expenditure that would exceed the firm's outlay.

We can then argue that productive equilibrium and efficiency must occur at the unique intersection, or tangency, of an isoquant and isocost line. Only when this is true will the firm be producing all that it can given its outlay on inputs. Al-

---

[11]For Figure 4.6, the equations of the isoquants are from Table 4.1, the equation of the isocost line is $K = 61 - 21 * L$. This equation was found by determining the slope of the isoquant at $K = 315$, $L = 15$, which is 21. The new price of labor is 42, and the new price of capital is 2.

though this result may seem a little forced and reliant on our graphical tools, the intuition behind it can provide an even greater understanding.

One property of geometry is that at the point where two curves intersect, their slopes must be equal. We have argued that the slope of the isocost line is equal to w/r, the price of labor divided by the price of capital. We have also shown that the slope of an isoquant is equal to MP_L/MP_K, the ratio of the marginal product of labor to that of capital. Mathematically, we may write this as

$$MP_L/MP_K = w/r \qquad (4.8)$$

some rearrangement yields,

$$MP_L/w = MP_K/r \qquad (4.9)$$

which we refer to as the *single firm condition of productive efficiency*. Efficient production requires that a firm choose the level of its inputs so that, for every input, the ratio of marginal productivity to input price be equal.

Each side of equation (4.9) identifies the amount of output provided by the last dollar spent on an input. Consider the left-hand side that refers to labor. The units of the marginal product of labor are $\Delta Q/\Delta L$, the units of w, the price of labor, are $\$/L$. If we ignore the Δs (which is appropriate if we consider the magnitudes fixed), the units of MP_L/w simplify to $Q/\$$, or units of output per dollar.

The *single firm condition of productive efficiency* maintains that the last dollar spent on each input must yield the same amount of output. What would happen if this were not true? Then the firm could reallocate its resources and increase output holding total cost constant.

Suppose for the sake of argument that the single firm condition of productive efficiency were not met. Let the marginal product of labor be 200, the price of la-

Figure 4.5 Isocost Lines, Increase W

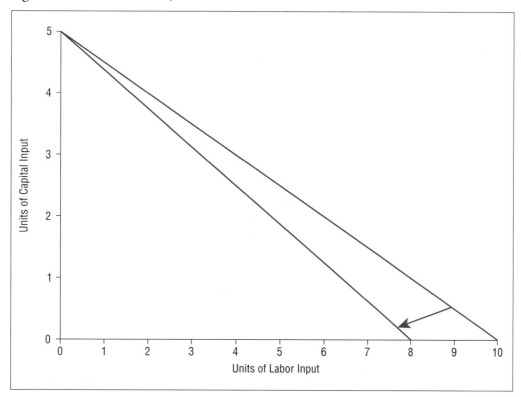

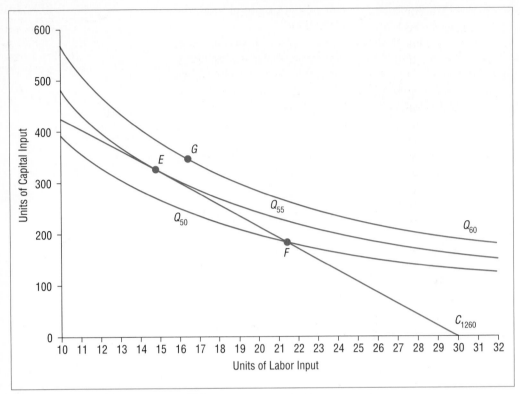

Figure 4.6 Production Equilibrium

bor 50, the marginal product of capital 125, and the price of capital 25. At these values, the equation becomes

$$MP_L/w = 200/50 < MP_K/r = 125/25 \tag{4.10}$$

From this point, the firm can increase output without incurring any additional cost. Let the firm eliminate one unit of labor, effectively freeing up $50. Eliminating this unit of labor will cause output to fall. By how much? By 200 units since this is the marginal productivity of labor. With the $50, now let the firm purchase 2 units of capital, which will cause output to increase by 250 units (2 units of capital times the marginal product of 125). Clearly, more is added to output by the extra capital than is lost by the reduced labor. We can conclude then that the single firm condition of productive efficiency must imply efficient production.[12]

As a brief review, we need to take a look at what we have recently accomplished. We began with a production function of a single producer and determined guidelines to lead this firm to producing efficiently. The tools we relied on were isoquants and isocost lines. In one sense, the output of our discussion is embodied in the single firm condition of productive efficiency. What we now need to do is determine what efficiency, as a requirement, implies for the input choice of more than one producer. This will prove invaluable in our understanding of pro-

---

[12]Note also that this rearrangement by the firm moves it closer to meeting the condition of productive efficiency so long as marginal productivity declines. Fewer units of labor raise the marginal product of labor. More units of capital increase the marginal product of capital. Thus, these adjustments occur until the condition of productive efficiency is met.

ductive efficiency and enable us to continue in our efforts in describing general equilibrium behavior throughout the economy.

What we need is a tool that will enable us to examine the production problem facing two firms simultaneously. For this purpose, we adopt an **Edgeworth Box,** as shown in Figure 4.7.

This diagram combines the isoquants of two producers into one device. There are two producers, food and clothing, each using two inputs, capital and labor. The food producer's graph emanates from the bottom left corner of the box. As you move rightward from the food origin, the number of units of labor devoted to food production increases. As you move upward from the food origin, the units of capital devoted to food production increases.

The isoquant graph of the clothing producer emanates from the upper right-hand corner of the box. Notice that the clothing producer's graph has been rotated 180 degrees so that it sits catty-corner to the food producer's origin. Also note that the labor and capital axes for the clothing producer are drawn thicker. If you begin at the clothing origin and move down toward the bottom of the box, you increase the amount of capital devoted to clothing production. Likewise, if you begin at the clothing origin and move leftward, the amount of labor devoted to clothing production increases.

This description brings one of the primary assumptions of the Edgeworth Box into the light: the total amount of productive resources is fixed. Figure 4.7 has been drawn assuming that there are 12 units of capital and 14 units of labor available. The Edgeworth Box in Figure 4.7 is then 14 labor units wide and 12 capital units high. Each point in, or on, the Edgeworth Box represents the amount of labor and capital going to both the food and clothing producers.

101

Chapter 4
*Efficiency,
the Price System,
and Organizations*

Production
in the Edgeworth Box

Figure 4.7 Edgeworth Box

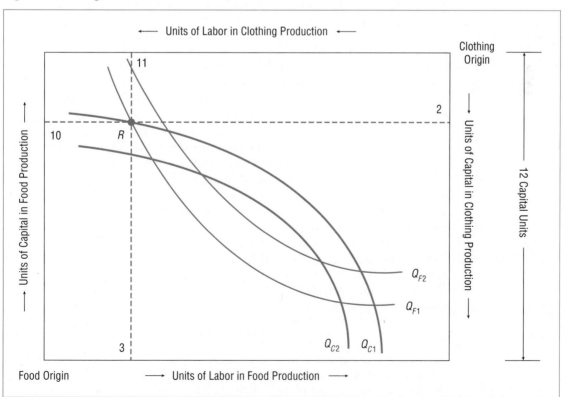

Point R, for example, has the food producer using 3 of the 14 units of labor available and 10 units of the available capital. Likewise, under the division implied by point R, the clothing producer has 11 units of labor and 2 units of capital.

Two isoquants for both the food and clothing producers are also shown in Figure 4.7. The food producer's isoquants, Q_{F1} and Q_{F2}, appear with the latter showing a larger output of food. Two isoquants are also shown for the clothing producer. To clarify the diagram, the isoquants of the clothing producer have been drawn thicker. Output of clothing increases as we move from Q_{C1} to Q_{C2}. Again, what we have essentially done here is to rotate the clothing producer's isoquants 180 degrees and superimposed them on the figure in such a way that the box formed has the specified dimensions of 14 units of labor and 12 units of capital.[13]

For productive efficiency necessary for general equilibrium, we must find the various combinations of inputs chosen by the food and clothing producers that specify a particular criteria. A particular allocation of inputs into the production process is economically efficient if the output of one good cannot be increased without decreasing the output of another good. Inputs are allocated inefficiently if reallocating the inputs generates more of one or both goods.

Consider Figure 4.8, which reproduces Figure 4.7 with some slight modifications. Since we are familiar with point R, let us begin there. Recall that at point R, the food producer has 10 units of capital and 3 of labor while the clothing producer has 11 units of labor and 2 units of capital. The clothing production level is shown by the isoquant Q_{C1} and the food production level is that consistent with Q_{F1}. If point R represents an economically efficient allocation of the inputs for the two producers, then output of one producer cannot be increased without reducing the output of the other producer.

Unfortunately, the allocation of capital and labor shown by point R is not efficient. Output of one good, or both, can be increased without reducing the output of the other good if we consider point R as a starting point. If one unit of labor is removed from clothing production and reallocated to food production while one unit of capital is taken away from the food producer and added to that available to the clothing producer, output of clothing is increased while that of food is unchanged. These movements take us to point S at which food production is unchanged (we remain on the isoquant Q_{F1}), and clothing production has increased as we move to the clothing isoquant Q_{C2}.

A similar argument reveals that point S is not efficient either. Clothing output can be increased again with no loss in food output. The requirement in the Edgeworth Box for productive efficiency is that we be at a tangency of two isoquants such as that shown as point T in Figure 4.8. Only when the isoquants of the two producers are tangent is it impossible to rearrange the allocations of capital and labor to the two producers so that neither is harmed by the lower output and at least one is helped.

Now we must ask what the structural requirement common to all efficient allocations of resources is. Recall the property from geometry that when two curves are tangent, their slopes must be equal. We know that the slope of an isoquant is the marginal rate of technical substitution of capital for labor. Formally, we may then write:

$$^{F}MRTS_{lk} = {}^{C}MRST_{lk} \qquad (4.11)$$

---

[13]F. Y. Edgeworth, *Mathematical Physics: An Essay on the Application of Mathematics to the Moral Sciences* (New York: Augusta M. Kelly, 1953).

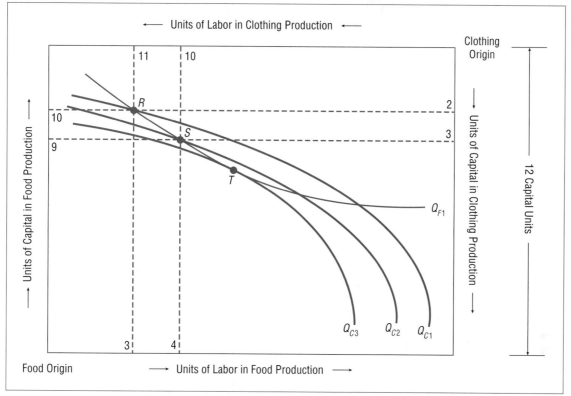

Figure 4.8 Edgeworth Box: Multiple Firm Efficiency

In Figure 4.9, we produce a number of tangencies for which the marginal rate of technical substitution is equal for the two producers. Theoretically, there are an infinite number of tangencies. If we connect these points of tangency, the resulting curve is called the **contract curve.** In Figure 4.9, the double-lined function connecting the food and clothing origins is the contract curve for our two producers. We can conclude that every point on the contract curve is efficient and that every point off the contract curve is not efficient.

In a competitive market system, resources are allocated efficiently if wages and capital rents are determined in active, free markets such as those described in Chapter 2. Individual producers act efficiently, and maximize profits, if they equate their own marginal rates of technical substitution to the ratio of input prices. In competitive equilibrium, production occurs at a point where the marginal rate of technical substitution between every pair of inputs is the same for all producers who use both inputs. If input markets clear, then the following condition must be met:

$$^{F}MRST_{lk} = w/r = {}^{C}MRTS_{lk} \qquad (4.12)$$

By mapping the contract curve from input space into an output space, we can derive the production possibilities frontier. The **production possibilities frontier** is one of the first, and most important, concepts to which students of economics are introduced. However, the connection between this very simple analytical tool and general equilibrium is seldom made. The production possibilities curve shows the various combinations of food and clothing that the economy can produce by fully utilizing all of its labor and capital with the best technology available. We show a typical production possibilities frontier in Figure 4.10.

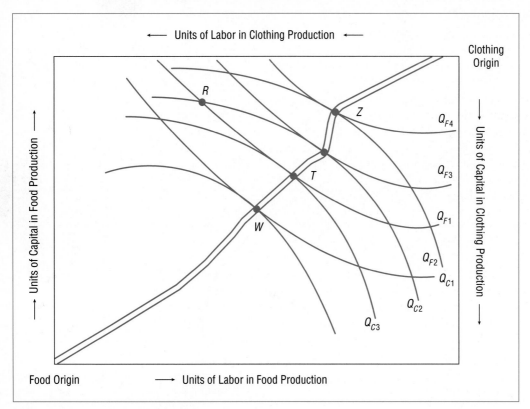

Figure 4.9 Contract Curve

Figure 4.10 Production Possibilities Frontier

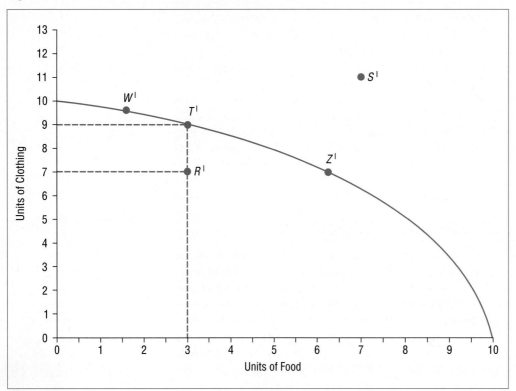

In Figure 4.8, we identified point T as an efficient allocation of resources (labor and capital) between the clothing and food producer. The allocation indicated by point T implies that the clothing producer is on Q_{C3} and the food producer is on Q_{F1}. Suppose that these isoquants represent 3 units of food and 9 units of clothing produced. Notice that since the allocation of labor and capital indicated by point T is efficient, point T also appears on the contract curve in Figure 4.9. The corresponding point on the production possibilities frontier T' represents the "mapping" of the information from the Edgeworth Box to the production possibilities frontier.

By the definition of productive efficiency, all points on the contract curve correspond, or map, to a point on the production possibilities frontier. This is true because productive efficiency requires that the output of one good can be increased only by reducing the output of another good. Points W and Z on the contract curve shown in Figure 4.9 likewise map to the points W' and Z' on the production possibilities frontier. Notice that, relative to point T and T', points Z and Z' correspond to more food and less clothing produced.

Notice that if an allocation of resources is off the contract curve, then it maps to a point inside the production possibilities frontier. Point R in Figures 4.7 and 4.8 was seen to be inefficient. The allocation of capital and labor implied by point R can produce, say, 3 units of food and 7 units of clothing. Notice also that points T and T' correspond to 3 units of food and 9 units of clothing. In the production possibilities frontier shown in Figure 4.10, point R' corresponds to the allocation of capital and labor shown by point R in Figures 4.7 and 4.8.

Points outside the production possibilities frontier are beyond the reach of the economy given the available technology and organization schemes. Point S', for example, involves 7 units of food and 11 units of clothing and is, although desirable, unattainable.

There are several important features of the production possibilities frontier. It is downward sloping. The slope of the production possibilities frontier at a particular point gives the marginal rate of transformation of food for clothing MRT_{fc} at that point. It measures by how much this economy must reduce its output of clothing in order to release enough labor and capital to produce exactly one more unit of food. If we want to produce more food, we must switch inputs from clothing production to food production. This in turn lowers clothing production. The production possibilities curve is concave. This implies that the law of increasing relative costs prevails. It measures the amount of clothing that has to be given up to produce one additional unit of food. As we move down the production possibilities frontier, the rate at which clothing has to be sacrificed to produce an additional unit of food increases. We then say that the marginal rate of transformation of food for clothing (MRT_{fc}) increases at an increasing rate as we move down a given production possibilities frontier.

■ GENERAL EQUILIBRIUM OF PRODUCTION AND EXCHANGE

Production efficiency is only the first step on our journey to understand efficiency. Products must also be produced in combinations that match consumers' willingness to pay for them. An economy reaches general equilibrium only if production efficiency is matched with exchange efficiency.

We would now like to bring together two concepts: efficiency in production and efficiency in exchange. For an economy to be efficient, first it must produce goods at minimum cost and second it must produce those goods at prices that people are willing to pay. This idea is captured in the concept of *product mix efficiency*.

Market Coordination

The logic and necessity of attaining product mix efficiency are apparent. Structurally, what has to happen is that consumers choose the optimal point on the production possibilities frontier to consume. If this happens, then producers are providing the goods that consumers want at the right prices. If producers are at one point and consumers desire another, various markets do not clear, prices change, and the economy moves along its production possibilities frontier.

Economists speak of the **marginal rate of substitution (MRS)** as being the rate at which consumers are willing to trade two goods in the market place. In Figure 4.11, we have a production possibilities frontier along with a social indifference curve,[14] which is derived at the end of Appendix 4A. In Figure 4.11, the social indifference curve, SIC_1, reflects the tastes and preferences of consumers. Only one point on a production possibilities frontier reaches the highest attainable social indifference curve. In Figure 4.11, this point is labeled point *E*.

The slope of the social indifference curve equals the marginal rate of transformation of the goods on the horizontal and vertical axes. Since product mix efficiency requires a tangency between the social indifference curve and the production possibilities frontier, the slopes of the two functions must be equal. Put another way, product mix efficiency requires that

$$MRS = MRT \qquad (4.13)$$

Thus, at point *E* in Figure 4.11, productive and product mix efficiency are achieved. This implies that there is a common rate at which consumers and producers are willing to trade the two goods.

Informational Efficiency

For general equilibrium to be achieved, the above condition must be achieved not for just one consumer for two goods but for all consumers for all goods in the economy. A key problem in achieving effective coordination is that the information needed to determine the best use of resources is not available to everyone. Efficient choices require information about individual tastes, technological opportunities, and resource availability. This information does not reside with any one individual or organization, no matter how large or powerful, in any society. Instead, this information is localized and dispersed throughout the economy. Because this knowledge is dispersed, no one has the knowledge needed to make the calculations of what to produce, how to produce it, and for whom to produce it.

There are two solutions to solving the information problem. One is to transmit the dispersed information to a central authority that will solve "the economic problem." The second solution is to develop a system of coordination that leaves much of the decisions with those who possess the information. Which system works better? Frederick Hayek suggested over 50 years ago, "which of these systems [central planning or competitive markets] is likely to be more efficient depends on the question under which of them we can expect that fuller use will be made of the existing knowledge."[15] We have just seen that under certain conditions, the price system achieves this result of coordination of individual prices while economizing on informational demands. In other words, a well-

---

[14]An indifference curve shows different groupings of goods (bundles) that yield consumers the same level of satisfaction, or utility. Basically, indifference curves are very similar in shape to isoquants discussed earlier in this chapter."Higher" (up and to the right) indifference curves show bundles that yield greater satisfaction. For a complete discussion of indifference curves and consumer tastes, please see Appendix 4A.

[15]Friedreich Hayek, "The Use of Knowledge in Society," *American Economic Review* 35, 1945, pp. 519–530.

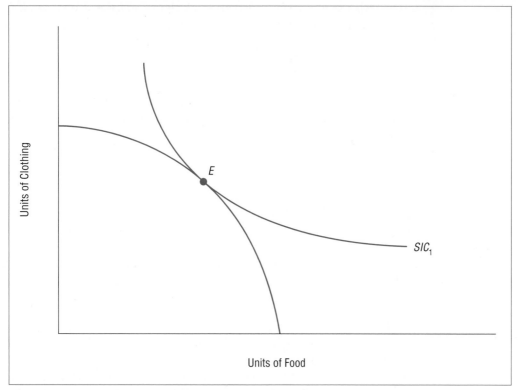

Figure 4.11 General Equilibrium

functioning market economy achieves coordination at a minimum cost, at least in theory.

◼ ASSUMPTIONS OF GENERAL EQUILIBRIUM THEORY

This chapter has brought together the pieces of the basic competitive model. We have shown how a competitive equilibrium in an ideal economy is achieved. To the extent that conditions in the real world match the approximations of the basic competitive model, there will be economic efficiency. This sounds almost too good to be true. Coordination of the economy is achieved at almost no cost. However, before we celebrate, let's stop and take a look at the assumptions that we had to make for the system to be competitive. There are two crucial assumptions. First, all agents in the economy are price takers. In all markets—product, labor, and capital—agents are price takers and take prices as given. For example, both the prices of GM cars and the wages of autoworkers are set by the market. The second assumption is that **perfect competition** prevails in all markets. Economists strongly disagree about the extent to which the competitive model describes reality. A group of economists referred to as *free market economists* believes that the competitive model provides a good description of most markets most of the time. Most other economists agree that the general equilibrium model is extremely powerful. But many are not quite so sure that it provides an accurate description of the real-world economy. These economists are known as *imperfect market economists*.

Still other economists contend that the assumptions that firms have perfect information about the quality of their workers or that investors have perfect information about the returns to different investment opportunities are not good assumptions, and that **incomplete information** results in capital and labor markets functioning in ways different from that described by the general equilibrium model.[16]

MARKET FAILURE

Efficiency is the central concern in economics. In our example, the economy is producing efficiently when it cannot produce more of one good without producing less of another—when it is on the contract curve in Figure 4.9. Up to now we have assumed that the economy is producing on the contract curve and is on the production possibilities frontier in Figure 4.10.

One way to have an economy operate inside its production possibilities frontier and still to be on the contract curve is to have unemployed resources in an economy. Unemployed resources may arise because of a lack of effective demand for some outputs or because of some disturbance in the competitive functioning of the input markets.

To fully understand the effect of unemployed resources on the production possibilities frontier, we must consider two cases: in the first, the unemployed resources do not cause changes in the input prices; in the second, input prices change because of the unemployed resources.

Regarding the case in which input prices do not change, first we must recognize that the dimensions of the Edgeworth Box change. This is shown in Figure 4.12. The upper right-hand corner of the box (the clothing origin) moves toward the lower left-hand corner (the food origin). Because of the unemployed resources, one, or both, producers has fewer inputs to work with. Thus, one producer or both producers are moved to a lower isoquant. It follows then that the maximum output obtainable declines and the production possibilities frontier shifts inward as shown in Figure 4.13.

Regarding the case in which the unemployed resources cause one or both input prices to change, remember that every firm in the economy is assumed to obey the single firm condition of productive efficiency described earlier. Each firm equates the ratio of the marginal product of its inputs to the input price ratio. All firms must do this. If a large number of firms are out of equilibrium, then those firms must expand their use of some inputs and reduce their use of others. These adjustments are also further constrained because the resource "pool" is smaller economywide. The changes in input level usage alter their market-determined equilibrium prices, which will cause adjustments by other producers. The changed conditions in the input markets result in changed market prices for productive resources that, in turn, cause further changes by producers as they attempt to hire inputs so that they obey the single firm condition of productive efficiency.

Graphically, the manifestation of these changes is shown in Figures 4.13 and 4.14. Figure 4.14 shows an Edgeworth Box that has shrunk in response to unemployment. The contract curve in the original Edgeworth Box is shown as the solid curve *CC'*. The contract curve in the smaller Edgeworth Box is shown as the dashed curve *CD'*. The new shape of the contract curve reflects producers changing the relative amounts of inputs they use in production.

In either case, it is worth pointing out that an economy can produce efficiently with unemployed resources. In both Figure 4.12 and Figure 4.14, the firms still choose resource allocations that are on the respective contract curves. What-

---

[16] See for example, Joseph Stiglitz, *Economics* (New York: W. W. Norton, 1992), ch. 14.

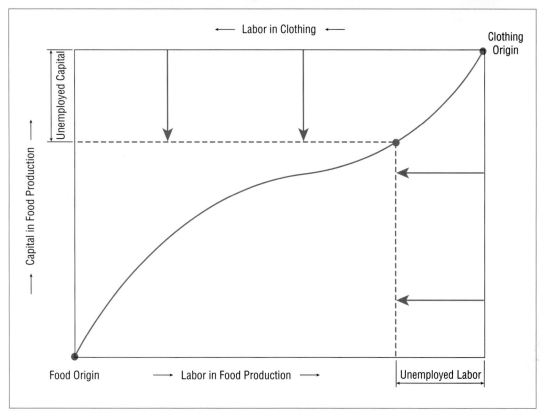

Figure 4.12 Edgeworth Box: Reduction in Resources

ever output is produced is produced efficiently. However, we are not on the production possibilities frontier since there are unemployed inputs. The cause of this problem may be a lack of effective demand, not organizational inefficiency.

If an economy is inefficiently organized at any level, it may be off the contract curve and well short of the frontier too. We saw such a case after the breakup of the Soviet Union. Ukraine in 1994 was inside its production possibilities frontier as the price system broke down. Political turmoil pushed Ukraine inside its frontier.

Less dramatic, but no less important, are cases for which an economy is inside its frontier and off the contract curve when it is riddled with monopoly or inefficient regulation, or when a command economy is subject to arbitrary decrees by inept bureaucrats. Competitive markets fail basically for four reasons: imperfect information, missing or incomplete markets, externalities, and increasing returns to scale. We would like to discuss each one of these with reference to the contract curve in Figure 4.9 and the production possibilities curve in Figure 4.10.

The competitive model assumes that firms and households are well informed. Imagine knowing every good and service sold at every store and the price at which it sold. If information were perfect—complete and accurate—problems of how to allocate resources would be relatively easy to solve. But information is imperfect—less than complete and accurate—and costly to acquire. If decision makers had perfect information concerning the consequences of their decisions, decision making would be a relatively easy matter.

Imperfect information can flaw the tendency toward an efficient equilibrium such as predicted in the standard competitive model. Consider the single firm

Imperfect Information

109

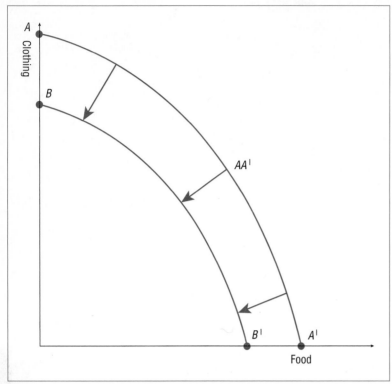

**Figure 4.13 Production Possibilities Frontier
with Unemployed Inputs**

productive efficiency condition. The firm may not know exactly what the marginal products of its inputs are. Further, attempts at estimating them may be flawed for a number of reasons. We will take up this very issue in Chapters 7 and 8.

Imperfect information regarding prevailing wage rates for labor (or rental rates for capital) can also create problems leading to inefficiencies in production. Workers' individual wages are often negotiated on a case-by-case basis. In many instances (most notably government employment), wages are determined by institutional factors such as pay grades or seniority rules. In either of these instances, wages may not be as closely tied to productivity as suggested by the competitive general equilibrium model presented in this chapter.

Each of these situations of imperfect information may lead producers to a point off existing contract curves such as point *R* in Figures 4.8 and 4.9. From a general equilibrium perspective, these particular sources of inefficiency are even more damaging since there is no tendency for change, even in the long run.

Incomplete Markets

One particular example is often referred to as one with asymmetric information. That is, the seller has more information than the buyer. One of the consequences of asymmetric information is that there may be relatively few buyers and sellers, far fewer than there would be with perfect information. In some situations, the market may be so thin as to be nonexistent. With nonexisting or incomplete markets, it may be impossible to move to the contract curve from point *R*.

Externalities
Increasing Returns

Externalities arise when an individual or firm takes an action but does not bear all the costs or receive all the benefits. Externalities can also be associated with missing markets. They represent goods or services that consumers or producers would want to buy. However, since they are not traded in markets, prices cannot be attached to them. Therefore, the market fails to guide their allocation. Again, we cannot move from point R to the contract curve.

In some industries, it may be impossible to have an equilibrium because supply and demand may not intersect. There may be no price at which supply and demand will equilibrate. Without a price, we cannot move from point R to the contract curve. This failure is especially likely when there are significant scale economies in some production process, so that it is less expensive to produce many units than to produce few.

For example, economists did not observe that scale economies in resource-based industries necessarily led to increasing returns. A resource-based industry is one in which the main inputs are labor and capital. Sometimes large plants have proven more economical; often they have not. Knowledge-based parts of the economy, on the other hand, are largely subject to **increasing returns.** In knowledge-based industries, the main inputs are research and development, for example, software. Products such as computers, pharmaceuticals, missiles, aircraft, software, or fiber optics are complicated to design and manufacture. They require large investments in research and development. As production increases, unit costs continue to fall and profits increase. Moreover, experience gained with one product or technology can make it easier to make new products incorporating similar or related goods. In these cases, the competitive market fails.

Market failure is defined as a malfunction in a market mechanism that results

Figure 4.14 Edgeworth Box: Changed Input Prices

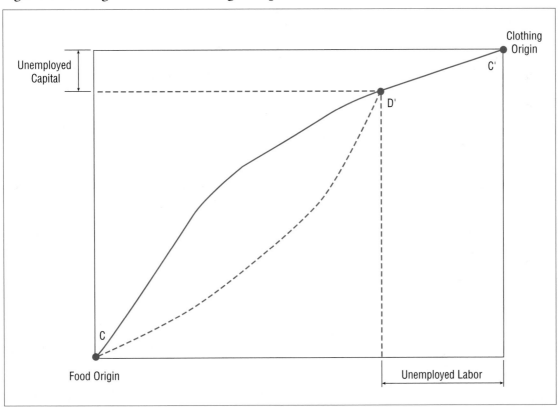

in a misallocation or an unproductive use of resources. How to achieve efficiency when markets fail is an important question. One approach is to try to reproduce the conditions of the competitive model in the economy. Therefore, you break up large firms—AT&T, IBM, GM—to create ones with less market power. Most traditional textbooks take this approach. This book takes another tact. Since we are unlikely to replicate the competitive model, we should concentrate on how to deal with market failure. For example, the information problem is at the heart of understanding how organizations function.

■ MARKET FAILURE AND ORGANIZATION

If competitive equilibrium did provide a complete description of how markets work, there would be no need for other economic organizations. However, when people have found markets inefficient, they have organized firms. As we saw in Chapter 1, the firm has evolved over time. In the 18th century, business in the "New America" consisted of a large number of very small firms. In most instances the unit was the family. By the early 1800s, new forms of specialized enterprises had sprung up to facilitate trade and transportation from the farms into the interior of the cities. The growth of industry continued along these lines into the first decades in the 19th century as large enterprises emerged that specialized in finance, transportation, marketing, and distribution.

Transactions Costs

In economics, like in all social sciences, asking the right questions counts. Ronald Coase in his classic 1937 article asked why companies exist if production can also be organized as a chain of individual market transactions among people who are buying and selling everything from the labor to mine the iron ore to a finished car. Or, simply, why are there firms? According to Coase, there are costs to carrying out transactions, and these costs vary from transaction to transaction. Firms eliminate uncertainty and costly one-time transactions costs by creating stable contractual relationships—firms.

For example, when a firm wants to buy an input, it has two alternatives. When Ford needed steel, it could have bought the steel from another firm or produced the steel itself. But there are transactions costs involved. If the firms use the market, they have to have salespeople and buyers and lawyers to negotiate contracts. In some markets, the transactions costs can be high. Thus, Ford decided to produce its own steel at the River Rouge Plant in Detroit. At its peak, iron ore and coal entered the plant at one end and finished cars rolled off the assembly line at the other end of a giant building. Was this arrangement efficient?

**Efficiency
of Organizations**

Most production in the economy, both in the United States and the Ukraine, takes place in organizations. In fact, about one-fourth of U.S. manufacturing takes place inside the 50 largest manufacturing corporations. Much of the production in the Ukraine takes place in even fewer factories and on huge collective farms.

Our initial concern about efficiency was with allocative efficiency. *Our other concern about efficiency is with the efficiency of organizations themselves.* People are concerned about the outcome of organizations, and the organizations are to be judged on the basis of these outcomes.

How do we know whether an organization is efficient? One way is to evaluate each organization on a case-by-case basis. The problem with the case-by-case method is that it is expensive and there is no adequate yardstick by which to measure efficiency. IBM used to be efficient. Is it still efficient today? Ought it to be? Milgrom and Roberts suggest a positive principle to evaluate organizational efficiency. They start with the premise that people wish to make their organization more efficient rather than less efficient. We therefore need an organizing principle to help evaluate efficiency in organizations. This is found in the efficiency principle:

> efficiency principle: *If people can bargain effectively and can effectively implement and enforce their decisions, then the outcomes of economic activity will tend to be efficient.*[17]

Many familiar business relationships and economic institutions are framed by efficiency. The concept of efficiency is important because it provides a minimal set of rules for governing behavior of economic agents. Much of what we will learn in the rest of this book is about the outcome of efficiency in organizations. However, before we can discuss the efficiency of organizations, we must develop the concepts to deal with efficiency in the face of market failure. We will see in the next chapter that ownership can provide the incentives necessary to promote efficient dealings between buyers and sellers.

▓ CHAPTER SUMMARY AND KEY IDEAS ▓ ▓ ▓ ▓ ▓ ▓

This chapter has been concerned about efficiency in a general equilibrium framework. Efficiency is the process of getting more for less. Efficiency is to be judged by the ability of the system to satisfy the wants and needs of individual human beings. Efficiency is therefore important for resource allocation.

Ever since Adam Smith it has been known that wealth can be increased if people specialize in production and then exchange their output for the actual goods and services they need. However, when each person specializes, the economy must either be planned or there must be some other mechanism that accomplishes the same goal. The market provides one mechanism for coordinating economic activity. The market also provides for individuals to help themselves in a socially beneficial way.

The basic assumptions of the model are that rational, perfectly informed households interact with rational, profit-maximizing firms in competitive markets and in an environment free of market failure.

Production efficiency looks at the economy from the perspective of inputs into the production process. When production is efficient, output is on the contract curve. We can map the contract curve from input space into an output space. The production possibilities frontier maps the various combinations of two goods that can be produced. For general equilibrium to be achieved, the economy must achieve both production efficiency and product mix efficiency. The slope of the social indifference curve equals the marginal rate of transformation of the two goods. Since product mix efficiency requires a tangency between the social indifference curve and the production possibilities frontier, the slopes of the two functions must be equal in equilibrium. The assumptions of general equilibrium are that firms are price takers and that perfect competition prevails in all markets.

When markets fail, the economy will not be efficient. For example, when externalities arise, individuals or firms take actions that do not bear the full cost or receive all the benefits of their actions. If competitive equilibrium did provide a complete description of how markets work, there would be no need for other economic organizations. However, when people have found markets inefficient, they have organized firms. Firms eliminate uncertainty and costly one-time transactions costs by creating stable contractual relationships.

---

[17]Milgrom and Roberts, *Economics, Organization & Management*, p. 58.

KEY TERMS

budget line	isoquant
contract curve	marginal rate of substitution
Edgeworth Box	marginal rate of technical substitution
efficient	market failure
exchange efficiency	partial equilibrium
externalities	perfect competition
general equilibrium analysis	product mix efficiency
imperfect information	production efficiency
incomplete information	production function
increasing returns	production possibilities frontier
indifference curve	resource allocation
isocost	specialization
isocost line	

FURTHER READINGS

Arrow, K. J., and G. Debreu. "Existence of an Equilibrium for a Competitive Economy." *Econometrica* 22, 1954, pp. 265–290.

Edgeworth, F. Y. *Mathematical Psychics: An Essay on the Application of Mathematics to the Moral Sciences.* New York: Augusta M. Kelly, 1953.

Ferguson, C. E. *Microeconomic Theory.* Homewood, Ill.: Richard D. Irwin, 1972.

Hayek, F. "The Use of Knowledge in Society." *American Economic Review* 35, 1945, 519–530.

Milgrom P., and J. Roberts. *Economics, Organization & Management.* Englewood Cliffs, N.J.: Prentice Hall, 1992.

Pindyck, R. S., and D. L. Rubinfeld. *Microeconomics.* New York: Macmillan, 1992.

Salvatore, D. *Microeconomic Theory.* New York: McGraw-Hill, 1974.

Sinn, G., and H. Werner Sinn. *Jumpstart.* Cambridge: The MIT Press, 1994.

Smith, A. *The Wealth of Nations.* Chicago: The University of Chicago Press, 1976.

Stiglitz, J. *Economics.* New York: W. W. Norton, 1993.

QUESTIONS AND PROBLEMS FOR REVIEW AND DISCUSSION

A. Suppose that I use two inputs, K and L, to produce output, Q. Input K is purchased at a price of $5 per unit. Input L is purchased at a price of $10 per unit: $MP_K = 100$ and $MP_L = 250$.

  1. Is this situation one of efficiency in production? Why or why not? *Hint*: transfer one dollar's worth of one input to purchasing the other input and see if output is increased while costs remain constant.

  2. Explain exactly how you move the inputs around to achieve productive efficiency. For each input move, explain fully the effect on output.

B. Consider the production possibilities frontier shown in Figure 4.10. Assume that a curve with such a slope and shape exists for a hypothetical student, Steve Isberg, a junior at the Coffee School of Business. Instead of having food and clothing on the two axes, place two goods of more direct concern to Steve on them. On the vertical axis place the good "social life" and on the horizontal axis place "good grades."

  1. Explain what the slope of this function shows regarding the allocation of Steve's time.

  2. Begin at a point on the production possibilities curve near the vertical axis. Are good grades expensive or cheap at this point? Can you explain why?

3. Begin at a point on the production possibilities curve near the horizontal axis. Is it expensive for Steve to consume the good called "social life"? Can you explain why or why not?

C. One explanation for market failure and the general failure of a competitive market system to operate on a production possibility frontier is the problem of missing markets. Determine a good or service that you consume for which there is not a market (remember this is for a mixed, family audience).

APPENDIX 4A   Efficiency in Exchange

Exchange efficiency requires that whatever the economy produces must be distributed among individuals in an efficient way. Exchange efficiency is best understood in four steps. The first step examines consumer preferences. The second accounts for the fact that consumers have budget constraints. The third puts the two together and determines consumer choice. The fourth studies exchange between two individuals.

CONSUMER PREFERENCES

The theory of consumer behavior begins with four basic assumptions regarding individual preferences for one market basket versus another. We assume that each consumer has complete information on all matters pertaining to its consumption decision.

1. The first assumption is that preferences are *complete*. This means that consumers can rank all market baskets. A consumer either prefers *A* to *B* or *B* to *A* or is indifferent between the two. By indifferent, we mean that the consumer would be equally happy with either basket.
2. The second assumption is that preferences are *transitive*. This assumes that if a consumer prefers basket *A* to *B* and *B* to *C*, he or she will prefer *C* to *A*. Indifference curves cannot intersect each other, for this would violate the assumption that consumers are rational.
3. The third assumption is that preferences are *nonsatiable*. That is, consumers always prefer more than less of the good.
4. The fourth assumption is that preferences are *convex*. The term *convex* implies that the rate at which consumers are willing to substitute between two bundles of goods diminishes along the same indifference curve.

The decision to consume an individual commodity is seldom made in isolation. Instead, products are consumed as parts of a market basket of goods and services. Take an imaginary household and give it bundles of two goods, food and clothing. This gives the household a certain level of utility or satisfaction. Households can hold the level of utility constant and substitute between food and clothing. Different combinations of food and clothing can give the same level of satisfaction. Assume that after the household runs through several trials, a number of bundles have been identified. These are shown in Table 4A.1.

Different bundles of commodities that yield the same level of utility can be represented by an **indifference curve**. In general, *an indifference curve shows all combinations of goods and services that yield the same satisfaction to the household*. A household is indifferent between the combination indicated by any two points on one indifference curve. Figure 4A.1 plots the information from Table 4A.1. An indifference curve is constructed by connecting all the points representing consumption baskets that provide the same level of utility. Points *A, B, C,* and *D* are on the indifference curve. The consumer is equally happy with either one of these

Indifference Curves

Table 4A.1	**Alternative Market Baskets**		
Bundle		**Clothing**	**Food**
A		30	5
B		18	10
C		13	15
D		10	20
E		8	25
F		7	30

bundles of goods. The consumer would prefer any combination of goods to the right of the indifference curve, for example *G*. Consider, for example, the combination 20 food and 18 clothes, which is represented by point *G*. Although it may not be obvious that this bundle must be preferred to a bundle *A*, which has more clothing but less food, it is obvious that it will be preferred to bundle *C* because there are both less clothing and less food represented at *C* than at *G*. Inspection of the graph shows that any point above the curve is obviously superior to some points on the curve. But since all points on the curve are equal to the consumer, the point above the curve must be superior to all points on the curve. By a similar argument, all points below the indifference curve represent bundles of goods that are inferior to bundles represented by points on the curve.

Figure 4A.1 Indifference Curve

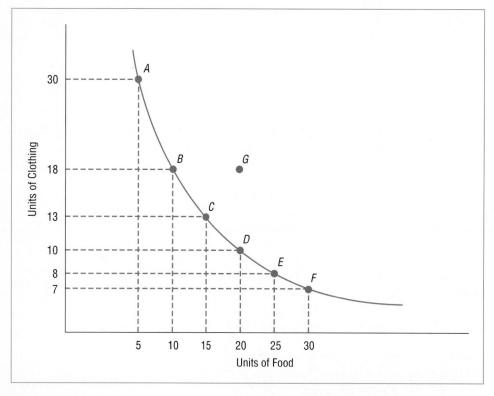

Households face trade-offs when comparing different bundles of commodities. How much clothing would a household be willing to give up for an additional bundle of food? The indifference curve depicted in Figure 4A.2 illuminates this situation. The consumer is indifferent between the bundles represented by points A and B. Starting at point A and moving to point B, we see that the household is willing to give up 6 units of clothing to get an additional unit of food. That is, decreasing clothing consumption from 24 to 18 units is equivalent to increasing food consumption from 5 to 6 units. A similar situation exists moving from point B to point C. When the household starts at point B, it is willing to give up only 4 units of clothing to get an additional unit of food. Indeed, it is true that the more clothing and the less food a person consumes, the more clothing he or she will give up to obtain additional units of food. Similarly, the more food a person possesses, the less clothing he or she is willing to give up to obtain food.

The marginal rate of substitution (*MRS*) is the amount of one commodity a consumer would be willing to give up to get one more unit of another commodity. The MRS_{fc} of food for clothing is the maximum amount of clothing that a person would be willing to give up to obtain one additional unit of food. If the *MRS* is 4, the consumer is willing to give up 4 units of clothing for 1 additional unit of food, and if the *MRS* is 2, the consumer is willing to give up 2 units of clothes for one unit of food.

The *MRS* is defined as $-\Delta C/\Delta F$, where ΔC is the change in clothing and ΔF is the change in food. The negative sign is included to make the *MRS* a positive number. As a result, the *MRS* at any point on the indifference curve is equal in absolute value to the slope of the indifference curve at that point. For example, moving from point A to point B on the indifference curve in Figure 4A.2, the MRS of food F for clothing C is $-C/F = -(-6)/1 = 6$. When starting at point B, however, the MRS falls to 4. Therefore, the indifference curves are convex and the slope of the curve increases as we move down the curve.

So far we have constructed only a single indifference curve. However, there must be similar curves through all other points in Figure 4A.2. To describe a person's preferences for all combinations of goods, we can graph a family of indifference curves called an *indifference map*. The farther any indifference curve is from the origin, the higher is the level of utility given by any of the combination of goods indicated by points on the curve. When economists say that a household's tastes are given by assumption, they do not mean that the household's current consumption pattern is given, but that its entire indifference map is given.

What a household does is determined by both its tastes and income. A household's indifference map describes what its preferences are for goods and services. The budget line shows what the household can do—the choices it can make given its money income.

THE BUDGET LINE

Consider a very simple model in which a household is faced with a choice between only two goods, food (F) and clothing (C). Let P_F be the price of food and P_C the price of clothing. Therefore, $P_F F$ is the amount of money spent on food, and $P_C C$ is the amount of money spent on clothing. Assume that the household has a certain money income denoted by Y. The amount of money spent on food plus the amount of money spent on clothing will add up to household income. We call the relationship between the prices of the goods consumed, the number of units of the goods consumed, and household income the **budget line**. The budget line shows all combinations of goods that the household can purchase

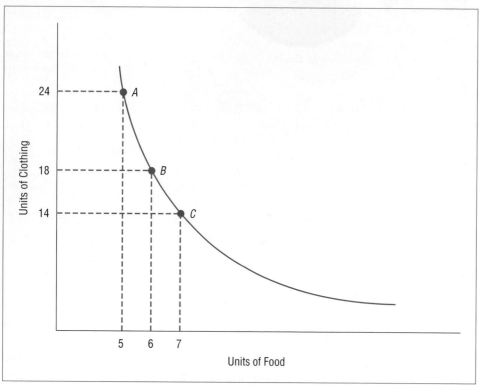

Figure 4A.2 Marginal Rate of Substitution

given prices and income level. The equation for the budget line facing a household is:

$$P_F F + P_C C = Y \tag{4.14}$$

As shown in Figure 4A.3, assume that the household has an income of $80 a week and that the prices for food and clothing are set at $2 a unit for clothes and $1 a unit for food. The household does not save: its only choice is how to spend on food and clothing. It could spend all of its income on food and obtain 80 units of food or spend all of its income on clothing and obtain 40 units of clothing. For each unit of food the household gives up, it can obtain an additional one-half unit of clothing.

The budget line facing this household with $80 in income is shown in Figure 4A.3 and L_1. Notice that line L_1 intersects the vertical (clothing) axis at 40 units of clothing and the horizontal (food) axis at 80 units of food.

In terms of the equation of the budget line, we can see how much of C must be given up to consume more of F by dividing both sides of the equation by PC and then solving for C:

$$C = (Y/P_C) - (P_F/P_C)F \tag{4.15}$$

This is the equation for a straight line; it has a vertical intercept of Y/P_C and a slope of $-(P_F/P_C)$.

What happens to the budget line when money income changes? If the household's money income is halved from $80 a week to $40 a week, prices being unchanged, then the amount of goods it can buy is also halved. Changes in income shift the budget line from L_1 to L_2. The vertical intercept of the budget line changes, but it does not change the slope of the budget line. If income is halved, the budget line shifts to the right from L_1 to L_2 as shown in Figure 4A.4. As long

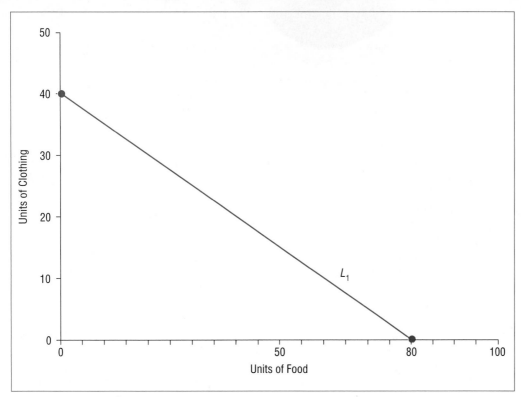

Figure 4A.3 Budget Line

Figure 4A.4 Change in Income

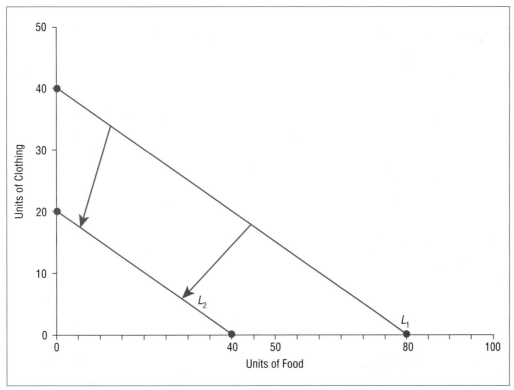

as the price ratio remains the same, the shifts are parallel to the original budget line.

Absolute price, or money price, is the amount of money that must be spent to acquire 1 unit of the commodity. A relative price is the ratio of two absolute prices. The statement that the price of food is $2 refers to the absolute price. Saying that the price of food is twice the price of clothing refers to a relative price. A change in the relative price can be accomplished by holding one price constant and changing the other.

What happens to the budget line if the price of one good changes but the price of the other good does not? We can use the equation $C = (Y/P_C) - (P_F/P_C)F$ to describe the effects of a change in the price of food on the budget line. Suppose that the price of food falls by half from $1 to $0.50. Then the vertical intercept of the budget line remains unchanged, but the slope changes from $-PF/PC = -\$1/\$2 = -1/2$ to $-\$0.50/\$2 = -1/4$. In Figure 4A.5, we obtain the new budget line L_2 by rotating the original budget line L_1 outward, pivoting from the C-intercept. This rotation makes sense intuitively because a person who consumes only clothing and no food is unaffected by the price change. However, a man who purchases a substantial amount of food greatly increased his purchasing power. In fact, the maximum amount of food that he can purchase has doubled in response to the decline in the price of food.

Consumer Equilibrium

Indifference maps describe the preferences of households. Budget lines describe the possibilities open to the household. To predict what households will actually do, both of these sets of information must be put together. Households maximize the satisfaction they can achieve, given the limited budget available to them.

Figure 4A.5 Change in Relative Prices

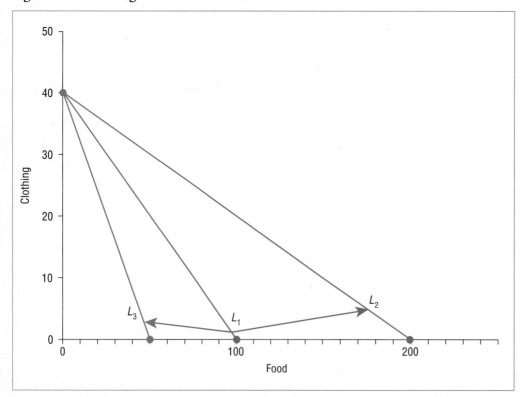

For the household to maximize satisfaction, two conditions must be met. The first is that it must reach the highest level of satisfaction. That is, the household wants to be on the highest indifference curve possible. The second condition is that the consumer must be on its budget line. It cannot spend more than it has. As shown in Figure 4A.6, only when the basket of goods represented by an indifference is tangent to the budget line is the consumer maximizing its utility. At point E, it is impossible for the consumer to move to a higher level of utility, given the current budget constraint.

At point E the slope of the indifference curve, the *MRS* of food for clothing, equals the slope of the budget line, or the ratio of the price of food to the price of clothes:

$$MRS_{fc} = P_F/P_C \qquad (4.16)$$

Consumer utility is maximized when the marginal rate of substitution of food for clothing MRS equals the ratio of the prices of food for clothing P_F/P_C. The common sense of this result is that if the household values goods at a different rate than the market does, there is room for profitable exchange.

If people specialize in production, they must trade. Adam Smith recognized this over 200 years ago when he wrote,

> This division of labor, from which so many advantages are derived, is not originally the effect of any human wisdom, which foresees and intends that general opulence to which it gives occasion. It is the necessary, though very slow and gradual, consequence of a certain propensity in human nature which has in view no

Exchange
Between Two Parties

Figure 4A.6 Consumer Equilibrium

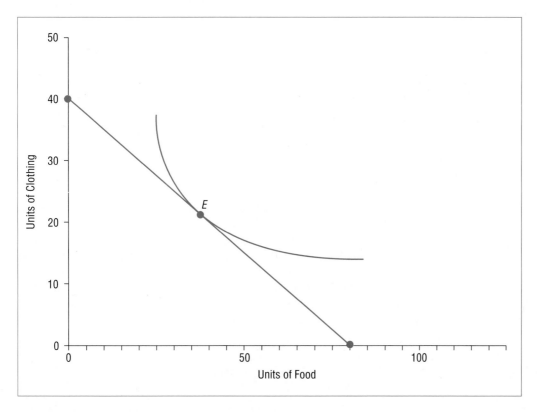

such extensive utility; the propensity to truck, barter and exchange one thing for another.[18]

To see how trade can increase efficiency, let us look at a very simple model. Assume there are two people Dan and Diane, and two commodities food and clothing; both individuals have complete information about each other's preferences; transaction costs are zero. Suppose that Dan and Diane have 10 units of food and 6 units of clothing between them. Initially Dan has 7 units of food and 1 unit of clothing, and Diane has 3 units of food and 5 units of clothing. To determine whether trade between Dan and Diane would be advantageous, we have to know their preferences. Suppose that because Diane has a lot of clothing and little food, her marginal rate of substitution of food for clothing is 3. On the other hand, Dan's *MRS* of food for clothes is only 1/2. He will give up only 1/2 unit of clothing to get 1 unit of food. Thus, there is room for mutually advantageous trade since Dan values clothing more highly than food, and Diane values food more highly than clothing. Dan would be willing to trade up to 3 units of food to get more clothing. Diane will give up only 1 unit of food for 1/2 unit of clothing. Among the possible outcomes are a trade of 1 unit of food by Dan for between 1/2 and 3 units of clothing from Diane. The actual terms of trade depend on the bargaining process with only two individuals. If Dan offers Diane 1 unit of clothing for 1 unit of food, and Diane agrees, both will be better off. Dan will have more clothing, which he values more than food, and Diane will have more food, which she values more than clothing.

Whenever two consumers' *MRS* for two goods differ, there is room for mutually beneficial trade because the allocation of resources is inefficient; exchange will make consumers better off. Even if a trade from an inefficient allocation makes both people better off, the new allocation may not be efficient. To achieve efficiency, two consumers' *MRS* must be equal.

We can use the indifference curve analysis developed earlier to answer the question concerning how much better off consumers will be after trade. Suppose that Dan and Diane possess together a combination of 14 units of clothing and 16 units of food. Suppose also that Dan's tastes are represented by indifference curves 1′, 2′, 3′ in Figure 4A.7, while Diane's tastes are given by indifference curves 1, 2, 3. What we have done here is essentially rotate Dan's set of indifference curves by 180 degrees and superimpose them on the figure of Diane's indifference curves in such a way that the box formed has the specified dimensions of 14 units of clothing and 16 units of food. This is known as an Edgeworth Box.[19] Every point inside or on the box represents a particular distribution of the 14 clothing and 16 food units between Dan and Diane. For example, point *C* indicates that Dan has 12 clothing and 1 food units, and Diane has 13 food and 2 clothes units.

Is there a basis for mutually advantageous exchange between Dan and Diane? The answer is yes because the *MRS* of food and clothing is not equal for Dan and Diane. Starting from point *C*, if Dan gives up 3 units of clothing in exchange for 6 units of food to Diane, Dan would move from point *C* on his indifference curve 1′ to point *S* on his indifference curve 3′, and Diane would move along indifference curve 1 from *C* to *S*. Dan would gain all of the benefit from the exchange while Diane would lose nothing, since she would still be on her indifference curve 1. At point *S*, indifference curves 3′ and 1 are tangent and so their slopes are equal. At point *S*,

---

[18]Adam Smith, *The Wealth of Nations*, book 2, ch. 2, p. 17.

[19] F. Y. Edgeworth, *Mathematical Psychics: An Essay on the Application of Mathematics to the Moral Sciences* (New York: Augusta M. Kelly, 1953).

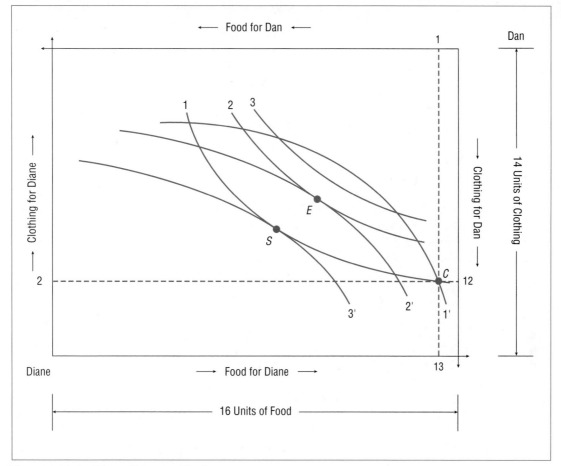

Figure 4A.7 Two-Person Exchange

the MRS_{fc} for Dan equals Diane's MRS_{fc}; therefore, point S is said to be pareto efficient. Economists say that an exchange outcome is *pareto efficient* if no trading partner can be made better off without making a second trading partner worse off.

To further clarify matters, again start from point C, and assume that Dan and Diane make the exchanges necessary to move to point E. Each party is willing to make this exchange since each moves to a higher indifference curve: Dan from 1′ to 2′ and Diane from 1 to 2. Notice that a tangency between indifference curves 2 and 2′ occurs at point E; point E is also pareto efficient. To see why, ask yourself the question, "Would Dan and Diane be able to trade from point E to point S?" No, because although the trade would make Dan better off (moving him from indifference curve 2′ to 3′), it would make Diane worse off (moving her from indifference curve 2 to 1).

Both allocations S and E are efficient, and the theory cannot predict which will emerge from a bargaining process begun at point C. All theory can do is predict that from point C, further exchange is possible. The exact outcome depends on considerations outside the realm of theory, such as Dan's and Diane's personalities and their trading skills. It is clear though that at least one of the two trading partners can be made better off through exchange without lowering the well-being of the other.

We can now summarize the conditions for consumer equilibrium and efficiency in competitive markets as follows:

$$MRS_{fc} = P_C/P_F = MRS_{fc} \qquad (4.17)$$

First, the marginal rate of substitution between consumers is equal. Second, the marginal rate of substitution of food for clothing is equal to the ratio of the prices of the two commodities. This is perhaps the most efficient way to illustrate Adams Smith's quote on the propensity to truck, barter, and exchange.

Until this point, we have focused on decision making by a single consumer and extended this concept to cover exchange between two parties. We now adopt some of these ideas as we provide a brief introduction to the way in which economists view the mechanisms involved in decision making by society as a whole.

Social Indifference Curves

Basically we assume that the social preferences obey the same four properties as consumer preferences: completeness, transitivity, nonsatiableness, and convexity. Society views all of the possible combinations of goods and services available and ranks them, much the same way that individuals do. The result of this ranking process can be represented with a set of indifference curves greatly resembling those of individual consumers. The only difference, of course, is that the resulting set of social indifference curves represents the tastes and preferences of society as a whole.

Property Rights, Ownership, and Efficiency

Economic growth will occur if property rights make it worthwhile to undertake socially productive activity.[1]

CHAPTER OUTLINE AND STUDENT GOALS

The general equilibrium concept presented in the previous chapter was supported by a variety of rather restrictive assumptions. One reason that competitive markets might fail is the presence of externalities. In this chapter, an alternative tool available to economists for analyzing efficient outcomes in the presence of externalities—the Coase theorem—is presented. The assumptions supporting this type of analysis are far less restrictive than those supporting the neoclassical competitive equilibrium. The Coase theorem is also important because it gives insights into efficient arrangements even when it doesn't strictly apply.

In this chapter, we consider the impact of market externalities once again. Externalities in an economic system may be viewed as distortions preventing the attainment of efficient arrangements between buyers and sellers. We then turn our attention to the provision of public goods and examine market failure in these cases. To further clarify the issues surrounding externalities, we apply our economic analysis to pollution, one deadly externality.

Once the problems externalities create in traditional markets are clearly laid out, we discuss the Coase theorem and how it solves some of these problems. Of course, other solutions will be summarily considered and evaluated.

In the last section of this chapter, we highlight the importance of Coase's ideas in a more managerial context. In these managerial applications, the basic theme is that ownership can provide the incentives necessary to promote efficient dealings between buyers and sellers. We raise many issues in this chapter: ownership of corporations, incentives facing employees, and the likely behavior of individuals purchasing insurance against various losses. More detailed explanations follow in Chapters 7, 8, and 9; but be aware that ownership is one theme that permeates much of the remaining material in this text.

---

[1]Douglas C. North and Robert Paul Thomas, *The Rise of the Western World: A New Economic History* (Cambridge, MA: Harvard University Press, 1973), p. 8.

After reading this chapter, you should be able to

* Define the concepts of ownership and property rights, in your own terms.
* Explain how externalities may be created in production and consumption.
* Understand how externalities prevent market exchange from creating efficient outcomes and how the assignment of property rights can lead to efficiency.
* State the Coase theorem and explain why the assignment of property rights removes inefficiencies if bargaining costs are low.
* Describe the *tragedy of the commons* and the reasoning behind assigning property rights.
* Examine other solutions to the problems posed by externalities on free, competitive exchange.
* Apply Coasian-type analysis in a variety of managerial contexts.

FIRM OWNERSHIP IN THEORY AND PRACTICE

One of the fundamental building blocks in our capitalistic economic system is the institution of **ownership,** or the rights to decide by whom, how, when, for how long, and under what conditions an asset will be used. The entrepreneur, a sole proprietor, is likely to put in longer hours in her business than is a hired agent. The reasoning is simple; it is very clear where the proverbial "buck" stops. **Property rights** is the term used by economists to describe ownership.

The issues of ownership and property rights are important on both the economywide and individual levels. The lack of individual ownership rights is one recurring theme cited as a factor in the failure of the socialist economies of Eastern Europe; in layperson's terms, nobody has reason to do anything. On an individual level, these concepts are equally important. When you rent a car from Hertz or Avis, you obtain certain property rights—the ability to drive the car subject to state regulations—but you do not own the car. Thus, you have no incentive to guard the car from theft or collision as well as you would if the car were yours.

Ownership and property rights are fairly clear concepts when applied to rental cars or the leases we commonly sign for apartments. There are, however, many settings in which one cannot easily determine exactly who owns a particular asset. The obvious cases are the corporations populating our economic landscape today. In Chapter 1, we presented a brief history of the institutional entity called the *firm*. The large, vertically integrated firms in U.S. manufacturing industries in the middle part of this century were clearly owned by whoever supplied the capital. In the 1990s, new organizational patterns emerged: networks, value-adding partnerships, and virtual corporations. Determining ownership of these firms is not all that straightforward.

One thing that we hope to make clear in this chapter is that ownership is an important issue because it presents economic agents with the set of incentives that promote efficiency in a wide variety of settings.

EXTERNALITIES AND MARKET FAILURE RECONSIDERED

**Decision Making
with Externalities**

Consider, for a moment, your decision to commute to work or school. A variety of options are open to you in a number of different dimensions. You might pick (subject to your requirements) the time of your commute, your route, and your mode of transportation. Let's focus on the mode dimension. Exactly how will you get there? You have several options: first, you may drive your own car; second, you may take public transportation; and third, you may opt to car pool with others living near you.

This decision is clearly yours, but your choice will affect others. It may even affect others in different ways than it affects you. Let's briefly examine the effects of your mode choice on all involved parties. If you drive, you maximize convenience (no coordination with others). You also add to traffic congestion, thus making everyone else on the road with you take a little longer. If you take public transportation, you deal with the inconvenience of being subject to an externally created schedule, and you may have to stand in a crowded aisle for a long period of time. By taking public transportation, you will have reduced the amount of congestion. If you car pool, you face a schedule over which you can presumably exert some influence and do a little more to reduce the amount of congestion on the road.

Once again, notice that the decision is yours, and you will make it in your own interests with perhaps no concern given to the effects of your decision on others. For most of us, the decision we make is to drive our own cars. Each of us then makes a contribution to traffic congestion. In economics, this is an example of an **externality,** a cost or benefit imposed involuntarily on another party that is not regulated by any system of prices. An externality is said to be a *positive externality* if a benefit is imposed on another party. A *negative externality* imposes costs on the related party. In the commuting example, by choosing to drive our own cars, we impose a cost on all users of the same road in the form of increased congestion.

Because of this, the outcome is not efficient because of a difference between our benefit from the choice to drive our own cars and the costs to society of our having made this choice. Inefficiencies typically occur with externalities because decision makers do not take full account of all the costs and benefits involved with their choices. Namely, they fail to recognize those costs and benefits that accrue to other parties.

The commuting mode choice example clearly points out two different types of costs to be considered in analysis based on efficiency. **Private costs** are the total costs borne by the initiator of some activity. **Social costs** are the total costs borne by all members of society. Since individuals decide on what type of transportation to employ, their actions are based on only the private costs of their choice. Clearly, in choosing to drive their own cars, the private costs to individuals are far less than the social costs of their actions. With the idea of externalities causing a difference between private and social costs, we now turn our attention back to markets, and supply and demand analysis.

Kimball is a small, relatively isolated, fictitious town in northeast Iowa. Kimball has several small manufacturing firms, but most economic activity there is in the agricultural sector. Cummings, Inc., is a national producer of ball bearings. In the last couple of years, it has become clear that Cummings needs to close its existing plants throughout the northeastern United States and, because of technological conditions in ball bearing production, consolidate manufacturing in a single facility. Cummings decides to locate in Kimball, Iowa, for reasons best understood only by its CEO, Mr. Stanley Beckwith.[2]

The townsfolk of Kimball, Iowa, are abuzz over the new decision, and many are overjoyed at the prospect of having a new industry in their town. Stanley

**Market Failure
in a Supply
and Demand
Framework**

---

[2]Although this tongue-in-cheek example may make some drastic simplifications to make its point, it is only fair to point out that firm location is often quite unpredictable.

Beckwith and Cummings, Inc., construct their new plant, bring many Cummings employees into town and also hire a very large number of Kimball residents. Business in Kimball is good; there are plenty of jobs to go around, and much infrastructure development and construction is taking place.

For Cummings, Inc. (which incidentally is a major player in the ball bearing market), the national price of the ball bearings is shown in Figure 5.1 as P_c, and at this price Cummings produces Q_c units of ball bearings. The supply curve in Figure 5.1 reflects the costs to Cummings of producing, distributing, and marketing its ball bearings in the United States.

After about a year, some of the other local employers begin to complain about the presence of Cummings in "their" community. Don Angeletti, the native farm equipment dealer, is quoted in the *Kimball Gazette*, the local newspaper, as saying

> I know that Cummings has brought a lot of good things into Kimball, but I have some concerns. Ever since the ball bearing plant has opened, it is harder for me to hold on to my staff. I'm a fair guy and would not begrudge somebody fair pay for hard work. You see, however, since the plant opened, I have had to raise my people's wages by about half to keep them.

Similar sentiments are voiced by the owners of the area brewery, bakery, grain elevator, and railroad.

The other employers in Kimball are impacted by an externality created by the presence of Stanley Beckwith's Cummings, Inc.: the higher wages they must pay to attract and keep workers. Make no mistake about the role of the price system in this example. The labor markets transmit the externality to local employers. The price system also fails in forcing Cummings to bear the full cost of the higher wages in the local area labor markets. It is true that Cummings' presence raises la-

Figure 5.1 Cummings, Inc.: Supply and Demand

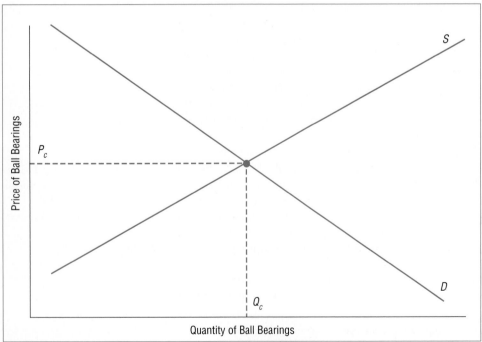

bor costs to itself, but this is a separate issue from raising the labor costs of other producers in the Kimball area.

Once again, the issue here is a difference between the private and social costs of ball bearing production by Cummings. If we define society here as all economic activity surrounding Kimball, Iowa (maybe not a bad assumption for a relatively isolated town), the social costs of Cummings' actions include the increase in wages experienced by other employers in the Kimball area because of the presence of Cummings. In Figure 5.2, the supply and demand curves of Figure 5.1 are reproduced. A second curve, above and to the left of the original supply curve, labeled S_C, also appears. The S_C curve includes the increased labor costs borne by other employers in the Kimball area. The socially optimal, and efficient, level of output for Cummings is found by the intersection of the demand and SC curve, Q_s.

This diagram illustrates one important very general result concerning externalities generated by producers. Under a market system, a negative productive externality results in overproduction of some good or service.

The situation is a little different but still not optimal if the production of some good or service generates a positive externality. As an example, consider the production of widgets, a hypothetical good. Because of the production of widgets, others in the economy benefit. Consider the market depicted in Figure 5.3. The supply function, S, accounts for all of the production costs incurred by the industry of widget producers. The demand function, D_1, shows the market demand for widget consumers. Recall from Chapter 2 that the height of the demand function at any point shows the value placed on that unit by the marginal consumer of widgets. The market will clear at the price P_m, and Q_m units will be produced and purchased.

The market demand function, D_1, does not reflect the total value placed on

Figure 5.2 Cummings, Inc.: Social Costs

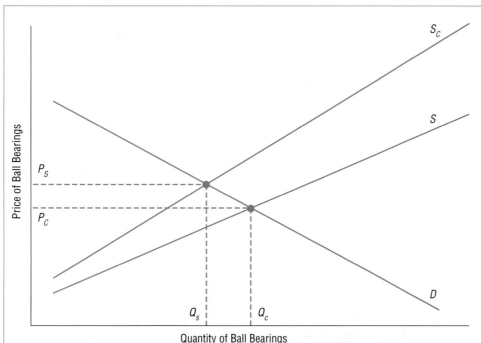

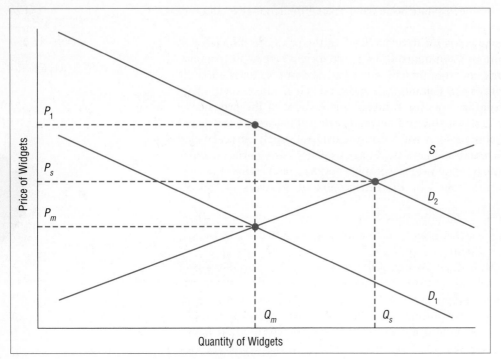

Figure 5.3 Positive Production Externalities

widget production by society. Because of the benefits to others in the economy who do not produce widgets and possibly do not even consume them, the total benefit of producing any quantity of widgets exceeds the amount shown by the demand function. The demand function labeled D_2 is drawn to represent these positive externalities. At the output level Q_m, for example, the marginal consumer (one willing to pay at most P_m for a widget) experiences benefits equal to P_m from consuming a widget or else he would not purchase it. However, there are other benefits. The production of the widget consumed by the marginal consumer created benefits for others in the economy; in Figure 5.3 these benefits are shown as the difference between P_1 and P_m, that is, $(P_1 - P_m)$. The socially efficient level of output in the widget market is Q_s, which would sell for a price of P_s.

When markets function in the presence of externalities, substantial distortions may exist precluding a socially efficient outcome. In the context of the general equilibrium ideas presented in Chapter 4, we say that *market failure* has occurred. This implies that the prices relayed to producers and consumers lead them to the "wrong" quantity sold at the "wrong" price.

With a negative externality in production, too large a quantity is produced. You may ask what the harm of this is. The answer is perhaps subtle. The injured parties would prefer less to be produced; if we add to the costs of production the value lost by the injured parties, we obtain the total social cost. Presumably, if some redistributive authority existed, the price that would equate the total social cost to the demand function could be charged, the socially optimal level of output would be produced, and the source of the externality could be made to compensate those injured by his actions.

With a positive externality, too small a quantity is produced. Society as a whole could benefit from additional production. Unfortunately, the only information acted on by producers is the demand function, which ignores these benefits.

Although externalities represent a rich field of exploration for economists interested in market failure, we end our discussion of them for now. Suffice it to say that some very prominent economists use externalities as a justification for increased government involvement in markets. Although this solution to the problems caused by externalities has its merits, we explore another solution in this chapter. Before we do, it will be helpful to explore another common source of market failure. After discussing this other reason that many markets might fail, we turn to a solution to these, and other, causes of inefficiencies in the functioning of markets. Of course, this solution is the much heralded Coase theorem.

■ PUBLIC AND PRIVATE GOODS

For a brief moment put aside the thoughts of school work, examinations, and term papers. Let's suppose that it is early July and you set off, blanket and cooler in hand, to the local fireworks display. You select the best spot, spread out the blanket, and wait. As you are waiting, an ice cream vendor appears, and you purchase a treat; after all, it has been a hot day. Pretty soon the fireworks are lighting up the nighttime sky.

Reflecting for a moment, you realize that you have consumed two goods that go very well together. Each is quite different, though. The ice cream was purchased in an organized market: you paid for it, and you have the right to determine who will consume it. The situation with the fireworks is much different; they may have been paid for by the local government or by some civic organization such as the chamber of commerce. Equally striking is the idea that while you are consuming the fireworks, plenty of other people are also. Goods such as fireworks present problems to a market-oriented approach to economic analysis.

A **public good** is a good that can be consumed by one person without diminishing the amount that other people consume of it and from which no individual can be barred from consuming. More technically, we may say that public goods have two very special features. First, they exhibit **nonrivalous consumption;** that is, one party's consumption does not detract from (rival) full enjoyment by other parties. Second, once produced, it is impossible to exclude others from consuming a public good; it has the characteristic of **nonexcludability.**

Public goods tend to be relatively indivisible; they often come in large units (or lumps) that cannot be broken into pieces that can be bought or sold. The two mentioned characteristics of public goods make them separate and distinct from private goods, which are most of the goods and services exchanged in the economy.

The supply and demand models described in Chapter 2 usually are applicable to the markets for private goods. The benefits and additions to utility from consuming a private good are directly assignable in a price-based system of exchange. At the fireworks display, you (or your designee) can consume the ice cream cone since you contracted with the vendor and provided payment.

The community fireworks display itself is clearly a public good. Up to an ambiguous crowd size limit, the rocket's red glare can be enjoyed by all. Other examples of public goods include national defense, parks, and the environment.

Many, but not all, public goods are provided by government. The reason is that the characteristic of nonrivalous consumption encourages the market mechanism to fail. Suppose that the fireworks were to be financed by asking everyone in the crowd to contribute whatever he or she wished. It is in your own interests to grossly understate the value you place on the fireworks. Being a business student, you clearly recognize that so long as others are more altruistic and generous than you, your enjoyment of the fireworks will not suffer. This reasoning embodies what economists call the **free-rider problem** and should ensure market failure, or the attainment of an inefficient outcome in the market.

As was the case with production externalities, the attainment of nonoptimal outcomes in the market with consumption externalities can be exhibited in a supply and demand model. The "market" for Fourth of July fireworks displays is depicted in Figure 5.4. In this diagram, the supply function shows the costs of providing fireworks. For simplicity, we assume that different quantities of fireworks are available, with larger quantities—better and longer displays—costing more to produce. We attempt to measure these attributes of fireworks displays in a single dimension. Thus, as we move rightward on the horizontal axis in Figure 5.4, we increase the quantity of fireworks.

The market demand in Figure 5.4 is the lower, downward sloping curve labeled D_1. It shows, for a given quantity, the maximum amount the crowd would be willing to pay in a market setting for the right to watch the fireworks. Herein lies the free-rider problem. Sound, rational (and perhaps shrewd) individuals would never let their true valuations of the fireworks become known. After all, once the fireworks are produced, individuals cannot be kept from consuming them. Further, their consumption does not detract from consumption by others.

The higher, downward sloping curve, D_2, is drawn to reflect the true, unknown, valuation placed on fireworks. Naturally, one could never actually construct a demand curve like D_2, because it would be difficult to induce consumers to reveal their true valuations of fireworks.[3] The implication of the fireworks example is well in accordance with standard economic theory: markets provide far too little of public goods.

Now that we have somewhat of an idea of what a public good is, we want to emphasize one way of examining market failure in the context of public goods, the related issues of ownership and property rights. Expressed somewhat parenthetically, in one sense, everyone owns a public good and has certain property rights to its use. However, it is also true that nobody owns a public good; that is, because of the free-rider problem, no one has any incentive to create a public good, to maintain it, or to provide it in sufficient quantity to maximize the welfare of all members of society.

National defense is clearly a public good. The federal government cannot protect one person in Delaware and fail to protect another person in Ohio. However, national defense is not provided by a market; it is provided by the U.S. government. Why is this the case? Everyone owns national defense once it is provided; would any individual, group of individuals, or firm voluntarily provide this service? Suppose one did. Also suppose that you decided not to contribute, reasoning that defense could not be provided to your neighbor but not yourself. Surely, the good would not be provided or would be provided in a limited quantity. The government provides the good; it can circumvent the functioning of the market by levying taxes and forcing you to pay them.

The ownership and property rights issues associated with public goods have

---

[3] A good discussion of this issue in a very different context can be found in John Silberman, Dan Gerlowski, and Nancy Williams, "Estimating Existence Value for Users and Nonusers of New Jersey Beaches," *Land Economics* (May 1992), pp. 225–236.

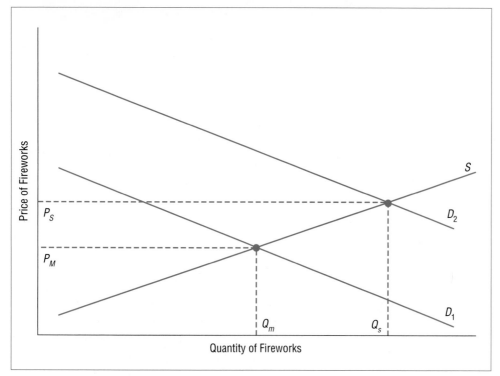

Figure 5.4 The Market for Fireworks

long been recognized by economists. One of the oldest and most widely used examples of property rights and the incentives of ownership is the tragedy of the commons, a situation experienced throughout England in past centuries.

Garrett Hardin describes the tragedy of the commons in this way.[4] There is a small town that is economically dependent on the agricultural sector for its economic and practical existence. Part of the output of this town is cattle; as a result of historical forces, there is a large pasture, or commons, freely available for grazing to each herdsman's cattle. The situation is good for years barring the occasional minor dispute between herdsmen.

As time passes, the town grows and develops. Stresses and strains emerge in the arrangement with the commons. Simply put, the commons is overgrazed, hurting each cattle owner. The reason for this failure is evident. Each herdsman advances his own interests by maximizing the size of his herd; it is rational for each to expect a positive gain by adding one more animal. The cost of adding each additional animal is, of course, the effect of overgrazing, borne by *all* cattle owners. Hardin states it more eloquently:

> The rational herdsman concludes that the only sensible course for him to pursue is to add another animal to his herd. And another; and another. . . . But this is the conclusion reached by each and every rational herdsman sharing a commons. Therein is the tragedy. Each man is locked into a system that compels him to increase his herd without limit—in a world that is limited. Ruin is the destination toward which all men rush, each pursuing his own best interest in a society that

---

[4]Garrett Hardin, "The Tragedy of the Commons," *Science*, December 13, 1968, pp. 1243–1248.

believes in the freedom of the commons. Freedom in the commons brings ruin to all.[5]

In this setup, which was prevalent for several centuries throughout England, the commons are clearly a public good. It is equally clear that externalities play a role in the allocation of grazing rights on the commons. Each individual rancher acts on the private costs of grazing his herd on the common land while ignoring the social costs of his actions. Here, the free-rider problem manifests itself bringing disaster to the community, the destruction of the common grazing land.

The free-rider problem also causes trouble in the fireworks example. In that case, however, the results were not as damaging. We do not need a detailed, highly technical study to determine whether or not communities across the United States regularly enjoy fireworks displays. These yearly celebrations anchor the events at many backyard barbecues but are seemingly never as long or as good as we wish they were.

The problems illustrated with public goods are some of the most severe incentive problems in economic management. When a resource is freely available to all, overuse likely results. It also stands to reason that when many people share the obligation to provide some resource, it will be undersupplied.

The Environment

The ultimate public good is perhaps what we have come to call the *environment*: the relatively thin layer of nitrogen, oxygen, hydrogen, and other gases that surround our planet, the salt and fresh water available for human use, and the large number of biological life forms found therein. Given that the environment exists, everyone has access to it (exclusion is viewed as equivalent to murder in most societies), and, within reason, one person's consumption of it does not impinge on another person's enjoyment of the same. Further, the environment is one of the greatest causes of concern in the world today.

For years, we discharged freon gas into the atmosphere; in the late 1980s, we learned that these discharges were causing a great thinning of the layer of ozone surrounding the earth that keeps us safe from the dangerous ultraviolet radiation caused by the sun. This is an example of a negative worldwide externality. The problem is that since nobody owned the atmosphere, no one party had incentive to curb the use of freon gas and its valuable commercial properties. Notably, a treaty was signed in 1990 calling for the eventual removal of these gasses from the marketplace.

A similar example is provided by the so-called greenhouse effect; the emissions of burning carbon are ultimately raising the average temperature on the planet. The list of environmental threats goes on and on: acid rain, water shortages, and oil spills on the world's oceans.

There is also concern, widely described, regarding a number of species of fish in the ocean. Of particular concern is the overfishing of cod by commercial fishers in a variety of countries, particularly Japan and Norway. Again, the problem is that nobody clearly owns the cod.

**Property Rights,
Ownership,
and Incentives**

In each of these examples of public goods, the story is the same. There is a lack of clearly defined property rights for certain resources. While all can enjoy the fireworks display, nobody holds the property rights enabling her to sell viewing rights to others. The payment issue seemingly dominates the example of national defense as a public good; only the government can force people to pay for it through taxation. If one cattleman owned the grazing resource called the commons, he would have incentive to ration its use, securing his own income next

---

[5]Ibid., p. 1244.

year. Similarly, no one person has the incentive to restrict access to the environment so as to preclude other individuals from damaging, or even destroying, it.

With the importance of property rights established, we next turn our attention to a solution to the problems of externalities and public goods in markets. These solutions are interesting in their own right, and they provide critical insights into managing economic organizations.

THE COASIAN APPROACH TO MARKET FAILURE

The 1991 Nobel Prize in Economics was awarded to Ronald Coase; the 1993 Nobel Prize in Economics was awarded to Douglas North. The work of both of these men is important to understanding managerial economics and organizations; we shall, however, mainly concern ourselves in this chapter with the work of Ronald Coase. In fact, we will pretty much focus on only one piece of Coase's work contained in an article written in 1960 entitled "The Problem of Social Cost."[6] A number of arguments made in this article have grown into what is now called the Coase theorem. Just how important can this one theorem be? Consider the purposes to which it may be put.

One of the most celebrated contributions to economics in this century is also one of the simplest. The **Coase theorem** states that if there are no legal, strategic, or informational barriers to bargaining and if property rights are clearly defined, then people can always negotiate to an efficient outcome. Furthermore, civil liability rules will have no effect on the allocation of economic resources.[7] The Coase theorem implies that if parties bargain to an efficient agreement, then the activities chosen do not depend on the bargaining power of the individuals and are not influenced by what assets each owned when the bargaining began. Efficiency alone determines the selection of the activity by the group.

Part of the appeal of the Coase theorem to economists is the minimal role allotted to government. The task of government is simply to assign clear property rights; theoretically, it does not even matter to whom the property rights are assigned.

In practical applications of the Coase theorem, there are two common stumbling blocks. First, in many cases, bargaining may be expensive. The costs of reaching agreements are commonly called *transaction costs*, a concept introduced in Chapter 1. Reflecting the importance of transaction costs, we devote an entire chapter, Chapter 6, to their discussion.

The second stumbling block in applying the Coase theorem is that the actual assignment of property rights will cause redistributive effects; that is, one party will end up paying another party.

To illustrate the application of the Coase theorem to an economic problem, we refer to the example provided by Ronald Coase himself in his article "The Problem of Social Cost." In advance, we apologize for the size of the numbers

The Coase Theorem

An Illustrative Example

---

[6]A full citation is Ronald Coase, "The Problem of Social Cost," *Journal of Law and Economics*, 3 (1960), pp. 1–45. This article is arguably the most often cited research work ever; its importance has been recognized not only by economists but also by legal scholars and, more recently, by management professionals. It is strongly recommended that you read this article as part of your general education.

[7]There is actually one additional assumption to the Coase theorem. This assumption is that there are no "wealth effects" in the implementation of decisions for the involved parties. A wealth effect occurs when changes in an individual's wealth cause a change in his or her behavior.

used in this example; we modified those used originally by Coase in order to facilitate the exposition.

Imagine a railroad that owns a pair of tracks passing through the middle of a farmer's land. The farmer must decide how much crop to plant on his fields and the railroad must decide how many trains to run per day along these tracks. The issue of concern is that each train, as it travels down the track, sometimes produces sparks, which can create fires that could destroy the farmer's crop.

Perhaps your immediate response is to recognize that the trains impose a negative externality on the farmer and to call for the railroad to reimburse the farmer for any damages caused by the passing trains. However, we can safely point out that there are two ways to solve this problem: either the railroad could run fewer trains, or the farmer could plant his crops further back from the tracks. At this point, more facts are needed before the most efficient solution is identified.

The basic facts are as follows. If the railroad runs one train per day, the total value of these transportation services to consumers is $300 per year. Two trains per day result in a total value of $500 per year, and three trains in a total value of $560 per year. The marginal cost of running each train equals $100 per year. If the railroad acts in its own interests, it will run two trains per day. The first train generates a profit for the railroad of $200. If a second train is run, revenues increase by $200 and costs by $100; since the marginal revenues exceed the marginal costs, the second train will increase profits. For the third train, however, marginal revenues are less than marginal costs and running it will decrease profits by $40 per year.

Consider the profitability of farming in this example. The market value of the crops produced by each of the farmer's two identical fields is, if there is no fire damage, $1,000. The marginal cost of putting one field into production is $700; the marginal cost of putting the second field into production is $980. Clearly, the farmer will choose, in the absence of the threat of fire damage, to plant and harvest both fields.

It is by no means certain that a fire will ever occur. However, if one does, on either plot of land, the value of the crops that remain is only $40. In the event of a fire, all other production costs are lost. This means that a fire causes a loss of $9,407 on each plot affected. Since it is random whether or not a fire will occur, we can only characterize the probability of one occurring. We will assume that the probability of a fire on either plot is the same and increases with the number of trains run each day. This probability is zero if no trains are run, 12.5 percent (1/8) for one train, and 25 percent (2/8 = 1/4) for two trains.

To determine the socially optimal number of trains to run and number of fields to plant, let's calculate the net expected social benefit from all of the possible combinations of number of trains and number of plots. If no trains are run and no plots are planted, the expected total social benefit is zero.

If one train is run and one plot is cultivated, the calculations are a little more involved. The net benefit to society of running one train is the market value of the services provided less the costs of providing that train for service, $300 − $100 or $200. To this figure we add the expected net social benefit of the farmer having planted a single field.

If the farmer plants a single field, the expected net social benefit reflects the net benefit if there is and if there is not a fire. To form the expected benefit, the benefit in each case is multiplied by the probability that each occurs. If there is no fire, the social benefit of one field's production equals $1,000, the market value of the crops produced, minus the costs of providing that one field, $700. The difference is $300. If there is a fire, the market value of the one field is reduced to $40, but the costs of cultivating that field remain at $700; the benefits are then negative, $40 − $700 = −$660. The probability of there being a fire, given that one train is run, is 12.5 percent; the probability of there not being a fire is 87.5 percent. The expected benefit of planting one field, given that one train is run then equals

$$(0.125)*(-\$660) + (0.875)*(\$300) = -\$82.5 + \$262.5 = \$180 \qquad (5.1)$$

The total expected net social benefit is then found by adding the net benefit of running one train to the expected net benefit of planting one field, $180 + $200 = $380. The total expected net social benefit for all possible pairings of number of plots cultivated and number of trains run is shown in Table 5.1.

With some of the facts of this example laid bare, we can see how each party can best participate in reaching the socially optimal, and efficient, outcome. Society is made as well off as possible when there is one train run per day and one plot of land cultivated. Two questions remain. First, can the farmer and railroad operator be expected to reach this conclusion on their own? Second, what are the property rights issues involved? Both of these questions are now addressed. We assume that the parties can bargain and that the costs of this bargaining are negligible. Concurrently, we make assumptions about which party has the property rights. What will be seen—and this is part of the attraction of the Coase theorem to economists—is that the efficient outcome will emerge regardless of which party is granted the property rights.

First, suppose that the farmer is granted the property rights, that is, that the farmer has the final say as to what happens in the field and that the railroad must reimburse the farmer's fire damages. What will the farmer decide: zero, one, or two trains, and zero, one, or two plots cultivated?

Since zero plots result in zero income for the farmer, this option may be ruled out. So let the farmer plant one plot. Now, we examine the number of trains chosen by the farmer. If there are zero trains, the farmer earns profits of $300. In fact, since the railroad is liable for any fire damage to the farmer's crops, her profits are the same regardless of the number of trains being run, always $300. Now, will the farmer permit one train to run? She would be willing to do so if it earns her more profits than $300.

If the railroad runs one train, its profits depend now on whether or not there is a fire, so we must construct the railroad's expected profit of running one train. If there is no fire, the railroad's gain in running one train is simply revenues ($300) less operating costs ($100), or $200. If there is a fire, the railroad's gain includes damages paid to the farmer. These damages equal the lost value of the farmer's crops, $960. Then if there is a fire, the railroad's gain is revenues ($300) less operating costs ($100) less reimbursement to the farmer ($960), −$760. Since

Table 5.1	**Total Net Expected Social Benefit**				
			Railroad		
			0 Trains	**1 Train**	**2 Trains**
Farmer	0 plots		$ 0	$200	$300
	1 plot		300	380	360
	2 plots		320	280	140

we know that the probability of a fire when one train is run equals 12.5 percent and the probability of there being no fire when one train is run equals 87.5 percent, the expected gain to the railroad can be calculated as

$$(0.125)*(-\$760) + (0.875)*(\$200) = \$80 \tag{5.2}$$

Will the farmer be willing to permit the railroad to operate one train? Well, the running of one train allows $80 of value to be created even when the fire losses of the farmer are covered by the railroad operator. If the parties are free to bargain, this $80 can be allocated between the two parties to induce the farmer to permit one train to run. Presumably, if the railroad pays the farmer $1 for the right to run one train under the liability rule, the farmer would then earn profits of $301 and the railroad $79. It is also possible that the farmer could wind up with profits of $379 and the railroad $1. So it is clear that social benefits can be increased to $380 when one train runs from the level of $300 when no trains run. The cause of this gain is the profit earned by the railroad operator.

At this point, the farmer holds the property rights concerning activities in the field. She may permit the railroad operator to run trains, if so doing raises the total value created and if some of this increase in value is paid back to the farmer. The source of this incremental value is the profit earned by the railroad. In Table 5.2, the profits earned by the railroad under all possible combinations of plots cultivated and trains run are shown.

The calculations behind Table 5.2 are somewhat cumbersome and are left as an exercise to the reader. The figures indicate, however, that the railroad's profits are maximized by running two trains if zero plots are cultivated; by running one train if one plot is cultivated; and by running zero trains if two plots are cultivated. When the railroad incorporates crop damage as a cost of doing business, the largest social value is created if one plot of land is cultivated and if one train is run. Recall that we showed earlier that this mixture was socially optimal.

An alternative arrangement would assign property rights to the railroad, making the farmer liable for any damage caused to her crops. In this arrangement, the railroad is guaranteed $200 by running one train and $300 by running two trains. The farmer could bribe[8] the railroad not to run any trains at all by paying the railroad $300. The farmer could bribe the railroad into running only one train by paying $100, the value to the railroad of the second train.

Under this alternative liability rule, the profits of the farmer now depend on the expected fire loss. To see how these profits are calculated, suppose that the railroad will be running two trains per day. If the farmer does not cultivate either of her fields, her profits are zero. If the farmer cultivates only one of the fields, her expected gains can be calculated. If there is a fire (the probability of a fire with two trains run is 25 percent), the net gain to the farmer is −$660 ($40 − $700). If there is no fire (the probability of no fire with two trains run is 75 percent), the gain to the farmer is $300. The expected gain to the farmer is then

$$(0.25)*(-\$660) + (0.75)*\$300 = -\$165 + \$225 = \$60 \tag{5.3}$$

The expected net gains to the farmer under all the possible combinations of number of plots and number of trains are shown in Table 5.3. The figures in Table 5.3 show that when the railroad owns the property rights, the number of trains run directly affects the costs to the farmer of doing business.

---

[8]*Bribe* is a very strong word; typically, economists prefer the term *side payment*.

Table 5.2	**Railroad Profits When the Farmer Holds the Property Rights**			
		Railroad		
		0 Trains	**1 Train**	**2 Trains**
Farmer	0 plots	$0	$200	$300
	1 plot	0	380	60
	2 plots	0	−40	−180

Once again, we can see how exchange will occur. To start, suppose that the railroad intends to run two trains. If it is in the farmer's interests to pay the railroad to eliminate one of its trains, will the railroad accept the bribe? If the farmer considers planting only one plot of land, her well-being increases by $120 as the number of trains is reduced from two to one. The railroad values the second train at only $100, so some exchange is possible. Perhaps the parties could split the difference with the farmer paying the railroad $110 to eliminate the second train. Can the farmer induce the railroad to go from one to zero trains? No, because the gain to the farmer from such a move does not exceed the loss by the railroad. Continuing our analysis of the bargaining situation described by the figures in Table 5.3, we point out that the farmer will not rationally ever plan to use both plots when two trains are run since she loses $160 in this situation and can lose nothing by planting neither of the fields.

We can now conclude what outcome will be chosen by the farmer and the railroad if the railroad is not legally liable for the fire damage caused by its trains. The farmer will plant one of her plots, and the railroad will run only one train. As shown in Table 5.1, this is exactly the outcome that maximizes the total expected social net welfare. The granting of property rights, in this case the right to use the fields, affects only the relative well-being of the farmer and the railroad operator.

There are several points central to this conclusion. First, we assumed that there were no large bargaining costs for the exchange between the farmer and the railroad. Communication was easy and cheap. Second, we assumed that somebody held the property rights. If both parties hold the property rights, then effectively neither of them does, and it would be impossible to predict the outcome. In practice, what would happen is that the railroad would run two trains and the farmer, if a fire occurred, would chase the railroad through the court system, a situation in which the emphasis could very well end up on bargaining costs in the form of legal fees.

Before moving to other ways of dealing with externalities, we need to make one more point with our farmer and railroad example: if the two entities were to

Table 5.3	**Farmer Profits When the Railroad Holds the Property Rights**			
		Railroad		
		0 Trains	**1 Train**	**2 Trains**
Farmer	0 plots	$ 0	$ 0	$ 0
	1 plot	300	180	60
	2 plots	320	80	−160

be joined under a common ownership, perhaps by a merger or by simultaneous purchase by some third party, the newly created organization would choose the socially efficient outcome. After all, the new entity's profits would be equal to the net total social benefit shown in Table 5.1. If, for some reason, property rights could not be assigned, or, if bargaining costs were too high, a merger would create total value for the concerned parties.

▧ OTHER SOLUTIONS TO THE PROBLEM OF EXTERNALITIES

Coasian analysis provides one solution to the problem of market failure in the presence of externalities and public goods. Three other approaches have been identified: cooperation, regulatory responses, and tax and subsidy measures.

Cooperation and Group Ownership

Cooperation involves, in one way or another, an element of group ownership. If all parties involved in the externality, or in the use of a public good, can effectively be joined in some fashion, they would be forced to equate the social and private costs of their actions. Consider the forces behind the ocean fisheries off the eastern coast of the United States. As a group, all fishers have an interest in preventing overfishing. As individuals, all fishers have more of an interest in their own incomes. If ownership of the current and future fishing harvests could be granted to all fishers simultaneously, the incentives would be in place to eliminate overfishing.

However, this level of cooperation, in practice, would fail for much the same reason as would the Coase theorem: namely, the involved bargaining would not be costless. Some issues that could be resolved only with great difficulty would be defining the relative shares of ownership across all fishers, identifying who should receive the shares, determining if the shares should be sold or given away, and policing members to see that cheating (in the form of overfishing) does not occur.

Regulatory Response

Regulatory responses to negative externalities are sometimes called the *application of the command and control approach.* In its strictest application, the government simply outlaws the negative externality. This approach may be appealing, but the example of the farmer and the railroad shows that it may be possible to increase social welfare if some agreeable amount of the externality is permitted.

The command and control approach applied to pollution typically defines some uniform standard that all sources of pollution must meet. Certain inefficiencies result, however, because of the different marginal costs faced by different firms. Furthermore, once a company meets the uniform standard, it has little economic incentive to find innovative ways to reduce pollution even further.

In 1993 the federal government began another approach to reduce pollution: a system of marketable permits. Firms can purchase (or are granted) a permit allowing them to emit a certain level of pollution. Enough permits are issued to take pollution levels in total to some desirable level. Under this system, companies are allowed to sell their permits. This program is clearly an attempt by the federal government to assign property rights, namely the right to pollute. This system provides many incentives to create the best possible antipollution devices rather than simply meeting the government-imposed targets for emissions.

Taxes and Subsidies

The third response to the presence of externalities in markets is some form of tax and subsidy program instituted by the government. Subsidies, in a sense, are the carrot used to drive firms toward some standard; taxes are the stick. Subsidies, in the form of tax credits for the purchase of pollution-reducing equipment, are fairly common and favored by businesses. Such subsidies do not affect firm output since they represent a change in fixed costs, not a change in firm marginal costs.

Since subsidies reduce the level of pollution, they lower the social marginal costs of production, driving them closer to the private marginal costs of production. In effect, the difference between the socially optimal outcome and the market outcome is diminished.

Economists tend to focus on the difference between social and private marginal costs as being the major cause of the inefficiency created by an externality and favor taxes as the appropriate policy response. Taxes equate private and social marginal costs and grant firms some leeway in deciding how to react to a demand for pollution reduction. In the best world, a per unit tax on pollution would be levied. In the absence of this, the tax would be placed on units of output at a rate sufficient to reduce pollution to some desirable level.

IMPLICATIONS FOR MANAGERS

Ownership, property rights, and the reasoning behind the Coase theorem provide managers with many useful tools to use in solving economic problems.

The concept of ownership for some assets is clear. You may own your car, giving you the right to operate as you wish subject to some legal restrictions; you also have incentive to take proper care of your car. The concept of ownership of organizations is not so clear but can be understood in terms of what are called residual rights.

The *residual rights* of control to an asset give the holder the opportunity to employ the asset as he or she wishes. In firms, the residual rights of control include the selection of suppliers, and the advertising medium as well as setting prices. In short, the holder of the residual right of control determines how the firm will act. In most large corporations, the residual rights of control belong, in large part, to chief executive officers (CEOs) and some levels of their management teams. In smaller enterprises, the residual rights of control belong to the owner.

The **residual claimant** has the rights to the residual returns. An organization may be seen as an entity that takes in revenues (determined in part by luck) and, out of these revenues, makes specified payments to the factors of production, or inputs. Any amounts left over are said to be **residual returns** and belong to the residual claimant. Under the corporate structures mandated by state and federal laws, the residual claimants in corporations are the stockholders.

The improper matching of the residual rights of control with the interests of the residual claimant forms the basis for one of the fundamental problems in managing economic organizations. In large corporations, the linkage between the stockholders and the CEOs is the corporate board of directors, which is supposed to pick a CEO and monitor her performance in light of the stockholders' interests. This linkage has been strained in many ways. In Chapter 8, we provide examples of what is called *shareholder activism*, when the stockholders begin to take a more active role in the management of their companies.

On a much lower organizational level, this mismatch is also apparent. It may not be practical to assign every employee a portion of the rights to the residual return. Thus, in the absence of the favorable incentives provided by ownership, employees must be motivated in some other way. One response is to monitor employee performance. In practice, however, this process might be rife with measurement errors.

One of the classic papers in organizational economics, by Armen Alchian and Harold Demsetz,[9] treats the very nature of firms as creating the linkage between

---

[9]A. Alchian and H. Demsetz, "Production, Information Costs, and Economic Organization," *American Economic Review* 62 (1972), 777–797.

residual control and residual claims. They consider an environment of team production, in which firm output is a joint effort of many individuals' efforts that cannot be uniquely identified. In a sense, the output of the team becomes a public good; a free rider in this context is a worker who decides to put forth little effort. This problem is discussed in detail in Chapter 8.

The Coase theorem is also important to understanding patterns of economic activity. The emphasis of the Coase theorem is the importance of costless bargaining. Even if markets fail, efficient solutions may be obtained regardless of bargaining position. The Coase theorem also provides essential insights when it fails to hold, for it emphasizes the importance of bargaining costs.

One area to which the Coase theorem is applied is the use of outside suppliers by firms. Quite often, markets fail to provide the intermediate goods needed by firms. What supplier will willingly commit, in a major way, to the needs of a particular customer? If we understand the cost of this commitment by the supplier and the total value created by this horizontal relationship, Coasian analysis may provide clues as to how this value may be shared by the involved parties.

The problem facing firms in lining up other firms as outside suppliers may be considered one of property rights. With some form of cooperation, the total value of the relationship may be increased substantially. The critical point of contention is who should lay claim to this value, or who has the property rights to it. If the bargaining costs prove too high, then there are two options: either the extra value will not be realized because the two firms will fail to come to an agreement; or one firm will try to purchase the other, thus internalizing the relationship. Recall that in the example of the farmer bargaining with the railroad company, some form of merger would result in the socially optimal outcome. These questions are addressed in great detail in the first two chapters of the next part.

▓ CHAPTER SUMMARY AND KEY IDEAS ▓ ▓ ▓ ▓ ▓ ▓

In this chapter, we have considered the impact of market externalities on efficiency. Externalities in an economic system may be viewed as distortions preventing the attainment of efficient arrangements between buyers and sellers.

One of the fundamental building blocks in our capitalistic economy is the institution of ownership. *Property rights* is the term used by economists to describe ownership. Property rights are important for the economy as well as for the individual. One of the oldest and most widely used examples of property rights and the incentives of ownership is the tragedy of the commons. Because the pasture is freely available for grazing, the commons are overgrazed.

One of the most celebrated solutions to the problem of externalities is the Coase theorem. The theorem states that if there are no legal, strategic, or informational barriers to bargaining, and if property rights are clearly defined, people can always negotiate themselves to an efficient outcome. The Coase theorem implies that if parties bargain to an efficient agreement, the activities chosen will not depend on the bargaining power of the individuals and are not influenced by what assets each owned when the bargaining began.

Ownership, property rights, and the reasoning behind the Coase theorem provide managers with many useful tools in solving economic problems. For example, the residual rights of control to an asset give the holder the opportunity to employ the asset as he or she wishes. In short, the holder of the residual right of control determines how the firm will act.

KEY TERMS

Coase theorem
externalities
free-rider problem
nonexcludability
nonrivalous consumption
ownership

private costs
property rights
public good
residual claimant
residual returns
social costs

FURTHER READINGS

Barzel, Y., *Economic Analysis of Property Rights*. Cambridge: Cambridge University Press, 1989.

Coase, R., "The Problem of Social Cost," *Journal of Law and Economics* (1960), pp. 1–45.

QUESTIONS AND PROBLEMS FOR REVIEW AND DISCUSSION

A. The amount of training that firms make available to their employees varies greatly across firms and across occupations. Some firms pay the employment and training costs or tuition for employees regardless of the content of the knowledge gained; others are more picky. Consider the following two individuals. Pete Simpson is a computer analyst for BigChip, Inc.; his job involves writing code to integrate multimedia capability throughout BigChip's operations. Mike Wallace also works for BigChip. However, he works as a sales representative.

   1. BigChip has offered to pay Pete Simpson's tuition as he pursues a master's degree in systems design from a major state university, BigState U. BigChip has denied Mike Wallace's request for tuition payment for an MBA degree program at BigState U. What can you say about BigChip's rationale behind paying for Pete Simpson's degree while denying Mike Wallace's request?

   2. Which degree, Pete Simpson's master's in systems design or Mike Wallace's MBA, has more characteristics of a public good to the pool of current and future employers?

II

Part I discussed the perfectly competitive neoclassical world from which many economic theories are drawn. Adam Smith's "Invisible Hand" sees to it that transactors are efficiently coordinated and motivated by the price system. One answer to the question of how society efficiently allocates its resources is with perfectly competitive markets. The problem with this approach is that markets are often less than perfectly competitive and may even fail.

The Coase theorem provides a heroic option predicting that an efficient outcome *could* happen even if the perfectly competitive market were to fail. To achieve this outcome, property rights must be clearly defined and bargaining costs must be zero. In Part II, we return to this line of inquiry by examining what happens to efficiency if bargaining costs are not zero. This is a unique perspective from which to study economic exchange. When we allow bargaining costs, two things happen. First, we move outside the perfectly competitive markets with which economists have become very comfortable. Second, we cannot strictly follow the Coase theorem.

Chapter 6, "Organizational Tools," begins with a question: "Do buyers and sellers freely interact?" In many instances, the answer is no for two reasons. First, all parties to the transaction may be less than perfectly informed. Second, parties to a transaction may have justifiable fears of agreeing to a deal in which the other parties may face few obstacles to simply walking away. This perspective provides a different viewpoint from which to examine the make-or-buy decision increasingly faced by firms. When transactions occur in well-developed, competitive markets, the actual agreements covering the exchanges are usually straightforward. In most transactions, however, much attention needs to be paid to the contract on which the exchanges rest.

THE ECONOMICS OF ORGANIZATION

II

Chapter 7, **"Contracts: Motivation Through Agreement,"** discusses the process of contracting as viewed by economists. What emerges is that most contracts leave much open to interpretation, mainly because writing a contract that leaves nothing open to interpretation is infinitely expensive. Further clouding the picture are informational asymmetries and the fear of making a commitment.

Chapter 8, **"Contracts: Issues of Discourse,"** addresses problems associated with imperfect measurement and misalignment of incentives. Transactions often take place in this type of environment when one party to the transaction can only imperfectly monitor the behavior of the other party. This line of inquiry is far reaching, and we consider many everyday settings for this common problem in deposit-taking institutions, insurance markets, and large corporations. Increased efforts on measurement may not be the optimal answer either. All measurement is imperfect, despite the resources dedicated to it, and, more important, open to several sources of randomness that we consider in great detail.

Chapter 9, **" Distribution, Rents, and Efficiency,"** concerns rents and distribution as they pertain to managing economic organizations. Rents represent extra payments to economic agents. Traditionally, economic analysis of rents has dealt with payments to fixed factors of production such as land. More recently, analysis has used rents as a reward for good behavior in economic exchange that can help to promote efficiency. There is, however, a dark side to rents. Given that they exist, parties expend resources to acquire them, even fighting over their distribution.

6

Organizational Tools

The normal economic system works itself. For its current operation it is under no central control, it needs no central survey. Over the whole range of human activity and human need, supply is adjusted to demand, and production to consumption, by a process that is automatic, elastic and responsive.[1]

The main reason why it is profitable to establish a firm would seem to be that there is a cost of using the price mechanism. The most obvious cost of "organizing" production through the price mechanism is that of discovering what the relevant prices are. The costs of negotiating and concluding a separate contract for each exchange transaction which takes place on a market must also be taken into account.[2]

CHAPTER OUTLINE AND STUDENT GOALS

Adam Smith and Specialization

Economic efficiency is enhanced and the opportunities for exchange are created by specialization in production. The idea of specialization, or division of labor, was first expressed by Adam Smith in 1776. Smith argued that specialization increases resource productivity, causes larger amounts of output, and, hence, raises standards of living. Since a finer division of labor reduces self-sufficiency, exchange is beneficial and indeed necessary to both producers and consumers.

In Chapters 2, 3, and 4, we discussed the perfectly competitive neoclassical world from which many economic theories are drawn. In this scenario, Adam Smith's "Invisible Hand" sees to it that transactors are efficiently coordinated and motivated by the price system. In the previous chapter, we saw how the Coase theorem predicts that an efficient outcome *can* happen even when the perfectly competitive market may fail. Of course, according to the Coase theorem, to achieve this outcome, property rights must be clearly assigned and bargaining costs must be zero. In this chapter, we return to this line of inquiry by examining what happens regarding efficiency if bargaining costs are not zero.

In standard economic analysis, very little is said about firms and why they exist. In the standard story, there is a mysterious thing called the firm acting to maximize profits subject to production and market constraints. The firm has been viewed as a car speeding down the highway. Economic theory could often predict

---

[1]Alfred Slater quoted in Ronald H. Coase, "The Nature of the Firm," *Economica*, Vol. IV, 1937, pp. 386–405, at p. 387.
[2]*Ibid.*, p. 391.

the car's destination; it could not, however, explain the body style, speed, or route selection.

Inside the Firm Looking Out

It is our task to examine the firm from the inside out rather than from the outside in. We hope that by looking under the hood of the car and understanding the functions of the engine, transmission, and brake system, we can see how the driver (the firm manager) can best coordinate and motivate the individual pieces under the hood to reach the driver's objectives.

This useful vantage point from which we view economic organization is not possible within traditional economic thought largely because traditional economic thought assumes away many of the basic issues we are concerned with. We begin our study of managing economic organizations by recognizing that there are significant, additional costs associated with transactions and, hence, all economic decisions. Using an analogy from elementary physics, these costs represent frictions restricting the free motions of economic agents.

Buyers and Sellers Freely Interacting?

Economists including Nobel Laureates Ronald Coase, George Sigler, and Kenneth Arrow have focused attention on additional costs, and Coase concluded that firms exist when a central coordinating authority is more efficient than market exchange. Oliver Williamson has continued this line of inquiry, and his work leads us to recognize that several significant differences exist between transactions handled entirely within a firm and those made between the firm and outside parties.

Information is costly, and limits exist on market-based transactions; thus, buyers and sellers do not freely interact. The additional costs incurred by economic interaction are called **transaction costs**—costs above and beyond contracted prices including the costs of acquiring costly information, monitoring performance, committing specific assets, and handling complexity. Out of the limitations of the price system, firms emerge to organize economic activity, efficiently handling these transaction costs.

After reading this chapter, you should be able to

- Explain, in your own words, what transaction costs are.
- Discuss various ways in which the task of coordinating economic activity gives rise to transaction costs.
- Interpret the necessity of motivating parties to contractual agreements and how this gives rise to costs.
- Understand the importance of asset specificity to contractual agreements and why commitment is a particular concern.
- Recognize that certain transactions occur frequently and that institutions emerge to lower the costs behind these transactions.
- Acknowledge that from an organizational perspective, some transactions are "stand alone" in that they affect only a small segment of the organization while others have a wide impact on many parties.
- Interpret the implications of complex transactions possibly involving great uncertainty.
- Recognize that it may be quite difficult for the parties to a contract or transaction to evaluate the performance of other parties.
- Apply information and transaction costs analysis to a variety of managerial problems, including the so-called make-or-buy decision of firms.

**Some Problems
for Business**

Two adages are often tossed about by successful entrepreneurs in business today: "Necessity is the mother of invention" and "If you build a better mousetrap, the world will beat a path to your door." Let's suppose that there is a brilliant inventor, Joe Zinpack. Joe is a man of modest means, supporting his wife, Rose, and two children, Ashley and Daniel, on his salary as a staff engineer at a large chemical corporation. Joe is deeply concerned about the environment and the prospects for a better life he can supply his two children.

Working in the basement of his family's home, Joe accomplishes some wondrous things. To his astonishment, he stumbles on a process that converts standard household waste, yard clippings, and old newspapers into clean-burning ethanol. Joe soon realizes that his discoveries have enormous implications for society. A single, and relatively simple process can reduce pressure on overcrowded landfills and nearly eliminate a major source of air pollution plaguing the world today—auto emissions.

In a nutshell, Joe's process works like this. Fifty pounds of standard household garbage are placed in a large metal container, called a *reactor vessel*, along with four gallons of a chemical mixture. The reactor vessel is sealed and then basically left alone for one week. One pipe allows a second chemical mixture to flow into the reactor vessel. A second pipe allows pure, clean-burning ethanol to continuously flow out of the vessel. At the end of the week, 30 gallons of ethanol have been produced, ready for use in the family car. At that time, the reactor vessel contains only water, which is available for household use or which can be safely dumped into any household drain.

Joe shares his news with his neighbor Doug, a venture capital specialist, who quickly outlines the financial benefits now possible for Joe, Rose, Ashley, and Daniel.

Not wanting to trust others with his significant knowledge, Joe sets out to produce and sell his device on what he envisions as a fairly large scale—1,000 units. Joe is brimming with confidence; after all, he has proven his technical competence and superiority. As he begins making arrangements, Joe becomes less enthusiastic and, as Rose confides to a family friend, begins to wonder if his dream will ever become a reality. Let's examine the sources of some of Joe's headaches.[3]

In his basement workshop, Joe fashioned a reactor vessel out of a standard metal garbage can and copper tubing available at any hardware store. Clearly, fashioning 1,000 of these devices in this way would not be possible. Joe contacts three local metalworking shops concerning the production of a suitable reactor vessel. The prices submitted by the metalworking shops vary considerably. None of the potential suppliers is overly enthusiastic about retooling their factories even temporarily to meet Joe's needs. Furthermore, despite his technical background, Joe is dumbfounded by the exotic-sounding materials and detailed quality assurance measures each potential subcontractor is proposing.

Production is not the only concern. To sell his invention, Joe has begun negotiating with four marketing consultant firms. Each has examined the relevant market data and, to Joe's consternation, four unique and separately distinct mar-

---

[3]In our example, we concentrate on certain aspects of Joe's problem and ignore financing at this time. The financial decisions are indeed complex and are introduced in Chapter 10. In a very practical way, financing would be, perhaps, Joe's biggest problem; we do not consider it here so that we may focus attention elsewhere.

ket assessments have been produced. A bewildering array of pricing schemes and advertising strategies adds to Joe's confusion.

Another possibility for Joe is licensing his technology to an established firm in a related line of business. He contacts two prospects but is dismayed when each seems less than enthusiastic about getting Joe's invention to market. It also becomes clear that with a new technology such as his, any licensing agreement would involve giving up control and ownership of his process for future products.

To avoid some of these issues, at least for a little while, Joe decides to do some yard work. His neighbor Doug comes over to borrow a rake and strikes up a conversation. Joe discusses the difficulties he is facing and conveys two deeper concerns to Doug. First, Joe is concerned about being taken advantage of in one or both of the relationships. Second, he is afraid of the opportunity cost of choosing any one supplier/consultant over any other. The opportunity cost of an action is the value of the next best alternative to that action. Joe asks, "How will I know that this supplier or that consulting firm did everything possible for me?"

A system of markets exists for Joe to exploit. Reactor vessels can be bought from any number of sellers. There is an even longer queue of marketing specialists eager, and probably even competing, to guide Joe through the effort of selling his wares. How close these markets come to the neoclassical ideals discussed in Chapters 2, 3, and 4 is not the real issue here. Even if the metal workshop and marketing services markets were perfectly competitive (or at least approximately so), in practical terms they still present some problems to Joe.

From a broad perspective, Joe faces two types of obstacles in reaching his goal of producing and selling 1,000 units of his invention. First, he must coordinate the activities of several parties. His design must be communicated to the reactor vessel producer whose production must be coordinated with the marketing firm. Second, Joe must motivate and evaluate three parties: himself in his role of entrepreneur, the reactor vessel maker, and the marketing firm.

Our hypothetical situation facing Joe may be simplistic in a number of ways, but it does pinpoint a central concern of many businesses and their managers. Like Joe, they may have a better idea, and they even may have proven their ability to produce or implement it. However, actually organizing the necessary resources may be too tall a task. Or put into the language of economics, transaction costs may be very high.

■ TRANSACTION COSTS: A BROAD PERSPECTIVE

Just How Informed?

The pursuit of economic goals across multiple parties involves numerous agreements made with various levels of knowledge available in different amounts to different parties.

Information, or the lack thereof, plays a central role in the theory of economic organization. A market is characterized as providing **perfect information** if every participant (and potential participant) becomes aware of every price, product specification, and buyer and seller location at no cost. Perfect information does not imply costless processing of this information but only that it is freely available to all who desire to have it. Agreement and exchange are said to occur under **imperfect information** if at least some buyer or seller has less than perfect information. Contracting parties operate under **informational asymmetries** if one party to the transaction possesses knowledge that other parties do not.

Information increases the efficiency of exchange and facilitates the market mechanism in smoothly handling transactions. Nowhere is the value of timely information more apparent than on the stock exchanges. Several major publications such as *The Wall Street Journal* and *Barrons*, facilitate the flow of information between buyers and sellers. On the stock exchanges, thousands of shares, involving millions of dollars, are commonly bought and sold on the faintest rumors and informed speculation.[4]

No market is likely ever to be characterized as having perfect information. The major stock and commodity exchanges probably come closest to this ideal. Two classic examples of the uneven distribution of information are the markets for used cars and the market for life insurance. A buyer of a used car cannot be expected to possess the same amount of information about the car as the seller. A number of states have enacted lemon laws designed to protect used car buyers that require the seller to provide certain information about the vehicle to the buyer. In most insurance markets, the situation is reversed in that the insured is likely to have better information concerning the risks he or she experiences.

**Expensive Information,
Poor Individuals**

Most exchanges in business today occur under conditions of imperfect informational availability. The reason is simply that information is costly to obtain and interpret. This fact has given rise in economics to the concept of **bounded rationality,** which states that since there are positive costs to gathering and evaluating all information, economic agents will always bear some kinds of uncertainty since eliminating it would be prohibitively expensive. Nobel Laureate Herbert Simon is the economist who developed the concept of bounded rationality and explored its implications for economic analysis.

The concept of bounded rationality seems straightforward, but its implications are far reaching and have caused economists to reconsider some of the basic assumptions made in their modeling efforts. Because individuals are boundedly rational, transaction costs exist; or, put another way, no agreement will ever be made under conditions of perfect information. This puts economic agents in the position of making a trade-off. Transaction participants must weigh the benefits of gathering information against the costs of doing so.

Organizing economic activity is generally a costly proposition. At a very abstract level, we can distinguish between coordination and motivation costs above and beyond the simple dollar costs of agreements. **Coordination costs** entail the determination of prices; the costs of acquiring information concerning the location, quality, reputation, and availability of different parties; and other costs associated with allocating workers to specific tasks and with bringing transaction participants together.

Motivation costs are less direct but arguably more important to business managers today. They arise on two broad fronts: informational incompleteness and imperfect commitments. **Imperfect commitment** is said to exist when the parties come to an agreement that one or both would later like to abandon. Consider, for example, a municipality that promises a major manufacturing concern that it will construct a four-lane highway to a site if the manufacturer agrees to locate a new facility and many jobs there. Once the road is built (in the absence of any enforceable guarantees), the manufacturing plant manager has ample incentive to attempt to extract further concessions from the municipality. The ability of the municipality to extract resources from the manufacturer may be limited if there is ample social and political pressure to create jobs or if the municipality is concerned about its reputation in future dealings with other firms wishing to locate there.

---

[4]Despite all the resources dedicated to the transmission and analysis of information, it is interesting to note that a randomly chosen portfolio of stocks often outperforms those selected by highly regarded market professionals.

TRANSACTION COSTS OF AGREEMENT
AND DISTINCTIVE DIMENSIONS

By now, we hope to have made you aware of the importance of transaction costs in the study of economic organization on both the theoretical and more intuitive levels. Until now, we have offered two very broad categories of such costs: coordination and motivation costs. In this section, we provide a more detailed terminology based on more specific exchange characteristics. We refer to this grouping as the distinctive dimensions of transaction costs.

To complete a transaction, at least one of the parties may be required to tailor some of its resources to very specific needs. **Asset specificity** refers to the degree to which an asset is committed to a specific task and thus cannot be redeployed to alternative uses without sacrificing the majority of its productive value.

Asset Specificity

When you pull your car into your favorite gasoline station, your commitment to the transaction is, in all likelihood, very low. By contrast, when Westinghouse's Nuclear Reactor Division signs a construction and 30-year service contract to supervise and maintain a nuclear electric generating facility, it must commit the services of an army of very specialized engineers and technicians. Likewise, when a coal-fired electric generating facility enters into an arrangement with a coal mine, each party commits assets in such a way to greatly lessen their value in any alternative use.

Because of the importance of asset specificity in our understanding of managing economic organizations, we will fine-tune our asset specificity dimension of transaction costs along the lines commonly made by economists[5]:

1. Site specificity.
2. Physical asset specificity.
3. Human asset specificity.
4. Dedicated asset specificity.
5. Brand name capital specificity.

Site specificity refers to an asset that becomes committed to a particular use owing to its location. A key consideration when General Motors chooses a site for one of its major production plants is the existing or future proximity of suppliers. As just-in-time inventory management has become more widespread, the geographical proximity of suppliers has become a major concern in locating large manufacturing plants.

As another example, consider site specificity from the demand side of the market. Certain retail concerns open stores only in the up-scale malls spreading through large urban areas and in prime downtown areas. In addition, antique stores rarely locate in depressed areas.

Physical asset specificity represents investment in machinery or equipment that has one narrowly defined purpose. Consider, for example, the construction of a movie set by a Hollywood studio that has contracted with a production company to produce a futuristic, science fiction movie. The set is likely to have only one use, unless, of course, the movie proves immensely popular and sequels can be made.

Human asset specificity arises when individuals develop skills with narrow applications as a result of learning by doing or taking specialized training. Economists refer to the experience, abilities, training, and knowledge held by in-

---

[5]These are summarized in O. Williamson, "Transaction Cost Economics," in *Handbook of Industrial Economics*, ed. R. Schmalensee and R. Willig (New York: North-Holland, 1989), p. 145.

dividuals as **human capital,** which like physical capital (plants, machines, and so on) may be committed to specific uses. For example, certain jobs in our economy limit their holders in terms of outside opportunities. The recession of 1990 to 1993 resulted in many corporate downsizings, and a well-publicized purging of the middle management ranks. These mid-level managers did not have a wide variety of jobs to choose from, and many were forced to significantly "retool" in pursuit of employment. Likewise, as the U.S. armed forces shrank during the early 1990s, many military personnel found themselves in a position of being very good at things that few employers needed.

Dedicated asset specificity entails investments in general-purpose plants that are made at the behest of a particular customer. The specificity here refers to committing funds to a specified transaction that might have been used elsewhere.

Brand name capital specificity refers to becoming affiliated with a well-known "brand name" and thus becoming less free to pursue other opportunities. Brand name capital specificity often affects actors on popular television shows. During the 1980s, *Dallas* was a very successful prime-time soap opera. Two of the main characters were the Ewing brothers, J. R. and Bobby, played by Larry Hagman and Patrick Duffy. The personage of these actors effectively became brands; this identification in the public's eyes limited these actors from being taken seriously in other parts.[6] Being so intimately related to *Dallas* significantly reduced their ability to find other acting work.

Asset specificity is a major theme of transaction cost–based economic analysis for a very basic reason. The more committed one becomes to a transaction, the more one stands to lose from unforeseen events and the possibility that contracting partners may find it in their interests to renegotiate more favorable terms from you given that you have committed (or sunk) assets. The various forms of asset specificity make transacting parties fearful of making a commitment that might later prove to be "one way." The other dimensions of transaction costs are more closely tied to the importance of informational availability.

Contractual exchange or relationship is made possible by all parties being convinced that they are made better off by the deal. In nearly every contract, party *A*'s well-being is tied directly to the actions of party *B*. In most realistic settings, party *A* will have doubts as to whether party *B* lived up to her promises. It is entirely likely that *A* will expend considerable effort in determining whether *B* has performed as promised in the contract when the results leave some room for ambiguity about the actions taken.

Consider, for example, your hot dog and soft drink purchase at the ball game. It is very easy for you to check to see whether the vendor had performed as promised. Of course, the bun is soggy, the drink is flat, and the hot dog is cold, but the vendor performed to your satisfaction and met or exceeded your (rather modest) expectations.

As another example, consider your hiring of a paid tax preparer. You are at first pleased with her services as she informs you that your refund this year will be $3,000. A part of you isn't happy, however. You ask yourself the question, "If she was able to get me a $3,000 refund, could I have been due for a $3,500 refund?" In short, you may never be completely sure that the tax preparer had done as good a job as she was able.

In assessing the benefits of a transaction, an economic organization faces dif-

---

[6]Some may argue that this is an example of human capital specificity, and this argument has some validity. However, this validity is questioned when it is recognized that it is not the skills of the actors that bind them to *Dallas* but rather the recognition by television viewers.

ficulties in three areas. First, participation in an agreement involves some form of opportunity cost. Regarding the hiring of a paid tax preparer, if you hire one accountant, you will always wonder whether another accountant would have gotten a larger refund (within the dimensions of the tax code, of course).

The second area of difficulty in assessing the benefits of a transaction lies in the organization's ability to identify the impact of that transaction on its performance. A great example of this is when a firm hires a single employee. One could reasonably ask what effect that single employee has on a large, complex organization.

The third area of difficulty in assessing the benefits of a transaction involves a mixture of not being able to perfectly monitor the actions of other parties to a deal and the incentives that those other parties face. To provide a clearer initial look at this difficulty, we briefly turn to the example of Janet Capocci.

Suppose that Janet owns a business and hires a manager, Barry Stein. Sure, Janet owns the business and is Stein's boss; but how can she be sure that he is advancing her interests rather than his own? Maybe he will pay himself far too generously. Maybe he will pursue short-term rather than long-term gains to make himself look good. It is even possible that he will put in very little time as manager and blame circumstances beyond his control when Janet's profits begin to fall.

The difficulties of assessing the benefits of a transaction greatly influence the underlying exchange and the agreement crafted to organize it. This dimension of transaction costs is, as expected, very problematic. We have barely hinted at its importance, instead deferring more detailed inspection to later chapters.

Given that individuals are boundedly rational, agreements are expected to be made in which the parties have not planned for every possible contingency. Within this context, economists say that in every transaction there is a degree of complexity and uncertainty that presents costs to the transactors.

Consider, for example, a standard futures contract for Treasury bills. The parties agree to exchange money today in return for a promise to provide a specified amount of Treasury bills at some future date. There is very little complexity in this transaction; the rights and responsibilities of each party are clearly stated. There is uncertainty about the outcome, however, and most of this uncertainty is the force behind the creation of the transaction in the first place (a differing perspective on the future course of interest rates). No unforeseen event is likely to cause ambiguity about the *terms* of the exchange.

In contrast, the contract between Rockwell, Inc., and the U.S. government in the early 1980s to provide a fleet of space shuttle vehicles was both complex and uncertain in many ways. Rockwell knew it would be put in a position to deal with many specialized subcontractors. Furthermore, Rockwell was often working with technology that it was actively developing as it constructed the space-bound vehicles we are so proud of today. Most important, Rockwell knew that it would be affected by changing political opinions if the public began questioning the massive spending on space exploration.

Some transactions such as daily shopping are repeated quite often and span a relatively short time period. Other transactions such as a contract for life insurance or marriage occur one time and are designed to last for many, many years. We would expect that the transaction costs for frequently repeated transactions, such as grocery shopping, are much lower than the transaction costs behind the "exchange" of marriage or life insurance. We would also expect that individuals have devised mechanisms, or institutions, to lower the costs of exchange for frequently repeated transactions.

If, in your household, you are responsible for the grocery shopping, you

**Complexity
and Uncertainty**

**Familiarity
with the Transaction**

probably have devised a routine. Using another, more technical-sounding word, we could say that you have created an *institution*. The institution may involve a designated shopping day on which your schedule and the expected crowd at the store provide the best mix.

The purchase of life insurance is quite different. We face a dazzling array of options: the amount of the insurance, term or whole life, cash value, survivability, and so on. Granted, agents can further explain your options and perhaps even make recommendations. However, any reputable agent will leave the final decision up to you. Very likely, you will devote much time to this single exchange.

Generally, when at least one party expects to be involved in many similar transactions, it is in that party's interests to acquire information and create an institution to manage the transaction. The major league baseball players and team owners provide a good case in point. When disputes arise concerning player salaries, a vast majority are turned over to approved arbitrators. The costs of this arbitration may seem large when viewed alone but are small in light of the large dollar amounts of baseball player contracts.

The familiarity of transaction participants with the transaction and with each other has another effect. In situations in which transactions are frequent and repeated over a long period of time, parties have motives and opportunities to withhold or grant favors, to help (or hinder) each other, in informal, implicit ways. The ability to cooperate and learn over time can reduce transaction costs and increase efficiency since parties will grow to understand what is expected of them and because the need for formal institutions to enforce arrangements may be greatly lessened. Further, within this scenario, parties may attain mutual trust and reputations that would be costly to jeopardize.

**Relationship
to Other Transactions**

Some transactions occur in relative isolation with little connection to other transactions. Others exert broad influences across the organization, being connected to other transactions. As transactions become more intertwined and interconnected, the cost of evaluating and enforcing them increases dramatically. These effects are thought to be magnified as the number of people involved increases.

The choice of industry standards for the high density television signals and transmission equipment is an example of a very connected transaction. The entire industry will be adversely affected by a poor choice today because future contracts for peripheral equipment will be affected.

■ EFFICIENCY AND ECONOMIC ORGANIZATIONS

The Idea of Efficiency

To best understand the role of transaction costs in economic analysis, it will prove useful to ignore them, for the time being. In this section, we first lay down some of the ground rules concerning the assumed behavior of economic agents and examine how these agents pursue a set of goals or objectives. Once this is understood, we consider the role of transaction costs and how these costs interfere with agents' pursuit of goals.

Economic analysis, as a science, follows a well-established pattern in explaining rational behavior by economic actors. First, assume that the economic agents strive to achieve some well-defined goal(s). Second, examine and operationalize the constraints faced by the economic agents. Third, produce behavioral statements by optimizing choices to best meet the goals in light of constraints. Consumers, for example, strive to maximize utility, or well-being, subject to well-defined budget and liquidity constraints. Likewise, in determining an optimal portfolio of financial investments, a financial institution diversifies and mixes investments of different risk and return.

In our study of economic organization, we have yet to formally state the goal of agents in our economic analysis. In standard business theory, there are a variety of goals for organizations. Our analysis is based on the premise that economic agents will act with **efficiency.** Recall from our discussion in Chapter 4 that an allocation of goods and services is inefficient if there exists another feasible allocation that lowers the well-being of no party and raises the well-being of (at least) one party.

Many familiar business relationships and economic institutions are framed by efficiency. Consider the role played by money in facilitating exchange. If money were absent, even the simplest transaction would take place by barter, the direct exchange of one good for another. Each party has a collection of goods to trade for objects that he or she desires to acquire; exchange takes place only if those who have the desired goods are willing to accept the goods offered in exchange. The Big Mac produced at the local McDonald's would trade for perhaps one video rental or two ice cream cones or any one of an almost limitless list of goods rather than for a well-defined dollar amount. The use of money obviously promotes efficiency despite several drawbacks: occasional counterfeiting, ability to be lost, and the practice of governments of issuing it in unpopular denominations.[7]

The concept of efficiency is important for at least two reasons. First, it provides a minimal set of rules governing the behavior of economic agents. We can always assume, at a minimum, that rational economic agents acting voluntarily will try to promote efficiency according to their knowledge and abilities. Second, it provides a decision criteria in ruling out certain outcomes. When faced with analyzing the decision of some group of economic agents, we may consider all the feasible possibilities and begin by ruling out those that are not efficient.

The role of transaction costs in reaching efficient agreements is probably a little unclear at this point. In the last chapter, we introduced the Coase theorem, which predicts the attainment of efficient outcomes in the absence of transaction costs. As a reminder, we outline this logic now.

If the parties are free to voluntarily bargain to a binding agreement and resulting allocation, it follows that this resulting allocation must be efficient. Suppose that bargaining resulted in an inefficient allocation; then, by definition, another allocation that is efficient could replace the first. Moving from the inefficient to the efficient allocation, nobody would be made worse off, and at least one person would be made better off. These gains could be awarded to the losers under the inefficient allocation, and then all parties would support the efficient allocation and voluntarily agree to it.

The existence of transaction costs and the property of bounded rationality may, strictly speaking, preclude the existence of an efficient outcome. However, the notion of efficiency remains important to us. We offer an alternative behavioral axiom.

**When the Coase
Theorem Won't Do**

> constrained efficiency postulate: *If individuals are able to voluntarily bargain to an enforceable allocation, the result of their efforts will tend to be efficient, subject to their generally limited information, resources, and bounded rationality.*

In one sense, what the constrained efficiency postulate does is to pick up where the Coase theorem fails in meeting the costly bargaining of the real world.

Transaction costs and the pursuit of efficiency are interesting concepts to help us understand firm behavior. These ideas are very far reaching and provide a rich vantage point from which to view exchanges as the building blocks of firms.

---

[7]As of the time this text went to press, Susan B. Anthony dollar coins and two-dollar bills were legal tender in the United States.

Efficiency is, however, one necessary component of a broader mosaic: **total value maximization.** We define **total value** as the complete set of benefits accruing to the participants of a transaction. It may include regularly defined profits of firms and consumer surplus; it may also include elements of risk minimization, strategic gains, and nonmarket benefits.

The relationship between efficiency, value maximization, and transaction costs is not clear and distinct. Strictly speaking, value maximization does not necessarily imply transaction cost minimization. Or, in other words, the allocation that minimizes transaction costs may or may not be the allocation that maximizes total value.[8]

Later in this chapter, we explore in detail the make-or-buy decision with an example of the use of outside suppliers by the large domestic automakers. The outside suppliers contribute expertise and skills associated with experience in making very specific components; basically, they contribute the benefits of specialization in production. The automakers contribute their ability to manufacture a complicated finished product for consumer use. Efficiency and, hence, value maximization in this example require more than the provision of low-cost components; they require a degree of trust and an environment of cooperation.

However, it is reasonable to argue that reducing transaction costs promotes efficiency and, hence, total value maximization. Thus, our approach is to examine the underlying exchanges and make recommendations on how the activities of the parties should be organized on efficiency and value maximization grounds.

■ FIRM ORGANIZATION AND TRANSACTION COSTS: A HISTORICAL EXAMPLE

Long-Term Changes in the Auto Industry

In 1921 General Motors was in dire straits. The recession that began in 1920 had decimated the market demand for automobiles. To make matters worse, a more efficient competitor, Ford Motor Company's Model T, was rapidly eroding GM's market share. Alfred Sloan was appointed to run GM in that year, and, as they say in the movies, "the rest is history."

Sloan envisioned a number of marketing and organizational improvements that would propel GM to the forefront of the automobile market at that time. He wished to capitalize on GM's size while offering a variety of products to different market segments. What Sloan accomplished was to coordinate many aspects of the different GM divisions (Cadillac, Buick, Oakland, Oldsmobile, and Chevrolet) from within a single corporate entity.[9]

Under the new organizational setting, GM moved to take full advantage of the large scale of its operations by including the same parts in many of the automobiles produced by the various divisions. When large numbers of such parts were required for the organization, **scale economies,** or the reduction in average unit costs as the number of units produced increases, became available for exploitation. This organization created by Sloan was also able to exploit **scope economies,** a reduction in unit costs due to the production of related goods. With almost unlimited access to capital, General Motors was able to achieve a high degree of **vertical integration,** or the control over various stages of production.

---

[8]An interesting example of this point is the use of "second sources" by computer chip manufacturers. This example is found in P. Milgrom and J. Roberts, *Economics, Organization & Management* (Englewood Cliffs, NJ: Prentice Hall, 1992), p. 34.

[9]See Alfred Sloan, *My Years With General Motors* (Garden City, NY: Doubleday, 1964); and Alfred Chandler, *Strategy and Structure: Chapters in the History of the American Industrial Enterprise* (Cambridge, MA: MIT Press, 1962).

Thirty years later, a relatively small Japanese manufacturer, Toyota, embarked on an entirely different path to challenge GM. Toyota lacked the "bigness" and ready access to capital that its U.S. competitors enjoyed. Thus, it developed a new organizational approach better suited to its needs.

Many believe that the rise of Toyota (and the other Japanese auto firms) to positions of market leadership was due to a favorable treatment by the Japanese government and lower labor costs relative to the United States. These advantages existed but were far from the only ones. The stark difference between the operations of U.S. and Japanese firms was that the Japanese firms relied heavily on outside suppliers for many of the parts used in their automobiles.

The important innovation was the development of a **kanban** or **just-in-time (JIT) manufacturing system**—a production system in which outside suppliers work closely with larger firms. A great amount of coordination and trust was required between Toyota and its suppliers as inventories were reduced to minimal levels. The effect of JIT was to eliminate much of the slack in the production process. The absence of inventories meant that Toyota had to be linked to suppliers on a day-to-day basis. At the same time, Toyota required that broken equipment be fixed quickly so that shortages did not occur at later stages of production. Toyota began training its workers to maintain and repair the machines they ran. Toyota and its Japanese counterparts were able to use their small size to promote flexibility for use against their larger, less dynamic competitors in the United States.

A number of interesting points concerning transaction cost analysis can be made by comparing General Motors' strategy in the 1920s and the strategy used by Toyota in the 1950s. When General Motors underwent the massive change under Alfred Sloan, the automobile industry was in its infant stages. Precision manufacturing at mass production levels was still a fairly new concept for firms in the economy. Many of the parts used by GM in its cars might have been available through market transactions, but it is likely that the transaction costs associated with this approach would have been high.

Difficulties would also be foreseen by the potential suppliers themselves. Given GM's size and the potential economies of scale available, supplying GM would require a massive investment in specific assets. As one of the corporate icons of industrial America, General Motors would enjoy an advantage in terms of cost of capital over its potential suppliers. Given this cost advantage in securing capital and the asset specificity required of suppliers, one could argue that the emergence of a vertically integrated firm was efficient and consistent with a desire to maximize total value by GM.

The situation would have been quite different in Japan in the 1950s for a number of reasons. Primarily, large amounts of technology and manufacturing know-how were available. The automobile industry was already established, providing a pool of information and resources. In this environment, entrepreneurs were able to harness this available technology and serve as outside suppliers, producing goods for Toyota. Furthermore, the Japanese culture with its emphasis on consensus and cooperation fostered a spirit of trust between Toyota and its suppliers under which the suppliers would be less afraid of engaging in highly specific investment.

▇ TRANSACTION COSTS AND OUTSIDE SUPPLIERS: ANALYSIS OF THE MAKE-OR-BUY DECISION

One of the purposes of this textbook is to provide some insights into the economic factors behind the organizational strategies of firms. Logically, this involves identifying which activities will be carried out inside the firm and which will be provided by the market. A quick look at business organizations today

Specialization and Specificity

When people think about what economists do, they are likely to conjure nightmarish equations and computer simulations and all manner of indigestible Greek-letter salad. For the most part, they are right.

But exceptions are often more interesting than the rules. And few are as interesting as the work of Ronald H. Coase, the 81-year-old retired University of Chicago Law School professor who last week won the Nobel prize for economics. His ideas have swept through legal scholarship like a fresh breeze. It is likely—some would argue, inevitable—that the Coasian way of thinking will influence policies ranging from access to transplant organs to the control of corporations.

Mr. Coase (whose name rhymes with dose) has made a career asking basic questions about the minuet of the markets—how people organize to advance their economic interests, and when government is needed to choreograph the dance. And what a career: his penetrating yet disarmingly simple answers have become the stuff of myth to a generation of scholars more at home in multivariate regression analysis than in English.

For a sample of vintage Coase, consider his 1974 article on lighthouses. For decades, textbooks used the lighthouse as an example of a "public good," a service that private markets could not deliver efficiently because there was no practical way to exclude consumers who refused to pay.

But the British-born Mr. Coase noted that lighthouses began as private enterprises in Britain, and that the system worked well. For in spite of the "free rider" problem, enough people who profited from the ship traffic through British ports were willing to support the lighthouses because they did not trust government to provide adequate service on its own. New Yorkers may note that what worked in Britain also works closer to home: hundreds of city block associations now pay for the extra protection the city's police department cannot or will not provide.

Mr. Coase reserved his broadest brush for an analysis of why business companies exist. Companies, he argued, are really contractual hierarchies that shelter collections of workers from the uncertainties and costs of relying on markets to meet their needs. When a professional wants a letter typed, she can hand it to her secretary rather than looking for typists on the street or in the Yellow Pages. And when a typist wants to sell his skills, he can trade flexibility, independence and perhaps a higher income for a guaranteed salary.

Businesses grow, Mr. Coase concluded, to the point that the costs of internal sources of inefficiency—the myriad conflicts between individual workers' interest and that of the organization as a whole—equal the costs of coping with the endless headaches of buying and selling what you need, when you need it. This may not seem an earth-shaking insight. But his ideas lurk behind serious analyses of contemporary business issues ranging from corporate control to workplace discrimination. Indeed, they have proved so fruitful that one of his disciples, Oliver Williamson of the University of California at Berkeley, may yet win his own Nobel prize for extensions of the framework.

For all its impact, however, Mr. Coase's theory of the firm must take a back seat to his 1960 article, "The Problem of Social Cost." When first submitted to the University of Chicago's Journal of Law and Economics, it evoked the wrath of the entire economics department, which was then home to giants including the future Nobel prize winners Milton Friedman and George Stigler. But in a famous seminar, Mr. Coase converted them one by one. Thirty years later it has probably become the single most cited article in modern economics.

Again, the point is simple. It had long been the conventional wisdom that markets generating "externalities"—costs not borne by producers—would inevitably be wasteful without a little help from government. If, for example, soot from a factory chimney ruined the paint on neighboring houses, some sort of tax or regulation would be needed to get the factory to take account of the soot damage in choosing a lowest-cost method of production.

Mr. Coase was skeptical. If the damage created by the soot exceeded the cost of curtailing it, why couldn't the homeowners bribe the factory to clean up its act? In a world where the practical problems of making deals (what economists call the transactions costs) were tiny, he concluded, government would not be needed to insure least-cost solutions to problems of externalities.

By the same logic, of course, pigs could fly if only they had wings. But as Guido Calabresi, dean of the Yale Law School, points out, Mr. Coase was not trying to make a practical case for keeping government out of regulating pollution. Rather, he was arguing the true source of market failure is not the externalities but the transactions costs that prevent waste-reducing deals. For purposes of clearer analysis, he was separating the problem of coping with the nuisance from the question of who was at fault. In a Coasian world of "causal agnosticism," Mr. Calabresi says, one could as easily speak of the paint getting in the way of the soot as the soot getting in the way of the paint.

Michael E. Levine, the dean of Yale's School of Management, offers an example of the way such analysis can change established legal thinking. In a hoary Minnesota case often cited in law texts, a Great Lakes steamer tied up at the nearest wharf to avoid sinking in a storm. The dock was badly damaged, and the owner sued to cover the repair costs.

At the time (1910), the court floundered its way through a logical thicket of assigning liability where common sense said no one was truly at fault. If Mr. Coase had been on the bench, however, he might well have focused on the next accident rather than the last.

A Coasian scholar would want to give both the owners of docks and the owners of boats the incentives to minimize the total damage to life and property. And that probably would have meant billing the boat owner, who was in the better position to weigh the risks.

The Coasian way of thinking, Mr. Calabresi says, offers opportunities for analyzing questions in everything from bankruptcy to environmental law. Even novel legal issues, like balancing the wishes of grieving families against society's interest in making body organs available for transplant, give way easily to Mr. Coase's brand of analysis. Such Coasian techniques have found a firm niche in legal scholarship.

But Richard A. Posner, a Federal appeals court judge and disciple of the Nobel prize winner from his days as a University of Chicago Law professor, thinks the best is yet to come. "Ideas filter gradually into the real law," he said. "It will be another generation" before the shock waves fully penetrate the system.

Source: Peter Passell, "For a Common-Sense Economist, a Nobel—And an Impact in the Law," New York Times *(October 20, 1991), p. 2E. Copyright © 1991 by The New York Times Company. Reprinted by permission.*

provides quite a mixture regarding in-house versus outside acquisition of goods and services. Clearly, no universal rules are followed, and recognizing that in some organizations entropy and historical precedence may be the only justifications, we analyze the problem from a transaction cost perspective. As usual, we suppose that in pursuit of value maximization, economic actors will pursue efficiency.

Perhaps the most obvious characterization of the in-house versus outside supplier choice involves the degree of asset specificity. This idea is so important to us that we spend a great deal of time on it in the next chapter.

Looking at the major metropolitan areas of the United States, we observe that most daily newspapers own their own printing presses and operate their own distribution process. However, the publishers of most textbooks liberally subcontract the actual printing process. Both textbook and newspaper publishers provide information and data via the printed page. The difference between them lies in the specificity of the content. For the newspapers, content is specific for a given day; for a textbook, the information will be relevant for a number of years.

Chrysler, Ford, and GM

A better example designed to show the many dimensions of transaction costs is the so-called make-or-buy decision in the automobile industry in the late 1980s and early 1990s. The most dynamic U.S. player in the market at this time was clearly Chrysler Corporation, which developed its new LH line of cars (Chrysler Concorde, Dodge Intrepid, and Eagle Vision). Like General Motors in the 1920s, Chrysler acted in response to a fairly desperate financial situation.

Chrysler's LH series of cars has a number of new features. For consumers, there is plenty of high-tech wizardry along with the new "cab forward" design, which moves the car's windshield farther to the front of the vehicle and moves the rear wheels back. This design change produces more interior space, provides better visibility, enhances aerodynamics, and yields a smoother ride for rear passengers owing to the vehicle's longer wheel base.

From the organization's standpoint, changes were equally drastic. Ford, in producing the Taurus and Mercury Sable, had followed Honda's example and used the team concept of production and design, allowing suppliers some input. Chrysler has carried the concept of teamwork the furthest by actually letting outside firms influence the design process. This level of cooperation had previously been unheard of in the industry. To facilitate speedy development, Chrysler established a $1 billion technology center for itself and its suppliers.

The larger role played by the outside suppliers was clearly evident as 70 percent of the LH series was made by outside suppliers. By contrast, Ford and GM bought 50 percent and 30 percent of their parts from outsiders.[10] Recognizing its critical dependence on outside suppliers, Chrysler has extended its partnership model outside its corporation.

Because the U.S. automakers faced severe global competition earlier than most industries did, executives at the Big Three were early converts to the partnership model. As far back as 1979, they were murmuring about switching to long-term contracts, taking advantage of their suppliers' know-how, and forging supplier relationships that valued more than just the lowest bid. By the mid-1980s, that murmur had become a chorus. To compete, the automakers needed higher quality, lower costs, and more innovation. In all of those things, they needed suppliers' help. So the car companies promised a new era of supplier relationships. On the one hand, the Big Three needed to reduce their supplier bases, but the companies they kept would be trusted. The trade-off would consist of us-

---

[10]See Alex Taylor III, "Can Iacocca Fix Chrysler—Again?" *Fortune*, April 8, 1991, pp. 50–54.

ing suppliers' ideas about improving product design and price cuts in exchange for long-term contracts. That was the theory. All three major domestic car companies did switch to long-term contracts with suppliers and did receive price cuts. However, when the U.S. recession deepened in 1990 and 1991, two of the Big Three requested bigger cuts. Chrysler, in a more cooperative mode, asked suppliers to come up with cost-saving suggestions.

Rather than simply demanding that their key suppliers cut costs overnight, as GM and Ford had done, Chrysler enlisted supplier support to make design and engineering changes that would add value and boost productivity. As a result, Chrysler's parts suppliers have turned in 3,900 suggestions that have saved the company an estimated $156 million in production costs.[11]

The transaction cost components of these contractual arrangements are illuminating. From a strict marginalist standpoint, the decision to use an outside supplier or rely on a more vertically integrated source is based on a consideration of costs and benefits. For the larger firm, the component can be made in-house or purchased on the market at a given quality and cost. Standard economic thinking dictates that if a better part is made by a supplier at a lower cost, in-house production should be curtailed. The transaction costs relevant for this decision cloud the issue and are missing from a strict marginalist interpretation of the situation.

Asset specificity is an issue for both the supplier and the larger firm. The supplier should have reservations about committing highly specific assets, machinery, and the human capital of engineers and technicians to the needs of the larger company. The larger company has reason to fear relying exclusively on the outside supplier for integral parts, believing that the outside supplier may withhold delivery at the last moment and desire to renegotiate the contractual relationship. Given the recession-battered state of the industry and the rough handling by GM and Ford, the suppliers may have been willing to trust the maverick Chrysler corporation, which may have been willing to trust the suppliers for the same reasons.

The complexity and uncertainty dimensions of transaction costs also came into play in the make-or-buy decision. The daunting task of building a car seemed to favor an in-house solution. However, given the new computer technologies and large pool of engineering talent in existence, there were incentives and opportunities for compartmentalizing the production and design process. Chrysler clearly sought to coordinate the activities and value-adding abilities of many bright, innovative companies rather than relying on its own, more static, resources. Chrysler knew that the use of outside suppliers would prove advantageous if they could provide cost reductions and quality improvements.

Chrysler was also in a position to assess the benefits from its contracts with its outside suppliers. With the required integration of the activities of many firms, Chrysler could easily monitor the performance of its contracting partners. Congruence to specifications could be checked through mechanical means and by seeing whether all the pieces fit together. It was also easy to determine whether the suppliers were putting forth their best efforts. Involving firms outside Chrysler meant letting them share in the risks and rewards of the LH line. Chrysler has shown a willingness to share the rewards with long-term contracts and by rewarding cost-saving suggestions. The suppliers must clearly recognize this for their transaction cost advantages to manifest themselves in the long run.

The truly startling thing about Chrysler's decision to rely extensively on out-

---

[11]For an interesting description of these events, see Martha E. Mangelsdorf, "Broken Promises," *Inc.*, July 1991, pp. 25–27; and William McWhirter, "Chrysler's Second Amazing Comeback," *Time*, November 9, 1992, p. 51.

side suppliers was not the technical challenges it successfully overcame but the implication that this form of organization was chosen over the more vertically integrated operation scheme of its U.S. counterparts. It must be believed that Chrysler was aware of all the alternative organizational arrangements, for its managers have often been both praised and criticized in the business press for ordering endless "what if" analyses when they tackle problems.

The coordination and motivation costs associated with extensive use of outside suppliers at first pass appear huge. Chrysler has taught us that these costs may be large, but, on balance, they may be far less than in-house production.

The greater reliance on outside suppliers is not tied exclusively to the automobile manufacturing industry. In the early 1990s many high-tech firms applied this organizational technique.[12] Hewlett-Packard had dominated the laser printer industry for a number of years in terms of quality, value, and durability. It did not, however, follow the leadership example of the two dominant U.S. computer-making firms, International Business Machines Corp. and Digital Equipment Corp. and rely on a high degree of vertical integration. Hewlett-Packard, in fact, obtains the heart of its printers, the laser engine, from Canon, Inc., of Japan.

The arrangement is clearly beneficial to both parties. Canon sells its own line of printers that competes with the Hewlett-Packard products. The U.S.–based concern has protected itself by denying Canon the rights to its printer software, termed PDL by the industry. Furthermore, Hewlett-Packard handles all production of its less expensive line of Ink Jet printers. Clearly, it is efficient and value creating for Hewlett-Packard and Canon to contract. Furthermore, mechanisms exist to overcome the transaction costs.

Hewlett-Packard is not alone in combining its relative strengths with those of other firms with complementary advantages. In the early 1990s, Apple Computer, Inc., had manufacturing pacts with two Japanese companies, Sharp Corp. and Sony Corp., to manufacture some of its hand-held and laptop computers.

For these firms in the computer industry, the pattern of exchange happens to follow nationalistic lines. U.S.–based firms typically are stronger in systems design and software creation. Their Japanese counterparts enjoy advantages in the more mechanical components, notably memory chips and monitors. Contractual exchanges permit each entity to add value in terms of what it does best.

■ THE VIRTUAL CORPORATION—A LIMITING CASE?

Corporations today are involved in many diverse activities. In many instances, teams are formed with competitors and suppliers alike all in an attempt to promote efficiency and maximize value through exchange. A new corporate model—the **virtual corporation**—has emerged; it is a temporary network of companies that come together quickly to exploit fast-changing opportunities.[13] In a virtual corporation (VC), companies can share costs, skills, and access to global markets, with each partner contributing what it's best at.

The possibility of opportunism, or misbehavior, by one of the contracting parties is minimized since companies team up to meet a specific market opportunity and then usually end the alliance once the need evaporates. An expanding

---

[12]A more detailed description can be found in G. Pascal Zachary, "Getting Help: High-Tech Firms Find It's Good to Line Up Outside Contractors," *The Wall Street Journal*, July 29, 1992, p. A-1.

[13]An excellent viewpoint on the purposes and scope of this organizational form are presented in "The Virtual Corporation: The Company of the Future Will Be the Ultimate in Adaptability," *Business Week*, February 8, 1993, pp. 98–102.

technology encourages the development of VCs as information networks link geographically dispersed entrepreneurs and enable them to work together. A VC form encourages excellence and efficiency since each partner offers what it does best. Potentially, a VC arrangement would be "world class," something that no single company could achieve. The VC relationship heightens the reliance between companies and requires far more trust than in the past. Most interesting, VCs redefine the boundaries between corporations by blurring them. More cooperation among competitors, suppliers, and customers makes it harder to pinpoint where company *A* ends and company *B* begins.

The possibilities allowable under a VC would be exceptionally attractive for small corporations and entrepreneurs. Significant start-up costs for manufacturing capacity and basic research results may be available from the market. Key components can be purchased from existing manufacturers, saving even more. Engineering services in particular can be purchased, saving the small firm large amounts in human capital development and/or hiring costs.

◼ OF PARTICULAR INTERST TO MANAGERS

Consider, once again, our definition of firms from Chapter 1.

> **firm:** *A conscious, willful effort to organize economic activity that consists of a collection of contracts when more than one party is involved.*

Of course, it is important to note that a firm is nothing more than a collection of contracts. Transaction costs are important to us because they are extremely relevant for the environment in which contracts are crafted.

Traditional microeconomics is concerned with things external to the firm such as the behavior of markets. The transaction cost view of economic organization, on the other hand, attempts to look at the situation from within the firm. Of course, this is a relatively new approach filled with scary sounding terms including *bounded rationality, asymmetric information,* and *asset specificity.* However, all of the ideas represented by these terms are very intuitive and will, we hope, move economics back into the realm of interest for business managers.

The most interesting problem we approached in this chapter with the tools provided by transaction cost analysis was the make-or-buy decision faced by firms. We are all well aware of trends in this area beginning with the breakdown of the mass-producing firms in the late 1970s. The prudent use of outside suppliers provides the benefits of specialization weighed against the transaction costs of market exchange. In the athletic footwear industry, this way of doing business is even more entrenched. One of the major players in this market, Nike, owns one small factory; Reebok, one of its competitors, owns none. In 1992 both Nike and Reebok earned a return on assets of 16 percent, placing fifth and sixth, respectively, in *Fortune* magazine's list of best service companies in that year.[14]

◼ CHAPTER SUMMARY AND KEY IDEAS ◼ ◼ ◼ ◼ ◼

The theme of this chapter is that economic exchange is often costly for the participants in that exchange. Every day we make very simple exchanges; for example, we purchase a cup of coffee. A number of factors cause us to think of this as a simple exchange: both buyer and seller are probably aware of other prices in the market; the market is very competitive; there are few complexities in the transaction; and the exchange does not involve a large degree of commitment by either party. For other ex-

---

[14]Shawn Tully, "The Modular Corporation," *Fortune*, February 8, 1993, pp. 106–111.

changes made by individuals and organizations, none of these things are true and some resources must be expended to provide a clearer picture of the environment in which the transaction takes place. We refer to these costs as *transaction costs*.

Individuals and organizations have the property of bounded rationality, which rules out the possibility of ever becoming completely informed because of the costs of doing so. As we study the principles of economic organization, we must keep this idea clearly in mind. There will always be costs to acquiring information and attaining commitment as individual parties try to coordinate and motivate economic exchange.

We have introduced five distinctive dimensions of transaction costs to further help our understanding of this important topic. Two of the most important ones are *asset specificity* and *assessing the benefits of the transaction*. As we continue into the next chapter, we begin thinking about how to deal with these types of transaction costs.

From the firm's perspective, the most important aspect of transaction costs may very well be the forces affecting the make-or-buy decision. This decision requires the firm to balance the potential gains from specialization in production against the costs of using a market (as opposed to an internal) source to fulfill certain needs. As more outside suppliers are used, the degree of vertical integration falls in the firm. Clearly, this is a trend prevalent in the recent evolution of corporations in the United States as they seek to become competitive in a global sense.

■ FURTHER READINGS

Coase, R. "The Nature of the Firm." *Economica* 4 (1937), pp. 386–405.

———. "The Problem of Social Cost." *Journal of Law and Economics* 3 (1960), pp. 1–44.

Holmstrom, B. R., and J. Tirole. "The Theory of the Firm." Chapter 2 in *Handbook of Industrial Economics*, ed. R. Schmalensee and R. Willig. New York: North-Holland, 1989.

Milgrom, P., and J. Roberts. *Economics, Organization & Management*. Englewood Cliffs, NJ: Prentice-Hall, 1992.

Smith, A. *An Inquiry into the Nature and Causes of the Wealth of Nations*. Oxford: The Clarendon Press, 1976.

Tirole, J. *The Theory of Industrial Organization*. Cambridge, MA: The MIT Press, 1989.

Williamson, O. "Transaction Cost Economics," Chapter 3 in *Handbook of Industrial Economics*, ed. R. Schmalensee and R. Willig. New York: North-Holland, 1989.

■ KEY TERMS

asset specificity	kanban
bounded rationality	motivation costs
brand name capital specificity	perfect information
constrained efficiency postulate	physical asset specificity
coordination costs	scale economies
dedicated asset specificity	scope economies
efficiency	site specificity
human asset specificity	total value
human capital	total value maximization
imperfect commitment	transaction costs
imperfect information	vertical integration
informational asymmetries	virtual corporation
just-in-time manufacturing system	

A. Suppose that your university is currently trying to fill two empty positions: Marketing Department secretary and professor of economics. The job description for the secretarial position lists the major duties as answering faculty phones; forwarding mail and messages to faculty; providing administrative support; typing letters, examinations, and research papers; and serving as departmental receptionist. The job description for the faculty position lists the major duties as work with existing faculty in a variety of research projects, collaborate with faculty of all departments regarding curriculum development, and serve and enhance the visibility and reputation of the university in the local and national communities. For which position would the university expect to incur more transaction costs? Frame your answer along the lines indicated by the dimensions of transaction costs.

B. There are basically two ways to directly purchase the stocks of U.S. corporations: through a full-service broker or through a discount broker. One of the main differences between them is that the full-service broker makes available to you advice by "market professionals." What is the role of transaction costs in the different services offered by the firms that buy and sell stocks for investors?

C. Suppose for the purposes of this problem in transaction costs analysis that a university very much like the one you are attending exists not very far, perhaps on the other side of town, from your own university. Parallel University is similar in size, function, mission, and quality to your own university. There are six divisions at Parallel University: Registration/Clerical, Library, Faculty, Pure Administration, Support Staff, and Secretarial Services. There is no central authority at Parallel U. The distinct divisions exist to permit specialization and the resulting productivity gains. The only interaction between the divisions, outside of functional communications, is a system of contracts binding them all. It is this system (or nexus) of contracts from which Parallel University exists.

   1. How many pairs of contracting partners are there at Parallel U?

   2. Comment on the efficiency of the Parallel U arrangement from a transaction cost perspective.

   3. Propose a second organizational scheme for Parallel U that would be more efficient. How does your proposed organizational scheme differ from that used at Parallel U?

D. The large consumer products corporations consume large amounts of business services to conduct their affairs. Three particular services come to mind: legal, advertising, and accounting/financial control. Most of the large, established firms contract out advertising, with little effort from in-house talent. The firms typically have their own legal and accounting/financial staffs, but some do use these services from outside firms.

   1. What factors could explain the use of both outside and inside legal resources by these firms?

   2. What does transaction cost analysis have to say about the differences in the outside provision of advertising services and the mixture of inside and outside firms used in legal and accounting matters?

Contracts: Motivation Through Agreement

Any attempt to deal seriously with the study of economic organization must come to terms with the combined ramifications of bounded rationality and opportunism in conjunction with a condition of asset specificity.[1]

CHAPTER OUTLINE AND STUDENT GOALS

Contracting: An Economist's Viewpoint

One of the most commonly used words in business is *contract*. Almost every issue of *The Wall Street Journal*, *Business Week*, or any other business publication contains mention of labor contracts, executive contracts, futures contracts, and T-bill contracts. Other references to contracts are more subtle: *merger*, *strategic alliance*, *hostile takeover*, and *production networks* are examples of contracts created by participating parties. Activities closer to your everyday course of events are also subject to contract. Subscribing to newspaper delivery, using utility services, purchasing gasoline with a credit card, and watching cable television also represent contracts. If you are a parent, there is contract with which you are even more familiar: you will do *it* (whatever *it* is) and your child expects *it* because you are the mommy (daddy).

From an economist's viewpoint, contracts are useful because they are the "stuff" that binds. But, even more important, from an organizational perspective, contracts serve to govern transactions defining relationships between parties. We analyze the crafting of **incomplete contracts,** agreements which fail to fully specify actions under every conceivable course of events. When a contract is crafted, the involved parties are forced to forecast future events and acquire costly information. Individuals will never become fully informed because doing so is prohibitively costly. In economic terms, we say that individuals possess **bounded rationality;** that is, they know that large transaction costs will prevent them from becoming fully informed.

Throughout this chapter, we emphasize transaction costs and the importance of eliminating opportunistic behavior. An understanding of these issues is essential in helping us to appreciate the importance of economic efficiency in organizing economic activity. Economic efficiency comes into play here because improvements in the contracting process through minimizing transaction costs increase organizational productivity.

---

[1]Oliver Williamson, *The Economic Institutions of Capitalism* (New York: The Free Press, 1985), p. 42.

Despite the wide usage of the term *contract*, and the even wider spectrum of activities that are undertaken to fulfill contracts, it is rather difficult to provide a working definition of what we mean when we use the term. Our working definition is very general and somewhat ambiguous so that it can be applied to a very diverse range of situations. A **contract** is an interlocking set of mutual promises that are enforceable and acknowledged by some disinterested third party. Generally, a contract specifies actions that each party will take and may assign decision-making powers.

This definition is workable, but it may create a certain amount of confusion through its ambiguity. To help further clarify the term *contract*, we list the properties common to most contracts.

Contracting, or economic exchange, is a process of voluntary exchange.[2] Although this property of contracting may seem obvious, it has an interesting implication. For any group to voluntarily reach an agreement, the expected result of that agreement must be both individually and mutually advantageous. All parties together and each individual party must expect to benefit for an agreement to be reached. Considering the voluntary nature of contracts, it is important to recognize that the parties expect to benefit, these expectations rely on limited information available in different amounts to the involved parties, the level of commitment of each of the parties, and the honesty of each of the parties.

Another property of contracts is that they attempt to provide motivation to the parties. Many contracts contain enforcement mechanisms outlining performance criteria and means for measuring that performance. Motivation also implies a specification of the reward structure identifying levels of payment if some minimum level of performance is achieved.

The set of promises composing a contract may be explicit or implicit. When dealings occur under an **explicit contract,** there is a written record of the agreement. With an **implicit contract,** there is no formal statement of the terms and conditions agreed to by the parties.

Contracts can be made highly transaction specific, with **fungible** terms; that is, they can be crafted to meet unique individual needs and circumstances. Standard-form contracts exist for frequently occurring transactions whose terms change little from transaction to transaction. Such forms exist as well for more complex dealings, like buying a house or purchasing life insurance. However, in standard business practice it is not uncommon for items in these standard-form contracts to be crossed out, or for the contracts to have blanks inserted where the dollar amounts or additional text are penciled in.

The final property of contracts is that they are relational and incomplete in nature. Rarely does a contract specify a mutually agreeable set of actions for every possible contingency that may arise over the life of the contract. This last property is important and gives rise to a number of contracting problems. A more detailed explanation of **relational contracting** will come shortly.

All of these properties of contracts indicate what you may have already guessed: that contracts are a basic tool used to organize economic activity. Do contracts replace markets? The answer is hidden in the slippery terminology. All

---

[2]There are, of course, situations in which agreement is involuntary such as the contract formed when the thief brandishes a gun and orders the victim to hand over his or her money and jewelry. The prison sentence imposed on the thief on conviction is likewise an involuntary contract between the court system and the thief.

market transactions are governed by contracts; although this is obvious, it must be remembered. The difference between contracts and markets is that relational contracting becomes important either when a market doesn't exist or when the transaction costs associated with market transactions are relatively large.

From a strict economic point of view, competitive markets provide many of the benefits of contracting through **market discipline.** A functioning, competitive market provides discipline if enough buyers (sellers) learn of a particular seller's (buyer's) poor behavior so as to curtail that seller's activities. Discipline under relational contracting is somewhat harder to identify.

Contracting problems fall into two general categories: those arising from imperfect information, and those related to **asset specificity.** In an environment of imperfect information and boundedly rational individuals, agreements must be crafted with some effort. Rational individuals will fear being taken advantage of by the situation itself or by other parties to the transaction. We define **opportunism** as the pursuit by individuals of their own interests at the possible expense of others. Opportunism may arise when a contract is being negotiated, within the contract, or by reneging on agreed upon terms.

Internal Versus External Contracts

It will be useful to distinguish between internal and external contracts. From an organization's perspective an **internal contract** governs an arrangement between the firm itself and an employee or owner of that firm. **External contracts** are those covering agreements between the firm and all other parties.

Opportunism and Reputation

It stands to reason that in an environment of imperfect information, individuals fear misbehavior or opportunistic trading partners. It also stands to reason that there should be some reward for good behavior. To organizations, reputation may be a valuable commodity. It is and does play a role in our understanding of economic organizations, and we investigate this role more fully in Chapter 9.

Establishing a reputation as an honest and fair trading partner can help an organization craft efficient contracts. Under an external contract, Craftsman tools, sold by Sears, are guaranteed indefinitely. Broken hammers, wrenches, and saws are replaced on demand. Because of this, Sears sells many, many tools. Under an internal contract, your employer most probably has an incentive to treat you fairly. If he or she imposes difficult work conditions or pays an unfair wage, attracting new employees and maintaining current employees may prove impossible.

After reading this chapter, you should be able to

- Explain, in your own words, what a contract is.
- Discuss, in layperson's terms, the concepts of relational contracting, incomplete contracts, and bounded rationality.
- Understand the problems associated with incomplete contracting in terms of the incentive structure facing parties to a contract.
- Appreciate the role played by truthfulness and reputation in reaching agreement.
- Identify the role played by private information in encouraging precontractual opportunism and strategic misrepresentation.
- Understand the problems created by adverse selection and the potential roles played by signaling, screening, and self-selection.

- Recognize the hold-up possibilities created by asset specificity and develop insights about the ways to achieve commitment.
- Acknowledge the presence of opportunities for pre- and postcontractual opportunism and identify strategies to mitigate their effects.

▩ INCOMPLETE CONTRACTING

Contributing Factors

Owing to bounded rationality and the associated transaction costs, most agreements framing behavior in the business world are incomplete and, as such, fail to exactly determine future actions. Four specific factors are identified by Coase[3] and Williamson[4] as contributing to the presence of contractual incompleteness. First, some contingencies that the parties may face are not predictable at the contracting date. Second, even if all contingencies could be foreseen, there may be too many contingencies to write into the contract. Third, checking that the other party abides by its terms (i.e., monitoring the behavior of others) may be costly. Fourth, enforcing contracts may involve considerable legal costs. Using our terminology, these four factors contributing to contractual incompleteness do so by creating transaction costs.

Summer Employment: An Example

To clearly illustrate some of the issues surrounding incomplete or relational contracting, we turn to an example you may have experienced. Most college students seek full-time employment during the months when school is not in session. Let's discuss, as an example, the experience of Becky, a full-time student at a major state university. Becky obtains a job for the summer at BigFood, a large grocery store near her home, as a stockperson/clerk. Becky's employment contract is an example of an internal contract.

No explicit contract details Becky's hourly wage rate or weekly schedule. In terms of documents, there is only a job application listing her education, work history, and personal information. Part of the application contains a paragraph stipulating that the information she provided was true and correct (to the best of her ability) and that asked her to agree to regular company policies. A second paragraph described company policies regarding pay, promotion, and scheduling disputes. According to policy, employee grievances are to be submitted in writing to the store manager, who must reply within seven (7) days. If an agreement isn't reached in the following seven (7) days, an outside arbitrator appointed by Big-Food will mediate the dispute. Her signature on the application recognized her agreement to these terms and her willingness to work.

Most of the agreement between Becky and BigFood was implicit and framed by a five-minute discussion with her supervisor prior to application. The two agreed that Becky would perform a variety of jobs: stocking shelves, checking out customer orders, bagging groceries for customers, assisting customers in getting their orders to their cars, and icing cakes in the store's in-house bakery. They also agreed on a wage and that Becky would fill in where needed as the store's regular staff went on vacation and during the extremely busy weekends and summer holidays. Any hours worked above 40 in any week would be compensated at time and a half.

Becky ponders the vagueness of her relationship with the store. There are a number of possibilities that are left unanswered; in fact, there are seemingly infinite possibilities that could cause problems. Becky realizes that some weeks she

---

[3]Ronald Coase, "The Nature of the Firm," *Economica* 4 (1937).
[4]Oliver Williamson, *Markets and Hierarchies: Analysis and Antitrust Implications* (New York: The Free Press, 1975).

will work more hours than other weeks; the number of hours in any one week depends on when the regular staff requests time off and the level of activity at the store. These, in turn, depend on many, many factors not included in the implicit agreement between herself and the store manager. Her exact duties are also unclear. Some of the tasks she will be quite good at, but at others she will experience difficulty. Further, she will enjoy some duties more than others. Becky does understand the procedure for settling disputes and is somewhat comforted that, in serious cases, an outside arbitrator will eventually be called in.

Becky comes to the realization that enumerating any significant portion of these things beforehand would require lots of thought and negotiation with the manager of BigFood. After her first day on the job, she does know one thing; a grocery store is a very busy place and neither she nor her manager has the time to discuss all of her concerns. In more formal terms, we could say that *Becky and the store manager are both boundedly rational and seeking an efficient way to organize this transaction.* She is partially appeased by the standard answer of her manager, "Don't worry, Becky; we treat our summer help well because we need you and we need to attract good people during the summer months when many of our year-round staff takes time off."

As the summer progresses, Becky receives a raise in her hourly rate, and her manager congratulates her for doing "a good job." Becky pauses for a moment and wonders on what this assessment was based. Her supervisor hardly seemed to notice her and never once actually watched her work. The supervisor was usually busy ordering items, programming the store's computer, or dealing with specific customers. She did notice that some of the other stockpersons took extended breaks or spent much longer than necessary with customers in the store's parking lot. They never seemed worried about being caught and had informed her that the manager was far too busy to know exactly what they were doing. Becky concluded that they were probably correct and, thinking back on her one economics course in college, realized that the opportunity cost for the manager of keeping close tabs on all the employees was much too high.

The contract between Becky and BigFood is clearly incomplete. As with nearly all employment contracts in the United States, her employment is termed "at will," she works voluntarily for an employer who employs her according to the employer's will. As Becky explains to her younger brother, it seems that her job is the result of cooperation between herself and BigFood, rather than the result of any highly specific list of job duties or activities.

The example of the relationship between Becky and BigFood illustrates some of the basic elements and causes of incomplete contracting.[5] The idea of foreseeing and unambiguously describing every contingency that may be relevant to the agreement between Becky and BigFood is obviously ridiculous. Neither Becky nor BigFood could possibly foresee every contingency in this environment. Furthermore, no language could be precise enough to describe all the eventualities, even if they could be foreseen. If we assume that either Becky or BigFood were omniscient and could, somehow, see every possible course of events, by the time Becky read through the reams of paper, the summer could well be over, and Becky would not have worked a single day.

In practice, the complete contracts of standard economic theory that specify what parties will do in every conceivable circumstance are impossible to negotiate and write. The ability of people to make plans and contracts is limited by

---

[5] There are some missing aspects that may appear in other transactions, however. In our example, there is no opportunistic behavior by either Becky or BigFood.

bounded rationality. Relational contracts emerge as a response to the many difficulties of writing complete contracts.

In our analysis of contracting, we will consider the contracting process as a sequence of three time periods. The first is the period of time prior to reaching agreement. Behavior in this period, the negotiating phase, is termed **ex ante,** a Latin phrase that translates roughly as "before the fact." Ex ante contracting issues concern incentives parties may have to exploit informational advantages, to engage in some sorting or selection activity, or to misrepresent their interests prior to signing the contract. The second event is the actual signing of the contract, or the contract date. The third period is termed **ex post,** again a Latin phrase that translates roughly as "after the fact." Ex post contracting issues are centered on the likelihood that one of the parties to the agreement may find it advantageous to fail to perform in agreement with the contract terms.

Ex Ante and Ex Post
Environments

■ EX ANTE OPPORTUNISM: PRIVATE INFORMATION

Prior to signing the contract, the parties involved (at a minimum) must reach a consensus as to what contingencies the agreement governs. There are said to be **informational asymmetries** when the amount and quality of information held by each party differs or is believed to differ. One contracting party may be better informed regarding the likelihood of each of several possible operating environments occurring after the contract date. Possibly, one party may have superior information concerning the net value of the contract to him- or herself and other bargainers. It is also conceivable that information regarding the alternative opportunities, costs of delay, and commitment possibilities of the involved parties may be imperfect. Informational asymmetries give rise to transaction costs and, as such, they hinder arriving at an efficient agreement.

Just What
Are Informational
Asymmetries?

We examine the effects of imperfect information in the form of informational asymmetries within an exchange setting. There is then a buyer (consumer) and a seller (provider). The setting of such imperfect information gives rise to incentives to engage in opportunistic behavior. In this section, we consider private information and the efficiency of markets; strategic misrepresentation; adverse selection; signaling, screening, and self-selection behavior; and measurement costs and investments in bargaining positions. Each of these influences gives rise to transaction costs and hinders efficient exchange. In certain situations, the presence of these transaction costs may be so compelling as to prevent trade all together.

The economic forces underlying exchange allow for analysis centered on the role of imperfect information in a market setting.

Private Information
and Market Efficiency

In the following example, we consider the pricing options of BigChip, a computer supplier in an environment in which private information affects the efficiency of transactions. BigChip has many identical computers for sale that cost $800 to build. Since BigChip has no direct competition, it need not sell at cost.

There are two kinds of potential buyers: those who value the computers at $832 and those who value them at $865. Half of the potential buyers place a high value on the computers; half place a low value. Thus, the probability that any given buyer is a high-value consumer is one-half. BigChip has no mechanism to distinguish between the two types of buyers even though its market research can show that two types of buyers exist.

BigChip must set a single price to all consumers in our example. This price is made as a take-it-or-leave-it offer. The risks to the seller are clear. If too high a price is set, sales will be lost to consumers with low valuations. If the price is set too low, profits are lost because some of the surplus of the high-value consumers is not captured by BigChip. So what price is appropriate?

BigChip will never set a price less than $832, so this amount provides a starting point. At a price of $832, every potential buyer makes a purchase, and the profit per potential buyer is $32. If the price is set at $833, only the high-valuation consumers purchase. If the price is set at $834, again only the high-valuation consumers purchase. In fact, for any price between $833 and $865, only the high-valuation consumers purchase and the profit per sale is the selling price minus $800. However, the profit per potential buyer is only one-half of this difference since the probability that a consumer is a high-value consumer is 0.5.

BigChip would then set a price of $865, selling only to high-value consumers so long as there were enough high-value consumers to purchase all of BigChip's stock. To understand why, consider the following. If a price of $832 is set, every consumer will buy, and profit per sale will be equal to ($832 − $800) = $32. However, if a price of $865 is set, only one-half of the buyers will purchase, and the profit per potential buyer will equal (0.5)*($865 − $800) = $32.50.

In a retail setting, this would amount to consumers appearing at the BigChip selling location and only half of them purchasing. The seller, ignorant of how highly any consumer values the product, rationally sets a price that excludes half of the potential buyers.

The efficiency loss is apparent. There still remain mutual gains from further trade; the lower valued consumers are willing to pay $32 more per computer than the cost of supplying those computers.

Strategic Misrepresentation

One party may try to benefit by being less than truthful about his or her assessment of an exchange situation. This **strategic misrepresentation** is an attempt to increase negotiating or bargaining power and arises out of an air of uncertainty that surrounds negotiations. If all parties' valuations of a transaction were known with precision, strategic misrepresentation would be impossible.

Consider labor contracts, for example. Negotiators expend significant resources to determine their opponents' objectives and to conceal their own. Effective labor union negotiators precede the bargaining talks with research to determine the production costs of the firm, the corresponding costs of competing firms, and the financial health of the firm. Concurrently, management's negotiators attempt to survey the subjective mood of workers and to determine the wage that workers could obtain elsewhere. Feigned anger, excessive friendliness, exaggerated impatience, and personal abuse are sometimes used in labor negotiations as a ploy to get the other side to reveal its true intentions and beliefs.

Strategic misrepresentation also occurs in more common settings. In most retail settings, prices are fixed. For big-ticket consumer items, however, haggling is common. One reason for the success of General Motor's Saturn Division in selling its automobiles was that its selling practices eliminated haggling.

Haggling over a sales price is an attempt by a buyer and a seller to strategically misrepresent their valuation of a transaction. It is possible given the basic economics behind exchange. Consumers buy an item because it yields positive utility. Implicitly, buyers place a valuation termed a **reservation price** on an item (given their preferences, their income, and the prices of other goods). The reservation price is equal to the maximum amount a consumer would pay for an item. In Chapter 2, we introduced the concept of consumer surplus; we can now see that for any given buyer, consumer surplus is equal to the difference between the reservation price and the actual price paid. Consumers strive to maximize the net value of their purchases by paying a price as far below their reservation price as is possible.

A similar option is available to sellers who have a minimum amount in mind when they place a floor on what they will charge for the good. This floor, termed a **minimum supply price,** may be determined by production costs or market conditions. In Chapter 2, we defined the idea of producer surplus, which is simply the difference between the price received by the seller and the minimum supply price.

Bargaining over a sales price typically involves the seller desiring a high price and the buyer offering a low price. Each party is thus attempting to maximize his or her surplus from the transaction. Clearly, the buyer has an incentive to make the seller believe that his or her reservation price is lower than it actually is. Likewise, the seller has an incentive to make the buyer believe that his or her minimum supply price is higher than it actually is.

In Chapter 2, we briefly discussed the practice of price discrimination by sellers. This occurs if sellers have some monopoly power, resale can be prevented, and different types of buyers can be identified. Under price discrimination, sellers attempt to appropriate some (if not all) consumers' surplus.

If buyers and sellers are less than truthful about the valuations they place on goods, it is possible that efficient exchanges may not take place. If the buyer claims too low a value, and the seller too high a value, the good will not be transferred from the seller to the buyer even though efficiency dictates that it should.

Negotiation often involves many factors and is at least partly an art. There is simply no way that economic theory can provide analysis general enough to be applicable in every case. Forces such as determination, interpersonal communication skills, and reputations for shrewdness or leniency could never be explicitly modeled. What economics *can* do is offer insights into that part of negotiation that is a science.

The question as to how much bargaining power does each of the bargainers have is, in effect, equivalent to the question of what does my opponent believe about my beliefs and willingness to settle. We can identify some propositions about how beliefs are formed. We recognize the limitations of these propositions, however, since they require one party to have some knowledge (that may be private) about the other parties.

An opponent with strong alternative opportunities fares better under a negotiated outcome. A standard tactic in corporate America is to use a competing job offer in negotiating for a pay raise. Knowing that production members lacked alternative employment opportunities, Caterpillar Tractor was able to end a strike by its employees who belonged to the United Auto Workers Union. By reminding the strikers that the unemployment rate in Illinois, where many of CAT's plants were located, was very high, they gained the upper hand. Since a bargainer expects to benefit by having a stronger fallback position, the investment in time, money, and energy in developing alternatives is rational. An understanding of the opponent's alternatives will strengthen your own bargaining position as well.

A second way to gain an understanding of your opponent's position is to understand the relative costs of delay to each party. To capture a larger share of the revenues generated by their efforts, the Major League Players Association voted to strike against the team owners in 1994, and earlier in 1980. In 1980 the players refused to participate in the preseason exhibition games, then agreed to play for the first six weeks of the regular season, and then refused to play again until their demands were met. Their rationale was clever. The players would lose less fan support than if they planned to strike continuously from the date of the first preseason game. The players also recognized that the revenues earned by owners were not uniform throughout the year. Attendance and fan interest are fairly low during the first part of the season and pick up markedly as the weather turns warmer, kids are out of school, and baseball begins to stimulate peaked interest by fans.[6]

---

[6]The facts behind the strike by players against major league baseball appear in Lawrence M. DeBrock and Alvin Roth, "Strike Two: Labor-Management Negotiations in Major-League Baseball," *Bell Journal of Economics* 12 (1981), pp. 413–425.

To minimize delay costs, most labor unions have strike funds, the purpose of which is to make payments to union members during a strike. Likewise, when anticipating a strike, many manufacturing firms stockpile product so as to not lose sales during a strike. In a bargaining situation, delay is a weapon and parties may take actions to diffuse this threat.

Another method to alleviate the possibility of strategic misrepresentation is to use commitment as a bargaining technique. Quite possibly, bargainers view a continuum of possible outcomes: any agreement may be favorable in one dimension and unfavorable in another dimension relative to some other feasible agreement. In short, parties may expect an agreement to represent simultaneous trade-offs in a number of dimensions. One of the bargainers may attempt to *manipulate the other's expectations*. The strategy here is to be the first party to make a "take-it-or-leave-it" offer. If the "leave-it" option is credible, and if the other party has limited alternative opportunities or cannot withstand long delays, this strategy may confer significant bargaining power. In short, refusing to bargain may represent the best bargaining strategy.[7]

■ EX ANTE OPPORTUNISM: ADVERSE SELECTION

The Role of Information

If one party to a contract has private information at the time of contract negotiation that potentially reduces the value of the contract to the other party, we say that the situation is one of **adverse selection.** The used car market provides a good setting to illustrate the efficiency effects of adverse selection.

**The Used Car Market:
Another Look
at Supply and Demand**

In the used car market, sellers typically hold private information during the negotiation or bargaining stage that potentially reduces the value of the transaction to the buyer. Two related aspects of used cars affect their market demand: quality and price. Of these, only price is clearly communicated to, and known by, the buyer, who must conjecture as to the quality of the car.

In this environment of asymmetric information, it is rational to expect sellers of high-quality cars to demand a premium for them. Thus, as quality increases, price rises. The higher price might reflect some subjective measure (a pleasing paint job or a "high-performance" appearance) or some objective measure (the amortized value of avoided repair bills). Buyers, however, are unable to accurately gauge quality and have no way to know whether the price of a given used car reflects higher quality or opportunistic behavior by the seller.

Consumers do, however, make inferences about the quality of goods being offered based on the price charged, since this is the only clear information they obtain. They know that, on average, if the price of a used car is low, the chance of getting a so-called lemon is high. Sellers know, of course, that consumers know this, and they try to take advantage of that information.

With imperfect information, sellers are not price takers; rather, they set prices based on their beliefs of consumers' expectations concerning the quality of their products. Lowering price may not increase sales, for a lower price might be an indication to consumers of low product quality. When the seller's offer price is an indication of quality, the market mechanics may operate in a somewhat perverse way.

When the supply of used cars is increasing in price, current owners are more likely to part with their cars, because the price at which the cars can be sold increases. One likely argument for a supply function increasing in price is the reason one usually sells a car: to buy a new one. The demand function may not, how-

---

[7]Of course, bargaining may completely break down if all negotiators have instruments to make a "take-it-or-leave-it" offer.

ever, have the standard slope. The reasoning is subtle and depends on the relationship between price and quality. In general, quality increases in price, but there may be diminishing returns. Or, in other words, quality increases in price at a decreasing rate: in the lower price ranges, price increases lead to large quality increases; in the higher price ranges, price increases lead to smaller quality increases. If we define *value* as the quality-price ratio, then a single price-quality ratio represents maximum value. We call the price at this combination p_o.

This price effectively becomes the market price for used cars. At any price less than p_o, the quantity demanded falls. The mechanics of this positive relationship between price and quantity depends crucially on the asymmetric information and the notion of value as a quality-price ratio. Lowering price indicates that a given car offers lower quality than similar cars, thus depressing the value of that car. A similar argument holds for price increases above p_o.

Causal empiricism indicates that the used car market is typically characterized by excess supply, confirming buyers' wariness when facing sellers with superior information.

In Figure 7.1, the graphical mechanics of this exchange situation are shown. As drawn, the used car market is characterized by *excess supply*. Note that the normal functioning of markets does not cause the markets to clear. Typically, excess supply is eliminated as competition forces sellers to lower prices. In the used car market, however, lower prices might actually increase market surplus since price also communicates quality to consumers. In a market such as this, we expect a price of p_o to emerge as the market price; however, the usual market clearing mechanism does not function properly, driving us toward this outcome.

Adverse selection is also a problem in insurance markets. The problem facing the insurance companies is fairly simple. Those most likely to file a claim against a policy are also those most likely to purchase insurance. Those who are least likely

**Efficiency
in Insurance Markets**

Figure 7.1 Used Car Market

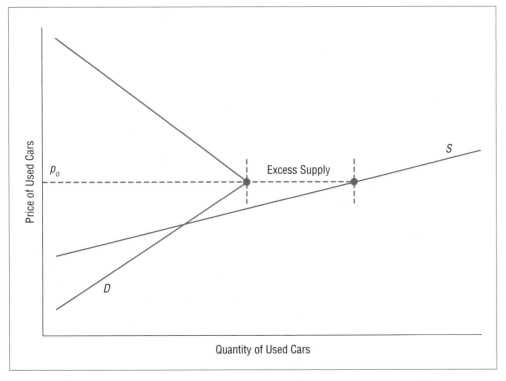

to collect, that is, those who are safety and health conscious may still buy some insurance but will not pay too high a price for it.

In insurance markets, the information regarding policyholder risk is asymmetrically held. The parties buying the policy have much more information regarding the potential risks they pose than does the insurance firm. This setting may present serious problems to insurance companies.

Suppose that an insurance company is earning losses; that is, revenues from policy premiums and investments are less than the amount paid out for claims. Can the insurer simply raise rates? Quite possibly, the answer is no. Increasing premiums results in a more serious adverse selection problem for the insurer. At higher rates, those customers who pose lower risks will either opt out of the market, contact another underwriter, or purchase less insurance.

High-risk policyholders, on the other hand, are less likely to opt out. The reasoning is subtle but very intuitive. Opting out means that a new insurer will have to be found who will want to independently assess the risks posed by the client. This examination may lay bare the true risks posed by the client and result in even higher premiums.

On balance, then, if an insurer wishes to raise premiums, the cost-benefit analysis of policyholders will be altered. Given that some current policyholders are low risk and some are high risk and that only the policyholders know for sure what risks they pose, low-risk policyholders are more likely than high-risk policyholders to abandon the company in face of higher premiums. Thus, the mix of high- and low-risk policyholders changes as high-risk policyholders compose a larger percentage of policyholders.

**Rationing Goods
and Services**

Adverse selection may also occur in markets as a rationing device when price increases are not permitted in order to reduce excess demand. A good example of this phenomenon is the market for loanable funds and credit rationing by banks and other lenders. In this setting of imperfect information, borrowers are more aware of the actual risks they pose than are lenders. An informational asymmetry exists preventing efficient exchange.

Banks are well aware of the risk-return trade-off characterizing most investment projects. Accordingly, higher returns can be earned only by bearing higher risk. The return on stocks, for example, is typically much higher than the return on government bonds. To a lender, this trade-off presents a unique environment. At low interest rates, potential borrowers representing different levels of risk are plentiful. Notwithstanding the efforts of the bank to identify the risks associated with each borrower, the odds of any borrower presenting a small risk are relatively high. At high interest rates, the pool of potential borrowers is smaller, and, further, a significantly larger percentage of these borrowers will pose higher risks. This is because of the aforementioned trade-off; only high-risk borrowers will anticipate the returns necessary to pay the higher interest rates.

The effects of this selection of borrowers are shown diagrammatically in Figure 7.2. There are two offsetting components to the expected returns for the lender. Higher interest rates will (in the low range of interest rates) increase returns to the lender. In the lower range of interest rates, risky borrowers compose a smaller percentage of the pool of potential borrowers. Thus, defaults are fairly low. In the higher range of interest rates, low-risk borrowers are conspicuously absent from the pool of potential borrowers. As interest rates rise within the higher range of interest rates, an even riskier pool of borrowers emerges.

Thus, at higher rates, the lender can expect more defaults. At some point, the gains from further increases in the interest rate are more than offset by the increased proportion of riskier borrowers attracted. This rate, labeled r_o in Figure 7.2, is the interest rate on the lenders' loans that maximizes its expected return.

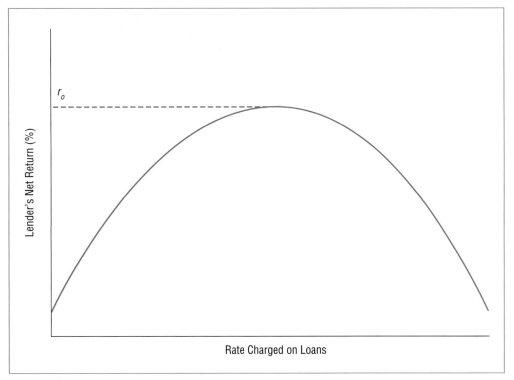

Figure 7.2 Credit Rationing with Adverse Selection

As in the used car example, it is assumed that lenders are not price takers; rather, they are price setters. There is no reason to suppose that the intersection of the market supply and demand curves will occur at or above r_0. Thus, as shown in Figure 7.3, the market may not clear and efficient exchanges may not take place. The credit market is characterized by *excess demand*.

Given that most markets are characterized to some extent by imperfect information, ways have evolved to promote efficiency in the face of adverse selection. In the next subsection, we concentrate on two more formal ways. Before proceeding to them, we consider the following less formal approaches to mitigating efficiency declines associated with imperfect information.

Outside appraisers may be called in to inform the information-deficient party. In the used car market, for example, some potential buyers hire a trusted mechanic to examine the car. In some of the larger metropolitan areas of the United States, firms exist solely to perform this function. Similarly, before banks lend money to real estate developers (and even home buyers), they often require input from an independent appraiser.

If transacting parties are fairly sophisticated and recognize that they are at an informational disadvantage, they may expend effort toward altering their selection of potential contracting partners. Credit card companies may target a specific demographic group—college graduates, for example—if they believe that the potential future earnings of recent graduates make them reasonable credit risks.

In some instances, however, companies have to expend effort to get a more random cross-section of customers. Most holders of health insurance policies in the United States are covered by employer-sponsored group plans. Furthermore, the premiums on group health insurance are markedly lower than the premiums on privately (and independently) purchased policies. There are two interesting

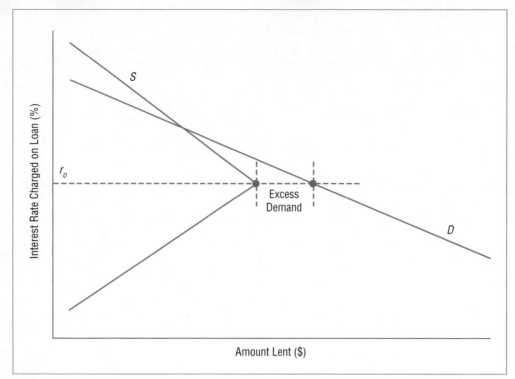

Figure 7.3 Credit Rationing

viewpoints to explain the price difference between private and group policies. On the one hand, insurers may believe that the employees of large firms represent a "true" cross-section of individuals. A second, more cynical viewpoint, is that insurers know that if they tie coverage to a job, the person holding the job is at least healthy enough to work and thus might pose a lower risk. Whichever point of view you deem more relevant, each admits to the importance of one contracting partner holding an informational advantage and exploiting it.

Credibility and reputation can also alleviate some of the inefficiencies posed by selection problems. Sellers of goods and borrowers of funds often go to great length to make their longevity and reputation for honesty known to potential buyers and lenders.

Other contractual and regulatory devices exist also to facilitate trade with imperfect information. Warranties are commonly offered with big-ticket consumer items. Not surprising, the fact that not all warranties are offered for free provides information to consumers regarding the underlying quality of the good being sold. In most states, Warranties of Merchantability specify basic minimums for performance. In addition, Underwriters Laboratories certify aspects of electrical devices, and Good Housekeeping's Seal of Approval is a sought-after label for many household items.

Signaling and Screening

In exchange situations with asymmetric information, one party is better informed than the other concerning specific attributes of the good being exchanged. Herein lies the problem: "If I am unsure about the characteristic of this good relative to other goods competing for my scarce resources, what price should I pay?" Economists have identified signaling and screening as two market responses that have emerged to facilitate information flows to the less informed party.

Consider, for a moment, all of the characteristics associated with a product. For most products, the list could get rather long. Divide these characteristics into

178

two groups: those characteristics that are desirable to a potential buyer and those that are observable by a potential buyer. With perfect information and completely efficient markets, each item in the desirable group would also be in the observable group. In practice, however, only some of the items in the desirable group are also in the observable group.

This feature of imperfect information is illustrated in Figure 7.4. Characteristics are either observable and in the lower box or unobservable and in the upper box. Also, characteristics are either desirable and in the circle or undesirable and outside of the circle. Buyers are limited to observable characteristics in their assessments and decision making.

Consider all the elements in the circle, that is, the desirable characteristics. Some link between the observable and unobservable items may be exploited. Suppose, for example, that a firm is considering hiring (that is, buying) a job applicant. The applicant may hold a master's degree from a prestigious university; that is observable and verifiable. The fact that he or she holds a master's degree may point to other desirable traits that are unobservable, such as perseverance, ability to work with others, and intelligence.

Signaling occurs when the better informed party makes certain verifiable facts known that, when properly interpreted, may indicate the presence of other unobservable but desirable characteristics. A job applicant may then signal his or her work ethic by pointing out that he or she earned the degree with honors while working full time as a salesperson. Similarly, a used car dealership may signal its standing in the community by building a permanent showroom (indicating that it would be costly for it to pack up and leave) or by making its long record of doing business known to prospective buyers.

For signaling to be effective, the receiver must believe that the signal is credible. That is, the observable characteristic must clearly point to the unobservable, desirable characteristic.

This concept is best illustrated in the context of the job applicant and the hiring firm example. Suppose that there are two types of workers: high ability and low ability. The exact level of ability predicts the ultimate productivity of workers but is, unfortunately, not observable. Educational attainment may serve as a signal to employers to differentiate between applicants if two conditions are prevalent within the context of the bargaining and contracting situation.

First, it should be generally true that only high-ability applicants are able to earn the degree marking educational attainment. If low-ability applicants could obtain the degrees, then they would do so and pass themselves off to unsuspecting employers as future high-ability workers. Second, it should be the case that all

Figure 7.4 Signaling and Screening

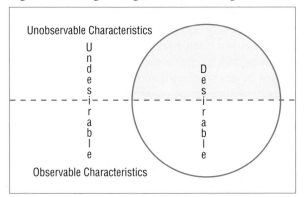

high-ability persons hold the degree; that is, it is in their interests to hold the degree. These conditions work to guarantee that any person with a degree is a promising hire to the firm and that there are no promising hires to the firm who lack a degree.

When the uninformed parties to an agreement undertake activities to cause the informed parties to distinguish between themselves, economists say that **screening** is taking place. In the context of Figure 7.4, screening means that one contracting partner demands certain elements in the set of observed characteristics that are correlated with unobserved but desirable elements. Screening then is a strategy sometimes available to an uninformed party, which, if successful, will get the better informed party to reveal information. To help operationalize our understanding of screening, we will consider two examples: screening in the labor market and screening used by sellers to privately informed buyers.

Screening is very prevalent in the job market for many types of workers. Salop and Salop[8] present a model in which screening is practiced by firms to reduce employee turnover. Having workers quit is costly for all firms. In the event of a sudden departure, the firm suffers two losses. First, if the employee has undergone training, the cost of that training is lost rather than offset against the future gains in worker productivity occasioned by the more productive worker. Second, there are positive costs involved in replacement; advertising, interviewing, and selection costs are fairly high. In many circumstances, firms have ample incentive to attract workers who are less inclined to change jobs.

Salop and Salop argue that employers may be able to alter the odds that an employee would consider leaving. One possible device is to announce a policy of continuous wage increases. Following this logic, a firm offers to pay relatively low wages initially but higher-than-market wages after the employee has been with the firm for an extended period of time. The positive relationship between wages and experience discourages workers who are likely to change jobs and encourages workers who plan to stay with the firm for a substantial portion of their careers.

Screening may also be used by sellers of goods if buyers hold private information concerning their true valuation of the good and if the costs of delay to the buyers are higher than the cost of delay to the seller.

Consider once again the used car seller example presented earlier in this chapter. The seller faces two kinds of buyers: those who place a high value on the good and those who place a low value on it. Assuming that the seller is a price setter, buyers have no incentive in revealing their true valuations. All buyers favor purchasing and having use of the car today over purchasing in two weeks. For simplicity, we assume that the seller has no costs of delay.

With the adoption of a price schedule rather than of a single price, the seller may be able to distinguish between the two types of buyers and to effectively price discriminate against the high-value buyers. One possible strategy for the seller is as follows: offer the car at a high price today and, if refused, offer it at a somewhat lower price two weeks hence. If a successful screen is created, the seller can be sure that only low-valuation consumers will come back in two weeks and purchase the car. The price in the second period will be the valuation of the low-value consumers. The first period price must be slightly less than (within several cents of) the price that equates the net return of first period buyers purchasing two weeks later adjusted for the costs of delay.

Bargaining typically consists of a series of offers and counteroffers, with the

---

[8]J. Salop and S. Salop, "Self-Selection and Turnover in the Labor Market," *Quarterly Journal of Economics* 90 (November 1976), pp. 629–649.

seller starting high and the buyer starting low. Eventually, it is hoped, agreement is reached somewhere in the middle. The previous exchange example shows, in a primitive way, an incentive for haggling. The seller is uncertain of any buyer's evaluation and starts with a high price and successively lowers it. Buyers with high valuations are relatively impatient to settle, for they lose more by waiting than buyers with low valuations do. By enduring the costs of holding out, low-valuation buyers credibly prove their starting valuation. Thus, at least in this example, the purpose of haggling is for the seller to get buyers to reveal valuable information.[9]

■ BETTER INFORMATION: IMPLICATIONS

Measurement Costs

As you have read through this chapter so far, you have undoubtedly become aware that the availability of information in exchange is a central issue in economics. To this point, we may not have added any ideas that are truly new to your knowledge base; we have, however, made two important contributions to your overall business education. First, we have provided a terminology for you to use in describing information problems. Second, by examining these issues from several vantage points, we hope that we have provided at least some new insights for you.

Strategic misrepresentation and adverse selection are two types of ex ante contracting problems. As we discussed these situations, it became clear that the best answer is to become better informed. The fear of exploitation by a contracting partner rationally leads all parties to become as informed as possible. Economists call the costs incurred by parties attempting to become fully informed **measurement costs.** We consider measurement costs to be a subcategory of the more general class of costs associated with exchange: transaction costs.

In the traditional supply and demand models, measurement costs are very small if not zero. Since there is a high degree of homogeneity among the wares of competing sellers, buyers have little incentive to assess the quality of a product themselves. Also, in the traditional supply and demand model, there is no incentive to invest in a bargaining position. Haggling does not occur since there is a fairly well-defined price known generally by all market participants. Overanxious sellers seeking higher prices quickly lose buyers. Exceptionally tight-fisted buyers do not find sellers at overly generous terms.

In the real world, however, market participants frequently cannot rely on competitive markets and the invisible hand. Consider, for example, hard-to-define goods that infrequently change hands, such as houses. For any given house, there may be no true "equilibrium" price. The seller must expend resources to determine the "fair market value" of the house. Buyers, in turn, attempt to determine the value of the house to them given their household size, tastes, and the house's location.

**Efficiency Aspects
of Measurement Costs**

From an efficiency perspective, these measurement costs represent a burden and a waste. When both parties seek to become better informed, the costs of gathering and analyzing the information are subtracted from the total value of the transaction to each party. The ownership of the asset changes, whether or not the information costs were borne, just as efficiency requires. It is true that the higher level of information results in an exchange price in line with the true value of the asset; however, to an outside party, price differences represent a transfer from (to) the buyer to (from) the seller.

---

[9]Haggling to achieve these ends may not always work, however. If, for example, the difference between high and low valuations is too large relative to the costs of delay, it will be impossible to determine a first period price that results in seller profits in excess of those earned by simply setting a fixed price.

**Reducing Measurement
Costs**

Strictly speaking, measurement costs are a loss to society as a whole and to transaction participants in particular. In some instances, contracting techniques have emerged to lessen the influence of measurement costs.

One strategy used in reducing measurement costs is called *block booking*. Roy Kenney and Benjamin Klein[10] identify block booking in several contexts. In each instance, **block booking** involves a price-setting seller, with some market power, grouping similar goods together and offering the package to buyers, who have little information. Sellers thus set, in effect, an average price. This practice eliminates duplicative search costs. Presumably, if a buyer could reject part of a package, he or she would do so after a critical (and costly) assessment of product quality. The seller would then have to verify this assessment and offer the once-rejected product at a lower price to another buyer, who would then incur the same measurement costs.

The practice of block booking does not require a perfect monopoly by the seller, but some monopoly power certainly helps provide the necessary framework. Competition by several sellers would not favor the practice of block booking. What is required is that both the buyer and seller recognize that the quality of each item in the package is somewhat random. They can then expect, on average, to get their money's worth. A definite contributing factor to this practice is that most arrangements of block booking involve many transactions over a long time period reinforcing the effects of bad "draws" being counteracted by good "draws."

Block booking has been common in the U.S. motion picture industry from as early as 1916. Kenney and Klein outline the following common scenario for many of the contractual arrangements made with theaters by Paramount Studios, Inc. A block booked group of films was offered prior to the films' actual production; thus, they were said to be "blind sold." Potential exhibitors had some information about production budget estimates; the past year's gross rentals of the studio's films; and the likely acting, writing, and directing talent. They could not, however, view the movies they were renting; further, if the exhibitor reneged, they were not contacted by the studio again. The potential for short-term opportunistic behavior was therefore large, placing an emphasis on the reputation and the brand name capital of the distributor.

Kenney and Klein also identify the marketing efforts of the Central Selling Organization (CSO) of the De Beers diamond group. Over the past decade, this group has directly controlled about 80 percent of the world's supply of new diamonds. Each customer regularly informs CSO of the kinds of diamonds it wishes to purchase. The CSO, in turn, puts together a "sight" of diamonds for the customer. Each buyer examines the sight for as long as he or she wishes before deciding to purchase or not. Negotiation over the price or composition of the sight is not permitted. If a buyer claims that one or more stones in the sight is incorrectly graded, the sight is adjusted if the sales staff agrees. These occurrences are said to be rare. Buyers rarely reject a sight, since in so doing, they are offered no alternative and deleted from the list of customers.

The economic rationale for the marketing practices of the CSO and Paramount Studios is clearly to avoid excessive bargaining costs. The transaction costs incurred in haggling over the price of diamonds and movies would be significant. It is interesting to note that De Beer's CSO pursues a different selling strategy for particularly large diamonds. Instead of being sold on a fixed average price basis, very large stones are offered to particular buyers on an individual stone

[10]Roy Kenney and Benjamin Klein, "The Economics of Block Booking," *Journal of Law and Economics* 26 (1983), pp. 497–540.

negotiation-based basis. The buyers of large stones suffer no consequences if they reject a stone on the basis of price or perceived quality. The rationale for the selling practice of large stones is arguably that estimates of value of larger stones vary significantly across buyers, since they can be put to many different uses.

Block booking, or average pricing, is also common in many less glorious aspects of economic life. Sports teams typically prefer to sell season tickets requiring customers to attend a number of home games or matches. Major college football programs have taken the idea one step further; tickets for home games against nationally recognized powerhouses are sometimes sold together with tickets for home games against less prestigious opponents.

A second strategy for reducing the measurement costs is to rely on other interested parties who may have incurred the measurement costs but whose observable actions can relay that information to others. As noted in Chapter 5, economists term this practice *free riding on the information of others.*[11]

If you can obtain costly information for free, through observation, it is in your interest to do so. In a retail setting, it is widely regarded that this practice is often used by fast-food chains in determining locations for their restaurants. Conventional wisdom has it that McDonald's is usually first into an area, after having done the necessary research on the site. Soon other competitors follow. In another context, free riding has been offered as an alternative to deposit insurance at banks and savings and loans. The argument goes as follows: large depositors have more incentive to monitor the financial health of the institution in which they have placed funds than do small depositors. Further, large depositors often have the resources and technical sophistication to conduct this monitoring. If the actions of the large depositors are made public knowledge, small depositors can mimic their actions and safeguard their investments.

■ EX POST OPPORTUNISM

Ex Post Disadvantages

The contracts crafted between individuals and organizations have a single purpose and a means of achieving this purpose. A contract is intended to benefit all agreeing parties. This benefit is achieved by aligning the parties' incentives and interests. With relational contracting, this alignment may be less than perfect. In particular, the possibility of being harmed by the other party's self-interested behavior may hinder efficient exchange. Opportunistic behavior occurs when one party selfishly pursues his or her own interests, possibly at the expense of other contracting parties. The threat of opportunism may seriously limit the degree of cooperation that can be expected, especially under bounded rationality and contracts.

In this chapter, we consider two forms of ex post opportunism: reneging and the hold-up. A third form of postcontractual opportunism arising out of imperfect information is reserved for the next chapter. **Reneging** occurs when one or more parties to a transaction simply refuses to honor the agreement. Holding up a trading partner involves exploiting the inflexibility or captiveness that may result from an agreement. The threats of falling victim to reneging or a **hold-up** problem sometimes present significant transaction costs to be overcome in the pursuit of efficient exchange.

These transaction costs arise from two sources: contract incompleteness and asset specificity. Before examining the second of these sources, we consider the role of contracts and their association with reneging.

---

[11]An interesting perspective of these issues is provided in a fairly sophisticated paper by Paul Milgrom and John Roberts, "Relying on the Information of Interested Parties," *Rand Journal of Economics*, 17, no. 1 (Spring 1986), pp. 18–32.

Contractual incompleteness and bounded rationality imply a trade-off in reaching agreements. On the one hand, relational (or in layperson's terms, *imprecise*) contracts involve a cost savings over perfect, highly detailed contracts. On the other hand, however, they leave much for interpretation ex post. Then it may be easy for one party to complain about the other's performance only to have the second party claim that it is doing as agreed and that no reneging is going on. Moreover, even if the other party fully believes that the first party is not living up to the agreement, the ambiguity of the contract means that it may be very hard for outsiders to determine exactly who is misbehaving and what actual behavior is appropriate.

In a well-publicized case in the early 1980s, Westinghouse failed to deliver uranium fuel to other utilities at prices set in a long-term agreement. The basis of Westinghouse's position was that appropriate contractual behavior indicated this to be the reasonable course of action.

If reneging takes the form of a failure to conform to agreed actions, efficiency is not directly sacrificed. For example, consider a magazine subscriber refusing to pay the subscription bill after receiving issues for six months. All that efficiency required was that the magazines be supplied; payments are merely an income transfer from one party to another. The threat of reneging may affect efficiency indirectly, however, by increasing the belief held by one party that he or she may be cheated or by tarnishing the reputation of a person or organization. If the magazine subscriber's name in this example is added to a "deadbeat" list, then he or she may have trouble subscribing to other magazines.

A second form of reneging termed *ex post renegotiation* may occur if at least one party wishes the contract to remain in force, only at altered terms. When contracts stipulate future behavior, different possible environments may not be stipulated. In fact, it may be impossible to know the environments themselves. If the parties understand at the time they are crafting the original agreement that they will later face these incentives, they may not be able to draft a contract.

Consider, for example, the practice of large corporations to reward key executives with stock options. An option gives the holder the right to buy the firm's stock at a specified point in time at a specified price. The executive will earn substantial profits if she is able to purchase the stock in the future at a price well below the market price and immediately resells it. This motivation scheme is, theoretically, a win-win situation. For the firm, it costs less than money paid today and provides incentives to the executive to enhance the profitability of the company. For the executive, she is essentially guaranteed a bonus in the future that is larger than the cash bonus she could get now.

One essential parameter, however, is the price at which the executive can purchase the stock in the future, the "execute" price relative to the future market price of the stock. If the execute price is set too high, the stock option may be viewed as an unreachable goal; if the market price turns out to be too low, the value to the executive falls. In this case, it might make sense, ex post, for the executive and the firm to renegotiate the option execute price. This is especially true when both sides agree that the stock price may have changed because of reasons far outside the executive's, or for that matter the organization's, control.

Certain contractual devices and separate institutions have emerged to help remedy some portion of the threat of reneging to individuals and organizations. By and large, these remedies involve introducing some flexibility into the relational contract. Sometimes penalty clauses in contracts are instituted if requirements concerning repayment, quality, and timeliness are not met. Further, some contracts guarantee a variety of options at some point in the future. In the home mortgage market during the early 1990s, for example, the relatively low interest rates encouraged both new home purchases and the refinancing of existing mortgages. Many borrowers opted for **adjustable rate mortgages (ARMs)** on which the interest rate changes in response to changes in some specified target rate. This aspect of ARMs makes them attractive to lenders, who have some protection for their earnings against a protracted increase in long-term interest rates. Consumers also have protection against higher mortgage costs in light of increasing interest rates; they often have the right to convert their ARM to a conventional fixed rate mortgage at some specified point in time.

When parties fear that their trading partners may renege on agreements made, they may rely on the **reputation** of those with whom they make deals. Economists view reputation as an institutional device that may be considered part of an organization's capital stock. Reputations are formed on past behavior, and, more important, on others' perceptions of that behavior. Choosing trading partners on the basis of their reputation is one defense against being exploited by a reneging trading partner.

You are probably aware of the importance of reputation and perhaps have some experience with devices created to provide information on a potential trading partner's reputation. One very common certifier of reputations is the local credit bureau, which may help determine whether a person is going to renege on his promise to repay. Local Better Business Bureaus and chambers of commerce often storehouse complaints against retailers, distributors, and contractors so that potential customers can assess their reputations. On a much larger scale, Standard Poor's rates organizations issuing bonds in an attempt to determine the possibility that they will or will not repay their financial obligations.

A different and perhaps larger problem caused by imperfect commitment arises when individuals or organizations are required to make significant investments that are (at least somewhat) specific to a particular purpose. **Investment** is the current expenditure of resources that produces a stream of benefits over future period(s). When a firm or individual invests, an asset is created. There are many types of assets, most usefully categorized by the created asset and its future stream of benefits.

**Asset Specificity
Revisited**

Financial investments purchase assets such as stocks and bonds, yielding a future flow of cash returns. For most people, the single biggest tangible investment they will make is in their home, which provides a stream of housing services over a long period of time. Although we most commonly think of physical investments such as houses, factories, or buildings, investments need not be tangible. Education is clearly not a physical asset, yet it is an investment we make in ourselves to reap future benefits. Economists term investments in education, skills, and training **human capital,** which it is hoped leads to higher future incomes, more meaningful lives, and better decision-making ability.

When considering the costs and benefits of investments, one problematic dimension concerns the asset specificity of an investment. Assets become specific when they are most valuable in one particular transaction or relationship. Physical assets may be highly specific, such as a large office building becoming part of an area or neighborhood. Asset specificity is not limited to physical assets, however. Human capital may be specific to a particular trade or discipline; for example, blue-collar manufacturing workers faced significant unemployment during the decline of manufacturing in the northeast United States during the late 1970s.

Asset specificity becomes a problem in designing efficient contracts when it puts one party at a disadvantage in potential future ex post bargaining situations. The disadvantage arises from a shortage of outside, alternative options.

The opportunities for ex post opportunism are especially important when the specificity applies to more than one asset. **Cospecialized assets** are most productive when used together and lose much of their value or productivity in the absence of the other(s). When assets become cospecialized, the value of the investment to one party depends crucially on the behavior of another asset owner with his or her own agenda and selfish interests. Thus, the door is left open for exploitative ex post opportunistic behavior. The determination of winners and losers in such exchanges is unclear and depends on unquantifiable factors such as the value of an organization's reputation and the alternative opportunities available.

An organization that places a high value on its reputation is less likely to attempt to exploit its position and hold up a trading partner. A damaged reputation may cause other future trading partners to think twice before committing to a joint effort. Cospecialization, like specialization, is a question of degree.

Asset specificity gauges commitment; formally, the specificity of an asset is measured as the percentage of investment value that is lost when the asset is used outside the specific setting or relationship. A higher degree of commitment implies a greater vulnerability to being held up. A higher degree of commitment by your partner is beneficial to you since it lowers the probability that he or she will attempt to hold you up (this would amount to cutting his or her own throat). Likewise, the lower the asset specificity, the more likely one party is to hold up the other.

Consider, for example, a municipality wishing to lure a manufacturing facility into its jurisdiction. Indeed, one common economic development strategy is for a state to promise a factory certain inducements: tax forgiveness, road networks, worker training, low interest loans, and so on. Suppose that an agreement is reached and the state government constructs a road linking the factory site to a major highway. Both negotiating sides have committed specific assets: the state has constructed a road with limited alternative uses, and the manufacturer has sunk development costs to construct its plant. In this case, the road and the plant are cospecialized assets.

In this example, either party could attempt to hold up the other; the specificity of the investments (the road and the factory) is determined by the owners alone. The factory manager could reason that once the state has laid the roadbed, he could make further opportunistic demands for, perhaps, further tax forgiveness or increased worker training. What factors limit the factory manager? Only two: the reputation of the plant in future dealings with the state; with suppliers, labor, and other state governments; and the true alternatives to the state for use of the road. If the state could still profit by extending the road to another site, then at least some of its value could be realized. Likewise, the state could notice that the constructed plant is highly specialized and, arguing economic hardship, prematurely end its tax forgiveness or worker training. This, of course, damages the state's reputation and hinders its attempts to draw additional employers and contributors to the tax base.

The hold up problem deserves our attention for two reasons. First, since it is most prevalent within an investment context, the affected transactions typically involve substantial sums of money. Second, and again because asset specificity is best exemplified in an investment context, the affected transactions typically span a number of time periods. Paul Jaskow, a well-known economist, has produced a number of studies examining the hold up problem in the context of the arrangements between coal-burning electric utility companies and the coal suppliers that serve them. A descriptive account of the bargaining situation facing the mines and the utilities and Jaskow's findings, which are consistent with the transaction cost approach, appears in the following box.

The transaction cost theory suggests that the incentives for firms to write long and detailed contracts increase with the lack of alternative ex post outside opportunities and with the specificity of investments. In a series of related articles, Paul Jaskow confronted the transaction cost approach with real-world evidence.

Jaskow chose to examine the specifics of the relationships between coal-burning electric-generating plants and the mines that provide the coal. The importance of this problem may not be apparent; however, in the mid-1980s, coal generated more than 50 percent of the electricity consumed in the United States. Today, that number may be smaller, given improvements and more widespread adoption of nuclear alternatives. For our purposes, this case is interesting, and the analysis is clear given the apparent and verifiable differences between the coal markets in different sections of the continental United States and the many specificities involved for both buyer and seller.

Coal mines (suppliers) must sink investments in mining capacity. The electric utilities (buyers) must commit specific investments in the amount of generating equipment and in the adaption of boilers to a particular type of coal.

Coal reserves are not distributed uniformly across the country in terms of either quantity or quality. We can roughly distinguish two polar geographic regions. In the East, topography and the nature of coal deposits support underground mining. Eastern coal is relatively homogeneous and there are no significant economies of scale in its production. In the West, strip mining is more common, providing large economies of scale in coal production. There is also more variation in the coal from different Western mines.

A large component of the effective price of coal to users is transportation or shipping costs. Again a regional difference emerges: given a more developed transportation infrastructure, and more shipping agents, transportation costs are much lower in the East.

Jaskow's findings are clearly in line with the predictions of transaction cost analysis. Contracts between buyers and suppliers are typically of much shorter duration in the East. In the Western region, Jaskow found the contracts to be much more complex and for much longer durations in the West. Furthermore, he found that the spot market for coal is very important in the East, but largely insignificant in the West.

In the language of this chapter, we conclude that specificity is an issue in this contracting situation. However, the degree of cospecialization in the eastern coal markets is much lower than the degree of cospecialization in the western coal markets.

Source: Jaskow, P. "Asset Specificity and the Structure of Vertical Relationships: Empirical Evidence," Journal of Law, Economics, and Organization, 4, no. 1 (1988), pp. 95–117.

GOVERNANCE STRUCTURES AND SPECIFICITY

Many economists have studied the role of transaction cost considerations in forming agreements between economic agents. The initial groundwork was laid by the Nobel Prize–winning economist Ronald Coase in his 1937 paper.[12] Coase intro-

The Contributions of Coase and Williamson

---

[12] Coase, "The Nature of the Firm."

duced the idea of transaction costs and argued that efficiency dictates that contractual arrangements be crafted in ways to minimize them. According to the Coasian logic, individuals and organizations choose a contractual format, termed a **governance structure,** from a wide variety of possibilities. On one extreme, transactions could take place within a "market." This extreme is the realm of most traditional theoretical economic analyses: there is perfect information, much competition, and little, if any, room for opportunism.

At the other extreme is the possibility that transactions occur entirely within an organization. If the transaction costs are too high in terms of informational asymmetries, selection problems, or asset specificity, organizations manage these transactions internally, avoiding markets altogether. In the previous chapter, we examined this same problem in terms of major manufacturing firms choosing to make components of their products in house or to rely on outside suppliers.

This train of thought was picked up by Oliver Williamson in his 1975 work, *Markets and Hierarchies.* Williamson sees a "comparative institutional" perspective in which there is a wide range of institutional arrangements that can be used to govern transactions between economic agents. Governance structures emerge in response to various transactional considerations. The boundary between a firm and a market provides a very rough distinction between the two primary institutional arrangements used by economic agents seeking to promote efficiency in defining the relationships between them. Williamson made it clear that firms are able to take on any one of a variety of different organizational structures.

Williamson also argued and provided a variety of examples showing that market transactions can be structured in a variety of ways. One type is the spot market transaction, for which buyer and seller come together at one point in time and exchange. A second alternative is for buyer and seller to craft their relationship with a complex long-term contract. For any given transaction, the chosen governance structure could be either of these two extremes or lie somewhere in the middle.

Of all the different sources of transaction costs, asset specificity has the clearest implications for the form of governance structure chosen by firms. In these instances, spot market transactions can be ruled out. When investment in cospecialized assets is required for efficient exchange and when these investment costs represent a significant portion of the costs of arranging and implementing the transaction, anonymous spot markets will fail. The reasoning relies on expectations of opportunistic behavior. Sinking a relationship-specific investment transfers an ex ante situation that may be competitive into an ex post bargaining situation that is not competitive and is, in fact, a bilateral monopoly. To induce the parties to make optimal investments ex ante, some contractual method is needed to constrain the ex post hold up problem. After ruling out spot markets, we are left with eliminating the opportunities for opportunistic behavior in one of two ways.

The transaction may be designed so that it is entirely within one firm, the vertical integration solution. Alternatively, a long-term relational contract may be written binding the parties together. Any long-term relational contract must preserve individual and joint incentives.

Examples

Logically extending the transaction cost analysis of Coase and Williamson, vertical integration is more likely the more specific the investments are. We revisit the work of Paul Jaskow, which was highlighted earlier in this chapter. Jaskow found that in the western United States, coal investments are effectively more specific than investments by mines and utilities in the eastern United States. Another feature of the coal market is that some utilities construct coal-burning electric-generating facilities at the entrance to a given coal mine. These so-called mine mouth plants are nearly completely cospecialized with the utility facility. As a result, the mine mouth plants and coal mines are always vertically integrated.

The question may be raised as to why more coal mines are not integrated into the utility firms. There are several reasons for this pattern of governance. First, coal producers are aware that energy prices fluctuate and change relative to each other. For example, during the OPEC oil crisis of the mid 1970s, coal prices relative to other competing energy sources declined. United States coal producers had to find new markets for their product. Second, the utility companies may not believe that coal is the permanent technology for creating energy. The utilities are surely aware that technological advances have increased the importance of nuclear energy and that future breakthroughs in solar- and perhaps even fusion-based processes may make them more practical.

Another example of cospecialized assets is provided by Klein, Crawford, and Alchian,[13] who examined the U.S. automobile industry in the early part of the 20th century. As of the early 1920s, General Motors purchased the automobile bodies used by its many divisions from Fisher Body. The threat of competition and the advance of automobile production technology pushed General Motors into constructing a new automobile assembly plant. GM desired greater cooperation from Fisher Body, arguing that product reliability would increase, production could be made more efficient, and massive savings in shipping costs could result if Fisher Body would likewise build a new plant adjacent to the new GM facility. In fact, one plan even suggested that Fisher Body not construct loading docks, road extensions, or rail spurs; instead, Fisher would directly supply GM on the production floor. Fisher balked at these ideas. GM eventually solved the obvious threat of the hold up problem by buying Fisher Body. Klein et al. offer other examples of firms that feared imperfect commitment and opted for the vertical integration solution.

Long-Term Relational Contracts

In his survey of contracts between coal mines and utilities, Jaskow found that future exchange prices were not usually stipulated but indexing was used. Under price indexing, future prices are tied to changes in some established market price. In the coal market, the spot market price is often used. This is a very familiar concept to many home owners who hold adjustable rate mortgages. Under the typical ARM arrangement, only the annual interest rates in the first or first and second years of a 15- or 30-year mortgage are stated. The interest rates in the remaining years are tied to changes in some index of mortgage loans or to changes in a long-term federal government bond rate.

It is also common for the buyer to agree to change prices in response to changes in the seller's (supplier's) costs. This practice is common in the construction industry in which the completion of large projects may take several years. A trade publication, *Engineering News Record*, publishes region-based indexes for the costs of different types of labor, cement, steel, and other inputs to the construction process.

An alternative approach that avoids the ex post hold up problem is to introduce ex post competition wherever possible. Farrell and Gallini[14] and Shepard[15] were the first economists to formally model this process in the context of transaction cost–based models of firm behavior. Suppose that the buyer invests in specific assets and the seller chooses, ex post, some ex ante variable (perhaps quality, deliv-

---

[13]Klein, B., J. Crawford, and A. Alchian, "Vertical Integration, Appropriable Rents, and the Competitive Contracting Process," *Journal of Law and Economics*, 21 (1978), pp. 297–326.

[14]Joseph Farrell and Nancy Gallini, "Second-Sourcing as a Commitment: Monopoly Incentives to Attract Competition, *Quarterly Journal of Economics* (November 1988), pp. 673–694.

[15]A. Shepard, "Licensing to Enhance Demand for New Technologies," Mimeo (New Haven, CT: Yale University Press, 1986).

ery lag, adaptability, or taste) that is not part of the contract. Ex post, the seller has an incentive to choose low quality; therefore, ex ante, the buyer invests little in the relationship. Dual sourcing consists of having two or more suppliers, who compete ex post on quality. This raises the equilibrium level of quality and the ex ante investment. Farrell and Gallini argue that this is a persuasive explanation of why Intel licenses its microprocessor technologies and why IBM adopts an "open architecture" policy in regard to its personal computers.

Reputation

We must also recognize the role of reputation in avoiding future contracting hazards. An excellent article by MacCaulay[16] found that relations between firms tended to be more informal than would be predicted by theory. In long-run relationships, reputation can sustain efficiency. Any firm that cheats (perhaps by making decisions that are not jointly efficient) runs the risk of losing future profitable deals with its partner. Reputation allows a firm to save on the costs of writing complete contracts and even from deciding on some distribution of authority.

▨ THE IMPORTANCE OF CONTRACTING FOR MANAGERS

A manager in today's firm faces a number of challanges. A firm understanding of the economic forces operating behind contracting can help today's manager face these challanges in a value-maximizing way. Whereas lawyers are most interested in what a contract is, the economist is most concerned with what a contract does, which is to organize economic activity.

The two themes of this chapter are the role of information and the likely effects of asset specificity. In a perfectly competive market, neither of these issues is very important or interesting and managers can act in the supply and demand framework taught in basic economics courses. In most exchanges, however, the invisible hand of Adam Smith is joined by other hands, and today's manager must be aware of things such as *bounded rationality*, *asymmetric information*, and *asset specificity*.

The possibility of strategic misrepresentation and adverse selection gives rise to significant transaction costs that can destroy value and impede efficiency. The manager must carefully weigh the costs and benefits of gathering more information and altering the selection of trading partners.

Specialized assets pose another problem more at the heart of today's corporations. The evidence indicates that relational contracts to which parties agree on broad goals, objectives, and some flexibility concerning the involved prices and costs can be a suitable answer.

▨ CHAPTER SUMMARY AND KEY IDEAS ▨ ▨ ▨ ▨ ▨ ▨

Economics is the science that studies the process of exchange. Traditionally, the functioning of markets has been explained within a competitive supply and demand framework. An alternative approach was pursued in this chapter. Our analysis focuses on the relevance of transaction costs in the crafting of contracts, or agreements, between parties that interact. Bounded rationality, contracting, information availability, reputation, and opportunism are the recurring themes in our analysis. If we accept the premise offered by Coase and Williamson, economic units should act to arrange their interactions with other economic units in such a

---

[16]S. MacCaulay, "Non-Contract Relations in Business," *American Sociological Review* 28 (1963), pp. 55–70.

way to minimize the associated transaction costs. We consider such behavior as a movement toward efficiency.

Bounded rationality implies that some uncertainty results in any contractual arrangement. Theoretically, it may be possible to remove the risks associated with contracting; however, the cost of doing so may quite well be infinite. Most employment contracts are largely relational, containing relatively few provisions in light of the nearly infinite possible environments that may occur ex post.

In exchange, information is a very valuable commodity. A number of problems emerge when one party to a transaction holds private information. Strategic misrepresentation is the economist's equivalent to successful bluffing in a poker game. Trade is not likely to be efficient when the threat of strategic misrepresentation exists; parties will expend significant resources to learn the truth about their partners. From an individual perspective, it pays to acquire information concerning your opponent's outside opportunities and costs of delay.

Insurance markets provide an excellent example of another efficiency-reducing aspect of private information. Adverse selection, to a trading partner, most generally means attracting the wrong type of people with whom to do business. Signaling and screening are two market responses to adverse selection.

Ex ante opportunism focuses on the availability of information; ex post opportunism centers on the idea of commitment arising from investments in highly specific assets. Market transactions involving highly specific investments are likely to be carried out with either a long-term contract or entirely within the auspices of a firm, that is, vertical integration.

A governance structure is a feasible way to manage a transaction. Major contributions by Coase and Williamson have emphasized the idea that firms have incentives to choose a governance structure that minimizes the costs of their interaction. Quite often that governance structure is a long-term relational contract.

The effective design of long-term relational contracts requires an alignment of individual and joint incentives that mitigates ex post opportunism (hold-ups or reneging) and is flexible enough to be lived out in an imperfect and unpredictable world. Economics cannot offer any single model of contract design under these conditions. Transaction cost analysis can, however, offer guidelines and suggestions.

◼ KEY TERMS

adjustable rate mortages (ARMs)
adverse selection
asset specificity
block booking
bounded rationality
contract
cospecialized assets
ex ante
explicit contract
ex post
external contract
fungible
governance structure
hold-up
human capital
implicit contract

incomplete contracts
informational asymmetries
internal contract
investment
market discipline
measurement costs
minimum supply price
opportunism
relational contracting
reneging
reputation
reservation price
screening
signaling
strategic misrepresentation

▨ FURTHER READINGS

Coase, R. "The Nature of the Firm." *Economica* 4 (1937), pp. 386–405.

Farrell, J., and N. Gallini. "Second-Sourcing as a Commitment: Monopoly Incentives to Attract Competition." *Quarterly Journal of Economics* (November 1988), pp. 673–694.

Jaskow, P. "Vertical Integration and Long Term Contracts: The Case of Coal-Burning Electric Generating Plants." *Journal of Law, Economics, and Organization* 1 (1985), pp. 33–79.

Jaskow, P. "Contract Duration and Relationship-Specific Investments: The Case of Coal." *American Economic Review* 77 (1987), pp. 168–185.

Jaskow, P. "Asset Specificity and the Structure of Vertical Relationships: Empirical Evidence," *Journal of Law, Economics, and Organization*, 4, no. 1 (1988), pp. 95–117.

Kenney, R. W. and B. Klein. "The Economics of Block Booking," *Journal of Law and Economics*, vol. 26 (1983), pp. 497–540.

MacCaulay, S. "Non-Contract Relations in Business," *American Sociological Review*, 28 (1963), pp. 55–70.

MacMillan, J. "Games, Strategies, and Managers." New York: Oxford University Press, 1992.

Milgrom, P. and J. Roberts. "Relying on the Information of Interested Parties," *Rand Journal of Economics*, 17 (1986), pp. 18–32.

Salop, J. and S. Salop. "Self-Selection and Turnover in the Labor Market," *Quarterly Journal of Economics*, 90 (November 1976), pp. 629–649.

Shepard, A. "Licensing to Enhance Demand for New Technologies," Mimeo, Yale University, 1986.

Williamson, O. *Markets and Hierarchies: Analysis and Antitrust Implications*. New York: Free Press, 1975.

▨ QUESTIONS AND PROBLEMS FOR REVIEW AND DISCUSSION

A. Discuss, in general terms, the value of reputation in a contracting environment. Be sure to indicate how reputation can mitigate the negative efficiency effects of

1. Strategic misrepresentation.

2. Adverse selection.

3. The burden of measurement costs.

4. Asset specificity.

B. Measurement costs may affect efficiency in a number of interesting ways. Consider, for example, the sale of a professional baseball team. Recently, some clubs have sold for tremendous amounts of money. In August 1993, for example, the Baltimore Orioles sold for $173 million.

1. What do you think some of the sources of measurement costs are in such a transaction? Do they involve significant funds being expended?

2. Quite often the sale of a professional sports club invokes a bidding war involving many diverse interests. As in any other form of a bidding war, there is a winner who gets the team and at least one loser who does not. What are the efficiency implications for the measurement costs incurred by the winner? What are the efficiency implications for the measurement costs incurred by the loser?

C. Indicate whether you believe that the following statement is true or false or you are uncertain. In a market characterized as competitive on both the seller and buyer sides, private information is not an issue.

D. In the previous two chapters, we discussed many of the issues surrounding asset specificity and its effects on agreement. Is there a direct efficiency effect of the hold up problem?

E. Adverse selection is a problem of precontractual opportunism; it arises because of the private information held by at least one party to a contract. Consider the market for used cars. There are *good used cars*, which provide a reasonably expected amount of service. There are also *lemons*, which provide far less than a reasonably expected amount of service. Explain how, in this situation, adverse selection may effectively close the market; that is, there will be no voluntary exchanges. An excellent source for the thinking needed to analyze this situation is G. Akerlof, "The Market for Lemons: Qualitative Uncertainty and the Market Mechanism," *Quarterly Journal of Economics* 84 (1970), pp. 488–500.

F. Suppose that I own a small manufacturing plant in central Maryland, Danger, Inc. Danger, Inc., specializes in finely milling specialty sheet steel to a variety of industrial uses. Business is good despite the recession. I am approached by a representative of General Motors concerning the possibility of supplying a local GM plant with product. Currently, all of the GM plants on the East Coast rely on a large parts supplier in western Tennessee. Mine is the only facility of its type in the area that can do the job GM wants done. My reputation and skills are well known. The GM deal would require me to add additional capacity to the point of nearly doubling my manufacturing capacity.

   1. If I accept the deal, what specific assets am I contributing?

   2. One dimension of transaction costs is asset specificity. Is this relevant here? Why or why not, for either or both parties?

   3. Suppose that I accept the deal. What are the aspects of the hold up problem that each contracting party could exploit?

G. Use the information in problem (F). What additional circumstances *could* reduce the Danger's exposure to being held up? What additional circumstances could reduce GM's exposure to being held up? For each of these, list three and be prepared to fully explain and/or defend each listed item.

Contracts: Issues of Discourse

[B]oats are pulled upstream by a team of coolies prodded by an overseer with a whip . . . an American lady, horrified at the sight of the overseer whipping the men as they strained at their harness, demanded that something be done about the brutality. She was quickly informed . . . "Those men own the rights to draw boats over this stretch of water and they have hired the overseer and given him his duties.[1]

CHAPTER OUTLINE AND STUDENT GOALS

Another Important Source of Transaction Costs

The two previous chapters have highlighted the importance of information and commitment in economic exchange. Strategic misrepresentation and adverse selection were seen to negatively impact efficiency in transactions. Asset specificity was shown to be another culprit in affecting efficient exchange. In this chapter, we remain in the realm of bounded rationality and incomplete contracting and examine another ex post contracting problem.

Before proceeding into the detailed analysis, consider these examples of agreements gone awry.

You are a business student at a large state university. To instill in you the ability to work in teams, your economics professor has placed you on a team of students charged with writing a report that will determine your grade for the semester. You notice that throughout the term, some of your team members fail to complete tasks that they agreed to do.

A child is given an extravagant looking toy train set featuring a complete layout of TinyTown, U.S.A. The picture on the box is breathtaking. When opened however, the cardboard cutouts provided seem hideous.

Banks and thrift institutions are just like any other business; they try to "buy low and sell high." They are unique, however, in that the commodity they trade in is money. Buying low means acquiring deposits at low interest rates. Selling high means loaning this same money at higher rates. Financial markets are characterized by a risk-return relation: higher returns are obtained only by incurring the expense of higher risks. Bank managers have incentive to make riskier investments than they otherwise would, putting the solvency of their institutions in jeopardy.

John Rockofellow examines the operations of Acme, Inc., and decides that he could make better (more profitable) use of Acme's assets. Rockofellow buys

---

[1]John McManus, "The Costs of Alternative Economic Organizations," *Canadian Journal of Economics* (August 1975), p. 341.

enough shares in Acme to gain control, fires most of Acme's management, spins off some of its assets, and sets the company in his direction.

You take your car to an auto conditioning specialist who promises to make your car "showroom new." One week later, your car seems to be just as it always was.

In neoclassical theory, none of these events would arise. In the perfectly competitive and fully informed world, competition prevents each of these occurrences. Each classmate on your team would put forth more effort; toy train sets would actually look like those pictured on the box they came out of; and very, very few banks and thrift institutions would ever fail.

The problems in these examples arise out of the arrangement of the exchange between individuals and/or organizations. They are examples of what economists call **moral hazard,** which occurs when one party's actions are imperfectly observable and impact the value of the exchange to other parties. It is common to anticipate moral hazard in situations with imperfect information and when there is a misalignment of incentives. In describing retail markets, consumer protection groups often use the phrase *caveat emptor*, or let the buyer beware. In many settings it may be impossible for buyers to monitor the quality of the goods and services they purchase. As such, sellers may often substitute lower quality and less expensive goods, components, or delivery systems without the buyers' knowledge. Economists have studied moral hazard in this and many other less obvious contexts.

Situations of moral hazard arise frequently in daily life. When you rent a car, you are likely to exercise more caution if you are responsible for damages than if you purchased the collision damage waiver. The prevalence of huge malpractice awards against physicians has led many to practice what is termed "conservative" medicine; that is, to avoid a malpractice suit, they order many tests that probably were not worth the cost.

The term *moral hazard* originated in the insurance industry; it describes situations in which an individual who is insured against certain risks will expend less effort in avoiding those same risks. This context serves to characterize many other situations as well. In the content of bounded rationality and incomplete contracts, a moral hazard framework is useful for analyzing firm organization, team production, shareholder activism, and certain financial characteristics of firms.

Shirking and the Principal-Agent Problem

From an organizational standpoint, moral hazard is a serious problem attributable to the absence of perfect and cost-free monitoring behavior. Employees may have incentive to **shirk,** or to put forth less effort than they otherwise might if their actions could be more effectively monitored.

Why might shirking exist? There are two ways to approach this question. One is to consider the question from an ethical perspective and to argue that shirking is morally wrong. This approach is not within the realm of economics and, thus, not a topic for this book. The question may also be considered from an economic standpoint, which would stress the likely costs and benefits of shirking. Employees recognize that work is distasteful and that the benefit of shirking is the avoiding of work, leaving them free to pursue other options. To the individual, the costs of shirking may be small depending on the employer response and the degree to which the work can be shifted to other members of the organization.

It will often be useful in our discussions to adopt the jargon used by researchers in this field, referring to moral hazard as the **principal-agent problem.** The principal hires the agent to act on the principal's behalf. The problem facing the principal is to observe the agent's actions to determine whether the agent has, in fact, acted to advance the principal's goals. Quite often, as suggested by the terminology, the principal is the authority figure: the owner of the firm, the employer, or the person whose car is being fixed. However, in some instances, this appearance vanishes and the principal is, for example, the depositor or an insurance company. It is important to keep straight who is to be acting on whose behalf rather than who is perceived as an authority in some connotative sense.

After reading this chapter, you should be able to

- Describe, in your own words, what is meant by moral hazard and how this problem emerges in transactions within an informational framework.

- Review and understand the concept of property rights and apply this concept to the organization of a value-creating firm.

- Explain the many problems of team production within a moral hazard context.

- Identify the factors contributing to moral hazard in an insurance setting.

- Recognize the characteristics of the banking industry in the 1980s, particularly the role of deposit insurance, that made it especially susceptible to principal-agent problems.

- Discuss the principal-agent problem in standard employment contracts and in the context of the ownership and control of a corporation.

- Explain the risks facing agents in writing incentive-based contracts.

- Discuss the conditions under which suitable contracting structures may minimize agent risk.

■ PROPERTY RIGHTS, TEAM PRODUCTION, AND ORGANIZATIONS

**Team Production:
A Public Good?**

In Chapter 5, we discussed the issue of property rights and argued that the establishment of well-defined property rights to resources subject to congestion could be seen as an attempt to achieve efficiency gains. The development of institutional structures such as firms can be viewed in the same light. In Chapter 6 we introduced the concept of transaction costs and argued that the firm is a device used to minimize transaction costs. We can add a new viewpoint to the purposes and functions of firms in this section as we emphasize that the contractual relations found within a firm may be viewed as establishing property rights concerning the use of the firm's resources and defining the ownership of what is produced.

This reasoning was first advanced by the economists Alchian and Demsetz,[2] who argued that the creation and allocation of property rights within a firm is a response to transactional problems in general and, in particular, to the problem of **team production,** which occurs when an output is produced by the simultaneous cooperation of several team members. The organizational device called the *firm* then allows people to function as one or more coordinated teams.

As early as Adam Smith, economists understood the benefits of specialization in production. Firms and organizations exist to collectively pool the talents of individuals. An organization may then be viewed as a team. Team production is not

---

[2]See A. A. Alchian and H. Demsetz, "Production, Information Costs, and Economic Organization," *American Economic Review* 62 (1972), p. 77. Another paper written from a finance theory perspective is Eugene Fama, "Agency Problems and the Theory of the Firm," *Journal of Political Economy* 88, no. 2 (1980), pp. 288–307.

a sequence of separate, identifiable stages by members; rather, it results from the simultaneous application of effort by team members. There are two complications facing team production. First, the input of individual members is not identifiable and distinguishable from that of others. Second, the productivity of any one team member depends crucially on the input provided by other members.

The property rights approach to analyzing team behavior shares many similarities with the analysis of public goods presented in Chapter 5. A **public good** is a commodity that has two unique properties. First is the nonrivalous consumption characteristic that says that one individual's consumption of the good does not detract from another individual's enjoyment of the good given its existence. The second property is nonexcludability, or, in other words, consumers cannot be stopped from enjoying the benefits of the public good once it is produced.

Recall that no individual has incentive to produce a public good; however, each individual has incentive to consume it once produced. Its production advances the interests of society. For this reason, public goods are usually provided as one of the functions of government. When asked to pay for a public good, individuals have incentive to strategically misrepresent their valuations of the good. Thus, public goods are generally financed by tax collections.

The concept of team production is subject to these same problems. An agreement by all team members to work harder to increase joint output will be difficult to implement and enforce. Individual team members have incentive to strategically misrepresent their intentions by agreeing to some level of performance that is beneficial to the group and then to shirk and lower their level of performance, knowing full well that their input into the joint output cannot be accurately determined. In the absence of perfect and cost-free monitoring, each person can rationally be expected to shirk and hope to free ride on the efforts of other team members.

A Monitor
as a Residual Claimant

Alchian and Demsetz pursue the property rights argument to provide a solution to the moral hazard inherent in team production. Their solution involves the use of a "monitor" who would be charged with checking on the effort level of members. In many cases, having a full-time designated monitor can alleviate shirking. In other cases, it is prohibitively costly even for a full-time monitor to assess the efforts put forth by team members.

If we assume that a monitor is able to gauge the efforts of individual team members, the problem of determining the pay of the monitor remains. If the monitor is simply a team member who is assigned the monitor role, then she will have the same incentive to shirk as other team members. In common parlance, this is equivalent to putting the "fox in charge of the henhouse."

To promote efficiency, the role of the monitor must be defined as having some property rights to what is produced. Efficiency dictates that the monitor be made a **residual claimant** to the benefits of joint production. Each member of the team receives a contractually determined wage for his efforts; after these and all other expenses have been paid, the monitor receives whatever residual is left. The more effectively the team operates, the bigger the residual will be. Thus, the monitor has a definite interest in promoting the efficiency of the team.

Ownership and Control:
A Connection

Recall our discussion in Chapter 5 of the tragedy of the commons. A single resource (grazing land) is allocated to multiple users. In the absence of established property rights, the land is owned by everyone, but effectively no one. The ruin of the commons could be prevented by assigning ownership to some party who would allocate its current use in such a way to guarantee its future existence. The monitor, in some capacity as a residual claimant, is effectively given property rights to the output produced by the team. If the monitor is also given control over the contractual arrangements, then, by pursuing her own selfish interests, she encourages efficiency in team production.

While seemingly intuitive, the logic that a strong connection exists between the owners of an enterprise and those who control the enterprise has far-reaching implications. In Chapter 1, we identified the separation of ownership and control as a major organizational problem to be overcome as firms attempt to organize economic activity to maximize value. This is the same problem as that facing the common grazing land in that famous example of a public good causing market failure.

There may be some doubt forming in your mind at this point. You may stand ready to question the relevance of our discussion of property rights and team production by pointing out that no one entity could ever simultaneously "own" and "control" a firm such as IBM or Intel. Actually, your point is right on the mark and well taken. No single entity could ever accomplish this task. The problem facing large and small organizations is to determine the best way to simulate, or approximate, this necessary connection between ownership and control.

In any joint production effort, suppose that one worker is thought to be performing poorly. His first reply is that he was adversely affected by some random element such as a mechanical defect, poor materials, or the receipt of bad data owing to some transmission error. His second reply is that other team members failed to perform to specification, reducing the effectiveness of his effort. Since both of these replies rely on the importance of random effects, they illustrate the nature of the risks involved in monitoring.

The complex web of contractual relations within an organization may reasonably be expected to exhibit instances of moral hazard. Firm production has been termed *team production* and presents several difficulties. Any team member's output is determined only at great effort. One solution that would promote efficiency is to appoint a monitor who is also made a residual claimant to the value created by the firm.

■ TEAM PRODUCTION: COORDINATION AND MOTIVATION

A More Managerial Look at the Issues

In the previous section, we discussed the issue of property rights and the organization of productive resources accomplished by firms in a team, or joint, production context. In this section, we continue along these lines, but now we examine the same situation in more of a managerial context. In addition, we expand the ownership and property rights line of reasoning into several applied dimensions. We now consider the incentive problem, the horizon problem, and the inalienability problem facing managers in team production situations in virtually all companies and organizations.

The Incentive Problem

For the selfish individual, team production presents incentives to shirk largely for two related reasons. First, it is impossible to exactly determine the effort put forth by any individual member; hence, management (or the principal) cannot determine exactly which individuals are shirking. Second, the individual reaps all the gains from her own shirking; the costs are distributed over all members of the group. The dilemma posed in providing motivation in these situations is termed the **incentive problem.**

Management's attempts to deal with the incentive problem can be categorized into two general techniques: the carrot method and the stick method. The **carrot method** covers all incentive packages that attempt to encourage individual responsibility by linking an employee's pay to performance. In a sense, commissions assign property rights to the employee to the output created by the team. If extra output is created, at least some of this additional value is passed along to the employee. In a limited sense, then, commissions or productivity bonuses assign the team member some property rights to the residual value of production.

To see why, consider the view of the firm offered by Alchian and Demsetz discussed in the last section. Under this view, the firm organizes productive activity and pays the factors of production a fixed wage. Any value remaining flows to the residual claimant. The main result of the work of Alchian and Demsetz is that an arrangement that places contractual rights in the hands of a so-called monitor promotes efficiency and alleviates some aspects of the principal-agent problem. Clearly, the carrot method of providing commission-based and other performance-based pay schemes is a step in that direction. Who better to fill the role of the monitor than the employee himself?

The **stick method** implies another less subtle approach. In its crudest form, the stick method may amount to a supervisor yelling at, perhaps even threatening to fire, employees in response to some perceived misdeed. Usually, the stick method involves a substantial set of work rules coupled with a great deal of monitoring or supervision.

The choice of either a carrot or a stick approach in designing incentive systems is usually a question of degree; although for a number of reasons, we expect one or the other to be predominant.

The **horizon problem** refers to the potential mismatch between the planning horizon of the decision maker and the planning horizon of those affected by the manager's decision. Put another way, the horizon problem highlights the possibility that planners are not inclined to impute into their decision calculus the costs and benefits that their current actions might have after they have left the business.

Analogous to the incentive problem, the horizon issue is also within the realm of property rights, only along a temporal dimension. The manager, or decision maker, has property rights that expire at some date known perhaps only by the manager. If the manager is a residual claimant today, it may be in her interests to alter the current and future stream of costs and benefits. If possible, she can cause the benefits to occur prior to the expiration of her property rights and the costs to occur after. In a more common language, the selfish manager may leave others "holding the bag."

Sometimes efficiency is affected in organizations when the net benefit flows from a business relationship cannot be sold by those who currently hold the rights to those flows. When this occurs, economists say that the manager faces the **inalienability problem.** There is a distinct difference between the inalienability problem and the horizon problem discussed earlier. The horizon problem involves situations in which property rights could be transferred by the current holder and concerns the value of those rights. The inalienability problem is relevant when those rights effectively cannot be transferred.

An individual's skills and reputation represent an excellent example of an inalienable asset that must be managed. The role played at Microsoft, the dominant software firm, by William Gates continues to astound business analysts. The popular business press has linked the success of Microsoft with the name of its energetic founder. In his role, Mr. Gates has rights to the future benefit flows earned by Microsoft into the next century. However, to a certain extent, these rights are clearly inalienable since if Mr. Gates were to leave Microsoft, the value of the future benefit flows would be tremendously reduced.

In any team production setting, the manager not only must be concerned with monitoring the actions of the team members but also must be made aware of the incentives facing each team member. What we have discussed in this section are managerial problems that occur within the broader realm of moral hazard. The incentive, inalienable asset, and horizon problems each concern not only the monitoring of team members but also the incentives faced by each team member.

The Horizon Problem

The Inalienability Problem

■ MORAL HAZARD IN INSURANCE MARKETS

Moral hazard arises in contracting situations for two reasons: positive measurement costs and misaligned incentives. Insurance markets provide a rich environment for moral hazard. In order to fully appreciate the role played in insurance markets by moral hazard, we must review the basic mechanics governing exchange in insurance markets.

With the exception of the gypsy fortune teller present at most carnivals and charity bazaars and a few shady characters who routinely are found near horse racing tracks, most individuals are unable to predict the future. Everyone faces future risks in the form of possible losses (and theoretically, gains). Families risk having their homes burgled or burned down; individuals risk death, poor health, or accidents requiring visits to doctor; multinational corporations risk changes in exchange rates; farmers risk the loss of their crops. We define **risk-averse individuals** as those who dislike risk and are willing to pay some explicit or implicit payment to have the risk removed.

In each of these situations, institutions that serve an insuring function have emerged to transfer the risk from one party to another. Property insurance eliminates a family's risk concerning fire and theft. Medical and life insurance eliminate individual risks of poor health and early death. A variety of financial contracts consisting of options, forward contracts, and futures exists to protect multinational corporations from sudden, unanticipated swings in the exchange rate and farmers from unforeseen bad (and good) weather.

In every insurance situation, there are a buyer and a seller of risk. In the preceding examples, the families and individuals sell risk to insurance companies. The multinational firm and the farmer effectively sell risk to investors in the financial markets. The gain to the sellers of risk is clear: they benefit from transferring their risk to another party. The gain to the buyer of the risk is not so obvious.

Insurance companies and other buyers of risk profit for one simple reason: the pooling of independent risks. Two events are said to be independent if the occurrence of one does not change the probability that the other will occur. For example, the fact that you won last night's card game will not influence the probability that you will win tomorrow's lottery drawing. More important, the fact that Mr. Jones, a policyholder of Bangup Auto Insurance Company, is filing a claim to cover a loss from an auto accident today does not influence the probability that Ms. Smith, a second policyholder of Bangup Auto Insurance Company, will file a claim today.[3]

The one basic truth behind the economics of insurance is that when several parties face independent risks, these risks can be shared, and the costs of bearing these risks can be reduced, if not technically eliminated. The **principle of risk sharing**—the sharing of independent risks reduces the total cost of bearing the risk—underlies all financial insurance arrangements.

Insurance companies can profit by bearing the risk of policyholders and effectively pooling them. Of course, if the risks are not independent, pooling may fail to reduce the risk to the insurance company. Property insurers in Florida made very large payouts in 1993 in response to the extensive damage done by Hurricane Andrew. Many insurers rightly argued that pooling the risks of Florida property owners was unprofitable given that the risk that any one policyholder would file a claim from hurricane damage was not independent from the risk that other policyholders would file similar claims.

---

[3]Unless, of course, it is known that Mr. Jones happened to bump into Ms. Smith.

Even if an insurer is able to pool the perceived risks in an effort to eliminate them, moral hazard problems in which the insurer is the principal and the insured the agent must be overcome. The insured (agent) can affect the benefits from the transaction received by the insurer (principal) in a number of ways. First, the agent can take more risks than he would in the absence of insurance. Second, the agent can lie to the principal concerning the terms of the insurance contract. This would be the case, for example, if the agent claims to have taken steps to minimize the risks to the insurer.

Moral hazard is present in insurance markets if two conditions hold. First, after purchasing an insurance policy, the insurance buyer (agent) must be able to take actions that alter the probability of the loss or the size of the loss. Second, it must be so costly for the principal (insurance seller) to observe these actions that monitoring the buyer's actions is economically infeasible. Because of these high monitoring costs, the insuring company cannot change the terms of the policy after the insured acts to change the risks she transfers. The insurance company is then exploited by a consumer.

In the insurance setting, it is hard to determine the efficiency impacts of moral hazard. Consider life insurance; it seems unlikely that a great many people would alter their behavior in such a way to encourage their own death simply so that their beneficiaries can cash in on their policies. A small percentage of individuals do, however, commit suicide. Insurance companies have taken steps to mitigate the impact of policyholder suicide. All life insurance policies issued in the United States contain provisions barring payment of claims for suicide before a specified amount of time has elapsed (either one or two years). Milgrom and Roberts report that life insurance statistics show that the probability that a policyholder commits suicide is lowest in the 12th or 24th month after the policy has been issued and highest in the 13th and 25th months.[4]

Regarding health insurance, again it is difficult to determine whether the moral hazard problem encourages inefficient behavior. In this context, we would expect individuals to visit doctors more than they otherwise would. At one extreme, some individuals will overuse this resource and visit the doctor for every little (normal) ache, pain, and sneeze. Clearly, any arrangement that encourages a healthier society has at least some efficiency characteristics and is not, by definition, socially inefficient.

From this perspective, moral hazard in certain insurance markets may not be wasteful, damaging, or evil. All it represents is that insurance coverages have lowered the cost of something that people value—medical care. Being that individuals are rational, they simply consume more of that good. Regarding medical insurance, it can even be argued that efficiency gains exist from this "overuse." In the next section, we discuss a particular financial insurance arrangement plagued by moral hazard. Federally sponsored deposit insurance programs are typically plagued by principal-agent problems, and it can be easily argued that these inefficiencies and "perverse incentives" *are* wasteful, damaging, and possibly evil from society's point of view.

■ THE FEDERAL DEPOSIT INSURANCE CRISIS

The prominent role of deposit insurance in our economic system is best understood by first reflecting on the history of deposit insurance schemes in the United States. The first step in understanding the problems with these programs unfortu-

---

[4]Paul Milgrom and John Roberts, *Economics, Organization and Management* (Englewood Cliffs, NJ: Prentice Hall, 1992), p. 178.

Chapter 8
Contracts: Issues of Discourse

Importance of Deposit Insurance in the United States

nately involves a very simple understanding of the balance sheets of deposit-taking institutions in our economy. Of particular importance are the items on that balance sheet that represent the position of the owners of the institution.

The second step in understanding the failure of federally sponsored deposit insurance problems in the late 1980s and early 1990s involves an appreciation of the forces at work in and around the banking industry. We can identify the severe moral hazard problems between the principal, the federal government (and all taxpayers), and the agents, insured deposit-taking institutions. As we shall see later, the agents' incentives were not consistent with the interests of the principal, a situation made worse by a failure of monitoring mechanisms.

The Federal Deposit Insurance Corporation crisis also shares a key element from the team production reasoning considered earlier: the agents do not share the full cost of their actions; rather, these costs are shared by other deposit-taking institutions and eventually by Jane and John Q. Public.

Sorry—A Brief History Lesson

In response to the Great Depression, the U.S. Congress created the Federal Deposit Insurance Corporation (FDIC) and the Federal Savings and Loan Insurance Corporation (FSLIC) in the 1930s. The purpose of these programs was to protect the savings and checking deposits of U.S. citizens in the event of institution failure. All commercial banks were insured by the FDIC; the FSLIC insured deposits in the nation's savings and loans. Deposit insurance was not a new idea in the United States. Between 1907 and 1924, eight midwestern states had enacted their own deposit insurance programs; each of these failed quickly and spectacularly.[5] In our discussion, we will not differentiate between commercial banks and savings and loan institutions, referring to each of them simply as banks. There is little harm in this simplification, and when we do focus on events in the savings and loan industry, we will drop this simple terminology.

For the first 50-odd years, the federally mandated deposit insurance systems seemed to work well. Banks rarely failed. In the mid-1980s, however, bank failures increased markedly; within several years, more banks had failed than in the preceding 50 years. The impact on the FDIC and FSLIC was enormous. The FSLIC went bankrupt in 1986; the FDIC followed in 1990. By *bankrupt*, we mean that the cost of bailing out failed institutions (claims against the insurance fund) exceeded the cumulative stock of current and past premiums. Differences are borrowed from the U.S. Treasury.

A Bank's Balance Sheet

Before we can fully discuss and explain the underlying forces behind the deposit insurance crisis, it is necessary to review some of the basic "mechanics" behind the operations of a deposit-taking institution if we are to fully develop the importance of moral hazard issues in the most direct way.

Consider the balance sheet of a bank. On the one side are the assets, things the bank owns: cash, the bank's deposits at the Federal Reserve, and loans and investments. On the other side are the liabilities of the bank, the funds the bank owes to others; for the most part, these are deposit accounts. A very important third component, owners' equity, represents the capital used by the owners of the institution to finance the operation of the bank. According to a basic accounting identity,

$$\text{Assets} = \text{Liabilities} + \text{Owners' Equity}$$

---

[5]A history of the deposit guarantee programs and evidence of regulatory involvement in their failure can be found in C. Thies and D. Gerlowski, "Bank Capital and Bank Failure, 1921–1932: Testing the White Hypothesis," *Journal of Economic History*, 53, no. 4 (December 1993), pp. 908–914; and "Deposit Insurance: A History of Failure," *The Cato Journal* (Spring/Summer 1989).

A bank is said to be solvent so long as the value of its assets and owners' equity exceeds its liabilities. Recall that a portion (in fact, a very large portion) of a bank's assets are the loans and investments it has made. Solvency requires then that if push came to shove and depositors demanded their deposits, the bank could pay them. Funds could be raised by selling off some of the bank's assets; if this were not sufficient, funds could be taken from the owners' stake in the institution.

The owners' equity represents the amount of capital invested in a bank or savings institution. The institution's charter is another source of value to the owners of the bank. No one can open and operate a deposit institution without obtaining a charter from either the state or national banking authorities. Obtaining a charter requires a substantial application process by which the authorities approve the major players in any proposed bank and by which minimum capital requirements and market definition are determined. In the managerial context, a bank's charter represents an inalienable asset, that is, one whose value cannot be transferred from the current holder.

Traditionally, the chartering agencies did not encourage "reckless" competition among banks and limited the number of charters in any one market. Thus, the charter became an entry barrier supporting profits for some lucky institutions and functioning much like the certification and license requirements for practicing medicine or law or for providing certain accounting services. These restrictions deter entry into the medical, legal, and accounting industries and, thus, safeguard the incomes of many doctors, lawyers, and accountants. In other words, the charter of a bank may have value. Owners may have incentive not only to protect their own capital but also to protect the value of their charter.

If depositors are fairly sophisticated and can determine that a bank's assets are quickly falling in value, they may fear for their deposits. This fear is taken away by the presence of deposit insurance. If the depositor knows that her funds are safeguarded by some party, then she will not fear bank failure. Deposit insurance is clearly in the interest of the depositor; it protects her vested interest regardless of the health of the deposit institution (up to some maximum amount, currently $100,000). The guarantee effectively removes any incentive depositors may have in monitoring the banks that hold their balances.

Although beneficial to the public, the existence of deposit insurance creates quite a different set of incentives for the bank owners. Bank management knows that because depositors' interests are guaranteed by the government, depositors will not carefully watch the actions of management, who will seek to exploit the risk return trade-off, trying to increase their profits. Their loans will become a bit more speculative. They may even reduce their equity to increase the rate of return on their capital. Remember that the owners' equity represents capital they have invested in the organization, and they will always act to earn as many rewards as possible.

In the late 1970s and early 1980s, the environment began to change at both commercial banks and savings and loans. Interest rates began to rise. Institutions that had previously made long-term loans at low interest rates (3 percent to 6 percent) were having to pay double that to attract deposits to support those loans. This proved especially difficult for the nation's savings and loans (or thrift institutions), which traditionally held a large portion of their assets in residential mortgages. New competitors emerged; life insurance companies and other financial intermediaries offered to lend money to what used to be the customers of banks and savings and loans. Some of the best corporate borrowers were lost to the emerging direct market for corporate debt.

At the same time, restrictions on markets were crumbling. Aggressive institutions appeared in geographic markets that had been profitable for years. Bank ex-

**The Environment
Begins to Change**

**Moral Hazard Rears
Its Ugly Head**

pansion was encouraged by economies of scale (the reduction in unit costs at higher levels of output) in banking services. Banks expand by increasing the size of their loan portfolios. Quick expansion means to take on more risk, either in terms of less diversification or lower probability of repayment.

For thrifts, the higher interest rates paid for deposits meant, in effect, buying high and selling low, given their emphasis on residential mortgages. Further, many thrifts had expanded their lending in commercial real estate: shopping malls, resorts, and office buildings. Many of these projects were large, glamorous, hyped by publicity, and unprofitable. Unfortunately, in some regions of the country (notably Florida, California, and Texas), land values began to fall, and many development schemes went belly up. Thus, the value of the assets of many thrifts fell drastically.

Using the preceding basic accounting identity, given that the value of the thrifts' assets had deteriorated, the value of the equity stake held by management fell as well.

A second, more subtle, factor also contributed greatly to the moral hazard problem faced by thrifts. When an institution is protected from competition, it has market power and earns significant economic profits. The increased competition fostered by regulations (ironically, these regulations were designed to help the industry) eroded the value of their charters.

These events undermined the incentives for the owners of thrifts to engage in safe banking. With little to lose and deposit insurance to cover the downside, thrift managers increased the risk of their loan portfolios. On the upside, if these risky loans paid off, the larger profits would earn them bonuses and restore profitability to their institutions. On the downside, if the new, riskier loans and investments failed, the owners would lose little more than they already had, and the risk would have been transferred to the deposit insurance program.

**Two Early Regulatory
Responses**

The regulators responded to this crisis in 1980 on two fronts. First was the policy of **regulatory forbearance,** which allowed insolvent thrifts to continue operations in the naive hope that continued operations would restore profitability. Most notably, the regulators allowed thrift institutions to change their accounting methods of evaluating assets to a way that overstated their values. The insolvent institutions became known as "zombie" thrifts.

The second part of the regulatory response was to allow thrifts to invest in assets that were previously unallowed. Thrifts were permitted to invest in more nonresidential real estate and, most notably, junk bonds.

The justification for these policies was that the cost of the clean-up was much too high. The General Accounting Office estimated in 1982 that, at that time, it would have cost $20 billion to close down all the insolvent thrifts and pay the insured depositors. Of course, by 1988, the actual cost of dealing with some of the thrift problem was close to $70 billion. Inflation alone accounts for only about six percent of the increase.

Clearly, neither of these responses served to mitigate the moral hazard problem facing the thrift owners. By 1988, the FSLIC was unable to keep up with the problem. Monitoring was difficult, given the large number of institutions becoming insolvent and because of staff reductions within the FSLIC caused by the federal budget cuts ordered by President Reagan.

The closer a bank is to insolvency, the more serious the moral hazard problem becomes. In the mid-1980s, the equity and charter values of many institutions were pretty much gone; as such, equity holders had little to lose. The delay in closing these institutions provided the motivation to gamble with depositors' money. The lax restrictions on allowable investments gave thrift owners something to gamble with.

By 1988, even the reluctant regulators were willing to admit to a problem. Their initial response was the passage of the Financial Institution Reform, Recovery, and Enforcement Act (FIRREA) of 1989. FIRREA abolished FSLIC and moved thrift institutions under the FDIC umbrella of coverage and regulation. The Federal Home Loan Bank Board, which was responsible for thrift supervision, was replaced with a new Office of Thrift Supervision housed in the Treasury Department. Deposits at thrifts were then insured by a new Savings Association Insurance Fund, a division of the FDIC. In addition to these organizational changes, regulatory changes were also instituted.

Under FIRREA, capital requirements at thrifts were doubled, putting them on par with those at commercial banks. Additionally, assets were grouped according to risk; higher risk assets could be held only if increasingly higher percentages of capital were held to support them. FIRREA also changed the pattern of loans and investments of thrifts. Savings and loans are now required to have 70 percent of their assets in mortgage-related investments; commercial real estate loans could be no more than four times capital.

Each of these changes was designed to force an institution's owners to have a larger stake in their business. Thrifts were allowed to make risky investments, but only if the owners set aside increasingly more capital to be available if the riskier investments were to fail. Obviously, the new standards are designed to provide incentives to thrift owners to pick their investments more carefully.

FIRREA and later legislation, the Federal Deposit Insurance Corporation Improvement Act (FDICIA) of 1991, did two additional things to eliminate the agency problems at banks and thrifts. First, all institutions were made subject to more careful (and, it was threatened, more frequent) audits by regulatory agencies. Second, this legislation gave the FDIC more powers to close institutions. The legislation prohibits zombie institutions. Additionally, current law phases out the ability of the FDIC to reimburse depositors over the stated maximum amount, currently $100,000. The effects of these laws, it is hoped, will be to remove more of the perverse incentives created by deposit insurance. Insolvent institutions will not be able to undertake undue risk, counting on the deposit insurance system to bail them out. Furthermore, large institutional depositors will have incentive to closely monitor the financial well-being of their institutions.

■ MORAL HAZARD: IMPACT ON THE ORGANIZATION

Employment relationships are essentially incomplete contracts written between employers and employees. Because of their incomplete nature, there are many implications of the vagueness of these relationships. Now we consider only one dimension of this vagueness, that associated with imperfect monitoring and the misalignment of interests of the principal and the agent. The worker recognizes that monitoring is imperfect and that she may enjoy the full benefits of her shirking while spreading the costs of her shirking around, to be borne by all team members.

Employee Shirking

The importance of moral hazard in employment situations is evidenced by the large number of incentive pay systems currently in use. As will be argued later in the section on contractual risks for the agent, perhaps the most efficient compensation scheme involves workers being paid for the effort they supply to their employer. The employee provides his intellect, charm, computer skills, knowledge, and the sweat off his back. It is, however, impossible to directly measure this effort, so employers often base pay on measured output, which itself is subject to random influences.

The problem within the employment relationship is how to motivate workers

The world in which the CEOs of major corporations live and work has long been special: large salaries, extremely high standards of living, and stability. For a number of executives, all of that changed abruptly in the last week of January 1993. During that week, many shareholders banded together and screamed "Enough," dismissing their CEOs in the process.

James D. Robinson, former chief executive officer at American Express, had apparently won a battle of wills with his corporation's board of directors. The board agreed to keep him in place. A number of stockholders who were quite unhappy with Mr. Robinson's accomplishments lobbied board members and other key executives at American Express. The actions of the largest stockholder, J.P. Morgan Bank, were instrumental in these efforts. Mr. Robinson soon resigned.

Similar changes took place at IBM and Westinghouse, two icons of corporate America that also announced during that week that their chief executives would be leaving. Paul E. Lego was replaced as chairman of Westinghouse. Lego had come to Westinghouse in July 1990 when the value of Westinghouse stock was $36 per share; at the time of his encouraged departure, the stock price had fallen to $13.

Shareholders had often criticized Sears, Roebuck, and Co.'s operations. The giant retailer responded by announcing that it would terminate its historic catalog operations and close 113 stores in an effort to boost profits and increase its stock price.

As late as 1990, many investor analysts viewed shareholder rights movements largely as an academic exercise. That attitude has changed drastically. Investors demanded tough answers during the recession and a bigger say in corporate operations.

Source: Much of this material is taken from "Shareholders' New Power Reshaping the Corporate Landscape of America," The Baltimore Sun, February 1, 1993, p. A1. The depth and breadth of the shareholder activism movement regarding the removal of CEOs are questioned in "Shareholder Activism, Despite Hoopla, Leaves Most CEOs Unscathed," The Wall Street Journal, May 24, 1993, p. A1. Reprinted by permission of The Wall Street Journal, © 1993 Dow Jones & Co., Inc. All Rights Reserved Worldwide.

whose actions the principal can only imperfectly observe. In Chapter 12, we focus on this issue in greater detail. For now, suffice it to say that one way of dealing with moral hazard problems in the employment relationship is for management to reward workers who do not shirk, but to withhold these rewards for some period.

Managerial Misbehavior: When the Bosses Shirk

Although most of us envision shirking as a response of the typical rank and file worker, it is not at all uncommon of employees at much higher levels in large organizations. We now discuss two aspects of **managerial misbehavior** that have attracted ample attention in recent years and that involve the tricky relationship between firm managers and stockholders. Within these organizations, the goals of upper management may be quite different from the goals of the shareholders; given that shareholders have limited ability to monitor the performance of CEOs, the framework is ripe for agency problems. A second source of managerial misbehavior became evident in the surge of corporate takeovers during the 1980s and early 1990s. The justification for many of these takeovers was simple. A target firm was viewed as having certain assets and a management team that did not make the best use of those assets. The acquiring firm would then have reason to purchase shares in the target firm and put the assets of the target firm to this better use.

The roles of upper management and boards of directors in large corporations are related. Senior executives are to advance the interests of the firm's owners (shareholders), and the board of directors is to supervise these managers. Thus, as is well known, in large corporations, there is a **separation of ownership and control.**

The difficult situation is compounded by the incentives of the owners. Frequently, ownership is spread over many different individuals and institutions, none of which may have the resources or interests in any one company in which they invest. Large institutional investors have traditionally taken a hands-off approach and concentrated their efforts on diversification.

Critics of this ownership system maintain that CEOs' interests are quite different from the owners' interests and that it has become quite difficult for the owners to discipline their management teams. The interests of the managers may well be served by keeping unprofitable operations, resisting takeovers, pursuing short-term profits at the expense of longer-term increases in firm value, and lavishing themselves with perquisites. Additionally, it became common practice at many large firms for the CEO to name some members of the board of directors.

Economists have concluded that it is not at all clear that upper management teams are disciplined when necessary. The interests of owners and managers may be aligned in two fairly subtle ways. First, the managers' compensation packages may provide stock in the firm they manage. Second, the reputation of the manager may serve to influence her behavior. The manager might recognize that ultimately her employment is at the will of the stockholders; it would be wise to maintain some interest in her own marketability. A manager who takes undue advantage of imperfect monitoring may find it quite difficult to pursue other employment opportunities.

The ultimate form of discipline occurs when a manager or CEO is displaced by unhappy stockholders. When shareholders take an active role in the firm's operations and attempt to secure drastic changes in the organization, they are said to participate in **shareholder activism.**

Shareholder activism is becoming more of a force in U.S. stock markets. Starting in 1993, many institutional investors got into the act to influence the decisions of managements in which they have a large stake. The ultimate form of discipline for the corporate managers is, of course, the threat of corporate takeover, the topic to which we now turn.

There is a strong efficiency argument behind corporate takeovers. Suppose that existing management of a firm has operated so that the value of the firm is approximately $2 million. The 50,000 shares of the firm in the hands of the public are routinely bought and sold at prices very close to $400 per share. An alternative management team may feel confident that it can make better use of the firm's resources, perhaps believing that it can raise the value of the firm to $3 million. The alternative management team would then be willing to pay as much as $3 million/50,000 per share to own the firm. The acquiring firm would, of course, attempt to keep its actual valuation of the target firm secret.

In this light, takeovers may be viewed as auctions. The shares of publicly traded companies are available for sale if their current owners can be induced to part with them. Efficiency dictates that the shares should go to the highest bidder for, in that case, the assets that compose the target firm will be put to their best use. Some market professionals talk of a **takeover market,** or, equivalently, of a **market for corporate control,** in which buyers actively identify and pursue firms they deem attractive.

The threat of a takeover provides an important disciplinary device even for firms not seen as potential targets. A well-managed firm is unlikely to be taken over since the acquiring party would be hard pressed to make better use of the firm's assets.

The efficiency-enhancing aspects of takeovers may seem to be obvious. The principal-agent problem may imply, in a large corporation, that members of the management team are taking advantage of the firm, acting in a way to enrich themselves at the expense of shareholders. The threat of takeover, or takeover itself, may be sufficient to correct this inefficiency, but it may create others.

Very often, takeovers involve a restructuring of the acquired firm: some divisions or facilities are closed, and others are sold off. The repercussions of these changes may be quite negative from the employee's view. Nobody likes to have his job dropped or moved to some distant location. Recall that behind the concept of efficiency is the idea that everyone can be made better off without making anyone else worse off. In the merger and acquisition game, a new corporate structure represents a different allocation of resources. Regarding this change, all involved parties do not typically get the chance to influence the outcome.

A second and more direct argument against the efficiency of corporate takeovers is the creation of poison pills by the acquiring firms.[6] A **poison pill** is a defense against corporate takeover under which the target firm agrees to allow its current shareholders to purchase additional shares in the firm once some designated third party acquires a set percentage of the ownership of the firm. This strategy raises the cost of acquiring the firm. Poison pills may seem to be a good way to prevent corporate takeover, but their value to shareholders is dubious.

First, recall that shareholders may favor takeover, preferring either to sell their shares at the higher price offered by the acquiring firm or to maintain share ownership and enjoy the larger profits earned by the acquiring firm (of course, this option requires a shared vision of future success). Second, notice that poison pills are clearly in the interest of the firm's current managers, who may use them to avoid market discipline for inefficient management. Michael Jensen[7] has collected evidence on the use of poison pills by large corporations and has come to some startling conclusions. Once a firm adopts a poison pill takeover defense, the value of the firm typically falls. Also firms that are more likely to adopt poison pill defenses are firms for which the managers and members of the board of directors typically hold very few of the company shares.

**Other Sources
of Agency Problems**

Another source of agency problems arising in modern corporations involves how the firm finances its activities. Typically, firms are financed through a combination of **debt** and **equity.** Debt holders have loaned the firm money without receiving an ownership stake in return: bond holders, suppliers who offer credit, and banks. Equity holders, on the other hand, are the stockholders in most corporate structures. Usually, the debt holders receive fixed, stipulated payments while equity holders are residual claimants on current and future profits.

In some instances, disagreement arises between those holding debt in the firm and those owning shares of stock. The reason is fairly straightforward. Debt holders have no say in the operation of the firm, but stockholders do. At times, the interests of these two groups diverge and the debt holders feel at odds with the stockholders. During the late 1980s and continuing into the 1990s, this situation

---

[6]More will be said in Chapter 11 on poison pills, white knights, raiders, greenmail, and golden parachutes in the context of corporate takeovers.

[7]Michael Jensen, "Takeovers: Their Causes and Consequences," *Journal of Economic Perspectives* 2 (1988), pp. 21–48.

began to change as debt holders began placing demands and restrictions on the firms that borrowed their funds. We will pick up this train of thought again in Chapter 10.

The crisis in federally provided deposit insurance is an excellent example of this in a somewhat related context, so we will not dwell on it again. Basically, the equity holders are those who own the bank; the debt holders are depositors.

ADJUSTMENTS AND ALLOWING FOR MORAL HAZARD

Relationship
Between Monitoring
and Efficiency

Moral hazard in a contracting environment creates so-called agency problems in relationships in which a principal basically hires an agent to pursue the principal's interests. If it were cost free to monitor the actions of the agent and the actions of many agents can be readily checked, then there are no implications for economic efficiency. In some cases, however, the actions of the agent are observed imperfectly and the agent and principal do not share the same incentives.

This section discusses some of the issues surrounding efforts taken to mitigate the efficiency-reducing effects of moral hazard. In all fairness, we point out that moral hazard cannot be eliminated in many situations but that the parties to a transaction simply adjust to its presence. We also make frequent use of the organizational, insurance, and ownership examples discussed previously.

The logical choice for eliminating agency problems is to improve monitoring activities by lowering their cost. U.S. corporations are required, for example, to have certain financial reports audited by independent accounting firms. Presumably, independent auditors would not share with the audited corporations any gains from the production of false or misleading financial statements.

In the instance of health insurance, most health maintenance organizations (HMOs) do not allow patients to see highly specialized doctors without a recommendation from a general practitioner. If market charges are any indication, the services of general practitioners cost much less than the services of a physician with a much smaller area of expertise. Requiring a referral is an attempt by the HMO to monitor patient behavior.

One of the major problems in the deposit insurance crisis was a lack of monitoring by the regulatory staffs of state and local governments. The alternative incentives of the typical CEO and her shareholders present problems that may be reduced by monitoring. If the shareholders are willing, their efforts may directly influence the actions of CEOs and corporate boards of directors. As previously noted, one interesting truth in the matter is that CEOs often demand to appoint at least some of the members of the boards of directors.

Monitoring is typically a costly behavior and may require good faith on the part of the agent in developing an appropriate measurement. Consider the deposit insurance crisis; the insurance-providing agency (the principal) depends on the accounting and other records kept by the insured institution (agent). It was not unheard of for banks to lie to regulators or to misrepresent the value of their holdings. The costs would have been extremely high for the regulators to reconstruct the banks' financial statements from transaction-level documentation; it also would have been exorbitantly costly for the regulators to truly ascertain the values of the banks' investments.

It might also very well be that principals expect a certain level of misbehavior by the agents and simply consider this a cost when conducting their decision-making calculus. Employers might rationally expect a certain amount of shirking by their employees and recognize that eliminating it would be prohibitively expensive. At most commercial research labs, for example, research scientists frequently publish their results in technical and scientific journals. The value of these publications to the labs themselves is questionable; the value to the scientists is clear: enhanced professional reputation and better mobility.

In some situations, monitoring may be provided by an established market. For corporations in reasonably competitive product markets, failure may come quickly. As already discussed, a competitive takeover market punishes poorly behaving CEOs and their management teams. Some proposals for reforming the deposit insurance crisis centered on a larger reliance on market discipline. Large institutional investors often had the resources to acquire the necessary information and the technical savvy to assess this information to accurately predict failures. If their actions were commonly known, then smaller depositors could be expected to follow suit.

Because of the nature of the moral hazard problem, monitoring may not alleviate (and may even aggravate) tension between principals and agents. This happens because measurement, no matter how costly, may be imperfect in a number of ways. These problems often come to light when the agent is motivated by some performance incentive, such as a sales-based commission.

Quite often, only the result is measured. There is no leeway for accounting for good luck that may have befallen the agent; likewise, there is no way to determine whether something outside the agent's control affected the result. Each of these is a source of randomness that may put the employer and employee at odds with each other.

■ CONTRACTUAL RISKS FOR THE AGENT

**Importance
of Avoiding Risks
to the Agent**

Two general characteristics are relevant for our current discussion:

1. Motivating agents through performance-based incentives enhances efficiency in the principal-agent relationship so long as the performance being rewarded advances the interest of the principal.
2. The measurements necessary in incentive systems are far from perfect; this creates an environment of risk for the agent.

The first of these general characteristics merely points out the benefits of aligning the interests of the agent with those of the principal and then rewarding the agent for success in pursuing those goals. Concerning the situation surrounding the deposit insurance crisis of the late 1980s, the interests of the bank manager were clearly not in line with those of the deposit insurer. The regulatory reforms (FIRREA and FDICIA) were attempts to align the interests of the deposit institutions with the interests of the deposit insurer. Currently, banks are rewarded for making safer loans and investments by having to keep less supporting capital. The environment surrounding deposit-taking institutions is clearly much safer now than in the past; the efficiency gains are well defined.

The second of these general conditions may not be as obvious as the first. Surely we would all agree that the compensation of agents, be they workers, deposit institutions, or CEOs, should be linked to their performance. However, actually measuring their performance is costly and, usually, imprecise. This imprecision creates risk for both the principal and agent.

Risk that is created because of faulty measurement practices is one source of inefficiency in the principal-agent relationship. Put in the simplest terms possible, one reason that some parties are agents instead of principals is that they are risk averse. Recall that we consider individuals to be risk averse if they dislike risk and are willing to pay some explicit or implicit payment to have the risk removed. When you graduate from your business program, you will have the basic skills necessary to compete in the business world. Notice, however, that very few business graduates become their own bosses upon graduation; most go to work for others. The obvious reason for this is that agents bear less risk regarding the stability of their future incomes.

This is not to say that being an agent completely eliminates risk. Rather, so long as monitoring is costly and imperfect, and so long as earnings are linked to performance, some risk remains. If principals are to monitor the behavior of agents, the transaction must recognize the risk imputed to the agent from imperfect measurements. In a contractual framework, the risk takes the form of a wider range of possible outcomes for the agent.

There are many ways that randomness might enter the picture and affect the process of contracting between principal and agent. We explore these in this section within the context of one particular principal-agent relationship: employer and employee. Our analysis is germane to the more general principal-agent scenario, but we focus on the employment relationship because of its familiarity and to help prepare us for the part of the text dealing with managing human resources.

To help set the stage for investigation into the risks involved in an employer-employee relationship, let's pretend that we live in a perfect world. It is not required that employees put forth full effort at their jobs. To a certain extent, workers are able to pick their position in the shirk–don't shirk spectrum. There is variation in wages expected by workers. Rational individuals decide, based on their own preferences (and also on how badly they need the money), how hard to work after they know their rate of compensation. Employers are able to determine the effort put forth by each employee and to adjust his wages accordingly.

Now to drop some of the veneer and move back toward the real world. Employers cannot identify the effort put forth by any single employee; at best, employers can observe only very general things: hours at work, work experience, training completed, number of sick days taken, and so on. Employers also have, at best, a limited idea of individual output but may be able to observe team output. The central problem in the employment relationship is that employers face significant obstacles in observing individual effort. The employer is in the position of assessing the efforts of any one individual from (usually) indirect evidence. This assessment along with imperfect indirect measurements forces the employee to bear some risk, no longer knowing for certain how his performance is assessed.

The first way that randomness may enter employee evaluations lies in the very nature of team production and is internal to the organization. Earlier we discussed this topic in detail. For now, we recall only the main points that the input of any one team member cannot be determined and that the output of any single team member depends crucially on the inputs of other team members.

A second way that randomness may enter into the assessment of employee productivity lies outside the organization. Factors outside the individual's control may affect her productivity. Consider the gasoline station on the corner; it is one location of a large national chain. Quite possibly, the station manager's paycheck may depend on dollar volume of sales. Gasoline sales at one location of a chain of stations may depend on the traffic flowing by the station, consumers' experiences with other stations of that chain, or the national advertising efforts of the parent company. Clearly, the manager does not control any of these factors.

A third source of randomness may be caused if the performance itself entails some subjective elements by a supervisor. The influence of subjectivities is internal to the firm only in the sense that they represent a human element in conducting transactions. A hostess in a restaurant must be pleasant, welcoming, and friendly to customers. Each of these terms involves a degree of subjective evaluation, one person's idea of friendly may, to another person, be insulting or even brash.

A final source of randomness arises when factors internal to the employee but external to the firm are recognized. Many organizations are willing to recognize that individuals may face problems affecting their performance. Some large organizations even go so far as to provide employee programs aimed at reducing drug dependency or dealing with other traumatic occurrences such as those related to poor health, divorce, or child care needs.

Basing pay on performance is not a risk-free proposition from an employee's point of view. In some situations, the entire risk is effectively shifted to employees. Sharecropping was commonly used in U.S. agriculture years ago and is commonly used today in many less developed countries. Under this arrangement, the tenant releases a set percentage of his crop to the landlord. Similarly, many telephone marketing workers are paid solely on commission. In these instances, there is no attempt to account for bad luck, and employees have complete responsibility for their actions. Most employment relationships are not like these, however; instead, at least some of the risk is transferred back to the employer. In the next section we consider the mixture of risks and incentives inherent when the employer shares some (if not the majority) of the risk with the employee.

■ IMPLICATIONS FOR MANAGERS

In a complex and changing business environment, moral hazard remains unfortunately as one of the few constants affecting contracts. Economists have been aware for years of the principal-agent problem yet have only recently become aware of its implications. From a managerial perspective, the two most interesting areas in which agency problems occur are the external world where the firm interacts in the financial markets and the internal dealings with employees.

When the laws were written outlining the basic corporate form featuring stockholders, boards of directors, and chief executive officers, great things were made possible. Because of limited shareholder liability, huge corporations could be created and financed to accomplish great things. The implied separation of ownership and control was probably not seen as a major issue given the existence of boards of directors. However, for many reasons, recent history has taught us that moral hazard problems between the owners of a firm (the principals) and the management running the firm (the agents) can poison the relationship. In this chapter, we argued that efficiency dictates a closer relationship between ownership and control interests.

All firms must pay their employees, and the employees must work for the firm. Efficiency seems clearly to indicate that an incentive-based scheme is necessary. However, measurement problems can become problematic. Essentially, the workers are risk averse, and employers (the principals) reduce some of the risks associated with variable incomes in definite ways. By introducing incentive pay systems, the principals may add risk back to the relationship. In the appendix to this chapter, a mathematical model highlights some of these issues and provides some guidelines.

The importance of a firm's dealings with its employees and its financial backers is hard to understate. We have begun to analyze these problems and will consider them in much greater detail in the following sections of this book.

■ CHAPTER SUMMARY AND KEY IDEAS ■ ■ ■ ■ ■

Moral hazard arises in a contracting environment because of incomplete and asymmetric information. This class of contractual frictions has come to be called the principal-agent problem; a typical characterization involves a principal hiring an agent to act on behalf of the principal. The quandary is created since the agent has better information concerning her actions than does the principal. For the principal-agent problem to become operationalized, the interests of the agent must differ from those of the principal. This misalignment gives the agent incentive to act counter to the interests of the principal.

One seemingly obvious answer to the problems associated with moral hazard is to have better monitoring. In many situations, this may simply prove to be impossible for two very basic reasons. First, monitoring may be a costly process and perhaps physically impossible to accomplish. Second, we cannot demand more monitoring without considering the opportunity cost of the principal's time. The principal must allocate time carefully; more time devoted to monitoring necessarily implies less time devoted to other activities.

A second, seemingly obvious, answer to the moral hazard problem is to write most contracts between principal and agent with very strong incentive clauses. The problem with this approach is that in most cases, it can be argued that the agent will be risk averse. When contracts are based largely on incentive schemes, the agent is exposed to a number of risks. One is from fluctuating demand for the output of the firm; the other is from faulty measurements that reflect things outside the agent's control. In short, these sources of risk may actually work to reduce efficiency.

When expressed as a form of ex post opportunism, one solution to the moral hazard problem is to rely on the reputation of trading partners. Where possible, information on reputations can provide potential trading partners with at least some guidance in whom to contract with and how. This solution may not be applicable to each and every transaction.

The term *moral hazard* originated in insurance markets, which provide much insight into the functioning of agents in the presence of moral hazard. In the basic insurance setting, the agent purchases some form of insurance to minimize his exposure to various risks. From the insured's point of view, it may be beneficial to expose herself to risks since her potential losses are covered by insurance. Of course, these actions are costly to the principal, and, thus, the potential for inefficiencies is created.

One of the most analyzed and well-known economic calamities of this century is the crisis in the federally mandated deposit insurance programs, particularly the outright failure of the Federal Savings and Loan Insurance Corporation (FSLIC). In this program, many savings and loan managers engaged in risky behavior as a response to a perverse set of incentives. Money could be lent under risky conditions, earning the manager and institution large profits if the investments came through. The downside (the loss to depositors) was effectively covered by the federal government. The situation was made worse by market conditions and relatively small capital requirements for owners.

In organizations, moral hazard can take many forms. One usually can easily identify instances of employee shirking. Managerial misbehavior by chief executive officers may occur since the standard corporate structure provides for a separation of ownership and control. Market discipline may present an effective control on managerial activities. The basic argument for efficiency in the ubiquitous large corporation is the analogy with Darwinian natural selection applied to competitive markets. In particular, the threat of takeover represents the ultimate constraint on managerial discretion and organizational inefficiency and so should enforce value maximization.

We are very nearly through presenting the organizational tools needed to analyze firm behavior. In the next chapter, we turn our attention to the last remaining tool. In subsequent parts of the text, we begin to apply these tools to better understand a firm in its dealings with the financial markets, its employees, and with its position as part of a larger group of firms composing a sector or industry.

KEY TERMS

carrot method	public good
debt equity	regulatory forbearance
horizon problem	residual claimant
inalienability problem	risk-averse individuals
incentive problem	separation of ownership and control
managerial misbehavior	shareholder activism
market for corporate control	shirking
moral hazard	stick method
poison pills	takeover market
principal-agent problem	team production
principle of risk sharing	

FURTHER READINGS

Coase, R. H. "The Nature of the Firm." *Economica* 4, 1937, pp. 386–405. Reprinted in *Readings in Price Theory*, ed. G. Stigler and K. Boulding. Chicago: RD Irwin, 1952, pp. 331–351.

Gerlowski, D. and C. Thies. "Bank Capital and Bank Failure, 1921–1932: Testing the White Hypothesis." *Journal of Economic History* 53, no. 4, December 1993, pp. 908–914.

Jensen, M. "Takeovers: Their Causes and Consequences." *Journal of Economic Perspectives* 2, 1988, pp. 21–48.

———. "Eclipse of the Public Corporation." *Harvard Business Review* Sept.–Oct., 1987, pp. 61–74.

Milgrom, P. and J. Roberts, *Economics, Organization and Management*. Englewood Cliffs, NJ: Prentice Hall, 1992.

Stiglitz, J. E. "Credit Markets and the Control of Capital." *Journal of Money, Credit, and Banking* 17, no. 2, 1985, pp. 133–152.

Williamson, O. E. "The Modern Corporation: Origins, Evolution, Attributes." *Journal of Economic Literature* 19, 1981, pp. 1537–1568.

QUESTIONS AND PROBLEMS FOR REVIEW AND DISCUSSION

A. Firms today are financed in a multitude of ways. The two largest sources of financing are debt and equity. Therefore, a firm's capital structure is largely determined by the amount of debt financing relative to the amount of equity financing. Suppose that Danbank is considering making two loans to different borrowers that are identical in all respects except for their capital structures. Danny, Inc., one potential borrower, has a capital structure featuring a low debt-equity ratio. Drew, Inc., has a capital structure featuring high levels of equity relative to debt. Which borrower, Danny, Inc., or Drew, Inc., poses a larger risk to Danbank? Fully explain why and incorporate concepts covered in this course.

B. In many countries, corporations whose shares are publicly traded are required to have their financial statements audited by independent accountants who check whether the financial information being provided by management to investors is accurate and has been prepared following accepted methods and procedures and who then publicly attest to their findings. The auditors are generally chosen by management (perhaps subject to nominal stockholder approval). Audit work provides a major source of income for accounting firms. Generally, each accounting firm has many clients that it audits. This is true even when it might be technically feasible for a relatively small accounting firm to audit a large corporation's records. There seems to be a reluctance for corporations to use audit firms when a single client would represent too much of the accountant's business. Instead, a handful of extremely large accounting firms typically do almost all the auditing of large corporations, with each having many corporate clients. How do you explain this?

C. The 1980s were clearly a go-go decade. Yuppies ruled the consumer markets, and many critics maintained that in some areas, one-half of the population got rich selling real estate to the other half. Quite predictably, there are now many people in those areas with their hats in their hands, so to speak. Another aspect of the 1980s was the invention and widespread use of the hostile takeover in corporate finance. A hostile takeover is the acquisition of enough of the shares in a company to gain a controlling ownership interest in the firm, which the target company's executives and directors oppose. Decide whether the following statement is true or false, and explain your position: Managerial moral hazard in the form of managers pursuing their own interests at the expense of others caused the surge in hostile takeovers during the 1980s.

D. In the United States, many workers use a computer as a part of their job. In many fields, these machines not only greatly enhance productivity but also are a necessity. One popular operating system is *Windows*, produced by Microsoft. A standard feature in most copies of *Windows* is a version of solitaire, a card game played by an individual. Games such as solitaire represent an opportunity to shirk. In fact, in 1993, Wes Cherry, the Microsoft programmer who wrote the solitaire application for *Windows*, boasted, "I like to think that I'm partly responsible for the recession."[8]

1. What types of monitoring costs do these games pose to employers?

2. A corporate policy that does not permit these games to be loaded onto company machines is passed. Is this likely to be successful?

3. *Tetris*, popularized by Spectrum Holobyte, Inc., is another popular game. One popular feature of *Tetris* is a boss key, which, when pressed, quickly displays a spreadsheet that looks like work. What is the effect of this boss key on the employer's monitoring costs?

▌ **APPENDIX 8A** **The Risk-Incentive Trade-Off**

A Second Efficiency Function for Employers

Employers play a dual role in our society. Naturally, they organize production and provide workers a paycheck. In the United States, we also tend to attribute to employers a function of providing a type of income insurance to employees. Just as fire insurance transfers the risks faced by a homeowner to the threat of fire, the employer effectively insures the employee against randomness in income caused by two factors. Fluctuating industry demand would create much larger swings in income than are actually observed. This is interesting in its own right, but we do not dwell on it now; rather, we turn our attention to the second source of randomness in employee income: measurement error.

As our analysis unfolds, you will undoubtedly try to relate our model to your own experiences or knowledge of wage agreements. This is to be encouraged with

---

[8]For an interesting background on this issue, see "The Games People Play in the Office," *Business Week* (October 11, 1993), p. 40.

some warnings. First, our model is intended to be quite general; its application to a given set of circumstances may greatly increase its complexity. Second, our model is constructed to emphasize certain aspects of employment relationships and, as such, other aspects are held constant and do not explicitly appear.

We are concerned with characterizing the risks faced by employees (agents). Our analysis considers these risks along with the measurement costs from which they arise. An efficient contract is an arrangement that balances the cost of shifting these risks from the employee against the incentive benefits that result.

In our analysis, we concentrate on one particular measure of risk, the variability in the outcome of employee assessment. Regarding the choice between buying government bonds and stocks of major corporations, both the expected net return and the variability of net return are relevant.

Toward a Simple Mathematical Model

The structure of our model is relatively simple. A firm is charged with organizing labor to produce output that is sold in response to a profit motive. To keep the model as simple as possible, we consider the simplest case imaginable: one firm selling a single product that hires only one employee. This assumption is clearly unrealistic, but it does not make the analysis unreasonable. Using a single employee as an example allows us to ignore different types of employees, which would increase the analytical content of our model exponentially.

The employee chooses the intensity of her efforts on the job. We characterize these efforts as the employee's level of application or intensity to the job, *I*. Worker intensity, or energy level, is a personal choice for the individual. In our model, work per se is not distasteful; however, the personal cost of working at a high intensity level is greater than working at a lower intensity level. The personal cost associated with each level of intensity is determined by our worker's own tastes, preferences, and attitude. We assume that a functional relationship exists and that we can write this relationship as:

$$PC = PC(I)$$

The firm in our model employs the worker and is somewhat sophisticated in that it realizes that profits depend largely on the quality of the effort put forth by the employee. Greater employee intensity implies larger profits. We write the firm's profit function, *PROF*, also as a function of *I*.

$$PROF = PROF(I)$$

The Components of the Wage

Next, it is necessary to impose some structure for the wage paid to our worker. We will assume that the worker's compensation is an increasing linear function of what the employer observes. This may seem a little vague now, and very soon we will become much more concerned with what the employer observes. For now, let's say that the employer observes a quantity called observed effort intensity, which we will write as *OEI*. In particular, assume that her wage payments in any time period are of the form

$$\text{Wage} = B_1 + B_2 * (OEI)$$

The logic of such a linear compensation formula is straightforward. The worker receives a base wage of B_1. To this base amount is added some component that depends on *OEI*. As *OEI* increases by 1 measurement unit, pay would rise by B_2. The parameter B_2 is termed the *incentive intensity parameter*.

We now turn our attention to a fuller specification of the quantity *OEI*. There are three components to *OEI*, and each adds some insight into the problems of efficiently designing wage contracts in the face of imperfect measurement of employee activity.

Of the three components of *OEI*, two are lumped together in a single entity that can be observed by the employee. The direct performance indicator, *DPI*, is a joint observation on *I*, the true employee intensity, and random influences. These random influences, *RI*, are factors that affect employee productivity but are not easily identified as being attributable to any specific cause. For completeness, we include an equation linking *DPI* to *I* and *RI*.

$$DPI = I + RI$$

It will be useful to remember that the firm observes only *DPI* and cannot disentangle either *I* or *RI*.

The remaining component of the observed effort intensity, *OEI*, is the strength of overall conditions, *OC*. Overall conditions might include the strength of the market for the firm's product, overall business conditions, or factors inside the firm that might affect employee productivity. We assume that both the worker and firm can observe *OC* without error.

It also seems reasonable that *OC* would receive some weighting in determining the observed effort intensity, *OEI*. This weighting could be either positive or negative, depending on the impact of the outside conditions. We use the notation for the weighing as $B_3{}^*OC$.

We can then write an expression for observed effort intensity as

$$OEI = I + RI + B_3{}^*OC$$

A negative value for B_3 implies that outside conditions were favorable to the employee performance. As such, some of the employee productivity is attributable to a healthy market or some external factor increasing the demand for the firm's output. Likewise, a positive value for B_3 implies that outside conditions were unfavorable to employee performance. This would be the case if, for example, the market for the firm's output was declining.

Much has gone on here, and it may be useful to briefly review this discussion of employee wages. We began with the idea that our hypothetical employee's wage ought to be linked to her productivity, which we called observed effort intensity, or *OEI*. We then broke *OEI* down into three components, two of which were jointly observed and indistinguishable from each other. This joint observation we termed *DPI*, which was the sum of *I* and *RI*. The third component of *OEI* was overall conditions to which we attached a weight. We can sum this development up with the following three equations.

$$\text{Wage} = B_1 + B_2{}^*(OEI)$$

$$\text{Wage} = B_1 + B_2{}^*(DPI + B_3{}^*OC)$$

$$\text{Wage} = B_1 + B_2{}^*(I + RI + B_3{}^*OC)$$

A fuller understanding of the last equation for wage is obtained if we make the rationality assumption commonly made in economic analysis. In the context of our model, the rationality assumption provides us with definite expectations concerning the three components of *OEI*. *I* is, of course, chosen by the worker; this choice will be explained in the next section. Both the worker and the firm expect *RI* and *OC* to be zero. That is, in their planning, random influences cannot be predetermined, and no outside influences (in terms of exceptionally strong or weak) markets for the firm's output are anticipated.[9]

---

[9]Exceptionally strong or weak overall conditions could be accounted for by revising the values chosen for B_1 and B_2.

What the Worker Faces

We now have some idea of the wage risk facing the employee and how this risk may affect her choice of I. The worker's job is to take the wage that she expects to earn for every value of I and compare this wage to the corresponding increase in her personal cost function, $PC(I)$. Thus, our worker compares the marginal benefits of increasing I, the higher wage, with the marginal costs of doing so. The level of I that equates, on the margin, the benefits and the costs is the one that she chooses. These marginal costs are determined by her own tastes and preferences and represent the value of what she gives up by increasing her intensity of employment.

While this may sound like a simple task for our hypothetical worker, she faces some things that are known and some things that are not. Both the worker and the firm know the exact values for B_1, B_2, and B_3. Being rational, she assumes also that RI and OC will be zero, but she also recognizes that this may not very well be the case. This uncertainty may very well lead her to provide a level of effort, I, that is not efficient.

If the employee puts forth greater intensity in her duties (i.e., increases I), she cannot be certain that her wage will increase. In fact, her wage may increase or even decrease. Payments increase if the combined effect of RI and OC do not counteract the effect of the larger I. Rather than viewing her income as certain, our employee can view it now only as a random entity.

As an example, suppose our worker manages (and operates) an ice cream store at the mall for an owner. She may increase her efforts substantially: being friendly to all customers, working longer hours, or explaining the beneficial nutritional implications of ice cream consumption to the clientele. However, if the mall is experiencing less foot traffic due to the completion of a new mall nearby (a negative RI) or if the economy is in recession (a negative OC), then her wage may not increase if tied to dollar volume of ice cream products sold.

Four Principles
to Help Efficiency

One way to reduce employee risk is to follow the *relevant information principle*, which states that efficient contracts include a combination of parameters (B_1, B_2, B_3) that reduce the measurement error associated with the agent's performance.

To put the relevant information principle into the context of our model, recall the employee's compensation formula:

$$\text{Wage} = B_1 + B_2 {}^* (I + RI + B_3 {}^* OC)$$

In our model, the employee treats B_1, B_2, and B_3 as fixed and reacts in her own self-interest in choosing I. Because of this, we can let these measures be fixed and observe that random variation in wages then enters from that part involving RI and $B_3 {}^* OC$.

In the interest of efficiency, we then seek the conditions under which the measurement risks caused by random influences and outside conditions are minimized. To do so, we have to identify common movements in RI and OC. We still expect, on average, RI and OC to take zero values; however, the parties to the employment contract may very well have ideas about what one of these quantities is likely to be given that the other is positive (or, negative).[10]

It is probably most likely, in practice, that RI and OC are positively related. This means that a positive (negative) value for RI tends to be caused by the same set of broad economic factors that make OC positive (negative) as well. In this case, risk in the form of variation in Wage is minimized and efficiency in the relationship enhanced if B_3 was negative. Suppose this was not true and B_3 was posi-

---

[10]For those with a firm understanding of statistics, you will be aware that what we are really talking about here is the covariance between RI and OC, two random variables.

tive. Then when times were "good," both *RI* and *OC* would tend to be positive and Wage would increase spectacularly. However, when times were "bad," both *RI* and *OC* would tend to be negative and Wage would decrease spectacularly. Such variation in Wage exposes the employee to larger risk.

The *incentive responsiveness principle* provides some managerial insights into how sensitive rewards should be to improved (or reduced) performance if an employment contract is to be structured to minimize risk to the agent.

Within the context of our model, our task is to determine factors that influence the size of B_2. While we do not include a formal mathematical proof, we do offer guidelines with some intuitive explanation.

The size of B_2 should depend on the effectiveness of the agent in causing changes in the firm's profits. If the employee is able, through her choice of intensity level, to increase firm profits greatly, then a large B_2 should be chosen. On the other hand, if there is not a clear link between employee efforts and firm profits, B_2 ought to be smaller. Production workers, for example, could be motivated by incentive schemes tied to amount produced, but only up to a certain level. Overproduction in one division may swamp other divisions with components that are not yet needed.

The responsiveness of wages to effort put forth should also depend on two characteristics internal to the employee. If the employee is strongly risk averse, that is, does not like risk, then an intense link between pay and performance is not desirable. If, on the other hand, the agent is a risk taker, then it is entirely appropriate to motivate with intense incentives.

The *competing activities compensation principle* is meant to apply when one employee is to be motivated to fill several functions that may compete for the employee's time. Suppose that the employer cannot determine how much effort an employee devotes to each of two separate activities. If the marginal benefits of the two activities to the employee are unequal, then the employee will optimally devote only time to the activity with the higher marginal benefit. The consequences of the competing activities principle are enormous for the design of incentive contracts. In particular, if an employee is expected to engage in an activity for which no performance measurement is available, then performance pay cannot be used for any other activities that the employee controls.

At almost every business school in the United States, faculty members are required to teach classes and are expected to pursue an active research agenda. The reason for the teaching duties is simple: without students, society would have little use for universities. The reason for expecting the faculty to conduct research is to benefit the business school, the faculty member, and the students.

In evaluating faculty members from different universities, teaching evaluations are of limited use; they have been shown to be highly subjective, and there is not a uniform evaluation system across campuses. For these reasons (and many others), a faculty member's reputation depends largely on his research productivity. Quite often, within a given university, raises and ultimate promotion depend crucially on research productivity and somewhat less on teaching abilities.

The typical faculty member must allocate his time among competing uses. The competing activities compensation principle can shed some light on the faculty member's choices and the university administrators' decision to permit this situation to exist. Given the great difficulty in obtaining an objective measure of teaching productivity across disciplines, and even across faculty members within a common discipline, too large a weight given to teaching presents undue risk to faculty members.

The *monitoring intensity principle* adds to the above some responsibilities of the manager, employer, or firm. The monitoring intensity principle dictates that if an agent's rewards are to be highly sensitive to her performance, then it will pay the principal to monitor that performance very heavily. If we consider two contracts between pairs of principals and agents that differ only in the size of B_2, the principal involved in the contract with the larger B_2 will expend more resources in measuring agent performance.

Distribution, Rents, and Efficiency

Low wages are by no means identical with cheap labour. From a purely quantitative point of view the efficiency of labour decreases with a wage which is physiologically insufficient . . . the present-day average Silesian mows, when he exerts himself to the full, little more than two-thirds as much land as the better paid and nourished Pomeranian or Mecklenberger, and the Pole, the further East he comes from, accomplishes progressively less than the German. Low wages fail even from a purely business point of view wherever it is a question of producing goods which require any sort of skilled labour, or the use of expensive machinery which is easily damaged, or in general wherever any greater amount of sharp attention of initiative is required. Here low wages do not pay, and their effort is the opposite of what was intended.[1]

CHAPTER OUTLINE AND STUDENT GOALS

Introducing Rents and Distribution

In the previous chapters, we encountered several issues. In Part I, we emphasized the traditional approach economists take in analyzing the organization of economic activity: markets. In Chapters 6, 7, and 8 the emphasis shifted away from markets since imperfect information and bounded rationality create transaction costs that prevent smooth and efficient functioning of the market mechanism.

In this chapter, we turn our attention to rents and distribution effects. We define these terms more fully later; for now, we offer only broad general definitions. *Rents* are benefits earned by an economic resource that exceed what the resource could willingly earn elsewhere. *Distribution effects* broadly refer to the resources available to the parties of a transaction both before and after the transaction is completed.

Economists became interested in rents long ago. Initially, analysis of rents focused on land and other fixed factors of production. This is not surprising since long ago most individuals earned their living from the land. In fact, the term *rent* today typically evokes images of a check sent to a landlord, a usage evolved from the concept developed by economists. This concept of rent has been greatly expanded to cover many interesting exchange situations.

Efficient behavior can generate rents, a fact that should not be lost on any

---

[1]Max Weber, *The Protestant Ethic and the Spirit of Capitalism* (New York: Scribners, 1925), p. 61.

business manager. Where they exist, rents can be traced back to the mutual benefits of the underlying exchange, which is why two parties would interact in the first place. In a sense, rents represent "something for nothing" or, at least, an unearned bonus. As such, rational individuals try to arrange things so that they capture these rents. When viewed in this light, rents have the potential of either enhancing or diminishing efficiency.

Distribution, in economic terms, refers to who has (or gets) what. Attention was first paid by economists to the macroeconomy where distribution referred to the allocation of gross domestic product (GDP) between the owners of land, labor, capital, and entrepreneurial ability. Within a transaction, *distribution* refers to sharing costs and benefits. Within an organization, which, we remind you, is really nothing more than a collection of transactions or contracts, *distribution* refers to how the benefits of production and the required efforts are shared by members of the organization.

It has long been thought by managers, economists, and business strategists that the distribution of rents in an organization was simple: they go to the group with residual control. In a changing business environment, rents have taken on a new meaning. This is especially true witnessing the reemergence of markets as the highly vertically integrated firms created in the first half of the 20th century are being replaced by the more nimble and responsive organizations created as this century comes to a close.

After reading this chapter, you should be able to

- Describe, in your own words, what is meant by *rent*.
- Differentiate between the types of rents considered by organizational economists.
- Describe how rents can be used to increase efficiency.
- Explain the importance of reputation and "good behavior" in overcoming threats of ex ante and ex post opportunistic behavior.
- Understand the importance of distribution effects in economic analysis of the organization.
- Explain what is meant by *rent-seeking behavior* and why it is not efficient.

■ ■ ■ ■ ■ ■ ■   ■ **THE MEANINGS OF RENTS
AND DISTRIBUTION EFFECTS**

Types of Rents

Economists refer to two different types of rents, economic rents and a slightly different and newer concept, quasi-rents. **Economic rents** are the benefits from an activity going to a resource in excess of what is needed to attract that resource to that activity. **Quasi-rents** are the benefits from an activity going to a resource that are in excess of the minimum needed to keep a resource in its current use.

The implication of getting something for nothing in terms of economic rents is fairly clear. Some tremendous examples of economic rents are provided by the earnings of some professional athletes in the United States. Star football players including Emitt Smith of the Dallas Cowboys, Dan Marino of the Miami Dolphins, and Jim Kelly of the Buffalo Bills earn millions of dollars per year.[2] When each of these players is interviewed, he often dwells on how he plays sports out of

---

[2]As of 1995, no professional football player had managed to earn more than $1 million per game; however, that boundary may have fallen by the time this book is printed.

love. If this claim is in fact true, then all of their earnings represent economic rent since, presumably, out of love, they would play the game for free.

Economic rents are relevant for an "entry" decision regarding some activity. If an individual or organization is attempting to pick one of several activities to undertake with some limited resources, it will always choose the activity yielding the largest economic rent. The concept of quasi-rent is somewhat different; it focuses on an "exit" decision.

Under the quasi-rent concept, a distinction between **sunk costs** and **opportunity costs** must be kept in mind. A cost is said to be sunk if, once paid, it can never be recouped. An opportunity cost of an action is the value of the next-best alternative. When an individual assesses the quasi-rents of some particular activity, she ignores any sunk costs and focuses instead on payments in excess of what she could earn elsewhere (the opportunity cost).

These definitions may be a little murky, and we offer two examples to help cement them in your thinking. The first concerns a firm's price level in light of the firm's average costs of production. The second considers various components of a wage earned by a hypothetical worker. In each of these examples, both economic and quasi-rents are easily identified and distinguished from each other.

Consider the analysis of the neoclassical competitive firm discussed in Chapter 3. The firm would enter an industry if so doing would yield positive profits. If p represents the market price in some industry and p_{atc} represents the firm's average total cost of production,[3] a firm will enter so long as p is greater than or equal to p_{atc}. In this case, the firm's profits are equivalent to economic rents. On a per unit basis, the economic rents are $(p - p_{atc})$.

It is not necessary for a firm to earn positive economic rents; recall that the long-run equilibrium condition for competitive industries involves zero profits. It is necessary, however, for a firm to earn positive quasi-rents. Regarding the competitive firm, quasi-rents are the difference between market price, p, and the average variable costs of production, p_{avc}. If the market price falls below p_{avc}, then a rational firm will shut down, that is, not produce since producing involves a loss on every unit sold. On a per unit basis, the quasi-rents earned by a competitive firm equal $(p - p_{avc})$.

Notice that in the simple example provided by the neoclassical competitive firm, the fixed costs are sunk. This is obviously a simplification since a firm's fixed costs, in reality, might be offset by some salvage value or might contain some maintenance cost component that is possibly avoidable.

The example of economic and quasi-rents being earned by a competitive firm is illustrated in Figure 9–1, in which the cost curves facing a firm are shown. At any price above P_{atc}, the firm is earning positive economic rents. At any price between P_{atc} and P_{avc}, there are no economic rents, but quasi-rents are still being earned. If the price drops below P_{avc}, then even the quasi-rents are gone; and the rational firm will not produce at all.

One implication of this discussion relevant for managers that is made clear by the preceding example is that quasi-rents are not less than economic rents. Even when economic rents are zero (such as for the neoclassical competitive firm in long-run equilibrium), quasi-rents are positive and may be allocated to members of the organization to fulfill numerous efficiency needs.

A second useful example in illustrating the related, but different, concepts of

---

[3]The average total costs given by p_{atc} are those associated with the optimal level of production found by equating marginal revenue, p, with the firm's marginal cost.

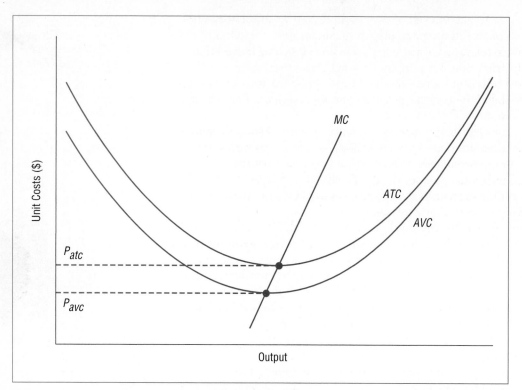

Figure 9.1 Competitive Firms, Entry Decisions

economic and quasi-rents is provided by the wage earned by a hypothetical factory worker, Noel Wheeler. Noel works for a wage of $15 per hour; we can assume for simplicity that there are no fringe benefits. We will denote this wage simply as w. Since Noel is a rational individual, she has a definite opinion regarding the highest wage she could earn elsewhere in a similar position. Suppose, in fact, that Noel believes that her alternative wage, which we will label as w_{alt}, is $12 per hour. Part of Noel's wage represents an economic rent, which is equal to $(w - w_{alt})$, or $3 per hour.

The rent component of her wage may seem large (20 percent), but her wage has an even larger quasi-rent associated with it. Define w_{keep} as the wage needed to actually keep Noel in her current position. It is important to understand why w_{keep} will be lower than w_{alt}. Associated with job changes are three categories of costs: worker search costs, skill acquisition costs, and adaptation costs.

Worker search costs are any costs associated with finding a new job. They may include the value of time unemployed, if any; costs of interviewing; and the actual costs of addressing letters and typing resumes. **Skill acquisition costs** reflect the sacrifices made by those in the job market to develop new human capital, that is, to retool in response to perceived market forces. **Adaptation costs** include any relocation costs and the value of any sacrificed employment benefits such as pensions.

The existence of search costs, skill acquisition costs, and adaptation costs is the reason that w_{keep} will be less than w_{alt}. Since w_{keep} represents the lowest wage necessary to keep Noel in her current job, it must be equal to

$$w_{keep} = w_{alt} - (\text{Search Costs}) - (\text{Skill Acquisition Costs}) - (\text{Adaptation Costs})$$

Noel's current employer doesn't have to pay her the alternative wage that she could earn elsewhere because she cannot earn that wage elsewhere "for free."

Noel earns quasi-rents equal to $(w - w_{keep})$. Worker search costs, skill acquisition costs, and adaptation costs will vary greatly by individual; as such, we refrain from putting hypothetical dollar values on them. It stands to reason, however, that within some occupations, these costs could be substantial.

Different kinds of decisions can be analyzed with economic rents and quasi-rents. In most of this chapter we will be concerned with quasi-rents. The rationale is that quasi-rents are what is lost, in competitive markets, if an agent is forced to exit. Although rents can exist only temporarily in a competitive economy, quasi-rents are much more common. Quasi-rents are created whenever specialized non-salvageable investments are made, for example, when an individual works for an organization and is asked to carry out a task that cannot be transferred outside the firm. Having made this investment, the individual will earn a higher wage than he or she can earn in the next best alternative. If an individual has invested in an activity that cannot be recovered if he or she leaves, this person is now earning a quasi-rent. Quasi-rents therefore have the potential to be widely useful for providing incentives.

Efficiency in exchange may also be affected by distributional effects, which refer to who has, or gets, what resources according to the terms of an exchange. Distributional issues manifest themselves in two ways. Some parties to a transaction may not be able to "afford" their part of an efficient allocation of resources. Also possible is a situation in which the benefits (or costs) of production are shared in such a way to lead to inefficient outcomes.

We can very easily contrive an example of how one party's ability to afford its part of an efficient transaction can have efficiency implications. Suppose that as a part of your job, you are required to use a laptop computer. Furthermore, both you and your employer are well aware that the performance, and perhaps the very survival, of your computer depends on how well it is cared for. The machine's performance may depend, for example, on how often the battery is permitted to run down completely or on how many times it is used as an umbrella by a forgetful employee. Both you and your employer recognize these facts; the only unresolved issue is who should own the laptop.

This situation is nothing more than the moral hazard problem encountered in Chapter 8. The efficient solution is probably for the employee to own the laptop, since only then can the proper incentives be created for the employee to be diligent in caring for it. Now, how can distributional issues affect this situation? Distributional issues become important if the employee lacks the financial resources to purchase the laptop. You see, it is not enough for the firm to purchase the computer for the employee, for if the machine breaks because of poor maintenance, the employee can rationally always ask for another one.

A second example of the importance of distributional effects and efficiency is provided by analyzing the wages paid to workers or, in other words, the way the benefits of production are shared between the factors of production.

Distribution is the mechanism by which the gross domestic product (GDP) is spread between individuals and groups in the economy. The functional allocation of income refers to the distribution of the GDP between the owners of land, labor, capital, and entrepreneurial ability. One of the first attempts to explain the distribution of income according to "natural law" was developed by the distinguished American economist John Bates Clark in 1899.[4]

This type of analysis rests on a supposition known as the **marginal productivity theory** of income distribution, a concept we will consider in greater detail in Chapter 12. This thinking suggests that an employer will not pay more for a

Distribution Effects

---

[4] John Bates Clark, *The Distribution of Wealth* (New York: Macmillan, 1899).

unit of input—whether a person or an acre of land—than it is worth to the firm. Economic analysis based on this theory ignores several distributional issues.[5]

In many developing countries, the marginal revenue product of workers may be very low, implying meager wages. In some cases, the pay may not be enough to sustain a worker, much less his wife and children. This was certainly the case in England during the Industrial Revolution when children as young as age six would be found working in the mills because their fathers did not earn a wage high enough to feed all members of the family. Similarly, in many developing countries, it is common to find children of a very young age working. If workers were paid higher wages, their children could go to school, eat a more nutritious diet, and ensure a more productive future.

Such practices certainly exist in today's world and are, in fact, perfectly consistent with the marginal productivity theory of income distribution. However, history has taught us that the long-run prospects of such economic and social structures are not good. Clearly, exploited workers in all nations are a sure sign that the interests of efficiency dictate a higher wage paid to workers.

Payments to Land

ECONOMIC RENTS GOING TO A FIXED FACTOR

In economic analysis, it is useful to think in terms of rents as being captured by some entity; both economic and quasi-rents are said to "go" to some factor of production or, equivalently, to some party of the exchange. Economists began studying rents by examining the "extra" benefits going to fixed factors of production. In later years, it became known that both economic and quasi-rents could be captured by nonfixed factors of production. In this section, our purpose is to explore rents going to a fixed factor. This will shed light on the nonfixed factor cases studied in the next section.

In a competitive economy, there are no economic rents. The reason is clear. In a competitive setting, positive economic profits attract entrants who eliminate all rents in the long run. The obvious exception is, of course, whether a factor of production is in inelastic (that is, fixed) supply, in which case rents may exist in the long run.

As recently as a century ago, virtually all economics texts devoted much space to land. This is easy to understand since most people worked the land for a living. David Ricardo, a leading economist of the 19th century, argued that land is both original and indestructible. His arguments were based on three assumptions:

1. The amount of land available is fixed.
2. Land used for growing corn (the generic term in England for all grains) has no alternative uses.
3. A landlord prefers to receive any payment for the use of land rather than to leave it idle and receive nothing.[6]

The supply curve of land is then perfectly inelastic or vertical. Its price is determined by the height of the demand curve. Rather than leaving the land to grow grass, the landlord willingly supplies the same amount of land at a lower price. In fact, the landlord would accept any price determined by the demand curve.

The resulting payment is an economic rent and will be determined by the productivity of land for farming. If demand rises, rents rise; if the demand de-

---

[5] This point is made much more eloquently in the quote at the beginning of this chapter.
[6] David Ricardo, *On the Principles of Political Economy and Taxation*, 3rd ed. (London: John Murray, 1821).

clines, rents decline. Notice that if the land truly cannot be converted to another purpose, then the payments received by the farmer are also quasi-rents.

Rents can also go to fixed factors other than land. In most other cases, what is required to earn a rent is **monopoly power** in the provision of some good or service. Every instance of monopoly power by definition can be traced back to some operative **entry barrier** or some device that keeps other firms out of the market.

Economies of scale, or continuous reduction in producer unit costs, represent a significant barrier to entry in many industries (see box in Chapter 1, "[still] The Importance of Size"). Usually, economies of scale involve large fixed costs in production. The functioning of economies of scale as an entry barrier is fairly easy to see: the large fixed costs keep potential entrants away.

Suppose that one firm producing in an industry is able to exploit economies of scale in production; it can then produce a large number of units at very low per unit costs. A second firm could hope, at best, to capture half of the industry demand if the second firm uses a similar production technology. Can the second firm expect to survive?

The first firm will fight (that is, compete on price) so long as it is earning quasi-rents, that is, charging a price higher than average variable costs of production. The second firm is competing for economic rents; its lowest price can be expected to be average total cost. Given the large fixed costs usually involved in economies of scale, the difference between average variable cost (AVC) and average total cost (ATC) is likely to be fairly large. In short, it will be very difficult for a second firm to enter the industry. Thus, economies of scale can represent a significant barrier to entry and earn the owners of the underlying capital significant economic rents and quasi-rents.

Economies of scope exist when the total cost of producing two related outputs within the same firm is lower than when the outputs are produced separately and represent an entry barrier in much the same way as economies of scale.

Many other legal and structural barriers to entry exist as well. Franchises play a critical role in assigning market territories to individuals. Evidence of these rents are the recent sales of the Baltimore Orioles for $176 million and the Philadelphia Eagles for $156 million. Patents and copyrights play the same type of role. In the United States, the patent system gives the inventor of a new product or process exclusive right to sell it for 17 years.

One commonly overlooked source of economic rents and quasi-rents concerns the old real estate adage, "Location is everything." The basic difference between two parcels of land is, of course, where they are located. Retail outlets prefer easily accessible sites; financial services firms prefer locations in central cities to facilitate face-to-face contact with others in their own and the legal and banking communities.

Each of these instances involves rents going to a resource that is in fixed or even "limited" supply and relies on some associated monopoly power. While instructive, these cases provide a limited basis for analysis because of their fixed nature. More managerial insights are provided when our attention shifts to rents earned by the nonfixed factors of production.

■ RENTS AND NONSPECIFIC INVESTMENTS

Mary Smith graduated from a New England liberal arts college in 1985 with an undergraduate degree in economics, soon landing a job with a major New York City bank. She was delighted. During the summer of 1985, she moved to New York City and rented a small but attractive apartment on the upper west side of

**Monopoly Power
and Barriers to Entry**

**Worker Shirking—
An Example**

Manhattan. Her job was in mid-town, and most mornings she walked to work past Lincoln Center.

Like most entry-level positions at financial institutions, Mary's job was demanding. She put in long hours learning the job, meeting deadlines, and learning her way around the office. After a few years, Mary was promoted, and her career at the bank looked bright. After a few years, now in her late 20s, Mary met Tom (a successful stockbroker) on a weekend in the Hamptons. Before long, they were married and moved into a larger apartment.

As Mary turned 30, she and many of her friends from college started thinking about having children. Mary became pregnant and had a beautiful baby boy. She took six weeks off from work—the legally allowable time in New York—plus her two-week vacation for that year. Then Tom and Mary found a day care center near home, and Mary returned to work.

Things became difficult for Mary and her family very soon. With a new baby at home, Tom and Mary found that time was constrained. Much of their time was spent caring for the infant, working, and keeping up their apartment. They had little time for each other, let alone for social and recreational interests. Up to a point, they managed. However, the demands on their time were tremendous. Tom and Mary soon began having difficult discussions on how they could improve their situation. One option was for one of them to quit his or her job, but this raised serious questions about having an adequate family income and about the large investments made in their human capital. They also considered other options.

Recently, the German magazine *Das Speigle*—a cross between the *Atlantic* and *Penthouse*—ran a story about working women. The article suggested that the German solution to Tom and Mary's problem was for Mary to shirk at work, saving her energy for her family. In other words, Mary should put in less effort at the office so that she would have enough energy to take care of the baby, her husband, and the apartment. The value of the extra energy and time devoted to her family would contribute to the economic and quasi-rents earned by Mary in her job.

Mary's employer had a choice of how to react to this situation. Moreover, this same situation was faced by millions and millions of employers as the female labor force participation rate of married women with small children exploded during the 1980s. How did employers and employees react to this situation? How can employers prevent workers from shirking?

As discussed in Chapter 8, one solution is to institute a pay-for-performance policy. We know the drawbacks to such a solution. First, all monitoring is very costly, especially at the individual worker level. It makes little economic sense to hire someone to monitor the efforts of a bus driver, a house cleaner, or a clerk. Second, while costly, monitoring is also imperfect and subject to random influences in a number of ways. These random influences may be so severe as to undermine the value of the agreement to both the worker and the firm.

**One Solution:
Efficiency Wages**

How might firms deal with the principal-agent problem when direct supervision is costly, difficult, and open to possible error? One approach, the **efficiency wage model,** is suggested by two economists, Carl Shapiro and Joseph Stiglitz.[7] The logic of the efficiency wage model is straightforward: pay workers an economic rent to reward good behavior. In all fairness, we must point out that the efficiency wage model is a working hypothesis in economics that provides one explanation for the determination of wages. The efficiency wage model is very

---

[7]Carl Shapiro and Joseph E. Stiglitz, "Equilibrium Unemployment as a Worker Discipline Device," *American Economic Review* (1984), pp. 433–444.

intuitive and allows us to illustrate how economic rents can be used by managers.

What the efficiency wage model does essentially is perform a benefit-cost comparison from the worker's perspective. More specifically, it isolates the decision of the worker: Should he shirk or not? The efficiency wage model attempts to identify the costs and the benefits of shirking and assumes that if the costs of shirking exceed the benefits, then the worker will not shirk. To conduct our analysis, we must introduce some notation.

Let w be the wage the employee is paid in his or her current employment ($35,000). Let W be the wage the employee could get if he or she looked for another job in the current employment market ($30,000). To keep our analysis focused, assume that W, the alternative wage, is already discounted to consider worker search costs, adaptation costs, and skill acquisition costs.

Let R be the amount that the employee could gain by shirking on the job. This gain might take the form of larger utility from increased leisure obtained by working shorter hours than agreed or simply reduced pressures from responding less diligently to demands at work (Mary and Tom considered this option earlier). Let p be the probability that shirking is detected and the employee is fired for his actions. Let X be the number of time periods over which the employment is expected to carry into the future. If the employee is hired for only one period, then X is 1. If there is to be continuing employment, then X can take any value greater than 1.

The basic outline of the efficiency wage model is quite straightforward. Monitoring is costly for the employer, so the firm knows that it can't always observe the actions of the employee. Knowing this, the rational employee must decide whether to shirk or not. This decision is made by the employee in a rational way in which the costs of shirking are compared to the benefits of shirking. The problem facing the employer is then to recognize this and offer the worker a wage such that shirking is not a rational employee choice.

The gains from shirking are the easiest to identify. We assume that these gains are given by R. The costs of shirking are a little harder to identify since they are not experienced by the worker with certainty. Before accounting for the probabilistic qualities of the cost of shirking, let's examine what is lost if the worker's shirking is detected and he is fired.

Put simply, the worker stands to lose the quasi-rents associated with his employment. These quasi-rents are given by $(w - W)$.[8] If the employment situation is to carry over X periods, then the cost to the worker of shirking, if detected, are

$$X * (w - W)$$

Now we turn our attention to the probabilistic aspect of getting caught shirking. Although the worker cannot be certain of getting caught and losing $X * (w - W)$, the worker does know the expected value of being caught and fired. The expected costs of shirking are then

$$p * X * (w - W)$$

In the worker's decision making, he will shirk if shirking is in his interests. Or, in other words, shirking will occur if the benefits of shirking, R, exceed the expected costs of shirking, $p * X * (w - W)$. Mathematically, we would then say that shirking will occur if

$$R > p * X * (w - W)$$

---

[8]Recall that we have discounted the alternative wage, W, to take account of the costs associated with changing jobs. If we had not adjusted W in this way, then our analysis would be based on economic rents rather than quasi-rents.

The possibility of earning the quasi-rent $(w - W)$ makes the job valuable to the employee and makes being fired an outcome to be avoided.

Even for most honest people, repeated and substantial temptation to cheat combined with ambiguity about what is right and wrong is likely to result in occasional cheating. What is an efficient response by an organization to this situation? There is one efficient approach suggested by the efficiency wage model.

Basically, the organization must consider what its options are. Only two variables in the preceding equation are under the firm's control: p and w. Each of these affects the expected costs to the employee of shirking; increases in either will raise the expected costs to the employee of shirking. Let's consider the effects of each of these decision variables separately, holding one constant while we consider the other.

The wage chosen by the organization can cause workers to choose not to shirk. Consider the preceding equation expressed as an equality:

$$R = p * X * (w - W)$$

If the wage set by the organization, w, is chosen so that the preceding equality holds, then workers will be indifferent between shirking and "behaving." If we solve this equality for w, then we have found the minimum wage necessary to encourage workers not to shirk. We call this wage the efficiency wage w_e.

$$w_e = W + R/(X * p)$$

Notice that the efficiency wage, w_e, exceeds the alternative or opportunity wage W (recall that we have discounted W to account for search and other "new job" costs) by the amount $R/(X * p)$. Thus, the efficiency wage contains a quasi-rent. Efficiency wages contain this quasi-rent to attract and hold workers in a particular employment, provided the higher pay is designed to induce higher produc-

EFFICIENCY WAGES AT THE FORD MOTOR COMPANY

In 1914 Ford Motor Company made headlines by offering auto workers $5.00 per day, up from $2.50 a day. This was at a time when average wages in similar industries were paying between $2.00 and $3.00 a day.

Before 1913, automobile manufacturing required skilled workers. However, the assembly line changed all of that. Now work was repetitive and boring. As the automobile plants changed, turnover increased sharply and productivity fell.

To reduce the high level of turnover, the company offered an efficiency wage. The rationale was that the higher wage rate would increase efficiency. Only workers who had been at Ford for six months were eligible for the $5.00 a day wage. Within a few days, 10,000 workers applied for work.

Although Henry Ford was attacked for it, the policy worked. According to historians, the $5.00 a day wage raised the value of the job to Ford workers. The labor turnover rate plummeted and in 1914 labor productivity at Ford was an estimated 50 percent higher. So the increased productivity more than offset the increased wage. In sum, Ford's experience with the $5.00 an hour wage is consistent with efficiency wage theory; that is, in some cases, efficiency wages may reduce principal-agent problems.

Source: Daniel M. G. Raff and Lawrence Summers, "Did Henry Ford Pay Efficiency Wages?" Journal of Labor Economics *(October 1987), pp. 57–86.*

tivity. By paying an efficiency wage when employer monitoring is costly, the firm establishes a financial reward for honest behavior from its employees and so discourages them from shirking.

The second option open to organizations to forestall cheating is to choose a different level for p, the probability of detecting and firing employees for exhibiting shirking behavior. A larger value for p will raise the expected costs of shirking for employees and encourage their good behavior.

Raising p, however, may be costly, perhaps exorbitantly so. Recall that in the setting of the efficiency wage model, monitoring is costly; if it were not, a performance incentive scheme could be used if it solved some of the measurement problems discussed in Chapter 8.

One clear-cut managerial interpretation from the efficiency wage model is that wages and monitoring may be substitutes. Recall the expression for the efficiency wage:

$$w_e = W + R/(X * p)$$

First notice that w_e and p appear on opposite sides of the equation. The second thing to notice is that p appears in the denominator of a term added to the right-hand side. The organization's goal is to encourage workers not to shirk. One way to accomplish this, holding monitoring effort constant, is to raise the wages paid to workers. A second way is to increase p. Notice that if p is increased, the expression $R/(X * p)$ gets smaller, implying a smaller efficiency wage. It is in this sense that monitoring and wages are substitute tools in the manager's toolbox to encourage proper behavior by employees.

The fast-food industry provides an interesting test of the efficiency wage model. The fast-food business, as every college student knows, consists of a number of chains, including McDonald's, Burger King, Kentucky Fried Chicken, Arby's, and Roy Rogers. Each of these chains has a large number of outlets, some of which are managed by the company; others are owned and managed by independent businesspeople under a franchise agreement.

MATHEMATICAL EXAMPLE OF EFFICIENCY WAGES

Assume that a worker is currently being paid $35,000 per year and that, if fired, his best wage is $30,000. This worker is earning a quasi rent of $5,000.

Does it make sense for the worker to shirk? For simplicity, assume that the employment situation is expected to last only one period so that $X = 1$. Let's suppose that the worker could gain $500 by shirking and that the probability of getting caught and fired is equal to 0.05. In terms of our efficiency wage model, then

$w = \$35,000$	$W = \$30,000$
$p = 0.05$	$R = \$500$

The expected costs of shirking are $0.05 * (\$35,000 - \$30,000) * 1$, or $250. The expected costs of shirking are less than the gains from shirking; in fact, the expected costs are one-half of the gains of $500.

What wage in this example will discourage shirking? We need to calculate the efficiency wage of w_e. This calculation is as follows:

$$\$30,000 + \$500/(0.05 * 1) = \$40,000$$

To the consumer, the ownership form of a McDonald's is unknown and of little importance. All stores within the chain appear similar. Each has the same architecture, featuring the "golden arches." The menu is identical, and quality is consistent. In fact, a Big Mac looks and tastes the same in New York, Tokyo, London, and Springfield, Illinois. Joe's diner may serve better food, but you know exactly what you get at McDonald's. Moreover, each outlet is similar to all others in another aspect: it draws employment from the local labor market.

These restaurants differ, however, in one crucial respect. The company-owned restaurants are managed by salaried employees; the franchise units are managed by their owners. The owner has no control over the menu, interior decoration, suppliers of food stuffs, or pricing policies.

The franchise store is managed by the owner who chooses the compensation packages and conditions of employment offered to employees. She is the one who decides to pay workers $4.75 an hour or $6.25 an hour. She also sets conditions for fringe benefits and hours of work and makes the hiring and firing decisions. Most important, she also is the residual claimant to the income generated by the organization. In other words, she is the one who will reap the profits or suffer the losses.

An important aspect of management's job is to monitor and train the supervisory and nonmanagerial staff. Traditional economic theory suggests that the franchisee who collects the residual income monitors more intensely and trains more effectively than does a salaried manager. As we saw, efficiency wage theory suggests an inverse relationship between monitoring intensity and the efficiency wage. Companies will pay higher wages in their outlets than franchisees in theirs. The higher wage makes the job more valuable and, therefore, the workers more productive.

Data from two fast-food surveys[9] suggest that in 1985, wages in company restaurants for a sample of supervisors were 8.9 percent higher and for full-time workers, 1.7 percent higher. In addition, company restaurants were less likely to hire workers at the minimum wage than were franchise restaurants. Company restaurants were also more willing to increase fringe benefits, for example, free meals. Preventing workers from taking free meals is very difficult, especially at restaurants like McDonald's where most marketing efforts are targeted toward the demographic group from which both employees and customers are drawn.

We can sum up our argument so far as follows. As an incentive not to shirk, workers must be offered a higher wage than the competitive wage. If workers are fired for shirking, they face a decrease in wages. If the difference between wages is large, enough workers are induced to be productive, and the firm will not have a problem with shirking. The wage at which no shirking occurs is called the *efficiency wage*.

■ THE IMPORTANCE OF REPUTATION

Contractual Honesty

For as long as traders can recall, successful commerce demanded that people honor their contracts. As Adam Smith wrote more than 200 years ago,

> When a person makes perhaps 20 contracts a day, he cannot gain so much by endeavoring to impose on his neighbors, as the very appearance of a cheat would make him lose. When people seldom deal with one another, we find that they are

---

[9]James A. Brickley, Frederick H. Dark, and Michael S. Weisbach, "An Agency Perspective on Franchising," *Financial Management*, 20, Spring 1991, pp. 27–35.

somewhat disposed to cheat, because they can gain more by a smart trick than they can lose by the injury, which it does to their character.[10]

According to Adam Smith, the greater a merchant's business volume, the greater the incentive to act honestly to protect his or her valuable business reputation.

In many business situations, conditions arise that were not anticipated. Transactions can be classified according to how decisions are made in these circumstances. In the short run, there are not long, involved contracts. Individuals buy fish in the spot market. When the fish "stinks," the parties bargain among themselves. An alternative to the spot market is to establish a long-run relational contract, stipulating a governance structure (such as that discussed in Chapter 7), in which some designated party has the final word.

When you accept a job, you agree to follow whatever direction is given within some socially acceptable limits in exchange for some fixed hourly wage or salary. If you take a job at McDonald's, you agree to cook hamburgers, make milk shakes, or clean the toilet, depending on what is needed. However, you should not have to clean the toilet every day and be the only one to do it. The supervisor can exercise discretion in assigning tasks, and the employee must rely on the supervisor to do it fairly.

The disputes that arise in these situations are often connected with ambiguity about what kinds of discretionary behavior are honest or appropriate. Let us assume that although it is not possible to write complete contracts to cover all situations, it is possible for parties close to the transaction to determine whether the person with authority has done the right thing. This is a basic requirement of any system of reputation.

Although it may be impossible to specify in advance how the decision maker should behave in every possible situation, it may nevertheless be possible for those involved to decide afterward whether the parties behaved honorably. In reality, however, perceptions of circumstances frequently come into conflict. Parties differ about what was the right thing to do. Even when people agree about the circumstances, they often disagree about each alternative. The problem is often compounded when a third party is involved because it is very difficult for outsiders to settle disputes. The cost and difficulty of making those judgments and the need for them to be made repeatedly by a series of outsiders undermines the effectiveness of a system of trust based on reputation alone.

Corporate culture is one way to enhance the efficiency of a system of reputation within an organization. **Corporate culture** is a set of routines for decision making and shared expectations that employees are taught and the stories and related devices used to convey those expectations. The corporate culture provides a set of principles and procedures for judging right behavior and resolving legitimate disputes. Because the principles to be communicated have to be simple and easily understood, no one culture can work well for all organizations.

Sometimes rules just evolve. The field of academics can offer some interesting instances of corporate culture. For example, at the University of Chicago, faculty spend 90 percent of their time on research. At Harvard University, if the professor puts a set of equations on the board and a student asks how to solve them, the professor responds that it is obvious and moves on to the next topic.

Retail businesses try to cultivate a corporate culture in which the customer is always right. In a small grocery store in Vermont, there is a sign outside the store.

Corporate Culture

---

[10]Andrew Skinner, ed., *Adam Smith, The Wealth of Nations* (New York: Penguin Books, 1974), p. 355.

It reads, "The customer is always right." The second line reads, "If in doubt read the first line again." Macy's, the department store chain, is famous for accepting returned merchandise without asking questions. In New York City, it became common during the 1980s for people to buy a dress for a Saturday party and then return it on Monday. During the 1950s, it was common to have a three-martini business lunch. There are some indications that, at many large firms, the practice became unfavorable in the 1990s, perhaps because of changes in the tax laws.

Why is it important to offer trust in business? Offering trust maintains a person's or organization's reputation for honesty. In the world of business, a reputation for honesty can be a valuable asset because it can attract trading partners. It is expensive and time consuming to write detailed contracts. A good reputation can often allow a business deal to be closed with only a handshake instead of incurring the expenses associated with crossing all the *t*s in a contract.

Reputation and Market Discipline

One interesting aspect of reputation is that in markets where the competitive model introduced in Chapters 2 and 3 may not be applicable, reputation can serve as a disciplining mechanism working against unscrupulous, or unable, producers. For example, in the absence of a trusted mechanic, people commonly ask their friends for the names of garages with which they have had some good experiences. Some corporations place great emphasis on their reputations and will go to great lengths to protect them. One advertising slogan used by Sears, Roebuck stores in 1994 was "Solid as Sears," an attempt to create an image of a trustworthy seller in the minds of consumers. In short, in markets where information is scarce, reputation is often relied on as a substitute.

Along these same lines, reputation can be seen as a potential solution to the ex ante and ex post contracting problems outlined in Chapters 7 and 8. With respect to moral hazard, reputation may serve to make a credible claim by the agent that "I will not shirk." Likewise, regarding the hold up problem arising under conditions of asset specificity, a reputation may amount to one party believing the others when they claim to be "committed."

Institutionalized Reputation?

We also see instances in which organizations attempt to "institutionalize" reputation. In urban areas, for example, it is not uncommon for there to be an association of used car dealers. On a broader scale, some professional organizations have, as a part of their functioning, a practice of certifying members as being qualified or competent, perhaps even developing criteria to rate the efforts of their members. The American Medical Association is one such organization. To practice medicine in the United States, it is necessary to be certified by the AMA. Similar institutions exist for accountants and lawyers.

These attempts at "institutionalizing" reputation potentially suffer in one critical incentive dimension. The individuals who certify professional practices often stand to gain from the very reputation their organization is trying to create.

■ RENT-SEEKING BEHAVIOR

A Dark Side to Rents

Up to this point, we have examined how rents can have a positive influence on organizations. In other words, they can be used to increase efficiency. There is also a negative side to the existence of quasi-rents in organizations. The presence of rents in an organization can create incentives to attempt to reallocate these rents. Quite often these attempts at reallocating rents do not increase total value and may even decrease it. Economists consider such activities as pure costs. Activities that serve no social function other than to transfer rents or quasi-rents have come to be called **rent-seeking behaviors** and **directly unproductive activities (DUP)**.

A very simple example can illustrate rent-seeking behavior. Suppose that the government gives out monopolies and that it gives them away free. For example, a contract to build fighter aircraft can be very lucrative. The company winning the contract stands to earn substantial rents because of its monopoly position. The lobbying for these contracts is extensive, and such efforts typically involve millions of dollars of expenditures trying to influence the decision makers.

Economists call these costs **influence costs,** which attempt to alter the distribution of rents in an exchange situation. Such influence costs are directly unproductive activities since they fail to create value. Influence costs refer not only to the costs incurred by trying to alter the distribution of costs and compensation in an organization but also to the costs associated with making inefficient choices when exposed to another party's influence.

Rent-seeking activities in private organizations have received much less attention than those in government. In neoclassical theory, there are no good jobs and bad jobs. The wages that workers can earn are the same in all jobs. If two jobs are the same, then they pay the same. If one job is less pleasant than another, it pays more. Thus, if it takes more education to be an engineer than a truck driver, and obtaining this education is not pleasant, then the engineer will make more than the truck driver. If wages were really determined in this way, there would be no problem of organizational politics. People would not care about these decisions because all changes would be compensated for in their wages and salaries. However, the world of organizations is much more complicated, as we have already seen. There are quasi-rents within organizations, and real resources are allocated as each group fights for a larger share of the organizational pie. When an individual is asked to make specific investments in a job quasi-rents are created. Firms will be led to offer higher pay when good performance is called for and monitoring is difficult. Especially talented workers may be given higher wages, and workers who go through a training program will receive higher wages.

For influence activities to take place, two conditions have to be met. First, the affected parties must have open channels of communication to decision makers. Second, decisions have to be made that will affect the distribution of costs and compensation in the organization. Your university is a good example of an organization that meets the first condition. Universities are organizations that pride themselves on being open to all parties concerned and seek consensus governance.

Consider General Motors, and the influence activities and rent-seeking behavior of its labor unions. In the early 1990s, the company had been plagued by expensive labor contracts, declining demand, sliding market share, negative press, big restructuring changes, and the loss of $2 billion in 1993. The company desired to close four of its assembly plants, forcing workers into early retirement. GM offered enormous inducements. Workers at the plants scheduled for closure were able to retire as young as age 50 and receive vouchers of $10,000 toward the purchase of a new GM car plus more than $3,000 in cash to cover taxes, according to union officials. Unlike a normal retirement program, these workers would be able to take another job without reducing their GM pensions.

However, the rank and file have resisted these efforts at every turn. Why? Because these severance benefits, seemingly generous, were substantially less than the economic and quasi-rents earned by continuing workers. The numerous labor laws that allow unionization and enforce collective bargaining meet the first condition for influence activities: open channels of communication. The second condition, that decisions affecting the distribution of costs and compensation in the organization be made, is met because of the recent financial problems faced by GM. In 1993, General Motors agreed to delay closing two factories and to cancel

Influence Activities

the sale of a UAW–represented unit. The Kalamazoo, Michigan, stamping plant, once scheduled to close in 1995, now won't shut until 1998. The Tarrytown, New York, assembly plant will stay open an extra year until 1996.

Influence activities are not limited to former employees. In 1993 International Business Machine Corporation (IBM) was in the midst of the worst business crisis in its history. Once the world's most profitable corporation, IBM has had to eliminate 180,000 of its 405,000 jobs because it lost $8.37 billion that year. However, IBM still maintained an elaborate system of perks for its employees, despite the losses. In May 1993, IBM staged its "Golden Circle," a celebration for 330 of its best salespeople and their spouses. The money-losing computer giant rented a museum and treated everyone to veal and salmon, a five-act circus, casino games, and a live performance by Liza Minnelli.

Should IBM employees receive such rents when thousands of people are being laid off and shareholders are asked to sacrifice through lower stock prices and dividends? IBM was long considered the safest of the blue-chip stocks. Its steadily rising share price and generous dividend made it the mainstay of thousands of investors' portfolios. IBM's stock lost nearly 75 percent of its value in the six years prior to 1993. In 1993, IBM further hurt shareholders by chopping its annual dividend by 79 percent to $1 a share. Management's decision to continue to reward existing employees with rents lowers the return to existing stockholders. Employees slated to be laid off from the company's mainframe computer spent time lobbying to change the rules that regulate the distribution of rents within IBM.

Two elements of influence costs must be balanced to arrive at an optimal decision in any situation. First, opening the decision process to individuals whose own interests are at stake increases influence costs. This is true of either the professor who has to teach more hours or the employees at IBM who will be laid off. Second, these influence costs must be balanced with the improved information that accompanies more participation. We now examine the way in which influence costs can be reduced in organizations. One is to limit communication in an organization; the other is to limit the distributional implications of decisions.

Minimizing Influence Costs

It is important to design organizations that minimize influence costs. For example, if the Economics Department wants to hire more faculty because all of its professors are too busy doing research to teach, the dean can say no. However, this does not preclude the chairperson from making an appointment with the dean and other university administrators to discuss the matter over and over, thereby increasing influence costs. What is needed in organizations is a formal or informal method to curtail these types of discussions. "Politicking" is an expensive process.

One effective way to control politicking is to limit information. For example, most organizations keep salary information secret. Without salary information, it is more difficult to build a case for yourself. However, such secrecy is difficult in a democratic society. For example, in most public institutions, salaries are public information. Likewise, the earnings of top managers in large publicly traded firms are commonly known. Controlling influence costs by limiting information is costly because useful information is often eliminated as well. In the former Soviet Union, copy machines were kept under lock and key to keep information that could be used against the system private.

One way to limit the impact of adverse decisions is to limit the distribution of rents across potential competitors as much as possible. An excellent example is provided by the higher education system in Germany. There most professors are civil servants and their salaries are determined neither by good teaching nor good research, but rather by years of service.

Such a pay system is frequently adopted in large corporations as well. Another approach is to offer employees group performance incentives; this approach can also foster cooperation and improve productivity.

Several detailed studies of Japanese firms support the notion that efficiency is enhanced by limiting influence activities. Some interesting characteristics have been institutionalized into Japanese organizations. These include long-term employment, flexible teamwork, narrow pay differentials across similar workers, and wages tied heavily to seniority. Plant-level union and cooperative nonadversarial bargaining allow flexible informal agreements, and long-term employment in large firms encourages specific skill and career development for blue-collar team workers.

Internally, Japanese firms and associated company unions maintain consensual, participatory labor and management relations, which substantially reduce supervision and hierarchical control costs associated with traditional U.S. firms. Less well known is the role of the implicit equity stake held by Japanese employees. High levels of firm-specific skill, together with much steeper age-earnings schedules than in the United States, and a substantial lump-sum payment on retirement all combine to reduce mobility and impose considerable losses on core employees in case of bankruptcy or dismissal for unsatisfactory performance.[11]

Sometimes companies attempt to involve their workers more deeply in decision making. One of the ways to lessen the differences in interests between workers and management is the **employee stock ownership plan (ESOP).** By making employees shareholders, firms with ESOPs hope to make the workers as a group more accepting of organizational changes, more willing to be flexible in accommodating labor-saving arrangements, and more forthcoming with suggestions about how to improve operations.

▓ CHAPTER SUMMARY AND KEY IDEAS ▓ ▓ ▓ ▓ ▓ ▓

In classical economics, the literature devoted much space to the issue of rent. Land is original and indestructible, and the supply and locations are clearly scarce. If demand rises, rents rise; and if demand declines, rents decline. Rent therefore is not a cost of production but a return in excess of total cost.

In neoclassical economics, *rent* is defined as a return in excess of what is needed to attract a resource into an activity. A competitive economy has no rents. In a perfectly competitive labor market, all workers are paid the equilibrium wage. This wage is required to get the last worker to supply his or her labor. The other workers earn rents because their wage is higher than what would be needed to get them to work.

Employment is often a situation of a double moral hazard within the context of the principal-agent problem. Pay-for-performance plans are most capable of solving the principal-agent problem in those circumstances in which individual output can be readily measured. But in many jobs, measuring and assessing individual output is at best difficult and at worst impossible. The efficiency wage model suggests that firms pay an amount above the market-clearing wage as a way to reduce employee shirking. The higher wage increases the relative value of the job as viewed by each worker. If workers are fired for shirking, they face a decrease in wages. If the difference between wages is large enough, workers are in-

Chapter 9
*Distribution, Rents,
and Efficiency*

A Japanese Approach

[11]Felix R. FitzRoy and Zoltan J. Acs, "The New Institutional Economics of the Firm and Lessons from Japan," *Japan and the World Economy* 4, 1992, pp. 129–143.

duced to be more productive, thus increasing efficiency, and the firm does not have a problem with shirking. The wage at which no shirking occurs is the efficiency wage.

The distinction between rents and quasi-rents is important. A rent is the portion of earnings in excess of the minimum amount needed to attract a worker to accept a particular job, or for a firm to enter an industry. A quasi-rent is the portion of earnings in excess of the minimum amount needed to prevent an agent from quitting her job. The crucial difference is that although rents are defined in terms of decisions to enter an industry or job, quasi-rents are defined in terms of decisions to exit a job or industry. In most of this chapter, we have been concerned with quasi-rents, which agents stand to lose if forced to exit an industry.

The existence of quasi-rents tempts people in organizations to compete for them. The attempt to reallocate economic rents between agents has no positive benefits. Activities that serve no social function other than to transfer rents are called *rent-seeking activities*. These activities have economic costs known as *influence costs*. Influence activities take place if two conditions are met. First, decisions have to be made that affect the distribution of costs and wages in the organization. Second, the affected parties must have information and open channels of communication to decision makers.

At least two elements of influence costs must be balanced. Opening the decision process to individuals whose interests are at stake increases influence costs. However, those influence costs must be balanced with the improved information that accompanies more participation. How to limit influence cost in organizations is an important aspect or organizational design.

One effective way to control politicking is to limit information. Controlling influence costs by limiting information is costly because useful information is often also eliminated. The other way to limit influence costs is to limit the impact of adverse decisions by limiting the distribution of rent across potential competitors. Participatory management is an attempt to do just that.

Japanese firms and their associated company unions practice participatory management. Key features include long-term employment, flexible teamwork, narrow pay differentials, limited outside opportunities, and job rotation. The workers also have an implicit equity stake in the company. High levels of firm-specific skill, together with much steeper age-earnings schedules than in the United States and a substantial lump-sum payment on retirement, all combine to reduce mobility and influence costs.

▇ KEY TERMS

adaptation costs	marginal productivity theory
corporate culture	monopoly power
directly unproductive activities (DUP)	opportunity costs
economic rents	quasi-rents
employee stock ownership plan (ESOP)	rent-seeking behavior
	skill acquisition costs
efficiency wage model	sunk costs
entry barrier	worker search costs
influence costs	

▇ FURTHER READINGS

Buchanan, J., R. Tollison, and G. Tullock. *Towards a Theory of the Rent Seeking Society*. College Station, TX: Texas A&M University Press, 1980.
Clark, J. B. *The Distribution of Wealth*. New York: Macmillan, 1893.

Kruger, A. B. "Ownership, Agency and Wages: An Explanation of Franchising in the Fast Food Industry." Working paper 3334. National Bureau of Economic Research, 1990.

Raff, D. M. G. and L. Summers. "Did Henry Ford Pay Efficiency Wages?" *Journal of Labor Economics* (October 1987), pp. 57–86.

Shapiro, C. and J. Stiglitz. "Equilibrium Unemployment as a Worker Discipline Device." *American Economic Review* 74 (June 1984), pp. 433–444.

Smith, A. *Lectures on Justice, Revenue and Arms*, ed. Edwin Cannan. New York: Augustus M. Kelley, 1964.

▆ QUESTIONS AND PROBLEMS FOR REVIEW AND DISCUSSION

A. Limits on a party's ability to pay cash damages are a common reason for distribution and efficiency to be linked. Criminals are usually punished for their crimes with prison terms rather than through a form of restitution. Some societies rely on whipping, ostracism, and even death. These forms of punishment result in a net reduction in total welfare.

  1. Evaluate the following claim: "Social efficiency should require that victims receive some financial compensation from those who have harmed them."

  2. Can you provide any rationale for the lack of legal support for victim remuneration for certain crimes?

  3. Can you provide any rationale for two systems of justice in the United States, one civil and the other criminal? Why are some offenses classified as civil and result in remuneration via law suits?

B. Consider an industry in which an existing producer exploits significant economies of scale. Usually, economies of scale are associated with very large fixed costs of production.

  1. Explain why these economies of scale represent a significant entry barrier.

  2. Explain how these rents can be protected from being captured by entrants. In your explanation, consider two firms, incumbent and entrant. Explain what the economic rents and quasi-rents are for each firm.

C. A common complaint of university students is that professors seem too remote and disinterested in teaching them. How do university systems of compensation, promotion, tenure, and pay raises contribute to the problem?

D. Firms that employ skilled workers are very conscious about the wages being paid by other employers and where they fit in the distribution of wages. In fact, there are many surveys done each year (and sold to business) of the compensation being paid in different geographic areas and industries to different types of employees.

  1. Is this consistent with the standard labor market story of classical economics in which workers are paid a wage equal to the value of their marginal products?

  2. How can this phenomenon be explained in the context of the model of efficiency wages?

E. Under what types of conditions would you expect a firm to pay its workers an efficiency wage as opposed to an incentive-based wage?

F. In your opinion, can repeated dealings solve the problems of moral hazard in a contracting environment?

The four major themes of this textbook are exchange, organization, the role of imperfect information, and contracting in an environment ripe with opportunism. In Part I, we focused on traditional approaches to exchange and organization. The latter two themes were, for the most part, assumed away. In Part II, we introduced an alternative vantage point, via transaction costs and contracting, from which to view the four major themes of this book. In Part III, we apply our knowledge of transaction cost economics to an integral component of firm existence: the financing activities of the organization. The emphasis here is on a sometimes imprecise relationship between the owners and those who control the firm. In this part, we extend the four major themes of this textbook into the interaction between organizations and those who finance their activities.

Chapter 10, "**Modern Financial Theory,**" concentrates on understanding some basic tools and issues of financial analysis. In the beginning of the chapter, we present one vision of a nearly utopian environment in which all involved parties share the same information and expectations. There is a striking resemblance between this theoretical setting and the traditional neoclassical analysis of economic markets. Not surprising, the outcome in this case is efficient, and we present a shortened version of the Modigliani-Miller theories. We then begin to drop some of the assumptions guaranteeing perfect information and attempt to analyze behavior when transaction costs cannot be ignored. We explain that the relationship between the owners and managers of the firm is one beset by moral hazard contracting problems. When these issues become so prevalent, ownership

ORGANIZATION, OWNERSHIP, AND CONTROL

interests must reassert their control; quite often, this implies ownership change, corporate restructurings, and the selling off of several corporate divisions.

Chapter 11, "Corporate Control and Economic Efficiency," is directly concerned with the establishment of an efficient relationship between the owners and managers of a firm. It centers on the issue of corporate control raised in the previous chapter but greatly enriches this concept in a number of ways. We directly consider the market for corporate control, discussing the efficiency aspects of mergers and acquisitions. Other, managerially useful concepts such as the use of debt and leveraged buyouts to enforce managerial efficiency are discussed. By and far, the most interesting aspect of Chapter 11 for managers is the model of corporate control. This model explicitly recognizes the existing moral hazard contracting problems and identifies explicit steps that can be taken to minimize their impact.

The material in this part of the text is not meant to replace fully developed courses in finance but to serve as an introduction or supplement to these courses. Transaction cost–based analysis can provide some useful and enriching insights in understanding the relationship between owners and managers of firms. With a good understanding of postcontractual opportunism in general and moral hazard in particular, we hope that the two chapters in Part III are not only educational but enjoyable as well.

Modern Financial Theory

After the crash, the media tried to explain it by talking about the country's budget deficits, trade deficits, and the possibility of new taxes. But economists pointed out that these factors had existed for a while, and still exist without causing continual stock market crashes. Examining the historical record and the experience of other countries showed that most of the explanations provided by journalists and Wall Street analysts simply did not hold up. A thorough economic analysis is not a list of anecdotes, but a systematic examination of all the relevant data.[1]

CHAPTER OUTLINE AND STUDENT GOALS

How do firms raise funds to sustain their operations? Given the options available, what are the implications of each for the organization? Firms at numerous points in their development face these two central questions. The answers to these questions are by no means simple and are best formed by recognizing the environment in which the firm conducts its financial transactions, the institutional forces at work in that environment, and the implications of the various financing options for organizational control and structure.

In this chapter, we attempt to gain an understanding of these issues and questions at a very intuitive level by considering some of the basic financial issues confronting firms today and illustrating the organizational implications of these financial issues. Toward this end, we hope to put these issues in the context of theoretical developments in corporate finance. On the organizational side, we also explicitly consider the roles played by transaction costs and imperfect information. One key issue in firms concerns the separation of ownership and control first introduced in Chapter 8 and the principal-agent context in which this separation is best viewed.

In Chapter 1, we introduced the three forms of corporate ownership: proprietorship, partnership, and corporation. The simplest legally recognized business form is the proprietorship, which has only one owner, a form best suited to very small business.

When at least one more ownership interest is added, the business becomes a partnership. The key feature of both proprietorships and partnerships is that, in each, all ownership interests are liable for debts incurred by the business. Conceptually, the unlimited liability in a partnership promotes efficiency in the relationship because it encourages any given partner to closely monitor the actions of all

---

[1] Joseph E. Stiglitz, *Economics* (New York: W. W. Norton, 1993), p. 271.

other partners.[2] Once a critical size is reached, however, the allure of a partner-ship may clearly diminish. Some of the largest accounting firms were organized as, and continue to be partnerships. Pominent examples include Arthur Andersen, with 1993 fee income of $6.02 billion; Deloitte Touche Tohmatsu, with 1993 fee income of $5 billion; and Price Waterhouse, with 1993 fee income of $3.89 bil-lion. When operations are spread across countries and continents, coordination and motivation costs may simply become too large to bear and another corporate form will be chosen.

Legally incorporated businesses circumvent the liability problem by featuring limited liability for ownership stakes; the firms' owners can lose only as much as they invest. Ownership of corporations is gained by purchasing the equities, or shares of stock, of that firm. The limited liability of corporations makes it possible for their equities to be sold in public markets, providing tremendous advantages in the capital markets for corporations.

Even though limited liability provides an advantage of creating markets in which the firm can issue stocks as a source of funds, it also poses a certain organiza-tional problem for the firm: although ownership may be clearly defined legally, in practice, control may be less easily determined. In a proprietorship, one owner must make all decisions based solely on her welfare. Ernst & Young, one of the "Big Six" accounting firms, had 5,300 partners in 1993. General Motors is one of the largest corporations in the world, with literally millions of stockholders. It may be quite difficult to say who is in charge in large partnerships, and even impossible in large corporations. The problem is further complicated when firms borrow funds directly from large lenders such as commercial banks; quite often, large pri-vate lenders insist on conditions that transfer a certain amount of control to them.

Here, once again, is the primary interest of corporate finance from an organi-zation perspective: the separation of ownership and control.

After reading this chapter, you should be able to

- Explain the difference between debt, equity, and retained earnings as in-struments for raising capital.

- Explain why a firm's capital structure is important for bankruptcy, corpo-rate control, and efficiency considerations.

- Understand the Modigliani-Miller theorems as they pertain to organiza-tional issues.

- Understand the role of moral hazard in the separation of ownership and control.

- Explain why the Modigliani-Miller theorems may not hold given numerous agency and incentive issues facing managers.

- Be able to explain net present value to a layperson.

SOME DIFFERENT FORMS OF CAPITAL

Corporations obtain the funds necessary to conduct their activities in three princi-pal ways: sale of stocks, borrowing (which may include the sale of bonds or bor-rowing privately), and "plowback," keeping some part of company earnings, termed *retained earnings*, rather than returning it to investors.

---

[2] A really good article about partnerships was "Partners in Pain," *The Economist* (July 9, 1994), p. 61. The gist of the article is that the partnership is losing some of its desirability as organizations become very, very large.

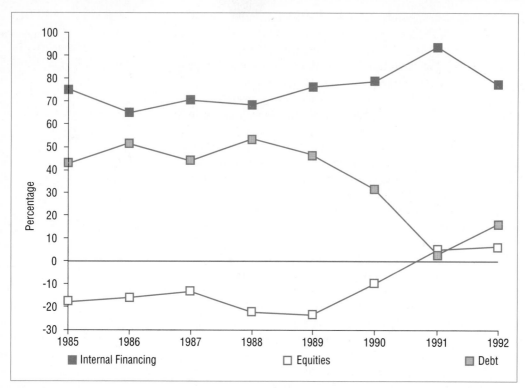

Figure 10.1 Sources of Corporate Financing

Figure 10.1 provides some idea of the mix between the three sources of corporate financing used by firms between 1985 and 1992.[3] Figure 10.1 shows the percentage of total financing attributable to each source. The upper line in the figure shows that, on average, firms provide the vast majority of their own financing from internal sources, including retained earnings. The middle line in Figure 10.1 shows the percentage attributable to the numerous forms of debt that fell in both relative and absolute importance from 1989 through 1992. Part of the change in sources of financial funds through the 1985–1992 period was a resurgence in the use of equities through the same time period.

Background on Stocks

The stocks of corporations are usually traded in one of the major exchanges. The New York Stock Exchange (NYSE) is the largest and best-known market for the equities of corporations, dealing with only 2,000 of the best known and widely traded companies. There are other exchanges including the American Stock Exchange and the National Association of Securities Dealer (NASDAQ) Exchange, which deal in smaller, lesser known firms. The leading U.S. brokerage firms hold "seats" on the NYSE, which permit them to trade directly on the exchange.

Someone who wants to buy a stock on the NYSE must use a broker who will deal with a firm that has a seat on the exchange. Suppose you live in Wisconsin and want to buy 200 shares of General Motors stock. The broker you approach may be employed by a firm that has a seat on the exchange, or she may work

---

[3] Figure 10.1 is based on *The Statistical Abstract of the United States, 1993* (Washington, D.C.: U.S. Government Printing Office, 1993), Table 853, p. 534. Internal uses of funds include domestic and foreign undistributed profits, inventory valuation, and capital consumption allowances. The data for debt are constructed using all external sources minus equity issues. The equity issues may be negative if a firm is a net purchaser of its stock in the market.

through another firm that holds one. In either event, your broker contacts a "specialist" who works on the floor of the NYSE and handles GM stock. This specialist may own enough GM stock to fill your order and may have limit orders of other investors permitting the specialist to sell their shares of GM stock at specified prices. The specialist takes your order to the floor and determines a price that more or less balances the supply and demand for GM stock. At this price, the specialist fills your order from one of his limit orders to sell (he must do so whenever possible), or he will fill it out of his personal inventory of General Motors stock.

Purchasing shares in a firm amounts to acquiring an equity interest in that firm. **Equity** represents a stake in a corporation made by an investor who obtains some rights to dictate the policies and operations of the firm. If there are 100,000 shares of stock in existence for a corporation, and an individual investor purchases 1,000 of these, that investor owns 1 percent of that firm. What does the investor receive for her investment in the stock of a particular firm? She receives two things: some degree of ownership and a claim on the earnings of that firm.

Ownership is important for two reasons. First, ownership implies some control over the firm's operations; as will be explained later in this chapter, control is a rather slippery concept in this context. Second, the investor may sell her ownership interest at some later date; if the firm's profitability increases, so will the value of her shares. In this scenario, the investor benefits by being able to capture a capital gain caused by appreciation in the stock price. Of course, part of the risk in investing in stocks is the fact that share prices may depreciate, resulting in a capital loss.

Earnings are simply funds that the corporation has left over from receipts after paying its workers, its suppliers, and other investors who have lent the firm money and hold debt in the firm. Shortly we will speak more about the debt holders of the firm; for now, it suffices to mention that the debt holders receive no ownership interest in the firm. Earnings are divided into two categories by the firm. Some portion, usually about one-third, of earnings is returned on a per share basis to stockholders in the form of a dividend. The bulk of earnings is usually "plowed back" into the firm in the form of retained earnings. Admittedly, this scenario is largely a simplification; one of the largest and most complex areas of corporate finance is determining the best dividend policy for firms. However, this simplification is useful for us because it does allow us to focus on issues more central to an understanding of organizational structure.

When a corporation sells shares to raise funds, the new issue is usually handled by a special firm called an *investment bank* and is not directly related to activity on one of the major exchanges. When new equities are issued, their trading does not occur on one of the exchanges but rather in a primary market.

The major role played by the major stock exchanges in the U.S. economy is to provide liquidity by creating a **secondary market** for the equities of existing firms. The established markets trade almost exclusively in equities held by individuals who bought them earlier and now wish to sell them. Liquidity is created because prices at which "secondhand" securities can be exchanged are determined. Investors then face less risk. The function of the market is to process information relevant to a particular firm in a given industry and enable existing shares to be exchanged.

This raises an interesting question for our discussion of corporate stocks: "Just how are stock prices determined?" If your answer is "randomly," there is much support for your reply. Before we explain why, let's consider a widely recognized determinant of stock prices. The price of any individual stock is largely determined by the return it yields to investors. Thus, one important component is the size of the dividend relative to the share price. A second, more volatile type of return to the investor results from expectations concerning changes in the share price that rely largely on beliefs about future firm profitability. If investors believe that the company will be more profitable in the future, they will see the option of holding stocks now as more desirable because current stock prices will rise.

On numerous occasions, economists have picked stocks for investment using completely arbitrary selection criteria; the most popular is to choose by throwing darts at a list of stocks on the wall. The darts identify the stocks to invest in, and they are included into a stock portfolio. The return to that portfolio (including accounting for dividends, stock splits, and capital gains) is calculated and compared against the returns on portfolios chosen by market professionals who used much more sophisticated techniques. It would be wrong to say that the dart method yields higher returns to investors. It would be right, however, to say that half the time the professionals do better.

There are two widely offered hypotheses—which are almost completely opposite to the other—as to why stock price movements are largely random. The first asserts that stock prices are random because market professionals are able to perfectly foresee every influence on corporate profitability that is not random. The professionals become immediately aware of any relevant change and buy or sell the stock in sufficient quantities to move the market price to the level they foresee as proper. Then the only thing for that stock price to do between the professional buyings and sellings is to wander randomly. Even this random wandering would not occur if professionals could somehow foresee random events.

The second view of random stock prices is that no investor has perfect information. In such an environment, ignorance is the only thing common to all investors; however, every investor holds an opinion. The net effect of this informational environment is that anything and everything can affect stock prices. Announcements of a new technology becoming available in an industry could cause some investors to see lower corporate profits ahead and some to see higher profits ahead. In this second view of random movements of stock prices, investors often characterize their strategy by considering what they expect other investors to do. An interesting perspective on this process was offered in 1936 by John Maynard Keynes:

> This battle of wits to anticipate the basis of conventional valuation a few months hence, rather than the prospective yield of an investment over a long term of years, does not even require gulls amongst the public to feed the maws of the professional;—it can be played by professionals amongst themselves. Nor is it necessary that anyone should keep his simple faith in the conventional basis of valuation having any genuine long-term validity. For it is, so to speak, a game of Snap, of Old Maid, of Musical Chairs—a pastime in which he is victor who says Snap neither too soon nor too late, who passes the Old Maid to his neighbour before the game is over, who secures a chair for himself when the music stops.[4]

Background on Bonds

As evidenced by the data presented in Figure 10.1, the **debt** of corporations represents an even more important source of funds for corporations. There are a number of different types of debt, but all share one important property: under any circumstance, the debt holders are paid before the stockholders. Corporate debt may take one of three forms: loans from commercial banks; loans from the so-called private sector, mainly large institutions such as life insurance companies and pension funds; or bonds.

---

[4] John Maynard Keynes, *The General Theory of Employment, Interest, and Money* (New York: Harcourt Brace Jovanovich, 1964), p. 155.

Beyond the legal ordering of stakeholders in terms of claims against the firm, bonds differ from stocks in several ways. Primarily, for our own purposes, we must point out that a bond is nothing more than a loan; there is no pretense of the bond holder having control of the corporation. Second, whereas stockholders have no idea how much they will receive for their stocks when they sell them, or how much they will receive in dividends each year, bond holders know how much money they will be paid regularly and how much they will receive when their bonds reach maturity, that is, when the underlying loan period has expired.

Although it may seem that bonds are less risky than stocks, this is simply not true; bond holders face large liquidity risks. If an investor holds a bond and needs her funds before the maturity of the bond, she can sell the bond. The price at which the bond is sold depends crucially on the current market rate of interest. To see why, we must recognize that a bond is basically an agreement in which the borrowing company agrees to give the lender fixed interest payments at various points in time. Being an investment, the bond must compete with other bonds and types of investments in terms of return. If market interest rates rise, then the fixed interest payment yielded by a bond is of lower value to any investor and the price of the bond falls.

When a corporation issues debt, it promises fixed payments of specified amounts occurring at previously determined dates. Long-term debt is either secured or unsecured. **Secured debt** is backed by an existing asset; in the event of default, the holder of the debt is entitled to the asset and may choose to either keep it or sell it. **Unsecured debt** is supported only by the general creditworthiness of the borrower; in the event of default, the lender must force bankruptcy and liquidation of the borrower's assets.

The most common form of secured debt issued by corporations is a **commercial mortgage,** which is secured by fixed property such as buildings. Commercial mortgages account for most of the lending activity of institutional investors because of their relatively low risk. A similar financial instrument is a **mortgage bond,** which is also asset backed and may be traded. Lending via the use of a **lease** is an avenue of issuing debt that has been growing in importance over the last 10 years. Suppose that a firm wishes to borrow money to buy a technologically so-

BOND PRICES AND INTEREST RATES

A negative relationship exists between bond prices and interest rates; if one increases, the other must decrease. For example, suppose that in 1994, Chrysler sold a bond with a face value of $10,000, which promised to make interest payments of $1,000 at the end of each of the next 10 years, and at the end of the 10-year period to return the purchase price of the bond, the investor's principal. The yield on the bond is then 10 percent.

Suppose that in 1996 market interest rates on investments of similar duration and risk as the Chrysler bond rise to 12 percent. If one of the Chrysler bonds needs to be sold, what will its price be? No buyer would be willing to pay $10,000 for the bond because higher yields can be had elsewhere. The price of the bond then must fall to guarantee an investor a 12 percent rate of return on his investment if he purchases the Chrysler bond.

When market interest rates in the economy rise, there must be a fall in the prices of previously issued bonds with their (lower) fixed interest payments. Likewise, when interest rates fall, the prices of previously issued bonds must increase.

phisticated piece of productive machinery; instead of handing the firm a check, the bank buys the machinery and loans it to the firm. Leasing may be mutually more attractive for two reasons. First, the bank maintains ownership rights to the machine: depreciation allowances and investment tax credits lower the cost of the "loan" to the bank by producing offsetting benefits for tax purposes.[5] Second, repossession in light of default may be easier.

For illustrative purposes we may divide unsecured debt into two categories: privately placed and that sold to the general public. Obtaining debt through a **private placement** amounts essentially to a long-term loan made to a firm by a large investor, which we will refer to loosely as a bank. The advantages to the borrower of a private placement are basically speed and secrecy. The increasing use of private placements results in large part from a new rule approved by the Securities and Exchange Commission (Rule 144a) that allows financial institutions of a minimum size to participate in trading of private placements. Thus, as with the stock market, a secondary market has been created to provide liquidity.

A **public issue** of debt is usually unsecured and results in bonds, or debentures, that are traded actively in established markets. Each time a new public issue is carried out, the firm must release large amounts of data to the public and to a firm that will rate the debentures, such as Standard and Poor's or Moody's. The sale of the debt itself is done by an **underwriter,** who purchases the entire issue and resells it to the public. A few firms handle most of the underwriting in the United States: Merril Lynch, Goldman Sachs, Lehman Brothers, Kidder Peabody, and Salomon Brothers are among the most well known.

**A Firm's Debt-
Equity Ratio**

With a background of equities, bonds, and retained earnings in place, we can now compare and contrast the aspects of each type of investment from the point of view of the corporation. What we are really talking about here is the capital structure of the firm. A firm's **capital structure** refers to the mix of debt and equity financing chosen by a particular firm. A firm's capital structure is represented by a debt-equity ratio: as debt plays a larger role in a firm, that is, as the firm becomes more leveraged, the debt-equity ratio increases. Similarly, as equity becomes more important for a firm, the debt-equity ratio falls.

For the most part, a firm can choose any capital structure it wants and can effectively change that structure as it deems appropriate. It could issue bonds, using the proceeds to buy back some stock currently held by investors, effectively increasing the debt-equity ratio. When a firm alters its debt-equity ratio without changing its assets, it is said to have experienced **financial restructuring.**

What is the best debt-equity ratio for a firm? This is a very general question with a number of highly technical and complex answers. *For now, suffice it to say that the optimal capital structure is the one that maximizes the market value, and hence, shareholder value in the firm.* We now turn our attention to actually comparing the alternative sources of financing through the eyes of the firm as it considers its relationship with the investors.

Tax considerations must enter into the firm's decision making. The firm must pay both types of lenders, bond holders and stockholders. The interest payments made to service debt are tax deductible; the dividend payments to the firm's stockholders are not. Other things being equal, it is cheaper for the firm to make interest payments than to pay dividends since the former reduces the firm's ultimate tax liability. Other aspects of the tax code impact the relationship between firms and their investors.

---

[5] These tax benefits may be more valuable to the bank than to the firm if the bank is in a higher tax bracket.

When dividends are paid, they are in effect subject to double taxation, as income for the corporation and as income for the individuals receiving them. Taken together, this double taxation problem seems to discourage individuals from holding stock, although its ultimate impact on the firm's choice of capital structure is probably negligible. From the investors' perspective, however, the current tax code features one important aspect for stockholders; capital gains are typically taxed at lower rates than are dividend and interest income.

These features of the tax code, when considered together, make debt more attractive than equity from the firm's perspective.

The ultimate fear for both firms and their investors is **bankruptcy**. Bankruptcies play an important role in our economic system from an efficiency perspective. If society does not pay a corporation to stay in business, then the resources of that corporation are better off, from society's point of view, in other uses. Along these lines, commercial banks and private lenders can provide an important service by carefully selecting those they lend money to and monitoring their behavior after the loans are made.

Even though some banks and other private lenders willingly keep lending to a firm if the rate of interest charged is increased sufficiently to compensate for the increased risk of business failure, rational firms place an upper limit on their borrowing. Despite its tax deductibility, debt still imposes interest costs on a firm that may prove difficult to pay during times of economic hardship. Bankruptcy imposes large costs on shareholders, creditors, and managers. Shareholders lose their investments; creditors must suffer through exceedingly long and potentially expensive legal avenues of debt collection; and managers may lose credibility and reputation, effectively precluding them from future jobs.

A firm's debt-equity ratio is also important because it may affect the market's beliefs about future profitability. Except for a few mythical market professionals who are "super" smart and able to interpret market signals better than everyone else, most investors believe that a firm's managers are in a better position to judge

MANAGERIAL BEHAVIOR: DEBT VERSUS EQUITY

Under a certain set of circumstances, a firm's managers can be expected to react differently according to the degree of firm leverage, the value of its debt-equity ratio.

If a firm is primarily financed by equity, managers may simply lack aggressiveness. As long as the company is making money and easily paying off its interest costs with enough money left over to give investors a reasonable dividend, managers may not be under suitable pressure to perform.

On the other hand, in a highly leveraged firm, managers are forced to be efficient and to work hard to avoid bankruptcy. In the 1970s, for example, the sharp increase in world oil prices brought many U.S. oil companies massive profits, much of which were retained. The investments made with these retained earnings proved unwise. As a result, people perceived that managers had failed to do their jobs well enough, and the market stepped in to correct the situation through threatened and actual takeovers.

The effect of these takeovers was ultimately to force better performance on firm managers. One very important lesson was learned, however. In all the firms, those taken over and those not, leverage was quite high and managers became better at making profitable investments.

the company's future well-being than they are. Since a firm's managers also wish to avoid bankruptcy, investors may view a high debt-equity ratio as a good sign. If the well-informed managers perceive little risk and are willing to borrow, investors can rationally be expected to tolerate, and possibly be encouraged by, a more highly leveraged firm. In a more leveraged firm, the fear of bankruptcy is incentive enough for managers to work hard, future prospective investors will be convinced of a rosy future, and the market value of the firm's shares will increase. In this way, a higher debt-equity ratio will lower the firm's overall cost of capital.

■ THE EFFICIENT MARKETS HYPOTHESIS AND THE MODIGLIANI-MILLER THEOREMS

In Chapters 2, 3, and 4, we applied economic concepts within the realm of the competitive world. Perhaps the most relevant feature of the competitive world is the widespread availability of information to all economic agents. Within a perfectly competitive economic system, prices characterize all relevant information. Modern financial theory began with a similar background in analyzing the relationship between firms and their lenders and investors by developing the efficient market hypothesis, the topic to which we now turn. To simplify our discussion, we focus on trading in the market with which most of you are familiar, the stock market.

**The Efficient
Market Hypothesis**

The price investors are willing to pay for a share of stock depends on numerous factors such as the size of the dividend, expected capital gains, liquidity, and expected future profitability of the firm whose share they purchase. Later in this chapter, we discuss the so-called dartboard theory of stock selection to illustrate why some investors may conclude that movements in stock prices are random.

In theoretical finance there is an abstraction that basically sums up the logic that there are no special deals or bargains to be had. The **efficient market hypothesis** (EMH) asserts that well-organized equity markets, such as the NYSE, are efficient markets, at least as a practical matter. In efficient markets, expectations concerning future profitability are formed, and stock prices reflect these expectations accurately. Thus, technically speaking, the EMH is a multiperiod concept with current stock movements tied to expected future returns. Advocates of the EMH might argue that although inefficiencies may exist in markets, they are relatively small and occur very infrequently. Efficient markets imply that there are no excess profits to be earned.

Competition among investors is the driving force behind enforcing efficient markets. Some individuals spend their entire working (and perhaps personal) lives trying to identify stocks that are not properly priced. They go to great lengths to identify equities that they perceive to be likely candidates for mispricing. They study what has happened in the past to the price of a particular stock and its dividends. They learn about past earning profiles, levels of debt, what new investments are planned, and how the firm's strategy is likely to react to future economic conditions.

Although this is a good deal of information, there is a powerful incentive for knowing it, for if a stock is priced too low or too high, exorbitant profits could be earned. If you know more about some company than other investors in the marketplace, you can profit from that knowledge by buying or selling that company's shares. If numerous individuals pursue such activities drawn by the profit motive, the logical outcome of all this information gathering and processing is that mispriced stocks will become fewer and fewer. Put another way, competition among investors will guarantee that just enough information is gathered. The competition generated by investors looking for that special stock, will, in practice, serve only to keep all market participants honest.

The efficient market hypothesis is probably the most discussed proposition of modern financial theory. As such, there are some misconceptions about what the EMH really is all about. First, efficiency is not an absolute question but one of degree. Second, the randomness of stock prices embodied by the so-called dartboard theory discussed earlier is often misinterpreted as implying that it doesn't matter which stocks an investor purchases. This is simply not true; most investors have definite preferences that should be reflected in their stock portfolio selections. One of the most well-known types of investing follows a "widows and orphans" strategy, investing only in the equities of large public utilities and blue-chip firms, which offer low risk and low return but also stability.

Efficiency implies that the price that a firm obtains when it sells a share of its stock is a "fair" price in the sense that it reflects the value of that stock given the information that is available about the firm and the costs of gathering and processing that information. Investors need not worry that they are paying too much for a stock with a low dividend or some other characteristic because the market has already incorporated that characteristic into the price. In stock trading terminology, we would say that all pieces of information have been *priced out*.

The concept of efficient markets can be further explained by addressing a supposed objection to the EMH. It is sometimes argued that because stock prices randomly fluctuate on a day-to-day basis, the markets must not be efficient. However, our discussion implies that these price movements are, in fact, consistent with the EMH. Given the amount of data generated by firms listed on major exchanges such as the NYSE and the many avenues for their distribution—*The Wall Street Journal, Business Week, Fortune, America OnLine*, the *MacNeil/Lehrer News Hour*, and so on—one would expect continuous price movements. At noon EDT on July 10, 1996, a piece of news about IBM may emerge that investors view favorably. At 5:00 PM EDT on July 10, 1996, a second piece of news about IBM may emerge that investors view unfavorably. Further complicating the picture is the possibility that either piece of news on IBM may later be shown to be false. Do stock prices fluctuate too much? You decide.

We turn our attention now to considering the options open to a firm in developing its capital structure. A great deal of research into this question resulted in theoretical propositions by Franco Modigliani of the Massachusetts Institute of Technology and Merton Miller of the University of Chicago. The Modigliani-Miller approach (hereafter referred to as *M-M*) does not require that the EMH holds, for, as we will see, the M-M approach is relevant for a single point in time when expectations are fixed. The M-M approach does assume, however, that debt and equity markets are competitive and free of friction caused by informational asymmetries and that managerial incentives are not altered by the firm's debt-equity ratio.

The approach yields two very broad and general propositions concerning a firm's debt structure and its total market value. A firm's **total market value** is defined as the amount of cash required to purchase a firm free and clear. If an investor wished to purchase and actually own a firm, she would have to pay current equity owners for their stakes and retire all outstanding debt. In this sense, the total market value of a firm is just like the total market value of a used car; the most one would rationally pay for a used car is the amount required to obtain the ownership rights plus the cost of any necessary repairs, which may be viewed as debts owed either by the car itself or its current owner.

The M-M approach features two separate theorems relating the total market value of firms to their capital structures. Earlier in this chapter, we discussed reasons that a firm may prefer one type of capital structure over another. For now, as we explore developments in theoretical finance, these concerns over taxation,

**The Modigliani-
Miller Approach**

bankruptcy, and managerial incentives are ignored and effectively put on hold until later.[6] As you learn about the M-M approach, we hope that you realize that it is about the smooth functioning of markets and has much in common with the perfectly competitive (and necessarily efficient) market economy studied by neoclassical economists and visited in Chapters 2, 3, and 4.

The first **Modigliani-Miller theorem** (M-MT1) states that ignoring bankruptcy, taxes, informational asymmetries, and managerial incentive problems, the total market value of the firm is independent of its capital structure. The first part of M-MT1 implicitly invokes the EMH and requires that changes in a firm's debt-equity ratio do not significantly alter firm profitability.

To begin to understand the logic on which the M-MT1 is based, consider the financing options open to XYZ Corporation seeking to build a new $50 million widget plant. Currently, XYZ has a number of shares outstanding in addition to an equal dollar value of debt; thus, XYZ's debt-equity ratio is 1.

If XYZ borrows the $50 million by taking on some form of debt, it will become more highly leveraged, and its debt-equity ratio will rise beyond 1. The insight provided by M-M is that in relatively efficient markets, the existing shares of stock in XYZ will become riskier and, thus, decline in value. Furthermore, the existing shares will decline in value just enough so that they are worth $50 million less than before the additional debt was taken on. Recall that we defined the total market value of XYZ to be equal to the value of outstanding stock plus the amount of debt. On balance then, the total market value of XYZ is unchanged.

If XYZ issues new equities to raise the $50 million required for the new widget plant, its total market value is also unchanged. It is true that as more shares are issued, people in the market "own" $50 million worth of XYZ, just as it is true that the underlying assets of XYZ increase by $50 million. However, the underlying value of the company is unchanged; on its balance sheet, the increase in assets is exactly offset by a corresponding and equal increase in owners' equity.

One frequently used analogy in describing M-MT1 is to say that the total market value of the firm is like a pie; its size is fixed. The debt-equity ratio simply tells what share of the pie is held by shareholders and what share of the pie is held by debt holders. MMT-1 is a powerful tool in corporate finance, for it argues that in highly competitive equity markets, the debt-equity ratio will not, by itself, affect firm value. If the amount investors are willing to pay for shares in a firm is likely to change in response to a changing debt-equity ratio, the underlying market mechanism is not to blame.

The M-M framework offers a second major proposition. M-MT2 states that when we ignore bankruptcy, taxes, informational asymmetries, and managerial incentive problems, the total market value of the firm is independent of the way in which it finances its dividends. Or, in other words, a firm's dividend policy does not affect its total market value. The reasoning behind M-MT2 is somewhat subtle but again relies on our definition of a firm's total market value as the sum of outstanding shares plus debt.

If a firm pays its dividends out of its earnings, nothing has happened that would alter either the value of its debt or outstanding equities. Suppose, however,

---

[6] For our purposes, taxation is *not* a major concern. There is a wide-ranging literature on taxation as it relates to the cost of the various forms of financing to a firm; see any of the finance texts listed in the additional readings to this chapter. Bankruptcy, as well, can largely be ignored. The role of bankruptcy in an economic system is to promote efficiency by acting as one way to encourage exit from an industry. As such, it is mainly a problem for small companies. While there have been some spectacular bankruptcies of large U.S. firms in recent years, these cases represent the exception rather than the rule.

that a firm finances a dividend by issuing new shares and forwarding the resulting cash to current stockholders. An investor who does not wish to consume his dividend in cash can simply purchase more shares in the firm, which, on average, keeps his ownership stake constant. If, on the other hand, the firm borrows to finance a dividend payment, investors are free to use their dividend income to purchase debt in the firm. By so doing, their expected return will be unchanged.

M-MT2 is also important in corporate finance because it argues that firm value does not depend on how earnings are divided. Using the pie analogy once again to describe total market value, as is commonly done in most corporate finance textbooks, the size of the pie does not change in response to how the pie is cut.

THE SEPARATION OF OWNERSHIP AND CONTROL

We first introduced the concept of the separation of ownership and control in Chapter 8, where we began to examine the problem in a moral hazard setting. We continue that discussion here. Along these lines, it will be useful to us to refresh our knowledge with some of the vocabulary and important concepts involved.

Moral hazard arises in a contracting setting where **monitoring** the actions of one of the parties involved is less than perfect. Also, it is important to keep in mind that the incentives facing each party are usually less than perfectly aligned. In the accepted terminology of economics, a **moral hazard** situation may also be called the **principal-agent problem,** or more simply, the agency problem. The principal hires the agent to pursue the principal's interests in some area. If monitoring is difficult, the agent can rationally be expected to shirk or to put forth less effort than what is required in pursuing the principal's interests.

As explained in Chapter 8, two devices are commonly used to control moral hazard. The first involves some element of incentive pay for the agent that is at least partly determined by his performance. In practice, this may be difficult to accomplish because the agent's performance is hard to observe and the possibility of inaccurate measurements results in inefficient risks to the agent. The second device to control moral hazard is ownership. If the agent has an ownership, or equity, stake in the transaction, she will behave quite differently. The problem with ownership is that the agent may lack the resources to pursue this option, a distributive effect as discussed in Chapter 9.

In a typical large corporation, three groups are involved in a discussion of the separation of ownership from control. Agency problems permeate the relationships between all three of these groups. The first group is the firm's stockholders. Legally, the ownership lies with stockholders because they are the residual claimants to the firm's income. The second group is the firm's board of directors. Corporate boards are appointed by equity owners, and it is their job to protect the interests of the stockholders by setting broad corporate policy and hiring and monitoring the third group, the chief executive officer (CEO) and her management team. Essentially, management is charged with taking assets owned by the firm and generating income with those assets to benefit the firm's stockholders.

In the relationship between the stockholders and the firm, the stockholders are clearly the principals who are often unable to monitor their agents, the firm's managers. Theoretically, the board of directors exists to facilitate this relationship and become agents to the stockholders and principals to the firm's managers.

If management fails in its task, it faces disciplining internally from the firm and externally via the stock market. Internally, the board of directors can communicate to management its dissatisfaction with current operations and, ultimately, can fire management. Recall that boards of directors must answer to stockholders. If a board seems unresponsive to shareholder desires, shareholders may take matters into their own hands, recruit new board members more responsive to their concerns, and, through these actions, replace CEOs and their management team.

The environment of the stock markets today raises many questions addressing the importance and practice of ownership to stockholders. More directly, we can ask the question, *"What incentives do shareholders have to monitor activities in the firms in which they have an ownership stake?"*

The first problem concerns the importance of any one shareholder in any one firm. Most of us would consider $1 million to be a good deal of money. Suppose that you had $1 million invested in the stock of ABC, a hypothetical firm included in the *Fortune* 500 companies list. ABC might very well have equities outstanding with a market value of $1 billion. As such, although your $1 million is a lot of money, it represents about one-tenth of 1 percent ownership in ABC. The largest shareholder for a typical *Fortune* 500 company holds a little more than 10 percent of the outstanding shares of stock. The degree of ownership required to obtain meaningful control is not certain. Even if there are a few large investors in a given firm with common preferences, they may control only 30 percent of the stock, which means that 70 percent of the stockholders might have different beliefs. If the remaining ownership is spread across a large enough number of people, more pessimistically, 70 percent of the stockholders simply may not care at all.

An additional complication is that most shareholders own a fairly well diversified portfolio of stocks. Thus, when an investor owns stock in nine corporations, the amount of effort required to monitor any one of them might be too great to warrant any meaningful ownership implications.

One important trend in the stock market over the past 15 years has been the increasingly larger roles played by institutional investors. Banks, pension funds, and insurance companies make large purchases of stock, and there is some evidence that these stocks are being held longer than previously. As of 1994, pension funds alone reportedly control 35 percent of the shares of publicly traded firms in the United States. This trend seemingly puts the large institutional investors in a position to more closely monitor manager behavior.

When managers act against the perceived interests of shareholders, this agency situation is termed one of managerial misbehavior and may take many forms. It may consist of huge salaries paid to top management or expensive perks provided to a select few in the firm. In Chapter 13, we document the generosity of these salaries and perks. Managerial misbehavior may consist of perceived poor managerial decisions resulting in lower firm profits and greatly diminished share value. Shareholder activism is the process through which enough shareholders become disenchanted with the management team to bring about significant change through a company's board of directors.

The Importance of Controlling Managers

Shareholder activism was responsible for causing changes in some major U.S. corporations in the early 1990s. Perhaps the most widely known instance of shareholder activism occurred at Westinghouse. As noted previously, in July 1990, Westinghouse's board of directors appointed Paul Lego to the position of CEO. At the time of his appointment, Westinghouse stock was selling for around $36 per share. By 1993, when shareholders had forced him out, Westinghouse stock was selling for $13 per share.

External discipline is provided through stock market transactions via the threat of corporate takeover. Shareholders entrust managers with their assets. Current shareholders and, more important, prospective shareholders may believe that this trust has been violated. They may believe that the assets are being used inefficiently or that new control over those assets will result in a more profitable use of them. Since there are potential profits to be made, above and beyond those currently being made, bidders for ownership may emerge and threaten a takeover.

As we explained in Chapter 8, at this point, a very interesting situation develops. Current managers begin to fear for their jobs as the market attempts to enforce efficiency. We devote most of the next chapter to the many implications of this issue; for now, it suffices to say that the threat of takeover is an attempt by the market at instilling efficiency in firms.

A second form of external control of managers is provided by lenders to the firm. Theoretically, at least, lenders have no ownership interest in firms and no legal right to access their management. In practice, the linkage is more than none but somewhat less than the control exerted by stockholders.

As with stocks, large, established markets exist for corporate bonds. These markets exert their influence via the establishment of liquidity through the setting of bond prices. Bond prices react not only to interest rate changes but also to perceived changes in the probability of repayment. To further facilitate exchange in bonds, several well-known rating agencies exist and attempt to categorize alternative bonds by the risks they pose to investors.

The input of private lenders (that is, commercial banks, insurance companies, and pension funds) into the firm's financing decision provides some mechanism for influencing the firm's managers. To a certain extent, this process is institutionalized in the lending process if lenders require attainment of certain target financial and accounting ratios to qualify for loans. Any general influence above and beyond that can be negotiated only on an individual basis. Firms must compete for funds and thus impress lenders. Lenders seek to find the exact mixture of risk and return that they deem desirable. Put simply, lending is voluntary and nobody will lend money to support what is viewed as a losing proposition; if some control over a firm's operations is necessary to achieve this, then so be it.

One characteristic of the market for loans is imperfect information, setting the stage for **adverse selection** as considered in Chapter 7. Summarizing that argument here, lending is viewed as a two-step process. Stage 1 occurs when a company decides to obtain a loan from a bank. In Stage 2, the company invests the proceeds of the loan. The only thing that the bank knows with absolute certainty is the rate at which the company is willing to borrow the money in Stage 1; the bank knows very little about the prospects in Stage 2. The bank does understand the risk-return trade-off facing the company in Stage 2.

Lenders may have in mind an optimal interest rate to charge on loans, say 10 percent. If they offer loans at less than this rate, they will attract a larger percentage of borrowers that wish to make low-risk, low-return investments. If they offer loans above 10 percent, they will attract a larger percentage of borrowers that wish to make high-risk, high-return investments with the proceeds of the loan.

The situation in the market for loans may be as appears in Figure 10.2, which represents a supply and demand model. Lenders prefer to lend at the rate r_o. They lend less below this rate because the proceeds from the loan to companies are invested in projects that yield too low a return. They also lend less at rates above r_o, because of the perceived risk of the investments made by companies in Stage 2. At the rate r_o, the market for loans does not clear; there is a shortage of funds; and those funds that are lent must be rationed using some device other than price, which in this case is the interest rate charged.

Individuals unable to obtain funds in such a market are said to be credit rationed. Credit rationing can occur in four ways. First, borrowers may receive loans for less than they requested. Second, some applicants for funds are denied, even though similar applicants are approved for loans. Third, some categories of applicants are simply denied credit. A fourth way that credit rationing may manifest itself occurs if banks, and other lenders, wish to obtain a degree of corporate control of the firms to which they make loans. Basically, borrowers must compete

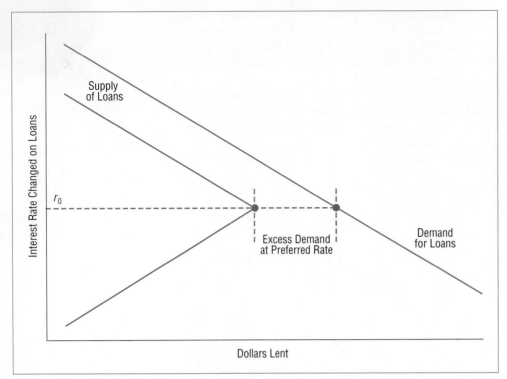

Figure 10.2 Lending Under Adverse Selection

for available funds in an environment in which funds are scarce; one aspect of this competition might very well be a degree of control.

In any event, credit rationing results in a situation of excess market demand resulting from information problems between lenders and borrowers. Regardless of how many data are provided by prospective borrowers via financial statements and references, lenders acknowledge that a residual amount of information is always missing.

Equity, as a source of funds, is also subject to rationing for two primary reasons. First, when new shares are issued, the existing shares are said to be diluted. In theory, the value of all of a firm's outstanding shares roughly equals the market value of that firm. If new shares are issued, each existing share is worth less simply because more shares exist. In practice, share values decrease by more than an amount proportional to the value of the new equity issue. As previously explained, investors may perceive debt as having a positive influence on a firm's managers. Furthermore, investors are well aware of the other positive features of debt; it is cheaper, and it does not usually threaten the existing ownership-control mix. Investors may then wonder why the firm needs to use equity, that is, why other lenders have turned down the firm. This can be interpreted as a sign of trouble; thus, investors purchase new shares only if they are priced lower than existing shares. On balance, equity may be rationed because of detrimental effects on current holders of existing shares and because of the signals it sends to the market.

THE MEANING OF STOCK PRICES

At this point, we have a fairly clear idea as to what is meant by the separation of ownership and control and how a firm's financial and managerial structures blend together in the organization. What is needed now is to return temporarily to our idea of total market value of the firm. Starting with this familiar concept, we add to our understanding of ownership and control by defining a more managerially important concept of firm value. We need to present one technical issue, net present value calculation, so that we may illuminate the connection between stock prices and expected future firm profits.

We defined the total market value of a firm as the amount of cash needed to purchase a firm free and clear, that is, an amount equal to the market value of the firm's equities plus all debt. From a managerial perspective, a more useful concept is **market value,** defined as the total value of all of the firm's outstanding shares, that is, the first broader concept less the amount of debt:

Market Value = Total Market Value – Amount of Debt

The rationale for turning to a more focused definition of value is clear, considering the lines of authority in most corporations. The owners of the firm are the stockholders; they have (or should have) final say over the affairs of the corporation. If stockholders are dissatisfied, they may wrestle the reins of control from a board of directors and obtain what they wish. If we focus on what is needed to control a firm, market value is the appropriate concept.

The obvious problem with discussing market value is that we must have some idea as to what determines stock prices. Earlier in this chapter, we considered the EMH and the dartboard theory of stock price determination. Taken together, these two ideas imply that stock prices are extremely volatile over the short term; the issue is how well the market processes information. Interestingly enough, we also argued that many short-term stock price movements were the result of "too much" information.

What we need to do now is to determine what value rational investors put on various stocks. Maybe this analysis is best interpreted as a long-run model of stock price determination or perhaps it is simply a model of what stock prices "ought" to be. In any event, it must be emphasized that the control aspects of stock ownership must be reflected in stock prices.

Nobody owns stock just for the sake of owning stock. The single incentive for owning stock is that stock ownership can produce income. In fact, there are two sources of income: dividend income and share appreciation. Since we are mainly concerned with the linkage between ownership and control, the dividend aspect of income can largely be ignored. The remaining aspect, share appreciation, depends crucially on the expected future profitability of the firm. If profits are expected to increase, share prices increase; unfortunately, the converse is also true.

Large future profits imply large future dividends, which make the shares of stock more attractive relative to other investments available to investors. Likewise, if it seems likely that a company will have diminished future profitability, its share prices will decline. We can conclude that expected future profitability is a large determinant of current share price. This concept is fairly easy to understand and hard to argue against. We do need, however, to add more details to this relationship.

Specifically, we need to develop the concept of net present value. A dollar today is worth more to us than a dollar next week, next month, or next year. Suppose that we are going to make a loan to our friend Roberta. Because she is a close friend whom we know well, default risk on the loan is zero. Roberta asks to borrow $1,000 promising to pay it back, with interest, after two years. In fairness to ourselves, we must charge Roberta interest for two reasons. First, during the time she has our money, we do not and we should be compensated for not having the funds to use. Second, inflation is likely to occur, making the dollars that Roberta

Net Present Value
and Discounting

gives us in two years worth less than the dollars we gave her. Put in a layperson's terms, we demand an interest payment from Roberta out of a sense of fairness to ourselves.

We define the **net present value** (NPV) of an amount of money received in the future as that amount that we consider equal if received today. In our two-year loan to Roberta, for example, the $1,000 given up today might be equally attractive to us as $1,200 received in two years. Notice that the future amount received is more than the current amount; this difference represents our earnings on the loan. In the jargon of finance, we say that the future amount is *discounted* to current dollars.

We might point out that if Roberta's loan had some default risk associated with it, the amount that we would find equally attractive increases, perhaps substantially. As we will soon see, the rate of interest provides us with necessary information to equate money at some future date with money today. The actual calculations behind *NPV* can be rather complex, and we will not go into great detail with them here. Basically, a mathematical relationship between *NPV*, *FV*, the future value received at some date *t* periods into the future, and the interest rate *i* is given by equation (10.1):

$$NPV = FV/(1 + i)^n \qquad (10.1)$$

If, for example, we wanted to know what value we placed on receiving $500 in one year at a 10 percent rate of interest, we would, in the equation (10.1), set $FV = 500$, $i = .1$, and $n = 1$. The calculation would reveal that the $500 received in one year is worth $454.55 today. Equivalently, we could say that $454.55, when discounted one year at 10 percent interest, is worth $500.

Often, as with the loan made to Roberta, we know the *NPV* and need to calculate the *FV*, which can be done by rearranging equation (10.1) to

$$NPV (1 + i)^n = FV \qquad (10.2)$$

Considering the two-year loan to Roberta, if the interest rate were 10 percent, we would calculate the *FV* by setting $NPV = 1,000$, $n = 2$, and $i = .1$, to arrive at a future value of $1,210.00. That is, after the two years, we expect Roberta to pay us back the $1,000 principal plus $210 in interest.

Whereas finance professionals can carry out these calculations in their heads, most of us rely on tables appearing in finance books to simplify the number-crunching process. The important things to note at this time are that a mechanism exists (called either *net present value calculations* or *discounting*) to equate dollars today with dollars at some time in the future and that this relationship depends on the interest rate.

For a given future value, *FV*, the *NPV* decreases as the interest rate increases. We saw this relationship earlier in this chapter when we discussed the relationship between bond prices and interest rates. A bond is nothing more than a promise to make a payment (or several payments) at some future date; if market interest rates rise, that future payment becomes less attractive and the price of the bond decreases, that is, the bond sells at a greater discount.

Figure 10.3 shows the future value of a dollar today at various interest rates at different times in the future. We show the discounted value of $1 for five alternative interest rates: 5, 7.5, 10, 12.5, and 15 percent. The upper curve shows the value of $1 after each of one through eight years at a 5 percent rate of interest. As you move to the lower curves, the interest rate increases in steps of 2 1/2 percent; thus, the lowest curve shows the current value of a dollar received in the future at 15 percent interest. At 5 percent, a dollar today is worth 95 cents one year from

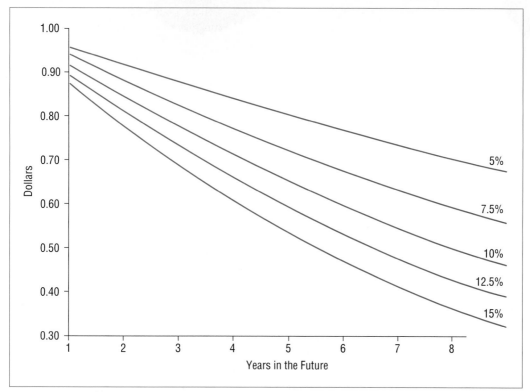

Figure 10.3 Discounted Value of $1, Various Interest Rates

now; at 15 percent, a dollar received one year from today has a discounted value of only 87 cents.

The net present value equation (10.2) equates a single payment made at some specified future date with today's dollars. In practice, most bonds and other investments promise to make a series of payments rather than one single disbursement. This technical complication does not really ruin the simple logic of net present value that we presented. If an investment makes a series of payments, its net present value is obtained by adding them up.

You may be wondering what all of this has to do with stock prices. As we argued earlier, the price of a stock depends on expected future gains in the form of dividends and appreciation in share prices (capital gains). Regarding our *NPV* concept, we assume that investors fix interest rates and that the *FV* represents gains in future years. Obviously, we have simplified the *FV* because stocks pay dividends at least every year, so there will be more than one future payment. However, this simplification doesn't really affect our conclusion; if we were really good at applying the *NPV* formula, we could simply do a calculation every year into the foreseeable future.

If the *FV* increases, then because of the expectation of larger future dividends and share appreciation caused by a perceived increase in firm profitability, the *NPV* must increase as well. The market value of a firm then must increase as the *NPV* of future expected profits increases and must decrease as the *NPV* of future expected losses increase. This view of stock prices is consistent with the ownership view of stockholders since profits eventually flow to the residual claimants. The importance of NPV of future profitability, stock prices, and control issues is discussed in much more detail in Chapter 11.

▧ CHAPTER SUMMARY AND KEY IDEAS ▨ ▨ ▨ ▨ ▨ ▨

This chapter discussed the basic question of how a firm raises funds and the implications of its decisions for organizational efficiency. Corporations raise the funds necessary to conduct their activities in three principal ways: selling stock, borrowing, and retaining earnings. Each of these has implications for the firm.

When funds are raised via a stock issue, control in the corporation is sacrificed, at least in theory. The major, established stock exchanges provide liquidity to stockholders, effectively lowering the risks of holding shares in a firm. Borrowing, through the issue of bonds or direct lending, may be a more attractive option to firms seeking to raise funds. Lenders have no legally imposed rights of control over borrowers, but they are becoming more and more an external disciplining device. Historically, retained earnings have been the most important source of funds for firms. Basically, retained earnings are profits that are not distributed to shareholders but are plowed back into the firm. Over the long run, we observe that firms typically disburse about one-third of earnings to stockholders.

The mix of sources of funding for a firm refers to its capital structure. The most common measure of a firm's capital structure is its debt-equity ratio. Different debt-equity ratios can elicit a range of behaviors from a firm's managers by altering the incentive structures that they face.

The efficient market hypothesis asserts that well-organized equity markets are efficient. That is, stock prices contain all relevant information that is available. The efficient market hypothesis implies that the price that a firm obtains when it sells a share of its stock is a "fair" price in the sense that it reflects the value of that stock given the information that is available about the firm.

The Modigliani-Miller theorems relate the total market value of firms to their capital structure. The first theorem states that the market value of the firm is independent of its capital structure. In other words, changes in a firm's debt ratio do not significantly alter firm profitability. The second theorem states that the total market value of the firm is independent of the way in which a firm finances its dividends. Given the moral hazard present in the relationship with stockholders and the incentives created for managers by a large debt-equity ratio, M-MT1 and M-MT2 are viewed by economists today as an approximation of reality. This view is very similar to the one taken by the neoclassical ideal of perfectly competitive markets.

Stocks imply ownership. This is important for two reasons. First, ownership implies control over the firm's operations. Second, the investors stand to gain from an increase in the value of shares and to lose their capital if the business fails. The stock market plays an important role in providing liquidity and processing information relevant to a particular firm in a given industry. The ultimate fear for both firms and their investors is the bankruptcy of the corporation.

The separation of ownership and control raises issues in a moral hazard setting. In a publicly owned corporation, three groups are involved in any discussion of agency: the stockholders, the board of directors, and the managers. External discipline is provided by the stock market and secondary control through the lenders to the firm.

▧ KEY TERMS

adverse selection
bankruptcy
capital structure
commercial mortgage

debt
efficient market hypothesis
equity
financial restructuring

lease
market value
Modigliani-Miller theorem
monitoring
moral hazard
mortgage bond
net present value
principal-agent problem

private placement
public issue
secondary market
secured debt
total market value
underwriter
unsecured debt

FURTHER READINGS

Brealey, R., and S. Myers. *Principles of Corporate Finance*. New York: McGraw-Hill, 1984.

Brigham, E. F., and L. C. Gapenski. *Financial Management: Theory and Practice*. New York: The Dryden Press, 1994.

Demsetz, H., and K. Lehn. "The Structure of Ownership: Causes and Consequences," *Journal of Political Economy*, 93, December 1985, pp. 1155–1177.

Saunders, A. *Financial Institutions Management: A Modern Perspective*. Homewood, IL: Richard D. Irwin, Inc., 1994.

Shapario, A. C. *Modern Corporate Finance*. New York: Macmillan, 1990.

Zeckhauser, R. J., and J. Pound. "Are Large Shareholders Effective Monitors? An Investigation of Share Ownership and Corporate Performance," in ed. R. G. Hubbard, *Asymmetric Information, Corporate Finance, and Investment*. Chicago: University of Chicago Press, 1990, pp. 149–180.

QUESTIONS AND PROBLEMS FOR REVIEW AND DISCUSSION

A. Consider a firm that needs $700,000 in capital to get started. In case A, think of this firm as a proprietorship in which you put up $100,000 and borrow the rest from a bank. In case B, think of this firm organized as a partnership, in which you and 10 friends put up $50,000 each and borrow the rest from a bank. Third, think about the firm organized as a corporation, in which you and 10 friends each buy $50,000 worth of stock and then borrow the rest from a bank. If the firm goes broke without earning any money, what are your personal losses in each case?

B. In the practice of law, much rides on reputation and performance. If more than one person is to be involved in any one firm, the activity needs to be organized via one of the three corporate forms discussed in the text.

1. Using the concept of *moral hazard*, explain why the partnership form is usually chosen for law firms.

2. Can you foresee any potential problems with the partnership form as law firms increase in size?

C. Suppose that a large corporation whose shares are publicly traded is financed with an equal mixture of debt and equity. Shareholdings are not concentrated; 90 percent of the shares are held by many, many investors each owning less than 1/2 of one percent of all the shares outstanding. The debt issued by the firm is in the form of loans; there are no bonds. All of the debt is held by a single bank. In this case, who may have more control over the activities of the firm, the bank or any single shareholder? Explain.

D. From the perspective of the firm, is debt preferable to equity as a source of financing?

E. The Modigliani-Miller theorems state that a firm's capital structure does not matter, that is, that its total market value is independent of its debt-equity ratio. Give at least three reasons why this may not be the case and explain each reason fully.

F. Is the following true or false? Explain your answer fully. The efficient markets hypothesis states that profits cannot be made in the stock market.

Corporate Control
and Economic Efficiency

The capital markets provide one mechanism for accomplishing change before losses in the product markets generate a crisis. While the corporate control activity of the 1980s has been widely criticized as counterproductive to American Industry, few have recognized that many of these transactions were necessary to accomplish exit over the objections of current managers.[1]

▰▰▰ CHAPTER OUTLINE AND STUDENT GOALS ▰▰▰

The previous chapter introduced some of the basic issues of modern financial theory. These included the efficient market hypothesis, the Modigliani-Miller theorems, the relationship between ownership and control in corporations, capital structure, and incentives in a principal-agent setting. This chapter examines mergers and acquisitions in the 1980s through the lens of modern financial theory.

The purpose of the present chapter is to examine the market for corporate control. The question we are interested in is whether the market for corporate control is an effective instrument of control in motivating managers to maximize the value of the firm. A more direct way to ask the question is: Do takeovers enforce efficiency? Much corporate behavior seems best understood in terms of myopic managers running the show largely as they please. If this is the case, then the question is: How can managerial behavior be controlled so that managers maximize shareholders value?

The response of Wall Street and the capital markets was harsh and clear: eliminate inefficiency in American industry. The financial restructuring of U.S. industry began with the steel industry in the 1970s, reached its zenith in the 1980s, and is continuing in the 1990s.[2] During the 1980s, takeovers, mergers, and leveraged buyouts restructured corporation after corporation. Takeovers have played an important role in facilitating exit from many unprofitable industries. This activity has been widely criticized, and it more than doubled the value of public equity from $1.4 to $3 trillion in just 10 years, reversed the decline in productivity, increased real income by one-third, and set record levels for research and development expenditures.

The role of mergers and acquisitions raises important questions about effi-

---

[1] Michael C. Jensen, "The Modern Industrial Revolution, Exit, and the Failure of Internal Control Systems," *The Journal of Finance*, July 1993, p. 851.
[2] Zoltan J. Acs, *The Changing Structure of the U.S. Economy: Lessons from the Steel Industry* (New York: Praeger, 1984).

ciency. First, do share prices accurately reflect the value of a company? If they do, then how do takeovers increase efficiency? If raiders have better information about the future of the company than managers, their activities may help raise share prices.

The restructuring of the 1980s also raises important questions about financial theory. The central tenet of modern financial theory is that firm cash flows are independent of capital structure (ratio of debt to equity) and dividend policy. In other words, when taxes are ignored, it does not make a difference whether a firm finances its activities with debt or equity. However, the evidence from the 1980s suggests that debt can be an effective substitute for dividends. Substituting debt for stock may affect managerial incentives, improve monitoring, and increase organizational efficiency.

This chapter does three things. First, it expands our analysis of the organization by examining the relationship between a corporation and its owners, that is, the principals and the agents. Second, by focusing on the market for corporate control, we can understand how mergers and acquisitions are restricting organizations in the information age. Third, the chapter examines corporate governance and makes suggestions for improving the existing system of governance based on evidence from leveraged buyout partnerships.

After reading this chapter, you should be able to

- Explain what corporate control is.
- Explain why a decline in stock price may lead to a takeover.
- Explain the role of the market for corporate control in the U.S. economy.
- Understand how efficiency may be encouraged by competitive capital markets.
- Explain what a leveraged buyout is.
- Understand what the evidence from the late 1980s and early 1990s means regarding corporate efficiency.
- Explain, in layperson's terms, why the forces unleashed by the capital markets will continue to affect corporate America well into the next century.

▪ THE RECKONING

The Radio Corporation of America, better known as RCA, was one of the premier technology corporations in the 1960s. It was by far the largest producer of color televisions in the United States, as well as black and white televisions, radios, record players, and tape recorders.[3] RCA owned the largest U.S. television network, NBC, and was a premier defense contractor supplying the U.S. armed forces with much of their technical wizardry. It even ventured into the conglomerate game by buying Random House Publishing and Hertz Corporation. In March 1985, after losing half a billion dollars, RCA was taken over by General Electric. Three years later, the RCA letters at the top of Rockefeller Center, a well-known New York City landmark, came down.

How does a company that in 1965 ranked as the 21st largest industrial corporation in the United States go out of business? It was quite simple. Although RCA had made a few tactical blunders, like most big companies, it had assembled a

---

[3] Today, most college students do not know directly what records are and may have never seen a black and white television set.

wide array of businesses under one corporate roof.[4] In the new economic climate with every business under siege, investors lost confidence in RCA management and the value of RCA stock fell to $17 a share in 1982, well below what it was trading for earlier. With the stock at $17, RCA was worth just under $2 billion. However, NBC was worth $1 billion, Hertz $500 million, and the company's other divisions $1.5 billion. RCA was worth more split up than together. This situation became worse, and by 1985 its liquidation value was twice its stock price. A deal was struck between Jack Welch, the CEO of General Electric, and RCA's board of directors, and the entity that was RCA simply disappeared much more quickly than anyone might have thought possible.

For most of the 25 years after World War II, the stock market was a pretty quiet place: trading of shares was low by today's standards and stocks generally rose in value. The equity markets on Wall Street merely reflected the stability and profitability of large, dominant U.S. corporations. Over this period, stock prices were actually higher than companies' intrinsic worth, as defined by the firms' book values. The **book value** of a firm is the accounting valuation of its assets including investment and depreciation. When we compare share price and book value, we are taking the corporation's total book value and dividing it by the number of shares outstanding.

Market share prices would exceed book, or intrinsic, value if investors anticipate substantial future earnings from the assets. A share of RCA might be worth, for example, $30 in book value terms but sell for more than $60 because of the appearance of stable future profits.

As the decade of the 1970s wore on, investors became extremely concerned about the future. There were the tenfold increase in oil prices and international competition, and new technologies seemed uncertain. Stock prices declined over time. The gap between companies' book value and market value began to converge. Many companies were selling for less than book value. According to John Case, stock prices got so low in the chaotic marketplace that

> if you could buy a company, particularly one that the stock market didn't like, you would acquire a bundle of debts and assets for a relatively modest amount. You could pay off the debts, and right away, never mind what you might earn in the future, you would have assets worth more than what you paid for the company. An environment more conducive to takeovers would be hard to imagine.[5]

Although managers can take actions that affect the value of their firms' stock, other factors influence stock prices. Included among these are external constraints, the general level of economic activity, taxes, and conditions on the stock market. Most important for the stock market as a whole are the external constraints. Working within the external constraints, management makes a set of long-run strategic policy decisions that chart a future course for the firm. These policy decisions, along with the general level of economic activity and the level of corporate income taxes, influence the firm's expected profitability.

*Book Versus Market
Value*

---

[4] One of the larger tactical blunders made by RCA involved a potential relationship with Sears, the dominant force in U.S. retailing at that time. For years Sears sold black and white televisions under its own brand name. In 1963 Sears asked RCA for permission to sell RCA color televisions under the Sears label. RCA declined, telling Sears to sell them under its label or not at all. Sears struck a deal with Sanyo, and between 1963 and 1977 sold 6.5 million televisions worth an estimated $700 million.

[5] John Case, *From the Ground Up: The Resurgence of American Entrepreneurship* (New York: Simon & Schuster, 1992), p. 62.

Table 11.1 shows one measure of the book value and the market value for the *Fortune* 500 companies between 1973 and 1992. In 1973, the book value of 475 industrial companies (firms that were listed in the *Fortune* 500 throughout the period) was $239 billion. The market value of these assets was $973 billion. These firms were trading in 1973 at four times book value. This represented the investment in the companies and the discounted present value of expected future earnings. The expected future earnings drove the stock price. The expected earnings reflected both the stability of the external environment and the soundness of existing management strategy in that environment.

Two trends are evident in Table 11.1. First, management strategy remained largely intact in the 1970s, at least as measured by the book value of corporate assets. These increased to $628 billion by 1992; however, most of that increase took place in the 1970s. The second trend is the market's valuation of this investment. Whereas the market value of these investments was $1,146 billion in 1992, most of the increase occurred in the 1980s. In other words, whereas the book value of corporate assets increased by 162 percent between 1973 and 1992, the market value increased by only 17 percent! The ratio of book to market reached a low of 1.3 in 1982, down from a high of 4.1 in 1973.

There was great variation in company performance. The pharmaceutical firms performed much better than steel companies. In both 1974 and 1991, the ratio of book to market for Bristol Myers Squibb was 5.8. During most of the two decades, it stayed well above 3.0.

Table 11.1	Total Book Value and Market Value for 475 Companies 1973–1992		
Year	**Book Value**	**Market Value**	**Ratio Market/Book**
1973	239,030	973,963	4.1
1974	265,353	630,953	2.4
1975	287,148	765,124	2.7
1976	321,432	871,757	2.7
1977	353,767	729,846	2.1
1978	390,183	718,384	1.8
1979	434,619	750,280	1.7
1980	494,763	863,436	1.7
1981	549,922	699,354	1.3
1982	570,142	738,034	1.3
1983	607,451	894,492	1.5
1984	603,921	811,854	1.3
1985	608,209	906,752	1.5
1986	609,199	1,007,105	1.7
1987	626,091	1,011,995	1.6
1988	651,645	984,932	1.5
1989	674,705	1,117,981	1.7
1990	701,590	1,006,676	1.4
1991	709,839	1,204,901	1.7
1992	628,053	1,146,223	1.8

We include 475 companies who were on *Fortune*'s list of the 500 largest companies throughout the period. Book value is based on fiscal year-end data and is calculated as follows: Common Equity – Liquidation Value. Market value is the close price for the fiscal year multiplied by the company's common shares outstanding and then divided by consumer price index (1982–1984 = 100).
Source: Data from Compustat, 1993.

Why was there such a sharp decline in stock prices especially in the 1970s? One answer is that changes in the external environment and continued investment created excess capacity. All of the investment in the post–World War II era resulted in capacity that could not be used in the 1980s. *Excess capacity* is the amount of capital stock that cannot be used to produce output. Therefore, it does not earn a rate of return but depresses the stock price. Decades of growth and expansion have led to excess capacity in many industries.

The easiest way to create excess capacity in an industry is for demand to fall, for example, in a recession, but this is temporary. A better example is what happened in the steel industry. Steel consumption per million dollars of GNP fell by 30 percent between 1965 and 1995. Technological change, which can expand capacity, can also make existing capacity obsolete.

The Need to Exit

The solution to excess capacity in an industry is exit. This is particularly difficult in industries that have enjoyed years of steady growth. In nearly every business school, the concept of a product life cycle is introduced as a strategic planning device. In the U.S. economy during the 1980s, the managers of corporations refused to acknowledge the inevitable for mature industries: technological change and fluctuating demand had created significant excess capacity in nearly all industries. Managers refused to downsize their corporations' activities, seemingly letting others worry about such things, and investment continued to increase.

Two important problems limit the exit of firms from industries. The first is the information problem. Firms often do not have good information. However, even if they have accurate information, they may not wish to exit. A manager who has spent an entire lifetime at a plant may not wish to close it. The second problem that may also inhibit exit is the contracting problem. As we saw in Part II, the security of property rights and the enforceability of contracts are extremely important to the growth of real output. For example, in labor markets, organizations make a commitment to workers about work rules, compensation, and tenure. However, with changing technology and markets, firms cannot adjust fast enough to maintain market dominance and must break contracts.

◼ THE ROLE OF THE MARKET IN CORPORATE CONTROL

We saw in the previous chapter that each type of financing had its own form of control on the firm. Lenders (commercial banks, insurance companies, and pension funds) have some control over the firm in the sense that if they view the firm as a money-losing proposition, they will not lend it any more money. However, they have little influence on the firm other than withholding additional funds.

What we are interested in is how society controls a corporation that is behaving in an inefficient manner with equity holders' funds. **Corporate control** is the process by which society exerts some control on the corporation through markets or regulatory means. Generally, four categories of control operate on a publicly held corporation: (1) the regulatory system, (2) product and factor markets, (3) the internal control system or governance by the firm's board of directors, and (4) the capital markets.

The Four Control Forces Operating on the Organization

Perhaps the best known form of corporate control is the regulatory system. It includes the regulation of the issuance and trading of securities by the Securities and Exchange Commission, rules on insider trading, and other anticompetitive activities. The legal and political systems are far too blunt as instruments to handle the problems of wasteful managerial behavior effectively. There are exceptions, however. The breakup of AT&T is one of the court system's outstanding successes. The breakup of AT&T created over $125 billion of increased share-holder value between AT&T and the "Baby Bells."

The second force is made up of product and factor markets. How many phonograph records do you own? Unless you are an antique collector, the answer may well be none. Records were played on record players, or phonographs, and there was a huge market for them. As consumer tastes shifted from records to tapes (and later to compact discs), the demand for record players declined since they were complementary goods. Being one of the largest manufacturers of record players, RCA went out of business. Many other factors were involved in the decline of RCA. However, as consumer tastes change, product markets have an important disciplinary force on firms. The decline in demand shifts the demand curve to the left, prices fall, and the quantity exchanged in the market declines.

Factor markets also play an important role in the process. As the demand for crude oil shifted to the right and the supply curve shifted to the left, the price of crude oil increased in the 1970s. The manufacturers of gas-guzzling automobiles almost went out of business. Chrysler had to go hat in hand to the government for guaranteed loans, which determined its very survival.

Product and factor markets will discipline corporate behavior in the long run. Firms that do not supply the product that customers desire at a competitive price and quality cannot survive. Unfortunately, this disciplining effect may take a long time to manifest itself. Firms have imperfect information about market conditions, consumer trends, and the desirability of substitute goods. To avoid a waste of resources, it is important for control forces to act much more quickly.

The third force operating on the corporation is its *internal control* system. The **board of directors** includes the representatives of the owners and has the responsibility to oversee the direction of the organization chosen by the corporation's managers. Substantial data support the proposition that the internal control systems of publicly traded corporations have failed to cause managers to maximize stockholders' value.[6] **Internal control** is the process by which the board of directors oversees the management of a corporation and the direction of the firm.

A good example of the failure of internal control systems is IBM. IBM failed to move away from its mainframe business following the revolution in workstation and personal computer markets. Today, IBM is a high-cost producer in a market with excess capacity. It began to change its strategy in 1991 after losses of $2.8 billion. Table 11.2 shows the value of assets and the market value per share for IBM. In 1973 IBM's total assets were $12,289 million, or $20.94 a share. Market value in the same year was $36,201 million or $61.69 a share. Between 1973 and 1992, the value of assets per share increased from $20.94 to $151.73. The market value of IBM stock also increased from $61.69 a share in 1973 to a high of $155.50 per share in 1985. However, since 1985, the price of a share of stock declined to $50.37 in 1992. The ratio of assets to market value declined to one-third (0.332) in 1992.

The fourth disciplinary force on corporations is the role of the capital markets. The capital markets provide a mechanism for accomplishing change before losses in the product markets create a crisis. The activities of capital markets have been widely criticized, but some economists are now coming to recognize that they were necessary to achieve exit from many industries. When Chevron acquired Gulf Oil for $13.2 billion in cash and debt in 1984, the net assets devoted

---

[6] Michael C. Jensen, "The Modern Industrial Revolution, Exit, and the Failure of Internal Control Systems," *The Journal of Finance* 48, no. 3 (1993), pp. 831–880.

			Ratio Share Price/
Table 11.2	**Asset (Book) Value per Share and Share Price of IBM**		
Year	Assets per Share	Share Price	Assets per Share
1973	20.94	61.69	2.9
1974	23.65	42.00	1.8
1975	25.91	56.06	2.2
1976	29.40	69.78	2.4
1977	32.17	68.37	2.1
1978	35.61	74.63	2.1
1979	42.03	64.37	1.5
1980	45.74	67.88	1.5
1981	49.95	56.88	1.1
1982	54.02	96.25	1.8
1983	60.98	122.00	2.0
1984	69.87	123.12	1.8
1985	85.53	155.50	1.8
1986	95.41	120.00	1.3
1987	106.67	115.50	1.1
1988	123.85	121.88	1.0
1989	135.26	94.12	0.7
1990	153.25	113.00	0.7
1991	161.94	89.00	0.5
1992	**151.73**	**50.37**	**0.3**

Assets are current assets plus net plant plus other noncurrent assets divided by number of outstanding shares. Share price is the closing share price for the fiscal year.
Source: Data from Compustat, 1993.

to the oil industry fell by $13.2 billion as soon as the checks were mailed to the stockholders of Gulf Oil. This payment to shareholders represented funds that were no longer available to the oil industry for exploration. However, it brought supply and demand in line with reduced demand for oil and gas. This was accomplished for all major oil and gas companies.[7]

Control is best viewed as a major component of the managerial labor market. It is the area in which alternative management teams compete for the right to manage corporate resources. Existing managers often have trouble abandoning strategies they have spent years devising and implementing, even when those strategies no longer contribute to the organization's survival. Takeovers generally occur because changing technology or market conditions require a major restructuring of corporate assets.

Gaining control over a firm's resources is typically achieved by purchasing alone or with allies a large percentage of the firm's shares. The purpose of attaining control of a firm is usually to change its corporate strategy, that is, its investment policy. Let us see how this works.

As we learned in the previous chapter, stocks are not just claims on income. They represent ownership interest in a corporation. With ownership come certain rights and responsibilities. For example, stockholders have the right to elect

---

[7] Michael C. Jensen and Jerold B. Warner, "The Distribution of Power Among Corporate Managers, Shareholders, and Directors, *Journal of Financial Economics* 20 (1993), pp. 3–24.

the board of directors. The board of directors represents owners in monitoring, motivating, and disciplining managers. They may also be involved in corporate strategy by deciding the type of business in which a firm should operate.

Let's assume that you own 100,000 shares of RCA purchased at $60 a share. You have invested $600,000. If the price falls to $30, your net worth has been cut in half. If you believe that the existing board is responsible for the fall of the stock price through poor performance, you have a dispute with the existing management. Owners have two choices **"exit"** or **"voice"**: (1) they can exit the corporation—that is, sell their shares of stock to someone else and take a capital loss—or (2) they can voice dissatisfaction at the annual board meeting. The latter may not be very fruitful because the existing managers and board members control the meeting.

Shareholders have other ways to voice their dissatisfaction. By working together with other shareholders, they can take control from the existing board and replace both the present board and management. This can be done in two ways. First, a person, usually a large shareholder, invites others to sell their shares of stock, allowing one individual to acquire enough shares to vote in a new board of directors, which will then fire the existing management.

Second, someone may organize a proxy fight. All stockholders have the right to vote at the annual stockholders' meeting when members of the board of directors are elected. Stockholders who do not attend the meeting can give their votes to another party; this is a **proxy.** The holder of the proxy votes then can try to oust the existing board and institute another. Proxy contests are difficult and expensive to organize.

Takeovers and Financial Restructuring in the 1980s

The decade of the 1980s was marked by a tidal wave of changes in corporate control. A change in corporate control almost always involved financial restructuring of the corporation. Financial restructuring, or financial engineering as it is sometimes called, involves changing the firm's financial structure. In many cases, financial restructuring was accomplished by changing the mix of debt and equity, or leveraging the firm. As was mentioned in Chapter 10 and will soon be greatly expounded on, increased debt in a firm serves as a motivating and disciplining device for the firm's managers.

During the 1960s, it was fashionable to use excess cash to acquire unrelated businesses. Many large conglomerates, as these corporations came to be called, contained more than one hundred separate and distinct businesses. There was a common ownership of these far-flung divisions in the parent company. The difficulty arose from the fact that the decision-making power is at the corporate executive level, but the managerial and technical expertise is at the division level.

During the 1980s, there was a return to fundamental lines of business in organizations; as a consequence, unrelated divisions were frequently spun off or sold. In many of the mergers and acquisitions of the 1980s, a conglomerate-style firm was acquired and pieces were sold off. This process came to be called **deconglomeration** because it represented a large-scale undoing of the conglomerate mergers of the 1960s. In Chapter 14 we will return to the practice of corporations refocusing their efforts in narrower, better defined ranges of business.

As shown in Table 11.3, in 1986 4,024 mergers and acquisitions were completed. The general methods for changing corporate control are through a merger, an acquisition, or a leveraged buyout (LBO). A **merger** is the process in which two firms are joined together. **Acquisition** is the process in which someone gains control of an entity.

A **leveraged buyout** (LBO) occurs when a group of investors acquires a relatively large portion of the outstanding stock of a firm. They obtain enough own-

Table 11.3 Mergers and Acquisitions Completed, 1979–1986

Year	Transactions	Percentage Change from Previous Year	Value[a]
1979	1,529	—	$ 34,177
1980	1,565	2.4	32,959
1981	2,326	48.6	67,209
1982	2,297	−1.2	60,402
1983	2,385	3.8	52,536
1984	3,144	31.8	125,693
1985	3,379	8.0	144,284
1986	4,024	18.4	190,512

[a] In millions of current dollars.

Source: Adapted from Frank R. Lichtenberg, *Corporate Takeovers and Productivity*. Cambridge, MA: The MIT Press, 1992. Copyright © 1992 The MIT Press. Reprinted with permission.

ership to force the firm to buy back most of its own stock from other stockholders at a price above market value by offering some cash, but primarily bonds, in exchange. This tender offer may be twice the current share price, and the bonds issued for the shares of stock pay interest at similarly inflated rates. Many of the mergers and acquisitions reported in Table 11.3 were formed as LBOs.

There were many variations to the LBO, the details of which are not important to us in our attempt to understand the economic management of organizations. In all cases, the effects on the firm and the underlying ownership and control issues were fairly clear. The investors who forced the LBO gained control of the firm. Within the firm, the debt-equity ratio increased substantially as the tender offer basically exchanged one type of financing for another. The group of investors effectively gained control of the firm in a somewhat ironic way in that it bought the target firm with borrowed money, pledging the assets of the firm as collateral on the loans.

The source of much of the financing of the corporate restructuring accomplished through LBOs was bonds. These bonds were used to increase the firm's financial leverage, the ratio of the firm's debt to its underlying equity. The $25 billion leveraged buyout of RJR Nabisco by Kohlberg, Kravis and Roberts (KKR) in 1986 resulted in RJR's having $23 of debt for each $1 of equity. It had to pay out $3.4 billion to service its debt in 1989. The exchange of cash and bonds for RJR Nabisco stock increased the amount of debt and released billions of dollars from the company.

Quite often the managers of one of the divisions in a conglomerate believe that the parent company, or its new owners, does not have good information concerning the profitability of their division. As a result, one of the best known ways to spin off a part of a firm is to have the existing management buy it in a transaction that has come to be called a **management buyout** (MBO) and run it as a privately held company. An MBO is the purchase of a division of a conglomerate parent primarily by its managers, usually also involving an outside group of investors. Often these transactions have resulted in highly leveraged firms because of the borrowing necessary to complete the purchase.

An MBO is, in some ways, similar to an LBO, although it differs in one critical dimension. In an LBO, the financing package is put together by "outsiders," those not involved in operation of the firm. In an MBO, a part of the financing package is supported by "insiders," those directly involved in the operation of the firm. What is important to note is that it is not so much the percentage of the financing put up by management that is important but how much management becomes personally committed to the new entity. Ultimately, an MBO is a chance for the management of a division to put "its money where its mouth is," so to speak.

In the 1980s there was an explosion of management buyouts. This was especially true with divisions that had strong management and good operating records. For example, Olin Corporations sold its Winchester sporting arms division; AMF sold its Harley-Davidson unit; Sperry & Hutchinson split off its Gumlocke unit and its Bigelow Sanford subsidiary; LTV sold Wilson Foods; Esmark sold Swift Company.

The financial structure of an MBO is usually a complex multimillion dollar package, supported by different layers of financing. Commercial banks generally provide the long-term debt financing, a line of credit pegged at rates above the prime rate. But the bulk of the financing typically comes from insurance companies that provide much of the long-term fixed rate debt. The MBO offers a unique solution to the general principal-agent problem arising in corporations due to the separation of ownership and control.

In an MBO, the managers likely have control over the newly created firm; after all, it is their know-how on which the likelihood of future success rests. Ownership is not so clearly defined, however. A group of investors likely holds much, if not most, of the debt of the new firm. Given the way in which the debt was raised and the highly leveraged nature of the firm, this debt may, in some sense, constitute an ownership interest. The management stake, as a portion of financing, may not be a majority of the capital invested in the new venture. It is important, however, that managers invest a large portion of their own personal financial holdings in the new entity. If they do, then outside investors can be assured that management has largely the same set of incentives as they do, the survival of the company. Rodney S. Dayan, partner of the New York law firm of Cadwalader, Wickersham & Taft, described what investors expect:

> Investors want managers to go in to their eyeballs. They want management to be committed, desperately anxious that it succeed and willing to work 18 hours a day. They tell management, "If it works, you'll be rich and if it fails, I won't be alone." These investors believe in the motivating power of money, that the golden rainbow is a powerful incentive.[8]

Hostile Takeovers and Takeover Defenses

The managers of a firm often do not want to be taken over, but they may have no choice. This results in a hostile takeover. A **hostile takeover** is initiated when the managers of one firm, the raider, make an offer for another firm, the target, that is resisted by the management of the target firm. As briefly explained in Chapter 8, there is an ongoing debate concerning the benefits of hostile takeovers. Clearly, if management in the target firm is operating that firm inefficiently, a takeover, whether hostile or not, can be beneficial. However, in the real world, it may be impossible to know for sure whether management is operating the firm inefficiently. What is certain, however, is that most managers fear takeovers because of the implied or direct threat to their jobs.

The majority of mergers and acquisitions during the 1980s were voluntary,

---

[8] Leslie Wayne, "Fleeing the Corporate Stable," *The New York Times*, November 15, 1981, p. 26.

but some were contested. For example, of the 4,026 transactions in 1986, only 40 were hostile tender offers. Perhaps management in some cases did not want to be held accountable, thought that they were on the right track, or perhaps just didn't want to work any harder. Various practices were spawned as the boards and management of potential target firms sought ways to defend their firms and themselves against hostile takeovers. A host of takeover defenses were developed in the 1980s. Some of these raised both ethical and public policy questions.

A firm thrown into a hostile takeover battle may engage in voluntary restructuring. To finance further restructuring or to purchase some of its stock in the market, the firm may sell a division or another part that the raider planned to eventually sell. The firm might also reduce corporate cash holdings to make itself more unattractive to a potential raider.

A firm may choose to make the takeover more expensive. The poison pill defense raises the cost of a takeover by giving current shareholders extra claims if a control change occurs or even if a single entity acquires a threateningly large holding of stock. This, in effect, raises the cost of the acquiring firm by transferring income from the purchasing firm to the current shareholders of the target company. Differential voting rights give some long-time stockholders extra votes. In this way, a recent buyer may have enough shares but not enough votes to take control.

Certain managers may give themselves preferential benefits—called **golden parachutes**—in the case of a takeover. The benefits are available no matter who controls the company. These golden parachutes were given to senior managers who had already made most of the investment in firm-specific capital. The main objection to golden parachutes is that they defend entrenched managers, not the firm, and that they are costly to stockholders. If they are too large, they may not make managers ready to fend off a hostile takeover.

Another questionable method to fend off a takeover is called **greenmail**, which is a corporation's payment to a potential corporate raider to induce him or her to abandon a takeover attempt. Greenmail usually involves a targeted share repurchase, in which the firm pays a premium over the market price to buy back the shares accumulated by the raider.

The results of the restructuring were predictable. The need to generate cash to service new debt led highly leveraged firms to trim staff and divest or close various parts of their businesses. They had to lay off long-time employees. Firms were forced to curtail investment, the purchase of new equipment, and perhaps even the development of new technology.

Intense controversy and opposition from corporate managers, in addition to charges of fraud, the increase in default and bankruptcy rates, and insider trading prosecution, caused the shutdown of the control market through court decisions, state antitakeover amendments, and regulatory restrictions on the availability of financing. The era of the market control came to an end in late 1989. In 1991 the total value of transactions fell to $96 billion from a high of $340 billion in 1988.

Of course, not all stakeholders shared this assessment of the takeover process. Why were savvy investors willing to pay 40 percent more than the market price of shares for the opportunity to replace existing management? The answer was that raiders and leveraged buyouts were shaking business out of its doldrums. For once, firms had to compete and to attempt to become efficient. These savvy investors believed that management had become complacent and that more aggressive management would lead to greater profitability.

Government to the Rescue

THE ROLE OF DEBT IN MOTIVATING ORGANIZATIONAL EFFICIENCY

One reason for the merger and acquisition activity of the 1980s stands out among many others. It is the **principal-agent problem** between owners and managers over the use of free cash flow. Managers and owners both act in their own self-interests. Managers are the agents of owners, who want the highest return for their investment. This is accomplished by **value maximization** of the firm. If managers pursue **wealth maximization** of the firm, there is a conflict between the two. The large size of a firm does not necessarily ensure that the owners are obtaining the greatest return possible. In other words, the largest company may not be the most profitable. According to *Business Week*,

> The issue is not whether companies should be bigger or smaller, but how they should be managed. Bigness in and of itself is neither good nor bad, and of course, bigness has important advantages: economies of scale, effective distribution, and marketing clout. Still, we know that these advantages frequently don't show up on the bottom line. The biggest companies are the most profitable—on the basis of return of equity—in only 4 out of 67 in the *Business Week* Top 1,000.[9]

Corporate managers may not be maximizing the value of the firm. And any serious conflict between managers and owners results in **agency costs,** which are the total costs that arise from the separation of ownership and management. According to Michael C. Jensen, when these agency costs are too high, takeovers or the threat of them can reduce agency costs.[10]

The conflict is a simple one. It evolves around expectations about the present value of future cash flow. What is cash flow? Cash flow is the actual amount of money that flows into (or out) of a firm during some specified period. Cash flow equals net income after taxes plus noncash expenses, usually depreciation. These funds are usually reinvested in the corporation to replace old plant facilities and equipment. However, assume that because of declining demand, there is no need to replace worn out plants and equipment. The firm is left with excess cash at the end of the year.

If the firm cannot invest this money in a project that has a positive net present value when discounted at the relevant cost of capital, it is in a sense **free cash flow.** For example, in the early 1980s, oil companies were the recipients of billions and billions of dollars in free cash flow because of the increase in oil prices on the one hand and the decline in the demand for gasoline on the other. The issue was what to do with the free cash flow. From the perspective of the owners, it should be paid to the stockholders. From the perspective of the managers, it should be invested in oil exploration. From the perspective of the government, it should be taxed.[11]

If the increased free cash flow is not paid to shareholders, the stock price of the firm may actually decline because the firm's owners do not believe that the strategies of existing managers will increase its value. The issue for corporate control is how to motivate managers to pay the free cash instead of investing it in projects that will earn less than the opportunity cost of capital. The answer is clear: *in a highly leveraged organization, management will not have the opportunity to*

---

[9] *Business Week*, "Big Is Not a Substitute for Smart," March 27, 1989, p. 64.

[10] Michael C. Jensen, "The Modern Industrial Revolution, Exit, and the Failure of Internal Control Systems," *The Journal of Finance*, 1993, pp. 831–880.

[11] The federal government passed a windfall tax in the early 1980s to tax away part of the free cash flow from the oil industry.

make "bad" investments with free cash flow because the cash flow must go out of the firm in the form of interest payments on the firm's debt.

The agency costs of free cash flow are the highest when stable divisions of large corporations are experiencing slow growth but have the potential for large cash flows. If this cash is diverted to acquisitions of businesses that management has no expertise in running, the stock price will fall. There are many examples of this in the steel, oil, chemicals, consumer products, and tobacco industries.

Is the market driven by short-term goals or long-run investments? If managers make investment decisions that undervalue future cash flow, they reduce the firm's net present value. The flip side of the coin is whether markets undervalue future cash flows and, if so, do they overvalue short-term cash flow? Is a bird in the hand worth two in the bush? There appears to be little evidence that the market values short-term decision making. The essence of a growing stock market has large investments yielding few short-term dividends but high future earnings.

The best example of this is the venture capital industry and the market for new issues of biotechnology stocks. These companies have had billions of dollars invested in them, and the payoff is years away. However, the stock price can be very high.

The role of debt as an instrument of motivation needs to be examined. If a firm substitutes $1 million of debt for $1 million of equity, the amount of capitalization of the firm has not changed. However, the interest payment on the bonds is an obligation that the firm is bound to make under the penalty of bankruptcy. Dividend payments are voluntary. Moreover, if the rate of interest on the bonds is significant, managers must pay a large percentage of free cash flow to bond holders. Debt reduces the agency cost of free cash flow because it reduces the amount of money that the managers have to spend. In other words, debt prevents managers from investing the firm's cash flow.

Debt actually binds management to pay free cash flow in a way that dividends do not. If managers do not pay the interest on bonds, bond holders can take the

Motivation and Debt

HARLEY RIDES ALONE

AMF and its $300 million Harley-Davidson division went their separate ways this year when it became clear that the only American motorcycle manufacturer needed to make a smaller medium-range cycle to meet the competition from Japan.

AMF knew that failing to make the capital investment would probably spell the end of Harley-Davidson. But AMF was also attracted to a promising new oil service project. In the end, the oil service project won out, and Harley-Davidson was sold for $60 million to management and a group of private investors.

"We've become a little more conservative in business decision," said Vaughn L. Beals, chairman and chief executive of the Harley-Davidson Motor Company. "You have to look at everything from the standpoint of 'Am I betting the business on this?' That was never a question when we were part of the parent. The most you could do was bet your job or something."

Source: "Fleeing the Corporate Stable," The New York Times, November 15, 1981, pp. 3–26. Copyright © 1981 by The New York Times Company. Reprinted by permission.

The High-Yield
Bond Market

firm to bankruptcy court. The same result could be accomplished by increasing the dividend rate. However, such an increase is not legally binding. Management could just as easily reduce dividends in the future.

The substitution of large amounts of debt for stock sets up organizational incentives to restructure what under normal circumstances would be more difficult to achieve. The large amount of debt is in fact a statement that the firm cannot do business as usual. It must work to reduce the debt by cutting expansion programs and selling divisions that are less valuable to it.

The incentive aspects of capital structure provide ample reason to challenge the Modigliani-Miller theorems introduced in Chapter 10. M-MT1 and M-MT2, taken together, lead to the conclusion that financial decisions cannot affect value. A firm's financial structure affects the incentives and behavior of its managers and equity holders. Changing the financing of the firm changes incentives. The resulting real changes in behavior affect the profits that the firm generates. These in turn determine what the firm is worth to outside investors and, consequently, what they will be willing to pay for the firm's stock.

Recall from Chapter 10 that a bond is nothing more than a loan. There is no pretense that bond holders have any control of the corporation, but they know how much money they will be paid regularly and how much they will receive when their bonds reach maturity. Most high-grade bonds can be traded in the secondary market, so investors do not have to hold them to maturity and liquidity is not a major concern.

High-quality corporate bonds have minimum risk, especially if held to maturity to ensure the stated return. In 1990, high-quality corporate bonds paid about 9 percent a year on the invested capital.

During the 1980s, Michael Milken and Drexel Burnham Lambert, Inc., created a secondary market for high-yield or so-called **junk bonds.** These bonds carry a high risk and therefore a high interest rate, which was as high as 14 percent in 1990. High-yield bonds are best viewed as any other bonds. They are commercial loans that can be traded in the secondary market. These loans will be paid back out of the proceeds of the venture. This is the essence of any stock or bond. They provide a claim on the proceeds of the venture.

Some thought that junk bonds might be riskier than common stock. However, remember that junk bonds are less risky by definition because the claims of stockholders are subordinate to bonds. Historical default rates on high-yield bonds have been low, but many of the bonds are so new that the experience could prove to be different in the next recession. Various opponents of high-yield bonds have backed regulation and legislation to restrict their issuance and their holdings by thrift institutions.

Part of the attack on merger and acquisition transactions centered on the high-yield bond market, which eliminated mere size as an effective deterrent against takeovers. This opened the management of the largest U.S. corporations to monitoring and discipline from the capital markets. Listening to the laments of entrenched management, Congress finally passed the Financial Industries Reform and Recovery Act (FIRRA) that forced savings and loans and insurance companies to sell their high-yield bonds, eliminating a large portion of the market demand for them.

How well have high-yield bonds performed? During the 1990 recession, they were among the best fixed income investments in the United States. While investors in blue-chip IBM stock lost some $70 billion in market value (Table 11.2) holders of high-yield bonds made over $100 billion. Junk bonds also helped provide capital for newcomers to compete with existing firms in product markets.

Today television viewers can tune in to as many as 100 different channels. Not too long ago, there were three networks: ABC, NBC, and CBS; cable television was just a dream. How is a cable network financed? Who builds it? Who took the risk and paid for the investments? Neither the traditional financial community nor established corporations did so. Much of the financing for the advanced communication systems that we take for granted today was provided by junk bonds.

Another positive side of junk bonds is that they were the financial instruments that financed the initial construction of the information highway. Perhaps one of the least known facts about the stock and bond markets is that it is extremely difficult to raise money in these traditional ways to finance risky projects. This poses a particular problem for technologically based projects that are relatively risky by nature. High-yield bonds were used to finance the information infrastructure that now connects our homes and offices around the country. This information highway was in large part financed with junk bonds.

■ EFFICIENCY GAINS AND FINANCIAL ACTIVITIES

Who gains from takeovers: raiders, stockholders, or society? Before the bidding war for RJR Nabisco, the stock was trading in the mid-forties, say $48. The final selling price of RJR Nabisco was $108. Why was someone willing to pay $60 over the market price for a share of stock? The $60 represents a takeover premium and goes to the sellers of the stock. The raiders didn't do badly either.

By one estimate, stockholders gains from 1977 to 1986 totaled almost $400 billion. What are we to make of this amount? Did it represent increased economic efficiency? Was it value created? Or was it, as James B. Stewart suggests in the title of his best-selling book—*Den of Thieves*—just plain old theft?

Some have argued that the gains to stockholders, especially in hostile takeovers, are merely transfers of corporate wealth from one group of stakeholders to another.

Nonvalue-maximizing behavior of managers transfers corporate wealth from shareholders to other constituencies in the corporation. Value-maximizing behavior by managers transfers wealth from the corporation to other entities, mostly stockholders. If employees and managers have no legitimate property rights to the cash flows of the firm other than their explicitly stated compensation during the time of their contract, the transfers from them cannot be judged as wrong. If managers take for themselves and for other corporate constituents what properly belongs to shareholders, takeovers correct this inefficient allocation of resources. This claim that shareholders have the unique property rights to all the firm's cash flows not allocated by an explicit contract is at the heart of any endorsements of hostile takeovers.[12]

Let us try to sort out this argument. Two essential arguments are from an economic perspective. The relevant question concerns the gains to the organization. In principle, the gains to the shareholders could be offset by losses to other stakeholders: bond holders, employees, customers, suppliers, and the Treasury Department.

An alternative hypothesis is that a change in corporate control tends to result in more efficient utilization of the resources employed by the firm. Hence, it moves the firm (and society) from a point inside the production possibilities frontier to a point on or closer to the frontier, and the gains to shareholders are social gains. This was discussed in Chapter 4. If the economy is inefficient, society is off both the contract curve and the production possibilities curve.

---

[12] Andrei Shleifer and Robert W. Vishny, "Value Maximization and the Acquisition Process," *Journal of Economic Perspectives* 2, no. 1 (1988), p. 16.

Michael Milken was head of high-yield securities at Drexel Burnham Lambert Inc., Beverly Hills, during the 1980s. At the height of his career, he made $500 million a year. He was convicted in U.S. District Court on six counts of insider trading and sentenced to a term in federal prison in 1990.

The claims that Mr. Milken's alleged crimes cost their immediate victims scores of millions have already been punctured. Federal District Judge Kimba Wood's experts appraised the damage at $318,082. Still, the heart of the case against Mr. Milken came not in specific legalities but in the larger charge that his entire enterprise was basically fraudulent.

But in 1993 the evidence presents its own clear verdict. Far from a Ponzi schemer, Mr. Milken was demonstrably one of the supreme investors in the history of finance. At a time when the air is full of talk of new investment in infrastructure, we can learn much from Mr. Milken's successful financing of the infrastructure for a new service economy.

Mr. Milken's largest commitment—some $21 billion—was to the information industry. The most important of these firms were MCI, Tele-Communications, Inc. (TCI), McCaw Cellular, Turner Broadcasting, Warner Communications, Twentieth Century Fox, and Metromedia Broadcasting. Virtually devoid of conventional collateral, none of these companies could have raised comparable sums from another source.

Perhaps the most visionary Milken investment was McCaw Cellular. When McCaw Cellular came to Mr. Milken in 1986, it was a localized cable and cellular company with small profits and a large, apparently foolhardy goal: competing with the giant regional Bell operating companies by creating a national network of wireless phones. Mr. Milken raised more than $1.25 billion for the company. As we enter an era when most telephones will be wireless, McCaw, together with Lin Broadcasting, was valued in the recent AT&T equity purchase at some $11 billion, and Craig McCaw speculated in *Forbes* about the possibility of taking over AT&T.

Source: "America's Best Infrastructure Program," Wall Street Journal, March 2, 1993, p. A18. Reprinted by permission of The Wall Street Journal, © 1993 Dow Jones & Company, Inc. All rights reserved worldwide.

Although looking at the increase in stock prices to acquired firms may be a good starting point, the ultimate answer to the question, "Who gains from takeovers?," cannot be determined in this fashion. The only way to answer the question is to examine whether a firm's total factor productivity was higher after a change in corporate control than it was before the change. **Total factor productivity** is the output produced per unit of input employed, where total input is an index of three individual inputs: labor, capital, and materials.

Lichtenberg examined the results of thousands of mergers and acquisitions in the 1980s concerning average annual rates of productivity increase.[13] His study is extremely useful because he examined productivity changes according to type of ownership change: all ownership changes, LBOs, and MBOs.

He found that, in general, plants that were losing money were the target of

---

[13] Frank R. Lichtenberg, *Corporate Takeovers and Productivity* (Cambridge, MA: MIT Press, 1992), p. 12.

Table 11.4	Rates of Productivity Gains and Ownership Changes		
	MBOs	LBOs	Total Ownership Changes
Before ownership change	4.3%	1.7%	−3.5%
After ownership change	**10.2**	3.9	−2.7
Total ownership change	5.9	2.2	0.8

Source: Adapted from Frank R. Lichtenberg, *Corporate Takeovers and Productivity* (Cambridge, MA: MIT Press, 1992).

corporate control. As shown in Table 11.4, if all ownership changes are examined, productivity changes were negative before the change in ownership, and they were still negative after, but by a little less (0.8 percent). If one isolates leveraged buyouts only, the gains are much larger: 2.2 percent over a six-year period.

This startling result concerns productivity gains for units that eventually experienced an ownership change via an MBO. Before any ownership change, productivity was increasing at 4.3 percent a year. After the MBO was completed, management incentives became more important and as its control of the firm increased, productivity increased 10.2 percent. Averaging the before and after ownership change shows a long-run growth in productivity in MBOs of 5.9 percent.

The major source of the productivity gains, Lichtenberg found, is that a change in corporate control significantly reduces the employment and wages of white-collar workers but not of blue-collar workers.

This evidence suggests that changes in corporate control, especially leveraged and management buyouts, were associated with significant productivity gains and, therefore, that these gains were social. Takeovers in fact do create value and increase efficiency. In other words, a change in ownership resulted in moving society toward its production possibilities frontier.

REVIVING INTERNAL CONTROL SYSTEMS

Perhaps the two most important decisions that a firm and, therefore, its board of directors make is what business to be in. A person wishing to be in a business needs to do two things. The first is to invest in research and development (R&D); the second is to invest in capital equipment, with both investments consistent with the chosen line of business. These investment programs should produce a stream of income in the future and be reflected in the price of the company's stock.

Table 11.5 compares the total investment in R&D and capital expenditure for

Table 11.5	R&D and Capital Expenditure for Five Major Companies, 1980–1990				
	GM	IBM	Xerox	Merck	Intel
R&D	42.7	36.8	7.1	5.4	2.5
Net income	24.5	25.4	2.7	1.8	1.8
Total	**67.2**	**62.2**	**9.8**	**7.2**	**4.3**
Value	26.2	64.6	3.2	34.8	13.5
Benchmark	(100.7)	(11.8)	(8.4)	28.0	3.2

Benchmark is defined as the actual value of the company as of December 31, 1990, less total value of benchmark strategy.
Source: Adapted from Jensen (1993).

five major corporations over a decade. It then compares this investment to the market value of the company and an alternative investment scenario. Under the alternative investment scenario, the firm invests its R&D funds along with its net income in an investment yielding a current market rate. The benchmark figure shown in Table 11.5 is calculated by subtracting the hypothetical investment in an alternative scenario—for example, putting the money in the bank—from the change in the market value of the corporation.

GM, for example, invested $67.2 billion in excess of depreciation and ended the period with a company valued at $26.2 billion. Although it is not possible with the tools that we have developed up to this point to determine why GM lost billions of dollars, in Chapter 15 we will be able to examine this in more detail.

If these losses are compared to a benchmark strategy of investing in a bank account at 10 percent, for example, GM lost $100.7 billion, IBM lost $11.8 billion, and Xerox, $8.4 billion; Merck made $28 billion, and Intel made $1.8 billion during the 1980s.[14] Let us examine the role of the internal control system in stopping these losses.

Let us start with the board of directors. The board is the apex of the internal control system, having final responsibility for the firm's functioning. Most important, it sets the rules of the game and controls the decision of hiring and firing the CEO. Few boards in the past decade have done this job well. This is particularly unfortunate because the very purpose of the internal control mechanism is to provide an early warning system to put the organization back on track before difficulties reach a crisis stage. Inferior CEOs are removed, but the removal often appears to be too late to prevent serious losses.

Problems arise because neither managers nor nonmanager board members typically own substantial amounts of their firm's equity. Encouraging outside board members to hold substantial equity interests would provide better incentives. Board members should have, at worse, an implicit and, at best, an explicit understanding that new members must invest substantially in the company's stock. This investment would force new board members to recognize at once that their decisions affect their own wealth as well as that of remote shareholders.

The board should be kept small. When boards go beyond 10 people, they are less likely to function effectively and are easier for the CEO to control. The only inside board member should be the CEO, but other insiders can be invited to the board meeting. Expanding the board to include various constituencies is likely to make its functioning less effective.

Active investors, such as the managers of pension funds and other financial institutions, have been kept out of board rooms by the legal structure, custom, and the pension funds' own practices. Active investors are important to a well-functioning governance system, and there is much they can do to dismantle the legal, tax, and regulatory apparatus that effectively limits the scope of activity investors.

It is common in U.S. corporations for the CEO also to be the chairperson of the board, whose function is to run board meetings and oversee the process of hiring, firing, evaluating, and compensating the CEO. Clearly, the CEO cannot perform this function apart from his or her personal interest. Without the direction of an independent leader, it is much more difficult for the board of directors to perform its critical function. Therefore, for the board to be effective, it should separate the CEO and the chairperson positions. We shall see in Chapter 17 that

---

[14] Michael C. Jensen, "The Modern Industrial Revolution, Exit, and the Failure of Internal Control Systems," *The Journal of Finance* 48, no. 3 (1993), p. 862.

in Germany and Japan, bankers, pension fund managers, and unions are a part of corporate governance.

281

Chapter 11
*Corporate Control
and Economic
Efficiency*

**A Model
for Corporate
Governance**

Well-functioning governance systems can be used as examples of how to create or rebuild the governance structure of the modern corporation. Below we present a guideline for the optimal design of organization structure. What is appealing about this guideline is that it recognizes traditional sources of agency problems and attempts to more closely align the incentives of the various stakeholders in the firm. Interestingly enough, many of the characteristics of this optimal governance structure were adopted from the very firms responsible for much of the reorganizations conducted in the 1980s: the leveraged buyout associations and the venture capital funds. These organizations are the premier examples of active management.

Venture capital firms tend to be organized as limited partnerships. The investors are designated to be active members of the management of the ventures. These governance systems are characterized by five features.

1. Subsidies from profitable divisions to unprofitable ones are suspect.
2. Members of the firm's board of directors should have a large equity stake in the firm. Furthermore, each member of the board should have an equity stake that should represent a significant portion of his or her financial holdings.
3. The board of directors should consist of a small number of individuals.
4. With the exception of the CEO, who should be a de facto member, there should be no corporate insiders on the board.
5. The CEO should not be the chairperson of the board of directors.

These venture governance structures solve not only some of the principal-agent problem but also many of the information problems facing typical boards of directors. For example, both managers and board members have extensive knowledge of all aspects of the business. In addition, these boards have frequent contact with the management, often weekly, even daily during difficult times.

▨ CHAPTER SUMMARY AND KEY IDEAS ▨ ▨ ▨ ▨ ▨ ▨

The purpose of this chapter has been to examine the market for corporate control. There are four categories of corporate control: the regulatory system, the product and factor markets, the internal control system, and capital markets. Corporate control is best viewed as a component of the managerial labor market. Gaining control over the resources of a firm is typically achieved by purchasing a large percentage of its shares.

Owners have two choices if they are unhappy with corporate performance. They can exit the firm by selling their shares, or they can "voice" their dissatisfaction. By working together, shareholders can take control from the existing board and replace both the present board and management.

During the 1980s, many organizations returned to fundamental lines of business. In many mergers and acquisitions, firms were acquired and the pieces were sold off. This process is called *deconglomeration*, which represented a large-scale undoing of the mergers of the 1960s.

The source of much of the financing of the corporate restructuring was accomplished through leveraged buyouts, in which the financing is put together by outsiders not involved in the operation of the firm. In the 1980s, this kind of activity exploded. The majority of mergers and acquisitions during the 1980s were voluntary, but some were contested. Various practices were spawned as the boards and management of potential target firms sought ways to defend their firms and themselves from hostile takeovers.

Among the many reasons for the mergers and acquisitions of the 1980s, one stands out: the conflict between owners and managers over the use of free cash flow. This conflict occurs because managers and owners act in their own self-interest, but managers are the agents of the owners. When their interests are misaligned, agency costs arise. When agency costs are too high, takeovers can reduce them.

Debt is an instrument of motivation. Debt actually binds management to pay out free cash flow in a way that dividends do not. The substitution of large amounts of debt for stock sets up organizational incentives to restructure the corporation. The management must work to reduce debt by cutting expansion programs and selling off divisions that are less valuable to the firm.

The efficiency gains from financial activities can be substantial. By one estimate, these gains to stockholders in the 1980s are almost $400 billion. Value-maximizing behavior by managers transfers wealth from the corporation to stockholders. If employees and managers have no legitimate property rights to the firm's cash flow other than their explicitly stated compensation during the time of their contract, transfers from the corporation cannot be judged as wrong.

KEY TERMS

acquisition	internal control
agency costs	junk bonds
board of directors	leveraged buyout
book value	management buyout
corporate control	mergers
deconglomeration	principal-agent problem
"exit"	proxy
free cash flow	total factor productivity
golden parachutes	value maximization
greenmail	"voice"
hostile takeover	wealth maximization

FURTHER READINGS

Case, J. *From the Ground Up: The Resurgence of American Entrepreneurship*. New York: Simon & Schuster, 1992.

Gilder, G. "America's Best Infrastructure Program." *Wall Street Journal*, March 2, 1993, p. 11.

Hirschmann, A. *Exit, Voice, and Loyalty*. Cambridge, MA: Harvard University Press, 1970.

Jensen, M. C. "Takeovers: Their Causes and Consequences." *The Journal of Economic Perspectives* 2, no. 1 (1988), pp. 21–48.

———. "The Modern Industrial Revolution, Exit, and the Failure of Internal Control Systems." *The Journal of Finance* 48, no. 3 (1993), pp. 831–880.

———, and J. B. Warner. "The Distribution of Power Among Corporate Managers, Shareholders, and Directors." *Journal of Financial Economics* 20 (1993), pp. 3–24.

Lichtenberg, F. R. *Corporate Takeovers and Productivity*. Cambridge, MA: The MIT Press, 1992.

Scherer, F. M. "Corporate Takeovers: The Efficiency Arguments." *The Journal of Economic Perspectives* 2, no. 1 (1988), pp. 69–82.

Schleifer, A., and L. Summers, "Breach of Trust in Hostile Takeovers," in A. Auerback, ed., *Corporate Takeovers: Causes and Consequences*. Chicago: The University of Chicago Press, 1988, pp. 33–56.

———, and R. W. Vishny, "Value Maximization and the Acquisition Process." *Journal of Economic Perspectives* 2, no. 1 (1988), pp. 7–20.

Wayne, L. "Fleeing the Corporate Stable." *The New York Times*, November 15, 1981, pp. 3–26.

▨ QUESTIONS AND PROBLEMS FOR REVIEW AND DISCUSSION

A. Explain what economists mean when they speak of "corporate control." In your answer be sure to include reference to each of the traditional stakeholders in the firm: workers, customers, suppliers, debt holders, and stockholders.

B. 1. What is meant by the "value" of a firm? What are two different ways to measure the value of a firm?

   2. Provide the reasoning that explains why these two ways are indeed best suited for different purposes.

   3. Hypothetically, what could be said if these two measures of firm value were equal?

C. In 1973, the market value of large U.S. companies was typically about four times their book value. By 1992, the situation was much different, with the book value of large U.S. companies typically about two times book value.

   1. What general reasons can you give for the substantial change in the relationship between market and book value over this time period?

   2. In Chapter 1, we provided a brief discussion of the evolution of industry in the United States, emphasizing the downfall of mass production. Can you provide an argument that a rough correlation exists between the changing relationship between the market and book values of large U.S. corporations and the demise of mass production?

D. Name the four forces operating on large, publicly traded corporations that should work to encourage an efficient use of the corporation's assets by its managers.

E. How can debt be viewed as motivating managers of a firm? In particular, how can debt levels provide a set of incentives consistent with efficiency enhancing behavior by a firm's managers?

F. What are the key components of the model of corporate governance provided by the venture capital firms?

People make up an integral part of every organization. Having already considered the impacts and issues surrounding the financial inputs used by firms, we turn our attention in these next two chapters to the problems of managing the human input in organizations.

We continue in this section with our emphasis on transaction costs and bounded rationality within a contracting environment. Of course, employment is nothing more than a contract, but the setting of the contract will be of paramount importance to us.

Chapter 12, "The Employment Relationship," considers two contracting environments existing between firms and workers. The first is that considered by traditional economic analysis: the marginal productivity–based model. In this model, workers are paid the value of what they produce, and equilibrium is determined by competitive forces within a supply and demand framework.

We propose an alternative framing of the contract between workers and firms that borrows the concepts of economic and quasi-rents from Part II of this text. A long-term relational contract, which we term the *employment relationship*, is agreed to between workers and firms. This contract has many desirable characteristics and efficiency-enhancing properties. Such a relationship will mitigate at least some of the transaction costs caused by imperfect measurement and the resulting principal-agent setting. Also, workers can be provided with ample incentive to make substantial investments in firm-specific human capital. Further, if this type of relationship is announced and the announcement viewed as credible by all concerned, in-

MANAGING HUMAN RESOURCES

fluence costs will be smaller and individuals will have institutional encouragement to become team players.

The employment relationship we describe is applicable to many instances in which the marginal productivity–based models are not and vice versa. In labor markets where firm-specific human capital is not important and where worker output is easily measured, we expect to observe a competitive supply and demand type model in operation.

Chapter 13, "**Employment Experience,**" begins to link together our understanding of the employment relationship with the labor practices of large organizations and firms. We make the argument that large organizations do act as predicted by the employment relationship in their dealings with employees. More specifically, it is not uncommon for wages to become tied to jobs and for workers to advance along some career path. This scenario worked rather well in corporate America for years until very recently when circumstances, at least temporarily, changed.

We also address the compensation packages given to the chief executive officers of corporations. It has become popular in the media to announce the earnings of CEOs, and these announcements generally cause an outcry over the large amounts of money involved. The debate on whether CEOs are paid too much is largely subjective, and very little can be said using objective economic principles. We can, however, put CEO earnings in perspective, providing the student with a unique vantage point from which to view this sensitive issue.

The Employment Relationship

No other decisions are so long lasting in their consequences or so difficult to unmake. And yet, by and large, executives make poor promotion and staffing decisions. By all accounts, their batting average is no better than .333: At most, one-third of such decisions turn out right; one third are minimally effective, and one-third are out right failures.[1]

CHAPTER OUTLINE AND STUDENT GOALS

How Important Are Our Jobs?

Suppose that you happen to run into someone that you had neither seen, heard from, or heard much about since your high school days. In some way, you will ask her what she is doing now. Her reply will most likely center on her occupation, as will yours in response to a similar question from her. In our society, we tend to define ourselves, at least partially, in terms of what we do for gainful employment.

There are many reasons for this. On the one hand, our jobs signify where we belong in the community in that they define our contribution to society. Our jobs also tell others information about ourselves; if a person is an accountant, we know that he has spent four or five years in a business school; if a person is involved in marketing, then we can guess that she has certain creative talents.[2] In short, in both social and economic terms, we tend to place much emphasis on our jobs.

Explanations for Labor Markets

Most economic analysis of wage determination and employment issues has, historically, been based largely on marginal productivity theory. This has resulted in a "traditional" economic view in which wages and employment levels are determined in competitive markets by the interaction of supply and demand. This view proves instructive and provides a starting point for our discussion, but the traditional view raises a number of questions.

We argue that the numerous transaction costs and the inherent bounded rationality of individuals will, in the interest of efficiency, replace spot employment markets with long-term relational contracting. The basic underlying mechanics of the long-term relationship between worker and firm are shown to be largely intuitive and, more important, in everyone's interests. The relationship itself addresses

---

[1]Peter F. Drucker, "Getting Things Done: How to Make People Decisions," *Harvard Business Review* (July–August 1985), p. 22.

[2]Stereotypes are also frequently attached to different occupations. In fact, one of the authors of this textbook recently overheard a conversation about him in which the comment, "He's a pretty funny guy, for an economist," was made.

numerous contracting problems, especially influence costs created by rent-seeking behavior in firms and by moral hazard issues.

This is not to say that the traditional view of labor markets is worthless: the point is that it should be applied only in certain circumstances. When employment occurs as a market exchange, via an external contract, the traditional view is relevant. However, when employment is viewed as a long-term relational agreement repeatedly made between the firm and the worker, it is an internal contract best conducted along the lines suggested in this chapter.

Consider an organization with two human resource needs. The first is a six-month position to fill in for a secretary granted a leave of absence to care for his elderly father. The second is a permanent replacement for one of the company's key executives who has retired rather suddenly. Filling the first of these involves participating in an external competitive market. Filling the second involves a long-term commitment to a sequence of internal transactions between the vice president and the organization.

The employment relationship offers three prescriptions for the development of efficient human resource policies. First, there may be efficiency gains to insulating workers from widely fluctuating demand in the product market. Or, put another way, one component of the employment relationship is a form of insurance for workers. Second, employee development is arguably a very important aspect for both organizations and workers. Third, recruiting the right type of employee is one of the central tasks of any organization.

After reading this chapter, you should be able to

- Intuitively explain the functioning of the traditional marginal productivity model of employment and wage determination.

- Understand the circumstances necessary for the application of the traditional marginal revenue product model of employment.

- Explain intuitively what the main features of the employment relationship are.

- Identify the transaction costs that frequently arise in all employment contracts and explain how their impact is mitigated by the structure of the employment relationship.

- Define idiosyncratic exchange and what it means to say that the employment relationship is self-enforcing.

■ THE STANDARD MARGINAL PRODUCTIVITY THEORY

An Idea
and the Environment

The standard, or traditional, approach in economics for analyzing labor markets is grounded in the concept of marginal productivity introduced in Chapter 3. **Marginal productivity theory** has existed for a long time; here we focus on its simplest form, seeking a sound intuitive understanding of it and its environment.[3]

We return to the competitive markets and firms discussed in Chapters 2, 3, and 4. Because each individual firm is a small part of larger markets, no firm can significantly affect market price. The role of each firm is simply to maximize profits, the difference between revenues and costs. To keep the mathematical compo-

---

[3]The reader interested in further exploration of the standard marginal productivity–based view of labor markets is referred to the textbooks by Pindyck and Rubinfeld, Nicholson, Hamermesh, and Devine and Kiefer listed in the further readings list in this chapter.

nent of our analysis as simple as possible, we envision the firm operating in the short run, where all factors of production are fixed except for labor.[4]

Profit-maximizing behavior by firms in this setting of competitive markets is neither tedious nor complex; in fact, it reduces to one very simple managerial rule. Consider the short-run decision-making framework of firms. Output price is determined by the market; the firm has no room to maneuver here. The first decision to be made is to identify the profit-maximizing, or optimal, quantity to produce given the market price of output and the firm's cost structure. This is accomplished by determining the quantity at which marginal revenue equals marginal cost. The second decision made is whether to produce any units at all. Recall from Chapter 3 the discussion of a firm's shut-down point: a profit-maximizing firm will produce so long as price exceeds average variable cost at the optimal quantity.

In essence, then, a single managerial rule tells a firm how many units to produce—perhaps zero, perhaps more. It is now time in our development of firm behavior to point out what you may have guessed already. In the short run, the decision on how many units to produce is *equivalent* to determining how many units of labor to hire at prevailing wage rates. The firm's production function relates output, Q, to the amounts of inputs. Following tradition, we label the inputs K and L. We let K represent the capital input to production, which we will assume to be fixed. We let L represent the labor input to production, which serves as the variable input to production. We then have

$$Q = f(K,L) \tag{12.1}$$

The functional form for the expression relating Q to the amount of inputs K and L means that if you specify the amounts of K and L used by a firm, the amount of output is given by Q. Given that K is fixed, there is a one-to-one correspondence between Q and L. If L is known, then so is Q. Likewise, if Q is known, then so is L.

As an example, suppose that beer is produced using two inputs: a capital input (K) representing the physical and technological characteristics of the brewery and a labor input (L) representing the number of brewery workers used in any week. Let the relationship be as follows, where Q represents the number of barrels of beer produced in any week:

$$Q = \sqrt{K} * \sqrt{L} \tag{12.2}$$

Now, because we know that the capital input is fixed, we can simplify the production function. Suppose that the brewery has 2,500 units of K, no more and no less, available for beer production. Then the above production function becomes

$$Q = 50 * \sqrt{L} \tag{12.3}$$

The total barrels of beer produced for alternative levels of L are shown in Table 12.1. If the brewery decides to produce 300 barrels of beer during the third week of July, 36 weekly brewery workers are required.

With the idea that the decision on how many units to produce corresponds to a choice of how many units of labor to hire firmly in place, we can now turn our attention to the broader framework of profit maximization. We approach the problem as a sequence of marginal decisions made by the firm. At every stage, it

---

[4]Although we do not formally model consumer choice, we require that households make a labor supply choice. For an excellent development of this aspect of consumer behavior, see Walter Nicholson, *Microeconomic Theory: Basic Principles and Extensions*, 4th ed. New York: The Dryden Press, 1989, chap. 22.

Table 12.1 Beer Produced with Variable Labor Input L

Number of Weekly Brewery Workers	Barrels of Beer Produced
33	287.2
34	291.5
35	295.8
36	300.0
37	304.1
38	308.2
39	312.2
40	316.2
41	320.1
42	324.0

is important to fully understand the marginal benefits and marginal costs of production.

For simplicity, suppose that the firm is already producing some amount of output.[5] A basic question emerges: Should the firm produce more output? Clearly, producing more output involves hiring (at least) one more unit of input, in our example, one more unit of the variable input, L. The question then becomes: Should the firm hire one more unit of the variable factor of production? For the sake of argument, suppose that it does. The change in costs to the firm is clear from this action: total costs increase by the amount that must be paid to hire this additional unit of L. In our competitive model, recall that all prices, including input prices, are determined by the market. We define the cost of each unit of L as w. On the margin, then, it costs the firm w to expand output.

We must also consider the marginal benefits of hiring that additional unit of L. On the margin, the benefit of hiring one more unit of L is equal to the market value of the output produced by that additional unit. Recall from Chapter 3 the concept of **marginal product:** the marginal product of an input is equal to the contribution of that input to total output, holding all other factors affecting output constant. All units produced are valued at the market price, p. Therefore, the marginal benefits of hiring an additional unit of L are equal to the price of output times the marginal product of that unit of L. We refer to these additional benefits as **marginal revenue product** (*MRP*).[6]

To determine whether the firm should expand output, the relevant comparison to make is between the market wage, w, and the *MRP*. If *MRP* exceeds w, expanding output will add more to total revenue than it will to costs; thus, total profits will increase. If *MRP* is less than w, expanding output will add less to total revenue than it will to costs; thus, total profits will decrease.

If it is in the firm's interests to expand output from its current level, will this expansion stop, or will it continue indefinitely? Because we know from our own

---

[5]Strictly speaking, we could begin our analysis at zero units produced and compare this outcome with producing one unit of output. However, this would be an intuitively unappealing way to proceed.

[6]If all units of output are not sold at the same price, then *MRP* is equal to the current marginal revenue times the marginal product. While this distinction is important, it somewhat clouds our analysis at this point.

experiences that there are no infinitely sized firms, we can conclude that at some point it is no longer in the firm's interests to expand output. Indeed, we have already developed the tools necessary to prove this observation.

The principle of eventually **diminishing marginal productivity** guarantees that at some point it is no longer in the firm's interests to expand output. The *MRP* is merely the price of output times the marginal product of the input; the second of these must eventually fall. Then, at some point, the marginal benefits of hiring additional units will begin to decrease. The rule, then, for our profit-maximizing firm is to expand output or to hire units of input until the marginal revenue product equals the wage. This rule can be expressed mathematically as follows:

$$MRP = w \tag{12.4}$$

We can illustrate some of these points using the brewery example discussed earlier. Suppose that the market price for a barrel of beer from the brewery is \$70[7] and that the going wage rate for workers doing jobs similar to those at the brewery are \$294 per week. We can easily demonstrate profit-maximizing behavior and our rule that $MRP = w$ is, in fact, true using the information in Table 12.2.

Begin with the possibility that the brewery initially produces 287.2 barrels of beer and employs 33 workers. Should another worker be added? The marginal cost of hiring that worker is the market wage of \$294. The marginal benefits of hiring that worker are the marginal product of the 33rd worker, 4.4 barrels of beer, times the market price of \$70. Then, the marginal revenue product, \$308, exceeds the wage of \$294. Hiring that worker increases profits by \$14, so that worker should be hired. The 34th and 35th workers likewise increase profits, each doing so by \$7. Further gains are exhausted, however, by hiring the 36th worker.

**Labor, a Derived
Demand**

A second interpretation of our rule is that a firm hires workers until the point at which wage equals marginal revenue product. This rule also can be used to derive a firm's demand function for labor. Recall that in Chapter 2 we defined the concept of **derived demand,** which is applicable when a good or service is bought not for final consumption but to be used in the production, marketing, or distri-

---

[7]This may seem to be a very high price for a barrel of beer, but remember two things: first, there is a good deal of beer in a barrel, and, second, it is very good beer.

Table 12.2	**Marginal Revenue Product at the Brewery**			
	Number of Weekly Brewery Workers	**Barrels of Beer Produced**	**Marginal Productivity of Brewery Workers**	**Marginal Revenue Product (\$)**
	33	287.2	4.4	308
	34	291.5	4.3	301
	35	295.8	4.3	301
	36	300.0	4.2	294
	37	304.1	4.1	287
	38	308.2	4.1	287
	39	312.2	4.0	280
	40	316.2	4.0	280
	41	320.1	3.9	273
	42	324.0	3.9	273

bution of some other good or service. The demand for labor is then a derived demand. All demand functions relate the amount that buyers are willing and able to purchase to alternative prices for the good, holding all other things constant. This is exactly the information contained in our rule that $w = MRP$.

Suppose that we were to ask a firm how much it would be willing and able to pay for an additional worker. As argued earlier, this amount would equal the price of output times the amount of output produced by that additional worker, or, in other words, the MRP. As we hypothetically added workers, the benefits going to the firm from hiring these "other" workers would decrease because of diminishing marginal productivity. Thus, our demand function for workers would slope downward.

The same type of logic and calculation would take place if we determined at this wage the number of workers the firm would hire. Again, the answer would depend on the marginal revenue product for each number of workers hired.

A hypothetical demand for labor, MRP, function is shown in Figure 12.1 along with the associated relationship between units of input, L, and the marginal productivity (MP_L) of those units. For 10 units of input, MP_L equals 50 and the MRP is \$75. Likewise, at a wage of \$60, the firm will hire 15 units of labor; at this level, MP_L equals 40. We now have an appreciation for how the demand of labor function for a firm may be created.

The extension from firm demand to market demand for a particular type of worker is straightforward. The market demand for any given type of labor is obtained by adding the quantity demanded by each of the individual firms at every wage rate. The market, or total demand, will basically look like the firm demand pictured in Figure 12.1 in that it is downward sloping. It too depends crucially on the marginal productivity of workers in their capacity at the firms. As interest-

Figure 12.1 The Demand for Labor

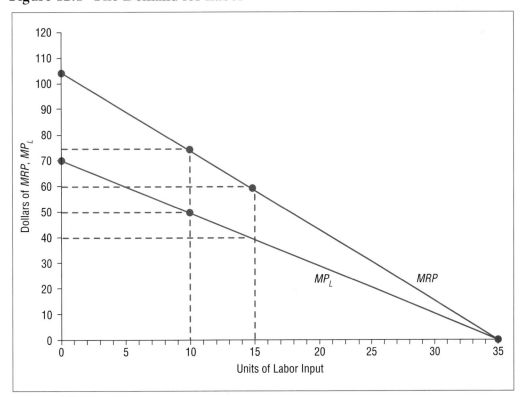

ing as it is, it represents only half of the traditional view of competitive labor markets.

Just as it takes "two to tango," we need to account for one other group of people active in the labor market, those selling their services. This second group is composed, of course, of consumers who are also the workers hired by firms. At one time or another, you have probably worked for an hourly, weekly, or monthly wage. In response to the offered wage, you made a decision about how much of your time would be devoted to work. This decision is the theoretical underpinning for the supply of labor, that relationship between the offered wage and the amount of time devoted to work. To fully understand the workings of optimal consumer behavior in determining labor supply, you are referred to a number of the readings listed at the end of this chapter. We focus, instead, on a more intuitive justification.[8]

Our primary assumption is that individuals believe that work is distasteful, or put another way, that there are other things that the workers would prefer to do. Given this premise, if workers are to be encouraged to voluntarily work more hours, they must be compensated an extra amount to get them to forgo the things they would rather do. Workers will increase the number of hours they work only if the reward for doing so increases. For every individual, then, there is a positive relationship between the wage rate and the amount of time devoted to work. By aggregating across numerous individuals, we can also claim the supply of any particular type of worker to a firm's increases in wages.

Economists view the competitive labor market much like they would any other competitive market. The interaction of the supply and demand of labor determines the equilibrium price, in this case a wage.

In Figure 12.2, the supply and demand for college teachers is shown.[9] The equilibrium wage is w^*, at which 20 college teachers are hired. Notice that at wages above w^*, such as w^+, the supply of college teachers exceeds the demand and there is a surplus of college teachers, implying significant unemployment. The opposite is true at wages below w^*, such as w^-, where there is a shortage of college teachers, and there is a tendency for their wages to increase.

The competitive labor market model features a demand curve based on the concept of marginal productivity and a supply curve that results from consumers (who are also the workers when they provide labor services) seeking to maximize their satisfaction. As with the demand and supply analysis in Chapter 2, some interesting comparative statics experiments are possible. Suppose, for example, that a large number of Mexican workers immigrate into the United States as a result of the open trade policies and cultural effects of the North American Free Trade Agreement (NAFTA) passed in 1993 by the Clinton administration. The resulting increase in the supply of labor will work to lower market wages in some occupations.

The traditional marginal productivity–based competitive labor market model has become fairly accepted by economists either directly or in one of its many variants. The evidence of this claim is the wide number of studies on which the model is based and its frequent appearance in most managerial economics and microeconomics textbooks. However, two facts must be acknowledged: first, the model is not directly applicable to all, or even most, employment situations; second, there is a substantial amount of statistical evidence that suggests alternative explanations for wage and employment determination.

A Competitive
Labor Market

---

[8]Although we do not formally model this aspect of consumer choice here, we require that consumers make this choice. For an excellent development of this aspect of consumer behavior, see Walter Nicholson, *Microeconomic Theory*, chap. 22.

[9]In Figure 12.2 the equation for the supply curve is $w = 5 + (9L)/4$. The equation for the demand curve is $w = 100 - (5L/2)$. They intersect at $L = 20$ and $w = 50$.

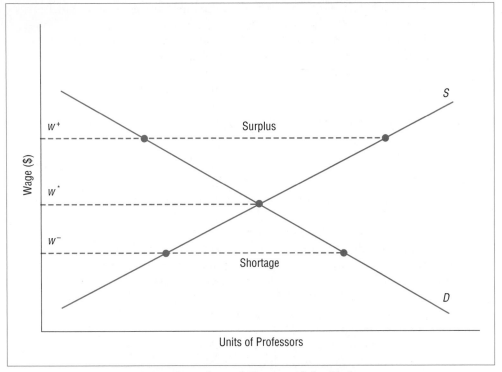

Figure 12.2 Competitive Supply and Demand for Labor

We now examine when the traditional marginal productivity–based model is applicable by addressing several stylized facts that have emerged. By addressing these issues, we hope to provide a better feel for when the model is applicable.

> Employees are, in most cases, not commodities that can be exchanged according to the rules created by a sometimes volatile spot market. The informational needs for the smooth and efficient functioning of such a market are prohibitive, a characteristic that would lead to significant transaction costs.

The standard marginal productivity–based competitive labor market model suggests, in a sense, that workers are largely undifferentiated commodities exchangeable in simple spot markets. More can always be bought and simply added to those you already have. Workers must be willing to progress from employer to employer, depending on who will pay them the highest wage. Such markets do exist. Itinerant farm workers who travel wherever the harvest is ready are one example. It might be argued that plumbers, electricians, and other construction workers also fall into this category. However, managerial and professional talent is far different. Likewise, given the renewed emphasis on employee development in the U.S. manufacturing industries, it can be concluded that many occupations are far less footloose than assumed in the standard model.

> The traditional model indicates a strong link between wages and productivity, a link that is neither clearly or widely observed.[10] These observations are strengthened by the prevalence of moral hazard.

---

[10]For an excellent review of these arguments and a review of the empirical evidence, see George P. Baker, Michael C. Jensen, and Kevin J. Murphy, "Compensation and Incentives: Practice vs. Theory," *The Journal of Finance* 43, no. 3 (July 1988), pp. 593–616.

A strict application of the standard model would predict that pay levels fluctuate a great deal. Recall that the marginal revenue product equals the price of output times the marginal product of labor. Demand may fluctuate greatly in the output market, implying swings in product price and quantity produced. However, actual pay cuts are not common for most workers. In fact, in many organizations, employees have become accustomed to gradually increasing wages with significant salary bumps resulting from internal promotions. Furthermore, firms commonly make some attempt to avoid laying off workers even when production falls to zero for short periods of time.

Perhaps the most significant obstacle to the standard marginal productivity model is the way in which firms and employees invest in employee development.

Employees often invest in **firm-specific human capital,** skills and knowledge that have value only to their current employing organization. They do so expecting to be rewarded and usually are. However, the firm in the standard model has very limited incentive to reward such investment by its workers. By definition, the firm-specific human capital cannot be used at other firms. As such, other firms will not lure away employees who have built firm-specific human capital. Since there is then no competitive pressure to reward the accumulation of firm-specific human capital, the standard marginal productivity model implies that it will not be rewarded.

Another complication in applying the standard marginal productivity–based competitive labor market model is the existence of set retirement wages.

These problems occur on two fronts. First, it is unclear why productivity should fall to zero just because a person reaches a certain age, say 65. Second, even if productivity is drastically reduced at some age, it is unclear why this hypothetical age should be the same for all workers.

The standard marginal productivity–based competitive labor market model is far from perfect. However, there must be a certain amount of truth to it. Before proceeding to the details of what we call the *employment relationship*, in the next section we review the ideas of incomplete and relational contracting and highlight its application in the employment context. In the following section, we describe the employment relationship. Certain aspects of the standard model are carried into this discussion, but we add many of the findings of our analysis of contracting from Chapters 7 and 8 and transaction costs from Chapter 6. What emerges is a richer description of employment that is relevant, we hope, for a wide range of occupations, perhaps even yours.

▓ EMPLOYMENT: RELATIONAL CONTRACTING

**Relational Contracting
Revisited**

Complete contracts are agreements that spell out actions to be taken under every possible eventuality. The employment contract is an incomplete contract because of the many unforeseen circumstances, costly calculations, and imprecise language involved. In the United States and in most other advanced economic systems, employment is voluntary on the part of each party. **At-will employment** implies that workers are employed by the will of the employer and that an employee works for a particular employer only because he or she finds it advantageous to do so. Workers basically agree (within certain moral and legal limits) to apply their backs, brains, and skills to complete the tasks directed by the employer. The employer agrees to pay the workers, who are free to leave at any time. Employers usually can terminate the worker if he or she fails to complete the assigned tasks satisfactorily. Naturally, this situation may seem somewhat vague, and you are undoubtedly questioning its reasoning. But that is precisely the point: because employment is largely a bilateral at-will situation clouded by uncertainties and complexities, *only relational contracting will do* (as considered in Chapter 6). The inherent transaction costs present an extremely large obstacle to the smooth or efficient functioning of the competitive spot markets required by the marginal productivity–based traditional model.

The employment relationship is a particular instance of relational contracting. It involves an agreement on the following criteria:

1. The goals and objectives of the individual employee and those of the organization.
2. General provisions governing each party's responsibilities.
3. The establishment of some criteria and, when possible, a procedure for dealing with unforeseen events.
4. Some agreed upon approach to dispute resolution.

Within these broadly defined criteria common to all forms of relational contracting, we can identify three specific areas that create the need for the relational nature of employment contracts: (1) the acquisition and development of firm-specific human capital, (2) imperfect measurement, and (3) producers' difficulties in perfectly predicting their future needs.

The Special Nature
of Labor

Most organizations have their own ways to get things done. As a part of your academic training in business, you are learning many fundamental skills: written and oral communication, spreadsheets, accounting, economics, and marketing, to name a few. Perhaps you were even taught, according to generally accepted accounting principles, how the accounts receivable entries should be handled. Quite possibly, once you are employed, you will learn that another approach—one that seems to work better than the "textbook" approach—is taken by your new organization. The approach must be superior to the "textbook" approach for that organization, or else it wouldn't take it. In fact, every organization may have its own unique way to handle accounts receivable. As you learn the approach taken by your new organization, you are building firm-specific human capital.

Firm-specific human capital is not unique to basic areas such as accounting or computer technology. It encompasses everything from communication with the varied and unique personalities in an organization to an appreciation for the corporate culture at any one firm and to an atypical understanding of the market position, or niche, of any one organization. In the 1990s we have experienced an emphasis in U.S. firms on being a "team player." Although people can transfer their willingness and inclination to be a team player to other organizations, the exact tasks and interpersonal relationships involved in being on a team are, almost by definition, unique to a single organization.

Whatever the nature of the firm-specific human capital, it is important for two reasons. First, there is some cost to the employee in building this capital. Learning is a difficult task, especially in the absence of any formal training. Second, once acquired, these skills or sets of information have little or no value in other organizations. Only under incomplete, relational contracting could these skills be built. The concept of being a team player is an excellent case in point. The exact duties of a team player could never be explicitly stated in any contract; what apparently matters is a largely subjective assessment by interested managers on whether or not a person "fits in" or "works with others." What is required is an understanding shared between employer and employee that frames the basis for their relationship.

In every transaction, it is important for the buyer to be satisfied. In fact, "getting your money's worth" has become a very often used phrase in the English language. In its employment decision, the firm is the buyer and must believe that it is getting its money's worth out of an employee. As explained in Chapter 8 when discussing the principal-agent problem, this may be quite difficult to determine under imperfect measurement.

The measurement may be imprecise for many reasons. When output is produced and sold through team production, it may be impossible and/or nonsensical to speak of individual output. Even in cases in which the output of an individual worker is measured, the effort put forth by the worker may not be identifiable. Further, the production process itself may be open to random (or external to the worker) influences and, hence, beyond the employee's control. In fact, attempting to monitor an individual worker and tie his or her pay to realized productivity creates a risky situation for the worker. These risks may create inefficiencies that serve to damage the value created by the relationship between worker and firm.

Clearly, relational contracting offers an attractive alternative to payment systems heavily tied to productivity incentives in many settings. Incentives must remain but are forced to take an alternative form. This can be accomplished in a relational contracting setting in which the worker and the firm agree on broad goals and objectives, valuing long-term rather than short-term results.

One incentive that can be offered within the relational employment contract is a certain degree of income security. In fact, in the United States, it is recognized that corporate employment provides some buffer against discontinuous periods of employment. Many workers choose either an entrepreneurial or corporate career path. An important aspect of this decision is the increased security of working for a large, diverse firm as a trade-off against the potentially larger wages the worker *may* make working for himself or herself.

The corporate restructurings of the early 1990s created a new class of jobless people who are well educated with extensive business experience. Many of these people had to make a simple choice regarding their careers: to seek work with an existing corporation or to take the big risk and become an entrepreneur hoping for a big payoff. Implicit in this decision is the observation that traditional employment offers a degree of safety lacking in starting one's own business.

The actions of every employee create value and risk. If you are your own boss, you have the exclusive rights to that value (minus the government's share). However, as your own boss, you are also your own head of marketing and must find somebody who values what you create. If you fail to do so, your payoff is zero. If you work for someone else, that person has the exclusive rights to the value that you create and is obligated to share it with you. However, your pay probably will not fall to zero every time your organization fails to find a buyer for your output. Presumably, most employees are willing to give up control over what they produce in exchange for a stable income.

Most employers in the United States are fairly reluctant to lay off workers for small, short, adverse fluctuations in demand. Many go to great lengths to keep people working in one capacity or another. Future levels of demand are impossible to forecast and firms are unlikely to know, for certain, how many workers they will actually need one or two years ahead.

Firms actually provide a type of insurance to workers, protecting them from wide variations in earnings. This has the effect of lowering the risks faced by the workers and creates value in the employment relationship. Clearly, a relational contract is necessary to accomplish this; the information requirements for anything approaching complete contracting would be prohibitive.

The contractual arrangement between worker and employer is, in actuality, rather imprecise and best accomplished through relational contracting. The benefits of this arrangement are that individuals can be provided with the incentives necessary to acquire firm-specific human capital shielded from the problems arising out of incentive pay and imperfect measurement and assured that wide pay fluctuations caused by random movements in the demand for firm output will not occur. In the next section, we develop the mechanics and structure of the relational contracts governing employment.

The allocation of **economic rents** and **quasi-rents** plays a central role in this relational contract. The idea that rents are used to reward good behavior by employees is not new to us; it was examined in Chapter 9 in the context of an efficiency wage model. What we offer now is a more complex arrangement spanning the career of a worker when rents are used to prevent shirking, encourage the development of firm-specific human capital, and build a sense of loyalty in both workers and firms.

■ THE STRUCTURE OF THE EMPLOYMENT RELATIONSHIP

To construct a model to explore the type of relational contract found governing employment, we must understand some of the model's analytical components. In this section, we first present its three main components: the age-wage profile, the long-run productivity profile (a concept that builds on the concept of marginal productivity), and the reservation reward profile. Each of these three pieces is an essential component of a model describing the employment relationship.

By an **age-wage profile,** we mean the relationship between the age of a typical employee at a given firm and that employee's wage. Undoubtedly, you have some expectation concerning the earnings you will make as you progress through your working life. In our analysis, we use the concept of an age-wage profile to show this progression.

To keep our analysis clear, we need to assume that wages change smoothly over an employee's career. This is not to say that salary "bumps," such as those caused by promotions, do not occur. We must visualize, however, an "averaging" of these discrete increases in salary such that wage gains are a continuous process as a worker matures. The final important thing to note is that we can speak only of "real" wages, that is, those adjusted for inflation. In the United States, by and large, rising prices paid by consumers (in the form of a general inflation) are usually more than offset by proportionate increases in earnings over the intermediate and long run.

To simplify our analysis, we assume that individuals become employed at age 23; this may be too early for some and too late for others, but it provides as good a starting point as any other. It is not unreasonable that wages rise continuously over the worker's career. To promote your understanding of the concepts behind our age-wage profile, we consider two versions. The first of these is a simplified one featuring a linear age-wage profile. The second is a little more involved since it permits wages to increase at different rates over the typical employee career.

Consider a hypothetical individual, Daniel Zinpack, age 23, soon to be a business graduate from a large state university. Having a minor in economics, Daniel has been exposed to various studies of wage determination and, after consulting with a number of executives who appeared at his university's career day, has a definite plan for his level of real earnings over his lifetime.[11]

In the first version of Daniel's age-wage profile, earnings increase at a constant rate over his career. We assume that Daniel anticipates a starting salary of

Age-Wage Profiles

---

[11]Despite all the benefits of this learning and others willing to speak of their experiences, Daniel has not given much thought as to how easily this money can be spent.

Table 12.3

Age	Wage	Age	Wage
Age	**Wage**	**Age**	**Wage**
23	$32,368	47	$44,272
24	33,192	48	44,768
25	34,000	49	45,264
26	33,856	50	45,760
27	34,352	51	46,256
28	34,848	. . .	
. . .		63	52,208
35	38,320	64	52,704
36	38,816	65	53,200

Table 12.3 Earnings by Age of Daniel Zinpack, Business Graduate, Simple Age-Wage Profile

$32,368 and an income at retirement, earned at age 65, of $53,200. A numerical and graphical representation of Daniel's linear age-wage profile appears in Table 12.3 and Figure 12.3, respectively.

The virtue of the simplified representation of Daniel's age-wage profile lies in its linear nature. This assumption may invoke too much smoothing, however, and may wipe away an important fact of the earnings experience of most individuals in white-collar occupations.

Wages may increase at different rates for younger and older persons. At

Figure 12.3 Daniel Zinpack, Simple Age-Wage Profile

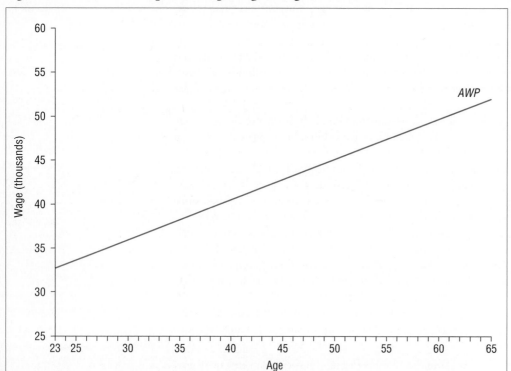

Table 12.4	Earnings by Age of Daniel Zinpack, Business Graduate		
Age	Wage	Age	Wage
23	$32,368	47	$47,728
24	33,192	48	48,168
25	34,000	49	48,592
26	34,792	50	49,000
27	35,268	51	49,392
28	36,328	. . .	
. . .		63	52,848
35	41,200	64	53,032
36	41,832	65	53,200

younger ages, wages rise more quickly than they do at older ages. This is not an assumption of our model but is, rather, an empirical fact. Incorporating this fact into our age-wage profile changes and somewhat complicates things. We show the actual expectations of Daniel Zinpack concerning his future earning potential numerically in Table 12.4 and graphically in Figure 12.4.

Notice that with this more complex representation, Daniel expects larger salary increases early in his career. After one year, he expects his largest raise, $824, which is somewhat smaller in the second year, $808, and continues to de-

Figure 12.4 Daniel Zinpack, Age-Wage Profile

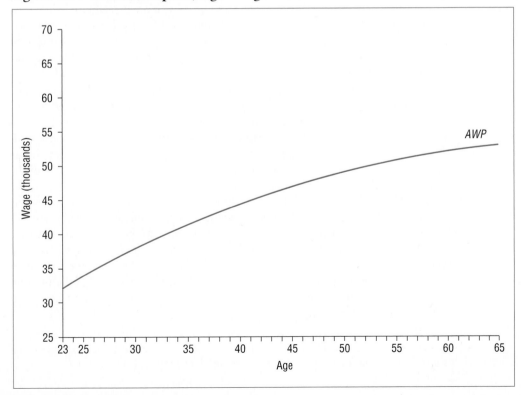

Long-Run Employee
Productivity

cline throughout his career. By age 35, his raises have fallen to $648. By age 64, Daniel's wage increase takes on its smallest value, $168.

We would expect age-wage profiles for many workers to be quite similar to that shown here. This type of relationship between age and earnings is, we argue later, appropriate in cases in which employees develop firm-specific human capital and in cases in which worker output is measured only imperfectly.

You may be wondering how our age-wage profile relates to the marginal revenue product concept with which we began this chapter. There is a link, but it is not one to one. Both workers and firms expect that employee productivity will increase as workers advance in their careers. Human beings have an innate ability and desire to learn, which makes workers more productive. Furthermore, the importance of experience cannot be ignored. Over the course of their careers, we expect then that learning and the benefits of experience raise worker productivity. What is missing from our age-wage profile is the concept implied in the traditional marginal productivity employment theory that worker output is continuously monitored and wages adjusted accordingly. We now assess the idea of a worker's long-run productivity.

For employment decisions to be made intelligently, both workers and firms must form expectations about the long-term (over the life of the employment relationship) ability of workers to produce output of value. This directly involves a determination of an employee's long-run productivity. A long-run productivity profile shows the relationship between a worker's age and the marginal productivity at that age. As with the age-wage profile, we present two versions of the long-run productivity profile depending on how productivity increases occur as workers mature.

If we assume that productivity increases linearly as an employee ages, we can construct a simple version of the productivity profile. Such an example is provided in Figure 12.5. As with the simplified age-wage profile shown in Figure 12.3, the function increases at a constant rate at every age.

To arrive at a more realistic representation of worker marginal productivity, we may assume that worker productivity changes at different rates, depending on the age of the worker. Initially, worker productivity is low but increases throughout the employee's career. It seems reasonable that marginal productivity increases relatively quickly at first as workers begin applying their skills and abilities and desire to learn how to act in their new environment. Productivity increases continue to take place, but at slower rates, as a result of the great deal of institutional learning that usually takes place in many occupations as workers begin to build and use firm-specific human capital. A productivity profile, showing a typical worker's marginal productivity at different ages, is shown in Figure 12.6. There are some connections between the traditional view of employment and the employment relationship that we must now consider.

Because labor is a derived demand—that is, it is demanded by firms not for its own sake but because it can be used to produce output valuable in the market—employers are concerned not with the marginal productivity of workers but with the marginal revenue product of workers. We now consider *marginal revenue product* to be the value of the output produced by a worker at each point in his or her career. In the simplest case, marginal revenue product is equal to the number of units produced by a unit of labor (at the margin) times the output price (for simplicity, assumed to be 1).[12]

---

[12]In some instances, not all units of output are sold at the same price. In these cases, marginal revenue product equals the marginal product times the marginal revenue at the current level of output.

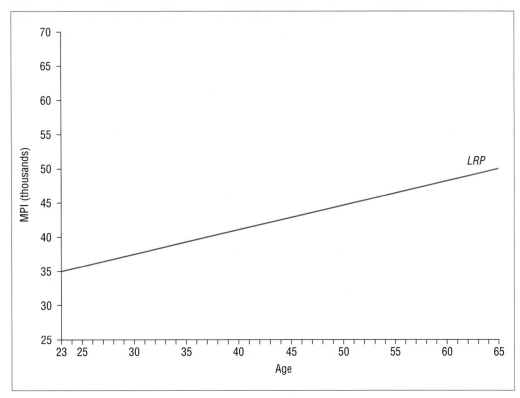

Figure 12.5 Long-Run Productivity Profile, Simple

Figure 12.6 Long-Run Productivity Profile

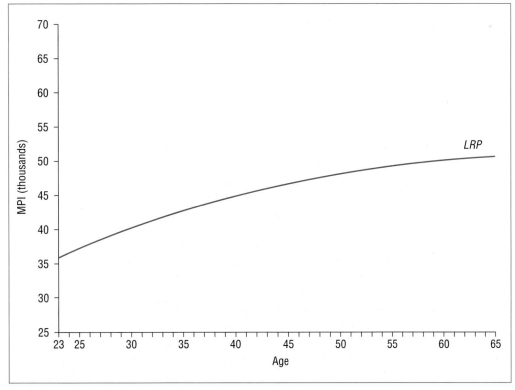

**An Individual's
Reservation Reward**

The other important structural variable in our model of the employment relationship relates to the individual's decision to supply (or not) his or her labor input to a particular organization. We assume that in every period, the individual has in mind an amount of pay that represents a price floor in the market for his or her services, or, in other words, a reservation price. This is to say, there is some minimum amount that the individual must be paid to entice him or her to put forth any effort at all. We call this amount the **reservation reward,** for if wages are offered below this amount, the individual will not willingly work.

It is rational to assume that the reservation reward increases as the employee grows older. As individuals mature and accumulate wealth, they tend to increase their consumption of leisure, which in our model is the only alternative to hours devoted to work. This greater propensity to consume leisure implies that it increases in value to individuals as they mature. In any one period, any difference between the wage received and the reservation reward represents a rent accruing to the worker such as those described in our discussion of efficiency wages in Chapter 8. Efficiency requires individuals to work only if their earnings exceed their reservation reward. If this is not true, efficiency is best served if individuals do not participate in the labor market.

As with the expected paths of productivity and earnings that workers anticipate over their lives, we envision a construct called the **reservation reward profile** linking an individual's reservation reward and his or her age. The reservation reward profile is upward sloping and its steepness increases at larger ages.

The long-run equilibrium condition on which the employment relationship rests shares one important similarity with the traditional model discussed earlier in this chapter. In each, firms are motivated to hire individuals because workers create value for the organization. This value represents an upper bound on how much firms will pay workers for their efforts. For the more sophisticated employment relationship, the condition does not rely on a "marginal" observation made at a single point in time; instead, it spans the worker's career at a given firm.

Over the course of a worker's career, employers benefit by selling what workers are able to produce. In any one period, this benefit equals the marginal revenue product of the employee. The total, long-run benefit to the employer is the sum of the benefits earned in each period. Thus, in determining the benefits to the organization of hiring a college graduate, the organization considers the likely benefits created over the next 40-odd years.

Long-Run Equilibrium

The long-run cost to hiring an employee likewise equals the costs per period aggregated, or summed up, over all periods. Long-run equilibrium requires that the long-run benefits equal the long-run costs for the organization. Technically speaking, the long-run equilibrium consists of a sequence of wages offered the employee in the form of an age-wage profile.

The concept of the employment relationship severs the *direct* link between pay and productivity. Earnings and output are linked only over the expected duration of the relationship. Technically speaking, pay received by workers only exactly equals marginal revenue product at some brief instant in time.

Under the employment relationship, pay is less than marginal revenue product in an employee's early years. Later in their careers, earnings exceed (on a per period basis) the employee's value to the firm as measured by the value of that employee's marginal product. The long-run equilibrium condition requires that the years of surplus balance the years of deficit. Put another way, organizations gain early in the employee's career in the sense that workers are paid less than their contribution to the value of output. Likewise, workers gain later in their careers in the sense that they earn more than their contribution to the value of output. It must be true, however, that the gains to the employee exactly equal the gains to the employer.

We present the equilibrium in both the simplified and more complete versions. Figure 12.7 shows the long-run equilibrium in the employment relationship for the simplified age-wage and productivity profiles. Figure 12.8 shows the long-run equilibrium in the employment relationship for the more realistic versions of the age-wage and productivity profiles. Keep in mind that in each figure, the productivity profile measures marginal revenue product, *MRP*.

In Figure 12.7, the curve labeled *AWP* shows a linear age-wage profile and the curve labeled *LRP* shows the long-run productivity. Early in the worker's career, marginal revenue product exceeds earnings: the *LRP* curve lies above the *AWP* curve. The situation is reversed, however, later in the worker's career. The long-run equilibrium condition implies that the area between the *AWP* and *LRP* functions before their intersection equals the area between the two curves after their intersection. Or, in other words, the triangular area *ABC* equals the triangular area *CDE*.

Figure 12.8 shows a comparable long-run equilibrium for the more complete (nonlinear) versions of the age-wage and long-run productivity profiles. Once again, early in a worker's career, the *AWP* is below the *LRP* curve. Also, the areas *A'B'C'* and *C'D'E'* must be equal.

Figures 12.7 and 12.8 stress the idea that the employment relationship is a long-term agreement between employer and employee. It spells out the costs and benefits to each party over a number of years. The long-run equilibrium condition regarding the triangular-shaped regions in Figures 12.7 and 12.8 implies that both employers and employees account for future payments in their decision making. A more formal treatment of the employment relationship would allow

Figure 12.7 Long-Run Equilibrium, Simple Form

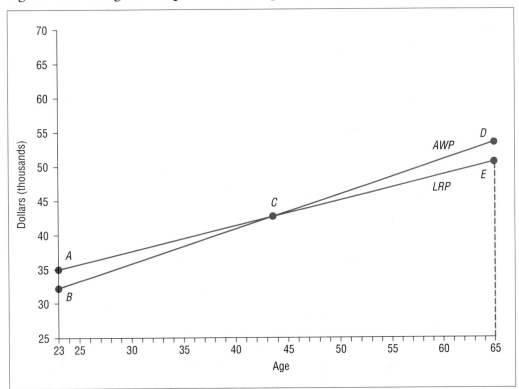

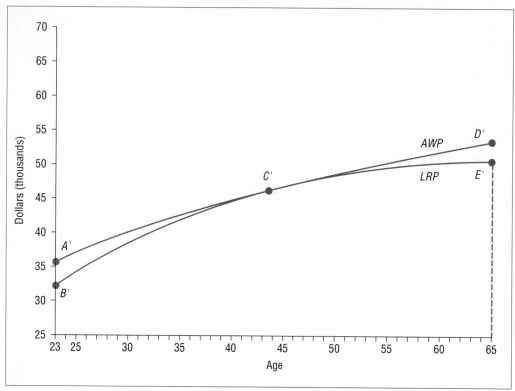

Figure 12.8 Long-Run Equilibrium

the parties to discount these payment streams to current dollars. That is, the dollars earned in the future must be made comparable to dollars earned today for rational decision making.[13] Including discounting in our analysis will not change the underlying forces framing the employment relationship. The consideration of the time value of money would, however, greatly complicate its presentation.

Until this point, we have not included an important piece of the employment relationship puzzle, namely, what happens when the relationship is over. A glib reply (that is not far off the mark) is to say that the employment relationship doesn't really end; however, it becomes rather one-sided after retirement. Today, in most occupations, U.S. workers can expect retirement income from two sources: privately funded pensions and Social Security. Because Social Security is available to nearly all retired persons, it does not play a role in our analysis. Privately funded pensions, however, play a major role in our analysis. In some occupations, privately funded pensions are collected only after the employee works to some specified age or, equivalently, after some number of years of service. In some occupations, employees become vested in their pensions after a few years of satisfactory service. It is indeed rare to find employees who are given rights to pensions immediately on being hired.

The addition of pensions changes our concept of long-run equilibrium in a predictable way. We require that over some long horizon, the costs of employment equal the benefits of employment to the firm. Pensions can be considered as a cost of employment, but their impact in this capacity is rather small. Most im-

---

[13]For a full discussion of net present value and the technique of discounting, see almost any introductory finance or accounting textbook.

portant, pensions provide large benefits accruing to the employee for years of good behavior. They represent significant rents earned by employees far into the future. Thus, they provide motivation for an employee to stay with his or her current employer.

The model of the employment relationship we have described is useful in a variety of settings, especially when workers require some reason (or incentive) to build firm-specific human capital, when measurement is imprecise, or when workers need to be protected from fluctuations in demand in the output market. Although the preceding discussion lays out the intuitive content of the employment relationship, we have, thus far, ignored one feature, namely, who should be in charge.

In Chapter 7, we considered the problem of team production and identified the efficiency gains in assigning authority to the residual claimant or his or her appointee. The employment relationship discussed allows us to shed more light on this issue. We rely on the nature of the employment relationship as it arises from an environment of relational, incomplete contracting. We also recognize that under the employment relationship, both employer and employee have good reason to focus on the value created by the relationship.

Having a single party hold the authority in the employment relationship enhances the efficiency and, hence, total value of the agreement for two very good, very basic reasons. Each of these involves efficiency-destroying transaction costs.

Suppose that no single party held the decision-making authority in a firm. Employment contracts are generally quite imprecise. Situations that are not explicitly covered by the contract are very common. Every time an event occurs that is not covered by the contract, there is a battle over who is in charge of the affected aspects of the employment situation. The bargaining costs in the form of

THE JAPANESE WINDOW SITTER

Implicit in our discussion of the employment relationship is the notion that employment is a long-term commitment by both workers and firms. This concept involves a certain loyalty on both sides. There is a fairly common conception that such loyalty is "new" to the U.S. workplace; however, it has long been a standard feature in Japan, where large corporations frequently implement policies of lifetime employment.

In Japanese corporations, unneeded late middle-aged workers are shunted aside, or shown the "window seat" in their organizations. Once there, they typically are permitted to hold onto their jobs but are given no assignments to complete. Within the Japanese culture, being labeled a *window sitter* causes great embarrassment but is seen as superior to having to rely on various forms of public assistance. The window seat is seen by some Japanese as a sacred entitlement representing a reward for decades of hard work.

Although a large part of the justification for such a policy may be cultural, there are important economic elements as well. The window seat represents a commitment made by employers to the employment relationship. It greatly enhances the corporation's reputation as credible to current and future workers.

Note: For an excellent discussion of window sitters and a number of colorful examples,
see Yumiko Ono, "Unneeded Workers in Japan Are Bored, and Very Well Paid,"
Wall Street Journal, *April 20, 1993, p. A10.*

Who Should Be the Boss?

eroded human capital, personal self-respect, and delays in reaching agreement are not negligible. It is unlikely, however, that any individual holds complete, absolute power, for the fear of opportunism and exploitation would be far too great. In the weakest case, the boss's decisions are usually subject to possible later review either internally or externally, perhaps even before a governmental board.

It also seems reasonable that the same party would hold the decision-making power in all events not explicitly foreseen by the underlying contract. If this were

---

GOLDEN PARACHUTES, SEVERANCE PAY, AND EARLY RETIREMENT BUYOUTS

A *golden parachute* is a device used by corporations facing the threat of an unfriendly, or even hostile, takeover. Typically, a golden parachute clause guarantees top management very generous payments if the unfriendly corporate suitor is successful and causes the current managers to leave the corporation. *Severance pay* refers to payments made to workers by firms in response to an abrupt termination of their employment. Early retirement buyouts are bonuses paid to workers in addition to pensions to encourage them to retire sooner than they otherwise would.

Each of these contractual devices, when standing alone, may seem to be an attempt by employees to extort funds from employers. However, using the economic theory of the employment relationship, we can argue that they are much more than that.

The common theme behind golden parachutes, severance pay, and early retirement buyouts is that they are payments to workers that provide some compensation in the event of a premature termination of the employment relationship. The entire point behind the employment relationship is that workers receive substantial rewards in the form of economic rents later in their careers in return for building firm-specific human capital and being loyal early in their careers. If the relationship is to end earlier than planned, the employee must be compensated in a way that will be considered "fair." Failing this, the organization will loose its credibility in dealing with current and future employees.

The size of the payments often seem rather large, which serves as empirical proof regarding both the value and existence of the relationship.

In late 1993, General Motors was coming to terms with the United Auto Workers on a new contract. One thorny issue was that GM was in the midst of a tremendous downsizing and a need to close plants operated by UAW personnel. The solution was an early retirement buyout policy with some incredible terms. Union workers would be able to retire as young as age 50, receiving vouchers worth $10,000 toward the purchase of a new GM vehicle plus more than $3,000 in cash to cover the associated taxes. Furthermore, union workers opting for the early retirement would have the right to take another job without reducing their GM pensions.

Young union workers at one particular plant received a seemingly even more generous offer. If they failed to qualify for the early retirement, they were offered bonuses of up to $100,000 to leave GM. Additionally, no workers, at any plant, were forced to leave GM.

not the case, contracts would have to specify who has what authority if various types of unforeseen events occurred. Given our implicit assumption that the future is very hard to predict with any degree of accuracy, the transaction costs in drafting and enforcing such an agreement would be huge.

We have then established that having a single person hold the residual decision-making authority may promote efficiency. What can we add to our thoughts of who this party should be? In Chapter 7, we discussed moral hazard and team production; in Chapter 5, we focused on the role of property rights in defining efficient market outcomes. The role of ownership in determining efficient actions is clear; by ownership, we typically mean the owners of the underlying capital. The only question remaining is to what capital do we refer, the physical or human capital? The efficiency argument dictates that the owners of the capital put at greater risk by unforeseen events are the appropriate choice for being the decision-making authority.

In a manufacturing plant, the greater risk is to the physical assets of the plant. The human capital required in manufacturing industries is relatively small, and workers are quite mobile, and, to a certain extent, interchangeable. In the partnerships commonly formed by doctors, lawyers, and accountants, the human capital is a more significant input and also more at risk. We would expect then that in these organizations, the partners themselves would hold the authority in the relationship.

GAINS FROM THE EMPLOYMENT RELATIONSHIP

Mutually Beneficial Gains

Idiosyncratic exchange refers to a particular type of relational exchange between contracting partners. It involves a relationship (usually long term) in which once the general nature of the relationship is established, neither party has incentive to engage in opportunistic behavior. Idiosyncratic exchange is then said to be self-enforcing. In this section, we argue that the employment relationship previously outlined qualifies as a situation of idiosyncratic exchange and that it represents an efficient way to arrange employment for both workers and firms. In a world in which transaction costs were zero, a different solution, namely the one predicted by the standard marginal productivity theory, would be efficient.

Gains to the Organization

The positive slope of the age-wage profile and its position relative to the marginal productivity of a worker at a given point in time offer many efficiency-enhancing incentives.[14] Firms benefit largely because the employment relationship induces workers to put forth full effort. Firms also benefit if they maintain the employment relationship and thus develop a reputation as being credible in their promises and fair to their employees. Employees benefit because of the implied income stability and avoidance of some of the risks involved in direct measures of output.

The employment relationship goes a long way to remove the incentives of employees to shirk. Because the difference between productivity and wages increases through time, the rents earned in the last periods of working serve as a "carrot" dangled in front of workers to entice full effort during their careers. If the employer detects shirking, the worker is punished, perhaps even fired, and fu-

---

[14]This argument follows many of the arguments developed by the economist Edward P. Lazear of Stanford University. We refer the reader first to his article "Labor Economics and the Psychology of Organizations," *Journal of Economic Perspectives* 5, no. 2 (1991), pp. 89–110.

ture gains are lost. It is worth noting that an abrupt, unplanned ending to the employment relationship usually results in a much reduced pension.[15]

Adopting the employment relationship concept provides substantial benefits to an organization in deterring employee shirking, and it benefits the firm in other ways as well. One of these benefits is the establishment of corporate loyalty among the employees of a firm. By and large, corporate loyalty depends on the reputation of the firm in its treatment of employees. If employees believe that the firm will do the things that it has (implicitly) promised, they are willing to trust the firm and not engage in opportunistic behavior. Corporate loyalty is a broad concept that covers many fronts. It may mean that employees are willing to temper their demands for wage increases when times are tough for the firm. Likewise, corporate loyalty may mean that employees refuse to "jump ship" and take their skills and abilities to a competitor in response to a slightly higher wage offer.

The third benefit of the employment relationship to the organization is that the long-term nature of the relationship with its emphasis on rewards received in the future provides workers with the incentive to build firm-specific human capital. This is especially important when technologies are rapidly changing in the goods-producing and service sectors of the economy. In Chapters 14 and 15, we will discuss the intra- and interfirm implications of the emergence of flexible production. For now, suffice it to say that flexible production involves specialization not in a single product but in a range of similar products. Obviously, in such an environment, large demands are placed on workers' skills.

Accumulating firm-specific human capital is expensive to workers because they could have spent the time required on building skills and talents that are transferable across firms. In a purely competitive spot market, employees would never build firm-specific human capital because firms have no incentive to reward them for doing so. Since, by definition, the skills are not transferable to another organization, the employer does not have to reward workers for acquiring them.

The establishment of an employment relationship with each of its workers will provide significant benefits to the firm in another dimension as well. By framing the relationship between worker and firm in this way, the negative impacts of rent-seeking behavior are likely to be made smaller within the organization. Both workers and firms will be able to avoid **influence costs** created when supervisors are lobbied by employees for special treatment in the form of raises, bonuses, and promotions. By leveling the playing field through the adoption of well-known terms, the employment relationship encourages an atmosphere conducive to a team approach to problem solving and production.

In discussing the gains of the employment relationship, thus far we have described only the gains experienced by the employing organization. The gains to employees are substantial, as they are to the firm.

Gains to the Worker

The primary gain to workers lies in the reduction of income variability promised by the employment relationship over other contracting forms. The largest source of risk to a person's income comes not from the income level but from unplanned deviations at some level. The employment relationship offers a slowly rising and steady wage. Given that employers value their reputation with current and future employees, they have incentives to shield their employees, at least partially, from price and demand fluctuations in the output market. The output level of most firms is not stable; there are periods of rising output and other periods of falling output. Further, as demand increases and decreases, the product

---

[15]In the federal and most state civil service occupations, the entire pension may be lost if workers are detected shirking.

price rises and falls. These factors imply short-run variations in the marginal revenue products of workers.

Risk-averse workers find this variation undesirable and are made better off under the employment relationship that provides a framework within which workers can trade off income levels for income stability. This trade-off is most obvious for younger workers who, at the early stages of their careers, are being paid less than their marginal revenue product (i.e., the value of what they produce). The difference between earnings and the market value of what workers produce represents an insurance premium of sorts. This interpretation is consistent with the common practice of firms laying off younger workers first in the event of a downturn in business. Notice that older workers pay less of an insurance premium because their risk of being laid off is less under this practice.

In all fairness, we must point out that firms will never completely insulate workers from income risk. Doing so would encourage rational workers to shirk continuously over their careers, destroying much of the value of the employment relationship.[16]

IMPLICATIONS FOR HUMAN RESOURCE POLICIES

A Long-Term View

The employment relationship we have described in this chapter has a number of notable properties. First, the agreements supporting the relationship are typically long term. Second, a certain amount of specificity is involved for both workers and firms: job searches (as you are quite likely to learn as you obtain your business degree) are an expensive proposition for workers; likewise, hiring an individual may impose considerable costs on firms. Once a commitment is made, each party has incentive to maximize the value of the relationship. Third, employers quite often are concerned with preventing shirking by workers, and workers are concerned with getting what they deem to be "fair" treatment by their employers. Fourth, and perhaps most important, we hope to highlight the importance to a firm's reputation of its labor relations.

Successful human resource policies provide a number of important benefits to firms. Primarily, once a firm establishes a set of ground rules governing its employment relationships and a reputation for not deviating from these ground rules, employees will have the incentives necessary for them to acquire firm-specific human capital.

There is a great deal of complexity underlying a typical employment relationship. Dealing with these complexities is the field of **human resource management,** which specializes in developing policies to satisfy firms and workers. An understanding of the benefits of a firm's employment relationship should not be limited to the members of the human resources department of a typical large corporation; every business manager should have an intuitive understanding of the forces that shape the employment relationship.

A full treatment of all the relevant issues in human resource management requires several separate graduate courses devoted entirely to this one topic. It is our task in this and the next chapter to discuss some of the more important aspects of human resource policies as they pertain to the idea of an employment relationship that we have developed. In this section of this chapter, we consider the importance of recruiting to organizations. We also discuss some issues behind

---

[16]An excellent, although somewhat technical, presentation of this issue can be found in Paul Milgrom and John Roberts, *Economics, Organization, and Management* (Englewood Cliffs, NJ: Prentice Hall, 1992), pp. 334 and 335.

**Getting and Keeping
the Right Workers**

successful retention policies by organizations. In the next chapter, we present a much fuller discussion of one of the main issues behind retention, a firm's policies toward layoffs.

As explained in Chapter 1, one advantage to the corporate form of ownership is that it allows economic organizations to outlive their founders. There is then an implicit need for organizations to recruit new members to guarantee corporate survival and to respond to the pressures caused by corporate growth. Many factors must be considered in developing recruiting plans and objectives. Fortunately, most of them are rather intuitive.

An organization's business strategy points to what types of individuals are needed to fulfill its mission. This involves a determination of what goods and services the organization will seek to supply over the next 10 or 20 years.

The firm's costs of firing or laying off workers also influence its recruitment decisions. In some instances, early termination of or interruptions in the employment relationship are quite costly to organizations. As this cost increases, firms may become concerned about adding permanent staff. As the decade of the 1990s began, a severe recession gripped the U.S. economy. In response to the economic downturn and a simultaneous rise in foreign competition, many U.S. firms cut employment as a cost-saving measure. This was certainly bad news for most sectors of the U.S. economy; one sector, however, experienced rapid growth: the market for "temps." It is certainly no accident that the largest private employer in the U.S. economy at that time was Manpower, Inc., a firm that specialized in providing firms with temporary workers.

The offsetting benefits to a higher cost of firing or laying off workers come in the form of promises of job security to workers. The publicized practice of large corporations such as Hewlett-Packard, IBM, and Lincoln Electric to avoid layoffs has undoubtedly helped them in the past with recruiting. However, this practice is ripe with the opportunity of a form of ex ante opportunism presented in Chapter 7, adverse selection.

Recall that adverse selection occurs in a contracting situation when information is distributed asymmetrically between the parties and the better informed party can behave opportunistically, reducing the value of the exchange to the other party. In a recruiting bargaining situation, the prospective employee has an information advantage over the firm. She possesses superior knowledge of her skills, abilities, attitude toward risk, and work ethic. If an organization is promising what amounts to lifetime employment, it may attract only very risk-averse applicants. In some situations, the managers of a corporation may not wish to do this or perhaps believe that a correlation exists between risk-taking behavior and ultimate performance.

In response to this adverse selection problem, firms may engage in **screening** behavior in an attempt to discourage certain types of applicants. When successful, this screening behavior encourages a **self-selection** by potential applicants. This means that certain aspects of a job announcement would cause some potential applicants not to apply. An excellent example of this occurs when an organization seeks to fill a sales position. If it desires an extraordinarily aggressive person, the organization may announce that the wage is almost entirely in the form of commissions.

It is hoped that successful screening and induced self-selection by potential applicants will provide the organization with a pool of desirable candidates from whom to choose. The problem of picking a single employee from the available pool remains. In this dimension of the problem, signaling is likely to be of some help in the recruiting process.

As explained in Chapter 7, **signaling** arises in situations of asymmetric information. In the context of recruiting, there exist a number of characteristics desirable to employers, only some of which are observable. The employer may not be completely unaware of the likelihood that an applicant has some desirable, but unobservable, characteristics, however. Quite possibly, at least some of the desirable but unobservable characteristics are correlated with observable characteristics. Potential applicants realize this and send what amounts to a signal to the employer. The signal is, of course, the observable characteristic that indicates that the applicant has a high probability of having the unobservable, desirable characteristic.

Consider the situation facing Janet Speelman, an accounting graduate of a state university who is looking for a job, and her perspective employers who are looking for workers. The employers want individuals who are intelligent, computer literate, energetic, hard working, ethical, and good team players. Of all these desirable characteristics, only the first two are easily verified and measured. Janet is well aware of this informational deficiency. On her resume she lists many nonacademic accomplishments: president of the accounting club, work with charities, and so on. Prospective employers will supposedly view Janet's nonacademic accomplishments and activities as indications that she has characteristics that are not directly observable but are desirable. In short, when Janet includes on her resume that she served two years as president of the accounting club, she is sending a signal to perspective employers that she hopes will be interpreted as evidence that she is energetic and hard working.

Recruitment efforts are likely to consume many of an organization's resources, and with good reason. Problems arise because of asymmetric information, and other problems exist as well. At the time of hire, organizations must estimate the likely productivity of the workers over their lifetimes. In some occupations, there are traditional "trial periods," which are really an extension of the organization's window on viewing employees. One example of employers taking a long look at prospective workers occurs at a university. Professors are typically granted tenure only after some minimum specified period of service.

One indicator of the importance of selection decisions by organizations is the cost of the hiring process. One study put this amount at $500,000 per hire, on average, of managerial talent in 1990. This figure may seem large, but the productivity differences between high and low corporate managerial performers is even more astounding. This differential has been estimated to be as high as 3 to 1. Efforts to select qualified employees can yield substantial benefits in each year that the employee is on the payroll.[17]

In any event, it is worth noting that if an employer understates the future productivity of workers, those workers will claim to be underpaid and will be reluctant to build the firm-specific human capital necessary to maximize the value of the relationship to all parties. If an employer overstates the future productivity of workers, the firm will lack incentives to exploit the relationship fully.

Once the right workers are attracted, retaining them may prove difficult. Employee retention enables both the worker and the firm to benefit from the firm-specific human capital created by the employees. Over their careers, workers create firm-specific and *general-purpose human capital*. **General-purpose human capital** is the stock of skills and abilities possessed by a worker that are usable by a number of firms. In a competitive labor market, such as that described in the first

**Retaining Workers:
A First Pass**

---

[17]See Vandra L. Huber, Gregory B. Northcraft, and Margaret Neal, "Effects of Decision Strategy and Number of Openings on Employment Selection Decisions," *Organizational Behavior and Human Decisions Processes* 45 (April 1990), p. 276.

section of this chapter, firms have no incentive to reward employees for their firm-specific human capital. General-purpose human capital, on the other hand, must be rewarded or the employee will leave the firm because he or she can command higher wages elsewhere.

In the absence of payment or reward for firm-specific human capital, the efficiency consequences are clear: no employee has incentive to create it. The obvious solution is to pay the worker for at least some of the firm-specific human capital he or she has acquired. The employment relationship provides workers with incentive to build firm-specific human capital. The reward for accumulating this capital is offered in the form of job security and earnings later in their careers that exceed workers' marginal revenue products and their reservation rewards.

Another important issue in employee retention is how organizations respond to outside offers. Firms follow a number of policies developed internally in response to outside offers. Unfortunately, economic theory cannot point to any one response that is efficient. As we will soon make more clear, a number of important forces characterize this decision for organizations: firm reputation, the value of the employee's firm-specific human capital to the firm, and the exact nature of the outside opportunity.

In an environment of symmetric and perfect information, efficiency would dictate that an employer consider matching an outside offer. Under these restrictions, the current employer would know the true value of the outside offer to the employee. If this value was, at most, as large as the employee's value to the current employer, the offer should be matched. In this situation, value maximization would prevail. The worker would end up working for the employer who would make the best use of his or her time; that employer would be the one willing to pay the worker the most.

The information requirements for this efficient, value-maximizing solution are tremendous, however. Any job involves, from the worker's perspective, a number of costs and benefits that are not easily expressed in dollars. Further, a worker may have very private views concerning the prospects of the new employer. A policy of matching outside offers may also lead to significant bargaining costs if it encourages employees to continually put themselves on the market simply to increase their wages with their current employer.

It is also conceivable that firms would completely ignore outside offers. For this strategy to be effective, the organization must pay essentially a fixed wage (or pay according to established and uniform age-wage profiles) to all employees. This wage, or wage stream, would then have to be higher than what the firm would offer employees in the absence of any threat of outside offers. The problem with the nonmatching strategy is that it requires commitment since its strength comes from the reputation of the firm. Any deviations, or special deals to certain employees, would serve to undermine trust within the organization.

CHAPTER SUMMARY AND KEY IDEAS

The single most important contract that most individuals will ever enter into concerns their jobs. It would indeed be convenient if this were a relatively simple transaction that was fairly well understood by all parties involved. However, in reality, nothing about employment contracts is simple. Throughout this chapter, we have highlighted many of the basic issues surrounding and forces affecting employment situations for a large number of workers in our economy.

The traditional view of employment held by economists is based on two primary notions: competitive markets and marginal productivity. It basically teaches us that through a supply and demand framework, an equilibrium is reached under which workers are paid their marginal revenue products. Although this approach has its merits, its applicability may be called into question on three fronts. First, workers are not interchangeable commodities. Second, worker incomes are much more stable than predicted by the traditional marginal productivity–based view. Third, numerous measurement problems and misalignments of incentives are simply not addressed.

To provide a more suitable explanation for employment arrangements, we appealed to our knowledge of relational contracting in the presence of transaction costs when participants have the property of bounded rationality. A very informal and imprecise form of relational contracting called the *employment relationship* was created.

Equilibrium in the employment relationship context involves an equality between the total payments made to workers over their careers and the total value of the employee to the employer over the employee's career. The idiosyncratic nature of the employment relationship largely lies in the position of the age-wage profile relative to the long-run productivity profile. Early in their careers, workers are paid less than their marginal revenue products. Later in their careers, the situation is reversed and workers earn economic rents in that their wages exceed their marginal revenue products.

The employment relationship may enhance efficiency in a number of ways. Shirking will be discouraged if the rents scheduled for the later part of an employee's career are credibly withheld. The employment relationship also will serve to minimize influence costs within the organization, to encourage a team atmosphere, and to foster the acquisition of firm-specific human capital. From the employee's perspective, the risks associated with variation in income resulting from imperfect measurement and fluctuating demand for the firm's output are, at least partially, eliminated.

The employment relationship is essentially a life-cycle approach used to describe the underlying mechanics of the arrangement between firms and their employees. Both the long-term nature of the relationship and the importance attached to organizations' reputations require that these relationships be entered into carefully. For employees, job-switching and search costs are likely to be significant. For employers, early termination of an employment relationship without employee agreement may be costly. The costs of the diminished reputation resulting from such an event could be very large in dealing with current and future employees.

▨ KEY TERMS

age-wage profile
at-will employment
derived demand
diminishing marginal productivity
economic rents
firm-specific human capital
general-purpose human capital
human resource management
idiosyncratic exchange
influence costs

marginal product
marginal productivity theory
marginal revenue product
quasi-rents
reservation reward
reservation reward profile
screening
self-selection
signaling

▨ FURTHER READINGS

Abraham, K., and R. McKersie. *New Developments in the Labor Market: Towards a New Institutional Paradigm.* Cambridge, MA: The MIT Press, 1990.

Baker, G. M., M. C. Jensen, and K. J. Murphy. "Competition and Incentives: Practice vs. Theory." *Journal of Finance*, 43 (1988), pp. 593–616.

Carmichael, H. L. "Self-Enforcing Contracts, Shirking, and Life Cycle Incentives," *Journal of Economic Perspectives* 3, no. 4 (1989), pp. 65–83.

Drucker, P. F. "Getting Things Done: How to Make People Decisions." *Harvard Business Review* 63, no. 4 (July–August 1985).

Devine, T. J., and N. M. Kiefer. *Empirical Labor Economics, The Search Approach*. New York: Oxford University Press, 1991.

Flanagan, R. J., L. M. Kahn, R. S. Smith, and R. G. Ehrenberg. *Economics of the Employment Relationship*. Glenview, IL: Scott Foresman, 1989.

Hamermesh, D. S. *Labor Demand*. Princeton, NJ: Princeton University Press, 1993.

Huber, V. L., G. B. Northcraft, and M. Neal. "Effects of Decision Strategy and Number of Openings on Employment Selection Decisions." *Organizational Behavior and Human Decisions Processes* 45 (April 1990), p. 276.

Industrial Relations Research Association. *Human Resources and the Performance of the Firm*. 1987.

Lazear, E. P. "Labor Economics and the Psychology of Organizations." *Journal of Economic Perspectives* 5, no. 2 (1991), pp. 89–110.

———. "Job Security Provisions and Employment." *The Quarterly Journal of Economics* (August 1990), pp. 699–726.

———. "Why Is There Mandatory Retirement?" *Journal of Political Economy* 87 (1979), pp. 1261–1264.

Milgrom, P., and J. Roberts. *Economics, Organization and Management*. Englewood Cliffs, NJ: Prentice Hall, 1992.

Nicholson, W. *Microeconomic Theory: Basic Principles and Extensions*, 4th ed. New York: The Dryden Press, 1989.

Ono, Y. "Unneeded Workers in Japan Are Bored, and Very Well Paid." *Wall Street Journal*, April 20, 1993, p. A10.

Pindyck, R. S., and D. L. Rubinfeld. *Microeconomics*, 2nd ed. New York: Macmillan, 1992.

Templin, N., and J. B. White. "GM to Attract Early Retirees with Cars, Cash," *Wall Street Journal*, October 27, 1993, p. A4.

Williamson, O. E., M. L. Wachter, and J. E. Harris. "Understanding the Employment Relation: The Analysis of Idiosyncratic Exchange." *Bell Journal of Economics* 6 (1975), pp. 250–278.

▦ QUESTIONS AND PROBLEMS FOR REVIEW AND DISCUSSION

A. Some of the more popular fast-food outlets in urban areas in the United States have great difficulty in locating and keeping good employees. It would seem that better information flows could help alleviate these problems. However, these establishments continually claim a shortage of able workers.

 1. Is the labor market for workers in these fast-food chains in urban areas best characterized by the traditional marginal productivity–based model? Why or why not?

 2. Is the labor market for workers in these fast-food chains in urban areas best characterized by the employment relationship? Why or why not?

 3. Many of these establishments offer employment contracts of the following form: a low initial wage but some significant wage increase after the worker has been at the establishment for a set time period. Is this practice explained by the traditional marginal productivity–based model? Why or why not.

B. Perhaps you are now searching for a new job. The want ad section of the local newspaper features postings for many different types of jobs. For some openings, the ad may feature a stated hourly, weekly, or monthly wage. For other openings, the ad may claim only a willingness on the part of the employer to pay a "competitive wage" or one "in line with applicant's qualifications and experience." For each of the following occupations, tell what type of ad you would expect to see and explain why.

1. Drywall installer
2. Secretary
3. Truck driver
4. Nurse
5. Accountant
6. Statistician
7. Management professor
8. Corporate CEO

C. In the context of the employment relationship, explain why the firm would never commit to a policy of making substantial severance payments to workers who are fired for a well-documented violation of organizational rules and regulations.

D. Consider two jobs requiring equal skills and effort on the part of employees. Each is to obey the employment relationship outlined in the text. In the first, workers receive a modest pension from the firm on normal retirement. In the second, workers receive a substantially larger pension on normal retirement. Competition for workers might imply that the starting salaries be equal. In which job would the age-wage profile of the employee be expected to be steeper? Explain why.

E. Early termination of the employment relationship results in employees being damaged in a sense. However, laying claim to these damages might prove impossible in a court of law. In your opinion, what effect does the financial status of the firm have on its decision whether to offer severance packages to employees who are prematurely let go?

The Employment Experience

This chapter serves two purposes in our quest toward understanding the importance of human resource management within organizations. First, it is concerned with extending and applying the concept of the employment relationship developed in Chapter 12. Within organizations there are fairly well-defined career paths and so-called job ladders for employees. Economists view these devices as **internal labor markets,** where wages are tied to jobs and employees are rewarded by moving up to higher-paying positions. We consider internal labor markets, the role of trust, and changes in internal labor markets that result from downsizing. Next we discuss internal labor markets in the context of the employment relationship, and we then discuss several issues related to the glamorous world of executive compensation.

Most economic analysis of employment is heavily influenced by the strong link between pay and performance predicted by the traditional marginal productivity–based model. This may explain, at least in part, why traditional economics has been consulted so infrequently by business leaders seeking guidance in this important organizational area.[1]

Applying the Employment Relationship

Economics has many useful contributions to offer managers interested in efficiently compensating employees. In Chapter 12 we presented the basic workings and intuitive appeal of the employment relationship, which is one of the newer and more powerful tools. Clearly, one of the most important factors affecting organizational behavior is the internal incentive structure, which is the management of human resources in general and compensation policies in particular.

Many organizational changes of the early and mid-1990s caused some of the underlying mechanics of the employment relationship to change. We consider these changes in this chapter and warn the student ahead of time that these changes are not part of a cold, uncaring decision calculus. Rather these changes are about quite softer topics such as trust, fairness, and beliefs. We show that in some cases, the use of downsizing precipitated a drastic shift in employment arrangements. In other cases, only temporary absences of trust are expected as the relationship between firms and workers moves to a new equilibrium path.

Addressing CEO Pay

Much of corporate America is quite concerned about the compensation packages that large corporations offer their CEOs. Some critics and disgruntled shareholders argue that CEOs' earnings are excessive. Although these attacks on the pay structure may have some merit, we hope to shed some light on not only the pay levels of CEOs, but also how they may come to earn these levels of pay.

---

[1]The reader is referred back to Chapter 1, the section on "Our Pathway to an Understanding of Managing Economic Organizations" and, in particular, to the box titled "Two Views of the 'New Way' of Doing Economics."

After reading this chapter, the student should be able to

* Comprehend the different dimensions of internal pay schemes found in organizations, including the competing ideas of pay-for-performance and egalitarian pay systems.
* Understand the general economic environment prevailing in the early to mid-1990s and the pressure this puts on businesses' dealings with employees.
* Explain in an intuitive way that it is necessary for employers and employees to interact in an environment of trust.
* Predict how current trends in arranging employment are likely to affect organizations in the coming years.
* Highlight some of the important ideas behind executive compensation and comment on the controversial issues surrounding executive pay plans.

▓ INTERNAL PAY SCHEMES

Most corporations in the United States rely on pay systems developed in the late 1940s by Edward Hay, who first applied these concepts at General Foods. Recall from Chapter 1 that this is about the same time in history that modern corporations featuring multidivisional forms were beginning to dominate the U.S. corporate landscape. The hallmark of this compensation system was the existence of many job "tiers," each with a well-defined pay range. Within such a system, wage levels become tied to jobs, not individuals. This hierarchical approach to wage determination has several efficient aspects, and a robust set of studies exists to empirically prove its adoption by organizations.[2] In most cases, such a well-defined compensation system based on gradual promotions to higher tiers fulfills many of the assumptions and characteristics of the theoretical employment relationship.

**Some Background
on Internal Labor
Markets**

Before we turn to this in more detail, we must reconsider the efficiency aspects of tying pay to observed performance. According to standard economic thinking, workers have a choice to make: they can supply effort to their employer or they can consume leisure. The choice is not necessarily binary; the worker can shirk and consume leisure while "working." Presumably, supplying effort creates output valued by the market. However, supplying effort is distasteful for workers who would rather consume leisure. If payments are tied to the amount of output, then workers can be induced to supply more effort. This argument is so simple and straightforward that it appears to be nonrefutable. However, complications arise at a number of different points.

In Chapter 8, we discussed many reasons that the linkage between effort provided and *observed* output may be less than perfect. In fact, such an arrangement exposes workers to potential sources of risk. Some of this risk is due to the imperfect measurement process and difficulties associated with uniquely identifying individual efforts in a team production context. An even larger source of randomness, and, hence, risk arises as the demand for the firm's output gyrates. Thus, a less than perfect linkage between pay and performance could be efficient for both the worker and the firm because doing so eliminates risk in the relationship.

**Pay for Performance:
A Human Dimension**

The fields of psychology and behavioral theory add some interesting input to this issue, arguing on two fronts that pay-for-performance plans might even be counterproductive. The first involves the logic behind a number of convincing

---

[2]See George M. Baker, M. Jensen, and K. Murphy, "Competition and Incentives: Practice vs. Theory," *Journal of Finance* 43 (1988), pp. 593–616 and many of the sources cited therein.

studies that have appeared in the more popular business press on this issue. One of these[3] offers three reasons as to why strictly merit-based compensation systems are counterproductive: "First, rewards encourage people to focus narrowly on a task, to do it as quickly as possible, and to take few risks. . . . Second, extrinsic rewards can erode intrinsic interest. . . . [Third], people come to see themselves as being controlled by a reward."

A second attack on performance-based pay systems focuses on the psychological impacts of singling out particular employees. The effects on employee morale may be devastating, especially in a team environment. The central notion is that other workers will feel slighted and unimportant if a co-worker receives a larger bonus. The net effect of aggressive pay-for-performance systems is to reduce employee morale and, ultimately, productivity. In practice, many organizations are searching for and finding ways to make wages more homogeneous across all workers. Such movements go by a number of names: **pay compression** and **horizontal equity** are two of these. Despite its prevalence in existing management systems, no sound and accepted economic explanation exists to explain why horizontal pay equity is desirable other than the fact that it avoids singling out individual employees.[4]

We believe that, if implemented, strict merit-based compensation systems as predicted by traditional economic analysis would do their jobs too well in organizations. That is, they would encourage workers to accomplish exactly what they are supposed to. Recall that employment relationships are, by their nature, extremely vague and only infrequently spell out exact tasks for employees.

The opportunities for unproductive rent-seeking behavior in such a situation are great. Employees who possessed certain skills and abilities would have huge incentives to nearly continuously lobby employers to tilt the incentive structures to their advantage. Similarly, employees who possessed skills that were in reduced demand in an organization would have even greater incentive to lobby for more favorable treatment.

Internal Markets to Address These Problems

Standard corporate practice skirts many of these issues by using internal labor markets in which wages are tied to jobs and employees are rewarded by moving "up" to higher-paying slots. Pay scales across much of corporate America are determined by "job evaluation systems," which identify the need to establish "internal pay equity."[5]

These plans set wage levels by conducting surveys within and across organizations to assess the value attached to any particular job, citing a number of determining factors such as the amount of training and education required, the total budget involved, the number of people supervised, and the extent to which independent decision making is incorporated into the job.

Such job evaluation systems could overcome some of the pitfalls of pay-for-performance compensation systems. Perhaps this is the reason that internal labor markets relying on promotion-based incentive systems dominate corporate America. As mentioned earlier, the promotion-based incentive system became popular in the United States around 1950. The central feature of this type of compensation system is that it has many different levels, each with a stipulated minimum

---

[3]Alfie Kohn, "Incentives Can Be Bad for Business," *INC*, January 1988, pp. 93–94.

[4]We can say for sure, however, that if individual employees are risk averse (as defined in Chapter 8), horizontal equity may be desirable. This argument relies on the logic that employees wish to avoid being identified when doing something "wrong" and that they are willing to pay the price of not being identified when they do something "right."

[5]Howard Risher, "Job Evaluation: Mystical or Statistical?" *Personnel*, September–October 1978, p. 24.

and maximum salary. Such systems are used by many large corporations and are even more prevalent in government employment, so much so that nearly every college placement officer is very familiar with the salary for category GS-12 (the level at which most college graduates enter the federal government's pay scheme).

Internal labor markets fit nicely into the employment relationship developed in the last chapter. They have no direct link to productivity, and workers in such a system usually receive gradually increasing wages. New hires come into an organization at a number of well-defined places. Once there, they can be moved to where they serve the organization best. Also, the long-run nature of the employment relationship is consistent with the observed functioning of internal labor markets.

**Fitting Within
the Employment
Relationship**

The long-term nature of the employment relationship and its practice in internal labor markets can be interpreted as efficient behavior on the part of both employers and employees. This type of relationship offers at least three types of benefits: the incentive to accumulate firm-specific human capital, an enhanced ability to offer rewards in the form of rents, and a longer horizon over which to evaluate employees and their contribution to the organization's long-term goals.

First, as explained in Chapter 12, an appropriately structured long-term relational contract can provide workers with incentive to build firm-specific human capital that the employer will value. Once this capital is built, the most productive use of workers' time is in their current organization. This argument applies to specific skills and abilities developed over years on the job and to interpersonal relationships that develop and enhance working with others in a team environment in less formal ways.

Second, one critical aspect of the employment relationship discussed in Chapter 12 was the timing of payments relative to the worker's productivity at any instant. This aspect of the employment relationship has some components of the efficiency wage model discussed in Chapter 9. Recall that an efficiency wage has two components, the portion of the wage that (1) covers the worker's opportunity cost in a given job and equals the worker's alternative wage and (2) is purely a rent. The rent is earned, in large part, by the employee's good behavior.

In the employment relationship, we can think of rents as being the difference between the value of the output of a worker (the marginal revenue product, MRP) and the worker's wage. The employer earns the rents early in the worker's career. Later in the career, the worker earns the rents, as a reward. In other words, in internal labor markets, rents can be used to coordinate and motivate employees. The most striking difference between the employment relationship and the efficiency wage model discussed in Chapter 9 is the horizon over which the rents are paid.

In the multitiered structure common to most internal labor markets, workers are promoted to higher-paying slots, at least in part as a reward for "good" behavior. Furthermore, workers typically believe that the harder they work now, the further up in the organization they will go (this situation can lead to a so-called rat race; we discuss this near the end of this chapter). We can then argue that there is a similarity between the employment relationship and an efficiency wage in that rewards are earned for working hard and not shirking. The added structure of an internal labor market and the longer time period available to the employer make an excellent opportunity for providing rewards to enhance organizational efficiency.

Under such an internal labor market functioning through promotions rather than wage increases, reputations become very important. Workers develop reputations for their ability to accomplish certain tasks that they carry with them over their careers. The employer will also develop a reputation and wish to be seen as credible by workers. After all, much of the incentive to employees is that their efforts today will be rewarded in the future. If workers do not hold this belief, they have a much diminished incentive to work hard and, theoretically, no incentive to invest in valuable firm-specific human capital.

Third, internal labor markets provide a long horizon over which employee accomplishments can be evaluated. When a person hires a copy service to produce 50 copies of a resume, the performance of the copy service can be immediately and easily checked by counting the pages and viewing the quality of the copy. At the opposite extreme, evaluating the performance of a CEO who is to make structural changes in an organization cannot be immediately and easily checked. The outcome of a large corporate merger or joint venture, in terms of the organization, may not be known for years.

Maryland's Internal Labor Market

An excellent example of an internal labor market and motivating through promotions is provided in Tables 13.1 and 13.2. Table 13.1 shows biweekly earnings by pay grade for employees of the State of Maryland in 1994. The entire system used by the State of Maryland for all of its employees is much more complex. Separate grade schedules exist for certain occupations (physician, nurses, and police). In the interest of brevity, only 13 of 22 grades currently in use are shown in Table 13.1.

A common practice in many organizations is to provide a number of overlapping salary grades, usually accomplished by introducing a number of "steps" for an existing pay grade. For State of Maryland employees, a grade is assigned to a particular job; workers are promoted either to a job with a higher grade or to a higher step within a grade.

In addition to a guide to determining pay grades and steps, the other component of the internal labor market is the set of jobs with defined duties and salary grades. For illustrative purposes, some of these jobs in the State of Maryland system are shown in Table 13.2.

Given that the various steps can overlap one or more grades, some confusion in determining pay on promotion is possible. Notice, for example, that grade 1, step 6 involves a biweekly gross salary of $562.61, a wage level at least as large as

Table 13.1	State of Maryland Internal Labor Market Pay Grades for Employees						
Grade	Base	Step 1	Step 2	Step 3	Step 4	Step 5	Step 6
1	451.76	471.06	491.88	516.62	543.05	552.49	562.61
2	474.62	495.18	518.73	545.12	574.58	585.13	595.87
3	528.55	553.56	548.79	576.96	608.68	619.92	631.39
4	528.55	553.56	581.79	613.78	647.69	659.58	672.01
5	560.20	588.89	619.61	653.90	690.68	703.96	717.46
6	596.06	626.82	660.11	697.59	737.52	751.67	766.17
7	633.04	665.94	702.34	742.70	785.42	800.54	815.92
8	672.58	708.98	748.95	792.10	837.86	853.89	870.38
9	719.26	758.50	802.26	848.64	897.54	914.91	932.60
10	770.85	814.00	860.95	910.70	963.63	982.23	1001.41
13	827.42	874.45	925.04	978.74	1035.66	1055.91	1077.05
12	888.33	939.46	994.04	1051.73	1114.87	1137.30	1160.01
13	954.46	1009.62	1068.84	1133.08	1201.09	1225.10	1249.53

Source: State of Maryland Salary Structure for Graded State Employees, Effective July 1994. In practice, there are 22 such grades; not all are listed.

Table 13.2	Jobs Classifications in the State of Maryland System, 1992

Classification	Grade
Accountant—Auditor I	9
Accountant—Auditor II	11
Accountant—Auditor III	12
Accountant—Auditor IV	13
Actuary I	12
Actuary II	14
Actuary III	16
Actuary IV	18
Administrator I	16
Administrator II	17
Administrator III	18
Administrator IV	19
Animal Autopsy Technician	6
Animal Health Aide	4
Animal Room Attendant I	2
Animal Room Attendant II	3

that can also be paid to a job ranked as grade 2, step 3.[6] In most organizations, a set of rules has evolved to circumvent this difficulty; for Maryland state employees, the rule is as follows:

> An employee who is serving in a classification compensated by a salary grade shall, at the time of promotion, be placed in the lowest step of the higher grade which provides for an increase of 6% of his present grade. The application of this percentage increase shall not, however, place the employee in a higher step in the new grade than the employee is receiving in his or her current grade.[7]

The salary grades listed in Table 13.1 and the job classifications listed in Table 13.2 document some of the more important characteristics of internal labor markets. First, the salary increases across steps and even across whole pay grades are fairly gradual. This characteristic gives managers some flexibility in assigning promotions as rewards. Clear evidence over several evaluation periods may justify promoting an employee into a new, higher-ranking position with increased pay. Second, earnings may fluctuate substantially within a given pay grade. An examination of the pay ranges for State of Maryland employees reveals that, relative to the base for any given grade, the maximum (step 6) salaries represent a 25 percent increase on average.

■ TRUST IN THE EMPLOYMENT RELATIONSHIP

Timing and Trust

Two features of the employment relationship enable an efficient arrangement to be crafted: the long-run equilibrium condition and the trust that workers and firms put in each other. The key analytical component of the employment relationship is the long-run equilibrium condition that states that the long-run costs

---

[6]In fact, the biweekly salary for an individual in grade 1, step 6 earns as much as a worker earning the base salary for a grade 5 position.

[7]*Salary Plan of the State of Maryland*, Maryland State Department of Personnel, 301 West Preston St., Baltimore, MD 21201, July 1, 1992.

of hiring an employee must equal the long-run benefit of hiring that employee. We can define the long-run costs of hiring a worker over T periods as the sum of the wage paid in any one of those periods, w_t. Likewise, we can define the long-run benefits of hiring a worker over T periods as the sum of the value of what that worker produces in any one of those periods, MRP_t. Equilibrium requires that

$$\sum_{t=1}^{t=T} w_t = \sum_{t=1}^{t=T} MRP_t \qquad (13.1)$$

where Σ is the mathematical summation.

The left-hand side of this equation adds the wage earned by the worker, w_t, in each year that the worker plans to be in the organization. The right-hand side of the equation adds the value of that worker's output in each year, MRP_t, that the worker plans to be in an organization. Put simply, the long-run equilibrium condition says that over the course of an employee's career, the benefits of hiring him or her must equal the costs of hiring that employee.

The intuitive appeal of the long-run equilibrium condition results from the lack of a requirement that wages and marginal revenue product be equal in any single period. We argued in Chapter 12 that this arrangement could be efficient if structured properly. In particular, early in the worker's career she or he is paid less than her or his marginal revenue product. Later in the career, the situation is reversed, and the worker earns rents in the sense that wages earned exceed the employee's contribution to the firm.

This arrangement enhances efficiency in two ways, each of which involves the reward seen by the employee at the end of her or his career. First, the firm holds the employee's rents "hostage" in the sense that the employee does not receive them if she or he shirks too much and is fired. Second, this same hostage situation provides motivation to employees to build firm-specific human capital, a practice that the firm views as desirable.

Figure 13.1 (based on Figure 12.8) contains a hypothetical age-wage profile, *AWP*, a long-run productivity profile, *LRP*, and a reservation reward profile, *RRP*. Several points are important. Efficient retirement occurs at time T. The area of the region *ABC* equals the area of the region *CDE*. Until year T_c (the time period corresponding to point C), the worker is paid less than the value of her output. After year T_c, the worker is paid more than the value of her output.

Now consider the employment relationship from the worker's perspective. She agrees to be underpaid early on in return for two things: continued stable employment and the promise of eventually becoming "overpaid." The only reason she agrees to this type of arrangement is that she elects to trust the firm. After all, the firm is, in effect, promising to provide stable employment and to pay the worker a bonus at some future date. Without this trust, the employment relationship drastically changes.

If Trust Goes Bust

What exactly happens when the trust is gone? In practice, this is not an all-or-none situation but one of degree. For argument's sake, let's assume, however, that all trust is gone. The employee then does not believe that her job is secure in future years, nor does she believe that her wages will continue to increase faster than her marginal productivity.

This situation for employees was common at some firms in the early and mid-1990s when most major corporations were announcing cutbacks and downsizings at an alarming rate.[8] The message to employees was clear: because there are fewer

---

[8]Whether these cuts were actually made in accordance with the announced magnitude is another matter. However, this matter is not relevant for our argument and analysis.

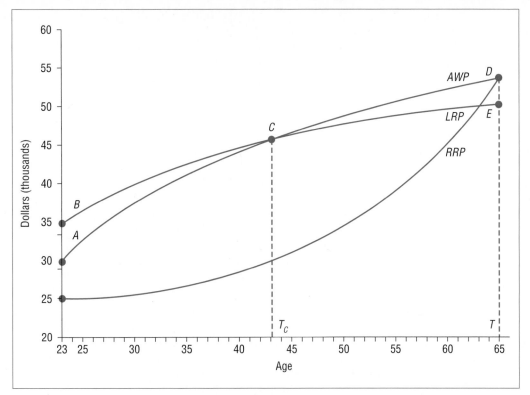

Figure 13.1 Mechanics of the Employment Relationship

employees, each one remaining will be asked to do more (that is, increase their marginal productivity). Employees also knew that this environment was hardly conducive to asking for a raise. Workers then had ample reason to doubt both their continued employment and the promise that their wages would someday exceed their marginal revenue products making up for the early, lean years.

In this environment, workers would foresee their employment arrangement as shown in Figure 13.2. Ignoring the position of the vertical scale, Figure 13.2 shows as the lower curves the "initial" age-wage profile AWP_1 and long-run productivity profile LRP_1. These initial curves show the relative position of the age-wage profile and long-run productivity profile under the employment relationship. The two upper curves in Figure 13.2 show the relative position of the employee's expected age-wage profile AWP_2 and long-run productivity profile, LRP_2, in the newer environment.

Notice that under the changed environment, the age-wage profile, AWP_2, is under the long-run productivity profile, LRP_2. As mentioned, there are two reasons for this. First, expected wages are lower as employees revise their expectations of future wages downward and account for the lower probability of being employed in the organization. Second, because organizations are cutting back the number of workers, those workers who remain must work harder, that is, must have higher marginal productivity without competitive pressures to increase their wages to their marginal productivity.

It should now become clear that the outcome of all of these changes to the employment relationship is devastating because the credibility of the organization in dealing with employees has been destroyed. Before the changes, firms could offer stable employment with a gradually increasing salary. After the various downsizings, the firm could credibly offer nothing of the sort.

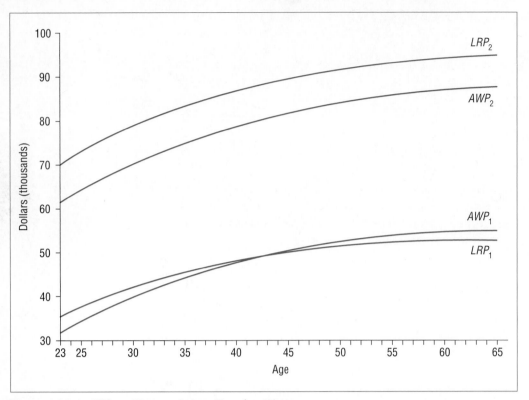

Figure 13.2 When Downsizing Erodes Trust

Rational employees will react to this vacuum of trust in three predictable ways. First, the incentives to build firm-specific human capital are gone. The reasoning is somewhat subtle: no firm has incentive to reward an employee for accumulating firm-specific human capital because no other firm will offer the worker more because of his or her investment in human capital. In the language developed in our analysis of transaction costs and contracting (Chapters 6 and 7), workers will be reluctant to invest in a specific asset for fear of being held up by their contracting partner (their employer).

Workers can also be expected to react to this vacuum of trust by eliminating (trashing) any regard for corporate loyalty. Workers have no incentive to trust their firms and every incentive to enhance their own marketability. This may amount to managers spending more time courting prospective employers than managing and making decisions in their own current organizations.

The third predictable response by workers to this vacuum of trust is for them to increase the amount and intensity of shirking. As we discussed in the section on Internal Pay Schemes of this chapter, there is a similarity between the employment relationship and the efficiency wage model: in both cases, rents serve as a reward. In the long-run scenario of the employment relationship, these rents also provide incentive for workers not to shirk. This shirking could take a number of forms: taking more sick days and/or more free time at work and using work time to try to secure a job at another firm.

The long-run losses from such an erosion of trust are potentially enormous. Firms lose because of lower worker productivity; workers lose because of the loss of security and increased exposure to risk.

In the long run, this undesirable outcome is not very likely, however. For any organization, long-run survival requires efficiency in a number of intrafirm dimensions. Human resource policy is one of these dimensions. The point of all of this is simply that the employment relationship offers an efficient method for compensating employees. Its primary ingredient is the mutual trust between worker and firm. Once this trust is removed, there is no real clear choice except to return to external markets. Henry Ford faced a very similar problem in the 1920s. His solution was to pay workers what amounted to an efficiency wage, which included a significant rent component that served to efficiently motivate employees.

■ THE POPULARITY OF DOWNSIZING IN THE 1990s

Growth and Then
Pink Slips

For corporate America, the decades of the 1980s and 1990s have been turbulent times. On the positive side, the economic expansion that began in 1982 and continued through 1989 was the longest economic expansion in more than a decade. Markets also grew because of the globalization of most economic activities. Corporations expanded and enjoyed growing markets and the adoption of new, cost-saving technologies.

On the negative side this period included the restructuring by many U.S. corporations as the large mass-producing firms faced new challenges. Also on the negative side was a prolonged recession beginning in early 1990, the impact of which was every bit as pronounced as the preceding economic expansion. Globalization proved to be double-edged sword as well, forcing corporations to produce more efficiently.

Many organizations responded to these changes by downsizing, a process that reduced employment and, at least temporarily, altered the employment relationship on which most workers had grown accustomed. In this section we provide some measure of the extent of these downsizings and discuss their ramifications in terms of employee reaction and corporate profitability.

In Table 13.3, some of the more spectacular corporate downsizings are presented. Two striking features are evident in Table 13.3. First, the list of corporations reads almost like a who's who of corporate America. It includes some of the largest organizations in the United States. Second, the magnitude of the cuts is enormous. IBM and AT&T alone revealed plans to eliminate nearly 170,000 workers. *Business Week* estimates that in the first quarter of 1994, employers announced an average of 3,106 cutbacks per day.[9] Because of the sheer magnitude of the announced cuts and their distribution throughout the economy, the corporate downsizings in the early to mid-1990s attracted much attention in the popular business press. With this attention came a great deal of confusion.

Just What Is
a "Downsizing"?

The use of downsizing is hardly new or exotic. In the simplest of terms, a corporation **downsizes** when it reduces the number of employees on its payroll. Downsizing may occur for a wide variety of reasons. We group these reasons into two categories: downsizing as part of a well-conceived plan to reorganize the productive efforts of an organization and as "slash and burn."

As markets and technologies change, organizations may seek to react to these changes to become more efficient organizers of economic activity. Additionally, there is a trend among corporations worldwide to return to the basics that these corporations do well, their core competencies. At the beginning of the 1980s, the United States had many conglomerates, organizations that had diversified into a wide variety of businesses. The competitive pressures of the global economy that emerged in the 1990s forced firms to abandon this strategy of risk minimization and seek efficiency through specialization.

---

[9]John A. Byrne, "The Pain of Downsizing," *Business Week*, May 6, 1994, p. 61.

Table 13.3	Major Announced Corporate Downsizings, 1991–1993	
Company	**Staff Cutbacks**	
IBM	85,000	
At&T	83,500	
General Motors	74,000	
U.S. Postal Service	55,000	
Sears	50,000	
Boeing	30,000	
NYNEX	22,000	
Hughes Aircraft	21,000	
GTE	17,000	
Martin-Marietta	15,000	
Dupont	14,800	
Eastman Kodak	14,000	
Philip Morris	14,000	
Procter & Gamble	13,000	
Phar Mor	13,000	
Bank of America	12,000	
Aetna	11,800	
GE Aircraft Engines	10,250	
McDonnell Douglas	10,200	
Bellsouth	10,200	
Ford Motor	10,000	
Xerox	10,000	
Pacific Telesis	10,000	
Honeywell	9,000	
US West	9,000	

Source: John A. Byrne, "The Pain of Downsizing." *Business Week*. Reprinted from May 9, 1994, issue of *Business Week* by special permission, copyright © 1994 by McGraw-Hill, Inc.

One aspect of these changes was discussed in Chapter 6, the make-or-buy decision concerning intermediate inputs. The increased use of outside suppliers was one organizational reply to the challenge of global competition. Another aspect of these changes in the 1980s was the trend of firms breaking up the conglomerates formed in the previous two decades. To the extent that these changes were part of a strategic action of organizations to redesign themselves, it is not clear that the employment relationship was permanently damaged.[10]

When downsizing occurred as part of a well-conceived plan to reorganize the productive efforts of an organization, the employment relationship with some employees was ended, possibly through outright firing, the encouragement of early retirement, or attrition. However, this change was not necessarily for the worse. Will the remaining employees trust the re-formed organization? Probably they will form this trust and revise their expectations concerning the form of the age-wage profiles and long-run productivity profiles. It is true that the firm "downsized" by letting go a number of their prior co-workers; however, it was the activities of these co-workers that were no longer in demand, not the co-workers themselves. By definition, the remaining workers will find themselves in demand

---

[10]We will have much to say on the related topics of business reengineering and organizational strategy in Chapter 14.

to the firm, perhaps not in a manner as generous as that prior to the downsizing, but in demand nonetheless.

In the analytical framework of our employment relationship, the effect of downsizing as part of a well-conceived plan to reengineer a corporation can be thought of as a shift in both the age-wage profile and long-run productivity profile. Given the great uncertainties involved, these shifts may take years to evidence themselves, leaving workers in short-run limbo. However, if the changes are accomplished in a more specialized, focused, and technically efficient organization, there is no reason to suspect that the employment relationship will be absent.

The real damage to the employment relationship occurred at organizations when workers perceived that the downsizings represented a "slash-and-burn" mentality on the part of management. In many of the downsizings, employees were cut seemingly only so that the firm could reduce operating expenses. These cuts were rationally viewed by workers as arbitrary and, perhaps, even capricious. A cost-cutting mentality often prevailed. Under these circumstances, workers have no reason to trust their employers.

The most important aspect of downsizing in terms of its effect on employee relations is not the size of the downsizing itself but the reason that it was done. Again, this issue is considered in more detail in Part V of this text; we merely intended to introduce it now.

Does downsizing work? This may seem like quite a simple question, but it is far too difficult to answer at this point. Downsizing, despite its cause, causes fundamental changes in corporate operations. The effects of these changes may take years to be felt. Many of the corporations listed in Table 13.3 had been experiencing difficulties for years prior to 1991. These "troubled giants" are hardly candidates for a quick turnaround.

A second reply to the question concerning whether downsizing works is the glib answer: "For whom?" After all, a corporation is a complex institution and involves many stakeholders: customers, investors and owners, managers, and employees. In theory, a downsizing inherently implies greater efficiency with the gains spread across all stakeholders of the firm. However, hindsight has taught us that some of the downsizing of the early 1990s resulted from the application of a "slash-and-burn" mentality, rather than from a comprehensive strategy. In these instances, it is doubtful that downsizing achieved its goals. Customers are the most likely winners from any successful downsizing; after all, greater efficiency should manifest itself in a higher quality product and better service at a lower cost.

Investors and owners typically take a long-term view and approve of downsizings despite the initial write-offs against current income that they generate. There are two primary sources of these write-offs: the severance pay and early retirement packages offered to employees, and the possible loss from the sale of corporate assets that are underperforming or simply not needed anymore. The investors and owners have a principal-agent relationship with the managers of the firms. The principals, investors and owners, are at an informational disadvantage in this relationship and rely on the agents, the managers, to keep them informed. The biggest fear of the principals is that their money is being wasted or spent inefficiently by the firms. When managers discuss plans for a potential reengineering or downsizing, they implicitly create fears in the owners and investors, thus causing an alliance between these groups. After all, the message is that the organization can more efficiently oversee their funds.

The fate of the firm's managers in any downsizing of the 1990s was mixed. As mentioned in Chapter 1 and will be detailed in Chapter 15, during the 1980s and early 1990s, most organizations became "flatter." Such organizational flattening amounts to an elimination of "middle" managers to facilitate communication between top managers and the functional units of a firm. Put simply, many middle managers lost their jobs in the downsizings listed in Table 13.3. Upper divisional managers and those whose positions were more closely tied with the central administrative unit of the firm fared much better. By and large, they were made part of the management "team" and spared layoffs. As previously discussed, another cushion against both the downsizing and the risks it created several years down the road for top managers was the existence in their contracts of golden parachutes, the promises of large payments in cash or stock if their employment was terminated.

Quite possibly, these three groups of stakeholders (customers, owners and investors, and managers) may view the situation as one in which some stakeholder has to lose and are happy that they are not the ones. The group that stands to lose the most, certainly in the short and intermediate term, are the employees.

Downsizings directly affect the decision calculus of the employment relationship in that they attack the basic trust on which the employment relationship rests.

Table 13.4 reports the results of a comprehensive survey recently appearing in *Fortune*. Obviously, the figures are correlated with the recessions of 1981–1983 and 1989–1991. When the economy turns down, workers fear for their jobs. However, despite this, the overall trend in the percentages shows that job security is clearly declining.

Whereas we would expect employee trust to form an integral part of the employment relationship in most companies, there is at least one example of a successful firm that avoided any implicit or explicit mention of job tenure in its employment offerings. Intel, the semiconductor and chip maker, is one of the dominant and most innovative firms in the U.S. computer industry. At Intel, there is no mention of long-term employment, yet Intel is widely considered one of the best firms to work for in the industry. The reasons for this are known only to those directly involved; however, we can hazard two, possibly related guesses. First, it may be that talented individuals see a certain amount of prestige in working for the industry leader. Second, Intel was founded and staffed by persons who had left other, existing computer firms.

The Winner's Curse: Glad to Keep Your Job?

Economics has a concept known as the *winner's curse*. This term was coined in the 1980s by economists studying the bidding wars for the stock of certain corporations. Suppose that two firms, Acme, Inc., and Bravo, Inc., were both interested in acquiring a controlling interest (that is, taking over) Comet, Inc. The announced intentions and stock purchases of Acme and Bravo would greatly bid up the price of Comet's stock. The ultimate "winning" bidder was often proven by hindsight to fall victim to the "winner's curse" because the actual value of the acquired corporation proved less than the final price that emerged from the bidding wars.

A similar concept may apply, at least to a certain extent, to those employees who kept their jobs in downsized corporations. Two things are known for certain

Table 13.4	Percentage of Workers Rating Their Job Security as "Good" or "Very Good"	
Time Period	**Management**	**Nonmanagement**
1980–1982	79%	75%
1983–1985	71%	72%
1986–1988	65%	58%
1989–1991	64%	61%
1992–1994	55%	51%

Source: Brian O'Reilly, "The New Deal," *Fortune*, June 13, 1994, p. 50. Data from Sirota & Alper Associates. © 1994 Time Inc. All rights reserved.

for those employees who maintain their jobs. They must work harder and usually longer hours, simply because there are fewer workers in the downsized corporations; and they are apt to lack a certain amount of faith in their employers. Psychological changes also occurred at many companies where significant portions of the workforce were let go. The generic name assigned to this phenomenon was *survival stress*. One official at AT&T cited an internal survey done after a large cutback in middle managers at the firm in the late 1980s, which examined 250 middle managers who retained their jobs and found that nearly half had more marital strains after the cutback. The popular business press in early 1994 was dotted with stories concerning the psychological impact in the form of increased stress for employees who managed to survive the massive layoffs common at many organizations at that time.[11]

The stresses placed on organizations in the early 1990s placed an emphasis on two characteristics: low cost and flexibility. A common response along with downsizing was the use of outsourcing and the employment of temporary workers, or temps. Many business analysts freely speak of the "contingency" workforce, individuals who are for hire in an emerging spot labor market. Contingency workers are hired for short periods of time and cost the employer typically 20 percent to 40 percent less than full-time employees do. Temporary workers always have played a role in U.S. labor markets, but since about 1990, that role has been increasing in terms of both numbers and the types of positions filled. Temp agencies exist to place secretaries and receptionists as well as doctors, engineers, lawyers, and even CEOs.

The largest single temp agency in the United States, as of 1994, was Manpower, Inc., employing nearly 600,000 workers. Currently, Manpower is the largest private employer in the United States. Its workers receive no benefits or training, and even lack certain legal rights such as complete protection from age and sex discrimination.[12]

Business analysts simply do not agree on the implications of this trend or on its current or future extent. As of 1994, by some measures, about one in four U.S. workers belonged to this contingency workforce. However, this figure is tremendously misleading for our purposes because it includes most independent professionals: doctors, lawyers, and accountants, as well as most independent contractors, such as the person you hire to remodel your kitchen. A more realistic current assessment of those temporarily employed in response to pronounced organizational change is much lower. Many management consultants shamelessly predicted that by the year 2000, one-half of the U.S. workforce would be made up of temporary workers. This assessment grabs ample headlines in the business press (and earns some consultants nice fat checks), but it is wildly unrealistic from any practical standpoint.

What is clear is that the growth in the contingency workforce and the temp agencies that peddle their services is impacting business to some degree. What it amounts to is a "return to markets," such as described in the first sections of Chapter 12. Workers of all sorts become commodities with wages tied exactly to expected productivity (signaled by the competencies, experience, and training) of the temporary worker. Two critical elements for long-term success are clearly absent, however: loyalty and the incentives to acquire firm-specific human capital.

---

[11]Joann S. Lublin, "Survivors of Layoffs Battle Angst, Anger, Hurting Productivity," *Wall Street Journal*, November 6, 1993, p. A1; and John A. Byrne, "Staying Power Has Rewards—And a Price Tag," *Business Week*, May 9, 1994, p. 67.

[12]See Janice Castro, "Disposable Workers," *Time*, March 29, 1993, p. 43; and Jaclyn Fierman, "The Contingency Workforce," *Fortune*, January 24, 1994, p. 30.

■ EXECUTIVE PAY: A NUMBER OF ISSUES

To many people, the most fascinating dimension of corporate business in the United States is the fantastic salary that organizations pay their CEOs. Chief executives are powerful people living lavish lifestyles seemingly worlds away from average Americans. In this section, we consider a number of issues surrounding executive pay. After describing the pattern and form of compensation packages, we refer to the moral hazard concept introduced in Chapter 8.

CEOs are paid large sums of money; we need to understand the form in which this income is received. Executive pay may be broken into two groups: direct compensation and in-kind compensation. *Direct compensation* consists of salary, yearly bonuses, and stock options. *Compensation in kind* varies considerably across individuals ranging from housing, education, and transportation allotments, the use of limousines, and memberships in professional and social organizations. In the mid-1990s, the direct compensation received by chief executive officers at U.S. corporations exceeded, on average, slightly more than $1 million.

Table 13.5 provides some insight into the dollars involved for the 15 highest paid CEOs in 1992, with the direct compensation split into two components, (1) salary and bonus and (2) long-term compensation (mostly stock options).

The statistics in Table 13.5 reflect that some CEOs are paid massive amounts of money for their efforts. An even more striking characteristic of CEO pay is that, for many CEOs, the bulk of their pay is in the form of stock options. This is a new development in corporate America. As corporations have come under increasing public scrutiny concerning their executives' pay levels, they have become more willing to issue stock options. Stock options serve two purposes: they reduce salaries per se, and they encourage executives to act to benefit the owners (stockholders, including themselves) of the firm. A variety of stock options are used.

First, a **standard option** is the right granted to an executive to purchase a specific number of shares of the company's stock at a specific target price. The incentives here are clear. If, for example, a CEO is offered a stock option with a specific target, or strike, price equivalent to that of the current stock price, then it is in the best interest of the CEO to make sure that the current stock price rises.

Second, **option swaps** are utilized often. An option swap occurs when a company issues a new stock option in exchange for a previously issued stock option. This type of stock option provides incentive when a company's share price falls for reasons that are not traceable to the CEO. Obviously, this type of stock option is voluntarily agreed on by the corporation's board of directors and provides incentives in a changed environment. An option swap is an example of efficiency dictating that all parties renege on the original contract.

Third, a relatively new type of option, a **reload option**, allows the CEO to collect the profits that he would have received had he exercised his option on the day during which the market price of the stock was the highest.

The fourth type of stock option is the **capped option**. In this case, an option is issued with a certain strike price and a limit on the share price he is able to obtain when he cashes the option. For example, if an option is granted with an upper limit of $55 per share, the CEO can sell his shares back only at that $55 limit, even if the current stock price is $60 per share.

It must be pointed out that the practice of linking executive pay with stock options can lead to some invalid conclusions. Stock options are typically issued yearly. CEOs rarely exercise their options nearly as frequently. Usually, a chief executive officer saves his stock options over a period of years and cashes them all in at once. A polar example is provided by Lee Iacocca, previously CEO of Chrysler Corp. Mr. Iacocca accepted a salary of $1 per year through much of the

Table 13.5 Executive Pay, 1992 (in thousands of dollars)

	Salary and Bonus	Total Pay
Thomas F. First, Jr. Hospital Corporation of America	1,068	125,934
Sanford I. Weill Primerica	2,752	67,635
Charles Lazarus Toys 'R' Us	7,025	64,231
Leon C. Hirsch U.S. Surgical	1,695	62,171
Stephen A. Wynn Mirage Resorts	1,505	38,005
Anthony J. F. O'Reilly H. J. Heinz	1,318	36,918
Martin J. Wygod Medco Containment	807	30,207
William A. Anders General Dynamics	7,849	29,015
Ronald K. Richey Torchmark	2,136	26,568
Louis F. Bantle UST, Inc.	2,701	24,602
Reuben Mark Colgate-Palmolive	2,002	22,818
Walter J. Sanders III Advanced Micro Devices	2,965	22,356
John F. Welch, Jr. General Electric	3,500	17,970
Lee A. Iacocca Chrysler	1,528	16,908
Eugene P. Grisanti International Flavors & Fragrances	900	16,475

Source: John A. Byrne, "Executive Pay: The Party Ain't Over Yet." Reprinted from April 26, 1993, issue of *Business Week* by special permission, copyright © 1993 by McGraw-Hill, Inc.

1980s, all the while accumulating stock options that he would eventually exercise to earn around $40 million.

It is also interesting to consider how CEO wages have changed over time. Table 13.6 can shed some light here. In this table, we show the percentage increases in average wages for the periods 1960 to 1970, 1970 to 1980, 1980 to 1990, and 1990 to 1992 for four occupations: engineer, school teacher, factory worker, and CEO. The numbers in Table 13.6 are nominal, that is, not adjusted for inflation. Thus, all of the percentage changes may appear a little large. Clearly, each of the four occupations shown in Table 13.6 experienced substantial wage growth over the period 1960 to 1992. The chief executive officer's wages increased much more quickly than any other occupation group.

The scenario facing most corporations regarding their CEOs is rife with moral hazard. To understand why, consider a typical organization's structure from a broad perspective. The owners of the corporation are its stockholders,

Agency Revisited

Table 13.6	Percentage Wage Increases by Occupation					
Occupation	1960–1970	1970–1980	1980–1990	1990–1992	1960–1992
Engineer	49.52	93.85	60.36	27.50	492.6
School teacher	72.87	84.94	75.38	21.74	582.6
Factory worker	48.79	116.33	44.62	12.36	423.0
Chief executive officer	188.25	13.89	224.08	89.70	1918.7

Source: William H. Shaw, *Business Ethics* (Belmont, CA: Wadsworth Publishing, 1991), pp. 82–87; and *Business Week*, April 26, 1993, p. 57.

those entitled to the residual claims. The shareholders own the firm, but they do not actually run it; this is the job of the CEO. To protect the interests of the shareholders, the board of directors exists with broadly defined supervisory powers over the CEO. In theory, the board then acts as a check or balance against a CEO pursuing her own interests at the expense of others.

A Seller's Market

This underlying structure changed drastically in the United States during the 1980s. A very active market emerged for CEOs, and, as a result, they moved from job to job, frequently bidding up their salaries along the way. The market for the services provided by CEOs became a "seller's market," and their negotiating power increased. With their improved bargaining position, CEOs began demanding, and receiving, a say in the composition of the boards of directors. These executives found themselves in the position of being given immense power and the ability to pick their own bosses.

Making It a Buyer's Market

This environment favorable for CEOs began to change in the early 1990s as corporations and shareholders often reasserted their control. This movement began in earnest in 1993 as the chief executives found themselves facing **shareholder activism.**

In the United States, shareholder pressure helped to depose the CEOs of very large but underperforming firms such as IBM (John Akers), Westinghouse (Paul Lego), GM Corp. (Robert Stempel), Digital Equipment Corp. (Kenneth Olsen), and Kodak (Kay Whitmore). Furthermore, many CEOs were forced to accept salaries more closely linked to performance.[13]

This surge in the activities of active, and sometimes hostile, shareholders represents a change in corporate governance. Recall from Chapter 7 the idea of a governance structure in a relational contract. By **corporate governance,** we mean the governance structure existing between the stockholders, boards of directors, and chief executives within an organization.

The most severe reply to managerial misbehavior is corporate takeover. The threat of a hostile takeover provides a stern discipline threat to CEOs who have squandered corporate resources because very few keep their jobs after a successful takeover bid. The threat of a takeover of their firms exemplifies an economic concept known as **contestability,** which argues that economic rents earned by one party can be eliminated only if others are able to secure them. Or, in other words, there will be a contest for economic rents unless something prevents one. For CEOs, what is contestable is control over their corporations. Managers who have eliminated internal discipline find that a ready answer to declining performance is the emergence of people who believe that they can do a better job with the corpo-

---

[13]The movement seemed to begin in the United States where the perceived abuses by executives seemed most prevalent, and it quickly spread to other countries, notably the United Kingdom.

NOW THAT'S ENTERTAINMENT

A very popular example of the use of pay-for-performance by a large corporation in dealing with its chief executive officer is the Walt Disney Co. and its chairman, Michael Eisner. Mr. Eisner earned a substantial bonus in each of his prior nine years at the helm of Disney Co. However, for the fiscal year ended Sept. 30, 1993, his compensation was limited to his $750,000 salary and a small insurance benefit. This was quite a change as Mr. Eisner's bonuses in 1992 and 1991 were $4.7 and $10.5 million, respectively. He did, however, earn nearly $190 million from the sale of stock options in 1992 and 1993. The compensation package includes a "straight" salary plus an annual bonus based on net income and return on shareholder equity.

Source: Richard Turner, "Disney's Eisner Got No Bonus in '93, Reflecting Firm's Financial Problems," Wall Street Journal, *January 4, 1994, p. A2. Reprinted by permission of the* Wall Street Journal, © *1994 Dow Jones & Company, Inc. All Rights Reserved Worldwide.*

ration's assets. The existence of a stock market in which enough of a firm's shares are traded for a bidder to obtain control ensures that CEOs are reminded of the need to please the owners.

The use of the stock market as a disciplining device is questioned, however, for a number of reasons. A study by Michael Jensen, a prominent corporate economist, found that between 1976 and 1990, hostile transactions, leveraged buyouts, and other sales of corporate control made shareholders more than $700 billion.[14] On average, however, shareholders in the acquiring firms gained nothing because of the deals.

The entire environment surrounding CEOs and the pay they receive attracts much media attention for several reasons. From an organizational standpoint, the arrangement is interesting because of the principal-agent characteristics present. The events of the 1980s created an environment in which CEOs experienced rapidly escalating salaries and less control by the boards of directors. In many cases, shareholder activism caused a rethinking of the relationship between shareholders, their corporations, and their executive officers. In some cases, CEOs were removed; in others, CEOs had pay-for-performance provisions added to their contracts.

◼ SOME IMPLICATIONS OF INTERNAL LABOR MARKETS

The Up Side and the Down Side

On the theoretical level, workers and firms agree to a construct called the *employment relationship*. The structure of this multiyear exchange evokes efficient behavior by workers—corporate loyalty and the building of firm-specific human capital—and by firms—steady employment and the credible delivery of withheld rents to workers.

In practice, the employment relationship occurs in large organizations within a well-defined internal labor market in which pay levels attach to jobs and a main vehicle for awarding raises is promotion. This process provides employers with long time horizons over which they can evaluate workers, eventually moving them

---

[14]Michael Jensen, "The Modern Industrial Revolution, Exit, and the Failure of Internal Control Systems," *Journal of Finance*, July 1993.

Congratulations
on Your Degree:
Welcome
to the Rat Race

into positions in which they add the greatest value to corporations. A number of interesting issues are associated with this practice with implications for both managers and students.

On the down side, such a promotion process creates what has come to be called in popular jargon *a rat race*. In some occupations, individuals put in heroically long hours, perhaps even 70-hour weeks, to keep up with the pack. The burnout rate for young accountants and lawyers, in particular, is rather high at the most prestigious firms. To keep up with the pack, individuals make great personal sacrifices in terms of family lives, social lives, and even health. From an efficiency point of view, we can ask whether those "extra" 30 hours per week generate sufficient value to justify the costs borne by the employees (and their loved ones).

A large part of one answer to this seemingly paradoxical situation centers on some of the contracting problems caused by imperfect information discussed in Chapter 7. From an efficiency perspective, employers want to hire, promote, and give raises to employees with the best ability. Ability, however, is an entity that is only imperfectly observed. In awarding promotions, employers must rely on past performance as an indicator. Knowing this, the employee may then engage in some

PAY-FOR-PERFORMANCE OR ULTIMATE MORAL HAZARD?

In June 1992, Robert Watson was appointed the new chief executive officer of Westinghouse Financial Services, a division of Westinghouse, Inc. The parent company had suffered financially for years from mismanagement. Of particular concern was the Financial Services division, which held a large portfolio of poorly performing real estate assets.

Watson's contract stipulated that he was to bring down the assets of the Financial Services unit from $8.8 billion to under $3 billion. His compensation system was not particularly attractive for executive talent but did offer payment over a long period. Watson received a signing bonus of $400,000 and an annual salary of $600,000. He was also guaranteed 10 percent raises in 1993 and 1994 and was guaranteed a pension reflecting 30 years of service, about $450,000 annually, after he left Westinghouse. The contract provided for six years of employment; however, on completion of his task, Watson could leave and still receive all six years of his salary.

Watson completed his task in a little over one year. By June 1993, the assets of the Westinghouse Financial Services unit showed $3 billion on paper.

How did Watson accomplish this? His contract did not specify exactly how the reduction in assets should occur. Some critics charge that in the environment of incomplete contracting, he engaged in postcontractual opportunism. He was able to write off half of the bad assets as uncollectible debts and asset depreciation. Further, he sold most of Westinghouse's commercial real estate holdings for $1 billion, half their original book value.

Was Watson engaging in managerial misbehavior, working against shareholder interests? When he sold the real estate assets at a loss, he sold them to a newly formed partnership consisting of Westinghouse and Lehman Brothers, Inc.

Source: Erle Norton, "Great Work If You Can Get It: Millions for an 18 Month Job," Wall Street Journal, March 2, 1994, p. A1. Reprinted by permission of the Wall Street Journal, © 1994 Dow Jones & Company, Inc. All Rights Reserved Worldwide.

signaling behavior by working long hours. On the one hand, if the employer measures only the performance of employees (and largely ignores the time required to achieve this performance), the worker is hoping that his or her heroic output will be noticed and interpreted as a signal of ability. On the other hand, a worker who is observed working an extraordinarily large number of hours may also serve as a signal of the employee's work ethic, attitude, and devotion to the organization.

While affecting workers of all ages, the rate race may be most severe on younger workers. Put simply, a young person hoping to climb a career ladder has more to prove to her superiors. The incentives reenforce this tendency because a promotion fairly early in one's career does in fact create more options later in that worker's career. Older workers lack incentive to drop out of the rat race and work a more reasonable number of hours. If an older worker cuts back on effort, the reduced performance, not the reduced effort, is noticed.[15]

The system of promotions in internal labor markets quite often resemble an athletic tournament, such as the NCAA basketball tournament held every year for men's and women's college basketball teams. In the men's tournament, 64 teams are selected from around the United States and divided into 4 regions. In the first round of the tournament, 64 teams play, and 32 lose and are sent home. The remaining 32 are allowed to stay and compete once again. The whole process culminates when a national champion emerges from the much heralded "final four."

This style of tournament is called an elimination tournament, in which the winners get to remain and play for even greater glory. Promotions in internal labor markets work much the same way, and it has been empirically documented that pay rises progressively faster the further up the "job ladder" one is promoted. Or, put another way, an employee who wins a promotion has even bigger incentives to compete for and win the next promotion.

These characteristics of internal labor markets functioning as tournaments have created much discussion in the organizational economics literature. There are also many critics of this system in the more popular business press. There are, however, some obvious good points to such systems. Basically, relative to the option of basing pay on measured performance, the tournament system typically allows managers to overcome measurement problems in principal-agent relationships discussed in Chapter 8.

Performance measures may not be consistent across employees, and the information available may need to be carefully considered and weighed against the environment in which it was generated. Suppose, for example, that you have a part-time job in an appliance store to finance your college education. You work in the television department and develop a performance rating based on sales and customer satisfaction. Your friend Barbara works in the computer department of the same store and likewise develops a performance rating based on sales and customer satisfaction. A position opens in the major appliance department, a position for which you and Barbara will compete. Both of you covet the new position because it will give you some respect among your fellow salespersons and because it will greatly increase your income (there are higher sales margins on big-ticket items).

Your manager looks at both of your performance ratings and awards the position to you despite Barbara's superior performance rating. The manager's logic was simple, and he explains it to you as follows, "Sure Barbara's sales numbers

**Promotions
and Tournaments**

---

[15]Many of these arguments are borrowed from Bengt Holmstrom, "Managerial Incentive Problems: A Dynamic Perspective" in *Essays in Economics and Management in Honour of Lars Wahlbeck* (Helsinki: Swedish School of Economics, 1992); and George Akerlof, "The Economics of Caste and of the Rat Race and Other Woeful Tales," *Quarterly Journal of Economics*, November 1976, pp. 599–617.

DOLLAR INCENTIVES FOR GOLFERS

Golf is a very popular game in the United States. Television coverage of major tournaments is widely watched and generates much advertising revenues for the networks. Further, the better the players involved, the larger the audience attracted. A recent empirical study examined the relationship between the prize money in a tournament and player performance. Not surprisingly, the more the prize money offered, the better the players attracted and the lower their scores. Increasing the prize money by $100,000 (in 1984 dollars) lowered each player's score by an average of 1.1 strokes over a 72-hole tournament.

Source: Ronald G. Ehrenberg and Michael L. Bognanno, "Do Tournaments Have Incentive Effects," Journal of Political Economy, *December 1990, pp. 1307–1324. Reprinted with permission of The University of Chicago Press.*

were better. But your numbers were biased downward relative to hers simply because computers are much more popular items than televisions." The manager was able to give you the promotion because within the framework of the tournament, he could weigh the environment in which you operated.

■ CHAPTER SUMMARY AND KEY IDEAS ■ ■ ■ ■ ■ ■

Managing human resources means coordinating and motivating a number of individuals to advance the organization's interests. In this chapter, we have taken the employment relationship into the organization through a device commonly referred to as *internal labor markets*.

The advantages of taking the employment relationship into an organization through the establishment of an internal labor market are clearly defined efficiency gains for both the worker and the firm. A reduction in influence costs, decreased incentives for shirking, the establishment of corporate loyalty, and the building of firm-specific human capital are some of the benefits. These gains are possible only when the involved parties trust each other.

Once the trust is gone, the employment relationship is seriously undermined and the efficiency gains could likely disappear. Such was the case at many U.S. firms in the early 1990s when downsizings were very common. Not all downsizings were necessarily bad however; we considered two types, those conceived as part of an overall strategy to produce a flatter, more flexible organization and those as part of a simple slash and burn strategy.

Interestingly enough, the well-being of one type of employee was eroded by downsizings while a second type of employee was actually prospering under them. During the 1980s, the salaries of chief executive officers rose tremendously and attracted much media attention. These high salaries also attracted the attention of stockholders, who very often instituted changes in corporate governance that put more power in the hands of the corporation's board of directors.

Internal labor markets may seem beneficial because we are very familiar with the efficiency-enhancing aspects of the employment relationship, but they are not without their costs. One particular example is the idea that every job is a rat's race. Individuals aggressively pursue career advancement at the expense of their social lives, their marriages, and even their health. A second interesting vantage point to look at internal labor markets is to view them as tournaments much like those in college basketball.

KEY TERMS

capped option
contestability
corporate governance
downsizing
horizontal equity
internal labor market

option swaps
pay compression
reload option
shareholder activism
standard option

FURTHER READINGS

Ansberry, C. "Hired Out: Workers Are Forced to Take More Jobs With Few Benefits. *Wall Street Journal*, March 11, 1993, p. A1.

———. "Steelmakers Find a Cost-Cutting Plan Yields Headaches," *Wall Street Journal*, March 17, 1993, p. B4.

Castro, J. "Disposable Workers." *Time*, March 29, 1993, p. 43.

"The Death of Corporate Loyalty." *The Economist*, April 3, 1993, p. 63.

Fierman, J. "The Contingency Workforce." *Fortune*, January 24, 1994, p. 30.

Prendergast, C. "The Role of Promotion in Inducing Specific Human Capital Acquisition." *The Quarterly Journal of Economics*, 107, no. 2 (May 1993), pp. 535–542.

Shelsby, T. "Westinghouse Chairman Quits on Heels of Losses." *The Baltimore Sun*, January 28, 1993, p. A1.

QUESTIONS AND PROBLEMS FOR REVIEW AND DISCUSSION

A. Explain how the use of internal labor markets in large U.S. corporations was consistent with the mass production framework.

B. Provide some reasons why incentive-based pay may not be efficient in all employee-employer agreements.

C. Define horizontal equity and provide three reasons why it might be adopted in U.S. organizations. Also provide two reasons why it may not be optimal in organizations in today's business climate.

D. What are three key aspects of internal labor markets that allow this system to function as an applied version of the theoretical construct termed the *employment relationship*?

E. Regarding the three features you identified in the previous question, what effect do you anticipate organizational change such as that witnessed in the early 1990s will have?

F. Explain what is meant in economics by the term *winner's curse* and how it is relevant in the context of business reorganization.

G. Can you explain so that a layperson would understand how a standard stock option as part of a CEO's compensation package would work?

H. Some analysts have termed the internal labor markets popular in many occupations the *rat race*. Can you provide an argument supportive of the rat race on efficiency grounds? Can you also provide an argument against it on efficiency grounds?

V

The overall purpose of Part V is to convey some understanding of how evolution of business entities occurs. We adopt a historical perspective, emphasize the importance of transaction cost considerations as they relate to economic efficiency, and focus on the major causes of organization and industrywide change. We hope, in this part of the text, to present an accurate picture of current organization structures in light of the pressures and changes that produced them both in the United States and abroad. We are thus fully prepared to consider how economic activity will be organized tomorrow.

Chapter 14, "The Evolution of the Modern Firm," begins with a review of the rise and fall of America's great mass-producing firms. The student will undoubtedly be reminded of the material in Chapter 1. However, we enrich the story by including the role played by transaction costs and the way that efficiency considerations affect organization structure. Significant changes in the business environment cause changes to occur in the way that firms choose to organize economic activity. The new environment is driven by global competition, technological innovation, and flexibility in production.

Chapter 15, "Core Competencies, Organization, and Strategy," presents a more detailed look at the way that corporations respond to environmental changes by crafting an appropriate organization strategy. In an ultracompetitive environment in which consumers demand customized products, firms must move their focus "back to basics," or, in other words, pursue their core competencies. Coupled with this movement toward an organization's fundamental strengths is the important role played by flexible manufacturing systems in today's industrial organization. A full model

ORGANIZATION STRUCTURE AS A DYNAMIC PROCESS

V

of the flexible manufacturing process sheds light on the effects of this manufacturing process within the organization.

Chapter 16, "Organizational Strategy and Strategic Alliances," applies some of the managerial tools developed concerning incomplete contracting and transaction costs to the logic supporting the use of strategic alliances by business. We argue that these increasingly common organization forms are consistent with the pursuit of efficient behavior by organizations. Strategic alliances represent a substantial departure from past methods of organizing economic activity and are becoming more and more prevalent as business goes fully global.

Chapter 17, "An International Comparison of Organizational Styles," compares and contrasts the patterns of organizing economic activities chosen by the largest competitors of U.S. firms. In this chapter, we pay extra attention to the way that cultural and demographic influences affect organization patterns in light of the problems and challenges facing U.S. firms.

As you read through this part of the text, you will undoubtedly become aware of the uniqueness of this material. Put simply, this material is an innovation in undergraduate business education drawn from the works of leading scholars in organization economics.

The Evolution of the Modern Firm

The fundamental impulse that sets and keeps the capitalist engine in motion comes from the new consumer goods, the new methods of production or transportation, the new markets, the new forms of industrial organization that capitalist enterprise creates . . . that incessantly revolutionizes the economic structure from within, incessantly destroying the old one, incessantly creating a new one. This process of Creative Destruction is the essential fact about capitalism.[1]

▌ CHAPTER OUTLINE AND STUDENT GOALS ▌

In this chapter, we examine the continuing evolution of business organizations by looking at the causes and consequences of organizational change. Put simply, many aspects of the environment facing firms as large as AT&T and Disney and as small as Beth's Machine Shop have undergone drastic recent changes. The broad themes of these environmental changes were discussed in Chapter 1; in this chapter, we provide a much fuller analysis of past and present changes by including the role played by transaction costs in organization evolution. We also adopt a historical perspective to foster a fuller appreciation of the evolutionary patterns exhibited by economic organizations.

In its early history, the United States had no real firms, but there was a large reliance on markets. By the mid-19th century, an infrastructure conducive to large-scale distribution was firmly in place. The next step in the industrial development of the United States was the spread of the large multiunit business enterprise across many different U.S. manufacturing industries.

The corporate form adopted by the mass-producing firms followed two principles: functionalization of work into specialized units and a managerial structure of hierarchical layers for coordinating activities of these units. The successful firms grew in size by diversifying into new lines of business and vertically integrating backward into their supply sources or forward into the distribution functions. With each increase in size and function, additional layers of management were required to coordinate the many different individual actions.

However, as we saw in Chapter 1, business today appears to be undergoing a second radical restructuring that is just as fundamental and important as the restructuring that created great mass-producing firms in the United States.[2] What are the "drivers" causing organizations to evolve?

The drivers of change are once again environmental: the emergence of the

---

[1]Joseph A. Schumpeter, *Capitalism, Socialism and Democracy* (New York: Harper & Row, 1950), p. 83.
[2]Zoltan J. Acs, *The Changing Structure of the U.S. Economy* (New York: Praeger, 1984).

world market, the revolution in microelectronics, and the development of flexible production technologies.

In practice, flexible production empowers workers, giving them more responsibility. As a consequence, it features an even increased importance on firm-specific human capital. From the perspective of the organization, flexible production often results in the replacement of middle management, flatter structures, and a speed up of the whole manufacturing experience, from customer ordering to follow-up, or after-sale, service.

Finally, we look at the impact of new firm entry on the evolution of the structure of industry. In a changing business environment, organizations must change their structure or perish under the competitive pressures exerted by those firms that have altered their structures. Sometimes the change is caused by innovative entrepreneurs. The U.S. steel industry was restructured in part by small-firm entry. The consumer electronics industry was restructured through large-firm exit. The result of environmental change on industrial organizations has been a larger variety in the size distribution of firms, more pervasive entry and exit of organizations, and a shift in the size distribution of firms toward smaller, more flexible firms and plants based increasingly more on applications of new technologies.

After reading this chapter, you should be able to

* Explain what mass production is and identify the environmental factors that made it the dominant form for organizing economic activity.
* Intuitively describe the drivers of industrial change that precipitated the downfall of mass production.
* Explain how the drivers of industrial change that made mass production inefficient are shaping organizations as they evolve today.
* Explain what flexible production is and why it is important.
* Understand and describe the differences between flexible and mass production.
* Explain how the differences between flexible and mass production caused organizations to restructure and the nature of the restructured industries.
* Explain the role of entry and exit in industry evolution.

▓ HISTORICAL PATTERNS OF FIRM EVOLUTION

In the 1790s, business in New England consisted of a large number of very, very small units. In most instances, that unit was the family. The most important economic sector was agriculture, and a large percentage of individuals lived in rural areas. The cities featured tiny shops selling a variety of goods: textiles, shoes, and even a limited supply of manufactured wares.

As the heartland of the United States became more heavily populated in the early 1800s, new specialized entities sprang up to facilitate trade and transportation from the farms in the interior of the young nation to the domestic and international markets accessible from the larger cities on the eastern and southern coasts.

The growth of industry continued along these lines into the first decades of the 19th century as large enterprises emerged, providing an industrial infrastructure by specializing in finance, transportation, marketing, and distribution.[3] Be-

Nature of the Enterprise

---

[3]It is interesting that in contrast to the way in which today's infrastructure is provided, many of the transportation firms running canals and turnpikes were privately owned.

342

Part V
*Organization
Structure
as a Dynamic
Process*

Multidivisional Firms

cause of the large sums of capital required to operate, the privately owned of these enterprises were typically organized as corporations, or "joint stock companies" in the vernacular of the day. In any event, a major portion of the infrastructure necessary to support the huge mass-producing firms was being developed at this time.

Developments in New England that would help establish mass-producing firms in later years also affected the structure of organizations, resulting in the creation of **multidivisional firms** in the manufacturing or goods-producing industries. The first multiunit firms emerged in the United States between 1810 and 1820. A classic example is Boston Manufacturing Company, which produced cloth by harnessing the power generated by a nearby river. This mill was the largest in the United States at that time and was the first textile operation to integrate the weaving and spinning functions of cloth production at a single location.

The multidivisional firm introduced a number of new ways to do business. A new class of entrepreneur, the owners of these large mass-producing facilities, was created. More important, two other classes of individuals, managers and workers, were also created. The managers fulfilled two functions in these enterprises. They acted on behalf of the owners, informing them on the state of their firms. Further, the managers were concerned with maintaining efficient production, a task that included monitoring the performance of the workers.

Becoming a worker in one of the multidivisional firms was quite a change for individuals because of the degree of specialization. Individuals who became factory workers were no longer part of society's effort to produce food but had to rely on others to fulfill that basic need. Further, having a factory job meant having only one job as opposed to often working at small family operations in addition to engaging part time in agriculture or another small concern.

The first truly modern business enterprises were the railroads. The new railroads were quite different from the already established firms that managed the canals, turnpikes, and smaller railroads. Becuase of the safety and efficiency elements of railroads, these organizations required detailed managerial structures that could coordinate and monitor the geographically and functionally dispersed components of the company.

By the 1880s, the great railroad companies learned, and provided a model for, corporate cooperation and competition in U.S. business. The new management practices and technologies of the individual companies were arguably efficient, but when considered as a system, they had many drawbacks. The industry learned how to cooperate and when to compete to eliminate the problems in the system. Cooperation was necessary to operate a true transportation system spanning the entire country. Alliances of individual carriers and system building through mergers and acquisitions became the norm.

The next step in the industrial development of the United States was the spread of the large multiunit business enterprise across many different industries. The manufacturing industries were a little slower than the distribution industries because the former needed to overcome technical obstacles before large quantities of output could reasonably be produced.

Throughout the 19th century, a number of developments occurred that essentially made mass production possible in the next century. From a social perspective, a working class capable of operating the factories, fields, and mines emerged during this time period. A transportation infrastructure was developed, linking the geographically dispersed regions of the country. Specialized entities came into being to facilitate distribution and to provide financing. U.S. companies began experimenting with multidivisional structures and fairly sophisticated production technologies. The introduction of the so-called American system of manufacturing using interchangeable parts first appeared in gun making around 1800. Firms in the United States soon established themselves as world leaders in manu-facturing, replacing those in Great Britain, which continued to rely on more handicrafted methods.

To economists, the key organizational point is that mass production required a reliable input and output market. The railroads, steamships, canals, and tele-graph contributed to the establishment of each. Business enterprises often pur-chased their suppliers or distributors if contracting relationships became strained because of postcontractual opportunism, such as the threat of being held up or moral hazard problems.

The corporate form adopted by the mass-producing firms followed two prin-ciples: *organization* of work into specialized units of activities and *hierarchical layers* of management, necessary for coordinating activities of the units. The successful firms always grew in size by diversifying either into new lines of business or in a vertical manner by integrating with their supply sources or means of distribution. With each increase in size and function, additional layers of management were re-quired to coordinate the many different individual actions. Within this structure, the role of managers and workers was well, and narrowly, defined.

The role of managers in this new paradigm was to facilitate production, dis-tribution, and sale of output. **Scientific management,** or **Taylorism,** came to be the way in which the human component of these massive firms was organized and supervised. The three underlying rules for management under Taylorism were (1) each job should be specialized through the simplification of individual tasks, (2) management should devise predetermined rules coordinating the separate tasks, and (3) individual performance should be evaluated by management through a de-tailed monitoring system.

From 1920 through 1970, and especially during the postwar years, mass pro-duction was at its zenith, engineered by the scientific management within the cor-poration, protected by government regulation of the external environment, and supported by the prevailing social institutions. This was the world of countervail-ing power so aptly described by Galbraith[4] in which virtually every major institu-tion in society acted to reinforce the stability needed for mass production.

In addition to the dominant firms of the period 1900 to 1970 being multidivi-sional, most of the corporate giants were also multiproduct firms, producing a mixture of products. Some firms pursued an approach of producing a product line or a collection of related products; others created products for different, unrelated markets. The firm strategies existing then were revealed in this choice and, over the next two decades, the ultimate success of one of these strategies was verified.

When producing an entire product line, firms were better able to exploit economies of scale and economies of scope and defend established markets. The term **economies of scale** refers to continuous reductions in unit costs of produc-tion over a very large range of output. **Economies of scope** refer to reductions in the unit costs of producing one good because the firm produces a related good. The relationship between the production of related, but different, goods then yields a cost advantage to the single producer who can capture these benefits within the organization. We would expect to see, for example, a firm such as Sony produce both televisions and stereos. Undoubtedly, Sony has some cost advantage in producing televisions because of its ability also to manufacture stereos. One such advantage may be a discount, on the basis of quantity ordered, that Sony can

Multiproduct Firms

---

[4]John K. Galbraith, *American Capitalism: The Concept of Countervailing Power* (Boston, MA: Houghton Mifflin, 1957).

344

Part V
*Organization
Structure
as a Dynamic
Process*

secure from a supplier of a component used in both products. Another advantage may be the physical and human capital in place for the production of each good.

It was, and is, fairly common practice for large firms to produce related product lines to forestall entry into their markets. One interesting example of this practice concerns developments in the ready-to-eat breakfast cereal industry.[5] Between 1950 and 1972, the six leading producers introduced over 80 brands into the market. The large degree of brand proliferation was seen as an attempt to forestall further entry into the market. Basically, the existing, oligopolistic firms intended to deny entry by filling every market niche with one or more of their own brands.

An alternative strategy pursued by some multiproduct firms was to produce unrelated goods. The rationale here is to eliminate risk to the organization resulting from changes in consumer demand. In this scenario, firms produce unrelated goods under the logic that diversification in the product market will lead to a more stable and, hence, more attractive earnings profile for the firm. A firm might choose, for example, to acquire the capability to produce chocolate bars and tomato sauce. Such diversification provides stability so long as trends in the candy market are unrelated to trends in the spaghetti market. It is interesting to note that many studies examining the stock markets' response to a firm's decision to minimize risk with a product diversification strategy have failed to identify any significant gains as a result of this strategy.[6]

This diversification strategy led to the formation of many conglomerates in the United States during the period 1950 to 1970. These conglomerates seemed to dominate at first. However, as explained in Chapter 1, during the intense stock market activity in the 1980s, there was a trend to "deconglomeratize" U.S. business; many of the conglomerates were broken up and parts sold off via equity transactions.

Over the 100-year period between 1870 and 1970, U.S. business came to be dominated by truly large corporations. These organizations were multidivisional and multiproduct, requiring the services of many levels of management to coordinate the wide range of activities pursued by the various components of the organization. In the next section, we begin to explore the details of how this structure was necessary to support the mass production carried out at that time. In that discussion, we emphasize the importance of transaction costs, relational contracting, and bounded rationality. As the mass production came to be the dominant organization form of economic activity, the use of markets to obtain inputs and allocate output was diminished.[7]

■ THE INTERNAL STRUCTURE OF THE FIRM

The multidivisional firm structure that dominated the U.S. corporate world beginning around 1900 was able to perform and manage a much wider set of activities than would be possible under a less vertically integrated and decentralized organization governance structure. This form helped organizations create the stability necessary in input and output markets to support the mass production system.

Evidence of the increased reliance on multidivisional structures in U.S. indus-

---

[5]See Richard Schmalensee, "Entry Deterrence in the Ready-to-Eat Breakfast Cereal Industry," *Bell Journal of Economics*, pp. 305–326.

[6]One reason may be that investors prefer to diversify by choosing an appropriate mix of individual firm stocks for their portfolios rather than having the firms themselves diversify.

[7]After 1970, many large corporations also became international. See John H. Dunning, *Multinational Enterprises and the Global Economy* (Reading, MA: Addison-Wesley, 1993).

tries is shown in Figure 14.1. This figure clearly shows an increase in the share of manufacturing activity taking place in multidivisional firms.

We can explain these developments concerning the internal structure of firms using many of the important tools and concepts discussed in Part I of this book.

Recall our definition of a firm from Chapter 1.

> firm: *A conscious, willful effort to organize economic activity that consists of a collection of contracts when more than one party is involved.*

Each of these contracts involves an exchange between at least two parties. Because many of these exchanges are not made in established competitive markets, they create many transaction costs for the firm and its workers, suppliers, and customers to overcome. Because of bounded rationality, parties had reason to fear exploitation through pre- or postcontractual opportunism (primarily via hold-up and moral hazard problems).

Organizations have two choices in conducting these transactions: **internal** or **external contracting.** Transactions are internalized through ownership and the establishment of an employer-employee relationship. External transactions are conducted in the market. One key decision variable for an organization to make is the degree of vertical integration. As the internal mode of exchange is chosen over the external, a higher degree of vertical integration is established. Making the choice between internal and external transacting for a particular commodity or service involves comparing the relative costs of each transaction mode. As Ronald Coase, the 1991 Nobel Laureate in economics pointed out over 40 years ago, the costs of administering transactions internally versus the transaction costs of conducting them through markets determine the boundaries of the firm.

Vertical integration occurs when one business enterprise gains control over more than one stage in the production of finished goods. In short, firms could se-

Vertical and Horizontal
Integration

**Figure 14.1 Percentage of U.S. Manufacturing
Employment in Multidivisional Firms**

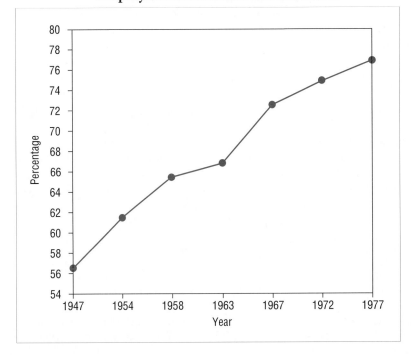

346

Part V
*Organization
Structure
as a Dynamic
Process*

cure reliable deliveries of large quantities of inputs and have ready access to large outputs.

A broad, multidivisional structure was adopted when significant transaction costs existed and threatened the input and output stability necessary for mass-producing firms. A perfect example is provided by the relationship between General Motors and the Fisher Body Company in the 1920s, as noted previously. Automaking technology was changing at the time: wooden car bodies were being replaced by steel ones. When GM was designing a new auto plant, it asked Fisher Body to build a body plant directly connected to GM's factory floor. Fisher objected, fearing that a commitment to such asset specificity would leave it vulnerable to various forms of postcontractual opportunism by GM, and was reluctant to take this risk. GM also feared being held up in production by Fisher Body Company. Because of the highly cospecialized assets, the efficient solution was a high degree of vertical integration: GM purchased Fisher Body Company.[8]

As another illustration, consider the structure chosen to provide multimedia and information-processing services. At one theoretical extreme, a fully vertically integrated firm, CompAll, would have full responsibility. In manufacturing computers, CompAll would own plastics factories to create the "box," metal factories and fabricators to create the wiring and other metal components, a glass factory to manufacture the screens, and a large piece of desert property from which they would obtain the silicon (from the sand) with which to construct the microprocessor chips. There would be large CompAll stores selling the finished product and legions of programmers to write the billions of lines of code necessary to fill the professional, personal, and entertainment needs of users. Further, CompAll would have employees to handle marketing functions, lawyers to protect CompAll in litigation, and finance specialists to handle CompAll's relationship with the capital markets. And, of course, when one of its machines breaks, a CompAll service center would repair the problem.

At the other extreme, each activity might be carried out by separate firms, coordinated and motivated by a single CompAll employee through a complex system of relational contracting. In the mass-producing world of U.S. business in the 20th century, this market-based form was rarely chosen, for it posed too many drawbacks to the stability necessary in input and output markets.

The issue of vertical integration of a company seems pretty simple. The issue is how the transactions between successive stages are managed through the spot market; through administration after integration into a single company; or through a more complex governance structure. The organization's choice of the degree of vertical integration is somewhat similar to the three basic questions facing whole economies: what to produce, for whom to produce, and how to produce.

Horizontal integration is perhaps the most important dimension of business strategy because it determines the horizontal boundaries of the firm. Horizontal integration addresses the issue of what business a company should be in. Generally, firms seeking profitable expansion are most likely to be successful by identifying the areas of their own special competencies, investing to build those competencies, and introducing products for which the competencies give the firm a cost and/or quality advantage with current and future product offerings. Most horizontal expansion takes the form of mergers or acquisitions. The impact of vertical and horizontal integration on firm size has been pronounced: the average firm size grew steadily throughout the 20th century.

---

[8]See Benjamin Klein, Robert Crawford, and Armen Alchian, "Vertical Integration, Appropriable Rents, and the Competitive Contracting Process," *Journal of Law and Economics* 21 (1978), pp. 297–326.

As with vertical integration, horizontal integration is not a question of yes or no, but of degree, depending on the governance structure chosen by a particular organization. Successful horizontal integration usually involved a multiproduct firm supplying goods related either in use by consumers or related in that they share a common set of inputs. The firms in the ready-to-eat cereal industry are an example of the former. A chemical firm producing fertilizer to farmers, plastic resins to toy producers, and various prescription drugs to the health industry is an example of the latter.

One important limitation on firm size is the challenge posed by coordination. As the size of the firm increases, either each division becomes bigger or the number of divisions increases. In the latter case, the amount of information flowing to the head office increases. Top managers become overloaded. They may respond by adding staff to support them or by further decentralizing, pushing more decisions to lower levels and perhaps adding levels of management between the top executives and the divisions. Both of these responses create additional transaction costs for management to contend with. Providing staff with proper incentives is difficult because their performance is hard to measure.

Decentralizing more decisions means sacrificing control and coordination across these decisions, and the additional layers of management slow decision making, act as filters on information transmission, and are themselves directly costly. Apart from the difficulty in efficiently processing a large amount of information, multiple layers of management create a situation rife with moral hazard and a misalignment of incentives between principals and agents throughout the organization.

As the large, mass-producing firms emerged in the first half of the 20th century, they internalized many of the aspects of production. For some inputs, this internalization replaced external markets because of transaction cost considerations. For other inputs, neither the inputs themselves nor the markets in which they were traded existed; the most favorable option in light of these missing markets was internalization.

We have just argued that during the post–World War II era until about 1970, there was a very stable environment in place in U.S. business that nicely supported the mass producers. This stability provided smooth flows of inputs and outputs as well as de facto barriers to entry (that is, U.S. producers were mostly immune from competitive pressures exerted by foreign producers). In many oligopolistic manufacturing industries, firms did not have to rely on product and process innovation to remain competitive. As Robert Reich, who has served as secretary of labor in the Clinton administration, described the situation,

> Individual firms did not need to worry that their competitors might suddenly introduce a new innovation that would render current technologies obsolete since they already knew what their rivals were planning. Firms, therefore, felt less compelled to invest in the development of radically new products or processes. As a result, while the unit costs of production continued to decline, there were few breakthroughs, and industries were often slow to apply new technologies.[9]

In the absence of competitive pressures, average costs of production not only increased but also failed to decrease as they would have done in a more innovative environment (either entrepreneurial or routinized regime). Three separate factors worked to increase costs. Higher wages and benefits were paid to workers because of the firm's secure and profitable market position. Managerial waste and

How Big
Should Firms Be?

The Legacy
of Oligopoly

---

[9]Robert B. Reich, *The Next American Frontier* (New York: Times Books, 1983).

348

Part V
*Organization
Structure
as a Dynamic
Process*

x-inefficiency were common in these firms. Nonprice competition such as through advertising and providing ancillary services was an expensive substitute for firms seeking a competitive edge when price competition had been suppressed.

A schematic representation is presented in Figure 14.2. The market demand function is shown in Figure 14.2(a) as a downward sloping function of market price. Figure 14.2(b) shows three average total cost functions—$LRAC_1$, $LRAC_2$, and $LRAC_3$—for a typical firm in the industry. The competitive cost function for producers given their technologies is $LRAC_1$ (the middle curve), which has a minimum unit cost of C_1, which corresponds to an industry price of P_1 in Figure 14.2(a).

The combined, cumulative effects of x-inefficiency, managerial waste, and nonprice competition raise the unit costs from this competitive level to a cost structure like that shown as $LRAC_2$ in Figure 14.2(b). Imposed by these inefficiencies, the higher costs translate into a higher market price shown as P_2 in Figure 14.2(a).

The real damage of the oligopolistic structure refers not to what occurred but to what might have been. In the absence of market power and the related economic and social structure encouraging stability, increased technological progress presumably would have lowered the firms' cost structures from $LRAC_1$ to $LRAC_3$. The competitive level of costs is shown as $LRAC_1$. X-inefficiency, managerial waste, and nonprice competition increase costs to $LRAC_2$. Subsequently, the oligopolistic price rises from P_1 to P_2.

In the output market, the effects of technological progress would have been to lower market price toward P_3. In this sense, consumers and society suffer increased market prices, P_2, rather than P_3 and a reduced level of output (compare Q_3 and Q_2).

The substantial profits earned by oligopolistic firms eventually attracted en-

Figure 14.2a Inefficiency of Oligopoly

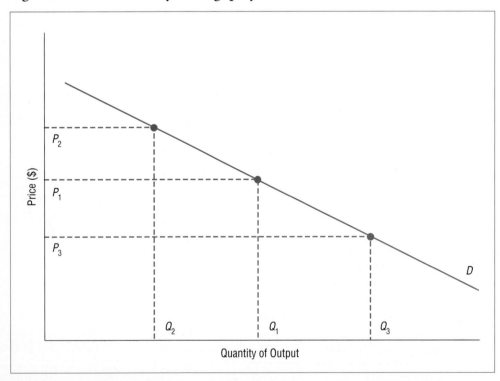

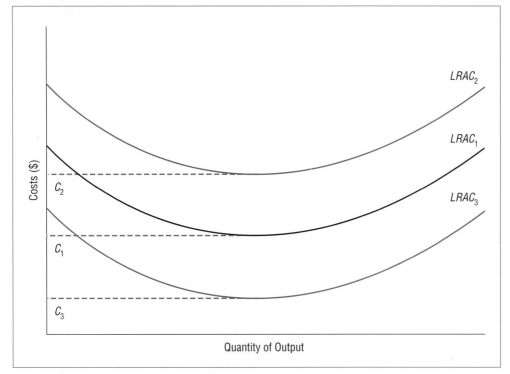

Figure 14.2b Inefficiency of Oligopoly

trants both from within the United States and from abroad. The other structural changes that worked to bring about the decline of mass production made entry for firms much easier and even encouraged it. These other structural changes, described in Chapter 1 were destandardization of consumer demand, elimination of trade barriers, input price shocks, and shrinking of the minimum efficiency scale (MES) because of technological advances. As the inefficiencies resulting from government protection and oligopolistic market structure drove up costs, entry became more attractive.

In this sense, then, economists often say that the legacy of oligopolistic mass producers was essentially their demise. Or, put another way, we can claim that the system of oligopoly was endogenously unstable, meaning that the very nature of its existence contributed significantly to its downfall. Domestic and foreign competitors could exploit newer and cheaper technologies to produce the varied products demanded, and they could do so free of the rigid cost structure that had solidified in many industries. In the following section, we highlight the changes in environment that created these corporate giants and the more recent changes that aided their demise.

▨ CURRENT DRIVERS OF CHANGE

Schumpeter's theory of creative destruction provides a potent descriptive model of the actual operation of capitalism. Its emphasis on the dynamics of new firm formation and growth concurrent with existing firm decline and termination makes it a central component of evolutionary economics. Three points about capitalism are important. First, in dealing with capitalism, we are dealing with an evolutionary system. Second, capitalism as a system is never stationary. Third, as suggested in the introduction, the fundamental impulse that keeps the economy in

350

Part V
*Organization
Structure
as a Dynamic
Process*

Globalization
and Internationalization

motion comes from new goods and methods of production, new methods of transportation, as well as new forms of organization.

In the late 20th century, we are witnessing a series of changes in the business environment. The first is the emergence of the world market replacing the national market of the last century, and the second is the modern industrial revolution. As a result of the developments in transportation, information, and communications technologies, we have seen a convergence of national and international markets for goods, investments, and technology.

Organizations change when their environments and the technologies they use change. As they accumulate the information and experience about what kinds of organizations work best for particular tasks, the speed of change quickens.

In the 19th century, the key environmental change was the development of a unified national market. The unified national market favored large-scale production technologies in highly vertically integrated firms. Goods were highly standardized but seemed to meet consumer needs. Perhaps consumers were willing to sacrifice variety for price, a situation conducive not only to mass production but also to mass consumption. The best example was the Model T, manufactured by Ford Motor Company, available in any color customers wished (as long as it was black).

In the late 20th century, markets have become much more international. International trade has grown more rapidly than output in all advanced countries in the post–World War II period. For example, the combined gross domestic production (GDP) of France, Germany, Italy, Japan, the United Kingdom, and the United States grew at an average of 5.5 percent per year from 1950 to 1973; their combined export volume increased at 9.7 percent per year. In the subsequent period from 1973 to 1990, which experienced substantially slower economic growth, the export volume continued to outrace GDP growth, with an average of 4.7 percent and 2.7 percent, respectively.

With changes in the world economy, industries that were national under mass production have become international. **Internationalization** implies that the demand for an industry's output is international. It is important to remember that firms, not industries or nations, compete internationally. The industry is the environment in which the firm competes, and that environment is becoming increasingly international.[10]

National markets have become even more integrated internationally than an examination of foreign trade figures would suggest. Investment has also become internationalized. **Globalization** implies not only that competition is developing on a global scale for industries but also that investment and technology are becoming global. This is illustrated by the fact that foreign direct investment has grown even faster than trade in recent years. As a result, an increasing share of world trade takes place among multinational corporations. For example, in 1988, 25 percent of U.S. exports involved sales of U.S. parent companies to their subsidiaries abroad and another 37 percent of U.S. exports represented sales of U.S. parent companies to unaffiliated buyers abroad.

Internationalization appears to have had two unforeseen consequences. The first is a growing demand for **differentiated products,** products that fulfill the same basic function but vary in at least one dimension. Product differentiation is not an absolute concept but one of degree. As the standard of living has increased, tastes and spending patterns have changed, and consumer demand has shifted from standardized commodities to more sophisticated and customized products. This change is reflected in the proliferation of the variety of products marketed.

---

[10]Michael Porter, *The Competitive Advantage of Nations* (New York: The Free Press, 1991).

The second is the high degree of *uncertainty* that has characterized the last several decades. After the breakdown in the Bretton Woods system of fixed exchange rates in 1969, many factors have contributed to this uncertainty: the oil price shocks of 1973 to 1974 and 1979 to 1980 and ensuing concerns about the reliability of supply, the enormous debt accumulation in many third world countries in the early 1980s, the increasing government budget deficits in several Western countries, the collapse of the former Soviet Union, the end of the cold war, and the concern about competitiveness.

The initial response to these changes was confusion regarding what was wrong and how to go about fixing it. Policy makers sought to blame macroeconomic events for the current problems.[11] This response had at least some justification; after all, the Vietnam War and the social spending efforts of President Lyndon Johnson's Great Society in the 1960s caused serious inflation. Nor was it accurate to conclude that U.S. businesses looked to the federal government for relief from what was perceived to be "unfair" foreign competition. Over the period 1980–1995, it became increasingly clear that the real source of the problems facing large U.S. producers was microeconomic rather than macroeconomic. The firms needed to change the way in which they did business.

According to Piore and Sable, two leading economic analysts, the economic crises of the 1970s resulted from the inability of firms and policy makers to maintain the conditions necessary to preserve mass production and the stability of markets.[12] Their claim is that the present deterioration in economic performance results from the limits of the model of industrial development: the use of special-purpose machines and of semiskilled workers to produce standardized products. The endogenous instability of the mass production model based on so many production and social rigidities over the past century has given rise to what Piore and Sable call an *industrial divide*.

An **industrial divide** is a moment in history when the path of technological development itself is at issue. In fact, if the Great Depression represented a macroeconomic crisis, the economic problems of the 1970s were a microeconomic crisis in that the focus was on the choice of technologies and the organization of firms, industries, and markets.

Electronic Technology

During the past 25 years, we have developed a revolutionary new technology, the microprocessor, which uses a silicon chip the size of a fly or smaller, with computing powers thousands of times greater than a million monks happily adding and subtracting for millennia. Like the technologies of the past—the steam engine and the internal combustion engine—the microprocessor does not operate within the confines of existing structures but makes possible a new one, in this case, the **Information Age.**

Each of the last three industrial revolutions and the current one can be characterized as a revolution that made (makes) possible the transportation of both raw materials and finished commodities to market. During the first Industrial Revolution (1780–1830), a system of canals in England made possible the transportation of goods at a fraction of the previous cost. In the last century, the second Industrial Revolution (1830–1850), the railroad provided cheap continent-wide transportation in England, Germany, and the United States, and the steamship connected the continents. Together, these developments made it possible to conceive of doing business on a scale never before possible. During the

---

[11]R. Dornbusch and S. Fischer, *Macroeconomics* (New York: McGraw-Hill, 1978).

[12]M. Piore and C. Sable, "The Second Industrial Divide: Prospects for Prosperity" (New York: Basic Books, 1984).

352

Part V
*Organization
Structure
as a Dynamic
Process*

third Industrial Revolution (1920–1940), the automobile, truck, and airplane made the transportation of goods and people inexpensive. The fourth Industrial Revolution beginning in 1955 and still in progress is also transportation oriented; however, this time, it involves the transfer of knowledge rather than the movement of people or goods.

The information revolution is providing less distorted information. According to Tom Peters,

> Hierarchies distort, abstract, and delay information processing by their very nature. The accelerator in an effective market economy is the increasing volume of unfiltered, "real-time" information about prices, and perceived values the world over, processed by those who can do something with the information in a hurry.[13]

A Time Line of Events

To keep these events in a proper historical perspective, we present in Figure 14.3 a time-line abstract depiction of events in the United States over the relevant time period. In regard to innovations, we recognize three as being central to organizational development: the steam engine, the internal combustion engine, and the microprocessor.

The top four time lines are an abstract representation of industrial development.[14] These lines begin in the early 1800s when industry was dominated by small cottage industries and crafters. In the mid-1800s, these craft industries were being supplanted by small-scale, multidivisional enterprises. Beginning around 1900 and continuing until around 1970, the mass-producing firms in their oligopolistic industries came to dominate U.S. industry. Into the 1980s, flexible manufacturing systems were developed and began to replace mass production as an organization strategy. The widespread adoption of flexible manufacturing systems, which took many years, began in 1975 when Japanese innovators coupled the microcomputer with numerical control techniques.

These organization changes were supported by changes in markets and transportation. The changes in transportation are represented by the bottom four lines in Figure 14.3. In 1800, transportation in the young United States centered on horses and canals. With the development of the steam engine, the great American railroads grew in importance as they provided a relatively low-cost way to ship large quantities of goods and people long distances. As the internal combustion engine was developed and applied to a number of new products, automobiles and trucks came to substitute for railroads due to lower installation costs and greater flexibility in use.

A new dimension to transportation was effectively added around 1955 as a result of the widespread use of information technology. The transmission of information became more important to many firms than the transportation of goods and people. Word processing and computer networks greatly reenforced the effect of the adoption of flexible manufacturing systems. As producers worried less and less about hold-ups resulting from asset specificity, markets developed. The widespread availability of information from advances in information technology helped create an environment more suited to competitive markets. Basically, with vast amounts of data available on goods and services and on providers of those goods and services, competition could work to eliminate many pre- and postcontractual opportunisms.

---

[13]Tom Peters, *Liberation Management: Necessary Disorganization for the Nanosecond Nineties* (New York: Alfred A. Knopf, Publishers, 1992), p. 567.
[14]The situation is clouded further by the fact that these innovations underwent great refinements, and the exact time such improvements rendered them useful in a particular setting is unknown.

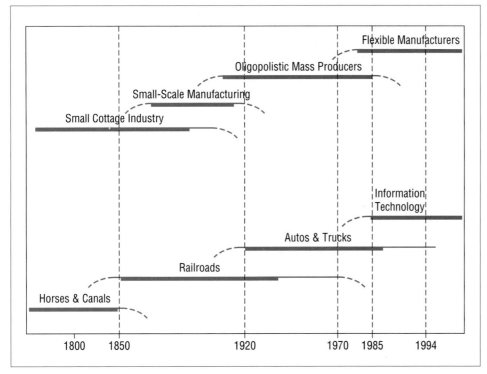

Figure 14.3 Time Line of Major Developments

Spurred on by the developments in transportation, which served to effectively make the world a smaller place in which to do business, markets changed as well. In the early 1800s, most markets were local in nature. Every town had its own bakery, brewery, and butcher shop. As the great American railroads linked cities and towns, the markets grew and became regional. However, given that manufactured goods could be shipped great distances without regards to spoilage, larger national markets were possible. The railroads permitted mass-producing firms to produce large volumes of output to serve the huge national market. The emphasis on national markets remained until around 1970 when economic development in other countries spawned new competitors eager for a piece of the huge markets available in the United States.

The course of events in U.S. manufacturing industries in the first three-quarters of the 20th century were, for example, guaranteed by the development of transportation and communication capabilities and by the emergence of technologies that permitted large-scale, or mass, production. A good example of the organization changes induced by technology advances was the first large-scale application of automation at the Ford engine plant in Brook Park, Ohio.

▓ DEVELOPMENT OF PRODUCTION TECHNOLOGY

Advances in computer technology not only have impacted the ways in which we transfer and analyze information but also have made possible an entirely new approach to how goods are actually made. The success of this new approach is leading to changes in firms and industries as we move from mass production technologies to flexible production technologies.[15] The impact on organizations has

---

[15]This section is adopted from Acs and Audretsch, *Innovation and Small Firms*, Ch. 6.

354

Part V
*Organization
Structure
as a Dynamic
Process*

**The Development
of Flexible Production
Techniques**

been enormous, and we devote the entire next chapter to a more thorough understanding of this impact. For now, we introduce the basic terminology and concepts in a historical context.

One of the major technological advances in manufacturing during the 1930s resulted in the introduction of transfer machines. **Transfer machines** consist of a number of machines or work stations, each for a separate operation such as drilling or milling, organized to work together in such a fashion that a piece of work is automatically put in place at one work station, operated on there, and then transferred to the next work station, and so on. Work is performed simultaneously at all work stations, and several operations may be performed simultaneously at each work station.

After World War II, the use of mechanization in mass production increased. The first large-scale application of automation was at the Ford engine plant in Brook Park, Ohio. Ford tied together several large stationary transfer machines into a continuous system. The system inspired a succession of improved engine plants in the United States and became known as **Detroit automation** or *Fordism*, which referred to several large transfer machines linked in a continuous system. Although the development of automation continued into the early 1970s, the most important technological progress in the last 30 years appeared in an entirely different direction: the development of machines that could be controlled numerically by a computer.

With the advent of numerical controls in the late 1940s, the potential emerged for reversing the 150-year technological trend in machine tools favoring large-scale production. The original development in numerical controls started around 1949, when the U.S. Air Force began to use machine tools in the aircraft industry to produce highly complex parts that were not only more accurate than those produced by conventional methods but also less expensive. Using the financial support from the government, John Parsons and the Servomechanisms Laboratory at Massachusetts Institute of Technology developed prototypes by 1951. The first commercial **numerically controlled** (NC) **machines** were displayed in 1955 by the National Machine Tool Builders Association.

Although the major technological inventions for NC machines occurred during the end of the 1950s, they were not commercially applied until the late 1960s. The extensive diffusion of NC machines tools did not really begin until 1975, when the Japanese introduced the microcomputer-based numerical control unit, thus enabling **computer numerical control** (CNC) to be used. At that point, two developments occurred that would forever change the organization of firms. First, the programmability and therefore flexibility of CNCs increased dramatically because of the development of more powerful computers. Second, cheaper and more flexible numerical controllers in combination with other changes led to mass production of CNCs, resulting in drastically reduced prices. Taken together, these two developments meant that better, more powerful CNC manufacturing systems were more readily available. The continued evolution of new flexible technologies has brought a host of various other flexible production techniques.

An **industrial robot** has three components. The first is a mechanical system of grippers or some other special-purpose device, such as a welding or painting mechanism. The second element is a "servo-system," which precisely controls the movement and positioning of the robot's "arms." Finally, a computer control system is required to coordinate and direct the robot. Industrial robots are primarily used for material handling and machine loading, as well as for specific process functions such as spot and arc welding, spraying, finishing, and assembling.

Computer-aided design (CAD) technologies involve an interactive computer terminal that designs product models as well as performs modifications and tests. In particular, CAD is used in computer graphics and simulation models.

Computer-aided manufacturing (CAM) systems typically involve applying CAD to control and actually perform the manufacturing processes. CAM enables the integration of systems comprising machine tools robots and other process machinery used in manufacturing. The mean cost of a CAD/CAM system fell from $400,000 in 1980 to $250,000 in 1985. However, smaller stand-alone CAD/CAM work stations using a microcomputer cost as little as $10,000 in 1982.

A **flexible manufacturing system** (FMS) typically consists of multiple workstations, an automated material-handling system, and a supervision system through computer control. In addition, an FMS may often rely on CAM technology as well as automatic tool changing, in-process inspection, parts washing, and an automated storage and retrieval system.

An FMS serves the same purpose as a conventional automated production system. However, it can be more easily reprogrammed and made compatible with CAD and CAM technologies, rendering the overall system of production substantially more flexible than transfer machines. Subsequently, the cost of small-volume production of complex parts has been reduced much more than that of large-volume production of standardized products. Such systems represent an enormous advantage for **small-batch production.** One of the properties of flexible manufacturing is the capability of inexpensive small-batch production. These can be as small as several hundred pieces.

Before we proceed to a detailed discussion of how flexible production technologies are altering the environment in many industries, we need to take a brief detour to address a more general topic concerning technological advances. Nearly every home in America has a videotape recorder (VCR) hooked up to a television set. At one time, there were two types of video recorders: beta and VHS. Each was an innovation that enabled home viewing of movies separate from the standard network offerings. However, the beta format is, at best, a distant memory. Why? This is a very general question concerning how the standards are chosen for a particular technology.

▨ A LOOK AT TECHNOLOGY STANDARDS

**The Importance
of Standards**

Technological advances typically present a number of options to the marketplace where the benefits and costs of each form of the new technology must be carefully weighed. The winner in the marketplace is said to set the standard for that particular type of technology. The importance of winning this competition cannot be understated. In the early 1980s, Bill Gates left IBM to found a new software company, Microsoft. Microsoft became the industry leader in PC application software when Bill Gates successfully set the standard for the exploding computer industry.

Economists have only recently become interested in the process of setting standards, and we hope to provide some insights into this process. Setting standards is neither new or trivial to organizational economists. In the 19th century, the development of large-scale manufacturing was made possible by the adoption of technological standards for interchangeable parts. The first application of this was in the manufacturing of armaments at the Harper's Ferry, West Virginia, Armory. Widespread adoption of this concept helped usher in a period of dominance for U.S. manufacturers.

Generally, a new technology becomes available in a number of formats. Consider the home video games offered today. What factors come into play as the market decides between 16-bit and 32-bit formats? As the new computer tech-

356

Part V
*Organization
Structure
as a Dynamic
Process*

The Economics
of Technological
Standards

nologies emerge in the business world, individuals are presented with options. Macintosh operating systems (platforms) feature user-friendly graphics and a "click and point" menu-driven system of commands. These platforms compete with Windows, MS-DOS, and Unix-based operating systems. In such situations, a single producer usually "wins" the competition and becomes the standard.

On closer inspection of the technology standards problem, it becomes clear that the competition is not between individual products but between **network systems,** a term that refers to collections of two or more components with an interface that allows the components to work together.[16] Some examples of systems are staplers and staples, which together bind papers; gas and cars, which yield transportation services; and computer hardware and word processing package, which together provide the service of transferring handwritten or typed information into a more presentable form. The key features of competition between network systems are the strong consumption complementarities between the components and the ability (or inability) to link together the components of different suppliers. **Consumption complementarities** refers to the process in which two related products or goods are used together.

The market competition between network systems, as opposed to more limited competition between individual products, features three important issues: expectations, coordination, and compatibility. Although it is not our purpose to explore this interesting area too deeply, a brief exposition of the central ideas should help to understand some of the issues important in shaping the technological environment in which firms operate.

Consumer expectations concerning the success of any network system are perhaps the most important force in the market. If a given network system, such as Windows software and its many applications programs, is thought to become popular, it is more likely to be adopted. Purchasers will be able to communicate with others by purchasing that software and are virtually guaranteed a "wide" market in the future with relatively inexpensive upgrades and enhancements. Another example of network system competition involves credit cards: VISA versus American Express. In the mid-1990s, VISA's main advertising strategy was to describe a popular place or event and then to warn, "But bring your VISA card; [the firm] doesn't take American Express."

Consumer expectations cause network systems to generate consumption externalities of the type described in Chapter 5. **Consumption externalities** are created when the consumption of a good by one party generates externalities that affect consumption of that good by other parties. Clearly, a decision to adopt a particular network system enhances its value to others who already have adopted (or yet may adopt) that network system.

Network systems pose coordination problems for relationships between firms, for the firms themselves, and for the relationship between a firm and its customers. A firm contemplating whether to develop a new computer architecture is forced to speculate on whether to provide software to work on it. Perhaps the most well-known example recognizing the coordination problem facing firms is IBM's strategy of allowing other software developers to write software applications that are compatible with its personal computers.

The compatibility problems facing providers of network systems also cause

---

[16]Three interesting articles recently appeared and serve the basis for this discussion. The articles are not overly technical and are written at a level that most undergraduates should understand. Each is contained in the Spring 1994 issue of the *Journal of Economic Perspectives*, pp. 93–133 and is listed in the Further Readings section of this chapter.

important decisions to be made concerning the future course of events in any market. *Compatibility* concerns whether a component designed to work in one system can also function in another system. Classic examples of incompatibility include railroad cars that do not fit the tracks, MS-DOS and Unix systems, and people speaking different languages.

A wide variety of solutions exist to the consumer expectation, coordination, and compatibility problems posed by network systems. If competing network systems exist or even are planned to exist, one obvious solution is cooperation. Throughout the 1980s and 1990s, two nations led the world in the development of high-definition television (HDTV): the United States and Japan. The Japanese committed early to an analog-based system.

In the United States, the Federal Trade Commission organized a competition between different firms vying to set the standards for the distribution of a digital-based HDTV signal. The result of this competition was a "grand alliance" of firms agreeing to share their technologies and split the licensing fees. Refer to the box, "High-Density Television—The Grand Alliance," in Chapter 1.

If cooperation is impossible to achieve, network systems will be largely incompatible. Some possible strategies have been observed by economists in such situations:

1. Firms may strive to build an "early" lead (or at least the perception of one) in the competition with other network system suppliers. This may involve heavy use of "penetration pricing," introductory classes and seminars, and consumer giveaways. Firms also often release very inflated sales figures showing an artificially high adoption rate.

2. Firms may attempt to obtain close and exclusive relationships with suppliers. In network system competition, a firm always wants complements for its product to be generously supplied, and complements for its rivals' products to be scarce. This suggests that firms may be more apt to vertically integrate suppliers to speed the adoption of product innovations while precluding others from enjoying them.

3. Firms may use elaborate product preannouncements. The effect of these highly publicized announcements is to make existing competitor's products less desirable.

In short, the adoption of industry standards for many of the technical advancements during the period 1970 to 1990 was usually not a straightforward process. Many of the difficulties arose because of the network system characteristic of these goods and services.

▧ INNOVATION, ENTREPRENEURS, AND INDUSTRY EVOLUTION

Beth owned a small machine shop in Cleveland, Ohio. For years, she made a modest living subcontracting for some of the large manufacturing firms in the area. Lately, business had been growing rapidly for Beth as many local manufacturing firms began outsourcing projects. As a result of this recent success, she envisioned even bigger and better things: her own product line. Following her dream, she decided to manufacture darts. This was a popular game, and Beth knew that there was a growing demand for high-quality darts. She designed a dart that was made of space-age steel, machined to tight tolerances. The dart had an innovative design that allowed the tip to swivel one-sixteenth of an inch when it hit the dart board wires. She wanted to manufacture a wide variety of darts with

From a historical perspective, there is a tendency to associate different eras with economic sectors and products that then dominated U.S. business. The 1800s were, for example, the age of the great American railroads. The late 1970s and 1980s are remembered as the eras in which service industries became central to the U.S. economy. As we move into the next century, we will look back and refer to the present as part of the information economy.

According to the principle known as Moore's law, at any given price level, microchips, the building blocks for the "brains" of a computer, double in performance every 18 months. As computers become more powerful, they also become less expensive. Advances in hardware lead to even more impressive and usable software, which, in turn, leads to increased communication capability.

With the ability to easily communicate between computers, networks may be created. A network consists of software for linking up multiple users at different locations. The term *information superhighway* refers to the linking of a large number of such networks. The applications of such capabilities in our businesses, schools, and personal lives are almost limitless.

As of 1994, four major groups of networks were widely available: Inter-Net, America Online, Prodigy, and Compuserve. Each has its own unique features; what they share in common is the ability to move data efficiently from one person to another.

different weights, styles, flights, and colors. In 1990 Beth invested $100,000 and bought one of the latest Japanese computer numerically controlled (CNC) lathes to make her dream come true right in her own machine shop.

Why did Beth decide to make darts? Perhaps she just enjoyed the game. Or perhaps she thought that she could make the product better and more cheaply than the existing suppliers. This seems rather unlikely, especially if the existing suppliers in the industry enjoyed the benefits of economies of scale in production. Beth could never compete on cost with an established manufacturer that was operating much further down the average total cost curve. Perhaps from a strategic (long-run) perspective, Beth thought that she could enter the industry with a superior product, learn how to compete quickly, take market share from existing producers, and grow larger and more profitable over time.

Firm Entry and Exit

Historically, small firms played an important role in industrial evolution. Alfred Marshall described this process of industry evolution by analogy, where one can observe "the young trees of the forest as they struggle upwards through the benumbing shade of their older rivals."[17] Marshall's view of industry dynamics is not so different from the prevalent view held by most economists studying industrial organization today.

Under the assumption that individual firms have identical U-shaped long-run average cost functions, a unique size distribution of firms exists for each industry. The number of firms would be determined by the number required to equate supply and demand, and changes in demand or factor prices would lead to entry or

---

[17]Alfred Marshall, *Principles of Economics* (London: Macmillan, 1920), p. 263.

exit, *but never both together*. As shown in Figure 14.4[18] when price P_2 is above *ATC*, existing firms in the industry earn economic profits and entry takes place. At price P_1, price is below *ATC* and firms in the industry do not cover the opportunity cost of capital and exit the industry.

However, this does not adequately explain reality. Between 1980 and 1986, the number of manufacturing establishments in the United States increased 38,000 from 448,000 to 486,000. On average, the increase was just slightly more than one percentage point per year in the number of establishments.

However, when the number of gross entry rather then net entry is examined, a considerably different picture emerges. Between 1980 and 1986, 205,000 new manufacturing establishments entered, representing a gross entry rate of 45.8 percent. At the same time, 173,000 such establishments exited from manufacturing, resulting in an exit rate of 38.6 percent.[19] In other words, what we see is that manufacturing is characterized by a high rate of simultaneous entry and exit. What is the explanation for this?

Much of entry of new firms is not about business as usual. Rather, the entrant is betting that she can do better than the incumbents by doing something differently. Thus, there are two fundamental functions of entry: (1) as the traditional model described earlier implies, entry serves to erode excess profits by increasing the amount of output in the market, effectively driving market price down and (2) entry serves as a driver of change; that is, entrants are engaging in innovative ac-

---

[18]In Figure 14.4, the equation for the *ATC* function is $ATC = 0.0048*Q_2 - 0.48*Q + 20$.
[19]U.S. Small Business Administration, *Small Business Data Base* (Washington, D.C.: 1980–1986).

Figure 14.4 Traditional Cost Structure and Entry

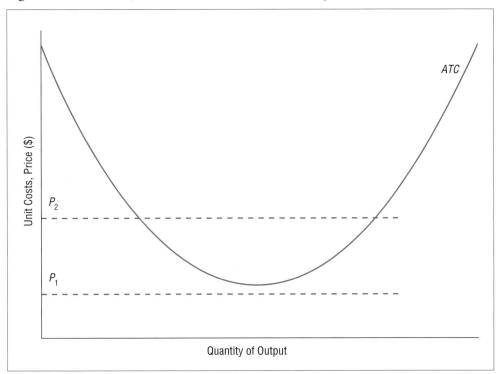

360

Part V
*Organization
Structure
as a Dynamic
Process*

**Innovation: Attempts
at Change**

tivity. The first function of entry is essentially equilibrating in nature; it restores the market back to the long-run equilibrium profit rate and price. The second function of entry is basically disequilibrating in nature and much more interesting to us.

To the extent that innovation causes both entry and change, it embodies Schumpeter's notion of creative destruction: for economic progress to take place, some of the existing organizations and institutions must be destroyed.

The extent to which firms are able to engage in innovative entry is determined to some extent by the type of information available to market incumbents and potential newcomers. Organizational economists speak of two types of regimes. An **entrepreneurial regime** is favorable to innovative entry but unfavorable to innovative activity by established firms. A **routinized regime** is unfavorable to innovative entry but favorable to innovative activity by established firms.

Assume that there are two different sources of information about new product technology. Also assume that information about new products is available from incumbent firms and firms outside the industry. The first information source is the product of experience and contains both transferable and nontransferable components. The accumulated stock of nontransferable information is the result of experience—learning by doing—and is not available to firms outside the industry. The greater the role played by the accumulated stock of nontransferable information, the greater will be the extent to which innovative activity emanates from the major incumbents.

By contrast, entry and growth by outside firms are encouraged when the second source of innovation-producing information is relatively more important. Under these conditions favorable to an entrepreneurial regime, information created outside the industry cannot be easily transferred to those firms existing within the industry; perhaps because of organizational factors, the holders of such knowledge must enter the industry to exploit the market value (appropriate the rents) of their knowledge.

The technological regime itself may be related to the **product life cycle.** The most complete version of the product life cycle describes four stages: introduction, growth, maturity, and decline. In the introduction phase, when the product is new, sales are increasing as is the rate of increase. In the growth phase, sales volume is still increasing, but the rate of growth is no longer increasing. Once the industry has evolved to the mature stage, sales are no longer increasing but have, for the most part, flattened at some sustainable level. Finally, in the last phase sales volume is declining.

To fully appreciate the life-cycle interpretation of innovation, we must consider separately process and product innovation. **Product innovation** refers to the design and creation of new products; it is possibly achieved by both existing firms and newcomers. It is the most competitive and risky type of innovation. Process innovation begins to occur in the second stage of the product life cycle and continues into the third. **Process innovation** refers to a refinement of production techniques, enabling cheaper production and distribution.

The amount of research and development (R&D) needed to enter the industry is relatively low during the earliest life-cycle stage and then subsequently rises until the product has been fully standardized. At the same time, however, the uncertainty associated with R&D is greater during the earliest phase before the product is standardized and then subsequently declines as the industry evolves toward maturity. Thus, the cost of innovation as a means of entry is relatively low during the early life-cycle stage but subsequently rises as the industry evolves toward maturity. Thus, the cost of innovation as a means of entry is relatively low during the early life-cycle stage but subsequently rises as the industry evolves toward maturity

An implication of this is that under the routinized regime, the source of innovation-producing knowledge tends to emanate from R&D laboratories of firms within the industry. This in not likely to be the case under the entrepreneurial regime. However, this is not to suggest the innovation-producing knowledge is unrelated to R&D under the entrepreneurial regime; rather, the knowledge is more likely to emanate from R&D laboratories outside the industry entered by the new firm.

This evolutionary view of markets suggests a considerably different economic function for entrants: agents of change. That is, by producing different products or employing different production techniques than the incumbent firms, entrants serve as a mechanism by which markets change over time.

**Innovation in Chips:
An Example**

This process of innovation can be illustrated in the semiconductor industry. The semiconductor industry began with a series of basic technological breakthroughs by a team of scientists led by William Shockley and Gordon Teal at Bell Laboratories in the early 1950s. Just as Teal departed Bell Labs in 1951 to join the fledgling Texas Instruments, Shockley left three years later to start his own firm. In 1957, eight of Shockley's former employees attracted enough venture capital to form Fairchild Semiconductor. The formation of Fairchild and the subsequent wave of entrepreneurial spin-offs fueled by venture capital proved to be one of the major catalysts underlying the formation of Silicon Valley.

As key employees developed their own specialized knowledge, they frequently left their employer and started their own firm to exploit the market value of their innovation(s).

Of the 23 semiconductor producers in Silicon Valley in 1971, 21 were started by former employees of Fairchild. By the middle of the 1970s, Fairchild had produced 41 high-tech entrepreneurial spin-offs. Table 14.1 lists the entrants into the semiconductor industry during this phase of the industry's development (1966 to 1976). Particularly noteworthy is the high concentration of entrants emanating from Fairchild that are found in the Silicon Valley area. Most of the start-ups were based on new technology and were founded by management and technical personnel from existing firms. At this early stage of the product life cycle, there was little product standardization.

By the mid-1970s, a new stage in the industry's development had been reached with the development of large-scale integration. With the introduction of the microprocessor by Intel in 1971, electronic systems began to be replaced with components. This led to the integration of computer firms into the world market. Toward the end of the 1970s, the semiconductor industry experienced a marked metamorphosis. Market share began to depend less on radical product innovation and more on the development of manufacturing techniques essential in the mass production of the more elaborate chips.

By the late 1980s with the industry concentrated in the hands of a few large firms, it was again ripe for entry by new firms that were innovating and competing with the large firms.

Entrepreneurship

During the early and mid-1980s, a new breed of corporate leader emerged as a powerful agent in bringing about change in U.S. industry. A discussion of the changing industrial structure of the United States would not be complete without at least mention of these people and the companies they started,[20] which is pre-

---

[20]The material in this section is based largely on "The New Corporate Elite," *Business Week*, January 25, 1985.

Table 14.1 Parentage in the U.S. Semiconductor Industry, 1966–1976

Year	Company	City[a]	Previous Employers of Founders
1966	American Microsystems	Cupertino	Philco-Ford (4)
	National Semiconductors	Santa Clara	Fairchild (3)
1968	Intersil	Sunnyvale	Union Carbide (3)
1969	Communications Transistor	San Carlos	National Semiconductor (3)
	Monolithic Memories	Santa Clara	IBM (1)
	Mostek	Carrollton, Tex.	Texas Instruments
	Signetics Memory Systems	Sunnyvale	Signetics (2), IBM (2), Hewlett-Packard (1)
	Advanced Micro Devices	Sunnyvale	Fairchild (8)
	Spectronics	Richardson, Tex.	Texas Instruments
	Four Phase	Cupertino	Fairchild (6), General Instruments (2)
1970	Litronix	Cupertino	Monsanto (1)
	Integrated Electronics	Mountain View	Fairchild (2)
	Varadyne	Mountain View	Fairchild (2)
1971	Exar	Sunnyvale	Signetics (3)
	Micropower	Santa Clara	Intersil (2)
	Standard Microsystems	Hauppague, NY	Four Phase (1), Electro-Nuclear Labs (1)
1972	Interdesign	Sunnyvale	Signetics (1)
1974	Synertek	Santa Clara	CMI (3), AMI (4), Fairchild (1)
	Zilog	Cupertino	Intel (2)
1975	Maruman	Sunnyvale	National Semiconductor (2)
1976	Supertex	Sunnyvale	Fairchild (1)

[a] Unless otherwise noted, the city is in California.

Source: U.S. Senate, Committee on Commerce, Science, and Transportation, 1978, *Industrial Technology*. Washington, D.C.: U.S. Government Printing Office, 1978, p. 91.

sented in Table 14.2. Many of the names in Table 14.2 are well-known today. What is spectacular about each of them is the impact they had in reshaping the way business is done in the United States. Some of those listed in Table 14.2 remain with their companies, but many have since changed industries or careers. What is truly amazing is that the innovations each individual made in the 1980s were considered drastic. Today, these changes are taken for granted.

Prior to 1980, American Telephone and Telegraph Co. held a monopoly on telephone services in the United States and was also perhaps the world's largest corporation. Sensing a definite change in the regulatory environment, William G. McGowan founded MCI and found tremendous success in doing so. MCI's move, and its success, started a revolution in the telecommunications industry in which competitive pressures encouraged lower customer costs and widely expanded services.

Joel Hyatt also caused a revolution, but in a different industry, the legal profession. Mr. Hyatt sought to reorganize the provision of legal services and greatly succeeded and helped usher in competitive pressures on the legal profession. A whole market for the low-cost overnight delivery of letters and packages was tapped by the innovative approach taken by Frederick W. Smith at Federal Express. Today it is very hard to imagine a world in which overnight delivery was available only through the U.S. Postal Service and at a cost that was high relative to today's standards.

Table 14.2	Corporate Elite of the 1980s

High-Tech Industries

James Coulker Contraves Goerz

Edson D. de Castro founder and president, Data General

William G. Gates III cofounder and chairman, Microsoft

Steven P. Jobs cofounder and chairman, Apple Computer

Sandra L. Kurtzig founder, Ask Computer Systems

Regis McKenna president, Regis McKenna

William C. Norris founder and chairman, Control Data, Inc.

Robert M. Noyce cofounder and vice-chairman, Intel

David Packard founder and chairman, Hewlett-Packard

H. Ross Perot founder, Electronic Data Systems

W. J. "Jerry" Sanders III founder, Advanced Micro Devices

Ray Stata CEO, Analog Devices

An Wang founder and CEO, Wang Laboratories

C. Norman Winnignstad founder and chairman, Floating Point Systems

John A. Young president and CEO, Hewlett-Packard

Service Industries

Donald C. Burr founder and chairman, People Express Airlines

Donald E. Guinn chairman and CEO, Pacific Telesis Group

Joel Z. Hyatt founder and senior partner, Hyatt Legal Services

David A. Jones cofounder, CEO, and chairman, Humana

J. Willard Marriott Jr. president and CEO, Mariott

Robert F. McDermott chairman, U.S. Auto Association

William G. McGowan founder and chairman, MCI Communications

Frederick W. Smith founder and chairman, Federal Express

R. David Thomas founder and senior chairman, Wendy's International

Financial Rearrangers

Herbert A. Allen, Jr. president, Allen & Co.

Sid Bass president and CEO, Bass Brothers Enterprises

T. Boone Pickens chairman and president, Mesa Petroleum

Source: Reprinted from January 25, 1985, issue of *Business Week* by special permission, copyright © 1985 by McGraw-Hill, Inc.

The actions of some of the people listed in Table 14.2 affected U.S. society in ways other than improved products at lower costs. T. Boone Pickens was an early player in the stock market boon of the 1980s, excelling as a corporate raider. In 1992, H. Ross Perot started a third U.S. political party to challenge the established Republicans and Democrats. The party carried no states in 1992; however, it won 17 percent of the popular vote.

SHIFT IN THE SIZE DISTRIBUTION OF ORGANIZATIONS

The view that the cornerstone of the modern economy is the large firm dates back to the onset of the (first) Industrial Revolution. Several lines of research have found that something happened to the centuries-old trend toward larger business;

Table 14.3 Small-Firm Share of Manufacturing Employment and Shift Over Time

Country	Year	Small Firm[a] Employment Share (%)	Year	Small Firm Employment Share (%)	Percentage Change
United Kingdom	1986	39.9	1979	30.1	9.8
Federal Republic of Germany	1987	57.9	1970	54.8	3.1
United States	1987	35.2	1976	33.4	1.9
The Netherlands[b]	1986	39.9	1978	36.1	3.8
Portugal	1986	71.8	1982	68.3	3.5
Italy[c]					
North	1987	55.2	1981	44.3	10.9
South	1987	68.4	1981	61.4	7.0
Czechoslovakia	1988	1.4	1954	13.0	−11.6
Poland[c]	1985	10.0	1937	33.0	−23.0

[a] A *small firm* is defined as an enterprise with fewer than 500 employees, unless designated otherwise.
[b] For the Netherlands, a *small firm* is defined as an enterprise with fewer than 100 employees.
[c] In the data for Poland and Italy, a *small firm* is defined as an enterprise with fewer than 200 employees.

Source: Zoltan J. Acs and David B. Audretch, *Small Firms and Entrepreneurship: An East-West Perspective*. New York: Cambridge University Press, 1993, Table 12.1. Reprinted with the permission of Cambridge University Press.

depending on the measure of business size examined, the trend decelerated, ceased, or reversed itself sometime between the late 1960s and the late 1970s.[21]

This shift in the size distribution of firms has occurred in the manufacturing sector of virtually every developed Western country. The magnitude of this shift varies considerably among nations, but the direction does not. As shown in Table 14.3, the shift ranges from an increase of 1.9 percent in the small-firm employment share in the United States between 1976 and 1986 to an increase of 10.9 percent between 1981 and 1987 in the north of Italy and to an increase of 9.8 percent between 1976 and 1986 in the United Kingdom.

There is a temptation to attribute this relative increase in the number of small firms and in small-firm employment to the obvious long-term transition of employment into services and out of the manufacturing sector. As we saw in Chapter 1, employment in U.S. manufacturing fell from 27 percent of the total workforce in 1977 to 17 percent of the workforce in 1991.

In fact, the shift in economic activity from large to small firms has been greater in manufacturing firms than in services or finance companies. As shown in Table 14.4 the small-firm share of employment is growing faster in the goods-producing sector—mining, construction, and manufacturing—than for other sectors of the economy. The small-firm share of employment declined in every major sector between 1958 and 1977. However, between 1976 and 1986, the small-firm share of employment increased in the goods-producing sectors and decreased in the other three sectors, as shown in Table 14.4.

The Survey of Manufacturers by the U.S. Bureau of the Census can be used to examine the extent to which plant size has increased or decreased within each manufacturing industry. As shown in Table 14.5, the percentage change in plant size can be measured by employment and value added, which serves as a measure

[21]Gary Loveman and Warner Sengenberger, "The Re-Emergence of Small Scale Production: An International Comparison," *Small Business Economics* 3, no. 1 (1991), pp. 1–39.

Table 14.4 Change of Employment in Small Firms[a] by Industry, 1958–1986

Industry	Percentage Change 1958–1977	Percentage Change 1976–1986
Mining	−16.8	7.8
Construction	−4.4[b]	3.5
Manufacturing	−8.2	1.8
Wholesale trade	−5.3	−0.8
Retail trade	−10.3	−7.5
Services	−8.4	−3.2

[a] Firms with fewer than 500 employees.
[b] For the construction industry, the early period is limited to 1967–1977 due to lack of data availability.
   Source: 1958–1977, U.S. Census Bureau, U.S. Enterprise Statistics for 1958–1977, as reported in Small Business Administration, 1984, table A2–24; 1976–1986: Small Business Administration, unpublished tabulations, 1987.

Table 14.5 Changes in Average Plant Size for U.S. Manufacturing Industries, 1979–1984

SIC Code	Industry Name	Employment	Value Added
	All Manufacturing Industries	−17.8%	−11.8%
20	Food and Kindred Products	−9.1	18.1
21	Tobacco Products	4.4	31.1
22	Textile Mill Products	−14.2	0.6
23	Apparel and Other Textiles	−12.1	4.1
25	Furniture and Fixtures	−16.6	−2.4
26	Paper and Allied Products	−6.7	2.6
27	Printing and Publishing	−11.8	−6.2
28	Chemicals and Allied Products	−12.6	−5.8
29	Petroleum and Coal	−15.4	−67.2
30	Rubber, Misc. Plastics	−19.9	1.4
31	Leather	−21.1	−1.5
32	Stone, Clay, and Glass	−17.4	−17.3
33	Primary Metals	−33.8	−29.1
341	Metal Cans, Shipping	−15.2	−18.4
344	Fabricated Structural Metal	−24.0	−22.7
349	Misc. Fabricated Metal	−26.7	−21.5
354	Metalworking Machinery	−27.3	−30.0
357	Office and Computing Machines	−27.7	−9.4
362	Electrical Industrial Apparatus	−28.2	−21.4
363	Household Appliances	−12.1	−2.4
364	Electrical Lighting and Wiring	−9.8	−10.3
365	Radio, TV Equipment	−26.7	32.5
366	Communication Equipment	−5.7	11.5
371	Motor Vehicles and Equipment	−28.0	−8.2
372	Aircraft and Parts	−20.4	−29.0
374	Railroad Equipment	−55.6	−63.6
376	Guided Missiles, Space Vehicles	23.5	31.0

   Source: U.S. Department of Commerce, Bureau of the Census, *Annual Survey of Manufacturers*. Washington, DC: U.S. Government Printing Office, 1979 and 1984.

"[t]hat the British tend to manufacture relatively standard products in long runs . . . German . . . manufacturers, by contrast produce a great variety of high quality goods in small batches. . . . Surprisingly enough, this strategy has involved no apparent sacrifice in productivity efficiency—German output per employee is roughly twice that in the U.K."

Paul Geroski, Sloan Management Review, *1990.*

"Despite ever-larger and noisier mergers, the biggest change coming over the world of business is that firms are getting smaller. The trend of a century is being reversed. Until the mid-1970s the size of firms everywhere grew; the number of self-employed fell. Ford and General Motors replaced the carriage-maker's atelier; McDonald's, Safeway, and W. H. Smith supplanted the corner shop. No longer. Now it is the big firms that are shrinking and small ones that are on the rise. The trend is unmistakable—and businessmen and policy-makers will ignore it at their peril."

"The Rise and Rise of America's Small Firms," The Economist, *January 21, 1989, pp. 73–74. © 1989 The Economist Newspaper Group, Inc. Reprinted with permission. Further reproduction prohibited*

of output. The number of employees per plant declined by about 18 percent in manufacturing between 1979 and 1984. Over the same period, value added per plant also declined by 12 percent. With a single exception, in the tobacco industry, the mean plant employment size declined in every two-digit Standard Industry Classification (SIC) category.[22]

◼ CHAPTER SUMMARY AND KEY IDEAS ◼ ◼ ◼ ◼ ◼ ◼

The existing structure and perceived boundaries of firms and the industries into which they are organized depend crucially on the prevailing environment and available technologies. In this chapter, we discussed their impact on industries in a historical perspective. The emergence of flexible production technologies presents a break point, or industrial divide, in the organization of U.S. industries and exerts an influence on organizations and industries that will be felt for decades.

The adoption of flexible production techniques, nearly continuous technological advances, and greater computerization led to many organizational changes best considered using the tools we developed in Part II. Most noticeably, these three advances caused firms to rely on outside suppliers and partnerships. Investment decisions held large amounts of risks for firms. If a firm purchased equipment that later proved to be different from what emerged as a technological standard, the firm could encounter difficulties in obtaining complementary goods such as spare parts, improvements, or software. Further, given that the technologies were rapidly changing, firms may have been reluctant to invest in equipment that they knew little about. Reliance on an outside supplier would shift most of

---

[22]Bo Carlsson, David B. Audretsch, and Zoltan J. Acs, "Flexible Technology and Plant Size: U.S. Manufacturing and Metalworking Industries," *International Journal of Industrial Organization*, 1994.

this risk completely to another party; identification of a suitable party for a joint venture would eliminate the risk.

Fewer but better-trained workers are required on the factory floor of the flexible producer, and the acquisition of firm-specific human capital is much more pronounced. More often than not, these workers are trained in a variety of tasks and are empowered to make certain decisions. In many organizations, the need for middle managers is sharply reduced because line workers at factories can report directly to top management.

▓ KEY TERMS

computer-aided design (CAD)
computer-aided manufacturing (CAM)
computer numerical control (CNC)
consumption complementarities
consumption externalities
Detroit automation
differentiated products
economies of scale
economies of scope
entrepreneurial regime
external contract
firm
flexible manufacturing system (FMS)
globalization
horizontal integration
industrial divide

industrial robot
Information Age
internal contract
internationalization
multidivisional firm
network systems
numerically controlled (NC) machines
process innovation
product innovation
product life cycle
routinized regime
scientific management
small-batch production
Taylorism
transfer machines
vertical integration
x-inefficiency

▓ FURTHER READINGS

Acs, Z. J. *The Changing Structure of the U.S. Economy*. New York: Praeger, 1984.

———. "Small Firms and Economic Growth." De Vries Lecture, Erasmus University, 1994 .

———, and D. B. Audretsch. "The Restructuring of U.S. Markets." *Wissenschaftszentrum fur Sozialforschung*, January 1986.

———. *Innovation and Small Firms*. Cambridge, Mass.: MIT Press, 1990.

———, and D. B. Audretsch. *Small Firms and Entrepreneurship: An East-West Perspective*. Cambridge: Cambridge University Press, 1993.

Beson, S. M., and J. Farrell. "Choosing How to Compete: Strategies and Tactics in Standardization." *Journal of Economic Perspectives*, Spring 1994, pp. 117–132.

Carlsson, B., D. B. Audretsch, and Z. J. Acs. "Flexible Technology and Plant Size: U.S. Manufacturing and Metalworking Industries," *International Journal of Industrial Organization*, 1994, pp. 359–372.

Chandler, A. *The Visible Hand: The Managerial Revolution in America*. Cambridge, Mass.: The Bellknap Press of Harvard University 1977.

Jovanovic, B. "Selection and Evolution of Industry." *Econometrica*, May 1982, pp. 649–670.

Katz, M. L., and C. Shapiro. "Systems Competition and Network Effects," *Journal of Economic Perspectives*, Spring 1994, pp. 93–116.

Liebowitz, S. J., and S. E. Margolis. "Network Externality: An Uncommon Tragedy," *Journal of Economic Perspectives*, Spring 1994, pp. 118–133.

Loveman, G., and W. Sengenberger. "The Re-Emergence of Small Scale Produc-

368

Part V
*Organization
Structure
as a Dynamic
Process*

tion: An International Comparison." *Small Business Economics* 3, no. 1 (1991), pp. 1–39.

Marshall, A. *Principles of Economics*. London: Macmillan, 1920.

Milgrom, P., and J. Roberts. *Economics, Organization and Management*. Englewood Cliffs, N.J.: Prentice Hall, 1991.

Nelson, R., and S. Winter. *An Evolutionary Theory of Economic Change*. Cambridge, Mass.: Harvard University Press, 1982.

Piore, M., and C. Sable. *The Second Industrial Divide*: *Prospects for Prosperity*. New York: Basic Books, 1984.

Porter, M. *The Competitive Advantage of Nations*. New York: Free Press, 1990.

Reich, R. B. *The Work of Nations*. New York: Knopf, 1992.

Schumpeter, J. *Capitalism, Socialism and Democracy*. New York: Harper & Row, 1950.

QUESTIONS AND PROBLEMS FOR REVIEW AND DISCUSSION

A. This chapter has discussed the factors important to the emergence of mass production. Consider these once again in terms of whether some were on the demand side and some were on the supply side. List and fully explain three factors that were on the demand side. List and fully explain three (separate) factors that were on the supply side.

B. We have also discussed the factors important to the downfall of mass production. Consider these once again in terms of whether some were on the demand side and some were on the supply side. List and fully explain three (separate) factors that were on the demand side. List and fully explain three (separate) factors that were on the supply side.

Core Competencies, Organization, and Strategy

Manufacturing is undergoing a revolution. The mass production model is being replaced by a version of a flexible multiproduct firm that emphasizes quality and speedy response to market conditions while utilizing technologically advanced equipment and new forms of organization.[1]

![] CHAPTER OUTLINE AND STUDENT GOALS ![]

The key lesson of the previous chapter is clearly that changes in the business environment have radically, and forever, altered the relationships that must be forged between and among firms, their workers, their suppliers, and their customers. On the demand side, competition is driving producers to provide innovative, high-quality, and very specialized goods and services. On the supply side, dramatic developments have taken place in the tools and methods available to producers. If there were a real-life Rip Van Winkle who had fallen asleep in 1960, on his awakening today, he would be amazed not only at the goods and services available but also at the way in which they are produced and sold in our marketplaces.

A great parallel was drawn in the previous chapter between the emergence of America's great mass-producing firms earlier this century and the emergence of flexible production today. In both cases, the drivers of change were environmental transformations on both the demand and supply side. As the technological foundations and marketplace dynamics were revolutionized, three things happened: some firms simply went out of business, unwilling or unable to successfully respond; new firms were created to take advantage of evolving opportunities; and existing firms were forced to restructure.

In this chapter, we move our analysis into the organizations of today and analyze the actions, alternatives, and strategies of today's successful firms that either evolved under or were born into the new business environment. We by no means want to imply that the metamorphosis of business is complete. Product and process innovations will likely continue, bringing even more changes in organization structures. Advances on the information technology front alone will probably easily eclipse today's machines. Recall Moore's law from Chapter 14: the cost of the most powerful computer chip available today will buy double that power in 18 months.

To survive and prosper in the new economy of the Information Age, firms have had to completely rethink the strategies that worked in the past. In the 1700s, Adam Smith, the father of modern economics, lectured on the importance of the gains

---

[1]John Milgrom and Paul Roberts, "The Economics of Modern Manufacturing: Technology, Strategy, and Organization," *American Economic Review* 80 (1990), pp. 511–528.

370

Part V
*Organization
Structure
as a Dynamic
Process*

from specialization. In Chapter 1 some of the painful lessons learned on specialization by major firms and industries were recounted.

The first aspect of modern manufacturing strategy is for the firm to position itself in the global marketplace and discover what it is best at. In a dynamic environment, a firm's capacity to innovate, to introduce new products quickly, and to manufacture them efficiently can be even more important than economies of scale.

The second aspect of the strategy prevailing in today's organizations is rebuilding the factory from scratch: introducing *flexible manufacturing systems, robots, computer-controlled machine tools, quality control equipment*, and much more. It also involves upgrading the labor force from semiskilled workers to a much more broadly educated workforce. The strength of the labor force in the Information Age lies in the fact that its firm-specific human capital is complementary to the physical capital used by firms.

The third aspect of this strategy is restructuring the organization itself. Much modern manufacturing technology cannot be fully exploited in yesterday's hierarchical organizations. Piecemeal changes are not enough; a complete overhaul of organizations is necessary. Many firms began this process (either wittingly or not) in the early 1990s, which usually and unfortunately involved a downsizing as described in Chapter 13.

In this chapter, we present a simplified version of a theoretical model developed by two economists from Stanford University, Paul Milgrom and John Roberts; the model addresses the issue of how the modern manufacturing firm should be organized. Theory suggests that (1) over an extended time period an organization should not have substantial volumes of both highly flexible and highly specialized equipment being used side by side; (2) because of complementarities, it is relatively unprofitable to adopt only one part of a modern manufacturing strategy when the other components have barely begun to be put into place; and (3) a flatter organization is better suited to modern manufacturing technology than a vertically integrated one.

The job of management in organizations is to ensure coordination. The survival and success of an organization crucially depends on effectively coordinating actions of the many individuals and subgroups in the organization. Managers must make sure that they all are focusing their efforts on carrying out a feasible plan of action that promotes the organization's goals and ensures that the plans are adjusted appropriately to remain feasible and appropriate as circumstances change.

After reading this chapter, you should be able to

- Explain why organization is important.
- Explain what organizational economists mean when they use the term *organizational strategy*.
- Provide a brief intuitive explanation of what is meant by *manufacturing strategy*.
- Explain what core competencies are.
- Explain the importance of complementarities in production as they impact various activities conducted by modern organizations.

■ INTERNATIONALIZATION, ORGANIZATION, AND COMPETITIVENESS

On November 9, 1989, the Berlin Wall collapsed and for the first time in nearly half a century, East Germany felt the winds of economic competition. This formerly communist nation must compete not only with West Germany but also with the United States, Japan, the four Tigers of Asia, and the whole developing world. Almost overnight, East Germany had to contend with a system of world prices for almost every known commodity from oil to bananas—prices that were absent in its former economic systems.

Production in East Germany was organized in large combines designed to emulate the large U.S. mass-producing firms that were successful when the blueprint for the Eastern European economies was created in the 1940s. The purpose of these economies was simple: take advantage of economies of scale. A deep underlying adherence to the principle that significant economies of scale can be reaped from large-scale production was embedded in the socialist world. Large units of production were viewed as the most efficient means to transform inputs into outputs, and any deviation from mass production was viewed socially and politically as a wasteful use of resources.

The economies of Eastern Europe face great problems in moving to a more market-oriented system. They need to redraft laws to allow for new forms of economic organizations and to determine property rights and who will be allowed to own the currently state-owned enterprises. These economies must find managers to run their enterprises and make decisions concerning competition and regulation policies.

For the first time since the end of World War II, the countries of Eastern Europe had to be concerned about competitiveness. *Competitiveness* is a popular term applied to a country's ability to compete with the rest of the world. In effect, in this case it refers to the ability to produce goods and services more efficiently than other countries for export.

In terms of a national economy, competitiveness is usually associated with certain industries or sets of them. For example, in the United States, competitiveness is usually associated with such industries as automobiles, semiconductors, aircraft, and agricultural goods and with certain services. When a country's industries are unable to compete internationally, organizations in that industry must be restructured to make them more competitive.[2] To put it differently, organization is an important aspect of competitiveness.

During Poland's communist era, the national shipbuilding industry was dominated by six shipyards.[3] The market served by the Polish shipyards was primarily determined by political forces, not competitive ones. The Polish shipyards' major customers were Eastern Bloc countries, particularly the former Soviet Union. The government's influence on shipbuilding operations was pervasive. The incentives faced by the communist managers at the Polish shipyards led them to be far more concerned with size and versatility than with product focus or cost control. By producing a variety of ships, they were unable to develop world-class expertise or manufacturing efficiency for any one particular model.

As a result of the collapse of the Soviet Union, government funding was withdrawn from state-owned enterprises throughout the region, and Eastern European shipping companies could no longer afford to buy ships produced in the Polish yards. By 1990, the shipyards' primary client, the Soviet Union, was in a state of economic disarray. The central government was bankrupt, and the country had

A Tale
of Two Shipyards

---

[2]When a country cannot compete internationally, it may use macroeconomic policies to increase competition. For example, lowering the value of the currency could stimulate exports by lowering their prices in other currencies. The United States pursued this policy in the early 1990s. Another example is the establishment of tariffs and other barriers to imports.
[3]This section is adapted from S. Johnson and G. Loveman, *Starting Over* (Cambridge, Mass: Harvard University Press, 1994), ch 1.

372

Part V
*Organization
Structure
as a Dynamic
Process*

been transformed into a conglomeration of republics. The disappearance of the Soviet market resulted in the demise of Comecon, perhaps the largest of Poland's six shipyards and wreaking output declines and staggering financial setbacks at Gdansk and Szchecin, two of Poland's larger shipyards.

The responses to this changing environment by the managers of the Gdansk and Szchecin shipyards were quite different. We briefly consider each. Important lessons on managing economic organizations can be gained by considering their responses to a changing environment.

The Gdansk Shipyard. Supported by government subsidies and Soviet clients, the 146-acre Gdansk shipyard in the 1970s was a self-contained industrial city. With a workforce of 17,000, the yard produced more than 30 ships a year. Its product portfolio was extraordinarily diverse. The yard not only assembled ships but also manufactured almost all internal components and even served as a supplier of diesel engines and boilers to other Polish shipyards. In other words, there was very little available in terms of outside suppliers; the highly vertically integrated structure encouraged by government pretty much precluded their existence.

In 1990, the Polish government and the Ministry of Industry recommended the privatization of the shipyard. Management continued to pursue a high-wage, high-employment managerial policy very similar to that used in the 1970s. New management was reluctant to make rapid reductions in the size of the shipbuilding operation. Moreover, management focused on a strategy of increasing revenues instead of profits because of the size of the facility. Fixed costs played a more important role than variable costs. The idea was that by simply producing more ships—that is, by increasing revenues—management would be able to spread the fixed cost over a larger production base, which would naturally increase the profitability of each project.

Because the plant was operating at less than full capacity, the idea was to build more ships, which was in line with management's reluctance to release labor. The high wages paid to workers were justified on the grounds that the work was demanding. The shipyard continued to operate a vast infrastructure of amenities for workers, including hotels, health spas, day care services, and a sports club.

The Gdansk management team argued that shipbuilding belonged within the realm of government rather than in the uncompromising world of a free market. It argued for a continuance of the government financial support it had received during the communist era. The shipyard had completed its contracts for ships ordered for the former Soviet Union, but they were never delivered because of the collapse of the Soviet economy. Gdansk management argued that the government should provide unlimited loans to cover the expenses incurred in building the ships for the reneged upon contracts. Moreover, they could not understand why the shipyard's main government contact had been with the Ministry of Privatization, not the Ministry of Industry.

The Gdansk management team believed that the shipyard would be unable to find investors. In sum, the new strategy for profitability was to build a complete product line, to focus on economies of scale, and to obtain government support. The only problem with this strategy was that although it had worked before, it was not consistent with the new environment facing the shipyard.

The Szchecin Shipyard. Events at the Szchecin shipyard closely mirrored those at the Gdansk shipyard prior to the introduction of economic reforms in Poland. However, the **restructuring** strategy pursued by Szchecin management resulted in fundamentally different operations and performance. Management pursued a strategy of reducing the company's massive debt and streamlining the yard's wasteful production operation by allowing the yard to pursue its core competency in container ships.

While trying to reduce debt, the company started to implement a sweeping change in production operations. The shipyard would try to become internationally competitive by deemphasizing its portfolio of products, minimizing its production cycle time, restructuring wages, and shifting markets from the East to the West. Management believed that it was important to develop a product niche with container ships.

This proved to be a wise choice. By 1993 almost all of the orders coming to Szchecin shipyard were for container ships. Once the product focus was set, management turned its attention to reducing the time required to build a single vessel. This strategy served two purposes. First, by reducing cycle time, the firm would have to borrow less money for shorter periods. Second, shorter production cycles would attract customers that needed ships to be delivered quickly, which was a growing population in the competitive marketplace. By restructuring the labor force, the firm was able to cut production time to less than a year.

A key component of management's strategy to reduce cycle time was to overhaul the shipyard's compensation system. A form of internal labor markets and teamwork was set up. Management assigned each shipyard worker to a professional qualification category that reflected occupational training and total years of work experience. An hourly wage was then assigned to employees in each qualification category, with higher wages allocated to more highly qualified workers. Employees could advance to higher qualification classes by passing a series of occupational exams. All workers were required to work eight hours per day, and no overtime was permitted.

The shipyard's production workers were divided into workers' brigades, each of which was directed by a supervisor and assigned specific tasks by shipyard management. Each job was carefully analyzed and a fixed number of hours were assigned. Workers' brigades were expected to complete their assignments within the time frame established by the engineering department. Tasks not finished in this specified time frame were completed on the worker's own time.

Besides restructuring its labor force, the Szchecin shipyard directed its marketing efforts westward, where there was a larger demand for container ships. By focusing on the single type of ship rather than on several types, the firm reaped gains from specialization and became even more efficient because of its larger experience base. Effectively, the Szchecin shipyard management chose to concentrate on building on what it identified as its core competency, container ships. Additionally, the shipyard cut nonproduction costs.

Gdansk and Szchecin embarked on the difficult path of restructuring with very different management strategies. The degree to which a restructured state-owned company can compete effectively in fiercely competitive international markets is perhaps the most important indication of the success of its restructuring program. By 1993, Szchecin shipyard had emerged as Poland's most successful shipbuilder. The success can be attributed to the firm's competitive advantage: container ship expertise, extraordinary rapid production cycle, and the relatively low cost of Polish labor.

■ THE ROLE OF MANAGEMENT IN COORDINATION

The study of organization is not about how boxes are arranged on a tree of authority but about how people are coordinated and motivated to get things done. Successful organizations share several features. Clearly, incentives are one important element. Another is the tendency to place authority for decisions in the hands of those individuals who have the relevant information. This practice encourages responsiveness and flexibility.

374

Part V
*Organization
Structure
as a Dynamic
Process*

Although delegating authority to those with the information needed to make good decisions is an important part of good organization design, it is of little use unless these decision makers share the organization's objectives. In the language of economics, incentives and delegated authority are complements: they are used together, and each makes the other more valuable. Evaluating complementarities—how the pieces of a successful organization fit together and how they fit with the company's strategy—is one of the most challenging and rewarding parts of organization analysis.

Strategic planning by organizations is a complex process that determines how the resources available to the firm should be allocated to best conduct the economic activity that the firm organizes. Strategic management therefore represents a drive for efficiency in organizations. The roles of management in encouraging efficiency are first to arrange the resources of the corporation in the best possible way and then to coordinate and motivate the pieces of the organization so that, as a whole, efficiency is maintained. **Organization strategy,** therefore, is a blueprint for accomplishing an efficient allocation of corporate resources.

A wide variety of inputs are available to managers to help determine the best strategic plan for their organization. Good strategic decision making virtually always requires that effective use be made of line managers' knowledge about how the operations actually work and what capabilities the business has. Additionally, decision making involves knowledge about the firm's environment in its industry: new technologies, new markets, new business partners, new forms of organization, and recent government regulations. Furthermore, strategic planning on an organizational scale also requires knowledge that is currently outside the organization.

We can characterize some of the problems faced in strategic decision making by the information available to the organization. Some aspects of the organizational puzzle have what organizational theorists call *design attributes*. Organizational problems have design attributes if two conditions hold. First, a great deal of information is available within the organization concerning the nature of the best organizational structure or optimal solution for the firm. Second, a small mistake made in specifying the solution can prove very costly because the effects of that mistake spread through the various activities of the firm. Other aspects of the organizational puzzle have what organizational theorists call *innovative attributes*, which occur when information concerning the best organization structure is not available within the organization.

Certain elements of fit are evidenced in a good strategy that recognizes both design and innovative decision attributes. The one common element in the solution to each of these types of problems involves sharing information throughout the organization. The **design attributes** involve spreading existing information. The **innovative attributes** involve one party in the organization acquiring the information from outside and distributing it within the organization. Only when the information is spread across the organization and all parties share a common view of the organization's goals can successful strategic planning be conducted.

When the strategic planning process is viewed as involving design and innovative attributes, two points become clear. First, all parties in an organization must be informed and their input considered. Second, all decision-making authorities must be encouraged to share a common viewpoint. Both of these factors point toward a centralized organizational structure on efficiency grounds. The use of prices (such as transfer prices) and other decentralized means of coordination will likely lead to a situation that is not manageable.

In our discussion of organizational strategy, we focus, for the most part, on the design attributes inherent in formulating strategy. Initially, we address two important design issues with which you already have some familiarity: economies of scale and economies of scope.

A good starting point for our discussion of design issues is with the concept of economies of scale. We developed this concept in Chapter 3. **Economies of scale** arise in the production of a good or service when average unit costs decline as output expands. Remember that returns to scale have to do with the slope of the long-run *ATC* curve. If long-run unit costs fall as output expands, we say that there are increasing returns to scale, or, more simply, economies of scale. Diseconomies of scale are said to exist if long-run average costs increase as output expands.

Within any given firm, two factors contribute to the presence of economies or diseconomies of scale. Within the context of production technology introduced in Chapter 3, some, or all, of the variable factors of production may be experiencing diminishing marginal productivity. This causes unit costs to change because, as additional units of variable inputs are added to the production process, costs (the numerator of average costs) increase at a constant rate and output (the denominator of average costs) increases at a decreasing rate. Average total costs also continuously change because of fixed costs: if fixed costs are large relative to variable costs, average total costs tend to decrease over a wide range of output.

If diseconomies of scale occur, any given increase in output can be obtained only by a proportionately larger increase in input usage. When production is characterized in this way, if demand is large, it is generally optimal to divide production among a number of smaller units to keep total costs relatively low. On the other hand, with economies of scale in production, efficiency generally dictates much larger plants or units.

For illustrative purposes, let's consider the case characterized by constant returns to scale. Constant returns to scale implies neither economies or diseconomies of scale; that is, any increase in output can be obtained by a proportionally equal increase in inputs. When production is characterized in this way, the slope of a firm's marginal cost function is zero, and marginal costs equal average variable costs at all levels of output. As shown in Figure 15.1,[4] the long-run average cost curve is a horizontal line at cost C_1. The minimum of each short-run average cost curve (representing plant sizes or number of plants in the industry) is tangent to the long-run average cost curve at all levels of output.[5]

When production results in economies of scale, the efficient level of output in a firm cannot be determined by prices alone. In that case, operational scale becomes a design variable. Depending on the volume of sales that a firm anticipates, it adjusts its production capacity, size of its sales force, order-processing technology, and administrative support offices accordingly. If the actions taken by the various departments of an organization are to be synchronized and harmonious, all of these units and individuals need a shared vision of the internal scale of operations. We would then say that the different groups in the organization are *coherent*.

---

[4]In Figure 15.1, the long-run average cost is a horizontal line at $Y = 1,030$. The first short-run cost function is $97*X^2/40 - 485*X + 25,280$. The second short-run cost function is $97*X^2/40 - 970*X + 98,030$. Some of the detail is lost because of the scaling of the vertical axis.

[5]At this point we should note that when the production function is homogeneous of degree 1, Elasticity = LAC/LMC is identical to unity. In this case, the elasticity of total cost is unity and the elasticity of average cost is zero. That is, total cost expands in the same proportion as output. The long-run average cost is consequently a horizontal line. Nonetheless, it is still the envelope of the U-shaped short-run average cost curves.

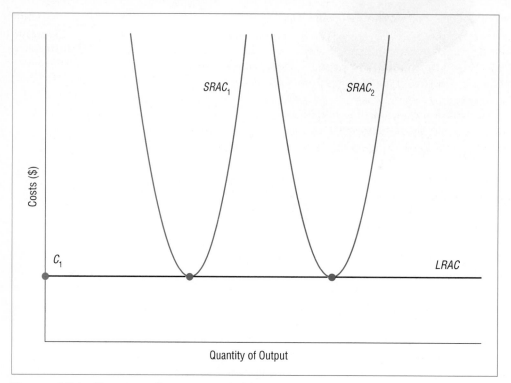

Figure 15.1 Constant Returns to Scale

Operational scale is a design variable because it meets two conditions. First, it has predictable implications for the various parts of the organization and, second, the cost of mistakes associated with incorrect perceptions of scale by other parts of the organization can be very high. By making sure that its managers share common expectations about what it is trying to do, the firm takes an important step toward coordinating its plans and behavior.

Most firms produce more than one good, choosing to produce a set of goods related in terms of their physical design or even sharing a common key component. **Economies of scope** exist in production if it is less expensive to produce a set of goods together than separately. The concept of economies of scope helps us understand why some firms often undertake different activities.

In the airline industry, most domestic carriers in the United States recognize that economies of scope exist in providing airline services. If scheduled flights converge in one city in a particular region in a hub and spoke pattern, certain economies of scope exist in serving other, smaller cities in that region. The economies of scope may arise in terms of reservations, scheduling, baggage handling, aircraft maintenance, advertising, and plane scheduling. Economies of scope are also apparent in industries more geared to production. General Motors and its divisions produce cars; they also produce trucks. The production of both cars and trucks relies on much the same technical expertise, shared components, and marketing know-how. Regarding the breakup of AT&T in the early 1980s, many economists argued against the breakup on the grounds that important economies of scope existed between local and long-distance telephone service and research in telecommunications.

From the managerial perspective, economies of scope offer both a blessing and a curse. On the positive side, even when a firm operates at an output too small to enjoy significant economies of scale for a single output, it may benefit from producing certain key components used in each of several products. On the negative side, economies of scope involve greater coordination within the multiproduct firm across its various product lines.

One of the basic building blocks in understanding international trade is the principle of **comparative advantage,** a concept that has much in common with the idea behind core competencies. Country A exports good X to Country B, which in turn exports good Y to Country A. At this point, every student knows why countries trade goods and services. The United States exports heavy construction machinery and computer programming services because it can produce them more cheaply than can other countries. Brazil and Colombia export coffee and cocaine because they are better at producing those things than, say, the United States and England. As heavy construction machinery becomes more advanced and powerful and as new blends of coffee are created, it is likely that the United States and Brazil (respectively) will continue to export these goods.

A similar concept exists for economic organizations: core competency. A key element in the "back-to-basics" movement involves having organizations identify their core competencies. The term **core competency** refers to an area of business in which an organization has a competitive advantage not only in producing a good or service but also in developing new and related products. It refers to the technological or organizational strength of the firm that allows it to do one thing cheaper, better, and faster than any other firm in the world and to build that one thing into a succession of high-quality, tailored products or services.

Core competencies affect corporate strategy as a problem that has both design and innovative attributes. In a dynamic environment, a firm's capacity to introduce new products and to manufacture them efficiently can be even more important than the economies of scale and scope it achieves in making its existing

MEASURING INNOVATIONS

Economists have begun measuring innovations in industry to understand both the process of innovation itself and the resulting changes in industry structures it helps to cause.

The process begins when firms spend money on research and development (R&D). The evidence indicates that the time lapse between expenditure and a new product brought to market varies greatly among innovations and across industries. On average, the time lag between R&D and innovation is about five years.

Empirical studies of this relationship focus on an equation such as the following one:

$$I_{i,t} = A \, \text{R\&D}^{\beta}_{i,t-5},$$

where $I_{i,t}$ represents innovations at firm i in period t; A is a mathematical constant; $\text{R\&D}_{i,t-5}$ is research and development spending at firm i in year $t-5$; and β is a parameter to be estimated and equals the elasticity of R&D spending (the percentage change in R&D divided by the percentage change in innovations).

β is interesting because it measures the sensitivity of the relationship. Most studies conclude that β is less than 1, meaning that as R&D increases the propensity to innovate increases at less than a proportional rate.

378

Part V
*Organization
Structure
as a Dynamic
Process*

product line. A strategy of developing scale and scope economies translates into one of *building the core competencies of a firm*. We saw the importance of this in the example concerning the Szchecin and Gdansk shipyards in Poland.

Recall from Chapter 7 that we introduced the concepts of **ex ante,** meaning before the fact, and **ex post,** meaning after the fact. The managerial challenges of core competencies are best illustrated by noting that core competency is an ex ante concept. When a firm is building core competencies to manufacture a set of products, it is doing so for a series of products that do not yet exist. In other words, *a firm is investing in key technologies, key people, and key machinery in a gamble that it can consistently develop a new product line*.

The notion of a core competency is an ex ante concept; we have to identify an ex post sign, or measure, proving that an organization indeed has a core competency in some line of business. Perhaps the best measure, after the fact, of a developed core competency is the number of innovations an organization produces.[6] We define **innovation** as a process that begins with an invention; proceeds by developing it; and results in introducing a new product, process, or service to the market. Innovation, thus defined, is a process that takes place over a period of time.

The ability to introduce a new product is not quite the same as the ability to manufacture the product in large quantities. The former is characterized as product innovation; the latter depends on process innovation. For example, a computer numerical control machine is a product innovation for the company that makes it. However, when a firm in Cleveland buys it to manufacture darts, it becomes a process innovation. The optical scanner was a product innovation for some company. As the product diffused throughout the economy from the supermarket checkout counter to the county library, it became a process innovation to reduce costs, ensure accuracy, and improve customer service for thousands of organizations.

As to **design decisions**, if rapid product innovation is important, a small firm may be much more efficient than a large firm in producing innovations (Table 15.1). Why would this be so? Factors favoring small firms with the innovative advantage generally emanate from the differences in management structures between large and small firms. The bureaucratic organization of large firms is not conducive to undertaking risky R&D. The decision to innovate must survive layers of bureaucratic resistance in which an inertia regarding risk results in a bias against undertaking new projects. However, the decision to innovate in the small firm is made by relatively few people. For example, Xerox Corporation invented the first personal computer. Its Palo Alto research center was lavishly funded, brilliantly staffed, yet Xerox, laden with bureaucracy, gained little from system after system that it invented first but did not capitalize on. The situation is much different in smaller firms where more flexibility exists and the decision to proceed with a proposed innovation is made by relatively few people.

The next design issue we are interested in is whether organizational design, other than size, makes a difference in the ability of firms to innovate frequently and continuously. In other words, is organizational design a key determinant of core competencies?

Table 15.2 compares the frequency of innovation for the 30 most innovative organizations in the United States in 1982 and provides three interesting observations. First, the distribution of innovations is apparently skewed, with a few firms making numerous innovations, and most firms contributing only several. This

---

[6]See Zoltan J. Acs and David B. Audretsch, "R&D, Firm Size and Innovative Activity," in *Innovation and Technical Change* (Ann Arbor: The University of Michigan Press, 1992).

Table 15.1 **Innovations in U.S. Manufacturing Industries, 1982**

Industry	Total Innovations	Small-Firm Innovations	Large-Firm Innovations
Electronic Computing Equipment	385	158	227
Process Control Instruments	161	68	93
Radio and TV Equipment	155	83	72
Pharmaceutical Preparations	133	120	13
Electronic Components	127	54	73
Engineering and Scientific Instruments	126	43	83
Semiconductors	120	91	29
Plastics Products	104	22	82
Photographic Equipment	88	79	9
Office Machinery	77	67	10
Electricity Measuring Instruments	75	28	47
Surgical Equipment	67	54	13
Surgical Instruments	66	30	36
Special Industry Machinery	64	43	21
Industrial Controls	61	15	46
Toilet Preparations	59	41	18
Valves and Pipe Fittings	53	20	33
Electric Housewares and Fans	53	47	6
Measuring, Control Devices	48	3	45
Food Products Machinery	49	37	12
Motors and Generators	49	39	10
Plastic Materials and Resins	45	30	15
Industrial Inorganic Chemicals	40	32	8
Radio, TV Receiving Sets	39	35	4
Hand and Edge Tools	38	27	11
Fabricated Platework	32	29	3
Fabricated Metal Products	29	12	17
Pumps and Pumping Equipment	34	18	16
Optical Instruments and Lenses	33	12	21
Polishes and Sanitation Goods	32	13	19
Industrial Trucks and Tractors	33	13	20
Medicinals and Botanicals	32	27	5
Aircraft	32	31	1
Environmental Controls	32	22	10

Source: Edwards and Gordon, "Characteristics of Innovations Introduced on the U.S. Market in 1982," as reported in Z. J. Acs and D. B. Audretsch, *Innovation and Small Firms* (Cambridge, Mass.: MIT Press, 1990), Table 2.1.

pattern indicates that some organizations are indeed more innovative than others. Second, given that there are tens of thousands of firms scattered throughout thousands of manufacturing industries in the United States, it is surprising that relatively few of these industries are included in Table 15.2. This is what economists call *technological opportunity*. Finally, no precise correspondence exists between R&D expenditures and innovative activity. This implies that just doing more R&D does not necessarily translate into more innovation. Moreover, R&D by itself is not adequate for core competencies.

The most innovative firm is Hewlett-Packard with 55 innovations in 1982.

Table 15.2 **Most Innovative Firms**

Firm	Number of Innovations (1982)	Sales (millions) (1975)	R&D Expenditures (millions) (1975)	R&D/Sales (%) (1975)
Hewlett-Packard	55	981.0	89.6	9.1
Minnesota Mining & Mfg.	40	3,127.0	143.4	4.6
General Electric	36	13,399.0	357.1	2.7
General Signal	29	548.0	21.2	3.9
National Semiconductor	27	235.0	20.7	8.8
Xerox	25	4,054.0	198.6	4.9
Texas Instruments	24	1,368.0	51.0	3.7
Pitney Bowes	22	461.0	10.5	2.3
RCA	21	4,790.0	113.6	2.4
IBM	21	14,437.0	946.0	6.6
Digital Equipment	21	534.0	48.5	9.1
Gould	20	773.0	23.1	3.0
Motorola	19	1,312.0	98.5	7.5
Wheelabrator Frye	18	332.0	2.0	0.6
United Technologies	18	3,878.0	323.7	8.3
Hoover	18	594.0	4.3	0.7
Honeywell	18	2,760.0	164.2	5.9
Rockwell International	17	4,943.0	31.0	0.6
Johnson & Johnson	17	2,225.0	97.9	4.4
Eastman Kodak	17	4,959.0	312.9	6.3
Data General	17	108.0	11.6	10.8
Exxon	16	44,865.0	187.0	0.4
Du Pont	16	7,222.0	335.7	4.6
Stanley Works	15	464.0	3.5	0.7
Sperry Rand	15	3,041.0	163.5	5.4
Pennwalt	15	714.0	15.7	2.2
North American Phillips	14	1,410.0	22.5	1.6
Harris	14	479.0	21.1	4.4
General Motors	14	35,725.0	1,113.9	3.1
Becton, Dickinson	14	456.0	17.8	3.9

Source: Z. J. Acs and D. B. Audretsch, "R&D, Firm Size, and Innovative Activity," in *Innovation and Technical Change* (Ann Arbor: The University of Michigan Press, 1991), Table 3.1, p. 43.

Hewlett-Packard is a large firm with sales of $981 million. In terms of R&D, it has one of the highest ratios of research and development to sales for any firm, 9.1 percent, almost three times that of General Motors. In terms of technological opportunity, it is well known that one of the richest industries to mine in the 1980s was the computer industry.

What can firms do to become more innovative? According to Jack Welch, chief executive of General Electric, "Speed is really the driver that everyone is after."[7] General Electric and other firms achieved success by emphasizing faster products, faster product cycles to market, and better response time to customers. The ability to get things done more quickly may in turn depend on how en-

[7]*Business Week*, Special Issue/Enterprise, 1993, p. 212.

trepreneurial an organization is. Another attribute is entrepreneurship. According to most experts in the field, the essence of an entrepreneurial company has little to do with size. The secret lies more in the company's mind-set than in its balance sheet, cash flow, technology, or other factors. How a company prepares for, engages in, and pursues its battles for the marketplace is what counts most. According to Marc Porat of General Magic, Inc., in Silicon Valley, "Make sure there is a vision in the company—a shared vision—that is so powerful that once a person joins the family, they barely have to be reminded of what to do."[8]

Several principles encourage entrepreneurship and innovation in both large and small companies. First, successful entrepreneurs find and exploit markets that others have missed or that new technologies have created. In entrepreneurial companies, these *idea champions* are encouraged; in other types of companies, they are thwarted by a bureaucratic maze.

Second, all decision makers must have an owner mentality. This is perhaps the most difficult task for an organization to accomplish. Every manager cannot be made an owner of the firm, he or she can be offered incentives to simulate that arrangement. Many companies have a compensation system that encourages managers to maximize the number of people working for them. One step to make a company more entrepreneurial is to divide the company into discrete units. This way managers have control of the whole process from start to finish. Effective entrepreneurial companies encourage managers to seize opportunities quickly and abandon losing ones. Finally, at entrepreneurial companies, status follows performance and faithfulness to the values and culture.

Achieving core competencies is one thing; turning them into a business strategy is quite another. Most strategic decisions require knowledge of new alternative production methods, detailed industry information, and innovative product designs that exist outside the firm. Acquiring and processing much of the informa-

---

[8]*Business Week*, Special Issue/Enterprise, 1993, p. 170.

UNLEASHING THE SPIRIT OF ENTERPRISE

"It's the fourth quarter. Budget time again. This year has been tough. Our group isn't even close to making budget. Corporate ordered a 10 percent across-the-board cut in expenses last month. No way I'll get much of a bonus. But Beth's group low-balled their budget this year, and they're maxing out on their bonuses. I heard they're pushing some sales into the first quarter. No sense in doing too well—it just makes things harder next year. Maybe we should try the low-ball routine.

"Uh oh, time for the weekly meeting. There's Bill, king of the yes-men, sitting right next to the boss. You can tell he's moving up fast. His new office has six windows, and they put in the oriental rug last week. And poor Jerry is hiding in the corner. Everybody has been avoiding him since that crazy idea of his cratered. We all knew it was a disaster six months before they pulled the plug. He'll be history soon. Just goes to show you've gotta keep your head down. New ideas are fine, but you'd better be damn sure they're going to work."

Source: "Summing Up," Business Week, Special Issue/Enterprise, 1993, p. 248.
Reprinted by special permission, copyright © 1993 by McGraw-Hill, Inc.

382

Part V
*Organization
Structure
as a Dynamic
Process*

tion needed in these areas represent a problem with innovative attributes for firms. Many aspects of this problem involve product and process innovations that can be accomplished only through an entrepreneurial environment. However, there is no established market for entrepreneurial services and no certain price at which they can be obtained. An additional difficulty is posed by the fact that there is no "market" for entrepreneurship, only the need. One thing is clear, however; solving the organizational problem requires conscious coordination by the organization.

MODERN MANUFACTURING STRATEGY

Defining modern **manufacturing strategy** is best addressed by putting it in the context of what it evolved from. Under mass production, the strategy was simply to get bigger, to achieve economies of scale, to produce a standardized product of average quality at the lowest possible price. As explained in Chapter 14, for many years the social and political environment in which U.S. manufacturing firms operated gave them the ability largely to ignore alternative organizational patterns. Put more simply, the U.S. mass producers probably believed that all of the attention on globalization was simply encouraging a foolish idea. Clearly, since industry belonged to the giants under this view, size was required to innovate and compete effectively against foreign rivals. Given the massive restructuring of organizations in the United States, one can conclude that too many corporate executives bought this idea.

We now know that the issue facing the U.S. manufacturing firms in the early 1980s is, in effect, the same issue facing businesses now: how companies should be organized and managed, not whether they should be bigger or smaller. Table 15.3 highlights the key difference between the so-called old economy and the economy that now prevails in the Information Age.

The relationship between firm size and function seemingly changed in the early to mid-1980s, and this change attracted much attention in both the academic and popular business literatures.[9] Years ago when foreign businesspeople visited the United States, they gravitated to Detroit and Pittsburgh. Today they trek to Silicon Valley and Boston's Route 128. The fact is that large U.S. companies had failed to maintain their international leadership. The biggest companies have been neither the most innovative nor the most profitable. In most industries, the largest corporations fail even to attain the average rate of return in their industry. To survive in the new economy, firms must rethink their existing strategy.

The first aspect of modern manufacturing strategy is for the firm to position itself in the global marketplace. This involves discovering what the firm is the best at. The firm must identify its core competencies. To become more competitive today, many firms are becoming more flexible. They are broadening product lines; increasing the emphasis on quality, both through frequent product improvement and new product introductions; and reducing defects in manufacturing.[10]

The second aspect of modern manufacturing strategy is rebuilding the factory from scratch. An important aspect of this strategy has been the adoption of flexible man-

---

[9]Perhaps the most widely quoted source for examining this issue is "Is Your Company Too Big?," *Business Week*, March 27, 1989, pp. 46–53.

[10]Total quality management, which many people associate with Japan, was invented in Bell Labs in the 1920s and became central to American war production. (The occupying Americans taught it to the Japanese in the 1940s, who then retaught it to their teachers in the 1970s.)

Table 15.3	Organizational Aspects of the Old and New Economies	
	Old Economy	**New Economy**
	Sprawling Plant	Small Plants
	Vertical Integration	Subcontracting
	Economies of Scale	Flexibility
	Hierarchical Organization	Flat Organizations
	Organization Employees	Entrepreneurs
	Grabbing Market Share	Creating New Markets
	Mass Marketing	Niche Marketing
	Quality	Total Quality Management

ufacturing technologies. This technology allows a firm to design products more quickly, have shorter production runs, and reduce inventories. The introduction of modern manufacturing equipment, robots, computer-controlled machine tools, quality control equipment, and much more has helped. Flexible production technology also involves upgrading a semiskilled labor force to a much more broadly educated workforce. When used together, these technologies allow the organization to run faster and leaner, thereby competing more effectively.

An important feature of the discussions in the business press about flexible manufacturing is the frequent assertion that success requires starting from scratch. To move toward the factory of the future, it is not enough to make small, marginal adjustments, like adding one or two more computers or combining two of your firm's 13 divisions. The adoption of computer integrated manufacturing requires the total overhaul of a firm's organization strategy. In other words, it must redesign the way in which it does business.

The third aspect of modern manufacturing strategy is restructuring the organization. Much modern manufacturing technology cannot be fully exploited in yesterday's organizations. Therefore, the firm must not only change the production technology but also overhaul the entire organization. However, the reengineering of organizations involves important complementarities both within manufacturing and between functions, such as marketing and engineering.

From an organizational perspective, three key organizational characteristics are behind the modern manufacturing strategy: more product differentiation, increased importance placed on subcontracting, and the use of highly skilled labor usually organized into teams.

The emergence of more flexible technology has enabled firms to accommodate the increased demand for more differentiated products. Firms today frequently offer a number of basic models based on an adaptable design and make each model available with a variety of features. In this way, an almost infinite variety of outputs can be produced. For example, Caterpillar's wheel loaders, wheel tractors, and compactors have many common components. With careful design, these components can be made interchangeable from a manufacturing point of view, and at the same time Caterpillar can offer the customer a choice of options.

Flexible production technology also gives the firm the option to produce in house or to subcontract all or some of the components of its output. Innovative outside suppliers may well have on-line electronic exchange of information with the contractor. This enables the outside supplier to make use of the design investment already made by the original contractor, providing a substantial efficiency

384

Part V
*Organization
Structure
as a Dynamic
Process*

gain. Further advantages of such an electronic exchange of information with the contractor would be the ability to make design modifications more quickly and less expensively as well as better coordination between production and just-in-time delivery systems. In effect, a flexible production system coupled with integrated electronic transfer of information can reduce the transaction costs in the exchange between a firm and its outside suppliers.

The complex equipment used in flexible production requires fewer workers, but those workers must have high skill levels. Teamwork and quality control require that workers take control of production and make decisions. Ford Motor Company is now hiring college graduates to make cars on the assembly line because they can more easily be relied on to take responsibility for quality.[11]

THE ECONOMICS OF FLEXIBLE MANUFACTURING

Nearly every student in every business school has heard about flexible manufacturing strategy. However, this exposure has been largely informal, based on examples, and presented in the absence of any rigorously derived theoretical background. By no means do we wish to downplay the importance of informal learning involving numerous examples, but we hope to describe a powerful theoretical framework enabling the student to sort out the important issues and to understand how these issues interact within the realm of modern manufacturing strategy. We do point out, however, that academic learning starts in the application of known theories and considers examples as empirical evidence in support of those theories.

In this section, we hope to help to correct this shortcoming in the business literature by presenting a simplified version of a complete formal model specified by Paul Milgrom and John Roberts.[12] One thing this model makes abundantly clear is that business strategies in the modern manufacturing environment address both design and innovative attributes. Their approach is a price theoretic supply-side one involving three major elements: exogenous (outside the firm) input price changes, complementarities among the production capabilities of the firm, and nonconvexities in the relationship between the different productive capabilities existing within a firm.

Technological Change

We can think of technological progress as lowering the price of certain inputs for a firm. Economists have long been concerned with the effect of input price changes on the mix of inputs chosen by a firm. In Chapter 4, we presented the traditional approach to this problem. Recall the single firm condition of productive efficiency, which states that the ratio of input marginal products to input prices must be the same for all inputs used by the firm. Consider the case of two inputs, K and L, and prices, r and w, respectively, having marginal productivities of MP_K and MP_L. The condition is then

$$MP_K/r = MP_L/w$$

If the price of capital were to fall, this equality would be violated, and the left-hand side of the equation would become larger than the right. Efficient firm behavior would require the firm to use relatively more capital and less labor to move the single firm condition of productive efficiency back to an equality.

---

[11]Neal Templin, "Auto Plants Hiring Again, Are Demanding Higher Skilled Labor," *Wall Street Journal*, March 11, 1994, p. A1.

[12]Paul Milgrom and John Roberts, "The Economics of Modern Manufacturing: Technology, Strategy, and Organization," *The American Economic Review* 80, no. 3 (1990), pp. 511–528.

The problems a firm faced when adopting a production paradigm based on flexible manufacturing systems were more difficult to analyze and solve than those created when a single input price changed. Given the advances in technology, several input prices changed and the single firm condition of productive efficiency could no longer be counted on to provide clear guidance. Even more important, technological linkages were forged between different divisions of a modern manufacturing organization. Marketing and sales are, for example, more closely tied to events on the shop floor to help coordinate the ordering of complex tailored products with the firm's ability to produce them.

The relationship between two activities in an organization is described as a **complementarity** if one of the activities experiences feedback from changes in the other activity. Marketing and manufacturing are examples of this type of relationship. A marketing strategy based on a certain degree of customization, speed of order processing, and after-sale follow-up by an organization with a manufacturing capability that allows only large batches has substantial costs in changing for variations in product and a high defect rate. In practice, complementarities usually extend over several activities. A collection of activities is mutually complementary if doing more of any one activity increases (or at least does not decrease) the marginal profitability of each other activity in the group. Put another way, in the new organizational structure, many effects of changing input prices caused by technological advances arise because of complementarities, which are said to exist between groups of activities in an organization if increases in the level of one activity cause an increase in the marginal returns to the other activities.

As an example, consider a firm with separate sales, design, and manufacturing divisions. Computer-aided design (CAD) equipment lowers the cost of the "design" input to the firm. Its impact need not stop there, however. Some CAD systems prepare actual computer-coded instructions that can be read by programmable flexible manufacturing systems (FMS). The CAD system and the programmable FMS are then complementary within the firm and the adoption of the CAD system lowers the firm's cost of installing and operating a programmable FMS. The adoption of integrated CAD and FMS systems will cause substantial changes in other operating units within the organization and, potentially, with outside suppliers. In fact, sales departments can use the CAD packages to create drawings and provide detailed technical information to customers.

It is one thing to understand that complementarities exist between the divisions of a firm; it is quite another to gain an understanding as to what form the complementarities actually take. One of the major contributions of the Milgrom and Roberts model of flexible manufacturing is that these relationships are not necessarily smooth and continuous; instead, they may be characterized as exhibiting nonconvexities. A **nonconvexity** implies that changes in one organization unit will significantly impact other divisions. These impacts may be so large as to be overwhelming.

Suppose, for example, that a firm invests in a customer ordering system using the latest information technology. It allows orders to be placed quickly and accurately, providing detailed information on just how the customer would like the company's product tailored to its needs. If the firm lacks sufficient manufacturing flexibility, the adoption of speedier, more tailored customer ordering capability may not be profitable for the firm. For example, if setup costs resulting from modifications of the base product are high in the manufacturing process, the ordering system would not add value. However, the firm may find investing in more manufacturing flexibility to be profitable. If we think of complementarities as linkages between the organizational units of the firm, nonconvexities imply that these linkages are extremely sensitive.

386

Part V
*Organization
Structure
as a Dynamic
Process*

Toward a Formal Model

We begin presenting the Milgrom and Roberts model by considering a firm producing and selling a product at a single point in time. We then move the firm through a number of time periods over which the firm receives orders for differentiated products and manufactures them. In this way, we will be able to build the model of the modern manufacturing firm, starting with a simple framework with which you are probably familiar.[13] Our model has two kinds of variables. Decision variables are the variables that the firm chooses after weighing the appropriate design and innovative attributes affecting corporate structure. In our notation, decision variables are represented as lowercased italic letters. Upper case italic letters represent functional relationships and parameters in the model. The firm's demand function is denoted D, for example, and T represents time. The firm cannot influence either the functional relationships or the parameters in the model.

Following along our stepwise plan to explore the Milgrom and Roberts model, we examine the firm producing output at an instant in time. The firm sells this output at a price of p and incurs a direct marginal cost of production of c. The net revenue per unit is then $(p - c)$. The number of units demanded depends on the base demand for the product, $D(p,T)$, and a demand shrinkage factor, $S(a,W,b)$. Base demand, $D(p,T)$, is defined as a function of unit price and calendar time. Demand shrinkage, $S(a,W,b)$, is a function of a, representing order receipt and processing time; W, representing expected wait for an order to be filled; and b, delivery time.

Base demand is assumed to be decreasing in unit price and increasing in calendar time; that is, base demand grows over time. The demand shrinkage is included to capture the importance of quickly filling customers' needs, and it is assumed that demand shrinks due to slower ordering, longer waits for production, and drawn out delivery times. The shrinkage factor $S(a,W,b)$ can be thought of as a fraction between zero and 1, speedier processing of orders, production, and delivery times push $S(a,W,b)$ toward 1.

For now, we can continue to ignore fixed costs of production and write out the firm's net incremental profits as equation 15.1.

$$(p - c)\, D(p,T)\, S(a,W,b) \qquad (15.1)$$

The importance of speed is clear from equation (15.1). A firm having faster customer ordering, processing, and delivery time will have increased revenues from any variant of the product sold. These "speed" variables, along with the direct marginal costs of production, are, in effect, chosen by the firm when it adopts a manufacturing system with certain capabilities. Shortly, we will consider the cost elements of the model that reflect the fact that these choices are not made for free by the organization. Before we do, however, we need to add some measures of flexibility to the model; we do so by jumping to the next period.

Equation (15.1) represents an approximation of net incremental revenues for the firm at one point in time as it produces one variant of its base product. Let's now suppose that the firm receives an order for a second variation of its base product. We explicitly consider the costs to the firm of changing production setup to produce the variant called for in the new order.

---

[13]It is only fair to point out that the presentation here is much simpler than that advanced by Milgrom and Roberts in "Economics of Modern Manufacturing." However, we maintain the essential components. The actual Milgrom and Roberts model is quite abstract and involves mathematical techniques far above and beyond the calculus-based techniques usually used in economic analysis. The interested reader will verify that the presence of non-convexities renders calculus techniques useless.

Producing a changed product causes the firm to incur costs related to setting up the machinery and to the design of the product variant. We define d as representing the design costs associated with producing a new product variant and e as the costs associated with changing the manufacturing machinery to produce the product variant. In our sequential development of the flexible manufacturing model, we consider how the expression in equation (15.1) changes when a new order is received and processed. Including these costs in our model changes the net incremental profit to

$$(p - c)\, D(p,T)\, S(a,W,b) - (d + e) \qquad (15.2)$$

Essentially, we have taken the earlier measure of net incremental profit and subtracted away additional design and manufacturing costs, which appear as additional variable costs (that is, they change as output changes).

At this point in developing our model of flexible manufacturing, we need to consider the firm's planning horizon. We assume that it is sufficiently long so that many variations on the basic product are ordered and produced.[14] The number of product variations in the firm's planning horizon is denoted by n, which affects the structure of our model in several ways.

First, n should be included in our base demand function D, which would become $D(p,T,n)$. Base product demand is increasing in n, implying that customers are attracted and demand increases if a firm is known to be more flexible. Second, because our firm plans several product variants and the expression in equation (15.2) deals with one product variation, we need to multiply this expression for a single product variant by the number of product variants over the firm's planning horizon. Third, n affects the expected wait for an order to be processed; basically, other things being equal, the higher the n (the more product variants), the greater the wait for an order to be processed. Then the function W is rewritten as $W(n)$. The effects of n on the firm's revenues over its planning horizon are somewhat offsetting. Revenues increase in n because of increased base demand and more production runs. Revenues decrease in n because the more setups the firm expects, the longer the expected wait for an order to be processed.

The number of product variations also affects the firm's variable cost structure because designing and manufacturing each product variant involve extra costs. According to our notation, each product variant costs d to design and e to actually produce; therefore, n product variants cost the firm $n(d + s)$.

The net incremental profit over the firm's planning horizon is then given by

$$(p - c)\,(n)\, D(p,T,n)\, S(a,W(n),b) - (n)\,(d + e) \qquad (15.3)$$

Considering the progression from equation (15.2) to (15.3), we can see the effects of n on net incremental profit as offsetting. As explained earlier, n can either increase or decrease firm revenues; additionally, n adds costs. The ultimate effect of the number of product variants on net incremental profit depends on the relative sizes of the effects of n on D and W and the sizes of d and e.

One important aspect of the net incremental profit expression of (15.3) is the presence of complementarities. A clear connection exists between the firm's marketing functions, manufacturing functions, and design functions. Ordering and

---

[14]We make two major simplifications of the Milgrom and Roberts model in this step. First, we assume that the number of different product variants produced equals the number of set-ups done by the firm. Second, we assume that the number of set-ups equals the expected number of improvements per product. This simplification is consistent with our second assumption, which is that the firm does not hold inventory but sells all that it produces.

388

Part V
*Organization
Structure
as a Dynamic
Process*

delivery speed directly affect revenues and are connected to both design activities (which cost e) and manufacturing activities.

The full effect of the integration of the different activities of the firm is illustrated when we add capital, or fixed costs, to the model. The fixed costs are incurred when the firm chooses from available technologies to be used in each division in pursuing its productive activities. The lower prices of the technological inputs implicitly appear within the fixed costs. We consider the fixed costs to be determined by the firm's choice of decision variables and time (T) rather than explicitly including the "amount" of the inputs times their prices.

Our expression for capital costs is $K(c,a,b,s,e,n,T)$. Lower values for c, a, b, e, and d raise capital costs. Thus, the desirable traits of lower direct marginal costs of production, speedier ordering and delivery, and smaller manufacturing design setup costs impose increased capital costs on the firm. Because capital costs increase according to the number of product variants the firm plans to produce, flexibility may be expensive. Finally, in time, technological advances tend to decrease capital costs as new innovations are available for use as inputs by the firm.[15]

As an example of the relationship between capital costs and decision variables, consider the following. A firm installs a computerized system allowing customers to place orders directly with little assistance from sales or marketing personnel; this system could transmit information directly to the factory or shop floor. The costs of installing such a system are capital costs; in our model, they allow the firm to enjoy lower values for a and e while increasing capital costs. CAD–CAM technologies have a similiar effect since they develop and exploit complementarities

---

[15]A number of extensions to this basic model suggest themselves. Milgrom and Roberts include a variable depicting wastage costs per setup and allow for inventory accumulation. Also interesting would be the representation of a firm's ability to raise capital to buy the newer technologies. Empirical results in this area are mixed. A truly complete model would explicitly consider the labor dimension in flexible manufacturing. This would prove tremendously difficult because it would involve a statement of the relationship between labor input, new technologies, and output.

DICTIONARY OF MODEL TERMS

Decision or Choice Variables

- p Unit price
- c Direct marginal costs of production
- a Order receipt and processing time
- b Delivery time
- s Setup costs for manufacturing
- e Design costs of setups
- n Number of product variations

Parameters and Functional Forms

- D Base demand for product (a function of unit price and time)
- T Measure of calandar time
- S Demand shrinkage factor, based on time for order receipt, processing, and delivery
- W Expected wait for a processed order to be filled

between design and manufacturing. Their adoption raises capital costs K and lowers s, c, and d.

The total profit expression for the modern manufacturing firm, then, is

$$(p - c)\,(n)\,D\,(p,T,n)\,S\,(a,W(n),b) - (n)\,(d + e) - K(c,a,b,s,e,n,T) \qquad (15.4)$$

Two striking differences exist between this type of model and that traditionally considered in economics. First, complementarities affecting revenues, variable costs, and fixed costs are explicitly included. In traditional economic analysis, fixed costs are created by resources devoted to organization, advertising, marketing, and product design, but this is not the case here. The second difference is that fixed costs are determined jointly with a firm's output decision. In the traditional model, fixed costs are largely ignored: for the perfectly competitive firm considered in Chapter 3, fixed costs play no role in determining the level of firm output.

Strategy is directly built into the model. We can use this model to identify and analyze many aspects of the trade-offs involved in the organization's choice of manufacturing strategy. The flexibility of design technology is modeled by the variable d. The introduction of CAD technology in the design function of the firm lowers d but also may put pressures on other aspects of the firm's operations such as sales and delivery, modeled by the variables a and b.

The flexibility of manufacturing equipment impacts the formation of a business strategy, some aspects of which are represented in the model. First, flexibility is often associated with low costs of routinely changing from producing one good to another. Here, this effect is represented by lower values for the variable s. However, adopting such flexibility might involve costs of changing machinery to produce new or redesigned products, thereby lowering the value of d.

The reader has probably already noticed that we say nothing about the effect of labor relations in this model. We point out, however, that an element of flexibility in modern manufacturing is associated with broadly trained workers and work rules that facilitate frequent changes in activities. In this context, we may interpret investments in flexibility in terms of worker education and in industrial relations efforts, as well as in purchases of physical capital. In this environment, flexibility in employees is complementary with flexibility in capital equipment.

Obtaining a solution for this model is very difficult, involving quite advanced mathematical techniques. Calculus-based constrained optimization techniques cannot be applied because of the nonconvexities in the complementary relationships between the activities of the various functional areas, or divisions, of the organization. However, tremendous insights that are in accordance with recent behavior by a variety of business organizations are contained in the solution. Thus, we can draw useful conclusions from the specified solution of the model of flexible manufacturing.

The model predicts that technological advances over time will cause a number of changes in organizations as they adopt numerous process innovations embodying advances in information technology. Because of the complementarities present in production, we would expect to see organizational changes reflect linkages between various areas of function within firms. In particular, the formal solution obtained by Milgrom and Roberts is consistent with the following:

- Lower prices of output and marginal costs of production.
- More frequent product redesigns and improvements.
- Higher quality in production with fewer defects in final products.
- Widespread use of information technology enabling customers to place detailed orders.

390

Part V
*Organization
Structure
as a Dynamic
Process*

- Smaller production batch sizes caused by more frequent setups in manufacturing and lower inventory levels.
- Smaller costs associated with product redesigns.

These characteristics of the solution to the model are interesting and useful in understanding organization behavior; they are even more useful concerning what the model implies about organizational evolution. Specifically, it suggests that even if environmental changes occur gradually, the adoption of new technologies will be erratic for two reasons.

First, the operating divisions are affected by complementarities. The theory suggests that we should not see an extended period of time during which one component of the firm's strategy is in place and the other components have barely begun to be put into place.

The second reason that adoption of new technologies will be erratic is that the complementarities discussed earlier are quite possibly governed by nonconvexities. Facing the problem of obtaining the optimal organizational structure, managers realize that the optimal solution may be discontinuous. This result means that it is unprofitable to be stuck with a mixture of highly dedicated and highly flexible production equipment. Explicitly, Milgrom and Roberts' theoretical model suggests that it will be unprofitable to operate with substantial volumes of both highly flexible and highly specialized equipment side by side.

Figure 15.2 illustrates the decision facing firms considering the adoption of flexible manufacturing systems. The technology needed becomes available at time t_1. Three possible paths for firm profits are shown. As a basis for comparison, the profit stream *ABG* represents expected future profits if the technology necessary for flexible manufacturing systems had not become available, that is, if the firm would continue with its present capabilities. If the firm adopts the new technology

**Figure 15.2 Effect on Profits of Changing Activity
in One Productive Unit**

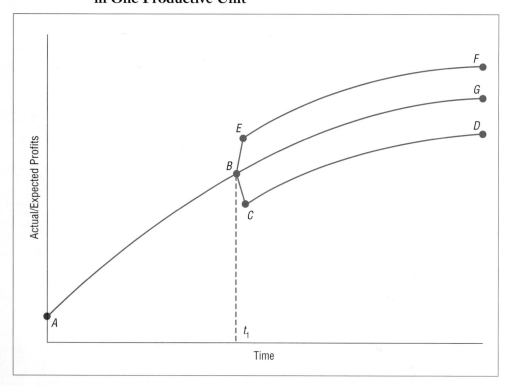

at time t_1 in all its divisions, then the expected profit stream would be as shown by *ABEF*. If, however, the firm adopts the new technology at time t_1 in only some of its divisions, then the expected profit stream would be shown as *ABCD*. The profit stream *ABCD* is shown below the profit streams *ABG* and *ABEF* to reflect the importance of complementarities and nonconvexities.

VERTICAL GOVERNANCE STRUCTURES

Many economists have studied the role of transaction cost considerations in forming agreements between economic agents. The initial groundwork was laid by the Nobel Prize–winning economist Ronald Coase in his 1937 paper. Coase introduced the idea of *transaction costs* and argued that efficiency dictates that contractual arrangements be crafted in ways to minimize them. According to the Coasian logic, individuals and organizations would choose a contractual format, termed a *governance structure*, from a wide variety of possibilities.

At one extreme, transactions could take place within a "market." This extreme is the realm of most traditional theoretical economic analyses and was summarized in Chapters 2, 3, and 4 of this textbook. In this ultracompetitive world, there is perfect information; much competition; and little, if any, room for opportunism.

At the other extreme is the possibility that transactions could occur entirely within an organization. If the transaction costs were too high in terms of informational asymmetries, selection problems, or asset specificity, organizations could be self-sufficient in some dimensions.

One of the major topics considered in Chapter 6 of this book was the role of transaction costs in firms' make-or-buy decisions. The back-to-basics approach being taken by many businesses today usually involves the innovative and design attributes in this decision. As an organization focuses its efforts more and more on what it perceives to be its core competencies, it must craft agreements for other organizations to conduct necessary, but ancillary, functions.

The large mass-producing firms that dominated U.S. manufacturing earlier this century had a highly vertically integrated structure out of necessity. Mass producers had to extensively exploit economies of scale because of the massive fixed investments required. This made stability in input and output markets a primary concern to the mass producer. The presence of transaction costs in many of the exchanges required to run the machinery of mass production directly threatened this stability. The easiest, and most efficient, solution was ownership, and a corporate governance structure emerged that featured a high degree of vertical integration.

In the 1970s, some economists began to conclude that the mass production system in the United States was soon to be tested by more efficient organizational patterns observed in other countries. This led to the exploration of alternative theories of the firm. One of these perspectives of firm behavior was based on transaction cost analysis. This train of thought was picked up by Oliver Williamson in his 1975 work, *Markets and Hierarchies*. Williamson sees a "comparative institutional" perspective in which a wide range of institutional arrangements can be used to govern transactions between economic agents. Governance structures emerge in response to various transactional considerations.

According to Williamson's view, the boundary between a firm and a market provides a very rough distinction between the two primary institutional arrangements used by economic agents seeking to promote efficiency in defining the relationships between them. One type is the spot market transaction for which buyer

392

Part V
*Organization
Structure
as a Dynamic
Process*

and seller come together at one point in time and exchange. A second alternative is for buyer and seller to craft their relationship with a complex long-term contract. For any given transaction, the chosen governance structure could be either of these two extremes or could lie somewhere in the middle.

Of all the different sources of transaction costs, *asset specificity* has the clearest implications for the form of governance structure chosen by firms. When specialized assets are required, spot market transactions can be ruled out. The reasoning lies on expectations of opportunistic behavior and on investments in bargaining position that are inefficient. Investment by firms is seen as creating, at most, a stream of *economic rents* and, at least, a stream of *quasi-rents*. The threat that these rents and quasi-rents may be appropriated by another party(ies) leads to investment at less than the efficient level, a level that would occur in the absence of any transaction costs. Sinking a relationship-specific investment transfers an ex ante situation that may be competitive into an ex post bargaining situation that is not competitive and is, in fact, a bilateral monopoly.

This leaves two forms of governance structure to consider: ownership and long-term relational contracting, as described in Chapter 7. In an environment in which technologies are rapidly changing—resulting in lower capital (fixed) costs of firms, demand for customized products is growing, and competition in quality is forcing firms to focus on their core competencies if ownership does not provide

MAKE OR BUY

The next manufacturing revolution is under way, and U.S. companies are bringing airplanes, cars, and even kitchen stoves to market faster and less expensively by leaning on their suppliers to help engineer and bankroll new products. This revolution goes far beyond the changes of the 1980s, when manufacturers attacked their high labor costs by shifting production to suppliers with lower labor costs. New manufacturers are slashing product development expenses by farming out the tasks to suppliers, in essence, evolving from being manufacturers to orchestrators that harmonize their suppliers' work.

Meanwhile, the suppliers, which once did little more than bang out parts as inexpensively as possible, are hiring hundreds of engineers to staff new research and development departments. Using the new approach, Whirlpool Corporation is cooking up its first gas range without hiring engineers to create the gas burner system; instead, the design work is being done by Eaton Corporation, a supplier that already makes gas valves and regulators for other appliance manufacturers. Whirlpool expects to get its new range to market several months sooner this way.

And Chrysler Corporation's skillful use of parts suppliers to design everything from car seats to drive shafts has enabled it to spend consistently less money than its competitors do to develop new vehicles. It is a key factor behind the automaker's strong comeback in the past three years.

Source: "Manufacturers Use Suppliers to Help Them Develop New Products,"
Wall Street Journal, *December 19, 1994, p. A1. Reprinted by permission of the*
Wall Street Journal, *© 1994 Dow Jones & Company, Inc. All Rights
Reserved Worldwide.*

what is necessary for organizations to efficiently organize economic activity. By its very nature, investment in new technology is a risky proposition for firms.

Uncertainties exist as to the applicability of the equipment; further, firms have reason to fear an even better application of technology being introduced that will make their recent investment unable to compete in terms of quality and cost. In this, the Information Age, capital costs are far less of a barrier to entry than they were in the past. In fact several studies have found that capital costs are less of a barrier to entry than advertising.[16] Thus, it is possible not only that an innovation will take place that eliminates a cost advantage but also that a competitor will likely be able to afford the innovation. In a sense, the same factors that raise the costs of ownership encourage the use of long-term relational contracts.

Any long-term relational contract must accomplish two things. First, it must maintain a degree of trust in the contractual relationship. Second, it must preserve individual and joint incentives. This is possible given the nature of flexible manufacturing technology, which, by its nature, represents both a far less specific, or specialized, investment and a smaller capital outlay. In terms of the contracting theory presented in Chapter 7, there is less fear that the stream of economic and quasi-rents generated by the act of investing will be appropriated via some form of ex post contractual opportunism.

The changing technologies and resultant emergence of the flexible manufacturing strategy then work to eliminate at least some, if not most, of the transaction costs associated with investing in specific assets. Given that markets are demanding high-quality, specialized goods, firms are able to concentrate on their own area of expertise in production by farming out the production of components to subcontractors or outside suppliers. The mechanics behind the make-or-buy decision has changed, and efficiency dictates that more firms pursue the buy option.

The implications for organization structure are fairly clear and general at this point in our discussion and consistent with what is observed in successful, flexible firms today. Firms concentrate on their core competencies. When cost or quality disadvantages exist, outside suppliers are asked to provide inputs or components. In such an organization, there must necessarily be a centralized managerial effort whose primary task (after identification of core competencies) is to coordinate the activities of the firm with the activities, expertise, and abilities of its outside suppliers.

Although mass production industries were highly vertically integrated, typically some room to maneuver existed as a firm determined the optimal amount of centralization in its decision making. Some firms were more centralized than others. However, with flexible manufacturing technologies, the modern organization must be controlled from the center in order to coordinate its internal and external activities.

In Chapter 16, we take this line of reasoning to the next logical level by focusing on the formation of strategic alliances. As organizations in the U.S. economy moved from mass production to the flexible manufacturing strategy with less vertical governance, the boundaries between firms became increasingly blurred. As we consider a number of relational contracts between firms in the next chapter, the boundaries between the firms will become increasingly blurred once again.

Make or Buy

---

[16]Zoltan J. Acs and David B. Audretsch, *Innovation and Small Firms* (Cambridge, MA: MIT Press, 1990), ch. 5.

394

Part V
*Organization
Structure
as a Dynamic
Process*

▓ CHAPTER SUMMARY AND KEY IDEAS ▓ ▓ ▓ ▓ ▓ ▓

This chapter has analyzed the strategies that modern manufacturing firms pursue to compete effectively in a global marketplace. Strategic planning by organizations is a complex process that must determine how resources should be allocated and organized within a firm. Organizational strategy is a blueprint for accomplishing an efficient allocation of corporate resources.

Certain elements of fit are evident in a good strategy. Only when information is spread across the organization and all parties share a common view of the organization's goals can successful strategic planning be conducted. These elements make it important to coordinate the actions of various parts of the organization closely through some centralized structure.

Modern manufacturing strategy causes the firm to rethink its existing strategy to survive in the new economy. The first aspect of this strategy is for the firm to position itself in the global marketplace. The second strategy involves rebuilding the factory from scratch. The third aspect of modern manufacturing strategy is restructuring the organization. Much modern manufacturing technology cannot be fully exploited in yesterday's organizations. From an organizational perspective, three key organizational characteristics are behind the modern manufacturing strategy: product differentiation, subcontracting, and highly skilled labor usually organized into teams.

This strategy is necessary because technological progress lowers several input prices simultaneously. There is no clear, easy decision for the firm to make under these circumstances because the existence of complementarities implies an intimate connection between the various activities taking place within the organization.

It is one thing to understand that complementarities exist; it is another to understand what form they will actually take. These relationships are not necessarily smooth and continuous. Nonconvexities imply that changes in one organizational unit will have large impacts on other divisions in the organization. Modern manufacturing strategy implies that we should see extended periods of time when one component of the firm's strategy is in place and the other components have barely begun to be in place. One implication is that it is unprofitable for a firm to have a mixture of dedicated and nondedicated equipment. One implication of the model is that firms will rely less on vertical relationship than they did in the past.

▓ KEY TERMS

comparative advantage	ex post
complementarities	imperfect information
core competency	innovation
design attributes	innovative attributes
design decisions	manufacturing strategy
economies of scale	nonconvexities
economies of scope	organization strategy
ex ante	restructuring

▓ FURTHER READINGS

Acs, Z. J., and D. B. Audretsch. *Innovation and Small Firms*. Cambridge, Mass.: MIT Press, 1990.

———, eds. *Innovation and Technological Change*. Ann Arbor: The University of Michigan Press, 1991.

Gifford, S. "A Review of Milgrom and Roberts' 'Economics, Organization and

Management.' " *Journal of Economics and Management Strategy* 3(2), Summer 1994, pp. 407–436.

Hamel, G., and C. K. Prahabad, *Competing for the Future*. Cambridge, Mass.: Harvard Business School Press, 1994.

Hayes, H. H., and R. Jaikumar. "Manufacturings' Crisis: New Technologies, Obsolete Organizations." *Harvard Business Review* 88, no. 5 (1988), pp. 77–85.

Johnson, S. and G. Loveman. *Starting Over*. Cambridge, Mass.: Harvard University Press, 1994.

Melcher, R. A. "How Goliaths Can Act Like Davids." *Business Week*, September 4, 1990.

———, special issue. Enterprise, 1993, 190–248.

Milgrom, P., and J. Roberts. "The Economics of Modern Manufacturing: Technology, Strategy and Organizations." *American Economic Review* 80 (1990), pp. 511–528.

Mitchell, R. "Masters of Innovation: How 3M Keeps Its New Products Coming." *Business Week*, April 10, 1989, pp. 58–63.

Toffler, A. *The Adaptive Corporation*. New York: Bantam Books, 1985.

Valery, N. "Factory of the Future: Survey." *The Economist*, May 30, 1987, pp. 3–18.

QUESTIONS AND PROBLEMS FOR REVIEW AND DISCUSSION

A. In the section concerning competitiveness, a brief narrative is given about the course of events at two Polish shipyards in the early 1990s.

   1. Give a brief description of the broad environment facing the Polish shipbuilding industry at the time.

   2. How did the response by the Szchecin yard differ from the response by the Gdansk yard?

B. **1.** In your own words, describe what economists mean by the term *complementarities* as applied to production. Give an example in line with your description.

   2. In your own words, describe what economists mean by the term *core competency*. Give an example in line with your description.

C. Consider equations (15.1). Describe each of the following pieces of the equation as fully as you can:

   1. $(p - c)$

   2. $D(p, T)$

   3. $S(a, W, b)$

D. One of the findings of the flexible manufacturing model presented in Chapter 15 is its prediction that firms adopting flexible technologies will have less formal vertical governance.

   1. What is vertical governance?

   2. Why is it a prediction of the material in Chapter 15 that firms will have less formal vertical governance?

E. Would we expect to see a more centralized or more decentralized management style in a flexible manufacturing firm? Explain why.

Organizational Strategy and Strategic Alliances

The core corporation is no longer a "big" business, but neither is it merely a collection of smaller ones. Rather, it is an enterprise web. Its center provides strategic insight and binds the threads together. Yet points on the web often have sufficient autonomy to create profitable connections to other webs. There is no "inside" or "outside" the corporation, but only different distances from its strategic center.[1]

CHAPTER OUTLINE AND STUDENT GOALS

One of the surprising findings of the flexible manufacturing model presented in Chapter 15 is its prediction that firms adopting flexible technologies will have less formal vertical governance. Organizations structured in this way will make extensive use of independently owned suppliers and subcontractors. In this chapter, we emphasize the economic underpinnings of these supplier relationships.

Each organization must decide where to place itself in the make-or-buy spectrum concerning the inputs it needs for a smoothly operating production process that exploits its core competencies. At one theoretical extreme, a firm can be completely vertically integrated, making all necessary components. A position opposite to this would be taken by a firm that purchases all inputs in spot markets using arm's-length transactions. In practice, firms fall somewhere between these two extremes in choosing how to best organize economic activity.

Recently, a whole host of production arrangements have developed as alternative governance or organizational structures to both vertical integration and market procurement models. These alternatives blend certain characteristics of both vertical integration and market-based transacting. Led by advances in technology, increasing globalization, and changing consumer demands, these production arrangements emerge as organizations pursue efficiency through specialization in an environment that has changed to reduce the transaction costs associated with the newer organizational forms. Producers now have many ways in which to structure their relationships with suppliers. Perhaps the most famous of these is the relationships the Japanese auto firms have with their suppliers. Other examples can be found in the garment district of New York, the Emilia-Romagna region of Italy, and in Silicon Valley.

These production arrangements are much more flexible than the hierarchical mass production system of the past, and they allow firms to achieve goals more easily and quickly. These goals might include gaining access to new markets, over-

---

[1]Robert B. Reich, *The Work of Nations* (New York: Alfred A. Knopf, 1992), pp. 95–96.

coming trade barriers, or introducing new products. The building blocks of these production relationships are strategic alliances. We offer the following working definition of a strategic alliance:

> **strategic alliance:** An association to exploit the unique strength of two or more companies whose core competencies are complementary when neither partner has the ability or the desire to acquire the other party's unique strength.

Given that our task in this textbook is to explain the behavior of economic organizations, we may not be happy to learn about strategic alliances, for they make it very difficult to identify where one firm "ends" and another firm "begins." In Part I of this textbook, we examined the economist's traditional view of firms, in which their boundaries were clearly distinct, marked by their market exchanges. The arrangements between firms in a strategic alliance are much more complicated than simple market exchanges; instead of focusing on competition, strategic alliances focus on cooperation. A strategic alliance may take many different forms, including equity purchases, licensing and marketing agreements, research contracts, on-line information exchanges, and joint ventures.

A strategic alliance is a relational contract by which both parties commit to a common goal, expect to learn from the alliance, and have a vested interest in it because it is related to their survival strategy. In other words, a strategic alliance becomes an essential ingredient in corporate strategy because it represents a choice for a firm's corporate governance.

Strategic alliances share the most important requirement of all relational contracting: a high degree of trust. Reputation between firms is important. Strategic alliances share one aspect with a market-based procurement scheme: discipline is provided through reputations in a setting similar to markets. Furthermore, each company in a strategic alliance must believe that the other company will not try to acquire it.

A system of related strategic alliances forms a production network. The purpose of these networks is to produce with the flexibility of a market but without the permanence and rigidities of vertical integration. We define production networks as follows:

> **production network:** A form of production that exists between markets and hierarchies.

A production network features a large number of related producers linked in some way. They emulate a market in the sense that within the network, some competitive elements are present. They also emulate a vertically integrated firm (hierarchy) in that they coordinate the productive activities of many highly specialized assets. Production networks allow firms to assemble the best inputs from all over the world in one place and to use these inputs without the coordination and management costs incurred in a highly vertically integrated firm.

Production networks may themselves be part of a larger system or culture. A production system includes not only the relationship between the internal organization of two or more firms but also their connection to the social and political institution of a community or location, including its history. The most famous production systems are Silicon Valley and Boston's Route 128 in the United States, and the Emilia-Romagna region of north-central Italy.

After reading this chapter, you should be able to

* Explain what a strategic alliance is, by showing it to be a way of organizing economic activity.

398

Part V
*Organization
Structure
as a Dynamic
Process*

* Understand what is meant by the statement that "production networks exist somewhere between markets and hierarchies."
* Explain what a joint venture is.
* Explain what a production system is.

▊ THE THEORETICAL UNDERPINNINGS OF STRATEGIC ALLIANCES

Throughout this entire textbook, we have stressed that firms exist as a collection of contracts whose purpose is to organize economic activity. Accordingly, the fundamental building block of firms is the contract. Difficulties experienced in crafting these contracts—transaction costs—prove interesting to us not in and of themselves but because of the way in which they influence the format of the contracts crafted by firms to organize themselves.

Alternative Governance Structures

We term the organizational form chosen by a firm to be its **governance structure;** at the heart of which lies the make-or-buy decision facing the firm. We argued in the last chapter that spot market transactions, as a form of governance structure, fall victim to contracting problems arising from various asset specificities. We also argued that as the successful corporations in today's internationally competitive business environment heeded Adam Smith's advice and specialized in production according to their perceived core competencies, ownership became a far less attractive option as a governance structure. Additionally, ownership was also made less attractive because the new flexible manufacturing technologies were not only less specific but also less expensive. This lower cost enables other organizations that can specialize in their own areas of core competencies to emerge.

According to these reasons, efficiency leads to an arrangement of firms similar to the concept of a network in which producers band together with suppliers through strategic alliances. This development is in accordance with established economic theories: *the Coase theorem* of Chapter 5 and the *constrained efficiency postulate* from Chapter 6. One loose paraphrasing of the Coase theorem is that if transaction costs are zero, individuals will be led to act efficiently. The constrained efficiency postulate is somewhat weaker, arguing that individuals *tend* to act efficiently given their limited information, resources, and bounded rationality.

Strategic Alliances and Transaction Costs

Strategic alliances do not eliminate transaction costs; instead, they represent a form of organizing economic activity that represents a *tendency* to efficiency. Strategic alliances are chosen today as the most efficient way to organize economic activity because of fundamental changes in the business environment: the widespread adoption of flexible manufacturing technology and the firms' back-to-basics movement toward their core competencies.

As firms specialize in production, they become more innovative, more cost efficient, and produce higher-quality goods. When Adam Smith spoke of the gains from specialization in the 1700s, his comments referred to activities within a single firm. Strategic alliances are the governance structure that permits this specialization to happen across firms.

Strategic alliances represent incomplete relational contracts as described in Chapter 7. Trust is an essential building block in these relationships. Thus, as in the structure of the employment relationship outlined in Chapter 10, a reputation for fairness and honesty is desperately crucial. However, additional stability is added because of the environment in which these relationships are developed. The incentives in the environment of the new economy and the trust work together to overcome many of the transaction costs that typically cause contracting problems. We next consider some of the main types of contracting problems and the way in which strategic alliances minimize their impact in the new economy to allow the benefits of specialization to occur.

For the large mass-producing firms, stability of inputs and a reliable output market were primary concerns; thus, the optimal governance structure featured ownership and a large degree of vertical integration. Outside suppliers were leery of making highly specialized investments for fear of being held up or made victim of other *postcontractual opportunism* by the contracting firm. Ironically, the contracting firms held the same fears about their outside suppliers. In modern manufacturing, the threat of being held up is much smaller because the underlying investments are far less specific.

In general, in a production network composed of numerous strategic alliances, any form of reneging is not likely to occur because of the importance of reputation. In the network, firms become specialized so that their long-term survival requires a steady stream of contracting partners. Once a reputation for being "dishonest" or "unfair" is established, that future stream of contracting partners is no longer guaranteed. In the examples to come describing organizations in Silicon Valley and Japan, we see evidence that institutional devices exist to develop and spread reputations.

A second major form of postcontractual opportunism was the topic of Chapter 8, which described moral hazard in the principal-agent relationship. One general solution to the moral hazard problem is market-disciplining device. In strategic alliances, reputation is one form of market-disciplining device. A second is offered by the typical widespread availability of information within productive networks and the fact that strategic alliances are by no means exclusive. By this, we mean that a company may have a strategic alliance with Firm X in which Firm X produces a key component of that firm's output. Very likely, Firm X has a similar relationship with other firms producing similar components. Furthermore, both contracting firms will know about Firm X's relationships and may discuss its performance. Any indication that Firm X is shirking in its duties will be quickly spread between and by the two contracting firms.

Another aspect of strategic alliances that may help prevent transaction costs from arising because of the agency nature of these relationships is that *bounded rationality* may be less of a problem than in simple arm's-length contracting. Both the contracting firm and the subcontractor have knowledge of the other's manufacturing processes and of the technological questions that arise in fulfilling the contractor's request. It is unlikely, then, that the subcontractor will be able to stonewall or mislead the contractor by claiming problems with some terribly advanced technological issue.

The use of strategic alliances has two clear implications for the management charged with formulating the corporation's strategy. First, the *intrafirm* coordination costs will decrease. The firm is not required to purchase as many assets and hire the workers to operate and manage them if organizations outside the firm play an increased role in designing, producing, and shipping the output. What this implies is that *interfirm* coordination becomes more important, which leads to the second implication for organizational management.

As explained in Chapter 15, today's flexible organizations need a more centralized corporate hierarchy than was common in dominant corporations even 10 years ago. Only a centralized management scheme can consistently gather and process the information required to develop an organization's strategy that advances its interests. The issues facing management are large and broad: What are the firm's core competencies? What should it produce? Who should it seek as partners at what terms? The answer to any one of these questions clearly depends on the answers to all of the others. Thus, an efficient, coherent reply can come only from a centralized management scheme.[2]

■ STRATEGIC ALLIANCES IN BIOTECHNOLOGY

Marteck Biosciences is a biotechnology company headquartered in Columbia, Maryland. Originally spun off from Martin Marietta, Marteck went public in 1993 and is traded on the NASDAQ stock exchange. The company has 70 full-time employees and is working in several product areas. Marteck's mission is to be the leading biotechnology company in the world based on its core competency, growing algae, commonly referred to as *seaweed*. Its corporate strategy is to exploit its core competency in developing algae-based products and to form alliances with other companies to complement its own strengths.

Breast feeding is good for babies. Certain amino acids (the building blocks of protein) in mother's milk are not available in infant formula. Studies of childhood development have shown that these particular acids are directly linked to intelligence in children. The market problem is that not all mothers are able, due to physical or time challenges, to breast feed their children and must rely on infant formula. Adding the amino acids to infant formula found in mother's milk could be a multimillion dollar market. Marteck has developed an algae-based derivative that replicates the amino acids in mother's milk.

Like most biotechnology companies, Marteck was not able to exploit its core competencies by itself. The company did not have the financial, regulatory, or marketing skills needed to capitalize on its ability and grow. Therefore, like many young biotechnology companies, Marteck's corporate strategy was to rely on strategic alliances to achieve its goals.

A major hurdle in the production of the infant formula additive is that it has to be manufactured in large enough quantities to satisfy global market demand. Marteck did not have the facilities to do this. Therefore, it entered into a strategic alliance with a large fermentation company in the Midwest to manufacture the product in large quantities. It formed a second strategic alliance to market the product with several large producers of baby formula. The product will be directly added to infant formula, and Marteck will receive a royalty from each bottle and can of infant formula sold.

Marteck did not make one of the major mistakes that many biotechnology companies made. It never licensed, or let others use, its proprietary technology. The company maintained proprietary control of its core competency and cooperated with other organizations that complemented its unique strengths.

Marteck will continue to develop its core competencies in algae and to develop new products that will find a place in the global market. In each case, it will seek partners with core competencies that complement its own.

In the biotechnology industry, strategic alliance is the name of the game. Many U.S. biotech companies form strategic alliances with both domestic and foreign companies. As of 1989, 46 publicly traded biotechnology firms had an average of six corporate partners each. The search for suitable partners that truly allow biotech companies to integrate core competencies is not confined to the United States. The average number of foreign alliances for each U.S. biotechnology company in 1989 was 3.5, which included an average of 2.1 alliances with European firms, and 1.4 with companies based in Asia, usually in Japan.

---

[2]For an interesting perspective on how production networks compete, see "Group Versus Group: How Alliance Networks Compete," *Harvard Business Review*, July–August 1944, pp. 4–11.

Half a dozen biotechnology companies have forged an extraordinary number of foreign ties; Chiron, Biogen, and Genentech lead the way, as seen in Table 16.1. The companies use several different strategies for foreign strategic alliances: some U.S. firms have emphasized European accords while others have stressed Asian over European alliances.

Three common types of strategic alliances are equity arrangements, joint ventures, and marketing deals. Because of the risky nature of their specialized businesses and their small size, biotechnology companies are always looking for capital. Selling equity to major U.S. and foreign corporations has always been an important part of this fund-raising, often accompanying strategic marketing or distribution arrangements. Equity investment gives a corporation much needed cash in exchange for part ownership. For example, Nova Pharmaceutical Corporation headquartered in Baltimore, Maryland, sold $10 million worth of its shares in 1987 to Celanese, Inc., for partial ownership.

With the exception of complete acquisition, the most intimate relationship two companies can have is a joint venture. In most cases, such an arrangement consists of a core competency contributed by each party. In biotechnology, the genetic engineering company invariably contributes the necessary technology while the partner contributes financing, marketing skills, and possibly even production capacity. This type of arrangement is common even today in the U.S. biotech industry and is perhaps necessary as many of the newer innovative firms lack financial, marketing, and production resources. For most new biotechnology companies, joint ventures are almost always preferred over licensing arrangements because they give the start-up firm an opportunity to finance its internal infrastructure and to share profits. In a standard licensing arrangement, the start-up

Table 16.1	**Alliances Made by U.S. Biotech Firms with Foreign Partners**	
U.S. Company	**European Alliances**	**Asian Alliances**
Amgen	1	4
Biogen	8	7
Bio-Response	0	0
Bio-Technology General	0	4
California Biotechnology	3	2
Centocor	4	4
Chiron	12	4
Cytogen	1	0
Damon Biotech	1	0
Ecogen	0	0
Genentech	7	6
Genetics Institute	6	3
Genex	3	1
Immunex	5	0
Plant Genetics	1	3
Repligen	4	1
Synergen	1	0
Vestar	3	0
Xoma	3	0

Source: U.S. Office of Technology Assessment, *Biotechnology in a Global Economy*. Washington, D.C.: U.S. Government Printing Office, 1992, p. 59.

402

Part V
*Organization
Structure
as a Dynamic
Process*

would avoid some of the business risk of the partnership but would receive a smaller reward in the form of a small royalty on eventual sales.

Licensing agreements are also very popular in biotechnology companies, but they do not receive rave reviews from biotechnology executives. These arrangements, if made exclusively to raise cash before the product is ready, put the company at a negotiating disadvantage from the beginning. However, if a firm has already created a product that has potential, such as the one Marteck has developed, licensing can be of great benefit to the firm because it guarantees a stream of income in the future, but the firm does not have to give up either technology or equity.

PRODUCTION NETWORKS IN THE COMPUTER INDUSTRY

For years, the large computer manufacturers in the United States, such as IBM, had structures featuring a high degree of vertical integration.[3] This method of production, which survived well into the 1980s, was characterized by slow-moving technology and stable product lines. The firm designed and produced in house not only the final product but also all of its technologically sophisticated components and subsystems. Subcontractors were used only to meet surges during boom times and to provide only standard inputs.

Competitive conditions in the computer industry have changed drastically since the 1970s. The cost of bringing new products to market has increased while the pace of new product introduction and technological change has accelerated. In this newer, more competitive market, products have to be brought to market in a matter of months instead of years. This change in the business environment forced IBM to rely on outside suppliers to an unprecedented extent in the early 1980s in order to bring a personal computer to the market rapidly.

Increasing technological complexity has raised the cost of developing new products. Computer systems today include central processing units, operating systems, power supplies, storage systems, and much more. Customers seek increased performance in all aspects of the product, making it virtually impossible for one firm to stay at the forefront of all these technologies.

Out of necessity, firms must focus on what they do best—their core competencies—and acquire the rest. This represents a fundamental shift from vertical integration. When Sun Microsystems was established in 1982, it decided to focus on designing hardware and software workstations and to limit manufacturing to prototypes, final assembly, and testing. All components for the workstations were purchased. The management of Sun Microsystems understood the issues quite clearly. A vertically integrated structure was possible, but Sun would face great difficulties remaining competitive in a number of separate areas. Sun recognized that hundreds of specialty shops in Silicon Valley invested heavily in staying at the leading edge in the design and manufacture of microprocessors, disk drives, printed circuit boards, and other pieces of computer hardware. Relying on outside suppliers reduced Sun's overhead and ensured that the firm's workstations used state-of-the-art technology.

Sun's guiding principle, like that of most new Silicon Valley systems firms, is to concentrate its expertise and resources on coordinating the design and assembly of a final system. This is the *core competency* of many of these firms, and Sun was able to advance only those technologies critical to its main line of business.

---

[3]This section is adapted from A. Saxenian, "The Origin and Dynamics of Production Networks in Silicon Valley," *Research Policy* 20, no. 5 (1991), pp. 423–437.

During the 1970s northern California's Silicon Valley and Boston's Route 128 attracted international acclaim as the world's leading centers of electronics innovation. Both regions were widely celebrated for their technological vitality, their entrepreneurship, and their extraordinary economic growth.

The enchantment waned in the early 1980s, when the leading producers in both regions experienced crises. Silicon Valley chip makers relinquished the semiconductor market to Japan, while Route 128 minicomputer companies watched their customers shift to workstations and personal computers.

The performance of these two regional economies diverged, however, later in the decade. In Silicon Valley a new generation of semiconductor and computer companies, such as Sun Microsystems, Conner Peripherals, and Cypress Semiconductor, as well as the region's established companies, such as Intel and Hewlett-Packard, experienced dynamic growth. The Route 128 region, by contrast, showed few signs of reversing its decline. The "Massachusetts Miracle" ended abruptly, and start-ups failed to compensate for continuing layoffs at the region's established minicomputer companies.

Why has Silicon Valley adapted successfully to changing patterns of international competition, while Route 128 is losing its competitive edge? Because, despite similar origins and technologies, the two regions have evolved distinct industrial systems since World War II. Their responses to the crises of the '80s revealed variations in local economic structure and organizational philosophy whose significance was unrecognized during the rapid growth of earlier decades. Far from superficial, those variations illustrate that local factors play an important role in determining how well a company will adapt to changes in an industry. And it's possible to pinpoint the factors that enable one region to capture and nurture the entrepreneurial spirit—and allow another to let it slip.

Silicon Valley has a regional-network-based industrial system—that is, it promotes collective learning and flexible adjustment among companies that make specialty products within a broad range of related technologies. The region's dense social networks and open labor market encourage entrepreneurship and experimentation. Companies compete intensely while learning from one another about changing markets and technologies through informal communication and collaboration. In a network-based system, the organizational boundaries within companies are porous, as are the boundaries between companies themselves and between companies and local institutions such as trade associations and universities.

The Route 128 region is dominated by a small number of relatively vertically integrated corporations. Its industrial system is based on independent companies that keep largely to themselves. Secrecy and corporate loyalty govern relations between companies and their customers, suppliers, and competitors, reinforcing a regional culture that encourages stability and self-reliance. Corporate hierarchies ensure that authority remains centralized, and information tends to flow vertically. The boundaries between and within companies, and between companies and local institutions, thus remain distinct in the independent-company-based system.

The performance of Silicon Valley and Route 128 in the past few decades provides insights into regional sources of competitiveness. Far from being isolated from what's outside them, companies are embedded in a social and institutional setting—an industrial system—that shapes, and is shaped by, their strategies and structures.

Understanding regional economies as industrial systems rather than as clusters of producers, and thinking of Silicon Valley and Route 128 as examples of the two models of industrial systems—the regional-network-based system and the independent-company-based system—illuminate the different fates of the two economies.

Consider two pairs of comparable companies, one pair located in Silicon Valley, the other on Route 128. The comparison of Apollo Computer and Sun Microsystems—start-ups in the same market, the former on Route 128 and the latter in Silicon Valley—shows how small companies benefit from external sources of information, technology, and know-how in a decentralized network-based industrial system. And the case of Route 128's Digital Equipment Corp. (DEC) and Silicon Valley's Hewlett-Packard—the leading computer-systems producers in the two regions—shows how regional networks facilitate the reorganization of large companies.

The experiences of Apollo and Sun show how the isolating structures and practices of Route 128's independent-company-based system put start-ups at a disadvantage in a fast-paced industry. Apollo pioneered the engineering workstation in 1980 and was enormously successful. By most accounts, the company had a product that was superior to that of Sun (which was started two years after Apollo, in 1982). The two companies competed neck and neck during the mid-'80s, but in 1987 Apollo fell behind the faster-moving, more responsive Sun and never regained its lead. By the time it was purchased by Hewlett-Packard, in 1989, Apollo had fallen to fourth place in the industry, while Sun was number one.

Apollo's initial strategy and structure reflected the model of corporate self-sufficiency that had been followed by its region's large minicomputer companies. In spite of its pioneering workstation design, for example, the company adopted proprietary standards that made its products incompatible with other machines, and it chose to design and fabricate its own central processor and specialized integrated circuits.

Sun, in contrast, pioneered open systems. The company's founders, then all in their twenties, adopted the UNIX operating system because they felt that the market would never accept a workstation custom-designed by four graduate students. By making the specifications for its systems widely available to suppliers and competitors, Sun challenged the proprietary and highly profitable approach of industry leaders IBM, DEC, and Hewlett-Packard, each of which locked customers in to a single vendor of hardware and software.

That strategy allowed Sun to focus on designing the hardware and software for workstations and to limit manufacturing, choosing instead to purchase virtually all its components off the shelf from external vendors. As Sun grew into a multibillion-dollar company, that focus enabled it to rapidly introduce complex new products and continually alter its product mix.

As a result, the Sun workstations, while vulnerable to imitation by competitors, were significantly cheaper to produce and priced lower than the Apollo systems. Apollo, like the Route 128 minicomputer producers, was slow to abandon its proprietary systems and as late as 1985 still refused to acknowledge the growing demand for open standards.

Sun's strategy succeeded because it drew upon Silicon Valley's sophisticated and diversified technical infrastructure. Apollo not only failed to respond quickly enough to industry changes but also suffered from a more limited regional infrastructure. Its commitment to formality, hierarchy, and long-term stability—typical of most Route 128 companies—could not have offered a greater contrast to the "controlled chaos" that characterized Sun.

The successes of the '80s generation of start-ups were the most visible sign that Silicon Valley was adapting successfully, but changes within the region's large companies were equally important. Established producers such as Hewlett-Packard decentralized their operations, creating intercompany production networks that formalized the region's social and technical interdependencies and strengthened its industrial system.

Adaptation in the Route 128 economy was constrained by the isolating organizational structures and practices of its leading producers. The region's large minicomputer companies adjusted very slowly to the new market conditions, and by the end of the decade they were struggling to survive in an industry they had once dominated.

By 1990 both DEC and Hewlett-Packard were $13-billion companies, and they're now among the largest civilian employers in their regions. Both faced comparable challenges, but each responded quite differently: Hewlett-Packard gradually opened itself by building a network of local alliances and subcontracting relationships, while strengthening its global reach. DEC, in spite of its formal commitment to decentralization, retained a substantially more self-sufficient organizational structure and corporate mind-set.

The lessons from Sun and Apollo, DEC and Hewlett-Packard are clear: local economies with industrial systems built on regional networks are more flexible and technologically dynamic than those in which learning is confined to individual companies. Sun and Hewlett-Packard are not unique in Silicon Valley—the region is home to hundreds of specialty high-tech producers that adjust to one another's needs through shifting patterns of competition and collaboration.

Since 1980 Route 128 has continued to generate new companies and technologies, but its companies have failed to commercialize their technologies rapidly or consistently enough to sustain regional prosperity. The regional economy continues to flounder today as cuts in defense spending compound the difficulties caused by ongoing layoffs at DEC and other minicomputer companies.

What can be done to promote local health? Our comparison suggests that networks flourish in supportive regional contexts. To survive, networks need a region's institutions and culture to ensure the repeated interaction that builds mutual trust while also intensifying rivalries. When industrial networks are embedded in such a supportive local environment, they promote a decentralized process of collective learning and foster the continual innovation that is essential in the current competitive environment.

Yet the clustering of companies in a given area does not by itself create such mutually beneficial interdependencies. Companies in an industrial system may be geographically clustered and yet have limited capacity for adaptation if the area's leading producers are independent-minded. As in the case of Route 128— and many of the older industrial regions of the United States and Europe—the legacies of a history of economic self-sufficiency that are passed on to the institutions and infrastructure of a regional economy mean that the prospects for regeneration are neither easy nor fast. Adopting an industrial system that breaks down the institutional and social boundaries that divide companies represents a major challenge for Route 128; it's a challenge that will be even more daunting for regions with less sophisticated industrial infrastructures and skill bases.

Source: AnnaLee Saxenian, "Silicon Valley Versus Route 128," Inc., February 1994, pp. 25–26. Reprinted with permission, Inc. magazine (February 1994). Copyright 1994 by Goldhirsh Group, Inc., 38 Commercial Wharf, Boston, MA 02110.

406

Part V
*Organization
Structure
as a Dynamic
Process*

This is not to say that the principle of bounded rationality did not apply to Sun; rather the limits of Sun's bounded rationality were reduced because of changes in the underlying technologies and industry structure.

In fact, some firms explicitly recognize their reliance on suppliers and foster their development. Apple Computers' venture capital arm makes minority investments in promising firms that offer complementary technologies.

This trend toward more reliance on decentralizing activities in the firm and on production networks is not limited to small or new firms seeking to avoid fixed investments. Even Hewlett-Packard, which designs and manufactures chips, printed circuit boards, disk drives, and many other peripherals, has restructured to gain flexibility. The reader's attention is directed to the box "ReDoing Hewlett-Packard" in Chapter 1.

The production network of integrated computer producers extends beyond the system firms and their immediate suppliers. Silicon Valley's suppliers of electronic components and subsystems are themselves vertically desegregated to spread the risks of chip making. The cost and risks of developing new computer systems are spread across networks of autonomous but interdependent firms in Silicon Valley. In an environment that demands rapid new product introduction and continual technological change, no one firm has the core competency to design and manufacture all components of computers on its own.

The more specialized these computers and their components become, the more organizations are drawn into partnerships with their suppliers. Because they are increasingly treated as equals in a joint process of designing, developing, and manufacturing innovative systems, the suppliers themselves become innovative and capital-intensive producers of differentiated products hiring their own outside suppliers. In other words, another layer is added to the productive web of firms.

Silicon Valley system firms now view their relationships with suppliers more as long-term investments rather than short-term procurement relationships. They recognize collaboration with suppliers as a way to speed the pace of new product introductions and improve product quality and performance. To keep the interfirm coordination and management costs low, most organizations build relationships with a few suppliers to supply most of their components.

These relationships are based on shared recognition of the need to ensure the success of a final product. Epitomizing the trust between partners, long-term business plans are commonly shared as are confidential sales forecasts and cost information. The sharing of sales forecasts allows suppliers to plan investment levels. Spreading the knowledge concerning cost structures encourages a fair negotiation of prices high enough to yield suppliers a fair return on their investments and low enough to keep the systems firm competitive.

These relationships obviously transcend simply handling an order placed by a customer. In the early stages of product development, engineers from the systems firms and parts suppliers explore issues of technical feasibility and share product visions. Throughout the whole process, communication is vital as the boundaries between firms become increasingly more and more blurred. Interestingly enough, in these strategic alliances, firms interact with each other in a way not much different from departments in a vertically integrated firm. The key difference is that in a strategic alliance, the systems firm and the suppliers treat each other as customers, not as corporate overhead.

In many of these alliances nondisclosure agreements and contracts are normally signed, but few believe that they really matter. What does seem present is a mutually shared concern for the long-term health of the other firms. According to Apple Computers' manager of purchasing:

We have found you don't always need a formal contract. . . . If you develop trust with your suppliers, you don't need armies of attorneys. . . . In order for us to be successful in the future, we have to develop better working relationships, better trusting relationships, than just hounding vendors for price decreases on an annual basis."[4]

While these relationships are often remarkably close, both parties are careful to preserve their own autonomy. Most Silicon Valley firms will not allow their business to account for more than 20 percent of a supplier's product and prefer that no customer occupy such a position. Suppliers are thus forced to find outside customers, which ensures that the loss of a single account will not put them out of business.

PRODUCTION NETWORKS IN THE JAPANESE AUTOMOBILE INDUSTRY

The international competitiveness and preeminence of the Japanese automobile industry has given rise to careful examination of that industry. The subcontracting system used by Japanese producers has been singled out as one of the main reasons for high production efficiency. One of the pillars of the subcontracting system in Japan is the role of small- and medium-sized firms in the production process. Over three-quarters of industrial production in Japan is carried out by small- and medium-sized firms.

The second pillar is the medium and small subcontracting promotion law, which defines subcontracting as the production of goods that are to be used as intermediary processed goods such as parts and raw materials. Japan has a high level of social interest in medium and small firms.

The automobile parts industry especially benefited from the 1965 passage of the law on temporary measures for promoting the machinery industries. Through this law, the Japan Development Bank lent funds to first-tier automobile parts firms, and the Small Business Finance Corporation assisted secondary suppliers. The purpose of the legislation was to establish a rational production system to modernize facilities and develop new technologies.[5]

In Japan the role of the subcontracting system has its origins in the economic boom of the 1950s. The initial role of the subcontracting firms was to allow the parent firms to expand their production. This was achieved by investing in the subcontracting firms. To utilize exclusively a specific subcontracting company, it was necessary to take care of the full operation, equipment, capital, employees, and so on. In the expanding economy, however, capital was plentiful and specialized producers grew rapidly.

During the expansion of 1965 to 1973, the make-or-buy decision of parent companies was reexamined. The strength of the system was further increased by the reorganization of subcontracting management through the creation of a tight relationship between the production and planning management departments, as well as the introduction of computers. At this time, value analysis was introduced; it focused on the availability and integration of parts in production. As a result, the number of parts decreased and the assembling function was simplified, as was the processing function of subcontracting companies.

Between 1974 and 1983, the subcontracting system was again restructured. Marginal firms were forced to leave the system and the rest were reorganized into

---

[4]M. Cohodas, "How Apple Buys Electronics," *Electronics Purchasing*, November 1986.
[5]Rebecca Morales, *Flexible Production* (Cambridge, Mass.: The Polity Press, 1994), p. 105.

408

Part V
*Organization
Structure
as a Dynamic
Process*

the now well-known *Kanban* method of production management. This system forced a combined enterprise group on subcontractors, including strict management of just-in-time delivery. The proportion of subcontractors in the manufacturing sector increased from 53.1 percent in 1966 to 65.5 percent in 1981.

The Japanese subcontracting system is defined by extreme specialization. Among parts makers, parts assemblers, and special processors, parts processors' specialization proceeds at different degrees at different levels. The degree of specialization in Japan is not found in other developed countries.

There are several levels of subcontractors, with subcontractors themselves subcontracting. The system is a dynamic one. The small and medium firms have freed themselves from restrictions set by large companies, and the new system is much less hierarchical than in the past. Subcontractors have tended to increase the number of large firms with which they have subcontracting relationships; on average, each has a supplier relationship with four contracting firms. This gives the small firm bargaining power and leverage over the large firm. Finally, one of the most important reasons for using subcontracting in Japan is the high level of technical knowledge of the subcontractors.[6]

Organization of the Subcontracting System

The guiding principle of Japanese auto firms, like most Silicon Valley systems firms, is to concentrate their expertise and resources on coordinating the design and assembly of a final system, to advance critical technologies with respect to the firm's core competencies. The firm spreads the cost of production and the risk of new designs through a system of strategic alliances with suppliers.

Japan has an asymmetric but nevertheless close relationship between assemblers and the first-tier supplier based on long-term interaction and information sharing. For the system of just-in-time production to be effective, it must have certain characteristics, including long-term relationships; close geographic proximity; and tight interorganizational linkages characterized by personnel sharing, joint participation in product development, and regular communication and interaction.[7]

Figure 16.1 shows the main subcontracting relationships in the Japanese automobile industry. The organization of the subcontracting system is broken down into three levels. The first level consists of the assembly operations of the parent company and its subsidiary relations with 12 first-tier subcontractors. These subcontractors supply unit components, for example, engine parts, body parts, electrical parts, and brakes. Like systems firms in Silicon Valley, the assembling firms primarily engage in research and development, design, and final assembly.

Each of these subsidiary firms is served by a second tier of subcontractors that produce finished parts and a third tier of subcontractors that produce semifinished parts. For example, in the production of body parts, the second-tier subcontractors, of which there are up to several hundred for each firm, work with thousands of third-tier firms that machine and supply the small plastic and metal parts. Each level has its own machining, stamping, finishing, and inspection unit.

The division of labor in the Japanese automobile industry is consistent with the new form of industrial organizations discussed in Chapter 14. In the new industrial organization, small- and medium-sized firms have a much increased role. The tendency is for the large firms to focus on design and assembly while subcontracting the others functions.

---

[6]Masahiko Aoki, "The Japanese Firm in Transition," in *The Political Economy of Japan*, vol. 1: *Domestic Transformation*, ed. Kozo Yamamura and Yashukichi Yasuba (Stanford: Stanford University Press, 1987), p. 283.

[7]Martin Kenney and Richard Florida, *Beyond Mass Production* (New York: Oxford University Press, 1993), p. 130.

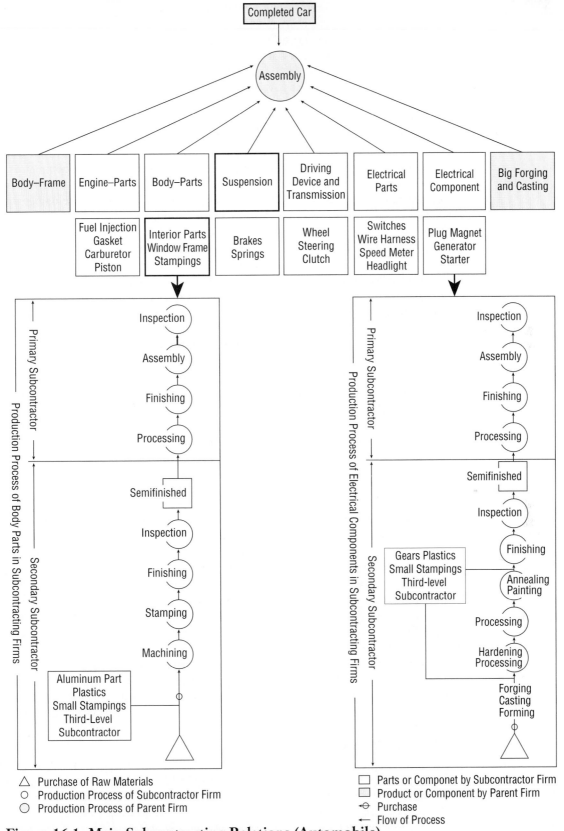

Figure 16.1 Main Subcontracting Relations (Automobile)
(White Paper on Small and Medium Enterprises 1982, p. 173.)

410

Part V
*Organization
Structure
as a Dynamic
Process*

**Comparison of Japanese
and U.S. Firms**

As a consequence of pursuing a strategy of working with subcontractors, the Japanese auto firms have been much less vertically integrated than the U.S. automakers. Japanese firms are quasi-integrated while the U.S. firms are fully integrated. *Quasi-integrated* implies that the supplier firm has its own research and development, manufacturing, and assembly operations. The difference between the two is that the Japanese firms have purchased fully assembled systems from a relatively small number of suppliers. For example General Motors used some 35,000 different suppliers in 1986; in the same year, Toyota used only about 224 second-tier suppliers, which in turn used about 30,000 third-tier suppliers. Whereas the Japanese assemblers contract out about 70 percent of the entire value of the car, U.S. manufacturers have traditionally used well under 50 percent of subcontractors.

The Japanese system differs from the U.S. one in several important ways. The Japanese system relies much less on competitive bidding and more on performance evaluations than do U.S. firms. Japanese suppliers have a powerful incentive to perform well—additional contracts with the parent company. In this setting, a long-term relationship is established marked by a succession of contracts for subcontractors who behave "properly." This is conceptually similar to the employment relationship described in Chapter 13. The economic rents that serve as rewards to discourage shirking and other types of opportunistic behavior in the Japanese subcontracting system are, of course, the future contracts.

In this environment, bidding on contracts can take place only after detailed design work has been completed. In this regard, the Japanese system of parts suppliers is similar to the **production network** seen in Silicon Valley. The most sophisticated suppliers are trusted to design their own parts, subject to general design specifications provided by the manufacturer. In other words, the system requires a certain amount of knowledge sharing.

This system has advantages and disadvantages.[8] Of the two disadvantages, one involves performance appraisal; the second is the hold-up problem. The performance appraisal problem has two dimensions: price and quality. Basically, the assembling firm needs to be reassured that it is getting a quality input at a fair price. On the quality dimension, the first-tier suppliers provide entire units to the assembling firms. Put in the simplest terms possible, either the part works, or it doesn't. If it doesn't, the supplier firm is held responsible. There is no room for endless technical discussions on which small part didn't work and which supplier is to blame; the unit is clearly the first-tier supplier's responsibility. If a supplier makes transmissions for Honda Accords, that supplier is responsible for them. This economizes on bargaining costs for the assembling firms, effectively shifting the costs to specialized producers that may have a better information base with which to deal with the problem.

To manage the price dimension of performance appraisal, Toyota has adopted a two-supplier policy under which different first-tier suppliers make the same unit for different Toyota models. One supplier makes the body parts for the Camry, and a second makes the body parts for the Tercel. In the absence of any collusive agreement between the two firms supplying body parts to Toyota (a practice that goes against Japanese culture), Toyota has information on what constitutes a "fair" price.

In the Japanese system, as noted, the reward for good performance is to be given more contracts. This practice further reinforces close ties between assembling firms and their suppliers.

Suppliers fear that after making a relationship-specific investment with an assembling firm, the assembler will demand unfair concessions on price. Even in a close relationship, "closeness" in and of itself does not resolve real differences of

---

[8]Paul Milgrom and John Roberts, *Economics, Organization and Management* (Englewoods Cliffs, N.J.: Prentice Hall, 1992), pp. 567–568.

opinion. The Japanese system takes several steps to minimize the likelihood of this occurrence. The approach commonly taken is for supplier and assembler to share cost information, forming expectations of the initial price. Profits for the supplier are then based on its ability to lower production costs through innovation. Additionally, suppliers earn bonuses if their more efficient production methods can be routinized to facilitate sharing with the other suppliers of the assembler. The result of all of this sharing is lower costs for the assembling, or core, firm.

A second device to mitigate the threat of a hold-up or other postcontractual opportunism is the formation of associations of parts suppliers, formalizing communication between them. This practice is a direct attempt to institutionalize information flows.

The advantages of the Japanese system of supplier relations over the vertically fully integrated system might not be clear at first. Both systems allow for the protection of firm-specific assets, with the Japanese system relying on reputation (quasi-market) and the U.S. system on ownership (vertically integrated). However, one advantage of the Japanese system is that it may be easier to break relations with a supplier that consistently does not meet quality or some other specification than to close a division that is performing badly. GM has had a very difficult time trying to close several underperforming parts divisions. The costs incurred in attempting to influence others' decisions in closing a division and going to outside suppliers might be substantial.

▓ THE GLOBAL AUTOMOBILE INDUSTRY

Japan's rise to market leadership in the international automobile industry sent multiple signals throughout the industry. Perhaps the clearest signals were the decline of U.S. dominance in the global automobile market and the beginning of a new international order.[9] Indeed, U.S. firms would drastically restructure their operations, becoming more efficient as a matter of survival.

Since its inception, the automobile industry has evolved through several phases. The first, beginning in the 1890s and continuing to the 1920s, consisted of the craft era. Initially, the scale of manufacturing and structure of markets favored European producers. The second phase, lasting from the 1920s to the end of the 1970s, came with the rise of mass production. As markets broadened and large-scale manufacturing predominated, U.S. firms took the lead. The third and current period is characterized by international competition and flexible production. In this era, Japan is clearly the driving force.

As shown in Table 16.2, motor vehicle production in the United States actually declined between 1975 and 1990; in Japan, it increased from 6,941,591 to 13,486,796 cars and trucks during the same period. In West Germany, it increased from 3,186,208 to 4,660,657 vehicles. These figures do not tell the complete story, however. If we look at the production of passenger cars only, the United States produced 634,000 fewer passenger cars in 1960 than in 1990, while total world production increased by 172 percent! Clearly, while passenger car production in the world was increasing, U.S. production was decreasing in both absolute and relative terms.

The internationalization of the automobile industry has led to two quite different strategies on both sides of the Pacific. In the 1970s, the U.S. automaker embarked on a strategy of avoiding unionization and moved assembly operations to the South and parts production to Mexico. This global plan had parts manufactured overseas and assembled in the southern United States to lower costs. The policy was a failure; between 1979 and 1991, U.S. car makers closed 66 plants.

Japanese Transplants
in the United States

---

[9]Morales, *Flexible Production.*

Table 16.2	World Auto Production, 1950–1990		
North America	**1950**	**1975**	**1990**
United States	8,005,859	8,896,513	9,888,036
Mexico	21,575	360,678	820,558
Western Europe			
(W) Germany	306,064	3,186,208	4,660,657
Italy	127,847	1,458,649	1,874,672
United Kingdom	783,672	1,648,399	1,295,611
Sweden	17,553	366,753	335,853
Asia Pacific			
Japan	31,597	6,941,591	13,486,796
South Korea	0	36,264	1,321,630
Eastern Europe			
Yugoslavia	0	205,567	342,727
South America			
Brazil	0	930,235	914,576
World	**10,577,426**	**32,998,363**	**44,165,033**

Source: Motor Vehicle Manufacturers Association, *World Motor Vehicle Data (1991)*, cited in Rebecca Morales, *Flexible Production* (Oxford: Blackwell, 1994.)

As early as 1970, Japanese automobile companies saw the need to expand into the U.S. market. These efforts intensified after the oil crisis of 1974 to 1975, because small, fuel-efficient Japanese cars were in great demand. Every component of the U.S. automaking industry—manufacturers, parts suppliers, and unions—began to call on both the public and the federal government for protection against imports. Negotiations between the U.S. and Japanese governments began and proceeded slowly. Eventually, an agreement was reached under which Japanese producers agreed to voluntarily limit the number of Japanese cars exported to the U.S. market.

In early 1980 United Auto Workers President Douglas Fraser lashed out at the Japanese assemblers, stating that voluntary restrictions "are not enough, we want firm, solid commitments [to establish U.S. production] this time."[10]

By 1980, it was clear to the Japanese auto assemblers that they would have to establish a U.S. production base. Japanese automakers were quick to set in motion plans for U.S. production. Toyota announced that it would build a truck assembly plant and Honda announced construction of a $200 million, 100,000-car-a-year plant in Marysville, Ohio.

Since 1980, the major Japanese automobile parts suppliers have set up a dozen high-capacity automobile assembly plants in North America. These **transplants** produce an estimated 2.4 million cars annually in the United States, roughly 20 percent of total U.S. production. The transplants employ more than 30,000 U.S. workers; and Honda, the largest employer, currently employs an excess of 8,000 workers in the United States, a number that is expected to increase to 11,000. For additional information on specific Japanese automakers plants in the United States, see Table 16.3.

Japanese Subcontractors in the United States

The arrival of Japanese assemblers in the United States in the early 1980s was followed by suppliers. More than 300 Japanese or Japanese–U.S. venture automo-

[10]Kenney and Florida, *Beyond Mass Production*, p. 97.

Table 16.3 Japanese Automakers in the United States

Company	Location	Start Year	Projected Capacity	Employment at Full Capacity	Investment Outlay[a]
Honda	Marysville, OH	1982	500,000	8,000	2,000
Nissan	Smyrna, TN	1983	450,000	5,100	1,700
NUMMI	Freemont, CA	1984	300,000	3,400	500
Mazda	Flat Rock, MI	1987	240,000	3,400	750
Toyota	Georgetown, KY	1988	400,000	5,000	2,000
Diamond-Star	Normal, IL	1989	240,000	2,900	700
Subaru-Isuzu	Lafayette, IN	1989	120,000	1,700	600
Ford-Nissan	Avon Lake, OH	1992	130,000	1,300	700
Total			2,380,000	30,800	8,950

[a] In millions of current dollars.

Source: Martin Kenney and Richard Florida, *Beyond Mass Production: The Japanese System and Its Transfer to the U.S.* Copyright © 1993 by Oxford University Press, Inc. Reprinted by permission.

bile parts suppliers have been established; these ventures have taken jobs from auto assemblers in the United States. These transplanted suppliers include a large number of wholly owned Japanese companies in addition to a sizable number of joint ventures between Japanese and U.S. automotive parts companies. Transplanted suppliers have invested at least $8 billion in U.S. production, creating a virtual second automobile industry in the United States.

Transplant suppliers are building an integrated supplier complex in the United States by providing the broader just-in-time industrial infrastructure for automobile production. The transplanted automobile suppliers are mainly concentrated in the Midwest in the same states in which the transplanted assembly facilities are located. Ohio is home to 65 transplant parts companies; Michigan has 44. In the South, Kentucky has 42.

▪ CHAPTER SUMMARY AND KEY IDEAS ▪ ▪ ▪ ▪ ▪ ▪

Every organization must take a position as to the make-or-buy decision. It must decide to what extent the firm will be vertically integrated. Between the two extremes of vertical integration and pure market lie strategic alliances. Recently, a host of production arrangements have developed as alternative governance or organizational structures to both vertical integration and market procurement.

These arrangements are more flexible than the hierarchical mass production system of the past and allow firms to achieve goals more easily and quickly. A system of related strategic alliances forms a production network. The purpose of these networks is to produce with the flexibility of the market but without the permanence and rigidities of vertical integration.

Strategic alliances do not eliminate transaction costs, but they represent a form of organizing economic activity that tends toward efficiency. Strategic alliances represent relational contracts in which trust is an essential building block and reputation serves as a disciplining device.

Another aspect of strategic alliances is that bounded rationality may not be as large a problem as in a pure market arrangement. Two implications of strategic alliances are that intrafirm coordination costs will decrease, and interfirm coordination becomes more important.

414

Part V
*Organization
Structure
as a Dynamic
Process*

KEY TERMS

business unit strategy	international joint venture
cooperation	production network
corporate strategy	strategic alliances
governance structure	transplants
industrial system	

FURTHER READINGS

Besanko, D., D. Dranove, and M. T. Shanley. *Economics of Strategy*. New York: John Wiley (In press).

Cohodas, M. "How Apple Buys Electronics" *Electronics Purchasing*, November 1986.

Geringer, M. J. "Strategic Determinants of Partner Selection Criteria in International Joint Ventures." *Journal of International Business Studies*, 1991, pp. 41–62.

Gerlach, M. *Alliance Capitalism*. Los Angeles: University of California Press, 1992.

Kenney, M., and R. Florida, *Beyond Mass Production*. New York: Oxford University Press, 1993.

Lie, D., and J. W. Slocum Jr. "Global Strategy, Competence-Building and Strategic Alliances." *California Management Review*, Fall 1992, pp. 81–97.

Mason, J. C. "Strategic Alliances: Partnering for Success." *Management Review*, May 1993, pp. 10–15.

Milgrom, P., and J. Roberts. *Economics, Organization and Management*. Englewood Cliffs, N.J.: Prentice Hall, 1992.

Morales, R. *Flexible Production*. Oxford: Blackwell, 1994.

Robert, M. "The Do's and Don'ts of Strategic Alliances." *The Journal of Business Strategy*, March/April 1992, pp. 50–53.

Sato, Y. "The Subcontracting Production (Shikauke) System in Japan." *Keio Business Review* 21, no. 1 (1983), pp. 1–25.

Saxenian, A. "The Origin and Dynamics of Production Networks in Silicon Valley." *Research Policy* 20, no. 5 (1991), pp. 423–437

U.S. Office of Technology Assessment. *Biotechnology in a Global Economy*. Washington, D.C.: U.S. Government Printing Office, 1992.

QUESTIONS AND PROBLEMS FOR REVIEW AND DISCUSSION

A. In the United States, most automobile firms were highly vertically integrated. What are the advantages of the Japanese system of supplier relationships over the more fully vertically integrated systems found in the United States?

B. Strategic alliances do not eliminate transaction costs: instead they typify a form of organizing economic activity that represents a tendency toward efficiency.

1. Why is trust important in a strategic alliance?

2. Is it important for just-in-time inventory systems?

C. One of the major organizational decisions made by corporations today is the amount of vertical integration to pursue in their corporate structure. A good example is provided by the automobile producers. G.M. typically makes a large portion of its cars, as does Ford (to a somewhat lesser extent). The newer Chrysler cars—the LH series—feature a large role played by outside suppliers. Provide a list of three (separate) factors that may influence a corporation in its choice of degree of vertical integration.

An International Comparison of Organizational Styles

▨▨▨▨ CHAPTER OUTLINE AND STUDENT GOALS ▨▨▨▨

The Importance of a Global Understanding

In the new global economy, isolation is not a viable option even for the most powerful single country in the world. We need to consider organizational practices in other countries for two major reasons. First, a firm understanding of business practices in other nations can provide the basis for a better understanding of organizations in the United States, especially as they continue to evolve and grow more competitive in the international arena. As indicated in Chapters 15 and 16, this evolution might make U.S. organizations more similar to organizations in other nations. Second, as interaction with organizations in other countries increases, U.S. firms must understand the practices and culture of foreign countries, for logistical purposes as well as for establishing an environment of trust and understanding that is necessary for relational contracting. In this chapter, we emphasize the organizational patterns found in Germany and Japan with corresponding patterns in the United States.

Intellectual isolation and ignorance of how the economies of trading partners function imply major costs. Increasingly, U.S. managers have to travel and interact with partners in foreign countries. Given the reality of today's global corporations, U.S. managers must frequently work overseas on joint ventures or in subsidiaries connected with the rapidly growing flow of foreign direct investment. Although foreigners usually speak English and have some idea of U.S. business, U.S. managers need to know the institutions and the customs of the economies in which they are active. The success of Japan, in particular, has generated enormous interest among U.S. managers in the way the Japanese do business and organize their economy.

Reflecting this widespread interest in learning from Japan, we have referred to practices of Japanese firms throughout this book. Germany is another major international trading country; it is the dominating economy in the European Union (EU). Germany represents a distinct European tradition, located somewhere between the U.S. and Japanese modes. The United Kingdom is perhaps familiar to many Americans, and is similar in many ways to the United States; German and other continental European institutional structures are in many ways closer to those of Japan. In other important and interesting ways, German and Japanese production and economic affairs are organized somewhat differently.

Areas of Comparison

In this chapter we highlight the key country-specific areas of interest and the similarities and differences between the U.S., German, and Japanese economies. We point out at the beginning that, as with any comparison, we must make some gen-

416

Part V
*Organization
Structure
as a Dynamic
Process*

eralizations. After all, economic activity in each country is dynamic and constantly evolving. Our characterizations of U.S., German, and Japanese practices reflect the most accurate assessment of activity in each of these countries today.

We begin with the organization of production in these three countries. In the United States, we have a strong tradition of mass production. German production organization has more emphasis on small and medium-sized owner-managed entrepreneurial firms in which labor has much more say concerning managerial decision making. Even though strategic alliances and long-term relationships with subcontractors are common in Germany, they are not as clearly marked as in Japan.

The most striking differences in organizing economic activity among the three systems are apparent in the area of labor relations. The U.S. tradition of adversarial, conflict-ridden labor-management relations becomes increasingly dysfunctional as U.S. companies strive to implement flexible manufacturing. Germany, by contrast, has a long tradition of institutionalized cooperation. The Japanese system of lifetime employment for core employees in large corporations is a purely informal arrangement. Employment at Japanese and German firms is more stable, although the mechanics in each case differ.

Financing activities and corporate control also differ across the three countries. The U.S. practices are vastly different from those in Japan and Germany; however, significant differences between the Japanese and German modes cannot be ignored.

Differences in scientific and technological progress have captured popular imagination and attracted much attention from policy makers in government and industry. The U.S. system offers enormous rewards for breakthroughs in basic research. However, the United States lags Japan in its ability to translate these breakthroughs into marketable and competitive products. Although Japan has a remarkable record of marketing new technologies, basic research in Japanese universities and industries has been relatively undistinguished. Germany has lagged both countries in the high-tech arena. We can attribute this performance to some institutional factors.

After reading this chapter, you should be able to

- Describe the way the traditional methods of organizing production in Japan and Germany differ from those in the United States.

- Recognize the differences in labor-management relations among the three countries.

- Acknowledge the significant differences and similarities in financing activity for organizations in the United States, Japan, and Germany.

- Describe the different trends in high-tech economic activity in the three countries.

- Explain what economists mean when they speak of the "breakthrough illusion" and the impact of this on U.S. industry.

- Understand how labor-management relations, patterns of corporate control, and innovative economic activity in each country have affected the evolution of organizations to date in the United States, Japan, and Germany.

- Forecast how changing labor-management relations, patterns of corporate control, and achievement of innovative economic activity in each country will affect the evolution of organizations in the United States, Japan, and Germany.

PATTERNS OF PRODUCTION AMONG GERMANY, JAPAN, AND THE UNITED STATES

Although technology knows no frontiers and advanced products are made by all developed economies, the organization of production varies to a surprising degree across countries. We have already described the evolution and partial demise of mass production in the United States beginning around 1970. By this time, however, Toyota and other Japanese manufacturers had begun to develop flexible manufacturing systems and teamwork that would replace the U.S. model as the globally dominant method of organizing production. Between these opposite methods, a different environment in Europe drove organizations into a pattern of production resembling, yet different from, each. In Germany, a strong craft tradition and a large sector of small- and medium-sized firms, the Mittlestand, helped to propel that country from the ruins of World War II to the European continent's leading economic power.

Henry Ford's introduction of the assembly line in 1914 must rank as one of the great industrial innovations of the 20th century. Mass-producing firms were able to capture the huge domestic market given the superb transportation infrastructure and the absence of foreign competition. **Economies of scale** allowed mass-producing, or Taylorist, firms to provide goods at low prices, albeit at the cost of repetitive and mind-numbing work for the employees. Workers were kept at these jobs by the highest industrial wages in the world, which included an element of rent sharing by oligopolistic producers.

The stable macroeconomic environment necessary for the smooth functioning of this system was disturbed by a number of shocks beginning in the 1970s. These were discussed in great detail in Chapter 14 and will not be detailed here. As Japanese and other imports conquered one U.S. market after another, standards in production technology came to be set by Japanese-owned and managed subsidiaries, or transplants, in the United States. The success of these transplants shows that Japanese productive organization is not culture bound but could be competitive while employing U.S. workers, even in the old U.S. industrial heartland.[1]

As we discussed in Chapter 15, U.S. firms have begun to adopt principles of flexible manufacturing and new Japanese-style work practices. Just how far this process has gone is shown by a 1992 survey on the use of flexible work organization.[2] Some 35 percent of establishments with more than 50 employees made substantial use of teamwork, job rotation, and total quality management (three pillars of Japanese business practice). More interesting, these practices were particularly common in internationally competitive sectors and among manufacturers that emphasized product variety and quality rather than simply competing on the basis of low costs.

The success of major German corporations such as Mercedes, BMW, and Siemens in international markets has made their names synonymous with German quality and artisanship throughout the world. Much less well known is Germany's relatively large and stable sector of small and medium-sized firms, the **Mittlestand**. These firms are usually privately or family owned and have frequently established a world leadership in niche markets, particularly in the fields of engineering and metalworking.

U.S. Firms

German Firms

---

[1]See the excellent book by Richard Florida and Martin Kenney, *The Breakthrough Illusion* (New York: Basic Books, 1991).
[2]See P. Osterman, "How Common Is Work Place Transformation and Who Adopts It?" *Industrial and Labor Relations Review* 47 (January 1994), pp. 173–188.

418

Part V
*Organization
Structure
as a Dynamic
Process*

The concentration of these small and medium-sized firms is particularly strong in southwestern Germany, where they have flourished with the support of industrial policy by local governments. This policy includes an excellent system of technical and vocational education and training, government-supported research institutions, and selective grants for promising research and development projects. Entrepreneurial families cooperate with each other and with labor unions or as subcontractors (outside suppliers) for larger companies on the basis of trust and personal reputation.

Germany's Mittlestand is much more stable than corresponding industrial sectors in the United States. New start-ups are relatively rare in Germany because of a more regulated labor market and an underdeveloped venture capital market. Managers in large German corporations have secure jobs and are reluctant to leave and face the risks associated with new ventures. The flow of managerial and scientific talent, which has fueled the formation and growth of small entrepreneurial start-ups in the United States, is thus largely absent in Germany. Small-firm exit is also far less prevalent than in the United States, perhaps because of less activity in the market for control of German corporations.

The craft tradition has remained remarkably strong in industrialized Germany and has retained a fairly dominant influence on organizing production there. Reasons for this may be found in Germany's late industrialization, the important role of scientific education and training, and centralized bargaining with strong labor unions. At a political level, support for the craft tradition is strong, as evidenced by the technical training made available. This tradition-bound system has been criticized for being bureaucratic and inflexible. Craft-based qualifications and regulation of entry have often failed to keep up with technical progress.

On the positive side, there is little doubt that the combination of the craft tradition with heavy government involvement in the training system has produced what is probably the most highly skilled blue-collar labor force in Europe, if not the world. Some two-thirds of the workforce possess vocational qualifications, compared with one-third or fewer in the United States. In Germany, most teenagers are either in a full-time academic program or combining apprentice training in industry with part-time schooling. Skilled workers who obtain certification as master crafters frequently move on to take responsible positions in lower-level management, positions that would be reserved for college graduates in U.S. firms.

If what is sometimes called *lower education* (what corresponds to a U.S. high school diploma with vocational qualifications) in Germany clearly leads the United States, it must also be emphasized that higher education in Germany suffers a disadvantage. The once dominant state-run university system is now overcrowded, bureaucratic, and generally inefficient. Only a handful of small and undistinguished private universities compete with the state-run institutions.

Japanese Firms

The origins of what has become known as the characteristically Japanese organization of production can be found in two independent developments in post–World War II Japan. The first was the use of machines that stopped automatically in case of faults or defects and were arranged in configurations that enabled one operator, with the appropriate multiple skills, to tend more than one machine. Related to this was the **kanban**, just-in-time, or "order card" system for coordinating production. This system had considerable advantages over the top-down, command system of centralized production adopted by U.S. mass producers. These developments were pioneered by Taiichi Ohno at Toyota Motors but rapidly spread to other companies.

The other foundation of modern Japanese manufacturing grew, paradoxically, out of intense labor-management conflict. These battles led to the establishment

419

Chapter 17
*An International
Comparison
of Organizational
Styles*

of less radical enterprise unions and an implicit agreement to respect managerial rights to direct the enterprise. In return, workers gained job security. This **implicit contract** with labor soon turned out to possess important **complementarities** with the multiskill requirements of the technological organization.

The Japanese firms pioneered a variant of the **employment relationship** we described in Chapters 12 and 13. Employers learned that they could invest in training, imparting to workers the **firm-specific human capital** necessary to work under the kanban system. Such human capital refers to having workers learn several jobs in the factory, obtain the ability to spot defects in output, be able to make suggestions to upper management, and know not only how to run machines but also how to fix them.

Teamwork, transfer of workers, and job rotation (both within teams and throughout the whole plant) equipped workers with a range of knowledge that was unheard of in the Taylorist production methods in use in U.S. firms. Rapid response in coping with new products and developments in the production process became increasingly valuable to Japanese firms as the pace of technical change quickened. Workers also became empowered to contribute their production-related skills to a process of continuous improvement or **kaizen**. This strategy, based on an organization of flexible work teams, stands in stark contrast to the separation of planning and doing on which mass production in the United States was based.

Internally, Japanese firms are much more homogenous than their peers in the United States and Germany regarding separation of management and production. As many managerial tasks were devolved to the shop floor, blue-collar workers could rise into lower-level management positions. The integration of production and management was thus fostered by personnel movement rather than rigid specialization. Under the kaizen philosophy, suggestions for improvement were encouraged from all employees and discussed fully to reach a consensus before implementation.

Another important structural element of the Japanese system is the highly developed network of end users and suppliers that actually blur the vertical boundaries of individual firms. This is the famous tiered subcontracting process discussed in Chapter 16. As an alternative both to arm's-length market contracting and a vertically integrated hierarchy, the parent or core company acts as the final assembler. A high proportion of components is delivered just in time by closely located and often partially owned, first-tier suppliers, which, in turn depend on second-tier suppliers for their components. Numerous tertiary subcontractors serve the second-tier suppliers. Japanese production networks are typically rather extensively developed.

We recall two major advantages of this method of arranging production. Relations within the production network are the mirror image of the teamwork witnessed within the firm. The kanban or just-in-time inventory system puts a premium on reliability and accuracy. Long-term relationships, personnel sharing, partial ownership, joint product development, and intensive communication are commonplace and represent significant relation-specific investment. The long-term nature of these arrangements, as well as the usual practice of maintaining multiple suppliers and the importance of reputations, all work together to minimize the risk of **opportunistic behavior** of the type considered in Chapter 7.

The second major advantage refers to the internal working of firms. Because firms in the production network maintain separate identities, problems of bureaucracy and influence activity (or rent-seeking behavior) are minimized relative to what they are in a large, vertically integrated organization.

Small firms, with less than 100 employees, abound in Japanese industry. They

420

Part V
*Organization
Structure
as a Dynamic
Process*

account for about one-third of total Japanese employment and pay just over half of the average wages paid by larger firms. Small Japanese firms have the largest share of manufacturing employment among all advanced economies and enjoy much lower bankruptcy and exit rates than do their U.S. counterparts. This is largely due to the absence of arm's-length and lowest bidder contracting. Small subsidiaries can specialize without the risk of a hold-up or takeover that may accompany such specific investment in the more turbulent U.S. environment.

There are not only fewer exits from the small-firm sector in Japan, but also few new start-ups by disgruntled managers and engineers from large corporations, such as those that have become common in the United States. In this regard, a similarity exists between the Japanese and German firms.

■ PATTERNS OF LABOR RELATIONS AMONG GERMANY, JAPAN, AND THE UNITED STATES

International differences are nowhere more striking than in the area of labor relations and the operations of labor markets. In each of the three countries, labor market evolution was tremendously influenced by cultural, political, and organizational factors. Hiring, firing, and moving workers are simple managerial tasks subject to quite different constraints, conventions, and rules. Understanding these differences can help managers avoid major pitfalls in international business.

Historical Context of U.S. Labor Markets

Relations between management and labor are traditionally described as *adversarial* in the United States. This does not mean that more days are lost through strikes in U.S. industry than in Germany or Japan. Adversarial relations have many more subtle and perhaps even more important manifestations. A pervasive "them versus us" attitude in the U.S. workforce can preclude productive cooperation, teamwork, and the establishment of firm-specific human capital. Unfortunately, these are the essential labor components of modern flexible manufacturing strategies.

Mutual suspicion and lack of trust encourage closer supervision and more intense monitoring; which, in turn, may encourage greater shirking and elaborate scams to outwit managers. A well-known example concerns the setting of piece rates in a manufacturing context. Workers on piece rates, a form of incentive pay, may believe that rates will be lowered if their productivity and hence earnings become too high. Workers may then deliberately restrict output rather than choosing the optimal pace of work at the current pay. An individual who decides to break ranks and works harder than the rest might signal to management that output is being deliberately restrained. To avoid revealing this collusive strategy, social sanctions against "rate busters" have frequently been observed in response to performance-related pay of any kind.

One way to understand why the U.S. labor-management relations may be characterized as adversarial is to trace the development of labor markets and institutions in the United States. Early industrialization of the United States, near the beginning of the 20th century, was largely facilitated by a steady flow of immigrants from the Old World. Arriving in the United States with limited resources, they were willing and eager to work hard for low wages wherever the jobs were offered. Workers who quit or who were fired could be easily replaced given the competitive nature of the markets. Investments in firm-specific human capital were unlikely to be rewarded in this highly mobile setting. Instead, ambitious workers looked for professional qualifications that employers would recognize across the country. Following the Taylorist tradition, work was largely standardized, and workers with appropriate skills were hired when they were needed.

Ironically, many of these tendencies were reinforced by the growing power of

421

Chapter 17
*An International
Comparison
of Organizational
Styles*

unions in the decades of prosperity following tighter labor markets during World War II and the Korean War. The giant, mass-producing firms faced stable and growing oligopolistic markets for steel, automobiles, and other products. Labor unions offered a sense of stability to these large vertically integrated firms. They received the payment of premium wages (with a substantial rent component) and a measure of job security for their most senior members with the help of agreements that stipulated layoffs according to inverse seniority.

As the implicit price for these gains, unions conceded to management absolute rights of decision making in the areas of employment, work organization, and technology adoption. To be sure, formalized grievance procedures were established to deal with overt abuses of managerial authority. However, there was no attempt by even the most powerful unions to challenge employer authority with any kind of employee empowerment or participation in managerial decision making. The fundamental Taylorist division of labor between the planning and the doing of tasks was thus cemented in a highly bureaucratic and inflexible organization of labor. This lack of flexibility was not a handicap as long as mass production remained the dominant way to organize production within firms. However, adversarial labor-management relations took their toll in the form of unnecessarily high costs that accelerated import penetration and the demise of the mass producers.

To supervise workers with little loyalty or commitment to their organizations, U.S. firms needed a higher ratio of managerial employees to production workers than their emerging rivals in Germany and Japan. Product and process innovation was hampered by restrictive working rules and job classifications, originally designed to protect the craft-based jobs of the most senior union members.

The most damaging aspect of the environment prevailing in U.S. labor markets was perhaps that collective bargaining and labor-management relations were regarded primarily as a distributional conflict. In other words, big labor and big business were concerned over sharing a pie of fixed size rather than with increasing the size of the pie available for sharing. The goal of management was seemingly to maximize shareholder value (barring some corporate empire building and bloated compensation for themselves). As such, costs, including employment costs, were to be minimized. Employees were generally treated like any other factor of production, as expendable, mobile, and with no legitimate stake in the orginization's goals. There was little acknowledgment of the role of stakeholders such as customers and employees, whose interests dominate in Japanese organizations.

It is interesting to contrast this traditional view with two recent studies of the most successful U.S. companies today.[3] They are companies that emphasize the interests of all their stakeholders—employees, customers, and owners—and thereby do more for shareholder value than those firms that concentrate exclusively on the traditional goals of maximizing profits and stockholder value. A notable example is Hewlett-Packard, which by any standard is one of the most innovative companies in the United States or indeed the world. Hewlett-Packard has a long tradition of Japanese-style permanent employment and nonadversarial labor relations. Many other examples show that adversarial labor relations and distributional conflict can block or delay the transition to flexible manufacturing.

A somewhat different tradition in labor-management relations emerged in Germany. Allied occupational authorities introduced **codetermination** as a delib-

Codetermination
in Germany

---

[3]See Robert Waterman, *What America Does Right* (New York: Norton, 1994); and Jeffery Pfeffer, *Competitive Advantage Through People* (Boston, Mass.: Harvard Business School Press, 1994).

422

Part V
*Organization
Structure
as a Dynamic
Process*

erate attempt to impose democratic control on the traditional heavy industries in Germany. Compared to the traditional pattern of labor-management relations in U.S. firms, codetermination is less adversarial as workers are legislatively made stakeholders in firms. Codetermination has several components that we now consider.

The original and best-known institutional arm of codetermination was to give labor seats on the board of directors of large corporations. In German law, the **supervisory board**, or board of directors, is quite distinct from top management and consists of only outsiders. The main tasks of the supervisory board are to appoint top management and serve as a consultant for major strategic decisions such as new acquisitions or plant closures. The exact role of labor representation on the supervisory board will be described in full detail shortly.

The second institutional arm of codetermination is the **works council**, existing at the plant level (a corporation may have more than one plant), which has no counterpart in U.S. firm structure. The employees of any plant or business employing more than five people are entitled to elect a works council, which has well-defined and far-reaching legal powers. Although powerful, the works council is explicitly prohibited from participating in any way in wage bargaining.

The role of the works council is to receive advance information on all personnel-related matters including layoffs, short-time working, overtime working, and any technological changes or reformations of work. In addition to these information requirements, the works council must be consulted on any substantive changes in work practice and on any changes in employment. In the case of layoffs, management must negotiate an agreement with the works council on the individual workers affected and agree on severance payment for them, called a **social plan**.

Works councils and social plans might seem to an American manager to be a nightmare, but they have worked relatively well in Germany. In addition to their formidable rights under German law, works councils also have carefully defined legal responsibilities. Councils actually have the right to veto managerial decisions on personnel matters, but they are expressly prohibited from using their veto rights in any way that would endanger the prosperity or survival of their organization. Works councils were not designed to give workers extra leverage in a distributional conflict with managers and owners but to encourage workers' cooperation with managers toward the overall success of their companies.

The system is not perfect. German managers sometimes complain of the constraints imposed on them by codetermination. However, numerous studies have shown that managerial cooperation with works councils has been productive and beneficial in a number of ways. One explicit indicator is the very low incidence of overt conflict, such as strikes and lockouts, in German industry. Even more important, works councils have been facilitators for companies dealing with rapid technological change. Works councils that are trusted by labor are able to fairly implement changes that might otherwise have been blocked by adversarial attitudes.

In spite of the formal independence of codetermination and union organization, there is also a strong complementarity between the two institutions in Germany. In large corporations, at least, works councils are predominantly populated by union members. Unions, after all, are concerned with employment stability and working conditions in addition to wages. Agreed wage scales are determined for skill groups rather than for detailed job classifications. The most bitter labor-management conflicts have undoubtedly been with unions over wages and working time, rather than with the institution of codetermination.

In spite of the rhetoric by union officials about class struggle and redistribu-

423

Chapter 17
*An International
Comparison
of Organizational
Styles*

tion, most labor settlements in the history of postwar Germany have been regarded as moderate and noninflationary, at least in retrospect. Only after reunification in 1990 was moderation abandoned at least in the former East Germany as West German unions helped to push up the wages of workers from the former East Germany.

Another philosophical difference between German and U.S. labor concerns the logic of wage concessions. German labor (and workers in other continental Europe nations with similar labor markets) has resisted giving ailing firms concessions on wages. They regard such concessions as the "thin edge of the wedge" that would undermine the whole principle of centralized collective bargaining. The result has been much less growth in wage inequality than in the decentralized bargaining systems found in the United States.

Codetermination, in general, and works councils, in particular, are part of a philosophy of company law and business organization that differs significantly from the adversarial U.S. tradition. Top German managers are legally required to consider the interests of all their major stakeholders, not just those of the majority ownership group. The philosophy of cooperation among the major stakeholders in a productive organization under codetermination is so different from the U.S. tradition that it is frequently misunderstood by business academics, business leaders, and governmental policy makers.

Until now we have focused mainly on the benefits of the system of codetermination in Germany. There are also implicit costs created by this and other related policies that are borne by the German economy. Labor representation on the supervisory boards of large corporations forms perhaps the most visible part of the codetermination system. Initial legislation after World War II required half of the seats on the boards of steel and coal companies to be occupied by labor representatives. The chair of the board, representing owners, was given a second, or casting, vote, to break a deadlock in the event of an equally split vote. This system of **almost parity** was extended to all public companies with more than 2,000 employees in 1976. These changes, and indeed codetermination in general, may have generated some costs by delaying the adjustment of the labor force in the face of shifting or declining demand. As in Japan, German firms tend to react to sudden, short-run downturns in demand with shorter work weeks; temporary layoffs are rare. In the long run, however, German employment does tend to adjust much like U.S. employment.

Another problem with codetermination in the global economic environment concerns the adoption of new technologies. Legislation rooted in craft traditions has impeded entry by new start-ups and self-employment in the service sector. Legislation has also failed to keep up with new productive technologies that often render traditional skills and qualifications meaningless.

The overall level of labor market regulation is much higher in Germany than in other advanced countries. This is not generally a direct consequence of codetermination, but it is undoubtedly created by the same political forces. Taxes on labor to pay for social security, known as *nonwage labor costs*, form a higher percentage of total labor costs than in many other countries.

The former skilled workers who sit on Germany's corporate boards and cooperate with senior bankers and other outside directors represent the most visible pinnacle of the German system of industrial relations. However, they form only one of a number of complementary institutional components. Works councils are clearly much more important in the day-to-day conduct of business, and the role of unions cannot be ignored. Where labor mobility is often limited by strong local cultural traditions and where most blue-collar workers are well trained and skilled, it seems natural to include representation of all employee stakeholders in

424

Part V
*Organization
Structure
as a Dynamic
Process*

**Lifetime Employment
in Japan**

**The Japanese
Employment
Relationship**

Employees or Partners?

the management and decision-making processes of the firm. The German institution of codetermination provides many efficiency-enhancing aspects to the relationships between labor and management. Workers have ample incentives to accumulate firm-specific human capital, and much of the rent-seeking behavior and associated influence costs so common in U.S. organizations are much less present in German organizations.

In the West, perhaps the best-known distinguishing feature of the Japanese economy is the system of lifetime or permanent employment. The limitations of the system are less well known, but it is generally true that male employees, particularly of large corporations, start work after leaving their educational programs (high school or university) and expect to remain with the same employer until retirement at around 55. After formal retirement, many continue to work for associated companies or their subcontractors until they are 65 or older. No formal contracts for lifetime employment exist in Japan; the arrangement is implicit and covers only about one-third of the Japanese labor force. The basic incentives for the employees are clear: the arrangement (credibly maintained) provides the organization with workers making specific investments and a reduction in influence costs for all parties.

Most women and part-time and casual workers have no expectation of job security. These groups form the secondary labor market in Japan with variable employment, low wages, and usually manual work with little prospect of career advancement.

The severe recession of the early 1990s has put the system of lifetime employment under considerable strain (see the box in Chapter 12 on Japanese "window sitters"). Recruitment of new graduates by major employers is now a small fraction of what is had been. However, large-scale layoffs of the kind that are commonplace in the United States rarely occur. The result of this, according to critics of the Japanese system of labor-management relations, is that many white-collar workers are effectively underemployed, having become functionally superfluous.

Growth of the Japanese firm translates into career advancement for most employees and job ladders found in **internal labor markets** are commonplace. With less risk of job loss, Japanese employees can accept a steeper age-earnings profile than U.S. workers can. Young employees receive low rates of pay, but even blue-collar workers are offered extensive training and career development opportunities. Pay rises rapidly with seniority, with qualification, promotion, and outstanding performance bringing additional rewards.

A firm's bankruptcy or job loss is an unattractive option for Japanese workers for several reasons. First, the steepness of the age-wage profiles typically found in Japanese organizations means the loss of higher wages at the end of workers' careers. Second, on retirement, Japanese workers typically receive a substantial lump sum amounting to two or three years' worth of final salary. Another unique feature of Japanese employment is the twice-annual bonus payment averaging about 25 percent of annual earnings. This bonus is more closely related to current profitability than to regular wages or salary.

Wage levels themselves are determined by annual bargaining with enterprise unions. Wage bargains have generally been responsive to economic conditions and the prosperity of the employer. Wages are particularly flexible in the small and family firms, which in any case are more aptly described as partnerships than employers in the U.S. sense.

For all of these reasons, employees in large Japanese firms are closer to being residual income claimants than are typical employees in U.S. and German firms. Wage and bonus flexibility imply that all workers share firm-specific economic

425

Chapter 17
*An International
Comparison
of Organizational
Styles*

and quasi-rents with the stockholders who are the formal residual claimants. Relationships in Japanese employment are characterized by high levels of trust and cooperation, such as normally found only in successful partnerships in Western economies. There is no need for the hundreds of detailed job classifications found in U.S. collective bargaining agreements meant to protect workers from surreptitious downgrading and pay cuts by opportunistic managers.

High trust and worker commitment are fostered through long-term association of work teams and co-workers under lifetime employment. Decision making is consensual and decentralized, rather than authoritarian and centralized. Top managers circulate draft plans for major decisions through the hierarchy for comment and stamp of approval. Achieving agreement on an important issue in a Japanese organization can thus be a fairly lengthy process. This is in stark contrast to standard operating procedures in U.S. firms in which a chief executive has ultimate authority. The Japanese approach to corporate decision making seemingly implies large bargaining costs within the organization. However, given the long-term atmosphere and desire to build a consensus, gains from a cooperative attitude must outweigh those costs.

The economies of Eastern Europe, having dismantled centralized planning, are now faced with building new organizations more or less from scratch. The first generation of reformers, as well as their Western advisers, favored so-called shock therapy. This implied the quickest possible transition to a largely unregulated market economy where labor could be hired and fired at will with none of the long-term implicit agreements that shape labor relations in Japan. This approach has run into severe political opposition, particularly in Russia. Large-scale closings of too many former state-owned enterprises could, it is feared, generate mass unemployment and political anarchy.

Privatization in Russia has proceeded by giving employees of former state-owned enterprises vouchers for preferential purchase of new enterprise shares. Widespread employee ownership has established a legal basis for at least one aspect of Japanese organization: residual claimant status for Russian employees. This is not to say that employees will hold unchecked power. The Russian economy is starving for capital that must be imported, and foreign investors are likely to demand some say in the operation of the enterprises in which they invest.

The economy of Russia faces other long-term challenges as well. Widespread reallocation of labor from the former military and heavy industrial sectors will be necessary before long-term employment relations become possible. Remaining employees in former state-owned enterprises will have to make major and prolonged sacrifices before viable new production for a market economy is developed. It is perhaps not implausible that the long-term rewards offered by ownership status will do more to encourage wage restraint and enterprise survival than the conventional process of collective bargaining. The experience with the wage explosion in former East Germany following reunification in 1990 led to the demise of much of East German industry.

The adoption of U.S.–style adversarial labor relations in Eastern Europe would very likely fuel political instability and extremism. However, the informal consensus and high trust, which characterize Japanese labor relations, can hardly be created overnight in a fragile and very different environment. Elements of the German codetermination system previously described, mainly providing a more formal framework for cooperation, might help to ease the pain of transition in Eastern Europe. At the current time though, even cautious Eastern reformers will have to continue to walk a political tightrope; it is hoped that they and their Western advisers will not ignore the lessons from the development of labor relations in the postwar German and Japanese economies.

**Can Japanese, German,
or U.S. Organization
Work in Eastern
Europe?**

PATTERNS OF CORPORATE CONTROL AMONG GERMANY, JAPAN, AND THE UNITED STATES

Just as labor markets are more constrained by either law or custom in Germany and Japan, so too are capital markets and the market for corporate control. The stock market is less important in these countries, and banks have maintained a considerably more important role in corporate finance than they have in the United States. The traditional reliance on free markets in the United States has left the hostile takeover as the ultimate control on managerial behavior. By contrast, hostile takeovers are essentially unknown in Germany and Japan, and top managers in these countries earn only a small fraction of the total compensation paid to U.S. managers. Because there is no reason to suppose that top managers are less efficient in Germany and Japan, this comparison adds fuel to the debate over the role and effectiveness of the takeover mechanism in the United States.

The Role of Banks in Japan and Germany

Systems of corporate control and finance in Japan and Germany are usually described as bank based, in contrast to market-based systems in the United States. According to recent research by organizational economists, the role of banks in the German economy is much smaller than previously believed. Economists now recognize that the most significant differences between the market-based U.S. system and other systems lie in the differing patterns of ownership among countries. Banks play the most important role in Japan and are influential, although not as dominant as is often claimed, in Germany.

In Japan, the key position of major banks for individual companies or corporate networks, or **keiretsu**, has been well documented. Major banks in Japan maintain long-term relationships and supply a higher proportion of debt capital than they do in other countries. Banks also hold equity shares of their primary customers. Most important, major banks are likely to take an active part in restructuring or rescuing ailing firms at a time of financial crisis.

The extent of the relational association between Japanese banks and their customers is astounding by U.S. standards. Major banks supply a higher proportion of debt capital than in other countries; they also hold equity shares of their primary customers. Further, the long-term association and regular personnel interchange, including directors, gives the major bank an informational advantage over other outside sources of funds. The combined debt and equity holding makes the bank, in effect, a stakeholder. It also removes any incentive to favor one party at the expense of another, for example, by initiating bankruptcy proceedings that might satisfy senior, secured creditors, while expropriating junior debt and equity holders. Empirical evidence suggests that firms with a major bank connection are more likely to survive financial crises in some, perhaps restructured, form.

Until the major recession of the early 1990s, growing prosperity had steadily reduced the dependence of Japanese firms on bank finance, enabling them to fund an increasing proportion of investment with retained earnings. As a result of the recent recession, however, bank relationships have bounced back to assume considerable importance to Japanese firms. This is especially true given the tide of insolvencies and necessary restructuring during the recent recession.

In addition to banks, most large stockholders of Japanese firms are other companies with close trading relations. Their equity holdings are infrequently adjusted and are not held for short-term financial returns. Instead, they serve to align the objectives of trading partners and hence reduce incentives for opportunistic behavior. With a majority of their equity financing held in this way, Japanese firms are not threatened by hostile takeovers or corporate raiders. Long-term investment strategies can thus be followed with less risk of disruption.

Although there is some exchange of personnel, including directors, between

427

Chapter 17
*An International
Comparison
of Organizational
Styles*

banks and their customer organizations, most directors are insiders, drawn from the company's own top management. Thus, there is little formal outside control of chief executives of large Japanese corporations. However, the corporate culture of decision making by consensus does impose informal constraints on top management. Employee stakeholders have no explicit representation on the board of directors, but surveys suggest that their interests are usually put before those of outside stockholders by top managers in Japan.

Smaller firms and subcontractors in the production networks, or keiretsu, are partially owned by the parent or core corporations. Seemingly, these ownership interests are generally quite small with the exception of some first-tier suppliers. Again, such ownership patterns complement the primary trading relationship without incurring the costs of bureaucracy and hierarchy involved in a vertically integrated or completely owned subsidiary.

In some ways, the structure of German banking relationships is quite similar to that of the Japanese. Most companies maintain long-term connections with a particular bank called a **hausbank**. Bank directors sit on the supervisory boards of large corporations, and banks hold substantial equity stakes in many companies. In the aggregate, however, debt finance has been almost as unimportant in Germany as in the United States, with most investment being internally financed. Furthermore, German banks play only a minor role in restructuring companies experiencing financial distress. Banks have no involvement in the day-to-day management of their customers. Bank representatives are often influential in choosing the chief executive or chair of the supervisory board, which is the essential function of the supervisory board of outside directors.

Although in Germany board members have access to internal company data, they meet infrequently (once or twice a year) and largely depend on information provided by top management. In several well-publicized cases, a steady deterioration in corporate performance went unnoticed and unchecked for several years, leading to the takeover of ailing electrical giant AEG by Daimler Benz, or to the restructuring of insolvent metals conglomerate Metalgesellschaft. Top managers of the Big Three German banks, Deutsche, Dresdner, and Commertz, sit on well over 100 corporate boards. Sheer diversity thus precludes close monitoring, although the number of board seats involved lends support to the mystique of bank power.

Banks do control more of the votes at shareholders' meetings than is implied by their own stockholdings. The reason is that proxy votes are given to the bank by private stockholders, whose shares are held in deposit by the banks as part of their stockbrokering function. However, German law gives considerable power to minority holdings of 25 percent, which allows them to block or veto majority stockholders' decisions. Bank (or other) majority holdings are thus less decisive than under U.S. law.

This brings us to what recent writers have found to be the most important difference between the U.S. and the German-Japanese systems of corporate governance.[4] In Germany, only a relatively small proportion of companies is publicly quoted. Most German companies are privately held or family owned. However, most large, listed corporations except the banks have concentrated institutional ownership. That is, at least one (usually institutional) stockholder has at least 25 percent of the shares. In contrast, most publicly quoted companies in the United States have widely dispersed, mainly individual ownership.

---

[4]See Jeremy Edwards and Klaus Fischer, *Banks, Finance and Investment in Germany* (Cambridge: Cambridge University Press, 1994); and J. Charkham, *Keeping Good Company* (Oxford: Oxford University Press, 1994).

428

Part V
*Organization
Structure
as a Dynamic
Process*

The large banks in Germany are thus quintessential managerial corporations. Top managers of other big firms sit on their boards to form a system of interlocking directorships. Nonbank management is ultimately controlled by managers of the banks and other nonfinancial corporations with large equity stakes. Labor representation on German supervisory boards under German codetermination ensures that employee stakeholder interests are respected. The German system of corporate ownership does seem to avoid the major weaknesses of the stock market–based system used in the United States, although it does not always function effectively and has come under increasing criticism in recent years.

The classical problem of separation of ownership as residual income claim and control thus does not seem to exist to any great extent for nonfinancial institutions in Germany or Japan. It should be emphasized, however, that most corporate ownership in these countries is by other corporations. The incentives facing the corporate stockholders in Germany and Japan are quite different from those facing individuals holding equity stakes for purely financial gains. Under these systems, the threat of hostile takeover is practically nonexistent.

PATTERNS OF TECHNOLOGICAL PROGRESS AND INNOVATION AMONG GERMANY, JAPAN, AND THE UNITED STATES

Technological progress and innovation are important determinants of international competitiveness, productivity growth, and, ultimately, living standards. The rapid expansion of high-technology sectors and the pervasive impact of their products has focused intense academic, policy, and popular interest on the process of innovation. The race for scientific and technical breakthroughs now attracts media attention in the United States of the kind that used to be reserved for sporting events (except, of course, the Super Bowl).

A long history of successful pioneering discoveries or breakthroughs in many fields of modern technology in the United States contrasts with rapidly increasing high-tech products attained by Japanese companies. U.S. industrial supremacy was once based on pioneering innovation. This ability to translate breakthroughs into marketable products has been increasingly developed by Japanese manufacturers, but lost in the United States.

In this section, we relate these changing international patterns of innovation to the fundamental differences in productive organization already surveyed.

The Breakthrough Illusion

Numerous industrial research and development (R&D) laboratories were established in the United States in the early decades of this century. Their close links with manufacturing (they were often located on factory sites) were essential in developing advanced products such as the automatic transmission and color TV for mass production after World War II. However, the very success of the U.S. system of Fordist mass production contributed ultimately to the demise in the United States of what two leading experts, Florida and Kenney, have called the follow-through economy.[5]

The term **follow-through economy** means the ability to follow important scientific or technological discoveries, or breakthroughs, with the development of new products at competitive prices. The breakdown of the follow-through economy began in the 1960s and 1970s with increasing specialization and hierarchical division of labor in the R&D lab.

There were two dimensions of this apparently natural extension of Taylorist management principles from the assembly line to the production of innovation.

---

[5]See Florida and Kenney, *The Breakthrough Illusion.*

429

Chapter 17
*An International
Comparison
of Organizational
Styles*

The first dimension attempts to make R&D as standardized as possible. The second dimension involves moving the R&D "production sites" away from the factory floors.

By functional specialization, corporations sought to cast R&D in the same stable mode as all of the inputs used in the mass production paradigm. Professional, "scientific" management increasingly took control of research projects and forced scientists and engineers to communicate through formal, bureaucratic channels. Projects were moved from one specialist division to the next, on assembly-line principles, so that the creative freedom of each receiving group was constrained by prior decisions. To a certain extent, the intention of this policy was logical on the grounds that it permitted specialization of R&D talent and discouraged shirking. However, R&D is not like the assembly of automobile transmissions, and the specialization proved counter to the R&D "production process."

The other dimension of specialization was the physical relocation of R&D labs to suburban campuses away from production sites and their environmental degradation. Production was also gradually moved, first to the Sunbelt and then to low-wage, third world countries. This relocation was supposed to provide R&D scientists with a more favorable environment, far from the factory floor and more conducive to innovation. This may have happened, and the productivity of R&D scientists may have increased. However, the practice had at least one negative, if unintended, side effect. A lack of contact between white-collar R&D workers producing innovations and blue-collar workers making the firm's products made intrafirm coordination of activities rather difficult.

In retrospect, the disconnection of R&D from downstream production activities turned out to be disastrous. Corporations responded to emerging problems by adding new layers of management to the bureaucracies that were already stifling the creativity of fragmented, overspecialized R&D units. The application of standard financial criteria that accompanied the bureaucracy forcefully imposed a short-term orientation onto the long-term nature of most R&D. Job-hopping and high turnover among managers further handicapped long-term R&D projects that incurred costs currently but were only expected to yield returns after the responsible manager had moved on.

As manufacturing divisions of U.S corporations were evaluated by short-term financial accounting criteria, they lost interest in long-term developments. Distant R&D labs often no longer even attempted to deliver much needed incremental product or process innovations. Instead of being used in manufacturing, innovations were sometimes simply sold off to the highest bidder, which very often was a competitor and frequently from Japan. As Florida and Kenney summarized, "The path from R&D to manufacturing became a bureaucratic nightmare of 'it's not my job,' 'that isn't my department,' and 'we can't do that.' It became harder to get R&D projects going, more troublesome to complete them once they were started, and exceedingly difficult to transform innovations into products."[6]

The New Breakthrough Economy

The new breakthrough economy emerged from this situation to exploit profitable new technological opportunities and growth areas that bureaucratic Fordist organizations were unable to take advantage of. These trends were discussed in Chapters 14 and 15; we repeat them here from a somewhat different perspective. The increasing frustration of R&D scientists and managers encouraged small groups with promising ideas to leave large firms such as IBM and form entrepreneurial start-ups. The emerging new venture capital industry played a vital role; this industry arose precisely to fill the funding gap between conception and realization of new market products and technologies.

---

[6]Florida and Kenney, *The Breakthrough Illusion*, p. 26.

430

Part V
*Organization
Structure
as a Dynamic
Process*

The venture capitalist, often a wealthy individual or a small partnership, would supply a majority of equity or risk capital for the new start-up. Based on close personal knowledge of the individuals involved, financial and managerial advice was provided by venture capitalists with seats on the board and a close, hands-on relationship to the start-up. The entrepreneurial team itself then supplied the rest of the equity capital from personal savings or loans from family or friends.

Free from the labyrinthine bureaucratic maze of large corporate R&D, scientists and engineers developed interactive teamwork with intensive, informal communications at all levels in the new start-ups. Motivated by their ownership stake, peer group pressure from team members was sufficient to elicit high levels of effort with little formal or hierarchical monitoring. Innovation naturally blossomed in this "hot house" atmosphere of the new high-tech start-ups. Most of the major breakthroughs in computer technology, semiconductors, and the emerging field of biotechnology came from entrepreneurial ventures of this kind.

The most important breakthroughs have generated enormous and well-publicized gains for founding entrepreneurs and venture capitalists. Such "big hits" compensate the venture capitalists for the high incidence of start-ups that never take off or fail in their first few years. When start-ups are successful and go public, the founders are often tempted to sell out, move on, or retire. Process innovation and the creation of new products generally offer much less spectacular and rapid rewards than the breakthrough discovery itself.

The breakthrough economy has stimulated innovation, but it has not halted the relative decline of U.S. high-tech manufacturing. One problem is that the separation of R&D and production has remained or even increased as more and more production moves to low-wage countries in Asia or Latin America. The essential interaction between R&D and the production process that is required for continuous improvement as practiced by Japanese manufacturers is thus difficult to implement.

The breakthrough economy was made possible by the high mobility of U.S. employees, but this very mobility imposes costs on the system. Departure of one or two key team members can seriously disrupt a project or even destroy the value of past investment in R&D. With employee turnover rates of 30 percent to 50 percent common in Silicon Valley, long-term development projects are jeopardized, and even the survival of small firms is at risk when their most important human capital cannot be retained.

Cooperative teamwork gave new start-ups a significant innovative lead over the old corporate R&D bureaucracies. Without continuity, teamwork loses much of its efficiency. Specialization and fragmentation may return to limit the damage from defection of workers who are knowledgeable about all aspects of a project. It is thus difficult to realize the full potential of teamwork in this type of highly mobile environment.

The extreme mobility of high-tech workers at all levels mirrors the cut-throat competition and lack of cooperation between firms in the high-tech clusters of Silicon Valley, Boston's Route 128, and other areas in the United States. With no continuity even among key personnel, it becomes difficult for firms to establish enduring joint ventures or subcontracting agreements that are based on high-trust personal relationships.

Much competition in high technology involves patent races and other contests to establish priority legal rights over breakthrough discoveries. In this climate, arm's-length market exchange and formal contracts are hedged with legal safeguards to protect firm-specific information from leaking to competitors. This extensive exchange of technical know-how, customary in Japanese networks, is thus blocked.

431

Chapter 17
*An International
Comparison
of Organizational
Styles*

Certainly, Silicon Valley and other clusters benefit from an infrastructure of legal, financial, and other services geared to the requirements of the high-tech enterprise. New start-ups are thus encouraged to locate in these areas and benefit from the proximity of major research universities, such as Stanford, which in turn supply major scientific talent and consulting services. The most successful firms in Silicon Valley enter into strategic alliances and form joint ventures, often with Japanese companies, and have succeeded in following breakthrough with competitive production—all this in spite of hypermobility and low trust. But litigation, particularly against small and new companies for alleged theft of intellectual property, has also increased explosively. A leading economist, Bennett Harrison, has noted that Silicon Valley has many different faces.[7] In spite of all the problems that seem to be evident in U.S. industrial organization, Silicon Valley has survived recession and international competition in much better shape than its former rival district, Boston's Route 128.

The concentration of breakthrough R&D has also encouraged a new breed of **vulture capitalists**, however. These entrepreneurs specialize in personnel raids, hiring key individuals away from competitors to get ahead in the race for some promising new breakthroughs. Start-ups may be launched largely on the basis of raids that essentially transfer people and know-how from one enterprise to another, destroying nearly as much value as they create in the process.

It is often difficult for small firms, in particular, to match a raider's offer of increased compensation to a member of a cooperative team. Once a raider's offer is generally known, other team members will demand similar rewards or lobby their services in the same market that lured away their colleagues. No less damaging than the raids by outsiders are the flood of defections of employees from established high-tech companies. Too many "copycat" start-ups in a fashionable field may swamp the market and destroy most of the newcomers' and existing firms' viability.

The main social costs of the hypermobility of labor in the U.S. high-tech fields can thus be summarized as underinvestment in human capital and disruption of ongoing R&D teamwork. Extreme mobility also fosters arm's-length relations among suppliers, breach of implicit contracts whenever opportune, and low trust. The proliferation of small new start-ups pursuing every imaginable technological "holy grail" generates a few big winners and a multitude of losers.

Neglect of manufacturing by the breakthrough economy raises even more serious problems for the near future. Contracting out production to the third world countries lowers cost in the short run but actually transfers valuable know-how in the long run. By 1988, South Korea had overtaken West Germany to become the third largest producer of semiconductors, after Japan and the United States. Based on learning from subcontracting, South Korea is developing a major high-tech sector.

As the pace of technological progress and product cycles accelerates, continuous improvement of both product and production processes become critical for competitive success. An increasingly global separation of production from innovation precluding the interaction between the two has put high technology and other Japanese manufacturing far ahead of Germany and the United States. Interaction and communication require a skilled and empowered workforce that can contribute its own detailed knowledge of the production process to continuous innovation. Third world and even U.S. high-tech manufacturers have replicated the Taylorist division of labor between semiskilled routinized production work and professional teamwork to produce breakthrough innovation. Until this division is

[7]Bennett Harrison, *Lean and Mean* (New York: Basic Books, 1994).

432

Part V
*Organization
Structure
as a Dynamic
Process*

**The Japanese Capture
High Technology**

overcome and the functions of manufacturing and R&D are integrated, it seems unlikely that the problems of the breakthrough economy can overcome.

Japan's rise to preeminence in many branches of advanced manufacturing has been spectacular by any standards. Commercial R&D spending and employment grew by about 15 percent a year until the recession of the 1990s. Two-thirds of this expansion was funded by industry that represented the highest nonmilitary- and industry-financed R&D effort of any country.

Some evidence of the emergence of Japan as a high-tech powerhouse is provided in Table 17.1 and Figure 17.1. As recently as 1980, nine of the top ten semi-conductor equipment manufacturers were in the United States. In the following decade, this situation drastically changed; by 1990 five of the top ten semiconductor equipment manufacturers were Japanese firms. A similar conclusion is drawn by Figure 17.1, which shows that the world market share of U.S. manufacturers of data processing equipment was more than halved between 1980 and 1994. Simultaneously, the share of the world market held by Japanese producers of data processing equipment increased fourfold from just under 10 percent over the same period. Similar developments could be charted for many other high-tech products, many of which were actually pioneered and developed in the United States.

The previous section described the loss of follow-through capacity in U.S. manufacturing. The key to Japanese success has been the integration of R&D with production in large organizations, linked to stable networks that provide economies of scale and scope and synergy without bureaucracy. The role of government has been limited, but, as already indicated, the Japanese system of economic organization is far removed from the laissez-faire ideology that became popular in the United States during the 1980s. Instead of universal arm's-length competition between all firms, commitment and cooperation in work teams and supplier networks is the hallmark of Japanese economic organizations.

A surprising difference between the patterns of innovation in Japan and the United States is the dominance of large firms in Japan. In spite of a much larger

Table 17.1	**Top Ten Semiconductor Equipment Manufacturers**	
1980	**1985**	**1990**
United States	**United States**	**Japan**
Perkin-Elmer	Perkin-Elmer	Tokyo Electron Ltd.
GCA	General Signal	Nikon
Applied Materials	Varian	Advantest
Fairchild TSG	Teradyne	Canon
Varian	Eaton	Hitachi
Teradyne	Sentry	
Eaton	Schlumberger (includes	**United States**
General Signal	Fairchild TSG)	General Signal (Includes GCA)
Kulicke & Soffa	Applied Materials	Varian
	GCA	Teradyne
Japan	**Japan**	Silicon Valley
Takeda Riken	Tokyo Electron Ltd.	Group (includes Perkin-
(became Advantest)	Advantest (formerly Takeda	Elmer
	Riken)	

Source: VLSI Research, Inc., 1991. In *Beyond Mass Production: The Japanese System and Its Transfer to the U.S.* by Martin Kenney and Richard Florida. Copyright © 1993 by Oxford University Press, Inc. Reprinted by permission.

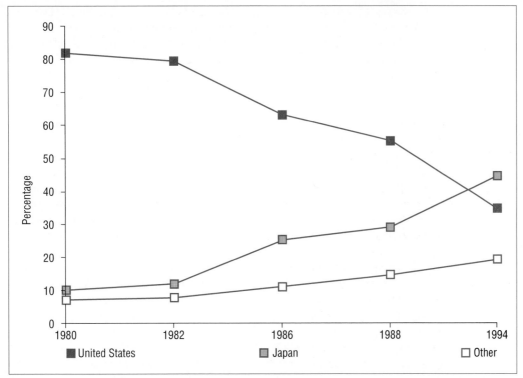

Figure 17.1 World Market Share, Data Processing Equipment

share of production by small firms in Japan, most innovation there is produced by giant corporations. As shown in Chapter 14, the relationship between firm size and innovation in the United States is much different. By 1988, the three companies receiving the largest number of U.S. patents were Hitachi, Toshiba, and Canon, all ahead of GE, IBM, and Siemens of Germany. These and other leading Japanese innovations have maintained a wide range of consumer and commercial product lines that are closely related to take maximum advantage of synergy in the application of their integrated R&D efforts. Japan now seems to have added a major breakthrough capacity to its successful follow-through capability.

Large Japanese corporations can utilize the full spectrum of R&D output in their diversified production. The situation is much different in the United States because breakthrough innovations are not able to be fully exploited by a small company. Synergistic benefits also occur from a single innovation in a large corporation in ready application in a wide range of products such as video displays in Watchman TVs and laptop computers.

Economies of scope also provide advantages in systems technologies. *Mechatronics* is a new synthesis that combines mechanical and electronic systems in flexible manufacturing systems, industrial robots, and semiconductor fabrication. Mechatronics is one instance in which specialized companies lacking any one of the component skills cannot fully exploit the benefits of the initial breakthrough.

At this point, we explore the crucial way in which the Japanese have avoided the stranglehold of bureaucratic Taylorist management that destroyed the follow-through capability of so many large U.S. corporations. As so often is the case when comparing Japanese with U.S. experience, the Japanese ability to do so lies both in the internal organization of firms and in the relationships between the firms of a productive network.

Why Is the Japanese Experience Different from That in the United States?

434

Part V
*Organization
Structure
as a Dynamic
Process*

Inside firms, decentralized management, and teamwork apply to R&D as well as to production. Most important, the two have remained integrated in various ways. In Japan, R&D facilities are usually located close to assembly plants, and R&D projects are systematically pursued in cooperation with production personnel. R&D scientists and engineers usually transfer to production after 10 or 15 years, where they help to maintain close links between the two activities, strengthening complementarities within the organization. The barriers erected between innovation and production by Fordist management in the United States are excluded by the most basic principles of production organization in Japan.

The other aspect of Japan's ability to avoid this stranglehold follows essentially from the long-term nature of links between parent and supplier companies common in Japanese production networks. Parent firms concentrate on core activities without the fear of hold-up by suppliers and without the necessity of totally owning or integrating with subsidiaries. In Japan, as new projects or products evolve beyond the core activities that offer the most synergy in the parent organization, they can be spun off to form associated but independent companies. Alternatively, new spin-offs can be created with personnel exchange and financial support from the parent until independence is attained in a permanent relationship, perhaps with part ownership.

This process is driven by consensus management in the parent company. It is thus the polar opposite to the creation of new start-ups by frustrated R&D scientists from U.S. corporations who can disrupt ongoing projects by quitting suddenly, taking irreplaceable human capital and know-how with them. Instead of cooperating with their parent in the United States, the new start-ups usually try to attract customers and business from their old employer and, in turn, can expect no assistance but perhaps costly litigation or other hostile reactions when they renege on implicit contracts.

By concentrating on related activities that promise synergy at some stage, Japanese corporations can dispense with the layers of bureaucracy and high manager-to-worker ratios that stifle large U.S. organizations. By simply downsizing, the latter can reduce costs in the short run, but they cannot reproduce consensus management and a commitment by all employees to continuous improvement without more far-reaching changes.

Japanese R&D teams are encouraged to use company resources to develop their own ideas. If these are promising, they can enlarge their budgets and staff and create an internal "start-up", without the costs of quitting the organization. Some of the most innovative U.S. corporations, such as Hewlett-Packard and 3M, have also encouraged internal **intrapreneurship** of this kind with some success. Suppliers and subsidiaries in Japan have their own R&D programs that also concentrate on product development. About 90 percent of total R&D resources in Japan are devoted to product development. Close personnel and organizational links with production divisions throughout the development process allow products to be designed for easy manufacture. Production delays are thus minimized so that new or improved products can be marketed more rapidly than in the United States.

The importance of "first-mover" advantages in marketing high-tech products puts tremendous pressures on R&D teams in Japan, as it does on U.S. start-ups. **Karoshi**, or death by overwork, has become a much discussed problem in Japan, matching the burnout of hypermobile R&D workers sometimes observed in the United States.

U.S. companies have attempted to emulate positive features of Japanese organization by forming strategic alliances with high-tech start-ups as a way to buy into new technologies without the uncertainties of the R&D process. With no ex-

435

Chapter 17
*An International
Comparison
of Organizational
Styles*

pectation of long-term cooperation in most cases, these alliances often collapse in mutual recrimination or lawsuits when the larger partner has effectively appropriated the start-up's technology. Direct acquisition of start-ups has also run into all the problems of overcentralized organization already discussed and frequently stifles creativity or leads to loss of key researchers. The competitive strength of Japanese networks depends on several complementary factors—decentralized internal organization, permanent employment, and links between suppliers—that allow optimal exchange of information and personnel without risks of hold-up or expropriation.

Given these comparative national advantages and failings, it is perhaps not surprising that U.S. companies seeking synergistic rather than opportunistic alliances are turning to Japanese corporations. Japanese investment in joint ventures and high-tech start-ups in the United States has been increasing, partly because U.S. breakthrough technology can often be manufactured most effectively with Japanese production expertise. Japanese high-tech manufacturing, in turn, benefits from access to important discoveries that may generate improvements and new products. This trend continues the Japanese tradition of learning from U.S. technology, but now it is on the basis of a formidable domestic R&D capacity that did not exist in the early postwar years of imitation.

U.S. companies have also began to imitate important aspects of Japanese organization; the most successful have integrated some of the key complementarities such as decentralization and long-term employment despite opposite prevailing trends in the U.S. environment. This process has been accelerated by the rapid development of Japanese transplants. High-tech automated steel works have revolutionized this traditional rust-belt industry. Japanese automobile-assembly transplants have generated hundreds of transplant and (more recently) U.S. suppliers using Japanese production and JIT delivery methods. Long-term relations, teamwork, joint problem solving, and other features of Japanese production networks have been replicated in the United States, demonstrating that these models of organization are not culturally determined, as some observers have claimed.

As transplants have grown in numbers and importance, R&D functions have increasingly come from Japan to maintain the close links between production and innovation that are so important in typical Japanese organization patterns. U.S. steel making and rubber and tire manufacturing have also been fundamentally restructured and transformed by the technology transplants. Early consumer electronic assembly has been followed by high-tech electronics, and basic research labs have been set up in various innovation centers to attract high-quality U.S. researchers.

Paradoxically, perhaps, Germany's very preeminence in traditional fields of manufacturing such as engineering, chemicals, and pharmaceuticals delayed recognition of, and entry into, the emerging new areas of electronics and biotechnology. The public sector in Germany reacted even more slowly than the manufacturers and continued to pour massive subsidies into commercial flops in nuclear energy, coal mining, and ship building.

Recognition of the problems, at least, has now swept through the European Union (EU). With a "domestic" market larger than that in the United States and a highly trained labor force, the EU is likely to reap tremendous gains from a unifying market. Strategic alliances and joint ventures are proliferating, not only across internal national boundaries but particularly with Japanese and U.S. leaders in the high-tech sectors previously neglected in Europe.

The rapid development of Eastern Europe with its low-wage, highly skilled labor offers much opportunity for outsourcing and applying competitive pressure on Western Europe's highly paid workers. These pressures and the deep reces-

436

Part V
*Organization
Structure
as a Dynamic
Process*

sion in the early 1990s have kept wage increases below productivity gains in Germany and other major European countries. Downsizing and outsourcing are contributing to an average level of unemployment of 10 percent to 12 percent in the EU; this is twice as high as that in the United States. This persistent unemployment in turn puts a brake on the rise in wages and nonwage costs that have reduced the competitiveness of German industry in particular.

A common hurdle for high-tech industries in the EU is the relative lack of cooperation between research universities and the business sector. The famous high-tech clusters centered around major universities such as Stanford or the Massachusetts Institute of Technology (MIT) in the United States have hardly been developed in the EU, except for that in Cambridge Science Park in England. There, as elsewhere, signs of change are evident as universities begin to overcome their traditional ivory-tower isolation under pressure from selectively targeted research funding.

An example of successful industry-government cooperation is the European Airbus, which is now catching up with the world's aerospace leader, Boeing. Airbus has pioneered innovations such as the wide-body, twin-jet engine design, and the two-person, all-electronic cockpit.

Perhaps the most fundamental factor predicting European companies' ability to catch up in high technology has been revealed in a major research project by the private Council on Competitiveness and the Harvard Business School. As Bennett Harrison[8] reports, two leading U.S. economists, Lawrence Summers, now undersecretary of the Treasury Department, and James Poterba of MIT interviewed CEOs of the largest firms in the United States, Japan, and Germany. These researchers found varied and striking evidence of the short-term orientation of U.S. management and of the much longer time horizon relevant for Japanese and German companies. In the United States, much higher rates of return on investment capital are required; it has been 12 percent in recent years. Potentially valuable investment projects, particularly long-term ones, are thus regularly rejected by these high "hurdle rates." The lower hurdles in Germany and Japan are matched by much higher proportions of GNP going into aggregate investment in these countries.

Most disturbing, even the nature of R&D projects reflects the short termism of many U.S. companies. Only 20 percent of R&D projects were classified as long term by the U.S. CEOs on average, while over 60 percent, or twice as many, were described as explicitly long term by top German managers. This proportion exceeded even the Japanese share of 47 percent long-term R&D projects and points to relatively increasing technical sophistication of German products in the future.

■ CHAPTER SUMMARY AND KEY IDEAS ■ ■ ■ ■ ■ ■

Taking a historical perspective, we can conclude that we certainly live in interesting times. Until about 1975, large U.S.-based mass-producing firms dominated their domestic and world markets. Technological progress and the opening of truly world markets caused this situation to change dramatically. Stable and profitable oligopolistic markets are gone, having been replaced by a highly competitive global environment in which speed and flexibility are seemingly more valuable than size.

It is now more important than ever for every manager to appreciate the

---

[8]Harrison, *Lean and Mean*, p. 184.

437

Chapter 17
*An International
Comparison
of Organizational
Styles*

means by which economic activity is organized in different countries. The reason is simple and has been touched on throughout this book. Mass production, based on economies of scale and scope, replaced craft production as the best way to organize economic activity for one simple reason: the mass production system was more efficient at the time.

It is too early to tell exactly what the dominant way of organizing economic activity will be in the year 2000. However, we can point to some important characteristics of the current leading candidates. In Chapter 15, we discussed the importance of, and formally modeled, flexible manufacturing systems; surely in a globally competitive marketplace in which product differentiation and customization are important, flexibility will play a key role. In Chapter 16 strategic alliances and production networks were seen as organizational devices that could potentially offer many of the benefits of both vertical integration and market transactions. Although these organizational traits are promising and observed in current business practice, another dimension is influencing organizations.

Our purpose in this chapter has been to examine patterns of economic organization, primarily in the United States, Germany, and Japan, in three key areas: production systems, labor relations, and sources of capital. Even though differences exist across countries in these three areas, it is important to recognize that within the countries, each of the three areas is consistent with the other two. The interesting question, in light of the success of Japanese firms in the past 15 years, is "Can one country's organizational scheme work in another country?" Judging from the record to date of the Japanese auto industry firms transplanted in the United States, the answer is, at least partially, yes. Thus, another dimension is added to explain various organizational schemes now arising that are attempting to become the most efficient pattern of economic organization tomorrow.

KEY TERMS

almost parity
codetermination
complementarities
economies of scale
employment relationship
firm-specific human capital
follow-through economy
hausbank
implicit contract
internal labor markets
intrapreneurship

kaizen
kanban
karoshi
keiretsu
Mittlestand
opportunistic behavior
social plan
supervisory board
vulture capitalists
works council

FURTHER READINGS

Acs, Z., and F. FitzRoy, "A Constitution for Privatizing Large Eastern Enterprise." *Economics of Transition* 2 (1994), pp. 83–97.

Charkham, J. *Keeping Good Company*. Oxford: Oxford University Press, 1994.

Edwards, J., and K. Fischer. *Banks, Finance and Investment in Germany*. Cambridge: Cambridge University Press, 1994.

Florida, R., and M. Kenney. *The Breakthrough Illusion*. New York: Basic Books, 1991.

Harrison, B. *Lean and Mean*. New York: Basic Books, 1994.

Osterman, P. "How Common Is Work Place Transformation and Who Adopts It?" *Industrial and Labor Relations Review*. January 1994, pp. 173–188.

438

Part V
*Organization
Structure
as a Dynamic
Process*

Pfeffer, J. *Competitive Advantage Through People*. Boston, Mass.: Harvard Business School Press, 1994.

Waterman, R. *What America Does Right*. New York: Norton, 1994.

QUESTIONS AND PROBLEMS FOR REVIEW AND DISCUSSION

A. Why has the United States fallen behind the Japanese in high-technology industries?

B. Discuss the concept of *lifetime employment* in Japan.

C. Compare the different ways in which Germany and the United States control corporations.

D. In light of the material you have learned this semester, can you provide at least two reasons why a better understanding of international trading partners of U.S. firms is necessary?

GLOSSARY

acquisition An arrangement in which the assets and liabilities of the seller are absorbed into those of the buyer.

adaptation cost Part of the implicit or explicit costs to workers to find a new job if it is necessary to relocate or to give up any employment benefits such as pensions.

adjustable rate mortgage A type of secured debt on private homes that allows the interest rate on the unpaid balance to vary through time according to some specified index or other criteria.

adverse selection A form of precontractual, or ex ante, opportunism in which one party has private information at the time of negotiation that potentially reduces the value of the contract to the other party.

age-wage profile The relationship between the wage earned by an employee at a given firm and various points in time (perhaps corresponding to that employee's age), typically assumed that higher wages are earned at higher ages.

agency costs A general name given to the costs involved in monitoring the behavior of some party acting on your behalf.

almost parity An institutional component of the co-determination system in Germany in which workers are granted by law one-half of the seats on corporate supervisory boards, "almost" because the chair of the board, representing ownership interests, is given two votes to break a deadlock.

arc elasticity A measure of the resilience to price changes measured over a range on a given demand curve.

asset specificity One dimension of transaction costs; refers to the degree to which a resource is committed to a specific task and thus cannot be redeployed to alternative uses without a substantial reduction in its value.

asymmetric information The relative holdings of data by individuals; when at least one party to an agreement has superior knowledge of some dimension of the agreement.

at-will employment Employment situations in free economies; workers are employed at the will of the employer and employees voluntarily work.

authority relationship An arrangement in which one party has the right, within reasonable bounds, to direct the behavior, punish, and reward other parties.

average fixed cost Fixed costs of production divided by the number of units produced.

average product The total product, or output, divided by the number of units of a given input employed.

average total cost The total cost of production including explicit and implicit components at any level of output divided by the number of units produced; equals average variable plus average fixed cost.

average variable cost Total variable cost divided by the number of units produced.

bankruptcy A situation in which a firm is unable to pay its bills and must go out of business, shareholders lose their investments, creditors have a long fight to recover debt, and managers may lose credibility.

block booking A pricing strategy in which sellers with some market power group similar goods together and offer them as a package to less informed buyers.

board of directors Shareholder elected officials who act in the interest of the owners in a corporation's internal control mechanism.

book value One way to place a value on a firm; the historical accounting valuation of the firm's assets including accumulated depreciation charges and owners' equity.

bounded rationality A property common to parties involved in economic exchange which implies that economic agents act with less than perfect information; arises because information is costly to acquire and process; that is, transaction costs will prevent parties from becoming fully informed.

brand name capital specificity A form of asset specificity that refers to becoming affiliated with a well known brand name and thus less free to pursue other opportunities.

business reengineering A form of business reorganization often embracing techniques such as teamwork, employee training in multiple skills, and worker empowerment.

business unit strategy The way the firm competes in a given line of business.

capital structure The mix of debt and equity financing chosen by a firm; the higher the ratio of debt to equity, the more leveraged the firm.

capped option A form of corporate executive compensation involving a standard option with a certain strike price and a limit on the share price the executive can cash in on.

carrot method A way to deal with the incentive problem facing managers by attempting to encourage individual responsibility by linking employee pay to performance.

change in demand A shift from one demand curve to another reflecting a change in one of the nonprice determinants of demand.

change in quantity demanded The movement along a given demand curve in response to a change in the good's price.

change in supply A shift from one supply curve to another reflecting a change in one of the nonprice determinants of supply.

change in quantity supplied The movement along a given supply curve in response to a change in the good's price.

Coase theorem A proposition that if legal, strategic, or informational barriers to bargaining are absent and if property rights are clearly defined, people can always negotiate an efficient outcome.

codetermination The process permeating every aspect of labor-management relations in Germany; the assigning of workers to seats on corporate boards and establishment of works councils at individual plants.

commercial mortgage A common form of debt secured by fixed property.

comparative advantage A theory used to explain international trading patterns; countries choose what to produce by determining those goods in whose production they have an advantage (in terms of the opportunity cost of other, lost outputs) over other countries.

comparative statics The comparison of two different equilibrium points.

complementarities The relationships between groups of activities in an organization in that one activity experiences feedbacks from changes in the other activity.

computer-aided design (CAD) The use of computers to speed up design involving an interactive computer terminal and product models and the ability to perform modification and tests.

computer-aided manufacture (CAM) The use of computers to speed up the manufacturing process by connecting computers to machine tools, enabling the integration of systems of numerically controlled machine tools, robots, and other process machinery used in manufacturing.

computer numerical control (CNC) A machine that has as its basis a minicomputer and occupies an intermediate position between transfer machines and conventional hand-operated machine tools.

concentration Economic term referring to the importance of large producers in a market, said to increase when fewer, larger producers dominate a market.

constrained efficiency postulate A hypothesis that states if individuals are able to voluntarily bargain to an enforceable allocation, then the result will tend to be efficient, subject to their generally limited information, resources, and bounded rationality.

consumer surplus The difference between what final users are willing to pay for a good and what they actually pay.

consumption complementarities The process in which two related products or goods are used together; use of one complements the use of the other.

consumption externalities Created when the use of a good by one party affects the use of that good by another party. See externalities.

contestability An economic concept stating that economic rents can be earned only if others are precluded from securing them by some process such as market bidding.

contract An interlocking set of mutual promises enforceable and acknowledged by some disinterested third party; generally specifies actions that each party will take; may assign decision-making powers.

contract curve The locus of points in a production Edgeworth box which represent tangencies of each firm's isoquants at the prevailing input price ratio.

cooperation In business terminology, partnerships with businesses in similar industries.

coordination costs A broad category of transaction costs entailing the determination of prices, the costs of acquiring information concerning the location, quality, reputation, and availability of different parties, and other costs associated with allocating workers to specific tasks and with bringing transaction participants together.

core competency An area of business in which an organization has a competitive advantage not only in producing a good or service but also in developing new and related products.

corporate control The process by which society through markets or regulatory means exerts some authority on a business entity.

corporate culture A set of routines for decision making and shared expectations that employees are taught as well as the stories and related devices used to convey those expectations; provides a set of principles and procedures for judging behavior and resolving legitimate disputes.

corporate governance The way in which the contracts are arranged which tie the individual units in an organization together; degree of vertical integration.

corporate strategy The determination of which business activities the firm will undertake.

corporation A legal entity recognized by and subject to the various laws in the state in which it is created; a dominant form of organizing economic activity because of the limited liability of its owners.

cospecialized assets Two resources that are most productive when used together and lose much of their value in the absence of the other.

cross-price elasticity of demand The percentage change in the quantity demanded of a good that results from a 1 percent change in the price of another good; all other things being equal.

debt A form of financing a firm; represents an agreement requiring regular payments; provides no element of corporate control to the providers of the loan.

decentralization A process taking place in corporations in which the functions of command and control are redistributed and more independent business units emerge.

deconglomeration The act of returning a firm to its original competencies; the breaking up of firms into many lines of business.

decreasing returns to scale When an X% increase (decrease) in all inputs causes output to increase (decrease) by only Y% where X is greater than Y.

dedicated asset specificity A form of asset specificity involving investment in general-purpose assets made at the behest of a particular transaction partner.

demand The quantity of a good or service that consumers are willing and able to purchase.

demand curve The graphical depiction of the relationship between quantity demanded and price holding all other factors affecting consumer behavior constant.

demand function An explicit mathematical or graphical relationship between the price of a good and the quantity demanded.

derived demand Requirement of a good or service not for itself but for what it can produce.

design attributes Some characteristics of a problem in formulating corporate strategy involving information that is generally available in the firm; an inefficient choice will have wide ramifications throughout the organization.

design decisions Choices made by organizations involving the way in which economic activity will be arranged when a small mistake will have large implications in future periods.

Detroit automation A method of factory mechanization pioneered by Ford Motor Co. at its engine plant in Brook Park, Ohio; linking several large transfer machines in a continuous system; also referred to as Fordism.

differentiated products Goods that fulfill the same basic function but vary in at least one dimension; concept is not one of absolutes, but of degree.

dimensions of transaction costs A breakdown of transaction costs into five types: asset specificity, assessment of the benefits of the transaction, complexity and uncertainty, familiarity with the transaction, and relationship to other transactions.

diminishing marginal productivity A generally accepted theory in economics stating that the marginal product of an input to the production process eventually declines as more units of that input are added to the production process.

direct demand Requirement of a good or service for the utility, or satisfaction, that good itself directly provides.

directly unproductive activities Actions that individuals take to change the allocation of rents within an organization; usually do not necessarily create value for the organization.

disequilibrium A situation in which quantity demanded and quantity supplied differ unleashing forces to bring then into equilibrium.

distribution effects A force affecting efficient exchange pertaining to who has, or gets, what resources; can refer either to a party's ability to "afford" its portion of an efficient allocation or to share the value created within firms.

division of labor Separation of tasks into a large number of different jobs.

downsizing A process by which a corporation reduces the number of its employees, leaves a line of business, sells off assets, or any combination of the three.

economic rents A term used by economists to describe "extra" payments going to a resource; more specifically the benefits from an activity going to a resource in excess of what is needed to attract that resource to that activity; in a sense representing "something for nothing."

economies of scale The result of physically combining inputs to form outputs that continually reduce producer unit costs over the relevant range of demand.

economies of scope The results of physically combining inputs to form outputs that produce two or more related outputs within the same firm; implies lower unit costs for each output than if produced separately.

Edgeworth box A graphical depiction of the total amount of two factors of production going to the production of two outputs.

efficiency A term describing the potential outcome of some exchange-based activity from which any change increasing one party's well-being necessarily causes a reduction in the well-being of one other party.

efficiency principle The proposition that people can bargain effectively to implement and enforce their decisions, resulting in outcomes that are efficient.

efficiency wage model A working hypothesis attempting to explain compensation patterns in labor markets; especially useful because it addresses measurement costs and predicts that managers will reward good behavior by workers with economic rents.

efficient An economic arrangement is said to be efficient if it is impossible, given available resources, to implement an alternative arrangement under which all parties involved are at least as well off.

efficient market hypothesis The proposition that prices in security markets fully and accurately reflect all information relevant to forecasting future returns.

elastic demand The percentage change in quantity demanded of a good in response to a 1 percent change in price that is higher than one in magnitude.

elasticity A general concept that measures the responsiveness of one variable to a change in another; an attempt to quantify sensitivity.

employee stock ownership plan When the employees of a firm obtain equities in their organization and actively participate in management.

employment relationship A long-term relational contract existing between a firm and its employees featuring gradually rising wages; intended to create incentives for workers to accumulate firm-specific human capital and develop loyalty.

entrepreneurial regime Describes the availability of information necessary for innovation; is said to exist if the information available to potential innovators exists outside of existing firms.

entry barrier Some device keeping other sellers from freely entering a market including economies of scale and scope, control of a key resource or location, or a patent or copyright.

equilibrium A state in an economic or physical system within which there are no forces affecting change; the price and quantity such that demand equals supply.

equilibrium price The single price at which the quantity demanded and the quantity supplied of a good or service balance.

equity A form of financing a firm; represents a stake in a corporation made by an investor who obtains some rights to dictate the policies and operation of that firm.

evolutionary economics A theory of economic organization and industrial structure that focuses on change; the primary assumptions are (1) firms satisfy rather than maximize, relying on routines and decision rules in doing so (2) the competitive environment rewards success and (3) any industry is not likely to be in equilibrium at any point in time.

ex ante A Latin phrase that translates roughly as "before the fact."

exchange efficiency Analyzes the behavior of consumers who can trade goods between themselves.

"exit" One choice that share owners have if they are unhappy with the performance of the company in which they have shares. To exit, they simply sell their shares.

explicit contract Dealings occur under a specified, existing contract.

ex post A Latin phrase that translates roughly as "after the fact"; used in describing contracting situations after the agreement has been reached.

external contract An agreement between the firm and parties lacking an ownership or employment interest.

externalities Costs (negative) or benefits (positive) imposed involuntarily on another party not regulated by any system of prices.

final goods Outputs produced in an economic system sold directly to consumers without further processing.

financial restructuring The alteration of a firm's debt-equity ratio without changing its assets.

firm A conscious, willful effort to organize economic activity that consists of a collection of contracts when more than one party is involved.

firm-specific human capital A term describing employee-acquired skills and knowledge that have value in only their current employing organization.

fixed cost A cost incurred by the firm that does not vary with output.

flexible manufacturing system (FMS) A process typically consisting of multiple work stations, an automated material handling system, and a supervision system through computer controls; often relies on computer-aided manufacturing technology.

follow-through economy The institutions that turn basic technological breakthroughs into marketable products.

free cash flow Funds existing in an organization that do not have to be paid out to workers, for materials, to suppliers, or to service debt.

free-rider problem The difficulty in eliciting true willingness to pay for a public good from which nonpayers' enjoyment cannot readily be prevented.

fungible An economic description of something with a very general purpose that can be crafted to meet very unique individual needs and circumstances.

general equilibrium analysis A method of inquiry that simultaneously determines the prices and quantities in all markets.

general-purpose human capital The stock of skills and abilities possessed by a worker that are usable in a number of applications.

globalization The process by which investment and technology occur on an international scale; is directly tied to direct foreign investment; most of the world's trade occurs within multinational corporations.

golden parachutes Contracts that promise large severance payments to employees who lose or leave their job shortly after and because of a change in corporate control.

governance structure The contractual format chosen to manage a transaction ranging from a simple spot market transaction to complex, long-term relational contracts to ownership.

greenmail Payment by a corporation to a potential corporate raider to induce him or her to give up the attempted takeover.

gross domestic product (GDP) The total money value of the goods and services produced by the residents of a country in a given time period; frequently used by economists to measure output in a national economy because it accounts for the "open-ness" of economic activity.

gross national product (GNP) A measure of the incomes of the residents of a country including incomes earned abroad but excluding payments made to those abroad.

hard science A physical science such as biology or chemistry.

hausbank A name given to the primary bank of a German corporation.

hold-up A form of ex-post opportunism arising because of asset specificity that involves exploiting the inflexibility of one party to a transaction.

horizon problem A potential mismatch between the planning horizon of the decision maker and those affected by his or her decision.

horizontal equity The concept in an organization that wages be similar across workers.

horizontal integration One dimension of firm strategy that determines the firms's horizontal boundaries which basically determines the business in which the firm should be engaged.

hostile takeover One firm taken over by a second without the cooperation of the management of the first firm.

human asset specificity When individuals develop skills within narrow applications.

human capital The amount of knowledge, skills, education, training, and experience held by an individual enabling that person to become more productive, earn higher future incomes, lead more meaningful lives, and have improved decision making ability.

human resource management A field specializing in developing policies to administer the relationship between firms and workers.

idiosyncratic exchange A particular type of relational interchange between contracting partners (usually long term) in which once the general nature of the relationship is established, neither party has incentive to engage in opportunistic behavior; said to be self-enforcing.

imperfect commitment A situation resulting in transaction costs; occurs when the parties come to an agreement that one or both would later like to abandon.

imperfect information Less than complete or accurate data held by at least some buyer or seller.

implicit contract A type of agreement with no formal statement of the terms and conditions agreed to by the parties.

inalienability problem A difficulty occurring in organizations when the net benefits from a business relationship cannot be sold by those currently holding the rights to those benefits.

incentive problem A difficulty in an environment facing the manager of a firm who must motivate and coordinate employees, possibly in a team production context.

income elasticity of demand The percentage change in the quantity demanded of some good resulting from a 1 percent increase in income.

incomplete contracts Agreements that fail to fully specify actions under every conceivable course of events.

incomplete information A situation where economic agents have data that are not accurate or complete.

increasing returns A relationship between costs and input usage by the firm in which additional units of input yield successively more to output resulting in declining average costs over a wide range of output.

indifference curve A depiction of all combinations of two goods or services that yield the same satisfaction to the household.

industrial divide That moment in history when the path of technological development itself is at issue; a "pointer" that demarcates a period before and after a significant change in the way firms organize economic activity.

industrial robot A machine typically composed of components: a mechanical special purpose device, a "servo-system" that controls movement of the device, and a computer control system that coordinates the machine within its industrial environment.

industrial system The relationship between a firm's internal organization and their connection to one another and to the social structures and institutions in their particular localities.

inelastic demand The percentage change in the quantity demanded of a good divided by the percentage change in price is less than one in magnitude.

influence costs Costs associated with rent-seeking behavior; occur when one party attempts to alter the distribution of costs and compensation in a contractual setting; or when decision makers make inefficient decisions because of their exposure to rent-seeking behavior.

Information Age A time period described by the replacement of traditional raw materials in the manufacturing process with knowledge.

informational asymmetries When the amount and/or quality of data held by parties to an exchange differs, or is believed to differ.

innovation A process that begins with an invention, proceeds with its development, and results in the introduction of a new product, process, or service.

innovative attributes Some characteristics of a problem in formulating corporate strategy involving information that is not available within the organization.

intermediate good Output subject to later processing before ultimately being sold to consumers.

internal contract An agreement limited to parties within a firm; typically vague with some amount of latitude given to each of the involved parties.

internal control One of the ways in which firms in a capitalistic economy face demands for efficient behavior; refers to the authority and conduct of that authority by boards of directors acting in the interests of stockholders.

internal labor markets Career paths and so-called job ladders within organizations where wages are tied to jobs and employees are rewarded by moving up to higher-paying slots.

international joint venture An undertaking in which one party is headquartered in a different country.

internationalization A situation in which the demand for an output is international as opposed to national or just regional.

intrapreneurship Entreprenerial activity within organizations.

investment The current expenditure of resources that produces a stream of benefits over a future period creating an asset.

isocost line The combinations of two inputs that cost the same amount.

isoquant The combinations of two inputs that yield the same output.

joint ventures Two or more legally distinct organizations, each of which actively participates beyond an investment role, such as in the decision-making activities of the mutually owned entity.

junk bonds Interest-bearing securities issued by corporations to finance their activities usually involving a merger or acquisition that have a very high risk of default.

just-in-time manufacturing system A production system in which outside suppliers work closely with large firms to provide parts on a rigid schedule eliminating the need for all firms to carry large inventories.

kaizen A strategy widely adopted in Japanese firms empowering workers to contribute their skills in an atmosphere of continuous process improvement; can include: teamwork, quality circles, job rotation, and flexible work teams.

kanban A characteristic of Japanese production that implies a high degree of coordination and communication between related units; emulated in the United States.

karoshi A Japanese word meaning roughly "death by overwork"; a particular problem in high-tech industries due to the importance of speed.

keiretsu The name given to a group of related firms in Japan that dominate the Japanese economy; usually consists of independent firms with close financial and technological links, possibly a shared name.

law of diminishing returns A premise that increasing amounts of a variable factor applied to a given amount of a fixed factor will add increasingly less to output.

lease When a resource is put in the control of a party without an ownership interest.

leveraged buyout Acquisition of a firm through heavy use of debt.

logical positivism A method of inquiry adhered to by most economists.

long-run equilibrium A situation in which the firm earns zero profits in competitive markets because the correct number of firms are active each producing at minimum average total cost such that industry supply and demand are balanced.

make-or-buy decision The choice a firm must make as to whether it should make an intermediate good in house or secure it in some market.

management buyout The purchase of a firm by its managers; often leveraged because they are accomplished with heavy debt.

managerial misbehavior The imperfect monitoring and conflicting incentives of the owners of a firm and its managers characterized by unjustifiably high salaries and maximizing something other than shareholder wealth.

manufacturing strategy A plan to position a firm in the global marketplace.

marginal cost The increase in the total costs of production resulting from raising output by one unit.

marginal product The change in total product, or output, resulting from the use of one more unit of a variable factor other things being equal.

marginal productivity theory A premise in economics stipulating that all factors of production be paid the value of their marginal contribution to output.

marginal rate of substitution The rate at which consumers are willing to substitute units of one good for another holding utility levels constant.

marginal rate of technical substitution (MRTS) Provides a measure of the amount of capital that must be added when one less unit of labor is used to keep output constant.

marginal revenue The change in total revenue resulting from the sale of one more unit of output is equal to price for perfectly competitive firms.

marginal revenue product The market value of the output produced when the firm uses one more unit of a variable input in the production process holding all else constant.

market The interaction of one or more buyers with one or more sellers.

market discipline A functioning, competitive market providing if enough buyers (sellers) learn of a particular seller's (buyer's) poor behavior so as to curtail that seller's activities; punishment for "bad" behavior.

market failure A malfunction in a market mechanism that results in an allocation of resources that is not efficient.

market for corporate control When investors try to become aware of and purchase corporations that are undervalued due to poor management or use of assets; theoretically promotes efficient behavior by the managers of a firm.

market power When a buyer or a seller can influence the market price by their actions.

market value The total worth of all of the firm's outstanding shares minus the amount of debt.

measurement costs In economic terms, expenses incurred by contracting parties attempting to become fully informed; a subclass of the broader concept of transaction costs.

merger An arrangement in which the assets and liabilities of the seller are absorbed into those of the buyer.

minimum supply price The smallest amount that a seller will accept in exchange for the good or service that he or she sells.

Mittlestand German industrial organization featuring a large sector of small- and medium-sized firms.

Modigliani-Miller theorems An approach to classical finance consisting of two theorems, the first states that a firm's market value is independent of its capital structure; the second states that the total market value of the firm is independent of the way it finances its dividends.

monitoring The act of observing the actions and behavior of contracting partners.

monopoly power Control held by a seller in economic exchange; if seller can, to any degree, ignore prices of other sellers in the market; demand curve has negative slope to it.

moral hazard An ex post contracting situation and source of transaction costs that occurs when one party's actions are imperfectly observable and when the incentives of the parties may be less than perfectly aligned.

mortgage bond A type of debt for firms secured by fixed assets.

motivation costs A broad category of transaction costs that have a basis in incomplete information; most important areas are imperfect monitoring of behavior and ensuring that others remain committed.

multidivisional firm A type of organization producing more than one output for market.

natural monopoly A market situation in which the minimum efficient scale is very large relative to the size of the market.

net present value An amount of money to be received in the future and considered equal to its value today.

network externality A term equivalent to consumption externality; refers to the value to one party of other parties' choice of a particular good or service.

network system In economics terms refers to two or more components of a system that are complementary, or work together.

nonconvexities A characteristic of the relationships between inputs or activities within an organization implying that small changes in one activity will cause increasingly larger changes in other, related activities.

nonexcludability The concept that once a good is produced, it is impossible to prohibit others from consuming it.

nonrivalous consumption The process by which one party's usage of a good or resource does not detract from its full enjoyment by other parties.

normative economics Questions with some moral or ethical basis.

numerically controlled machine A mechanical tool that can be controlled by a computer.

opportunism The policy of taking advantage of an informational asymmetry in your behavior; is a central assumption of transaction cost economics.

opportunistic behavior Action taken when one party to an agreement acts in his or her own selfish interests, even at the expense of other parties involved in the agreement.

opportunity cost The value of the next best alternative to an action.

opportunity cost of capital The rate of return measuring the next best return available for the funds a firm has for investment.

option swaps A form of compensating CEOs in the form of stock in the corporation; occurring when a company issues a stock option in exchange for a previously issued stock option.

organizational strategy A blueprint for accomplishing an efficient allocation of corporate resources.

ownership The right to decide by whom, how, when, for how long, and under what conditions an asset will be used.

partial equilibrium Economic analysis which examines events in one market in isolation from all other markets.

partnership A type of firm in the economic system that consists of two or more persons associating to conduct noncorporate business.

pay compression The concept that the wages in an organization are similar across all workers.

perfect competition An arrangement of buyers and sellers in which there is perfect information, a homogenous product, similar firms, and free entry and exit.

perfect information Every participant (and potential participant) in a market becomes aware of every price, product specification, and buyer and seller location at no cost.

physical asset specificity A particular investment in machinery or equipment that has one narrowly defined purpose.

point elasticity The percentage change in quantity demanded divided by the percentage change in price defined at a single point on a given demand function.

poison pill A defense against corporate takeover that can take many forms each of which increases the cost to the acquirer and decreases the value of the firm taken over.

positive economics The science of explaining what is and predicting what is to be.

principal-agent problem The recognition of the consequences of separating ownership and control in various transactions; the principal is the controlling authority, the agent is paid to act for the principal.

principle of risk sharing The concept behind every insurance policy and financial diversification strategy that the sharing of independent risks by a single party reduces the total cost of bearing those risks.

private costs Costs borne by the initiator of some activity.

private placement A way for a firm to raise funds by issuing debt to an identified investor; this type of debt is not made available to the general public.

process innovation A change in the way a product is made, or a service is provided, that improves quality and/or lowers cost.

producer surplus The area above the supply curve and below the market price; represents the difference between the minimum amount the seller will accept for any given unit sold and its actual price.

product innovation A concept closely affiliated with basic new knowledge and products.

product life cycle The series of stages experienced by an output: introduction, growth, maturity, and decline.

product mix efficiency A condition for overall efficiency and maximization of social well-being in an economic system; requiring that all products produced are sold, or, in other words, that all markets clear.

production function The characteristic behavior between the inputs of the production process and the resulting output; indicates the firm's maximum attainable output for every specified combination of inputs.

production network A form of production that exists between markets and hierarchies.

production possibilities frontier The combination of two goods that an economy can produce by fully utilizing all of its resources including technology.

productive efficiency A condition of production by firms that is reached when the production of one output cannot be increased without a corresponding reduction in the production of another good.

productivity A measure of output, or other result, per unit of effort expended in obtaining it.

profit maximization The process of achieving the largest profits possible; requires that the marginal revenue of the firm equal the marginal cost at a point where marginal costs are increasing; the goal of the firm in neoclassical economics.

property rights Ownership.

proxy When one's actions are taken for, or substitute for, another's, when stockholders grant others their voting rights for a limited time dealing with a specified issue.

public good An economic reality causing markets to fail and a perverse set of incentives to be created for parties consuming the good; two properties: nonrivalous consumption and nonexcludability.

public issue When a firm raises funds through the creation of new shares of stock and makes these issues available to the general public.

quasi-rents The benefits from an activity going to a resource in excess of the minimum required to keep a resource in current situation; in organizations relevant for analyzing the exit decision of a resource.

rationality The principle that individuals and firms act in a consistent manner.

real An economic measurement expressed in dollars defined in some base period; adjusted for inflation.

regulatory forebearance A policy of the U.S. federal government during the early 1980s that permitted economically insolvent deposit-taking institutions to continue to operate.

relational contracting Agreement incomplete in nature for failing to fully specify actions in every possible set of circumstances; typically include an agreement on broad goals and objectives and mechanisms for dispute resolution.

reload option A form of executive compensation in a corporation allowing the CEO and other executives to collect the profits that he or she would have received had he or she exercised his or her option on the day during the option period that would have earned him or her the highest profits.

reneging A form of ex post opportunism said by

economists to occur when one or more parties to an agreement simply refuse to honor it.

rent-seeking behavior An attempt by some interested party to alter the allocation of rents in a contractual agreement; in general, does not create value within the organization.

reputation Recognition viewed by economists as part of an organization's or individual's capital stock; based on past behavior and, more importantly, on others' perception of that behavior.

reservation price The maximum amount a buyer would be willing to pay, if forced, for an item given their preferences, incomes, and the prices of other goods.

reservation reward The minimum amount for which an individual will voluntarily work; thought to vary by an individual's age.

reservation reward profile The relationship between an individual's reservation reward and various points in time (perhaps corresponding to their age); typically assumed to be higher at more advanced ages.

residual claimant A person or organization that controls an asset and has the opportunity to employ the asset as he or she wishes; may be entitled to the economic rents or profits generated by that asset.

residual return Mandated by state and federal laws, are the payments to individuals who own stock in the corporation.

residual right of control A benefit given to stock owners by a corporation giving them some influence on the activities of the corporation through the election of a board of directors.

resource allocation The distribution of limited resources efficiently or in a way that maximizes some fixed objective.

restructuring The act of changing the resources available to a firm and/or altering the lines of business a firm is in; changing the way a firm chooses to organize economic activity, or those activities themselves.

returns to scale Refers the relationship between uniform percentage increases in the inputs available to a firm and the percentage change in output.

risk-averse A person who wishes not to face risks and is willing to pay some explicit or implicit amount to have the risk removed; a person who prefers a certain deal over an uncertain deal with equal expected value.

routinized regime Describes the availability of information necessary for innovation, if the infor-

mation necessary for innovation only exists in established, existing firms.

scale economies The results of some production processes when average unit costs decline as the number of units produced increases.

scientific management A management style for supervising workers featuring extensive task specialization, a detailed set of rules, and frequent evaluation of individual performance.

scientific method A way of thinking about problems and formulating a solution.

scope economies The results of physically combining inputs to form outputs that produce two or more related outputs within the same firm; implies lower unit costs for each good than if each was produced separately.

screening A potential solution to adverse selection that occurs when the uninformed parties to a contract undertake activities to cause the informed parties to distinguish between themselves in regard to some unobservable characteristics.

secured debt Form of financing backed by an existing asset that acts as collateral.

secondary market An institution allowing for the debt and equities of firms to be bought and sold.

self-selection A type of behavior usually in response to some screening activity that causes some percentage of a larger group of potential trading partners to identify themselves as desirable candidates for exchange.

separation of ownership and control A property of publicly held corporations; one group of shareholders owns the firm and a second group of managers runs the firm.

shareholder activism Vigorous action taken when shareholders become so dissatisfied with the actions of the corporation's management that they actively attempt to influence, or even eliminate management; occurs because of the separation of ownership and control.

shirking A form of ex post opportunistic behavior arising because of imperfect monitoring; one party puts forth less effort than it otherwise might if its actions were perfectly observable.

short-run equilibrium A situation in which the firm has no incentive to change its level, or mix, of outputs and the number of firms in the market is fixed.

shortage A situation in which the quantity demanded of a good or service is greater than the quantity supplied.

shut-down point   The minimum price that a firm will produce output for in the short run equal to average variable cost at the chosen level of output; further decreases in price cause losses larger than fixed costs.

signaling   A way to reduce inefficiencies caused by adverse selection; the better informed party may give indications of unobservable, but desirable, characteristics.

site specificity   A form of asset specificity, the condition of being limited to a particular location.

skill acquisition costs   The cost borne by workers as they gain new knowledge and skills to change jobs, that is the costs of building new human capital.

small-batch production   One property of flexible manufacturing when a very small number of units can be produced at a very low cost per unit.

social costs   The total costs borne by all members of society including those not directly participating in that activity.

social indifference curve   Shows all combinations of goods and services produced in the economy that yield society the same level of well being.

social plan   One element of co-determination in Germany requiring that the works council approve of all layoffs.

soft science   The study of the interactions resulting from human behavior.

sole proprietorship   A type of firm in the economic system owned by a single individual.

specialization   The division of tasks on the basis of comparative advantage.

standard option   CEO compensation that gives the holder the right to purchase a specific number of shares of the company's stock at a specified target price.

stick method   A way for managers to solve the incentive problem in a team production context by forcing the employee to act by making threats in a specified way.

strategic alliance   An association to exploit the unique strength of two or more companies whose core competencies are complementary when neither partner has the ability, nor the desire, to acquire the other party's unique strength.

strategic misrepresentation   A situation in which one party may try to benefit by being less than truthful about their assessment of an exchange situation; employed to increase bargaining power.

sunk costs   Costs that can never be recouped once they are paid; are irrelevant for decision makers.

supervisory board   The German corporate construct that best corresponds to a board of directors in a U.S. firm; comprised only of outsiders; hires top management.

supply   The quantity of a good or service that producers are willing to produce.

supply curve   The graphical depiction of the relationship between quantity supplied and price holding all other factors affecting producer behavior constant.

supply function   An explicit mathematical or graphical relationship between the price of a good and the quantity supplied.

surplus   An amount that remains when the quantity demanded of a good or service is less than the quantity supplied.

synergies   The combined effect of two activities is greater than their sum taken separately; agglomerations.

takeover market   Commercial activity by a number of investors seeking a corporation undervalued because of poor management to buy, replace management, and raise its value.

Taylorism   A management style for supervising production commonly used in mass-producing firms: (1) specialize each job through the simplification of individual tasks (2) devise predetermined rules coordinating the separate tasks and (3) evaluate the individual performance through a detailed monitoring system.

team production   A form of making output that requires the simultaneous efforts of more than one individual.

theory   An unproven explanation of observation.

total cost   Inclusive expenses (both implicit and explicit) of producing any given level of output; includes opportunity cost.

total factor productivity   Output produced per unit of input employed when total input is an index of three individual inputs: labor, capital, and materials.

total market value   The amount of cash needed to purchase a firm free and clear; an amount equal to the market value of the firm's equities plus all debt.

total product   A relationship between output and variations in one input.

total quality management (TQM)   A philosophy practiced by an entire organization working together with an interdepartmental collective responsibility for the quality of products and services.

total revenue Price times quantity.

total value The economic concept of a transaction as the total benefit of the exchange; may include regularly defined profits of firms and consumer surplus, elements of risk minimization, strategic gains, and nonmarket benefits.

total value maximization A goal of economic behavior to increase to a maximum the total value surrounding a transaction.

transaction costs Costs incurred in exchange, either explicit or implicit, above and beyond contracted prices including the acquisition of costly information, monitoring performance, and committing specific assets.

transfer machines A number of smaller machines or work stations committed to a specific task and organized so that a piece of work is immediately transferred to the next work station.

transplants Japanese owned and/or managed subsidiaries operating in the United States.

underwriter An entity who sells bonds in a public offering; often helps in many areas of issuing bonds.

unitary elasticity of demand The percentage change in the quantity demanded of a good divided by the percentage change in the price of the good are equal and their ratio equals 1 in magnitude.

unsecured debt Liability supported only by the borrower's credit worthiness.

value maximization When the management of a corporation acts to maximize the market value of outstanding shares (equities) so as to transfer the maximum value to the owners of those shares.

variable cost All costs incurred in production by firms that vary directly with output.

vertical integration The process in which either one of the input sources or output buyers of the firm are moved inside the firm.

virtual corporation A temporary network of companies that come together quickly to exploit changing market conditions under which companies can share costs, skills, and access to global markets with each partner contributing what it does best.

"voice" One choice that share owners have if they are unhappy with the performance of the company in which they have shares. They exercise voice if they express their dissatisfaction attempting to alter management style.

vulture capitalists Some entrepreneurs who specialize in raiding high-tech firms, hiring away their best talents as a basis for starting a new firm.

wealth maximization When the management of a corporation acts to increase the assets under corporate ownership; maximizes the book value of the firm.

worker search costs Expenses that employees incur when looking for a new job; including the value of time unemployed, interviewing, and efforts in contacting potential employers.

works council A group within the firm under codetermination in Germany which has certain decision-making powers in management issues.

x-inefficiency The operation of a firm far less efficiently than could occur given technical constraints.

INDEX